Industry and the Making of a Rural Landscape

Iron and pottery production at Churchills Farm, Hemyock, Devon

Edited by

Chris Smart

with contributions by

Tim Young, John Allan, David Dawson, M.J. Hughes, Roger T. Taylor, Sarah Newstead, Jens C.Ø. Andersen, Gavyn K. Rollinson, Dana Challinor, Julie Jones, Peter Marshall, Matt Tompkins, A.G. Collings, Laurence Keen, Graham Langman, Oliver Kent, Christopher Bronk Ramsey, Elaine Dunbar, Paula Reimer

BAR British Series 636

2018

Published in 2018 by
BAR Publishing, Oxford

BAR British Series 636

Industry and the Making of a Rural Landscape

ISBN 978 1 4073 1626 0

COVER IMAGE *Hemyock viewed from the Millennium Seat. Photograph, Katie Steed.*

Printed in England

BAR
PUBLISHING

BAR titles are available from:

BAR Publishing
122 Banbury Rd, Oxford, OX2 7BP, UK
EMAIL info@barpublishing.com
PHONE +44 (0)1865 310431
FAX +44 (0)1865 316916
www.barpublishing.com

Acknowledgements

We thank English Heritage, now Historic England, for providing the majority of post-excavation funding that enabled the analyses and this publication. Initial funding and staff time given by Devon County Council allowed the processing and sorting of the vast ceramic assemblage, as well as some early public outreach and dissemination. Historic England staff put considerable effort into the Hemyock project over a number of years, especially Vanessa Straker, Peter Marshall, Duncan Brown and David Dungworth. Without their support the analyses described in this book would not have been undertaken.

We pay tribute to the late Professor Harold Fox, who first noted the clay rents in the Arundell papers at the Cornwall Record Office and recognised that these indicated the presence of a major pottery, previously unrecognised, in Clayhidon parish – some years before any archaeological evidence was found to support his conclusion.

The following bodies and members of staff made comparative samples available for study: the RAM Museum and Art Gallery, Exeter (Tom Cadbury); the South West Heritage Trust (Steve Minnitt); the Admiral Blake Museum, Bridgwater with help from the Bridgwater and District Archaeological Society (David Baker and Jill Polack); Gill Selley and the churchwardens of St Swithun, Woodbury, Devon, and the Revd Preb. Alan MacDonald and Churchwardens of Cadeleigh, Devon.

In preparing the report on the floor-tiles, Laurence Keen writes, 'A special debt of gratitude is owed to John Allan for introducing the author to the finds from Hemyock, for providing facilities for their study, and for arranging for the chemical analyses included in this report. Additionally, he arranged for the tiles from Woodbury to be made available for study in the church, through the good offices of Gill Selley, and, with the helpful assistance of David and Butzi Brown, worked with the author in recording the tiles at Haccombe church. He has also provided helpful comments on the text. Peter Cox kindly provided a copy of AC Archaeology's report on work at Woodbury. Father Jerome Bertram has generously provided comments on the inscriptions. Jerry Bird has given much technical assistance'.

A group of volunteers helped make lighter work of the washing, sorting and quantifying of the vast pottery assemblage, particularly George Fox and Pamela Boyce, the latter of which has also been instrumental in marking and packaging the finds.

Contents

List of Figures

Chapter 4

Figure 57. Backscattered electron photomicrographs of samples from flow slags from non-slag tapping furnaces. (a) Typical slag texture with flow lobes marked by iron oxide rim. HCF10, SOI1 (1 mm-scale). (b) As (a) ,but with one rim cut obliquely to appear very broad in the section. HCF10, SOI2 (1 mm-scale). (c) Typical slag texture detail, showing poorly-formed, rounded, wustite dendrites, followed by fayalite plus hercynite cotectic and with dark leucite-rich interstices. HCF10, SOI8 (60 μm-scale). (d) Lobe boundary, lower lobe has very fine wustite (locally overgrown by hercynite) rather similar to that in the droplet in Figure 56 (c). HCF10, SOI10 (300 μm-scale).

Figure 58. Backscattered electron photomicrographs of samples from tapped slags from early medieval slag-tapping furnaces. (a) Montage showing several flow lobes, all with quench-textured of elongate, delicate, complex wustite dendrites, followed by fine fayalite. One lobe boundary is marked by oxide rim (see also (e)), the other solely by a change in the slag texture (see also (d)). The quench textures of the right two lobes, with lamellar fayalite (centre) and fayalite closely coating the wustite dendrites (right), resemble those of the later tapslags (Figure 59), but in neither case is iscorite present. HCF16, SOI3-5 (100 μm-scale). (b) Typical slag texture in a coarser-grained area away from the lobe margins. The early wustite is sparse and locally overgrown by euhedral hercynite. The subsequent elongate olivine contains abundant hercynite cotectic. The interstitial areas (dark) are dominated by a leucite-wustite cotectic. HCF23, SOI4 (600 μm-scale). (c) Detail of (b) showing interstitial areas, with leucite, leucite-wustite cotectic, wustite and apatite. The primary wustite is overlain by euhedral hercynite and fayalite-hercynite cotectic, with the outer parts of the fayalite also containing apatite. HCF23, SOI2 (40 μm-scale). (d) Cryptic lobe boundary demarked by change in the proportion of wustie (mid grey). The white overgrowth to the wustite in the lower lobe is iron. Both lobes show some large subhedral hercynite. HCF22, SOI2 (200 μm-scale). (e) Oxide boundary between lobes. First-formed lobe (lower right), shows inward –growing oxide dendrites from the rim (probably mainly wustite), the outlines of which suggest they were originally a spinel (they are now multiphase with wustite, bright, and duller spinel, probably magnetite). On both sides of the boundary the later-formed slag has fine, but elongate olivine with leucite-wustite eutectic. HCF16, SOI6 (40 μm-scale).

Figure 59. Backscattered electron photomicrographs of samples from tapped slags from medieval contexts. (a) Typical quenched tapslag, with variable, but mostly very delicate and long wustite dendritic arrays, followed by sheaves of elongate fayalite. HCF29, SOI2 (100 μm-scale). (b) Detail of coarser slag texture, showing the elongate fayalite to be rich in hercynite cotectic, with some hercynite also present as small early euhedral grains. The interstitial areas are filled by leucite-wustite cotectic. HCF29, SOI6 (40 μm-scale). (c) Detail of a flow lobe rim. The rim becomes more porous (and probably richer in magnetite inclusions), into the lobe towards the upper right (presumably the earlier), with the dendritic wustite of the lobe showing relationship with protrusions from the rim. The later coarse-grained lobe (now to lower left) shows nucleation of wustite dendrites onto the planar outer face of the rim, which is also coated in tiny euhedral hercynite. HCF25, SOI3 (100 μm-scale). (d) Detail of (c) showing protrusions from the (originally lower) face of the rim, which bear pores and act as nucleation sites for the subhedral hercynite. HCF25, SOI4 (40 μm-scale). (e) Example of a lobe boundary (in correct orientation) showing similar features to those of (c) and (d). The quenching of the lower lobe has produced thin fayalite coats on the wustite and hercynite dendrites. The upper lobe has abundant euhedral hercynite. HCF26, SOI8 (90 μm-scale). (f) Example of a lobe boundary in which the inner face of the rim has developed euhedral magnetite-rich spinels. The quench textured lamellae comprise fayalite and iscorite coating the wustite dendrites. HCF26, SOI4 (60 μm-scale).

Figure 60. EDS microanalyses of olivines, showing % calcium substitution against the % fayalite (where the olivine is expressed on the forsterite-fayalite solid solution). Calcium is preferentially taken up late in the development of the olivine. The upper diagram demonstrates the high levels of calcium substitution in a large furnace bottom from context (757), the fill of furnace [756]. HCF1 was a sample of dense slag from close to the pit wall, HCF2 was a low density, charcoal-rich slag from the distal part of the block. The middle diagram shows analyses from other non-tapping materials, including FB slag (HCF7, 8) and basal flowed slags (HCF9, 10, 14). The lower diagram shows analyses from tapped slags, showing (with the exception of unusual sample HCF16 from furnace [792]) a much lower degree of variation than for the non-tapped slag samples.

Figure 61. EDS microanalyses of olivines, showing % manganese substitution against the % fayalite (where the olivine is expressed on the forsterite-fayalite solid solution). Manganese uptake by the olivine declines slightly as it forms. The upper diagram demonstrates the continuity on manganese substitution in a large FB from context (757), the fill of furnace [756]. HCF1 was a sample of dense slag from close to the pit wall, HCF2 was a low density, charcoal-rich slag from the distal part of the block. The middle diagram shows analyses from other non-tapping materials, including FB slag (HCF7, 8) and basal flowed slags (HCF9, 10, 14). The lower diagram shows analyses from tapped slags, showing (with the exception of unusual sample HCF16 from furnace [792]) a much lower degree of variation in magnesium than for the non-tapped slag samples, but a greater variation in manganese.

Figure 62. EDS microanalyses of olivines, showing phosphorus substitution (in atoms per formula unit) against the % fayalite (where the olivine is expressed on the forsterite-fayalite solid solution). Manganese uptake by the olivine declines slightly as it forms. The upper diagram demonstrates the continuity on phosphorus substitution in a large FB from context

Chapter 6

Chapter 7

Figure 131 [right]. The extent of records for 'slag', 'slag heap', 'slag, quarry', 'ironworks' and 'iron working site' in the Devon County Council Historic Environment Record as of May 2016 in relation to the topography of the Blackdown Hills. It is noteworthy that the vast majority of findspots occur on the valley sides or lower slopes, rather than on the plateaux.

Figure 132. Map of pits shown on either the Ordnance Survey First Edition 25 inches to 1 mile (late nineteenth century) as claypit, marl pit, and/or those visible on Environment Agency 1 m resolution LiDAR data viewed as a hillshade model. The background mapping comprises late nineteenth-century Ordnance Survey First Edition 6 inches to 1 mile and British Geological Survey soil parent material dataset, sheet ew311 (© Crown Copyright and Landmark Information Group Limited (2016). All rights reserved. (1889)). It is unfortunate that there is not total coverage of LiDAR data (which focusses on valley floor) for the Blackdown Hills, which help us understand the broader pattern of mineral extraction (clay, marl, aggregates, iron ore etc).

Figure 133. Detail of a hillshade model of 1 m resolution Environment Agency LiDAR data for an area west and north of Hemyock, shown against a backdrop of late nineteenth-century Ordnance Survey First Edition 6 inches to 1 mile mapping (© Crown Copyright and Landmark Information Group Limited (2016). All rights reserved. (1889)). The data shows that there are many examples of extraction pits, possible for the digging of clay, marl or gravel, at the edges of fields within the historic landscape. Whilst undated, the form of those not also shown on historic mapping is more muted, perhaps implying that they are earlier in date.

List of Tables

List of Contributors

John Allan, Independent researcher, john.p.allan@btinternet.com

Jens C.Ø. Andersen, Camborne School of Mines, University of Exeter, j.c.andersen@exeter.ac.uk

Christopher Bronk Ramsey, Oxford Radiocarbon Accelerator Unit, Research Laboratory for Archaeology and the History of Art, christopher.ramsey@rlaha.ox.ac.uk

Dana Challinor, Independent researcher, dana.challinor@tiscali.co.uk

A.G. Collings, Independent researcher, tony.collings1@blueyonder.co.uk

David Dawson, Independent researcher, davidp@dawsonheritage.co.uk

Elaine Dunbar, SUERC Radiocarbon Dating Laboratory, Scottish Enterprise Technology, Elaine.Dunbar@glasgow.ac.uk

M.J. Hughes, Independent researcher, m.j.hughes222@btinternet.com

Julie Jones, Independent researcher, juliedjones@blueyonder.co.uk

Laurence Keen, Independent researcher

Oliver Kent, Bristol School of Art, kents@waitrose.com

Graham Langman, Independent researcher, gil1960@virginmedia.com

Peter Marshall, Historic England, peter.marshall@historicengland.org.uk

Sarah Newstead, Department of Archaeology, University of Leicester, srn6@leicester.ac.uk

Paula Reimer, CHRONO Centre, Queen's University Belfast, p.j.reimer@qub.ac.uk

Gavyn K. Rollinson, Camborne School of Mines, University of Exeter, g.k.rollinson@exeter.ac.uk

Chris Smart, Department of Archaeology, University of Exeter, c.j.smart@exeter.ac.uk

Roger T. Taylor, Independent researcher, taylor.rt@talktalk.net

Matt Tompkins, Department of History, University of Leicester, mllt1@le.ac.uk

Tim Young, GeoArch, tim.young@geoarch.co.uk

Abstract

Excavation at Churchills Farm, Hemyock, Devon, ahead of residential development, revealed an unexpected wealth of archaeological remains illuminating industry in the now tranquil setting of the Blackdown Hills in South West Britain. Twelve iron smelting furnaces were recorded, of both slag pit and slag tapping technologies, and an extensive program of radiocarbon dating places the use of these in a period of up to 65 years straddling the late ninth to early tenth centuries AD. Scientific analyses has characterised the output of these two technologies as similar and raises question over the normal narrative that slag tapping superseded slag pit methods by way of innovation. Iron production here is part of a much wider industry operating across the Blackdown Hills, the context of which is re-evaluated in the light of current evidence, with further chemical analyses demonstrating that multiple ore sources were employed. The metallurgical study and detailed radiocarbon modelling of the Hemyock early medieval smelting operation is presented alongside an exhaustive re-examination of chronology and technology of all comparative sites in Britain, with the Continental framework also reviewed.

The second major component to this work is the detailed analysis of 1.4 tonnes (*c.* 53,000 sherds) of pottery waste, representing a previously unknown kiln site of *c.* AD 1500-1550 and indicating a major new source of pottery for the domestic markets, notably Taunton and Exeter. The assemblage represents the largest individual find of late medieval pottery in Devon and is of great interest in showing on a grand scale the transition from medieval production (mainly jugs with only a few examples of other forms) to the much wider range of vessels typical of the sixteenth century. The assemblage also offers the most important evidence for the manufacture of floor-tiles in Devon, with products of the Hemyock kiln now recognised *in situ* in various churches in Devon and Somerset. An emphasis of the ceramic study was the development of scientific analyses using a combined approach, comparing and contrasting detailed petrological study, examination of chemistry using ICPS, and mineral mapping using the novel QEMSCAN tool.

The evidence for early medieval iron and later medieval pottery production are discussed within their local and regional historical and landscape contexts, and the interplay of these industries with the demand for raw materials on the Blackdown Hills considered.

Chapter 1

Introduction

Chris Smart

This publication presents the results of excavation, in 2008, of an early medieval iron production site and later medieval pottery, at Churchills Farm, Hemyock, a medieval village in the northern part of the Blackdown Hills in Devon. The stratigraphic account is presented in chronological order, though archaeological features and deposits are subsequently discussed by type, and this is followed by the specialist analysis of iron working remains and ceramic technology, as well as associated environmental evidence. A concluding chapter will review the broader landscape setting of these medieval industries, reviewing them each in a local, regional and national context. First, however, an introductory section will familiarise the reader with the location of the site, circumstances of the excavation, and the archaeological and historical background.

Situation and Topography

The village of Hemyock is located in the northwest of the Blackdown Hills in Devon, close to the border with Somerset. The medieval village was founded on the southern side of the River Culm, above a crossing of it, roughly halfway between Dunkeswell (Devon) and Wellington (Somerset). It is one of a network of known medieval settlements that follow the course of the Culm Valley northeast of Cullompton. The larger market towns of Tiverton and Taunton lay 20 km west and 14 km northeast, respectively. The excavation presented here took place on the grounds of Churchills Farm, which lay on the southern edge of Hemyock, adjacent to the High Street, and is now occupied by the modern housing development known as Churchills Rise (Figure 1). The site (SX 1364 1312) is positioned 130 m south of the parish church St Mary's, and 150 m south-southeast of Hemyock Castle which, as the manorial centre, was granted a licence to crenellate with walls of stone and flint in AD 1380.

The site occupies a gentle north-facing slope which extends from 145 m in the north to 150 m above Ordnance Survey datum in the south. Fields of pasture lay to the south and west, the latter delimited by a minor tributary of the River Culm, 160 m west of the site. The area is underlain by Triassic Mercia Mudstone (formerly known as Keuper Marl) and the resultant soils derived from this geology are of the Whimple 3 association, which are described as 'slowly permeable seasonally waterlogged fine loamy and fine silty over clayey soils' (Soil Survey of England and Wales 1983). Based on the inclement weather and resultant site conditions experienced in March and April 2008 this soil description seems quite accurate. In a broader setting, this geological and pedological sequence is part of the wider landscape of Upper Greensand plateaux within which nodular iron ore occurs.

Discovery and Investigation

A staged programme of archaeological investigation and recording was undertaken by the now defunct Exeter Archaeology in 2008 on behalf of Somerfield Homes Ltd, in advance of the construction of 23 houses, with associated access road, parking and garages, at Churchills Farm. The development took place adjacent to the extant farmhouse on ground formerly occupied by farm buildings and concrete yard surfaces. The work was required by Mid Devon District Council, following the advice of Devon County Council Historic Environment Service, as a condition of the grant of planning permission for the development. The planning reference for change of use and construction of Churchills Rise is 07/01005/MFUL.

An initial evaluation exercise was begun in February 2008, comprising the machine excavation of seven 1.8 m-wide trenches, representing five percent of the proposed development area (Figure 2). Whilst most trenches revealed a sequence of little interest – resulting from modern building terraces infilled with recent levelling deposits – two revealed archaeological features, including pits yielding late medieval pottery wasters and concentrations of iron slag. Accordingly, a new mitigation strategy was implemented and a programme of 'strip, map and sample' commenced immediately. The methodology allowed for the monitoring of all groundworks across the development area, but attention was focussed on those parts where heavy truncation was not already evident.

What follows describes the extent of industrial remains eventually recorded at Churchills Farm – and such was the size of the post-excavation task that analysis and the preparation of this publication was funded by Historic England (then English Heritage), to whom the authors are very grateful.

Historical Background

The earliest record for Hemyock is found in Domesday, which indicates that it was perhaps a long-held Crown lordship. Prior to 1066 it was held by Edward the Confessor and remained as part of the Royal estates after 1086. From the tenth century onwards, the importance of the royal manor is indicated by it being the centre for the

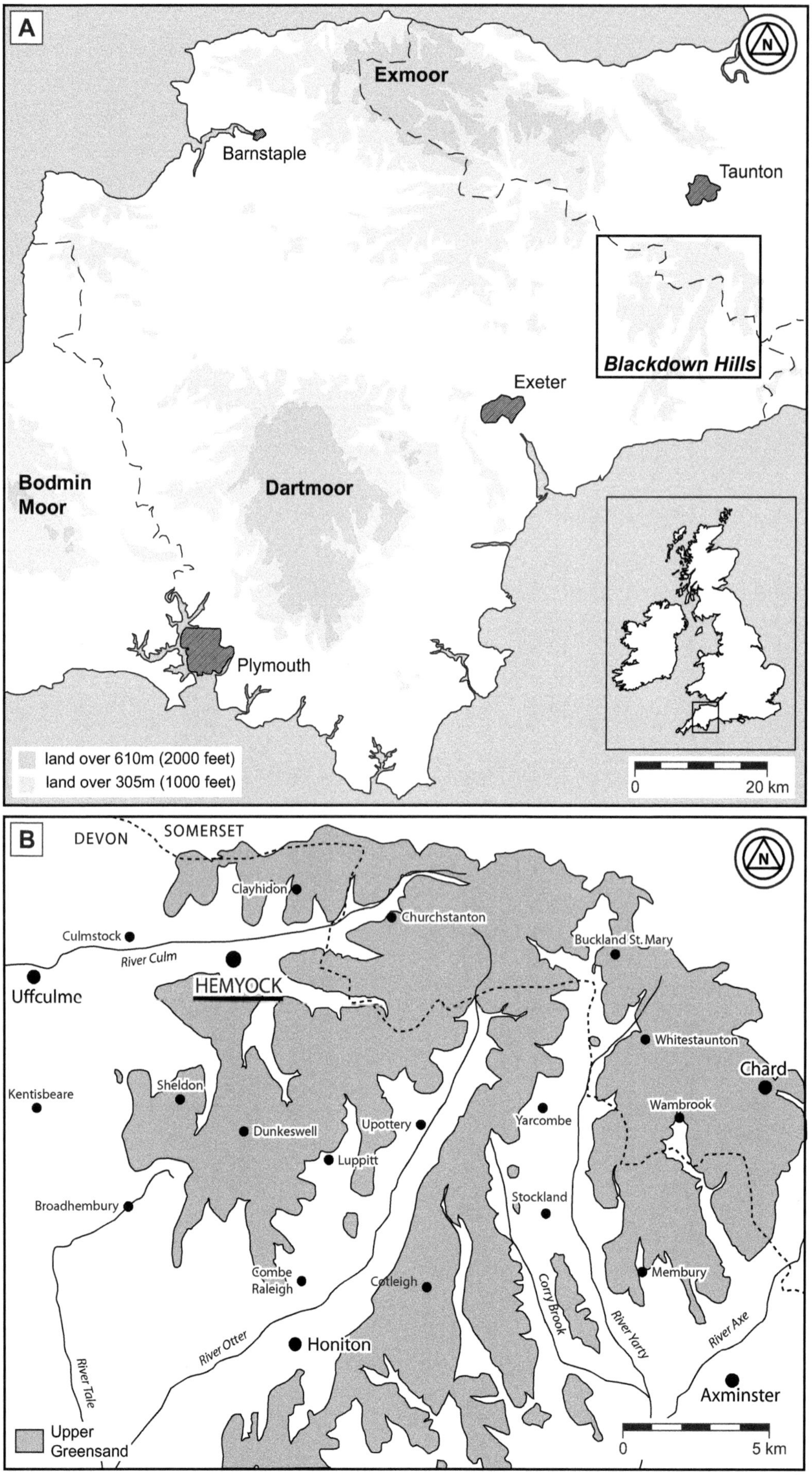

Figure 1. A: General location of the Blackdown Hills in South West England, and B: Location of Hemyock in relation to the settlement, rivers and greensand ridges and plateaux of the Blackdown Hills.

Figure 2. View northeast of the Churchills Farm site following demolition of the agricultural buildings and the machine excavation of archaeological evaluation trenches in 2008.

hundred of Hemyock. Despite earlier Anglo-Saxon land charters for this region being known (Finberg 1953; Hooke 1994), none make reference to Hemyock itself. Nearby, and within the hundred of Hemyock, charters record royal land grants in the adjacent manors of Culmstock and Culm Davy from King Cynewulf in the eighth century, King Egbert in the ninth century, and King Athelstan in the tenth century. Though a too literal reading of this distribution and chronology is unwise, there are perhaps indications that land within Hemyock was deliberately retained within the royal demesne.

At the time of Domesday, Hemyock is recorded as *Hamihoc*, with the next known iteration being *Hamioc* in 1204. The place-name is suggested to be the name of a stream derived from the British *Samiāco*, given to a brook which flowed all year (*samo-*, 'summer', never-dry) (Gover *et al.* 1932, 616).

The earliest available cartographic source for Hemyock is the tithe map of 1843, which shows Churchills Farm and three irregular-shaped fields between the High Street and stream (Figure 3). The First Edition Ordnance Survey map dated 1889 shows little change, though the southern end of the Churchills Farm building range has been extended with an east-west range. A small enclosure was created immediately southwest of these buildings. In the next fifteen years, the Second Edition map dated 1904-5 shows that the Churchills Farm building range was extended further, and a boundary created to divide it from fields to the south. This new boundary linked with the small enclosure and abutted the High Street. Both maps show that the fields immediately south of the farmhouse, covering the area excavated in 2008, were planted as orchard. By the 1960s, when the National Grid First Edition map was published, detached buildings had been built in the farmyard, opposite the farmhouse, and part of the adjacent field annexed for an agricultural building. This, and subsequent developments in the latter part of the twentieth century saw land to the south and southwest of the farmhouse being either built on, terraced, or turned over to hardstanding, and the truncation that occurred was evident during the evaluation phase of the fieldwork, where only two of eight trenches revealed *in situ* remains.

Archaeological Background

Exeter Archaeology's excavations at Churchills Farm in 2008 were not the first in the village, but the discoveries made there have prompted a surge in development-led investigations (Figure 4). The remains of iron production have long been recognised across the Blackdown Hills, since at least the nineteenth century, with an interim summary of the Blackdown Hills Ironworking Project (a Devon County Council/ Exeter Archaeology initiative begun in the 1990s and whose activity tailed off in the same decade) remaining the best summary of the evidence which shall not be repeated at length (Griffith and Weddell 1996). Finds of slag have been made across the region, often by local farmers, with some very significant slag mounds known – one such mound in Hemyock parish was apparently huge – 30 m long, 12 m wide and up to 3 m high – but was levelled in the twentieth century. This mound alone might have contained up to 1000 tonnes of slag, and demonstrates the truly industrial scale of production in the vicinity of the village (Crew 1993). Stuart Blaylock identified slag within the walls of the fourteenth-century Hemyock Castle, which hinted at a date for production of iron here (Blaylock 1989; Griffith and Weddell 1996, 31) but, with the benefit of the work at Churchills Farm, we know that there were pre-Conquest furnaces operating nearby and that it is possible that the slag used in the castle was already of significant antiquity. The present authors

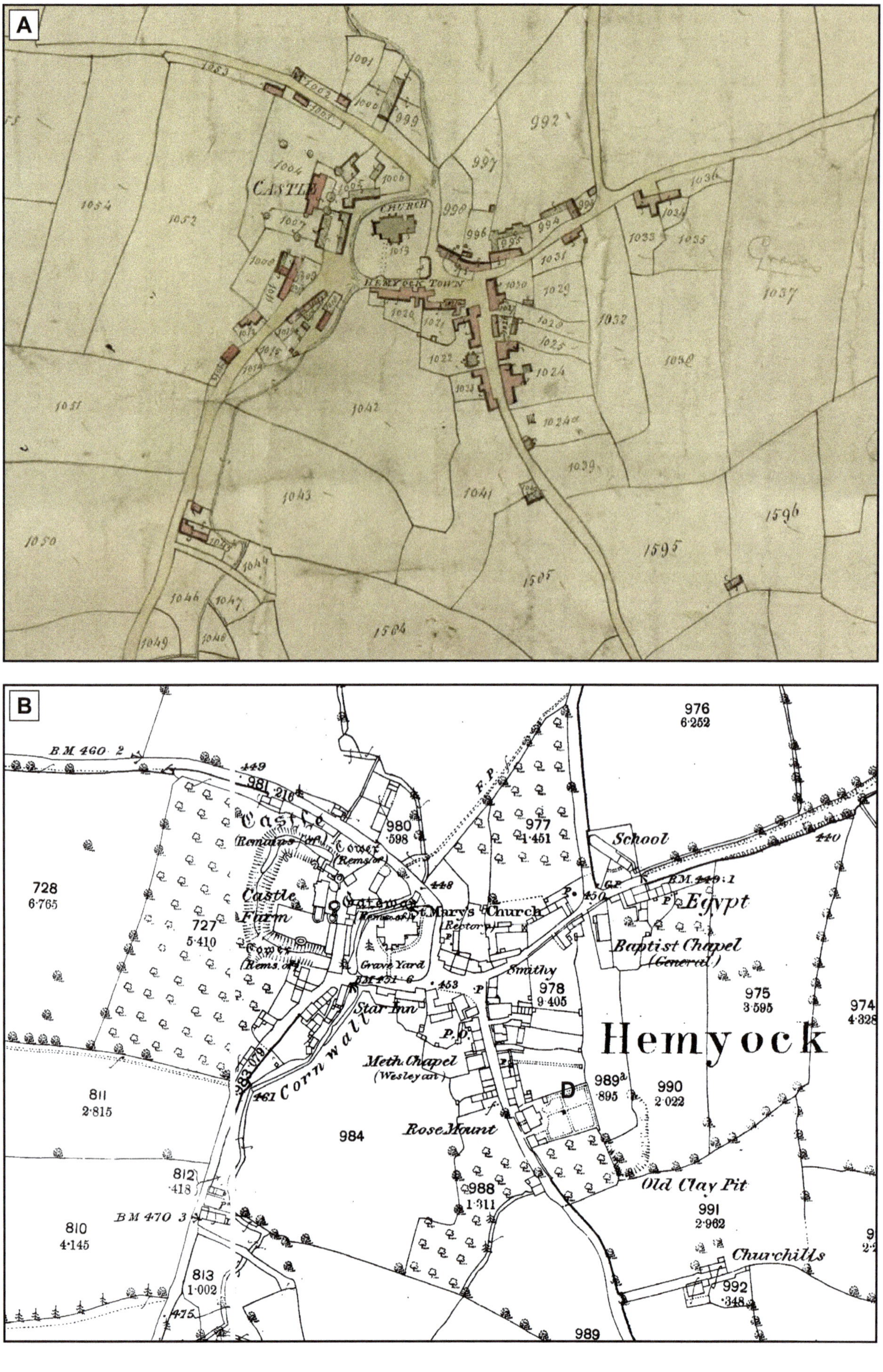

Figure 3 [left]. Historic map sequence of Hemyock village. A: 1843 tithe map; B: 1889 OS First Edition 25 inches to 1 mile (© Crown Copyright and Landmark Information Group Limited (2016). All rights reserved. (1889)).

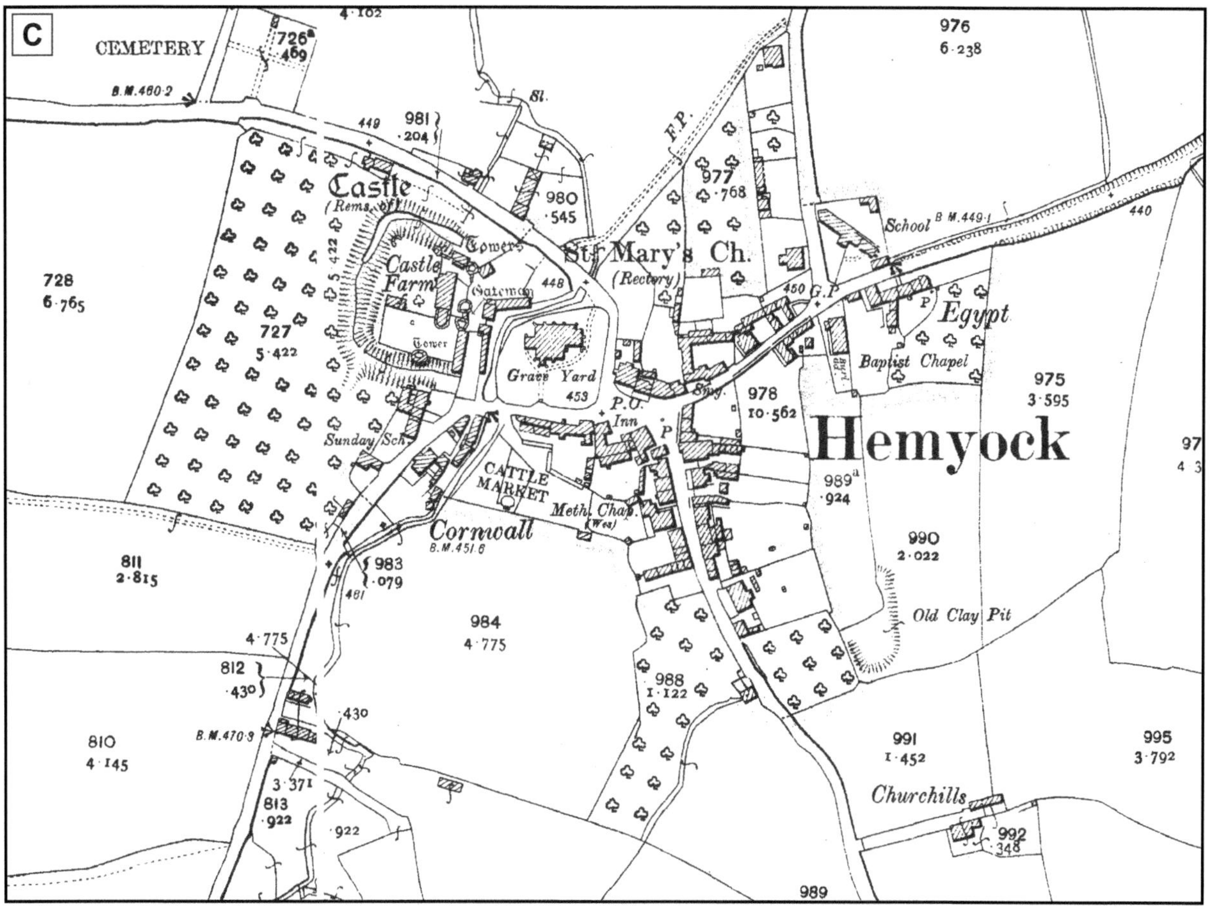

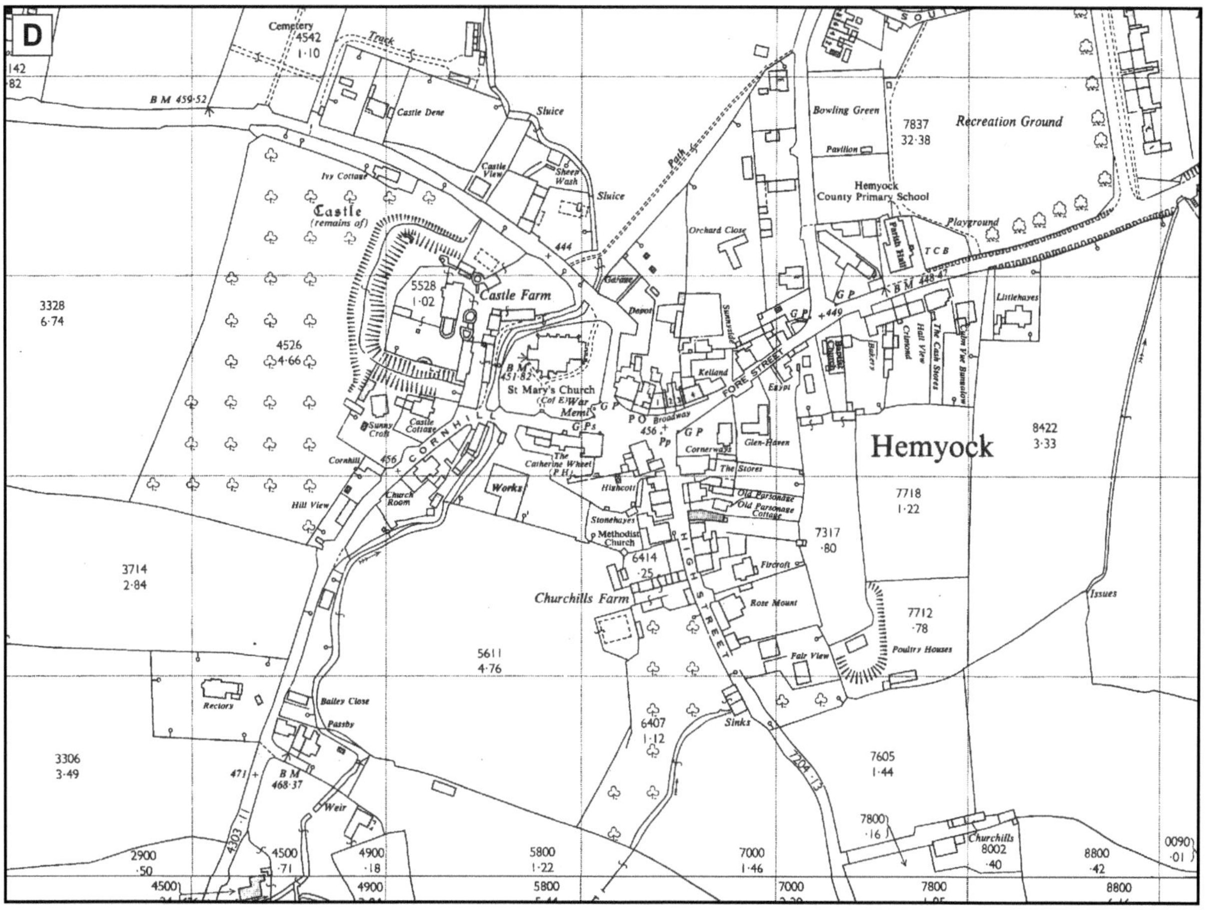

Figure 3 [right]. Historic map sequence of Hemyock village. C: 1904-5 OS First Revision 25 inches to 1 mile; D: 1964 OS First Edition National Grid 1:2500 (© Crown Copyright and Landmark Information Group Limited (2016). All rights reserved. (1904-5; 1964)).

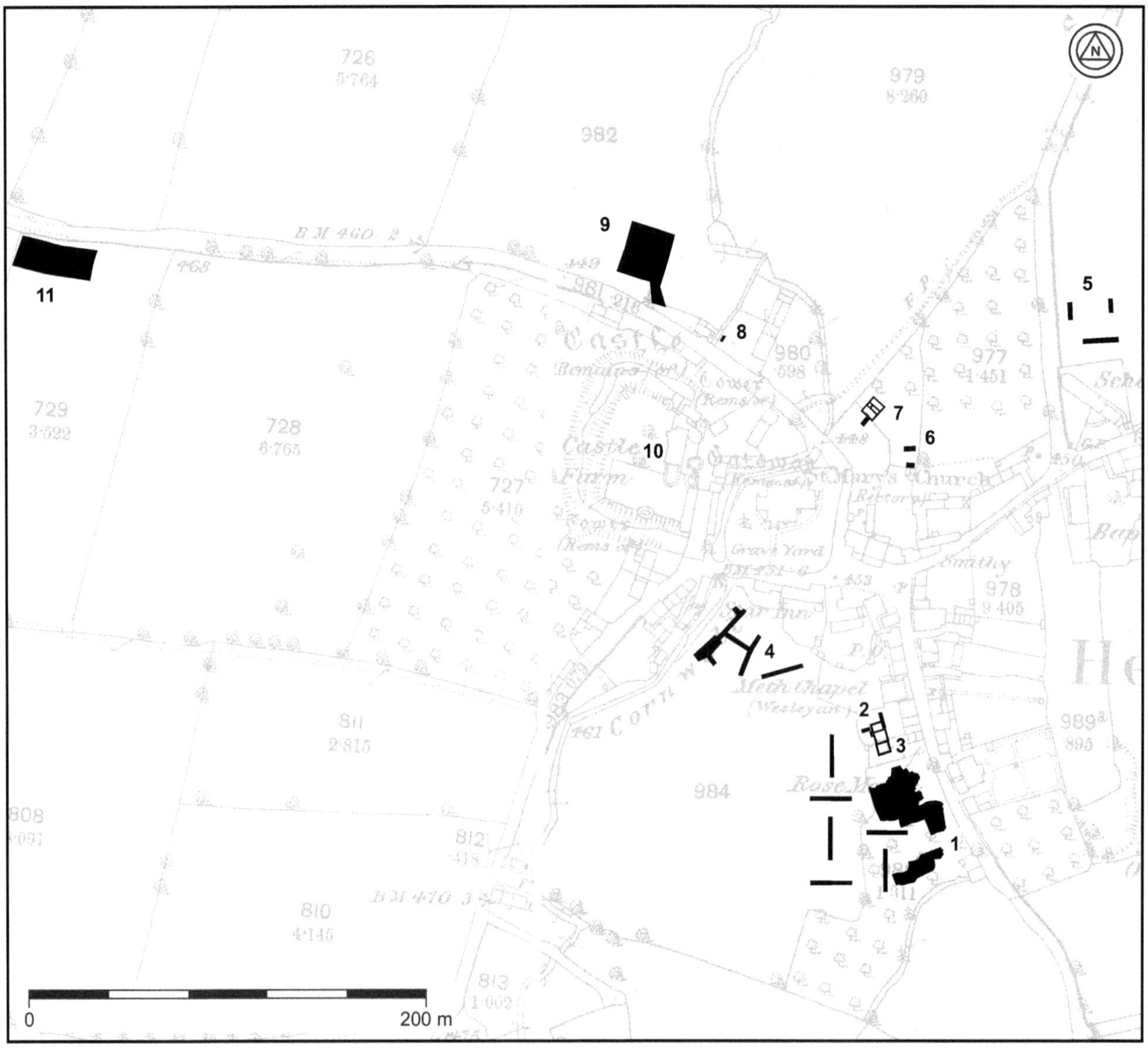

Figure 4. Location of all known archaeological interventions within Hemyock shown against a backdrop of the late nineteenth-century Ordnance Survey First Edition 25 inches to 1 mile mapping (© Crown Copyright and Landmark Information Group Limited (2016). All rights reserved. (1889)).1: Churchills Farm 2008 (this volume); 2: Land to rear of Churchills Farm (Hughes 2009a); 3: 12a Churchills Rise (Clarke 2012); 4: Former Halls Engineering Works (Exeter Archaeology 2005); 5: Old Tennis Courts Site (Hughes 2011); 6: 3 Broadway (Hughes 2009b); 7: Hemyock Motors Workshop (Jones and Hughes 2013); 8: Castle View (Austin 2011); 9: Land east of Castle Dene (Allum 2009; South West Archaeology 2005; Tabor 2010); 10: Hemyock Castle (Blaylock 1989); 11: Culmstock Road (Rainbird and Young 2015).

have also noted similar slag within the Norman tower of St Mary's church.

In October 2004 an archaeological evaluation was undertaken on the site of the former Halls Engineering Works, on the south side of St Mary's and within 50 m of Churchills Farm. It revealed numerous small ditches, some of which contained fragmented iron slag, though dating evidence was scant. In trench 5, a significant spread of industrial waste contained within a shallow depression was cut by three such ditches, suggesting that any major production phase may have predated subsequent land division (Exeter Archaeology 2005). In 2007/8 a programme of archaeological work, culminating in an open area excavation, was undertaken on land east of Castle Dene, to the north of Hemyock Castle alongside Culmstock Road (Allum 2009; South West Archaeology 2005; Tabor 2010), which identified traces of a medieval building oriented parallel with Culmstock Road, with a trackway demarcated by flanking ditches to the rear. The pottery recovered, which is of chert-tempered type and of a broad tenth- to fourteenth-century date, was suggested to indicate occupation later in that chronological range, between the twelfth and fourteenth centuries. The northern part of the site, including the building, was sealed by a dark humic deposit containing iron smelting slag and similar medieval pottery, sealed by a remnant clay bank, the latter of which was interpreted as a means by which Hemyock Castle further imposed itself on the landscape (Tabor 2010, 205). There was no evidence for *in situ* industrial processes.

No further investigations are known of until 2008, with the excavations at Churchills Farm revealing industrial-scale iron and pottery production. Whilst the archaeological remains from this site are only now being published, the discoveries have prompted Devon County Council's Historic Environment Service to attach conditions to most planning applications within the village which, as a result, have provided further archaeological observations on the periphery of the former Churchills Farm (Hughes 2009a; Clarke 2012) and in the centre of the village (3 Broadway: Hughes 2009b; Station Road: Hughes 2011; Castle View, Culmstock Road: Austin 2011; Hemyock Motors: Jones and Hughes 2013), with those at 3 Broadway and Hemyock Motors yielding further finds of iron slag and early post-medieval 'Hemyock' pottery. The most recent work, at Culmstock Road (Rainbird and Young 2015), has provided interesting comparative information with regard to iron production in Hemyock and is discussed at greater length later in this volume. Excavation at the site, located 350 m west of St Mary's church, and so outside of the historic village core, revealed a large denuded slag mound sealing *in situ* remains of slag-pit furnaces and ore roasting pits, with two radiocarbon dates suggesting production in the late eighth century, some 100 years before smelting is known at Churchills Farm.

Chapter 2

Excavation 2008

Chris Smart

Areas of Investigation

Excavation was focussed in four main areas that lay in the footprint of the eastern half of Churchills Farm (Figure 5). First stage evaluative work suggested that much of the western half had been lost during the construction of farm buildings in the mid-twentieth century and as such had low archaeological potential. The conditions under which the excavation was undertaken were not ideal and extremely wet weather caused severe waterlogging across the site. The work was phased in line with the schedule of the developer such that, for instance, by the time that Area B was stripped of overburden and archaeology recorded, a roadway had already been excavated in the adjacent part of Area A. The result of this was that at no time was a complete plan visible to those working on the site.

Area A (Figures 6, 7), which covered 430 m^2 was located on the northern edge of the site, closest to the farmhouse of Churchills Farm. After the removal of a thick overburden comprising recent demolition material it became evident that modern truncation had occurred in a number of places, resulting from the remodelling of the farmyard in the mid-twentieth century. Some small areas were left unexcavated as these coincided with the position of developer's benchmarks.

Area B (Figure 6) adjoined Area A to the south and covered 55 m^2. It was the second area to be stripped and recorded. Whilst it had been used as a store area for overburden removed from Area A it had suffered little obvious truncation.

Area C (Figures 6, 8) was situated in the sout-east of the site and lay adjacent to High Street on the south side of the new entrance splay created for the Churchills Rise development. It covered 158 m^2 and was the last area to be investigated following the removal of site Portacabins.

Area D (Figures 9, 10) was positioned at the southern edge of Churchills Farm, and was bordered by open farmland. It occupied the most elevated part of site and was separated from Area B by a substantial terrace cut that had been excavated in the mid-twentieth century to receive a large barn and yard surface. All archaeology within the footprint of this terrace cut had been lost. In total, Area D covered 176 m^2.

The total area excavated by Exeter Archaeology at Churchills Farm in 2008 was 819 m^2.

Archive

The site archive comprises written and drawn records, and black and white photographic negatives as well as digital survey files and photographs, artefactual, technological and environmental remains. At the time of writing all material is stored in the Department of Archaeology at the University of Exeter. A note should be made, for record, of the disposal of pottery and slag during the final stages of analysis. It had been clear from the fieldwork stage that the total volume of iron slag and pottery / ceramic waste was far in excess of what could reasonably be accessioned into the Royal Albert Memorial Museum and, as such, a proportion of the

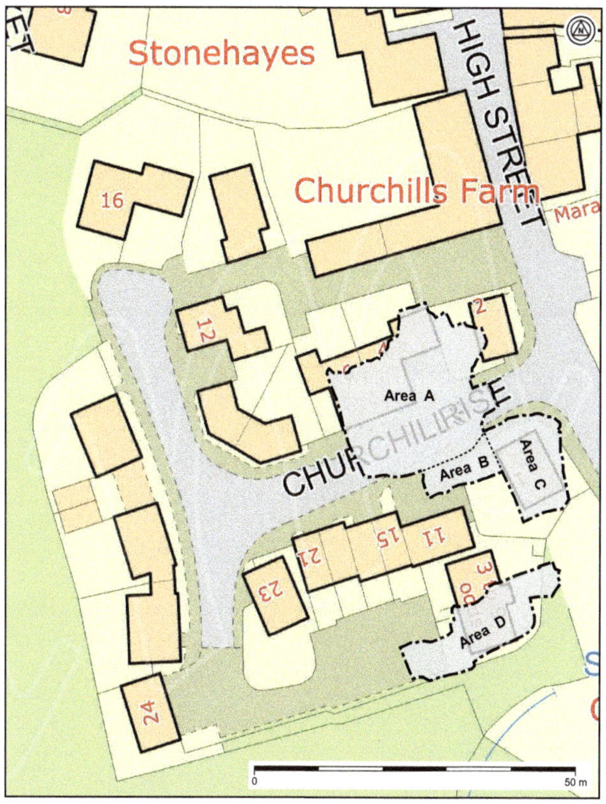

Figure 5. Location of the 2008 Exeter Archaeology excavations at Churchills Farm, Hemyock in relation to the present day housing development at Churchill Rise (© Crown Copyright and Database Right (2016). Ordnance Survey (Digimap Licence)).

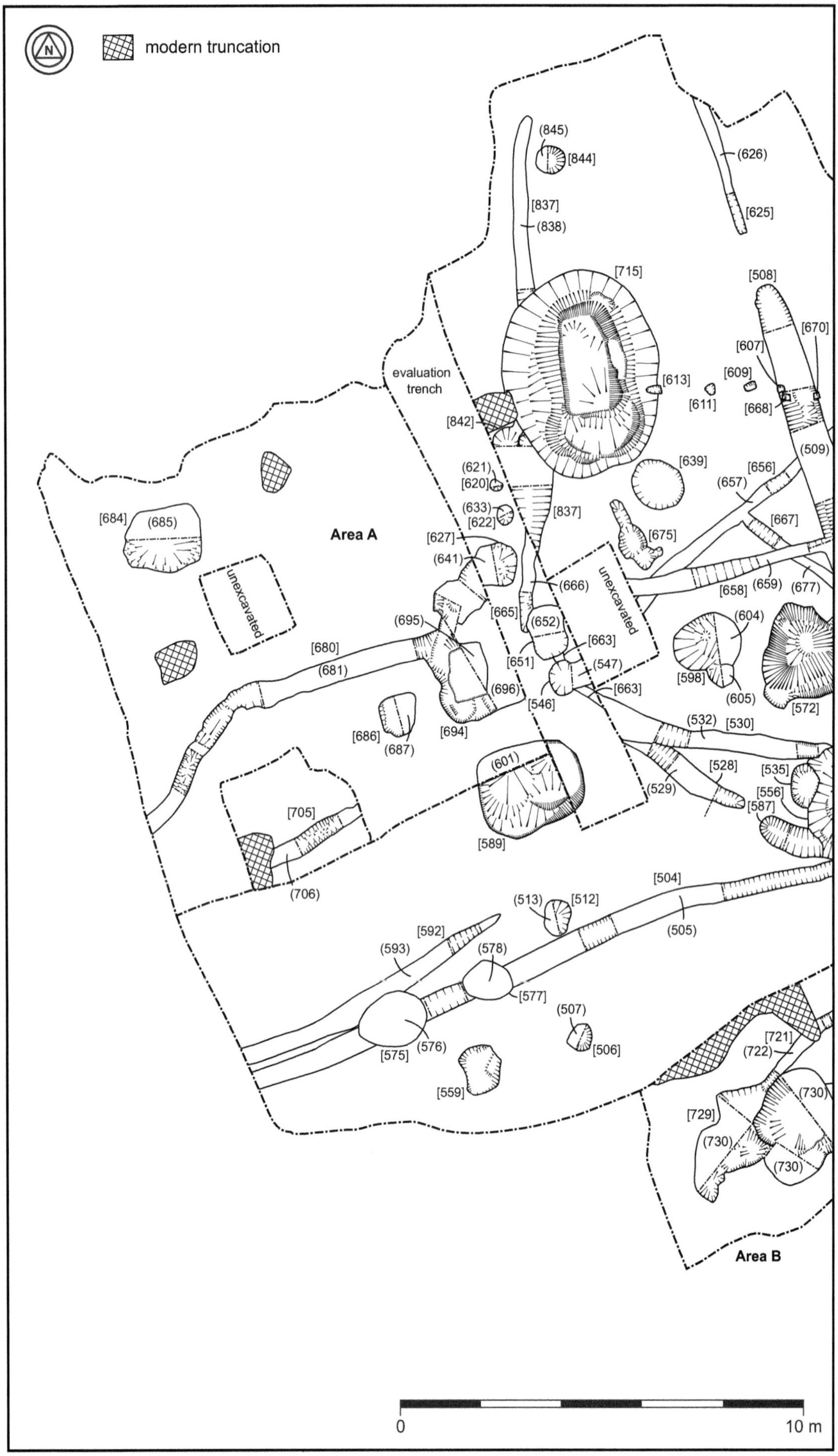

Figure 6 [left]. Plan showing all features excavated and recorded in Areas A, B and C, western half.

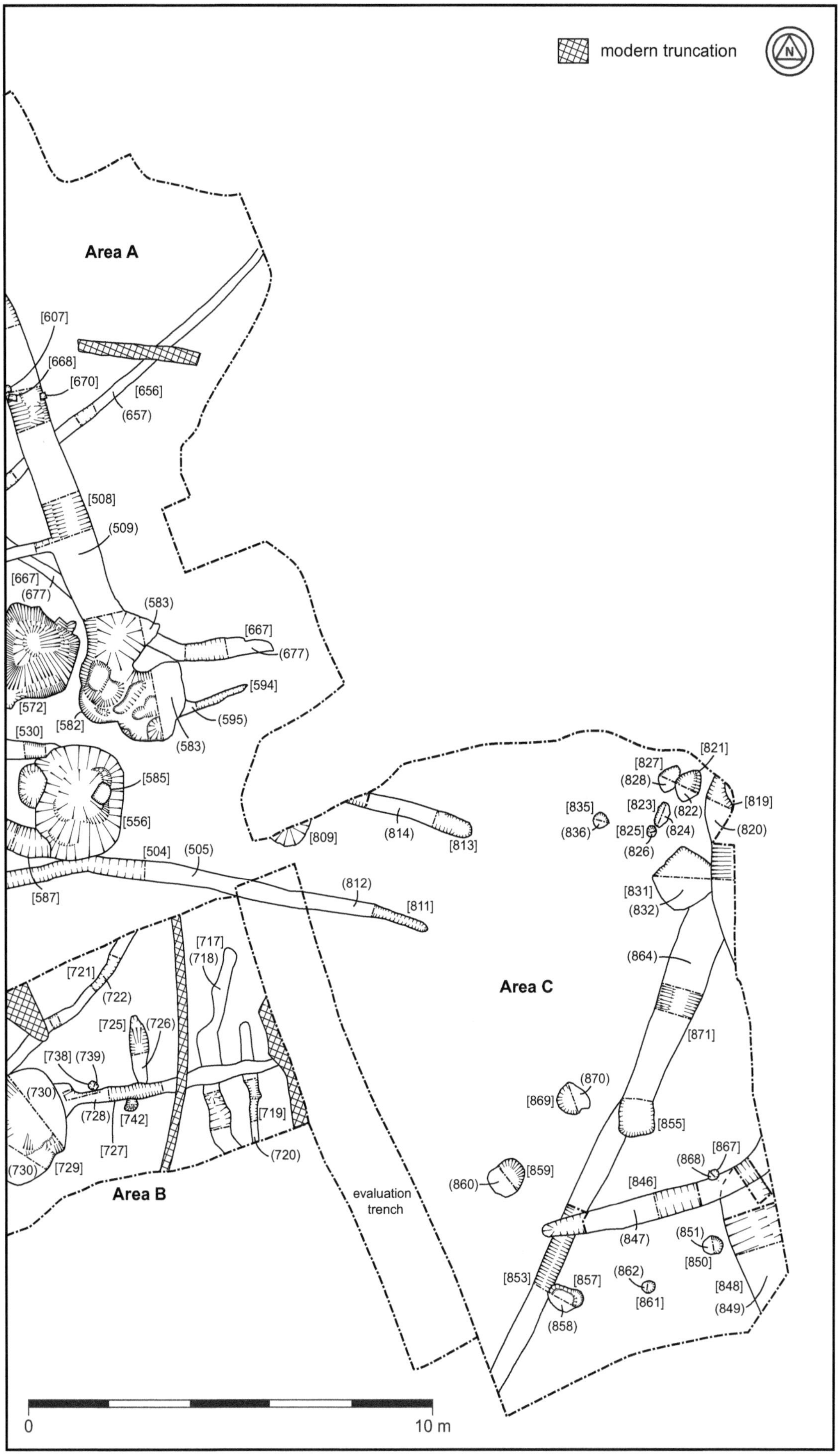

Figure 6 [right]. Plan showing all features excavated and recorded in Areas A, B and C, eastern half.

Figure 7. View looking northwest over Area A during the initial stages of excavation. The darker fills of pits and gullies stands out against the reddish brown clay subsoil.

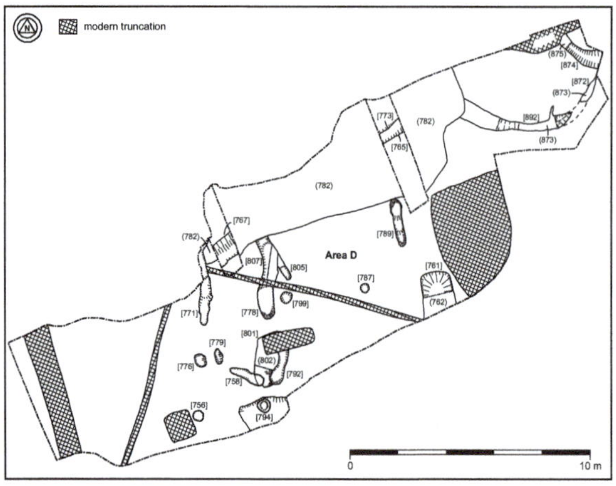

Figure 9. Plan showing all features excavated and recorded in Area D.

Figure 8. View looking east over Area C during the initial stages of excavation. The darker fills of pits and gullies stands out against the reddish brown clay subsoil.

Figure 10. View looking north over Area D during the initial stages of excavation. The darker fills of furnaces stands out against the reddish brown clay subsoil. Note the significant modern terrace cut behind the archaeologist – it is possible that additional furnaces and other features were lost when the farmyard was extended across this area (2m-scales).

material has been disposed of following full quantification and consideration. Undiagnostic iron slag from secondary contexts has, with the exception of a representative sample, been discarded. All iron slag from primary contexts, and that from secondary contexts subjected to scientific analysis, has been retained. The full ceramic assemblage has been quantified and the normal procedure for assessing vessel form and dimensions followed. Subsequently a large proportion of the undiagnostic sherds (of domestic vessels, kiln furniture, tile) was discarded. All sampled material i.e. thin sections have been retained and included within the broader collection held at the RAMM. The detailed digital results of all analysis will be included with the digital archive. The charred plant remains and wood charcoal have been retained in full. At the time of publication the archive is stored in the Department of Archaeology at the University of Exeter: the large volume of the archive presents a significant problem in terms of finding a suitable repository and so discussions over long-term storage are ongoing.

General State of Preservation of Deposits

In areas of the site that had not been previously developed, i.e. where agricultural buildings had not stood, the level of preservation was remarkably good. There were only moderate and localised disturbances within each of the four areas of excavation, with some modern services and stanchion pits for example. The shallow nature of some ditches and gullies recorded on the lower part of the site suggests that historic truncation had occurred, and this is most likely to have been as a result of the expansion of Churchills Farm northwards during the mid-twentieth century. A homogenous deposit of humic soil, containing late fifteenth-century pottery masked features in Areas A, B, and D, implying that no later truncation of underlying stratigraphy had occurred. The historic use of the site as an orchard (as can be seen on Ordnance Survey maps of nineteenth- and early twentieth-century date) is evident by the number of tree hollows and areas of root disturbance that were witnessed in Areas A, B, and C. Whilst these did not preclude the recording of archaeological features, root action had resulted in diffuse edges to some pits and ditches, and the impact in a number of cases was such that the relative stratigraphic sequence of features was indeterminable.

Stratigraphic Record

Ninth/Tenth Centuries

The earliest phase relates to a coherent area of iron production in Area D, dated to the late ninth/early tenth century AD (Figure 9). In terms of village topography, it is worth noting that this industrial activity is located on the very edge of Hemyock rather than in the core. Two technologies were employed for the production of iron at Churchills Farm – slag-pit furnaces and slag-tapping furnaces, analyses of which are presented in Chapter 4. Both types of furnace were recorded in the same area and there was no spatial distinction in where each occurred; the density of features suggests that this activity was confined to a specific area, which implies that other parts of the site were used for different purposes at that time. A magnetic gradiometer survey conducted by the author to the south and west of Churchills Farm identified two possible anomalies consistent with furnaces immediately south of the site, which indicates that iron production was not spread across a much larger area. It is possible that the area of iron production continued to the north of Area D where, in the mid-twentieth century, a barn had been terraced into the hillside removing several metres of ground.

Five slag-pit furnaces were identified (Figure 11). The remains of these comprised modest circular or sub-circular pits with evidence of *in situ* burning, and most retained a basal slag cake.

Furnace 756 had a diameter of 0.45 m and survived to a depth of 0.27 m. It contained a single fill, 757, comprising a matrix of dark grey brown silty clay surrounding a single slag cake that occupied nearly the entire pit.

Furnace 776 had a diameter of 0.4 m and survived to a depth of 0.17 m. It contained a single fill, 777, comprising a matrix of dark grey silty clay that contained several

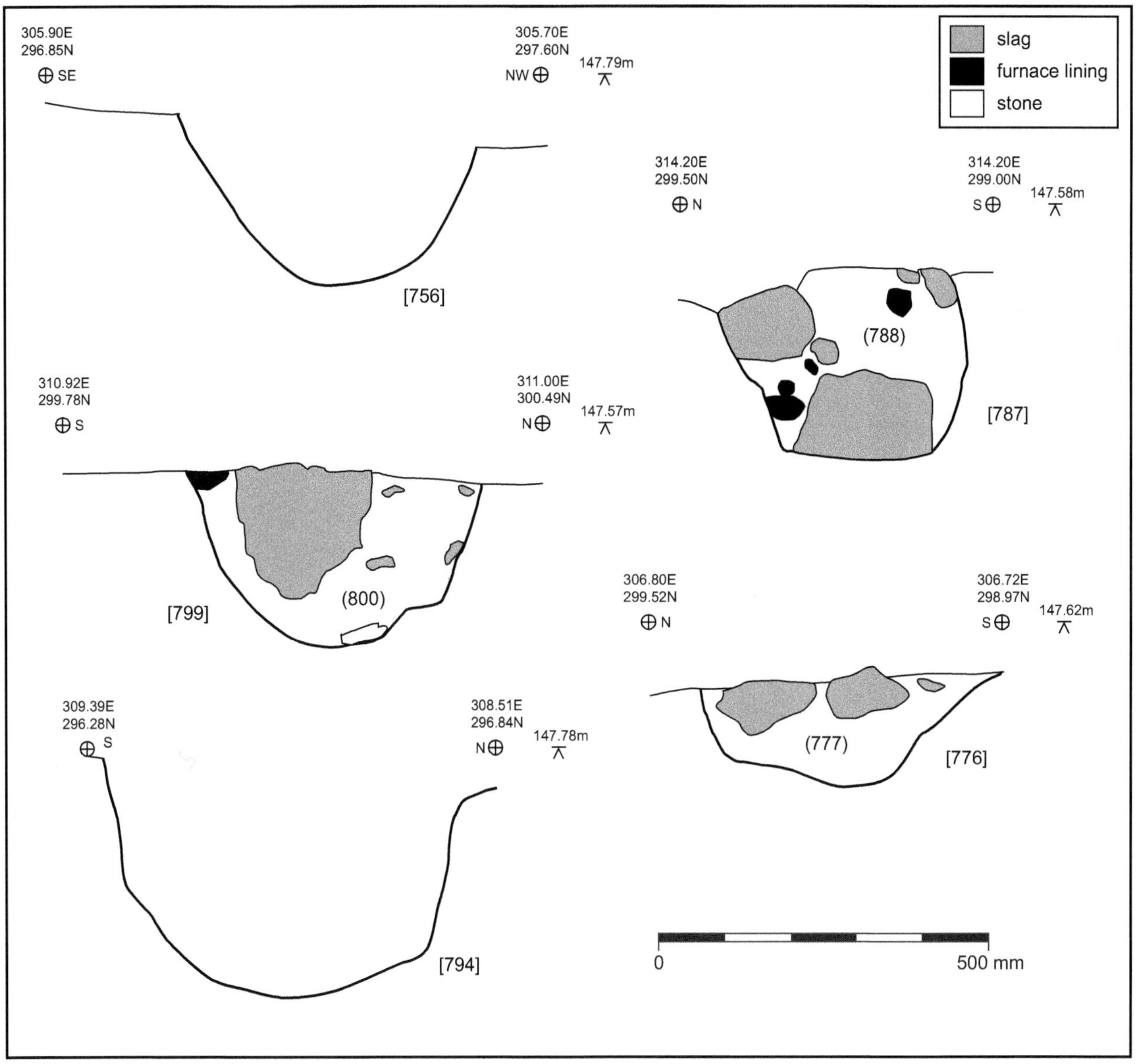

Figure 11. Section drawings of ninth/tenth-century slag-pit iron smelting furnaces excavated in Area D.

Figure 12. Photograph of west-facing section through slag-pit furnace 787 (0.25 m-scale).

Figure 13. Photograph showing slag-pit furnace 799 prior to excavation (south to top; 0.25 m-scale).

large fragments of slag and fragments of fired clay, which presumably derived from the furnace wall.

Furnace 787 had a diameter of 0.4 m and survived to a depth of 0.34 m (Figure 12). It contained a single fill, 788, comprising a matrix of dark grey brown silty clay, with patches of orange and yellow brown hue, and containing an *in situ* slag cake and quantities of fired clay furnace lining. It might be significant that beneath the slag cake was a thin ashy deposit over smaller fragments of slag, which might imply that this furnace was reused.

Furnace 794 had a diameter of 0.65 m and survived to a depth of 0.35 m. In plan, it was the largest of the slag-pit furnaces recorded at Churchills Farm. It contained a single fill, 795, comprising a matrix of dark grey silty clay that contained an abundance of iron slag and fired clay furnace lining. This furnace was recorded on the southern edge of Area D and had been established in a hollow, 801, and was sealed by an infill of that hollow, 796, comprising dark brownish grey silty clay with fragments of charcoal, furnace lining and slag. It is possible that this hollow was localised, or it may represent the northern edge of a larger area levelled into the rising ground, which extended beyond the excavation.

Furnace 799 had a diameter of 0.49 m and survived to a depth of 0.25 m (Figure 13). It contained a single fill, 800, comprising a dark brownish grey silty clay matrix mixed with charcoal, small fragments of slag and furnace lining. The furnace retained an *in situ* slag cake.

Four slag-tapping furnaces were identified (Figure 14). The remains of these comprised elongated channels with evidence of *in situ* burning at the upslope end, and most contained flow slags.

Furnace 758 was represented by a tapping channel with a pit at the south-east end. It measured 1.45 m long and had a maximum width of 0.4 m. The pit at the head of the furnace was 0.31 m deep with the tapping channel 0.1 m deep for most of its length. It contained a single fill of black silty clay, with patches of degraded furnace lining, 759. It contained a collection of tapslag, some of which appeared to be *in situ*.

Furnace 771 was represented by an elongated slag tapping channel, 3.17 m long, up to 0.4 m wide, and surviving to a depth of 0.2 m (Figures 15, 16). The northern end of the channel had been truncated by modern terracing between Areas B and D and therefore its original length is unknown. The base of the channel was flat, and had gently-sloping sides. There was evidence of heating along the channel and this was more pronounced at the southern end where the shaft of the furnace would have been located. The channel contained a single fill, 772, comprising a matrix of dark grey brown clay silt within which were pieces of flow slag. The runnels present on the surface of the slag were oriented with the downslope direction of the channel and were therefore considered to be *in situ* following the final operation of the furnace. It is interesting that the greatest concentration of charcoal within fill 772 was present at the southern end (upslope), which might suggest that much of the unspent fuel and packing material remained at the base of the furnace following tapping. The fill also yielded more and larger pieces of furnace lining at this end, which would be consistent with the location of the furnace shaft.

Furnace 789 was represented by an elongated tapping channel, 1.9 m long, 0.48 m wide and surviving to a depth of 0.19 m (Figure 17). As with the other tapping channels, the feature utilised the natural topography and sloped down to the north. The upslope southern end had been subject to intense heating, as evidenced by baking of the natural clay and cracking of stone within. The channel contained three fills, which each might represent a phase of material drawn out from the furnace base. The primary fill, 797, comprised black silty clay with charcoal and occasional pieces of slag. This fill had accumulated at the head of the channel, where

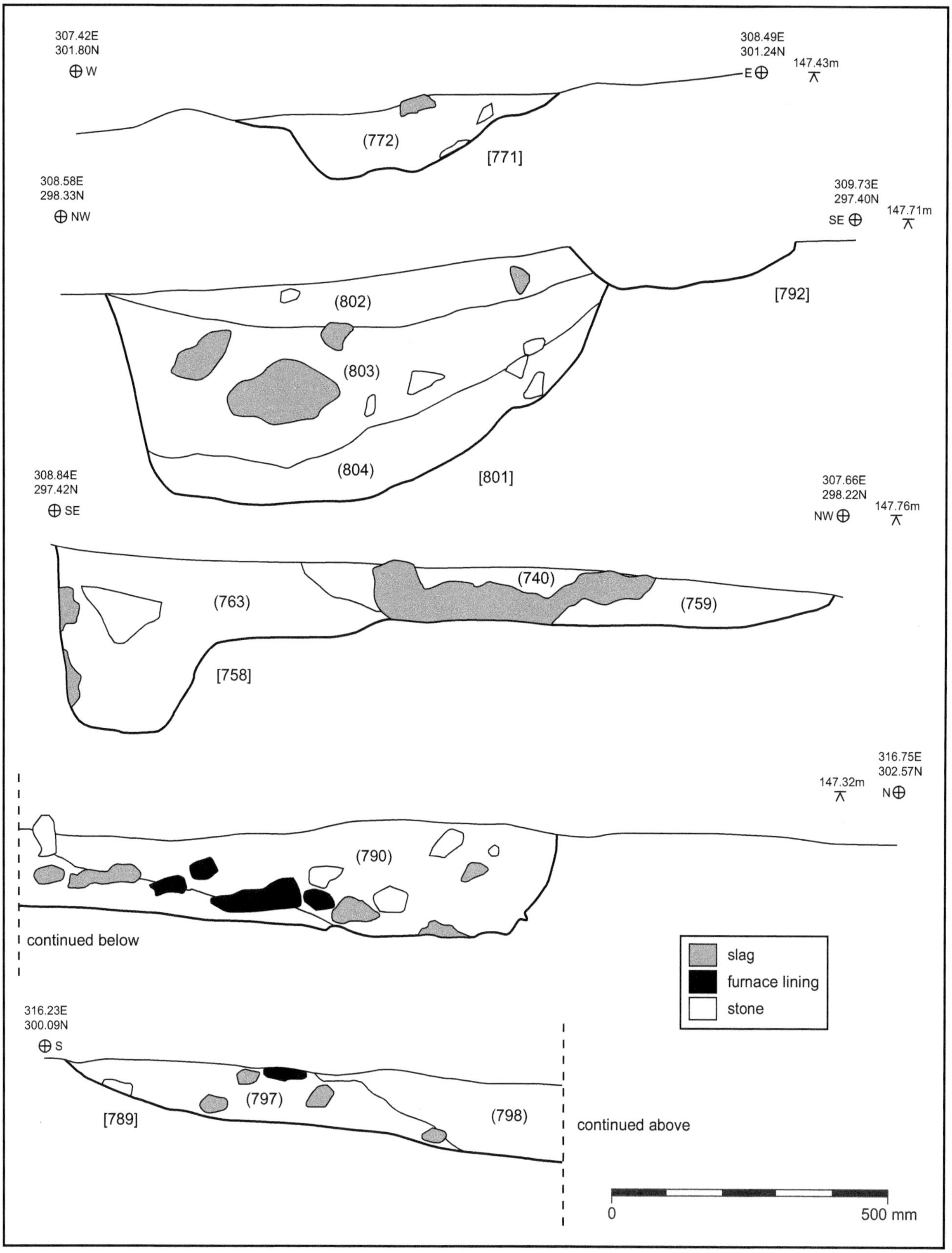

Figure 14. Section drawings of ninth/tenth-century slag-tapping iron smelting furnaces excavated in Area D.

the furnace shaft would have been. The secondary fill, 798, comprised a compact deposit of brown clay silt with a considerable amount of fired clay furnace lining and pieces of tapslag. This deposit is likely to represent the primary rake-out of the furnace. The formation of the tertiary fill, 790, is less certain. It comprised very dark greyish brown silty clay with some charcoal and slag fragments, but as it was later covered by a large area of terrace fill (782), there is a possibility that some of the material might derive from that later deposit.

Figure 15. Photograph showing slag-tapping furnace 771 in plan. Note that the flow direction of slag within the channel is towards the right of the image (south to top; 0.25 m-scale).

Figure 16. Photograph showing slag-tapping furnace 771 in plan. Note that the flow direction of slag within the channel is towards the right of the image (west to top; 1 m-scale).

Figure 17. Photograph showing half-section of slag-tapping furnace 789 (south to top; 0.25 m-scale).

Furnace 792 was represented by an elongated tapping channel, 1.5 m long, 0.4 m wide, and surviving to a depth of 0.13 m. The channel was oriented north-south with the wider end upslope, and it is as this end that the furnace shaft was located. The channel contained a single fill, 793, comprising a dark grey silty clay matrix surrounding *in situ* tapping slag, which had runnels flowing downslope. At the upper end of the channel were large fragments of 'spongy' slag which will have formed within the shaft of the furnace.

Three features in Area D might represent traces of additional furnaces but these were heavily disturbed and had no obvious *in situ* material (Figure 18). Channel 805 was 1.2 m long, 0.32 m wide, and survived to a depth of 0.18 m. The channel was oriented north-south and was broadly bowl-shaped at the southern uphill end. It contained a single fill, 806, which comprised dark grey silty clay, abundant with charcoal but with only small quantities of slag and fired clay furnace lining. None of the slag appeared to be *in situ* which suggests that the fill might represent backfilling of the open channel rather than a deposit formed through raking out of the furnace shaft. This channel had been cut by a second (807).

Channel 807 was 1.9 m long, 0.42 m wide, and survived to a depth of 0.27 m. The channel was oriented northwest-southeast and had been cut by possible slag-pit furnace 778 at its southern end. It contained a single fill, 808, comprising black silty clay which contained slag and furnace lining. Some of the slag pieces were large, occupying nearly the full width of the channel. Possible slag-pit furnace 778 was unusual in form and might not have served this function. As discussed in Chapter 4 the assemblage from this feature was solely of slag-pit residues. It measured 1.25 m by 0.65 m and survived to a depth of 0.41 m and had a single black silty clay fill (781).

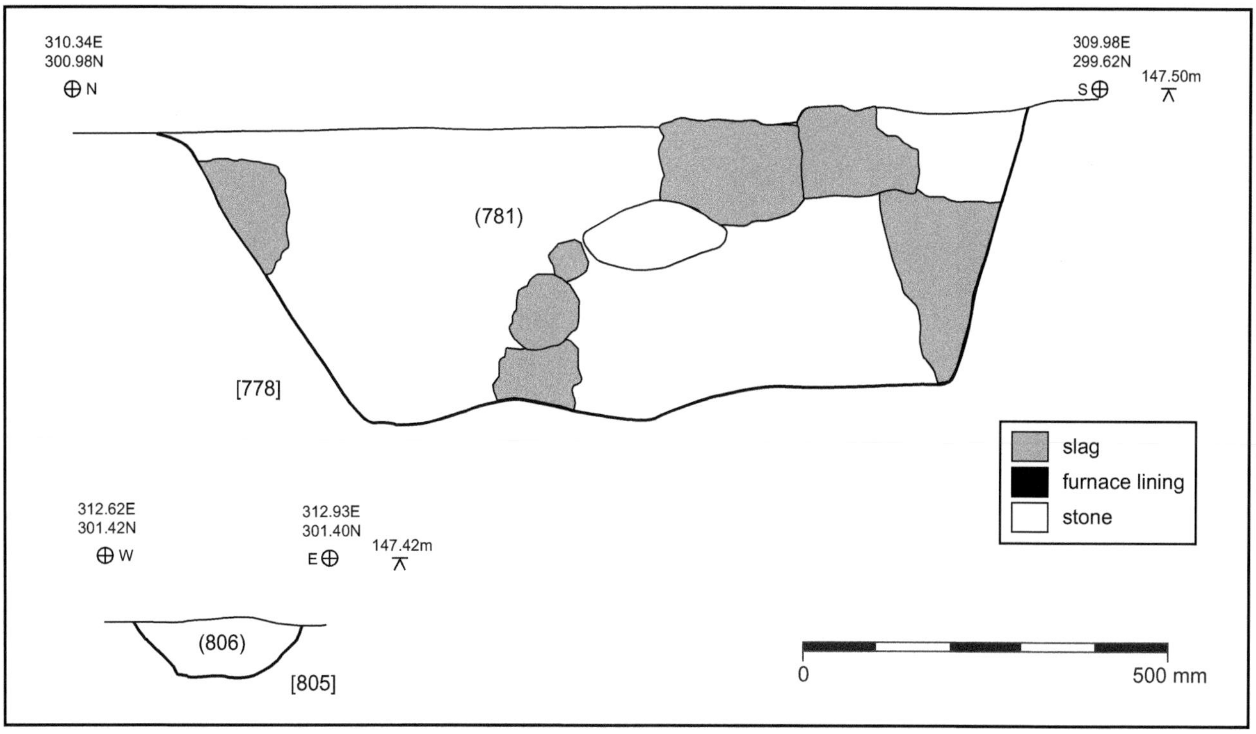

Figure 18. Section drawings of 'possible' ninth/tenth-century iron smelting furnaces excavated in Area D.

Tenth to Twelfth Centuries

Area A

Pits

A series of pits were recorded across Area A (Figure 19). We cannot be fully certain of the function of the pits – some might have simply been dug for the disposal of domestic refuse (though relatively low quantities of 'household' material were recovered from these contexts) – but given the underlying clay deposits targeted for potting clay in later centuries it might be reasonably argued that they were clay extraction pits. Features of this phase have been dated on the basis of Upper Greensand-Derived pottery from within their fills, dated broadly to between the tenth and thirteenth centuries AD. However, and as described by Peter Marshall *et al.* in Chapter 3, radiocarbon dating of charred material from pit 556 suggests that this ceramic was in use by *c.* 900-930 AD, and opens the possibility that other features containing the same ceramics were broadly contemporary.

Pit 556 was the largest that could be confidently ascribed to this phase. It was sub-square in plan and measured 2.72 m by 2.15 m across with a surviving depth of 0.85 m (Figure 20). The pit had irregular but steep sides and a flat base. There was no evidence of silting in the base of this feature and the two fills contained within it were consistent with deliberate backfilling and consolidation; the pit was not open for any length of time. The primary fill (558) comprised 0.35 m of dark grey silty clay that yielded small pieces of chert and iron smelting slag, as well as seven sherds (72 g) of Upper Greensand-Derived pottery. The tertiary fill (557), which comprised the majority of the pit's infill, had a similar matrix but contained significant quantities of iron smelting slag – 643 kilograms – as well as large pieces of angular chert. Also recovered were 61 sherds (616 g) of Upper Greensand-Derived pottery; two sherds (28 g) of fifteenth-century pottery from the surface of this fill were deemed intrusive. The context of this feature, if a clay extraction pit, deserves consideration. It is extremely likely, given the radiocarbon date for this feature and that the tertiary fill was dense with slag, that this and similar pits were contemporary with production of iron in the late ninth/early tenth century. In this regard we can anticipate the extraction of clay to form the superstructure of the furnace shaft and so it is plausible that these pits supplied the necessary material.

The western edge of pit 556 cut pit 535, which was significantly smaller. It measured 1.10 m by >0.68 m across and survived to a depth of 0.3 m (Figure 21). It was ovoid in plan, had a rounded profile, and contained two fills. The primary fill (537) comprised 0.15 m of brown silty clay matrix containing small amounts of angular chert and 2.7 kg of iron smelting slag. The tertiary fill (536) of dark grey silty clay was of equivalent thickness but included some large pieces of iron slag and two sherds (4 g) of Upper Greensand-Derived pottery. It is worth remarking that neither pit 556 or 535 showed any indication of *in situ* heating and they did not have a primary industrial function.

One metre north of pit 556 was another of similar proportions that belongs to this phase of activity. Pit 572

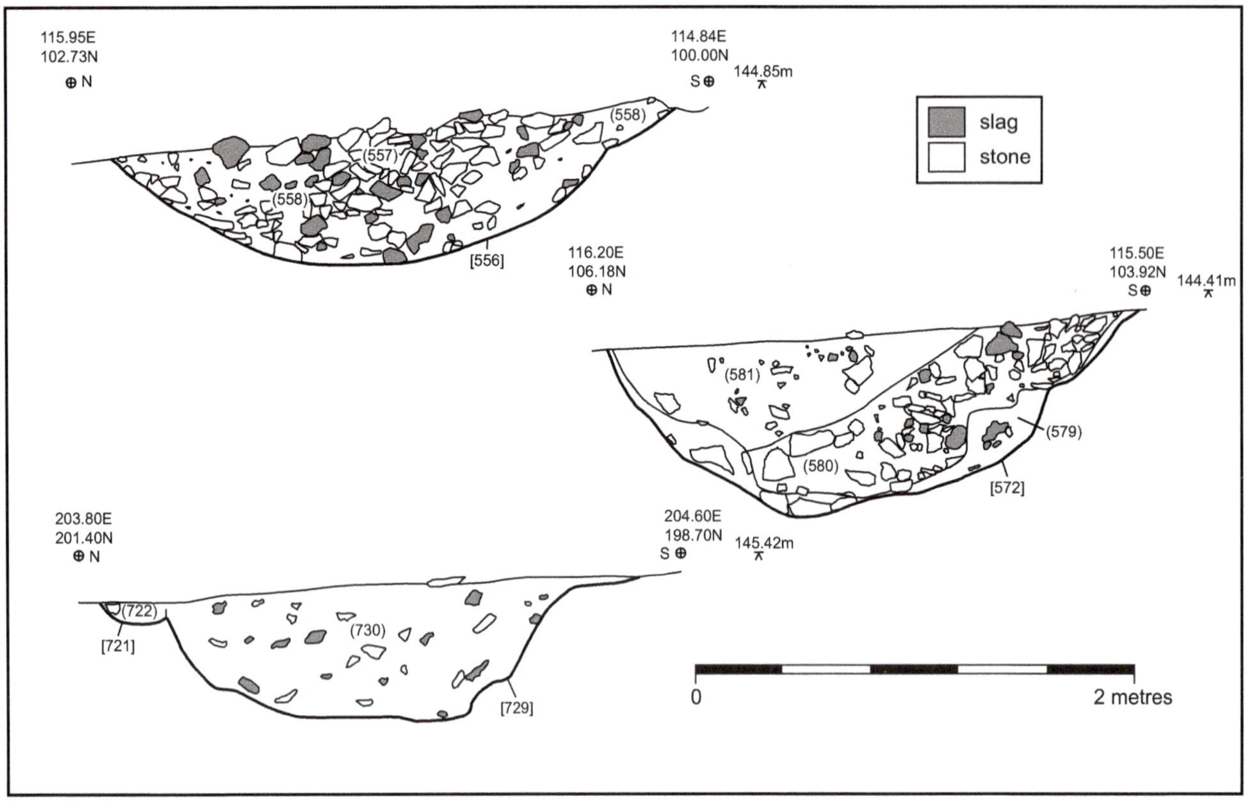

Figure 19. Section drawings of tenth- to twelfth-century pits excavated in Areas A and B.

Figure 20. Photograph showing a west-facing section of pit 556 (1 m- and 0.25 m-scales).

Figure 21. Photograph showing a west-facing section of pit 535 (0.25 m-scale).

was also sub-square in plan and measured 2.4 m by 2.2 m across with a surviving depth of 0.8 m. Again, there was no trace of gradual sediment accumulation at the bottom of this feature and so it is assumed that infilling occurred soon after its excavation. Three deposits were present within pit 572; primary fill 579, secondary fill 580, and tertiary fill 581. Fill 579 comprised up to 0.25 m of reddish brown silty clay matrix which contained large chert pieces and a moderate quantity of iron smelting slag. Fill 580 represented a second dump of material within pit 572 and comprised up to 0.5 m of dark grey brown silty clay matrix which, like the primary fill, also contained chert and iron smelting slag. Both fills yielded Upper Greensand-Derived pottery (six sherds, 54 g and eight sherds, 96 g, respectively), suggesting excavation of the pit and deliberate backfilling. The upper fill, 581, comprised up to 0.48 m of a dark grey brown silty matrix with only occasional pieces of chert and sparse iron smelting slag, and seemed more likely to derive from gradual in-wash of surrounding material. This fill also yielded a typologically later form of Upper Greensand-Derived pottery, which dates from the eleventh/twelfth centuries, indicating a later date for the deposition of this fill. Should this pit have remained partly open between the tenth and twelfth centuries, this might indicate a hiatus in activity in the immediate area at this time. A small elongated pit, 675, contained two sherds of Upper

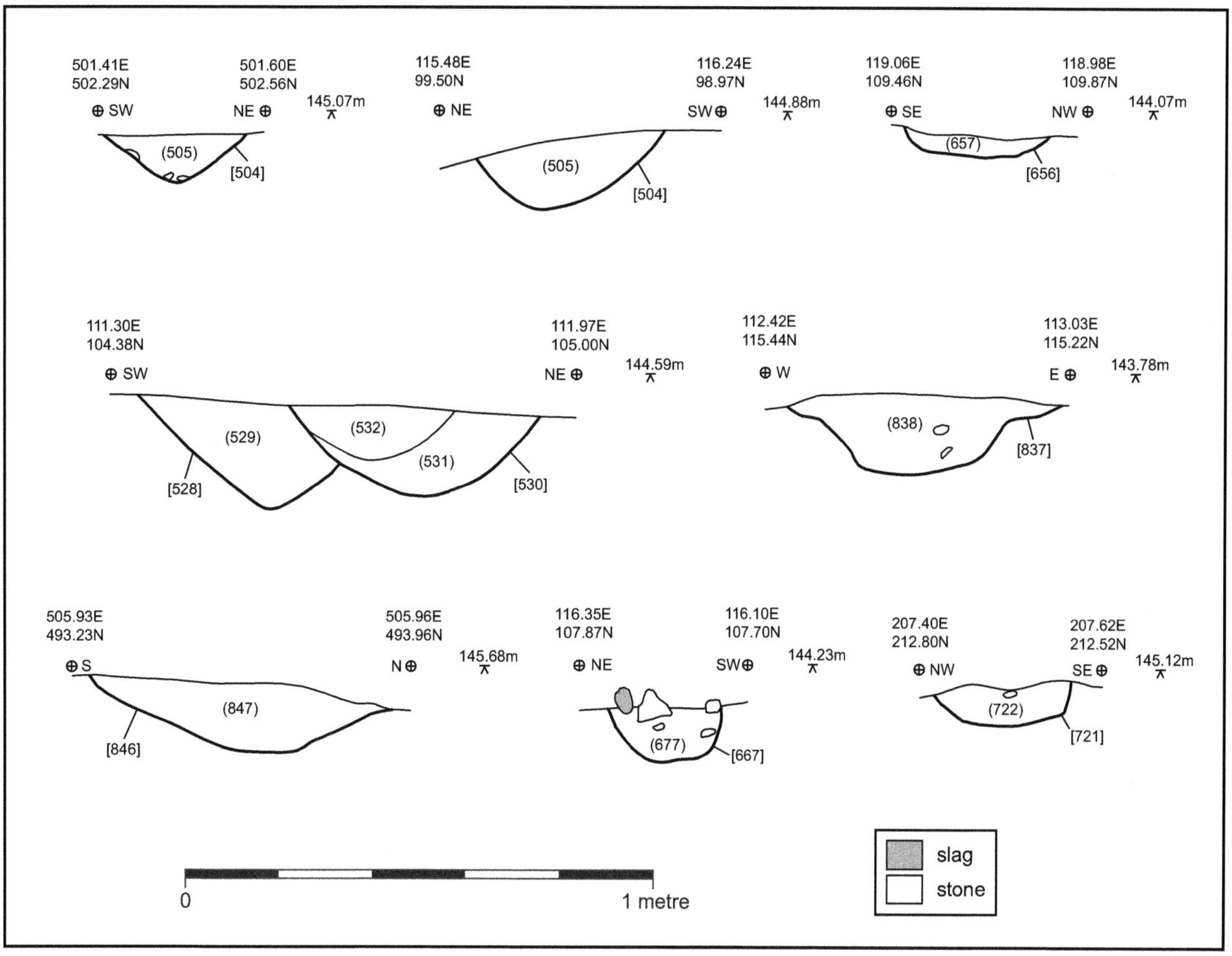

Figure 22. Section drawings of tenth- to twelfth-century gullies and ditches excavated in Areas A, B, C and D.

Greensand-Derived pottery and iron smelting slag was recorded north-west of pit 572. It was 2 m long, 0.68 m wide and 0.31 m deep, and contained a dark grey fill of silty clay flecked with charcoal, 676. Whilst initially regarded as a potential slag-pit furnace the character of the slags and the lack of *in situ* heating necessitated reinterpretation as a claypit backfilled with metallurgical waste.

Gullies

A network of gullies in Area A might have served as drains rather than boundaries (Figure 22). Perhaps the earliest linear features recorded at Churchills Farm are gullies 656, 667, 528 and 587, which are interpreted as land drains. Gully 656 was oriented east-northeast to south-southwest. It measured up to 0.33 m across and 0.14 m in depth. It contained a fill, 657, of dark blackish brown silty clay with an abundance of stone and iron slag. It yielded no dating evidence but was cut by ditch 508 and associated gully, 658. Gully 667 was oriented northwest-southeast and fed into gully 656 at its northwest end (Figure 23). It measured 0.3 m across and 0.12 m in depth and contained a dark brown silty clay fill, 677, which yielded a single sherd of Upper Greensand-Derived pottery. Gully 528 was oriented northwest-southeast and measured 0.51 m across and was 0.21 m deep. It contained a single fill of dark grey silty clay, 529, which had an abundance of slag within but no dating evidence. It ran parallel to gully 677 and appears to represent a continuation of gully 587. Gully 587 was on the same orientation as 528 and measured 0.7 m across and 0.27 m deep. It was only observed for a short distance as it had been truncated by the digging of pit 556. The fill (586) of gully 587 comprised dark grey silty clay which contained iron slag and two sherds of Upper Greensand-Derived pottery.

Gully 504 ran broadly east-west and was observed over a distance of about 23 m. It measured up to 0.4 m across and 0.16 m deep and contained a single fill of brown grey silty clay, (505) (Figure 24). Sample sections across this feature yielded eight sherds of Upper Greensand-Derived pottery and four sherds of later ‘Hemyock’ ware, which was considered to be intrusive.

A series of gullies and ditches had no dating evidence but, because of the stratigraphic relationships, their content of iron slag, and the fact they did not yield the abundant late medieval pottery, they are believed to belong to this phase. Gully 837 had a north-northeast to south-south west orientation and measured up to 0.3 m across and 0.17 m in depth. It contained two fills: a dark grey silty clay basal fill, 841, which showed oxidisation and was waterlogged, and

Figure 23. View southeast of gully 667 prior to excavation (1 m-scale).

Figure 24. View southeast of ditch 504 after removal of all fill (1 m- and 0.25 m-scales).

a dark greyish brown silty clay loam upper fill, 838, which contained small amounts of iron tap slag. This gully was also exposed at a lower level in evaluation trench 1, where it appeared to have been truncated during machining. No pottery or alternative dating evidence was found but the gully was cut by (i.e. it predated), later medieval pits 715 and 651. Gully 530 appears to form a continuation of gully 837 but turning ninety degrees in a southeast direction. The gully, which measured 0.6 m across and 0.17 m in depth, contained two fills: a dark grey silty clay basal fill, 531, and a lighter grey upper fill of similar texture, 532. Both fills contained chert, which would have provided a good drainage medium. The southeast end of gully 530 was cut by pit 556, which gives a date of origin in the early tenth century or before. The function of these gullies is not clear. It is possible that these formed part of a boundary enclosing a small rectilinear field. An alternative is that these gullies, like others recorded, served as land drains.

Area B

Pits

A single pit of this phase was revealed in Area B. Pit 729 measured 2.6 m by 2 m across and survived to a depth of 0.6 m (Figure 19). It was sub-circular in plan and had steep but irregular sides; the edges of the pit had been affected by extensive root action and the irregular hollows of a tree throw could be seen all around. The pit contained two fills. The basal fill, 731, comprised a thin lens of yellowish grey clay with flecks of charcoal throughout that might represent initial in-wash into the pit. The tertiary fill (730) was homogenous and represented the main infilling of the feature. It comprised a dark grey silty clay matrix containing an abundance of iron smelting slag and pieces of angular chert. A one metre-wide sondage cut across the pit, perhaps representing a *c.* 40 percent sample of the fill, yielded 322 kg of slag. The total amount of slag within the pit might be estimated to be about 800 kg. The fill also yielded ten sherds (196 g) of Upper Greensand-Derived pottery. The pit showed no signs of *in situ* heating and did not serve a primary industrial function; it is likely the pit was dug for the extraction of clay and then backfilled with available waste.

Gullies

Gully 721 was oriented northeast-southwest and probably once joined with the network of gullies in Area A. It measured 0.30 m across and was 0.13 m deep, and contained a fill of dark brown silty clay, 722, which yielded fragments of iron slag and a sherd of Upper Greensand-Derived pottery. It had been cut by pit 729.

Area C

Ditches

Investigation of Area C revealed three ditches of this phase. Ditch 819 ran parallel with the adjacent extant hedgebank for a short distance on the eastern edge of the site. It was exposed over a length of 2.3 m, and was presumed to continue beneath the hedgebank. It had a minimum width of 0.28 m, depth of 0.6 m, and contained a single fill (820) of grey brown silty clay which yielded fragments of iron smelting slag and chert. The only dating evidence was a single sherd of Upper Greensand-Derived pottery (4 g). A second ditch, 846, measuring 0.56 m across and surviving to a depth of 0.23 m, was recorded a short distance to the south; it ran east-west and potentially branched 90 degrees from ditch 819. It contained a single fill, 847, which comprised a mid brown silty clay matrix containing occasional iron smelting slag, and yielded two sherds (14 g) of Upper Greensand-Derived and fourteen sherds (634 g) of fifteenth /sixteenth-century Hemyock pottery which, given the extent of root disturbance was considered to be intrusive in the surface of the ditch. A third segment of ditch, 848, extended to the south of 846 and might represent a continuation of 819. Ditch 848 measured at least 1.2 m across, survived to a depth of 0.37 m and contained two fills. The primary fill, 852, comprised a deposit of chert pieces within a grey silty matrix, and probably represented slumping of the associated hedgebank into the ditch. The tertiary fill, 849, comprised mid brown clay silt with occasional stones and pieces of iron smelting slag, and likely formed through gradual silting of the open ditch. The latter yielded three sherds (74 g) of Upper Greensand-Derived, and thirteen sherds (338 g) of Hemyock pottery.

When viewed within the local context it is reasonable to suggest that the ditches recorded in Area C represent an opportunity to date the historic field pattern surrounding Churchills Farm, and in particular that the field boundary at the eastern edge of site, adjacent to High Street, may have been in place by the tenth century. This theme is discussed further in Chapter 7. It also suggests that at least one boundary contiguous with the historic pattern has been removed prior to the early nineteenth century, when the framework of the landscape is depicted by the parish tithe map.

Area D

Gullies

Apart from the late ninth/tenth-century furnaces described above, there were few other features recorded in Area D, perhaps indicating that it was deliberately set aside for the smelting of iron. It is also notable that, being higher than parts of the site covered by Areas A, B and C, the soil conditions were dryer. Not only does this raise the possibility that land drains were unnecessary here, but also that it would have been more troublesome to dig to a greater depth for clay. Two other features are worth mentioning; one is undated (gully 892) and is described below and the other is gully 874, which contained five sherds of Upper Greensand-Derived pottery. This gully, which measured up to 0.7 m across and 0.28 m deep, contained a dark grey silty clay fill (875) that yielded pieces of iron slag.

Late Medieval c. 1500-1550

Area A

Pits

A variety of features were associated with activity during the late medieval period which, based on the suggested date of Hemyock pottery, occurred between AD 1500 and 1550. The features are again of two types – pits (Figure 25) and shallow gullies (Figure 33). All pits are considered to have been dug for the extraction of clay and deliberately backfilled with waste from the iron and pottery industries.

Pit 715 was the largest recorded at Churchills Farm. It measured 4.8 m by 3.9 m across and survived to depth of 1.6 m. It was oval in plan with irregular sloping sides (Figures 26-29). The lower half of the pit's cut was different and comprised near vertical sides and a rectangular base. A sub-circular ledge was present on the southern side of the pit and may represent a separate feature cut through by 715. Alternatively, and given the overall depth of this feature, the ledge might have served a practical function as a step by which to get in and out. It is believed that, like others of this date recorded at Churchills Farm, pit 715 was dug for the extraction of clay for potting. As such, the variation in profile could result from the sporadic digging of clay in the same place but without sufficient lapses of time to allow for the accumulation of fills. The pit contained five fills.

The primary fill, 716, comprised a 0.9-m thick deposit of very dark grey firm silty clay with distinct lenses of yellowish red clay, large fragments of chert, and occasional sherds of Hemyock pottery. The material did not appear to have been the result of gradual in wash and appeared to derive from an episode of deliberate in-filling shortly after the pit was dug. The same fill extended into the hollow noted on the pit's southern edge.

Above this, fill 616 comprised up to 0.7 m of very dark grey silty clay loam with lenses of yellowish clay and charcoal, and contained an extraordinary abundance of ceramic waste, including domestic pottery, roof and floor tiles, and kiln furniture. In total, fill 616 yielded 20,055 sherds of ceramic. It is believed that the fill constitutes a single deliberate dump of material from multiple failed firings, probably removed from a waste heap near to the kiln(s).

The character of fill 619, which overlay 616, was very similar except that there was very little ceramic waste present. The 0.36-m thick deposit contained a greater quantity of chert and had thin lenses of charcoal, and it is possible that it accumulated through weathering of surrounding deposits rather than being a single-event in-fill. The tertiary fill, 618, comprised 0.19 m of very dark greyish brown silty clay, containing no ceramic waste but smaller chert pieces and some iron smelting slag. It is likely

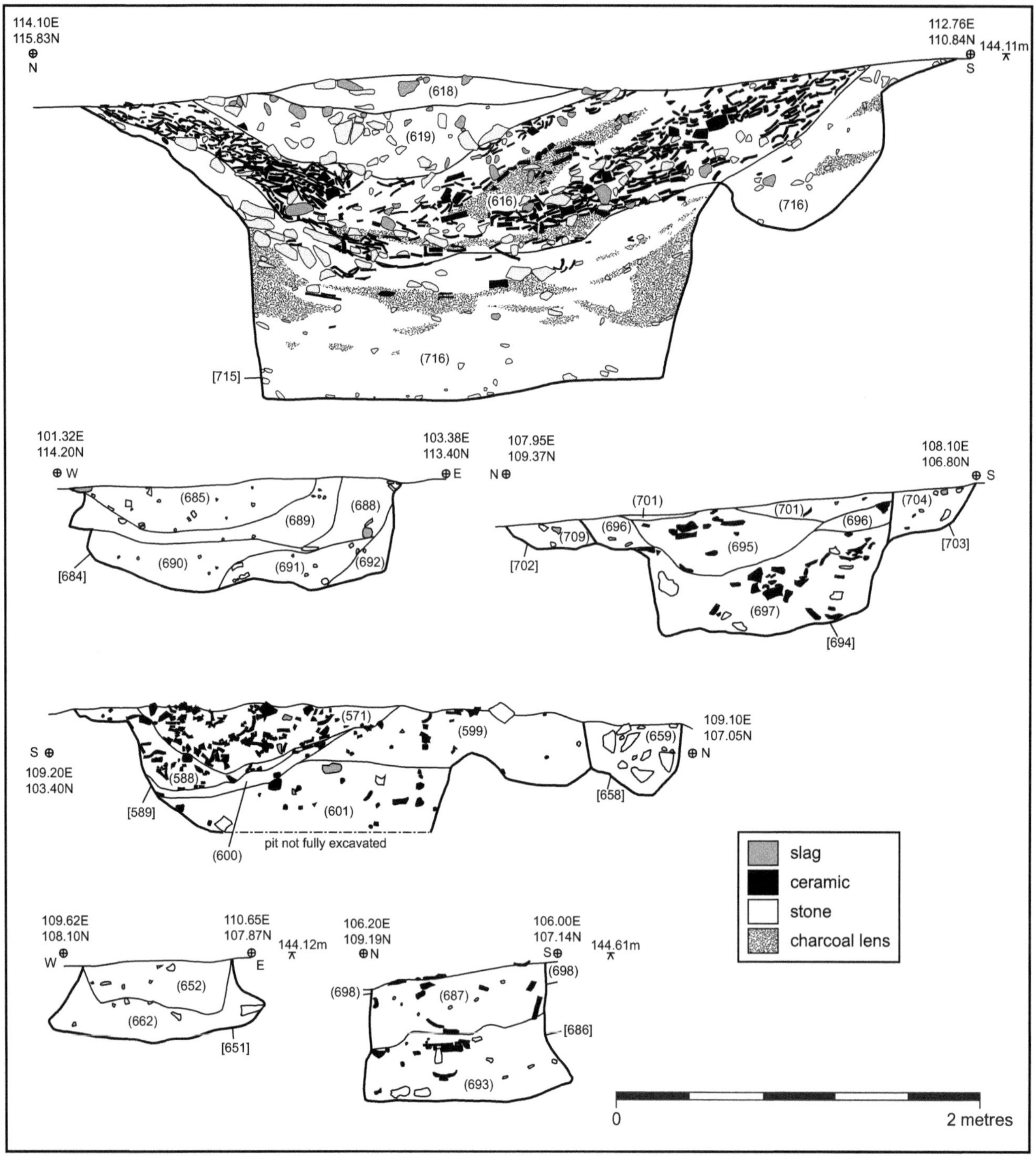

Figure 25. Section drawings of sixteenth-century pits excavated in Area A.

that this material accumulated gradually in the hollow left by the infilled pit and may derive from later overburden which spread across the site.

Pit 589 was roughly ovoid in plan and measured 2.6 m by 2.2 m across and survived to a depth of 0.98 m (Figure 30). The sides of the pit were steep and in places were slightly undercut, breaking to a flat base. A sequence of five fills were recorded, with the primary fill 601 comprising brownish grey silty clay, rich in fragments of chert, and yielding 'Hemyock' pottery and iron slag. This, and 599 that overlay it, appear to represent deliberate dumps thrown in from the east side of the pit. Fill 599 comprised dark reddish brown stony silty clay and yielded a significant amount of pottery waste. A thin layer of stony orange clay, 600, that overlay these might represent a short period of stabilisation where weathering of the surrounding natural occurred, or a lens of redeposited natural clay cast into the pit. The uppermost fills were extremely rich in ceramic and represented the final infilling of the pit using kiln waste. Fill 588 comprised dark greyish brown silty clay with patches of charcoal and yielded 14,081 sherds of ceramic (77% of the total from the pit) as well as some iron slag. The tertiary fill, 571, comprised dark greyish brown silty clay and further ceramic waste.

Figure 26. View south over large clay extraction pit 715 before excavation, showing the lenticular fills in plan (2 m-scale).

Figure 27. Photograph showing an oblique view of a west-facing section of pit 715 (1 m-scale).

Pit 684, which measured 1.85 m by 1.55 m across and survived to a depth of 0.55 m, contained a sequence of five fills whose position in the pit suggests infilling from the western side. The primary fill, 692, comprised dark brownish grey silty clay with patches of redeposited yellow natural clay. It contained no finds – pottery or slag – and the low quantities from within this pit are notable when compared to the fill of others. Fill 691 was similar in character though lacked the distinct patches of redeposited clay seen in 692. It yielded six sherds of Hemyock pottery. Fill 690 comprised brownish grey silty clay mixed with lenses of redeposited natural clay and yielded 50 sherds of Hemyock pottery. Fill 689 was more heavily mixed with redeposited natural clay and contained no pottery. The tertiary fill, 685, comprised mid brownish grey silty clay and produced no finds. This uppermost deposit might well derive from a final stage of infilling using contemporary topsoil.

Pit 651 was recorded within the footprint of an earlier evaluation trench, of which machine stripping of demolition rubble and overburden had removed the upper part of the feature (and others in its area). It was ovoid in

Figure 28. View east over large clay extraction pit 715 following removal of all fill. Note the square-cut base compared to the rounded upper sides (2 m-scale).

Figure 29. View south over large clay extraction pit 715 following removal of all fill. Note the square-cut base compared to the rounded upper sides (2 m-scale).

plan, measuring 1.21 m by 0.85 m across, and survived to a depth of 0.42 m. The sides of the pit had suffered slumping when dug, resulting in a bell-shaped profile (Figures 31, 32). The primary fill, 662, comprised a mixed deposit of dark brownish grey silty clay with redeposited natural clay, free of any finds, and possibly derived from the weathering and slumping of the pit's edge. The tertiary fill, 652, comprised a similar material but with only sparse patches of redeposited natural clay. This fill, by way of contrast, contained iron slag and Hemyock pottery.

Pit 627 was also recorded in the footprint of the earlier evaluation trench and so had suffered truncation. It was ovoid in plan, measuring 1.1 m by 0.98 m across and

Figure 30. View west over clay extraction pit 689 with nearly all fill removed. Note differential coloured banding within the clay natural (2 m-scale).

Figure 31. View east over pit 651 prior to excavation, with sherds of sixteenth-century pottery waste emerging from the tertiary fill (1 m-scale).

surviving to a depth of 0.36 m. The primary fill, 638, comprised black charcoal-rich silty clay which contained ceramic waste. The secondary fill, 628, was a mixed deposit of dark brownish grey silty clay and redeposited yellow natural clay, and also yielded ceramics. The tertiary fill, 641, comprised a similar material but it contained no ceramics.

Pit 694 was irregular in plan and profile. It measured up to 2 m across and 0.67 m deep and contained a mixed fill of silty clay and clay with hues of reddish brown, dark brown and dark grey. This deposit had within it 1224 sherds of sixteenth-century Hemyock pottery, as well as iron slag. The diffuse edges of this pit suggest later disturbance by root action.

Pit 582 was irregular in plan and profile, and might be the product of periodic clay digging prior to backfilling with a largely homogenous fill. It was cut on its northern side by ditch 508 which might have drained into it. At its greatest the pit measured 1.6 m from edge to edge and was 0.74 m deep. It contained a primary fill, 584, of a highly mixed nature, with clay of red, yellow and brown hues, and a small quantity of sixteenth-century pottery waste. This fill occupied much of the cut. The secondary fill, 583, comprised dark grey silty clay with frequent iron slag and a handful of sixteenth-century sherds. Curiously, a single sherd of Roman greyware cup was retrieved from this pit, pointing to occupation of that period somewhere in the general vicinity (exactly where depends on where the material used to backfill the pits originated).

Pit 686 was square in plan, measuring 0.94 m by 0.96 m across and 0.76 m deep. It had suffered slumping to the lower sides, suggesting that it had either been dug when the water table was high, or that it had remained open and suffered weathering prior to backfilling. The primary fill, 693, comprised grey brown silty clay with an abundance of 'Hemyock' pottery waste. The secondary fill, 687, comprised a mixed deposit of clay with hues of orange,

Figure 32. Photograph showing a south-facing section of pit 651, showing a distinct difference between the upper reddish brown clay and underlying blue-grey clay natural (1 m-scale).

brown and grey, and again containing large amounts of pottery waste.

Pit 577 cut ditch 504, which was dated to between the tenth and twelfth centuries. It was broadly circular in plan and measured <1.12 m across and 0.43 m deep. It contained a fill which comprised dark grey silty clay and a large quantity of iron slag, 505. A single piece of sixteenth-century pottery was recovered, hinting that the feature was of this period. It should be noted that other pits of sixteenth-century date contained an abundance of associated pottery and it is possible that this sherd is intrusive within a pit of earlier date. The large quantities of iron slag make its fill comparative with others dated to between the tenth and twelfth centuries, or that were undated.

Gullies and Ditches

A complex pattern of gullies and ditches was recorded at Churchills Farm, but the variable levels of truncation, site conditions, and limited dating evidence cause significant problems in phasing them (Figure 33). Nevertheless, there

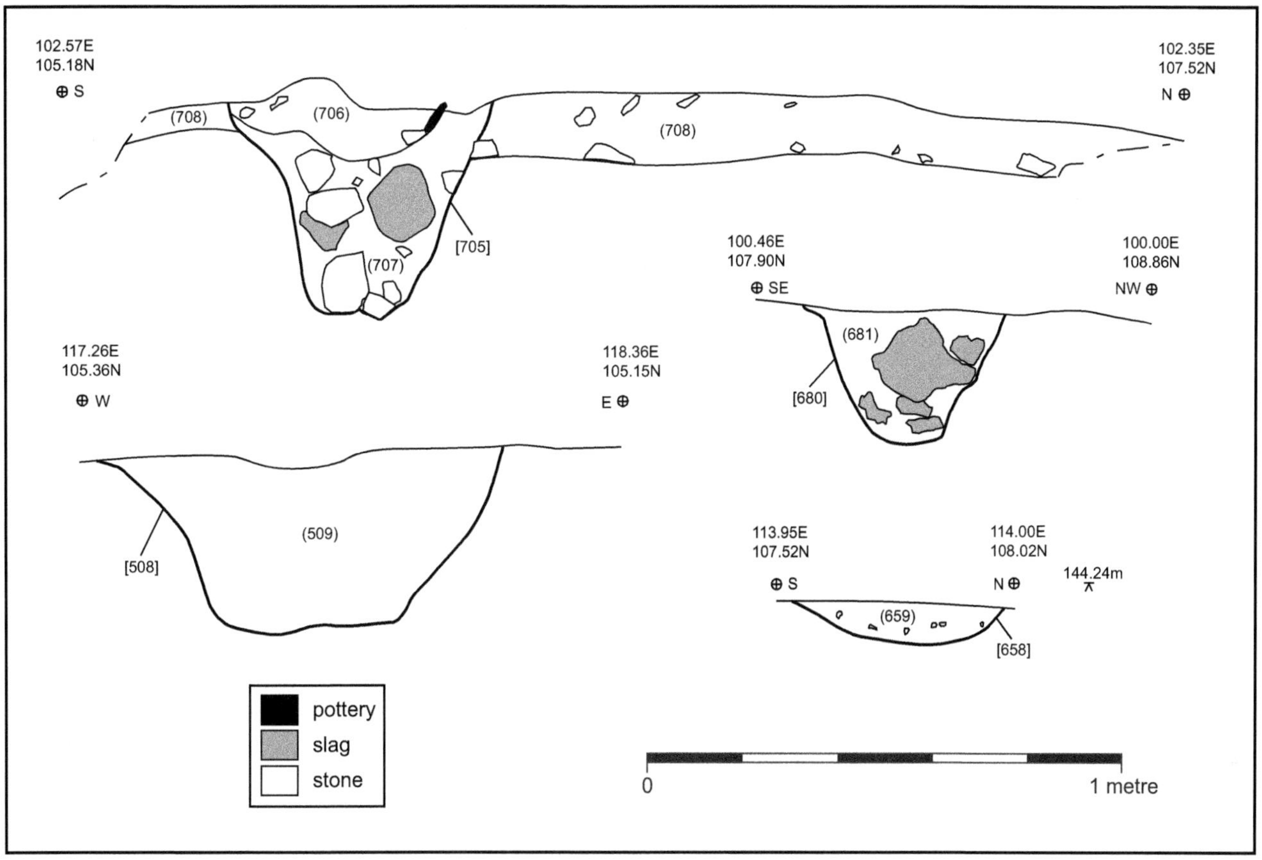

Figure 33. Section drawings of sixteenth-century gullies excavated in Area A.

are a few key stratigraphic relationships and finds groups allow us to propose a *terminus post quem* of the late medieval period.

North-south oriented ditch 508, which measured up to one metre across and survived to a depth of 0.4 m, cut through late medieval clay extraction pit 582. Three segments were excavated along the ditch and the fill was similar throughout, comprising dark grey silty clay and containing iron smelting slag and quantities of late medieval pottery. The two sherds of Upper Greensand-Derived pottery found within the fill were considered to be residual. A smaller gully met with ditch 508 and extended to the west. This gully, 658, which measured 0.45 m across and survived to a depth of just 0.08 m, contained a fill, 659, of dark grey brown silty clay. Whilst excavation of part of this gully yielded 11 sherds (only 12 g) of Upper Greensand-Derived pottery, it is probable that this is residual given the physical relationship with ditch 508, and the certainty that this has a late medieval *terminus post quem*.

Further west, gully 680, shares the same alignment as gully 658 and probably represents its continuation. It measured up to 0.48 m across and 0.38 m in depth and contained a single fill, 681, which comprised very dark grey brown silty clay with an abundance of iron slag. It is likely that the inclusion of large pieces of slag was a measure to aid drainage of the surrounding land.

Similarly, gully 625 extended north of ditch 508 on the same alignment and is logically coterminous with it. It measured 0.19 m across and survived to a depth of 0.08 m; it is likely to have suffered considerable truncation. It contained a single fill, 626, comprising dark grey silty clay that contained iron slag and sherds of abraded Upper Greensand-Derived pottery.

A short segment of gully had survived general ground disturbance on the western side of Area A. Gully 705 measured 0.41 m across and 0.4 m deep. It contained two fills – a primary fill of grey brown silty clay with abundant slag, 707, and a secondary fill of the same matrix but without slag. It was notable that the upper portion of the gully cut had been lined with sixteenth-century pottery wasters to the level of the primary fill (see section on Figure 33).

Area D

Whilst no cut features of sixteenth-century date were present in Area D, a layer of mid brown silty clay, up to 0.28 m thick and containing pottery of this date, covered a 6 m by 2 m area across its northern edge. A lack of later material within it suggests that it is unlikely to be dumped much later, and it is interpreted as a levelling deposit, perhaps with the intention of returning the land to agricultural use.

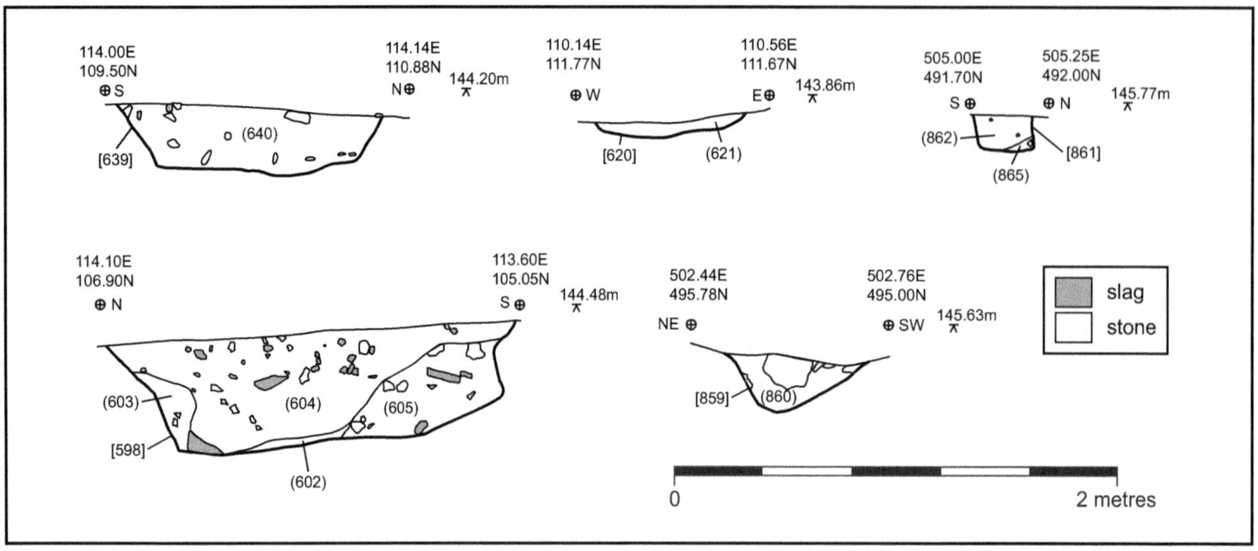

Figure 34. Section drawings of a representative sample of undated pits excavated in Areas A, B and C.

Undated (Figures 34, 35)

Area A

There were a number of pits and a single gully recorded in Area A that yielded no dating evidence. It might be argued, however, that the distinct lack of sixteenth-century Hemyock pottery pushes for a date earlier in the medieval period, or before. Gully 592 was oriented northeast-southwest and ran parallel with gully 504, the latter being dated to between the tenth and twelfth centuries. It measured 0.5 m across and 0.2 m deep, and contained a single fill, 593, of dark grey silty clay with an abundance of iron slag.

Slag was common within all but two of the undated pits in this part of the site, indicating that they are likely to be contemporary with, or post-date, the earliest phase of on-site smelting in the ninth/tenth century. Pit 559 measured <1.12 m across and 0.24 m deep and contained a dark grey silty clay fill, 560. Pit 575 cut gully 504. It measured <1.74 m across and 0.33 m deep and contained a dark grey silty clay fill, 576. Pit 512 measured <0.87 m across and 0.09 m deep and contained a mid grey silty clay fill, 513. Pit 506 measured <0.74 m across and 0.24 m deep and contained a fill of grey silty clay, 507. Pit 598 measured <1.8 m across and 0.5 m deep and contained a sequence of four silty clay fills, 602-5, in hues of dark grey and brown. Pit 639 measured <1.32 m across and 0.31 m deep and contained a single fill of grey brown silty clay, 640. The first undated pit to contain no iron slag was 844, on the northern edge of the site. It measured <0.77 m across and 0.4 m deep and contained a fill of grey silty clay. The second was pit 620, which was heavily truncated and measured <0.34 m across and 0.03 m deep. Its dark grey silty clay fill, 621, was like others containing slag. It is suggested that all of the undated pits were dug for the extraction of clay, and were deliberately backfilled with waste from iron production.

A row of six sub-square postholes, 613, 611, 609, 607, 668 and 670, measuring no more than 0.25 m across and 0.10 m deep, appear to trace a former fence-line running to the edge of pit 715, but cutting the line of ditch 508. The only dating evidence is from posthole 613, which cuts the edge of pit 715 and so the single sherd of ceramic might derive from its fill. It is thought that this row of postholes is very late in the sequence of activity.

A single short length of gully, 594, could not be closely dated. It measured 0.2 m across, 0.06 m deep and contained a fill of dark grey silty clay and iron slag, 595. The gully was cut by sixteenth-century pit 582. It is possible that this heavily truncated gully represents a continuation of tenth-twelfth century gully 530, a short distance west.

Area B

Undated features in Area B are most probably of medieval date, relating to occupation and activity in the ninth/tenth to twelfth centuries. Gully 727, which measured 0.37 m across and 0.15 m deep and contained a single fill, 728, of grey brown silty clay that had an abundance of iron slag within it. It appeared to have been cut by pit 729 at its western end and thus belongs to the same or an earlier phase. Given the presence of abundant slag within the gully, we might assume that it is broadly contemporary with pit 729 and iron smelting in Area D. Gullies 719 (0.18 m across, 0.04 m deep) and 717 (0.47 m across and 0.04 m deep) were undated and contained no slag, perhaps indicating that they predate the tenth century. However, given the fact that these features are very shallow and probably largely truncated, any slag within the original extent has probably been lost. Feature 725 is represented by a channel 1.75 m long, 0.49 m wide and 0.2 m deep, but its function is unknown. Its sole fill, 726, comprised dark grey silty clay which was abundant with iron slag. The lack of *in situ* heating or structure to the deposited slag suggests that it is not a primary metalworking feature. Two undated

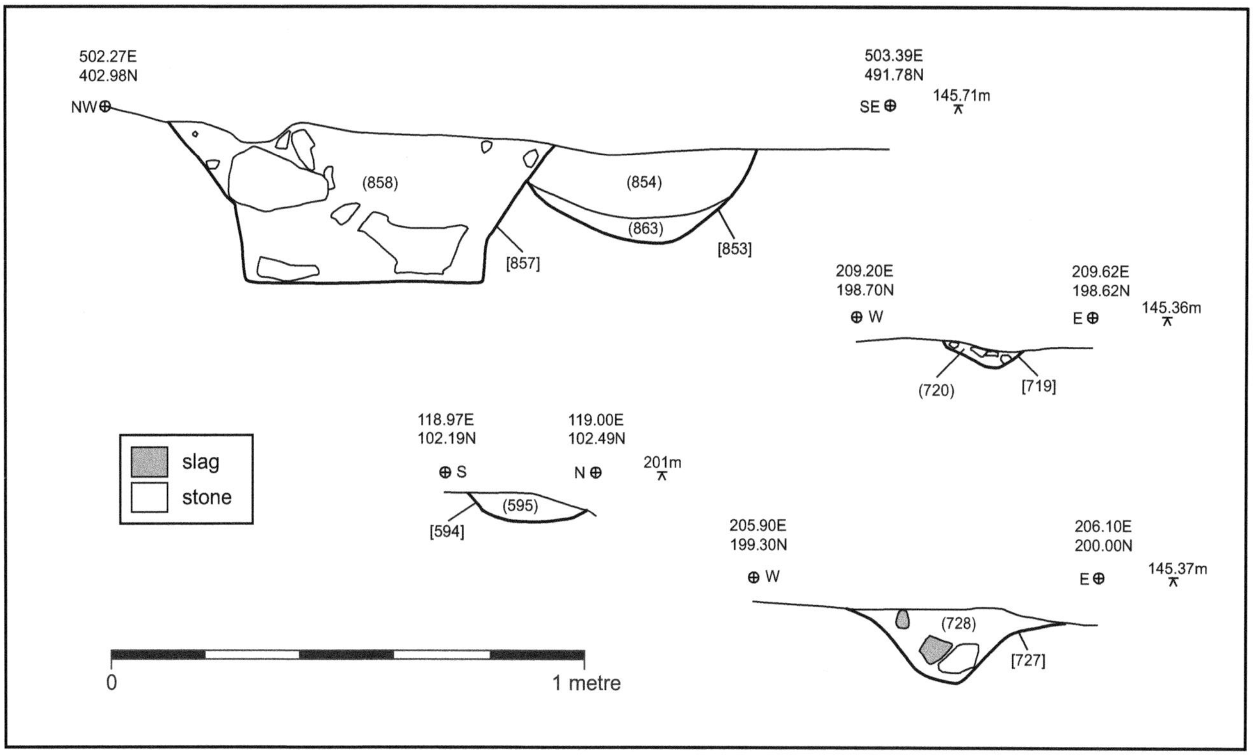

Figure 35. Section drawings of a representative sample of undated gullies excavated in Areas A, B, C and D.

postholes were also recorded here (738: <0.26 m across and 0.06 m deep; 742: <0.36 m across and 0.13 m deep) and both contained iron slag as packing.

Area C

Ditch 853 was U-shaped with a width of 0.5 m and surviving depth of 0.2 m. It had a southwest-northeast orientation, was truncated at the southwest, and disappeared beneath the extant hedgebank that bordered the eastern edge of the site. The primary fill, 863, comprised 0.08 m of brown silty clay with few inclusions, and which appeared to represent gradual silting in the base of the ditch. The secondary fill, comprising 0.22 m of light brownish grey silty clay, was waterlogged and had formed under similar conditions (i.e. silting/in wash). The tertiary fill, 864, might have been deliberated formed. It comprised 0.2 m of brown silty clay containing a moderate quantity of chert pieces, and in this regard could be viewed as a consolidation deposit. No finds were found during excavation of ditch 853 – no pottery or slag – which is notable on a site where most features yield iron smelting slag, Upper Greensand-Derived or Hemyock pottery. Whilst there is no firm evidence for the date of this ditch it is stratigraphically earlier than ditch 819 (tenth – twelfth century), and the absence of slag or Hemyock pottery (of which there is an abundance across site) might allow us to suggest a date of infill prior to the date of known iron production in the mid tenth century AD. From a topographical perspective, it is notable that the orientation of the ditch is *contra* that of the historic field pattern, which again suggests that it might have earlier origins.

Gully 813 was oriented east-west and is potentially a continuation of gully 530, which was dated to between the tenth and twelfth centuries. It measured 0.45 m across and 0.12 m deep and contained a single fill, 814, of dark grey silty clay. Unusually for the gullies across the site this section contained no iron slag.

Pit 809 was only partly observed, but measured 0.9 m across and 0.18 m deep. It contained a fill of grey brown silty clay, 810, with large pieces of iron slag.

Two clusters of undated pits/postholes were observed in Area C. The first forms a close but unstructured group on the northern edge and comprises cuts 821 (<0.7 m across, 0.06 m deep), 823 (<0.55 m across, 0.11 m deep), 825 (<0.36 m across, 0.12 m deep), 827 (<0.38 m across, 0.07 m deep) and 835 (<0.43 m across, 0.24 m deep). Some slag was recovered from within these features, indicating that they are probably of ninth-century or later date. The second group appear more regular in their distribution, and might describe a circular structure of about 5 m diameter. The seven postholes, 859 (0.9 m across, 0.74 m deep), 869 (<0.74 m across, 0.17 m deep), 855 (0.9 m across, 0.33 m deep), 867 (0.2 m across, 0.07 m deep), 850 (0.5 m across, 0.3 m deep), 861 (0.28 m across, 0.12 m deep) and 857 (0.87 m across, 0.32 m deep), contained evidence for the use of iron slag and stone for packing.

Area D

Curving gully 892 was recorded on the eastern side of Area D. It measured 0.55 m across and 0.1 m deep and contained a single dark grey silty clay fill, 893, which had iron slag within. Though it was undated its proximity and common orientation with gully 874 might suggest it relates to the tenth to twelfth-century phase of activity.

Chapter 3

Radiocarbon Dating

Peter Marshall, Christopher Bronk Ramsey, Elaine Dunbar and Paula Reimer

Aims of the Dating Programme

The primary aim of the radiocarbon dating programme was to determine the currency of iron production at the site and the chronology of the two types of furnace technology – the non-slag tapping (slagpit) furnaces and the slag-tapping furnaces. From this it was hoped to answer a series of specific questions:

1. are the furnaces, slag-pit and slag-tapping, contemporary representing a medium-scale industry, or are they temporally separated from one another representing repeated use of the same site over a longer period of time?
2. the slagpit furnaces consistently show evidence for the use of a grass/cereal pit packing. The more normal form of packing is of split wood, eg as at Hemyock: Culmstock Road (Rainbird and Young 2015) – are the grass/cereal remains contemporary with iron production?

In addition determining the age of Pit 556, that contained the largest group of chert-tempered pottery from the site, would provide a date for this ceramic series and also help in ascertaining whether ceramic and iron production was contemporary on the site.

Sample Selection

The first stage in sample selection was to identify short-lived material, which was demonstrably not residual in the context from which it was recovered. The taphonomic relationship between a sample and its context is the most hazardous link in this process, since the mechanisms by which a sample came to be in its context are a matter of interpretative decision rather than certain knowledge. All samples consisted of single entities (Ashmore 1999). Material was selected only where there was evidence that a sample had been put fresh into its context. The main category of material, which met these taphonomic criteria were fragments of carbonised wood and cereals that would have been used as packing in the furnaces. Given the quantities of fuel used in the iron smelting process and therefore the likelihood of residual fragments of charcoal being incorporated into the excavated features duplicate samples were dated from each feature were possible.

Radiocarbon Laboratory Methods

Twenty-seven radiocarbon measurements have been obtained on samples of charcoal and carbonised cereal grains from Churchills Farm. The 11 samples dated at The Queen's University Belfast were processed and dated by AMS as described in Reimer *et al.* (2015). Eleven samples were dated at the Scottish Universities Environmental Research Centre. The charcoal and carbonised grain were processed using an acid-alkali-acid pre-treatment as described by Stenhouse and Baxter (1983). CO_2 obtained from the pretreated samples was combusted in pre-cleaned sealed quartz tubes (Vandeputte *et al.* 1996) and then converted to graphite (Slota *et al.* 1987). The samples were dated by AMS as described by Freeman *et al.* (2010). Five samples submitted to the Oxford Radiocarbon Accelerator Unit (OxA) were processed as described in Brock *et al.* (2010) and measured using Accelerator Mass Spectrometry (Bronk Ramsey *et al.* 2004a; 2004b).

All three laboratories maintain continual programmes of quality assurance procedures, in addition to participating in international inter-comparisons (Scott 2003; Scott *et al.* 2010). These tests indicate no significant offsets and demonstrate the validity of the precision quoted.

Radiocarbon Results

The results (Table 1) are conventional radiocarbon ages (Stuiver and Polach 1977), and are quoted in accordance with the international standard known as the Trondheim convention (Stuiver and Kra 1986).

Radiocarbon Calibration

The calibrations of these results, which relate the radiocarbon measurements directly to the calendrical time scale, are given in Figure 36. All have been calculated using the datasets published by Reimer *et al.* (2013) and the computer program OxCal v4.2 (Bronk Ramsey 1995; 1998; 2001; 2009a). The probability distributions shown in Figures 36-41 are derived from the probability method (Stuiver and Reimer 1993).

Interpretation

Measurements on samples from six of the 11 dated features are statistically consistent at 95% confidence (Ward and

Table 1. Hemyock: Churchills Farm – radiocarbon results

Lab Number	Sample No	Material and context	Radiocarbon Age (BP)	δ13C (‰)
Area A				
UBA-22706	[675] <307> sample A	Charcoal, *Alnus/Corylus* (D Challinor), from fill (678) of iron smelting furnace [675]	912±32	−25.1±0.2
SUERC-45860	[675] <307> sample B	Charcoal, cf. Maloideae (D Challinor), as UBA-22706	909±34	−25.5±0.2
Area D				
Unknown technology				
SUERC-56923	[557] <301> sample A	Charcoal, *Fraxinus* (D Challinor), from fill (557) of pit [556]	1160±29	−25.8±0.2
UBA 27272	[557] <301> sample B	Charcoal Maloideae (D Challinor), as SUERC-56923	1045±30	−26.9±0.2
SUERC-45862	[778] <318> sample A	Charcoal, Ulex/Cytisus (D Challinor), from fill (781) of ?charcoal pit [778] containing slag blocks from a slagpit furnace	1084±34	−23.6±0.2
UBA-22705	[778] <318> sample B	Charcoal, Maloideae (strong roundwood with pith edge) (D Challinor), as SUERC-45862	1180±35	−28.1±0.2
SUERC-56927	(781) <318> sample A	Carbonised grain, *Avena* (D Challinor), SUERC-45862	1152±25	−25.0*
UBA 27275	(781) <318> sample B	Carbonised grain, *Triticum* (J Jones), as SUERC-45862	1112±44	−21.3±0.2
Slag tapping furnaces				
OxA-27977	[789] <326> sample A	Charcoal, cf. Maloideae (D Challinor) from central fill (798) of iron smelting furnace [789]	1124±25	−24.5±0.2
SUERC-45859	[789] <326> sample B	Charcoal, *Alnus/Corylus* (D Challinor), as OxA-27977	1170±34	−25.0*
OxA-27884	[758]<315> sample A	Charcoal, *Alnus glutinosa,* (D Challinor) from fill (763) of iron smelting furnace [758]	1136±24	−26.1±0.2
OxA-28004	[771] <327> sample A	Charcoal, *Alnus glutinosa* (D Challinor) from primary fill (772) of iron smelting furnace [771]	1202±25	−23.4±0.2
UBA-22707	[771] <327> sample B	Charcoal, *Acer camestre* (D Challinor), as OxA-28004	1129±32	−27.7±0.2
SUERC-56928	[793] <319> sample A	Charcoal, *Alnus/Corylus* (D Challinor), from primary fill (793) of iron smelting furnace [792]	1214±29	−26.2±0.2
UBA 27270	[793] <319> sample B	Charcoal, *Ulex/Cytisus* (D Challinor), as SUERC-56928	1212±35	−26.9±0.2
?Slag tapping furnace				
SUERC-56931	(806) <329> sample A	Charcoal, *Alnus/Corylus* (D Challinor), from primary fill (806) of iron smelting furnace [805]	1167±29	−26.2±0.2
UBA 27271	(806) <329> sample B	Charcoal, *Alnus/Corylus* (D Challinor), as SUERC-56931	1163±28	−25.9±0.2
Slagpit furnaces				
OxA-27885	[776] <317> sample A	Charcoal, *Alnus glutinosa* roundwood (D Challinor), from fill (777) of iron smelting furnace [776]	1142±24	−26.7±0.2
SUERC-45861	[776] <317> sample B	Charcoal, *Quercus* roundwood (immature – strong ring curvature) (D Challinor), as OxA-27885	1157±24	−26.5±0.2
SUERC-45863	[794] <322> sample A	Charcoal, *Ulex/Cytisus* (roundwood with strong ring curvature – 5yrs+) (D Challinor), from fill (795) of iron smelting furnace [794]	1142±34	−23.1±0.2
UBA-22704	[794] <322> sample B	Charcoal, *Corylus avellana* (roundwood with pith – 5yrs) (D Challinor), as SUERC-45863	1034±36	−25.4±0.2
SUERC-56929	(795) <322> sample A	Carbonised grain, *Avena* (D Challinor), from fill (795) of iron smelting furnace [794].	1095±29	−23.9±0.2

Lab Number	Sample No	Material and context	Radiocarbon Age (BP)	δ13C (‰)
UBA 27273	(795) <322> sample B	Carbonised grain, *Triticum* (J Jones), as SUERC-56929	1086±30	−22.6±0.2
UBA-22703	[787] <320> sample A	Charcoal, *Ulex/Cytisus* (roundwood with pith – 1 year old) (D Challinor) from fill (788) of iron smelting furnace [787]	1054±35	−25.3
OxA-27886	[787] <320> sample B	Charcoal, *Corylus avellana* (D Challinor), as UBA-22703	1172±24	−26.0±0.2
SUERC-56930	(800) <323> sample A	Charcoal, *Alnus/Corylus* (D Challinor), from primary fill (800) of iron smelting furnace [799]	1165±29	−27.5±0.2
UBA 27274	(800) <323> sample B	Charcoal, *Alnus glutinosa* (D Challinor), as SUERC-56930	1077±30	−28.3±0.2

*Assumed value.

Wilson 1978, table 2), three are not consistent at 95% confidence but are at 99% confidence, and two fail at 99% confidence. Although we would only expect one or two sets of measurements from the dated features to fail at 95% confidence if they contained material of the same actual age, the results do suggest that the incorporation of residual/intrusive charcoal is limited.

Statistically consistent results from features [778] and [794] (Table 2) indicate that the cereal packing in furnaces was taking place alongside the more common sole use of split wood.

Chronological Modelling

The radiocarbon dates from Area D associated with tapping and slagpit furnaces clearly fall into a coherent group (Figure 36); Pit [675] that contained tapped slag from Area A clearly represents much later activity and Pit [556] is associated with ceramic production. The measurements are not, however, statistically consistent (T'= 53.8; T'(5%)= 33.9; v= 22; Ward and Wilson 1978), and so they certainly represent more than one episode of activity.

The radiocarbon measurements on samples from the slag tapping furnaces are statistically consistent (T'= 12.3; T'(5%)= 12.6; v= 6) and so they could all be of the same actual age. The measurements from the definite four slag tapping furnaces ([758], [771], [789], and [792] are though not statistically consistent (T'= 24.1; T'(5%)= 16.9; v= 9).

Simple visual inspection of the calibrated radiocarbon dates does not allow us to assess the date of iron working activity at Churchills Farm accurately, since the calibration process does not allow for the fact that this group of radiocarbon dates are related – they all come from the same site. Bayesian statistical modelling is required to account for this dependence (Buck *et al.* 1992; Bronk Ramsey 2000; Bayliss *et al.* 2007), which we have undertaken using OxCal v.4.2 (Bronk Ramsey 1995; 1998; 2001; 2009b). The date ranges from these models are given *in italics* to distinguish them from simple, calibrated radiocarbon dates.

In order to ensure that independent estimates are obtained for the last use of each of the furnaces a single parameter (eg *Last_Pit_794;* Figure 37) has been calculated prior to the formal chronological modelling from the model shown in Figure 37.

The chronological model (Figure 38) shows good agreement (Amodel: 158) between the estimated dates for the last use of the ironworking furnaces (derived from Figure 37) and the assumption that this activity took place at a uniform rate over a period of time (Buck *et al.* 1992).

The model (Figure 38) estimates activities associated with ironworking on the site began in *cal* AD 865–935 (*95% probability*; *start_hemyock*; Figure 38), probably *cal* AD 875–910 (*68% probability*), and ended in *cal* AD 905–950 (*95% probability*; *end_hemyock*; Figure 38), probably *cal* AD 905–950 (*68% probability*).

Given that 'bulk' chemical analysis of the residues from both the non-slag tapping 'slagpit' style furnaces, and slag-tapping furnaces are very similar it is likely that the two technologies simply represent different ways in which to capture the phosphorus in the ore (Young; Chapter 4 in this volume). The chronological model (Figure 38) clearly show that the two technologies were in use at the same time.

The smelting of iron at Churchills Farm is estimated to have taken place over a period of *1–70 years* (*95% probability*; *hemyock*; Figure 39), probably *1–45 years* (*68% probability*).

Iron Working in the Blackdown Hills

Churchills Farm is one of a number of ironworking sites in the Blackdown Hills; the others being Culmstock Road, Hemyock (Rainbird and Young 2015), Town Farm, Burlescombe (Reed *et al.* 2006), and Dunkeswell (Griffith and Weddell 1996) that have provided samples for radiocarbon dating (Tables 3 and 4). A chronological model that incorporates the radiocarbon dates from Culmstock Road, Hemyock, Town Farm, Burlescombe, and Dunkeswell, together with estimates for the start and end

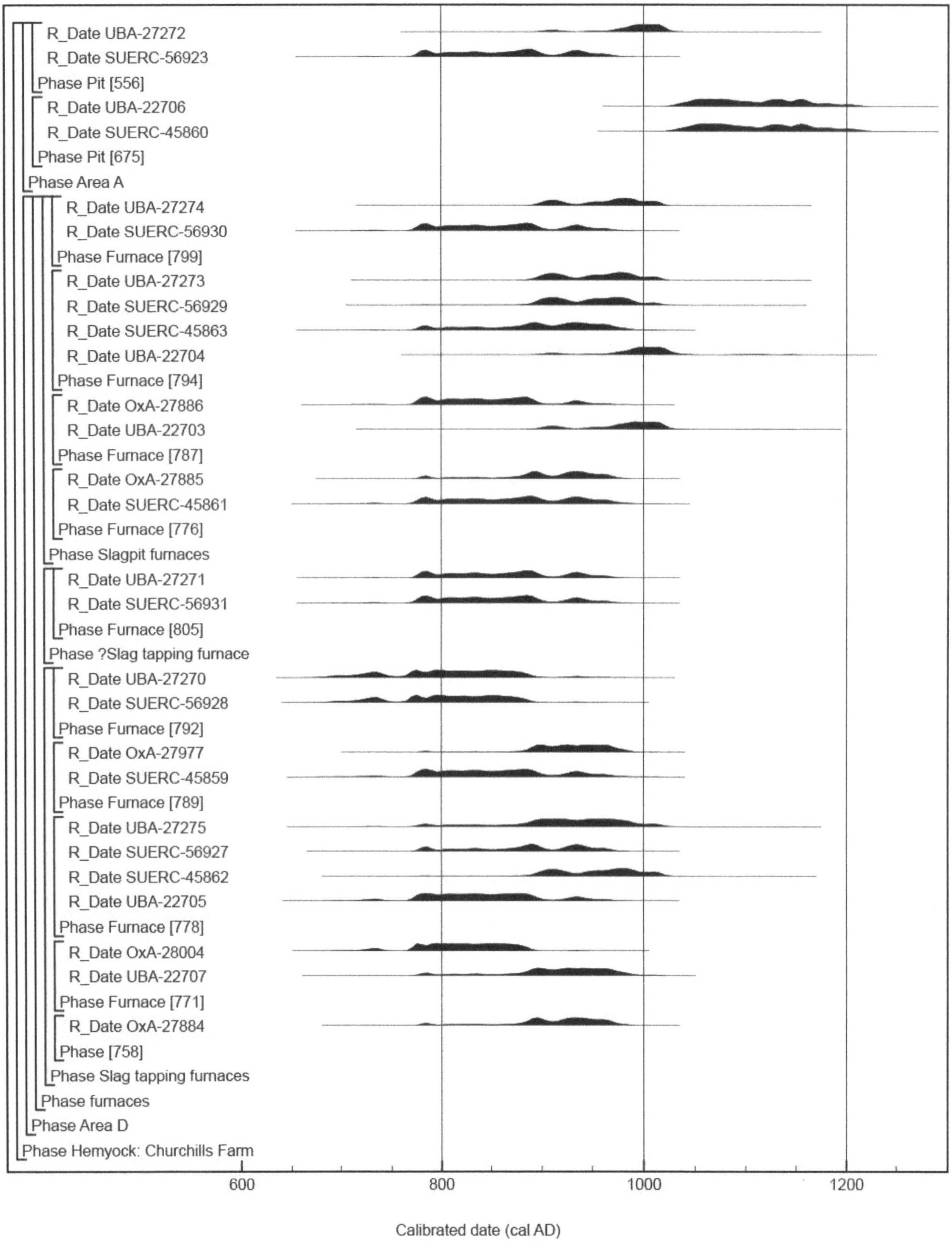

Figure 36. Probability distributions of dates from Hemyock: Churchills Farm. The distributions are the result of simple radiocarbon calibration (Stuiver and Reimer 1993).

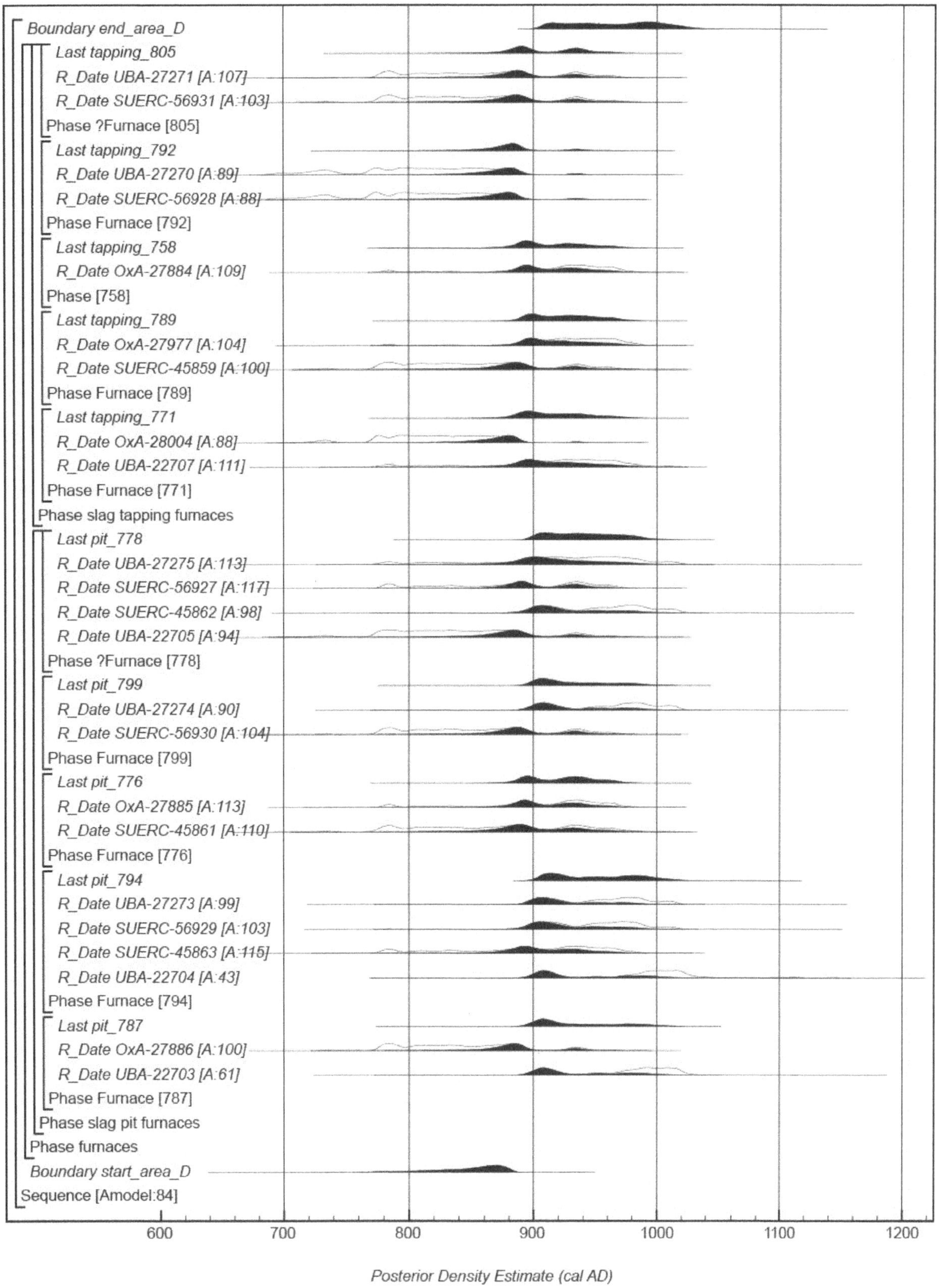

Figure 37. Probability distributions of dates from Hemyock: Churchills Farm, Area D. Each distribution represents the relative probability that an event occurs at a particular time. For each radiocarbon date, two distributions have been plotted: one in outline which is the result of simple radiocarbon calibration, and a solid one based on the chronological model used. The other distributions correspond to aspects of the model. For example, the distribution '*Last Pit_794*' is the estimate for the last use of non tapping furnace [794]. The large square brackets down the left-hand side of the diagram and the OxCal keywords define the overall model exactly.

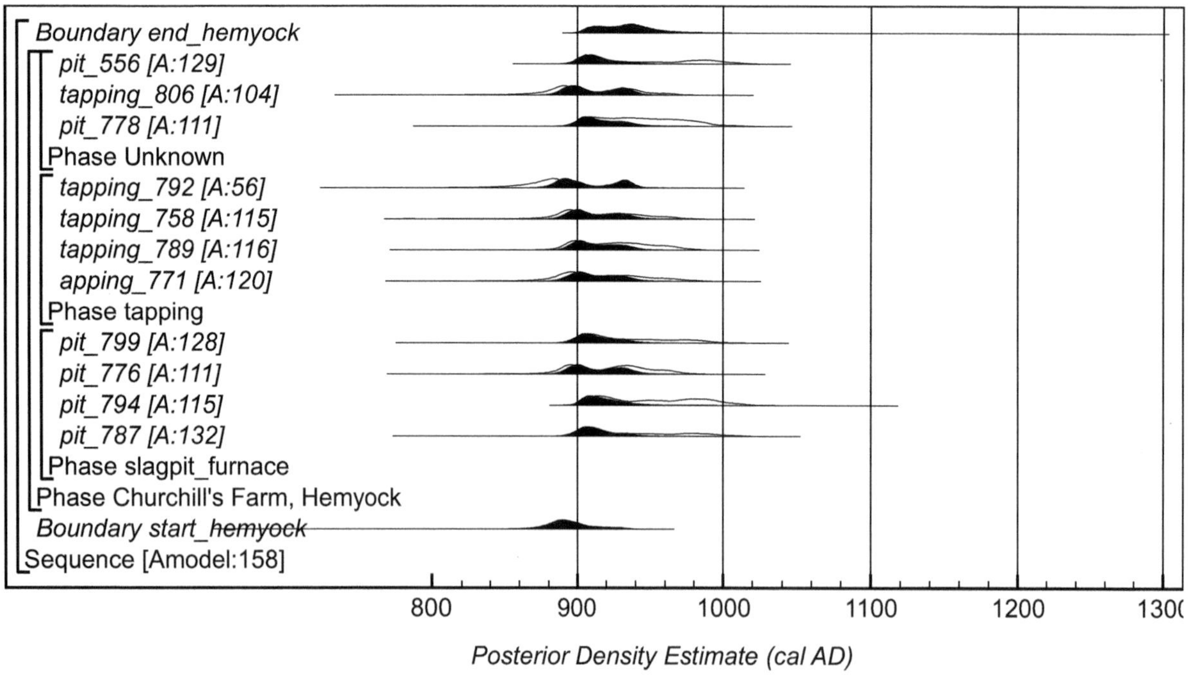

Figure 38. Probability distributions of estimated dates for ironworking activity at Hemyock: Churchills Farm. The prior distributions (eg *pit_778*) are derived from the model shown in Figure 37. The overall format is identical to Figure 37.

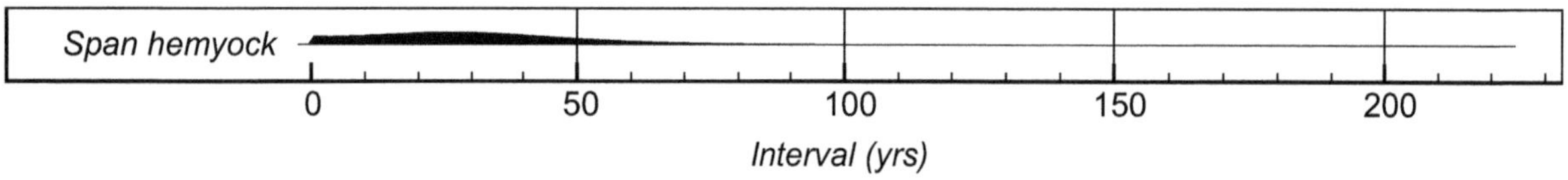

Figure 39. Probability distribution showing the number of calendar years during which ironworking furnaces were in operation at Hemyock: Churchills Farm (the distribution is derived from the model shown in Figure 37).

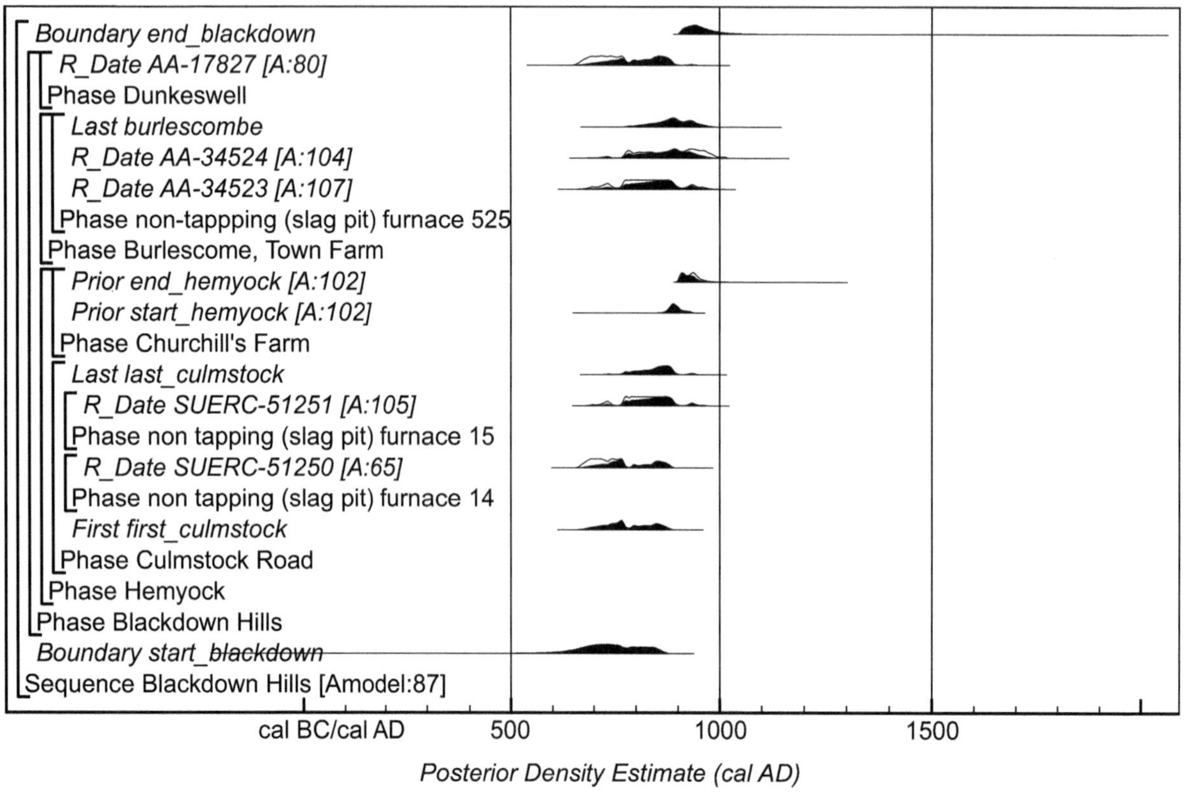

Figure 40. Probability distributions of dates for iron smelting on the Blackdown Hills. The overall format is identical to Figure 37.

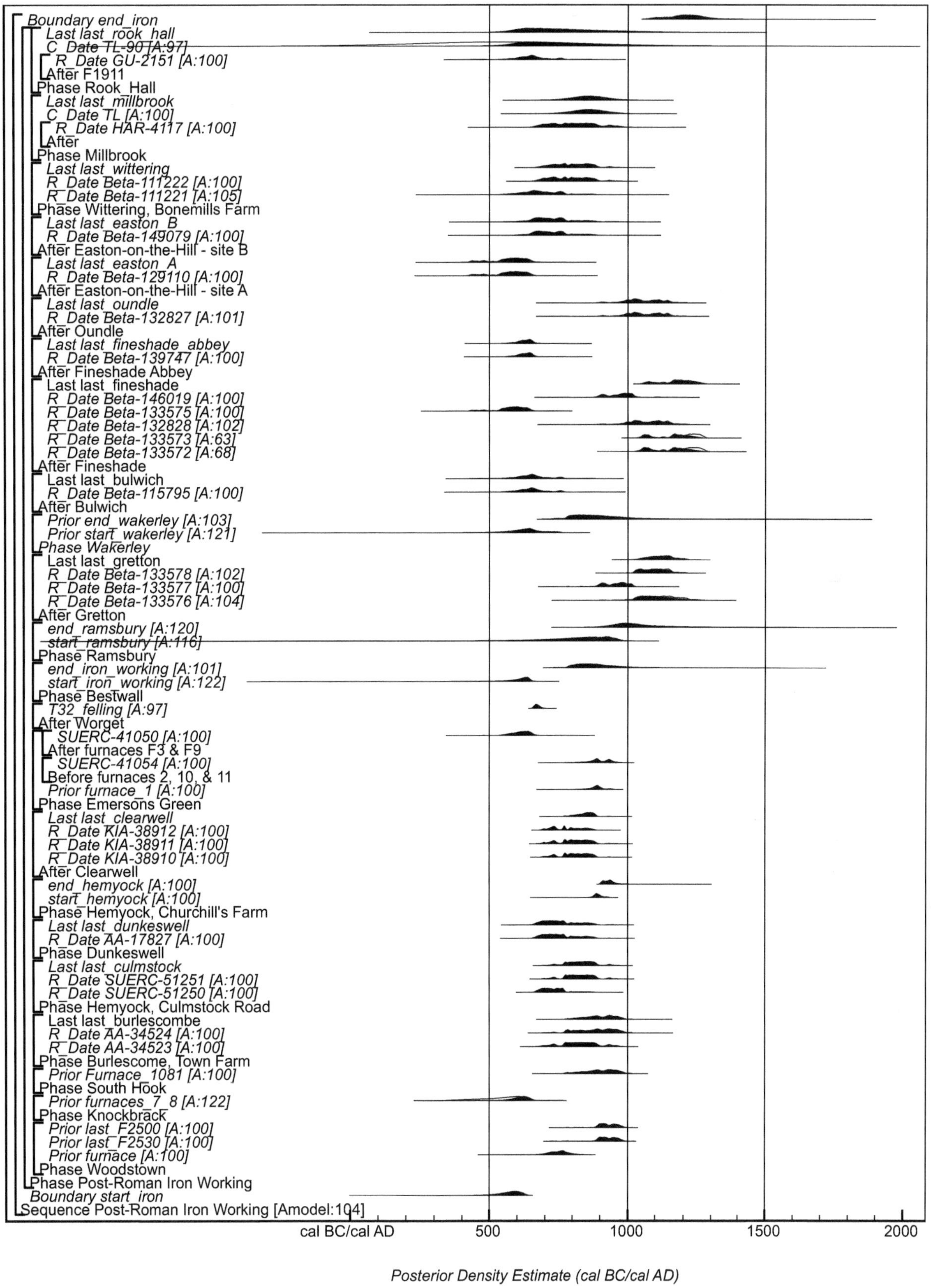

Figure 41. Probability distributions of dates for iron smelting and associated activities in England, Wales, and Ireland. The overall format is identical to Figure 37.

of non-tapping and tapping technologies from Churchills Farm (Figure 40) has good agreement (Amodel=87) and suggests that the earliest ironworking using a non-tapping technology happened at Culmstock Road (*96.0% probable*). The phase of iron smelting from these sites took place between the late eight–tenth centuries cal AD.

Table 2. Hemyock: Churchills Farm – statistical consistency of radiocarbon ages on samples from the same feature

Feature	Context	Laboratory Code	Radiocarbon Age (BP)	Statistical consistency (Ward and Wilson 1978)
Slag tapping furnaces				
771	772	OxA-28004	1202±25	T'=3.2; ν=1; T'(5%)=3.8
		UBA-22707	1129±32	
789	798	OxA-27977	1124±25	T'=1.2; ν=1; T'(5%)=3.8
		SUERC-45859	1170±34	
792	793	SUERC-56928	1214±29	T'=0.0; ν=1; T'(5%)=3.8
		UBA 27270	1212±35	
?Slag tapping furnace				
778	781	SUERC-45862	1084±34	T'=4.6; ν=3; T'(5%)=7.8
		UBA-22705	1180±35	
		SUERC-56927	1152±25	
		UBA 27275	1112±44	
805	806	SUERC-56931	1167±29	T'=0.0; ν=1; T'(5%)=3.8
		UBA 27271	1163±28	
Slagpit furnaces				
776	777	OxA-27885	1142±24	T'=0.1; ν=1; T'(5%)=3.8
		SUERC-45861	1157±24	
787	788	UBA-22703	1054±35	T'=7.7; ν=1; T'(5%)=3.8
794	795	SUERC-45863	1142±34	T'=4.8; ν=3; T'(5%)=7.8
		UBA-22704	1034±36	
		SUERC-56929	1095±29	
		UBA 27273	1086±30	
		OxA-27886	1172±24	
799	800	SUERC-56930	1165±29	T'=4.5; ν=1; T'(5%)=3.8
		UBA 27274	1077±30	
Other				
557	556	SUERC-56923	1160±29	T'=7.6; ν=1; T'(5%)=3.8
		UBA 27272	1045±30	
675	678	UBA-22706	912±32	T'=0.0; ν=1; T'(5%)=3.8
		SUERC-45860	909±34	

The Chronology of Post-Roman Iron Working: A Review

This review of post-Roman iron working is based on of 189 radiocarbon measurements, 13 archaeomagnetic dates, two luminescence ages, and one tree-ring date, from 22 sites. Details of all the scientific dates included are provided in Tables 1 and 4-7 (where the relevant information has been gathered from diverse sources: Table 3).

Here, all chronological modelling has been undertaken using the program OxCal v4.2 (Bronk Ramsey 2009b) and the atmospheric calibration curve for the northern hemisphere published by Reimer *et al.* (2013). The chronological models for each site are described below, and are defined exactly by the brackets and OxCal CQL2 keywords on the left-hand side of the technical graphs (http://c14.arch.ox.ac.uk/). The posterior density estimates output by the model are shown in black, with the unconstrained calibrated radiocarbon dates shown in outline. The other distributions correspond to aspects of the model. For example, *furnace* is the estimated date when the iron smelting furnace at Woodstown was last used (Figure 42). In the text and tables, the Highest Posterior Density intervals of the posterior density estimates produced by the models are given *in italics*, followed by a reference to the relevant parameter name and the figures in which the model which produced it is defined. Key parameters for the chronology of post-Roman iron working are listed in Table 5. So, for example, we estimate that iron working activity at Bestwall Quarry started in *cal* AD 570–660 (*95% probability*; *start_iron_working*; Figure 47), probably in *cal* AD 610–650 (*68% probability*).

Table 3. Summary of scientific dating evidence considered in the review of the chronology of post-Roman ironworking

Site	No. of ^{14}C results	No. of ^{14}C results (excluded)	No. of ^{14}C results (TPQ)	No. of TL ages	No. of TL ages (excluded)	No. of dendro dates	No. of archaeomagnetic dates	No. of archaeomagnetic dates (excluded)	References
Woodstown	35	1	10	-	-	-	-	-	Russell and Hurley 2014, tables 13.1–13.6
Knockbrack	3		2						Table 4; Hull and Taylor 2006
South Hook	15	3	3						Table 4; Crane and Murphy 2010
Burlescombe	2						2	2	Table 4; Reed *et al.* 2006, tables 11–12
Hemyock; Culmstock Road	2								Table 4; Rainbird and Young 2015
Hemyock; Churchills Farm	27								Table 1
Dunkeswell	1								Table 4; Griffith and Weddell 1996
Clearwell	3	3							Table 4
Emersons Green	8		1				4	4	Table 4; Young and Young 2013
Worgret	1	1				1			Table 5
Bestwall	63		1				6	6	Ladle 2012, tables 11–12
Ramsbury	6		3						Table 4; Haslam 1980
Gretton	3		3						Table 4; Bellamy *et al.* 2001
Wakerley	6	1							Table 4; Fell 2007
Bulwick	1		1						Table 4; Bellamy *et al.* 2001
Fineshade	5		5						Table 4; Bellamy *et al.* 2001
Fineshade Abbey	1		1						Table 4; Mudd 2006
Oundle	1		1						Table 4; Bellamy *et al.* 2001
Easton on the Hill	2		2						Table 4; Bellamy *et al.* 2001
Wittering	2								Table 4; Wall 2011
Milbrook	1		1	1			1		Tables 4 and 6; Tebbut 1982
Rook Hall	1		1	1					Table RCA1 and 6

Table 4. Radiocarbon results associated with post-Roman iron smelting activities from England, Wales and Ireland

Lab Number	Sample No	Material and context	Radiocarbon Age (BP)	δ^{13}C (‰)
Knockbrack – Site AR02, Hull and Taylor (2006) – NGR 107660 121267				
Beta-202182	3	Charcoal, *Quercus* from fill (60) of large pit (3) part of furnace complex (furnaces 7 and 8)	1790±50	
Beta-207372	8	Charcoal, *Corylus* sp. from fill (61) of large pit (3) part of furnace complex (furnaces 7 and 8)	1420±40	
Beta-210880	2	Charcoal, *Quercus* from fill (58) of large pit (3) part of furnace complex (furnaces 7 and 8)	1680±40	
South Hook, Wales, Crane and Murphy (2010) – SM 873062				
Beta-222371		Charcoal, gorse/broom roundwood, minimum 8 yrs old from charcoal deposit (1082) bottom of gully of furnace (1081)	1150±50	
Burlescombe: Town Farm – Reed *et al.* (2006) – ST 0790 1701				
AA-34523	678321	Charcoal, *Quercus* sapwood from *in situ* furnace slag (553) from slagpit furnace [525]	1195±45	–
AA-34524	678320	Charcoal, *Hedera* or *Sambucus* from *in situ* furnace slag (553) from slagpit furnace [525]	1145±50	–

Table 4 *continued*

Lab Number	Sample No	Material and context	Radiocarbon Age (BP)	δ¹³C (‰)
Hemyock: Culmstock Road Rainbird and Young (2015) – ST 132 133				
SUERC-51250	16	Charcoal, *Euonymus*, from context [16] a fill of slagpit furnace [15]	1271±35	−23.2
SUERC-51251	17	Charcoal, *Alnus glutinosa* from context [77] a fill of slagpit furnace [14]	1197±35	−26.6
Dunkeswell , Grififth and Weddell (1996) – ST 14 07				
AA-17827	BDH.HIS 547 529	Charcoal, birch from ironworking debris from the surface	1260±50	–
Lydney: Clearwell Quarry, Gloucestershire, Pine *et al.* (2009) – SO 5700 0660				
KIA-38910	25	Charcoal, unidentified from fill [155] of furnace [33]	1213±31	
KIA-38911	36	Charcoal, unidentified from fill [187] of furnace [42]	1215±33	
KIA-38912	44	Charcoal, unidentified from fill [268] of furnace [11]	1231±24	
Emersons Green, Gloucestershire, Young and Young (2013) – ST6705 7785				
SUERC-41050	1521 [1608]	Charcoal, *Quercus* sp. sapwood (single fragment) from a discrete spread of ash/charcoal-rich waste containing smelting debris and deposited prior to the construction of smelting furnaces F3 and F9	1430 ±35	−26.0
SUERC-41054	1522 [1606]	Charcoal, *Quercus* sp. roundwood (single fragment) from the fill of large pit P4, thought to have been a charcoal fuel preparation and storage area during smelting and subsequently backfilled with slag and smelting waste	1160 ±35	−25.9
SUERC-41055	1558 [1611]	Charcoal, Maloideae (single fragment) from a slag and charcoal-rich deposit immediately sealing the base of tapping pit P12 associated with smelting furnace F8	1150 ±35	−27.3
SUERC-41056	1563 [1665]	Charcoal, *Corylus avellana* (single fragment) from a discrete thin charcoal deposit lining the base of tapping pit P10 associated with smelting furnace F1	1105 ±35	−25.5
SUERC-41057	2109 [2300]	Carbonised grain, *Hordeum vulgare* (single fragment) from the second of four fills deposited in the northern of two pits that combine to form a large linear feature bordering the northeast side of the main smelting area	1140 ±35	−22.5
SUERC-41058	1517 [1604]	Charcoal, *Corylus avellana* (single fragment) from the fill of second large charcoal storage/preparation pit P5, which predates the construction and use of smelting furnace F1	1195 ±35	−24.2
SUERC-41059	1554 [1607]	Charcoal, *Corylus avellana* (single fragment) from one of two deposits sealing the in situ slag run at the base of tapping pit P10 associated with furnace F1	1070 ±35	−24.7
SUERC-41936	1527 [1600]	Charcoal Quercus sp. *sapwood* (single fragment) from the latest in the sequence used to to backfill tapping pit P10 associated with furnace F1	1159 ±24	−26.8
Ramsbury, Wiltshire, Haslam (1980) – SU 2723 7155				
HAR-1606	50	Charcoal, *Quercus* sp. from fairly large timbers and *Corylus* sp. – few firs – from slag and charcoal deposits, area B	1170±70	
HAR-1704	51	Soil with charcoal, *unidentified* from slag and charcoal deposits, area B	1070±70	
HAR-1609	83	Charcoal, oak and hazel, large timber from charcoal deposits in interior of furnace 3	1180±70	
HAR-1626	117	Charcoal, unidentified, from filling of hearth area C (associated with furnace 3)	1130±70	
HAR-1607	61	Charcoal, oak, *Salix* sp. , and ?*Acer* – large timbers – from lowest level of stake hole in furnace 4	1320±70	
HAR-1608	41	Oak, hazel and maple – large timbers – from soil, area B (later than furnace 4)	1090±80	

Lab Number	Sample No	Material and context	Radiocarbon Age (BP)	$\delta^{13}C$ (‰)
Rockingham Forest, Bulwick, Northamtonshire, Bellamy *et al.* (2001) – SP 9700 9485				
Beta-115975[#]		Charcoal, unidentified (radiometric measurement) from slag mound	1380±60	–
Rockingham Forest, Oundle, Northamtonshire, Bellamy *et al.* (2001) – TL 0125 8804				
Beta-13287[#]		Charcoal, unidentified (radiometric measurement) from slag mound	990±60	–
Rockingham Forest, Easton on the Hill, Northamtonshire, Bellamy *et al.* (2001) – TF 0205 0035				
Beta-129110[#]		Charcoal, unidentified (radiometric measurement) from furnace site (tap slag)	1470±60	–
Rockingham Forest, Easton on the Hill, Northamtonshire, Bellamy *et al.* (2001) – TF 0206 0034				
Beta-149079[#]		Charcoal, unidentified (radiometric measurement) from smithing site	1310±70	–
Rockingham Forest, Gretton, Northamtonshire, Bellamy *et al.* (2001) – SP 8943 9280				
Beta-133576		Charcoal, unidentified (radiometric measurement) from slag mound	920±60	
Rockingham Forest, Gretton, Northamtonshire, Bellamy *et al.* (2001) – SP 8949 9283				
Beta-133577[#]		Charcoal, unidentified (radiometric measurement) from slag mound	1080±40	
Rockingham Forest, Gretton, Northamtonshire, Bellamy *et al* (2001) – SP 8952 9285				
Beta-133578[#]		Charcoal, unidentified (radiometric measurement) from slag mound	940±40	
Rockingham Forest, Fineshade, Northamptonshire, Bellamy *et al.* (2001) – SP 9730 9800				
Beta-133572[#]		Charcoal, unidentified (radiometric measurement) from slag patch	810±60	
Beta-133573[#]		Charcoal, unidentified (radiometric measurement) from slag patch	810±50	
Rockingham Forest, Fineshade, Northamptonshire, Bellamy *et al.* (2001) – SP 9742 9827				
Beta-133574[#]		Charcoal, unidentified (radiometric measurement) from slag patch	940±60	
Fineshade, Northamptonshire, Bellamy *et al.* (2001) – SP 9724 9750				
Beta-132828		Charcoal, unidentified (radiometric measurement) from slag mound	980±60	
Fineshade, Northamptonshire, Bellamy *et al.* (2001) – SP 9765 9784				
Beta-133575		Charcoal, unidentified (radiometric measurement) from slag patch	1470±50	
Rockingham Forest, Fineshade, Northamptonshire, Bellamy *et al.* (2001) – SP 9740 9805				
Beta-146019[#]		Charcoal, unidentified (radiometric measurement) from slag mound/furnace	1060±50	
Wakerley, Northamptonshire, Fell (2007) – SP 946 980				
Beta-222901	Trench 12, 7	Charcoal, *Quercus* sp. sapwood (single fragment) from channel hearth [1217]	1270±40	
Beta-222902	Trench 54, 3	Charcoal, *Quercus* sp. sapwood (single fragment) from [5404] fill of furnace [5407]. The lack of iron slag and roasted ore, both within or near the feature has to make its interpretation as a furnace tentative.	1380±40	
Beta-222897	Trench 63, 37	Charcoal, *Quercus* sp. sapwood (single fragment) from [633] primary fill of furnace [6332]	2050±40	
Beta-222899	Trench 87, 44	Charcoal, *Quercus* sp. sapwood (single fragment) from channel hearth [8711]	1140±40	
Beta-222898	Trench 87, 47	Charcoal, *Quercus* sp. sapwood (single fragment) from [8710] fill of furnace [8709] (tapping slag)	1220±40	
Beta-222900	Trench 93, 2	Charcoal, *Quercus* sp. sapwood (single fragment) from channel hearth [9306]	1260±40	
Fineshade Abbey, Northamptonshire, Mudd (2006) – SP 973 979				

Table 4 ***continued***

Lab Number	Sample No	Material and context	Radiocarbon Age (BP)	$\delta^{13}C$ (‰)
Beta-13947		Charcoal, oak heartwood (radiometric measurement) from fill [92] of furnace [46] (tap slag)	1410±40	
Wittering: Bonemills Farm, Cambridgeshire, Wall (2011) –TF 0475 0153				
Beta-111221		Charcoal, *Quercus* sapwood from (1003) slag tapping furnace [1]	1350±80	
Beta-111222		Charcoal, *Sambucus* from ?bloomsmithing hearth or ?slag-pit furnace, pit (1013)	1230±50	
Millbrook, Sussex, Tebbutt (1992) – TQ 441 296				
HAR-4117		Charcoal, *Quercus* sp. ?mature timbers from non-tapping furnace	1220±70	
Little Totham, Rook Hall, Essex, (Adkins 1989) – TL 878 093				
GU-2151	F1911	Charcoal, maple and oak from slag tapping furnace F1911	1380±60	−24.7

Table 5. Key parameters for post-Roman iron working activities in England, Ireland, and Wales (`Courier font` **denotes OxCal commands)**

Parameter name	Parameter description	Posterior Density Estimate (95% probability unless otherwise stated) cal AD	Posterior Density Estimate (68% probability unless otherwise stated) cal AD
Woodstown			
furnace	`Date` parameter estimating the date of the furnace in boundary Ditch 1B	*680–830*	*715–790*
Last_F2530	`Last` parameter estimating the last dated event in F2530	*875–995*	*890–930 (41%) or 940–970 (27%)*
Last_F2500	`Last` parameter estimating the last dated event in F2530	*880–995*	*895–930 (40%) or 940–970 (28%)*
Knockbrock			
furnaces_7_8	`Date` parameter estimating the date of the use of furnaces 7 and 8	*535–665*	*590–650*
South Hook			
Furncae_1081	`Date` parameter estimating the date of the use of furnace 1081	*775–995*	*855–975*
Burlescombe			
last_burlescombe	`Last` parameter estimating the last dated event at Burlescome	*780–990*	*850–975*
Hemyock: Culmstock Road			
last_culmstock	`Last` parameter estimating the last dated event at Culmstock Road	*720–900 (92%) or 925–945 (3%)*	*775–780 (2%) or 785–885 (66%)*
Dunkeswell			
last_dunkeswell	`Last` parameter estimating the last dated event at Dunkeswell	*660–885*	*670–780 (63%) or 790–805 (3%) or 845–855 (2%)*
Hemyock: Churchills Farm			
start_hemyock	`Boundary` parameter estimating the start of activity at Hemyock: Churchills Farm	*865–935*	*875–910*
end_hemyock	`Boundary` parameter estimating the end of activity at Hemyock: Churchills Farm	*900–975*	*905–950*
Clearwell			
last_clearwell	`Last` parameter estimating the last dated event at clearwell	*765–895*	*820–890*
Emersons Green			
Furnace 1	`Date` parameter estimating the date of the use of furnace 1	*830–950*	*865–915*

Parameter name	Parameter description	Posterior Density Estimate (95% probability unless otherwise stated) cal AD	Posterior Density Estimate (68% probability unless otherwise stated) cal AD
SUERC-41054	`Date` parameter providing a *terminus ante quem* for the date of the use of furnaces 2, 10, and 11	*815–970*	*865–905 (41%) or 915–950 (27%)*
SUERC-41050	`Date` parameter providing a *terminus post quem* for the date of the use of furnaces 3, and 9	*535–680*	*585–660*
Worgret			
T32_felling	`Date` parameter providing a *terminus post quem* for the date of iron working	*650–695*	*660–685*
Bestwall			
start_iron_working	`Boundary` parameter estimating the start of iron working activity at Bestwall	*570–660*	*610–650*
end_ iron_working	`Boundary` parameter estimating the end of iron working activity at Bestwall	*775–1050*	*795–925*
Ramsbury			
start_ramsbury	`Boundary` parameter estimating the start of iron working activity at Ramsbury	*620–980*	*770–960*
end_ramsbury	`Boundary` parameter estimating the end of iron working activity at Ramsbury	*880–1195*	*935–1080*
Gretton			
Last_gretton	`Last` parameter estimating the last dated event at Gretton	*1035–1210*	*1070–1165*
Wakerley			
start_wakerley	`Boundary` parameter estimating the start of iron working activity at Wakerley	*570–760*	*595–685*
end_wakerley	`Boundary` parameter estimating the end of iron working activity at Wakerley	*730–1090*	*780–945*
Bulwich			
Last_bulwich	`Last` parameter estimating the last dated event at Bulwich	*550–770*	*595–690*
Fineshade			
Last_fineshade	`Last` parameter estimating the last dated event at Fineshade	*1055–1270*	*1065–1085 (6%) or 1155–1255 (62%)*
Fineshade Abbey			
Last_fineshade_ abbey	`Last` parameter estimating the last dated event at Fineshade Abbey	*565–675*	*605–660*
Oundle			
Last_oundle	`Last` parameter estimating the last dated event at Oundle	*895–925 (3%) or 940–1170 (92%)*	*985–1055 (40%) or 1075–1150 (28%)*
Easton-on-the-Hill site A			
Last_easton_A	`Last` parameter estimating the last dated event at Easton-on-the-Hill site A	*425–665*	*545–650*
Easton-on-the-Hill site B			
Last_easton_B	`Last` parameter estimating the last dated event at Easton-on-the-Hill site B	*610–885*	*650–775*
Wittering			
Last_wittering	`Last` parameter estimating the last dated event at Wittering, Bonemills Farm	*675–900 (93%) or 925–945 (2%)*	*725–880*
Millbrook			
Last_millbrook	`Last` parameter estimating the last dated event at Millbrook	*740–980*	*800–925*
Rook Hall			
Last_rook_hall	`Last` parameter estimating the last dated event at Rook Hall	*530–1105*	*585–876*

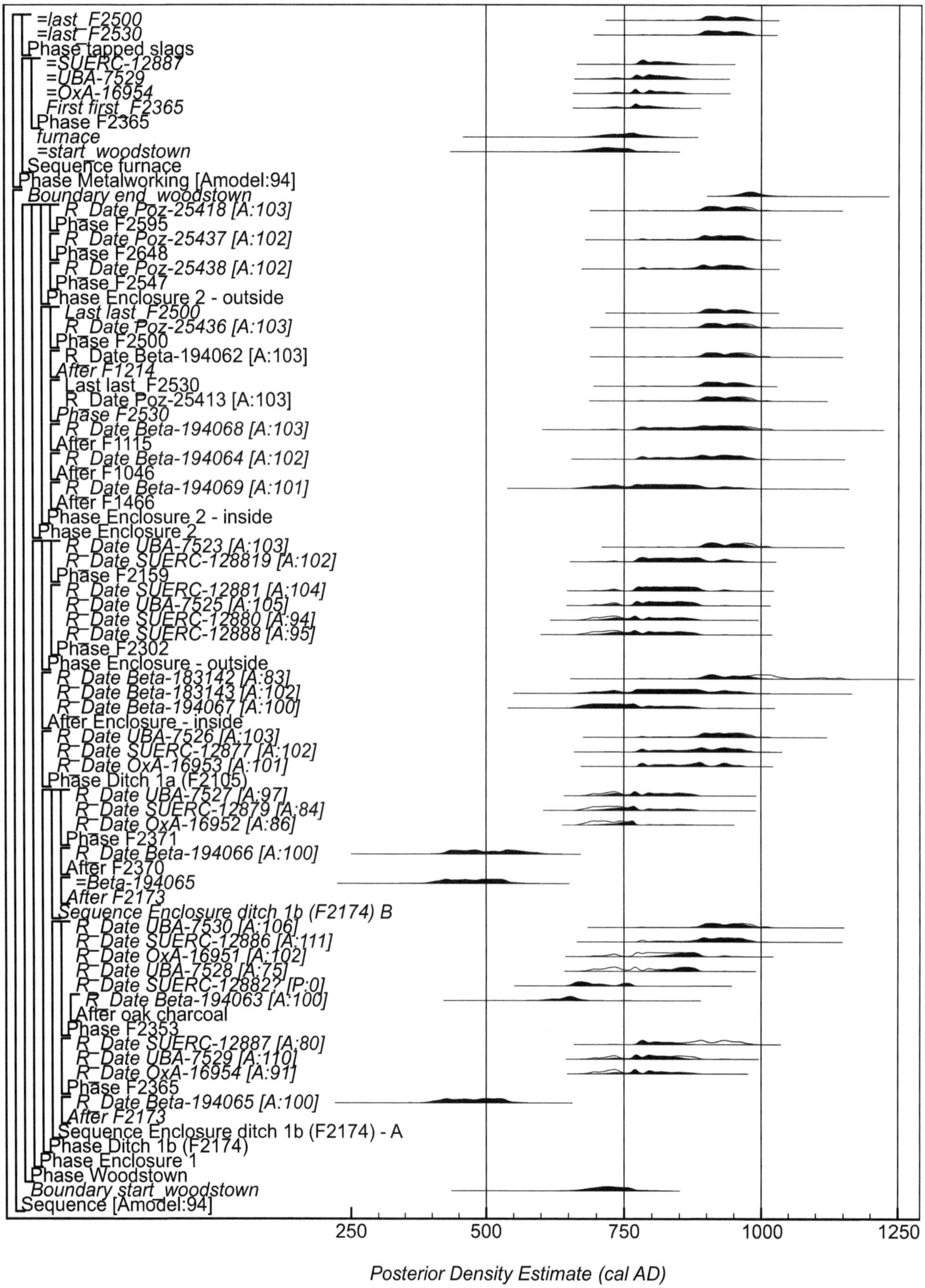

Figure 42. Probability distributions of dates from Woodstown. Each distribution represents the relative probability that an event occurs at a particular time. For each radiocarbon date, two distributions have been plotted: one in outline which is the result of simple radiocarbon calibration, and a solid one based on the chronological model used. The other distributions correspond to aspects of the model. For example, the distribution '*furnace*' is the estimate for the last use of the furnace in defensive Ditch 1b. The large square brackets down the left-hand side of the diagram and the OxCal keywords define the overall model exactly.

This review sets out the current understanding of the chronology of particular iron working sites, considering them from east to west across Ireland, Wales, and England.

Woodstown, Ireland

Between 2003 and 2007 archaeological investigations along the proposed route of the Waterford City Bypass on behalf of Ireland's National Road authority discovered the remains of a Viking settlement on the southern bank of the River Suir at Woodstown (Russell and Hurley 2014). A slag tapping furnace subsequently converted into a smithing hearth was constructed within the terminal of one of the defensive ditches (Ditch 1b) of the longphort at the northern entrance to Enclosure 1. In addition tapped slags occurred in the deposits associated with a building from the interior of Enclosure 2, 400m SW of the furnace.

Our model (Figure 42) that follows the stratigraphic relationships outlined in Russell and Hurley (2014) has good overall agreement (Amodel=94) and provides an estimate for the last use of the furnace of *cal* AD 680–830 (*95% probability*; *furnace*; Figure 42), probably *cal* AD 715–785 (*68% probability*).

Knockbrack, Co. Kerry Ireland

Fieldwork in 2004 as part of the National Roads Authority scheme for upgrading the N21 Limerick to Tralee Road between Castleisland and Abbeyfeale resulted in excavation of six archaeological sites (Hull and Taylor 2006). One of these in the townland of Knockbrack found evidence for an early medieval ironworking complex. This was composed of an iron smelting furnace as well as a number of pits. Three radiocarbon dates were obtained (Table 4) and the model shown in Figure 43 provides an estimate for the use of the two possible furnaces (7 and 8) of *cal* AD 370–660 (*95% probability*; *furnaces_7_8*; Figure 43), probably *cal* AD 490–645 (*68% probability*).

South Hook

Dyfed Archaeological Trust undertook an archaeological excavation on the site of the former Esse oil refinery at South Hook, near Milford Haven during construction of an Exxon Mobil liquid natural gas storage installation between 2004–5. The excavations revealed an early medieval settlement with an associated iron smelting site and crop processing complex (Crane and Murphy 2010).

Within Complex 1 were the remains of two iron smelting furnaces. The chronological model shown in Figure 44 excludes the three measurement (Beta-255067, Beta-255069, and Beta-255072; Table 4) that relate to Bronze Age activity and includes the dates as deriving from a single phase of activity. The model has good overall agreement (Amodel=94) and provides an estimate for the use of iron working furnace (1071) of *cal* AD 775–990 (*95% probability*; *Beta-222371*; Figure 44), probably *cal* AD 855–970 (*68% probability*).

Burlescombe

Excavations at the site of a proposed quarry extension near Town Farm, Burlescombe in 1996 uncovered the remains of three iron smelting furnaces (Reed *et al.* 2006). Radiocarbon determinations on two fragments of charcoal (Table 4) from slagpit furnace [525] provide a date for its last use.

Dunkeswell

During the early 1990s a programme of investigation into early working in the Blackdown Hills was undertaken by Devon County Council Archaeological Service and Exeter Archaeology (Griffith and Weddell 1996). Fieldwork including the use of documentary evidence, aerial photographic reconnaissance, field investigation and geophysical prospection demonstrated ironworking to have been carried out in the Blackdown Hills from the Roman–middle ages. A single radiocarbon measurement on a fragment of charcoal (Table 4) from the parish of Dunkeswell provides a date for iron working activity.

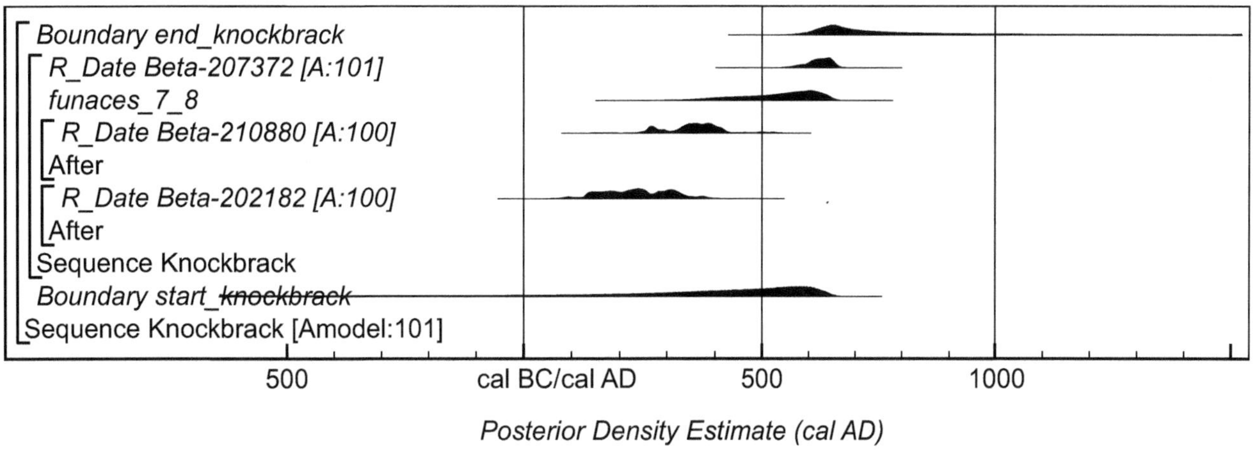

Figure 43. Probability distributions of dates from Knockbrack. The overall format is identical to Figure 42.

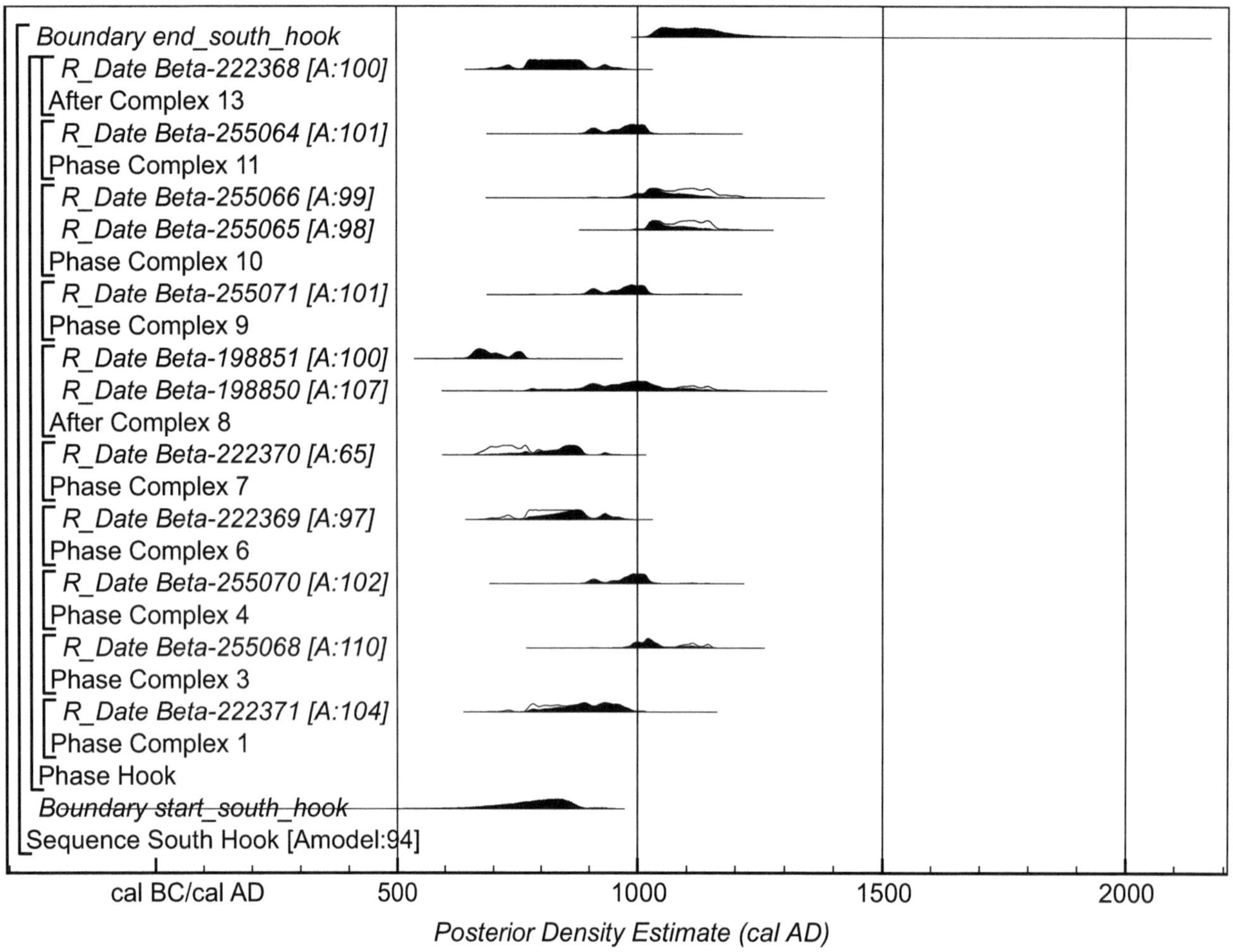

Figure 44. Probability distributions of dates from South Hook. The overall format is identical to Figure 42.

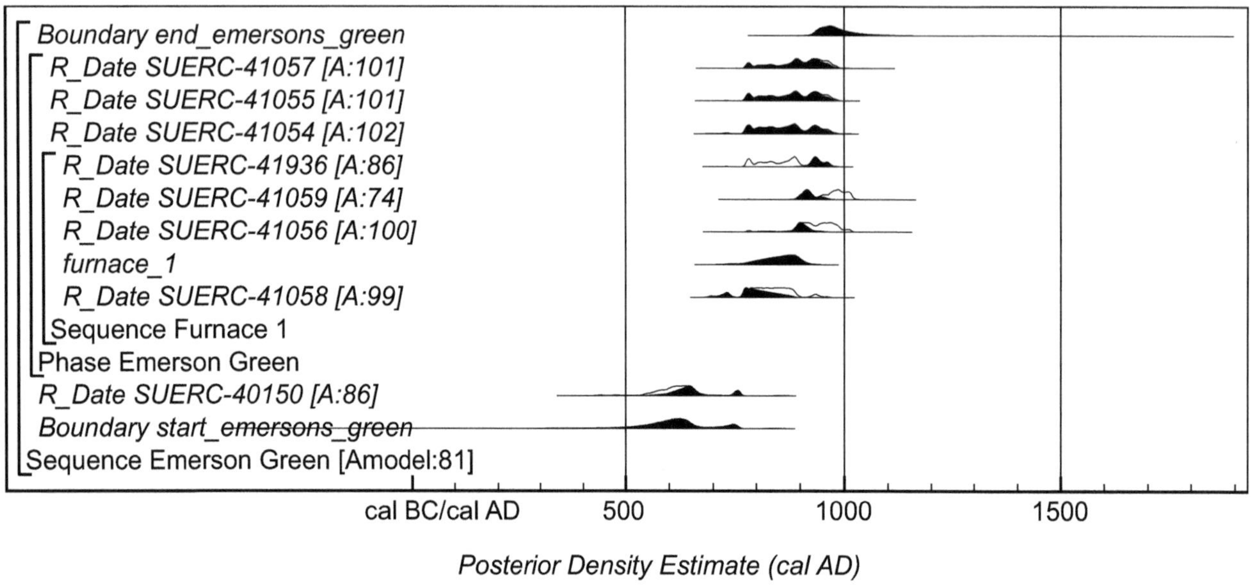

Figure 45. Probability distributions of dates from Emerson Green. The overall format is identical to Figure 42.

Culmstock Road, Hemyock

Excavations in 2012 on agricultural land to the south of Culmstock Road, Hemyock followed an earlier evaluation in advance of a residential development, which had uncovered a significant evidence for iron smelting activity (Rainbird and Young 2015). Two dated short-lived pieces of charcoal (Table 4) from slagpit furnace F14 and adjacent pit F15 give an indication of the date of smelting activity.

Clearwell, Quarry

Open area excavations in advance of limestone extraction at Clearwell Quarry revealed evidence for Saxon iron working activity, including 30 furnaces, 10 ore roasting pits and seven charcoal-clamps. Three samples of unidentified charcoal (Table 4) provide *termini post quos* for iron smelting (Pine *et al.* 2009).

Emersons Green, Gloucestershire

Excavations in advance of development for the new Bristol & Bath Science Park at Emersons Green, South Gloucestershire revealed evidence of a highly developed iron smelting industry dating to the late Anglo-Saxon period Young and Young (2013). A group of 13 iron bloomery furnaces were recorded, one with the *in-situ* tapping runs from the final smelting preserved in an associated tapping pit. Charcoal storage areas were also identified alongside significant quantities of smelting waste occurring as spreads or filling pits.

Eight radiocarbon determinations were obtained on short-lived single entity samples of charcoal or grain. The model shown in Figure 45 follows Young and Young (2013; fig 6.3.2) although we have chosen to not exclude SUERC-41050 as this provides a *terminus post quo* for the construction of smelting furnaces F3 and F9.

Worget

Excavations on the flood-plain of the River Frome at Worgret, 2km west of Wareham in 1988 produced evidence for ironworking activity in the form of iron-slag and furnace lining residues that had been used to fill the base of a wooden structure (Maynard 1988). Timber 32, a base-plate which unlike some of the timbers did not appear to be reused (Maynard 1988, 88; figs 4 and 10) produced a tree-ring date for the last ring of the 224 year sequence of AD 654 (Table 6; Hinton 1992). In order to estimate the felling date, the probability distribution of the number of sapwood rings expected to be missing from the sample has been applied, given the sequence ended at the heartwood-sapwood boundary to provide an estimate of the date of the felling of the timber. The methodology for this approach is described by Bayliss and Tyers (2004). The resultant estimate for the felling of Timber 32; *cal* AD 660–685 (*95% probability*; *T32_felling*; Figure 46), probably *cal* AD 650–695 (*68% probability*), provides a *terminus post quem* for the ironworking at the site.

Table 6. Tree-ring date associated with iron smelting activity from Worgret, Dorset

Sample	Material and Context	Date
Timber 32	*Quercus* sp. 224 rings, ?heartwood sapwood boundary, AD 431–654 base plate that appeared to have not been reused (Maynard 1988)	After AD 664

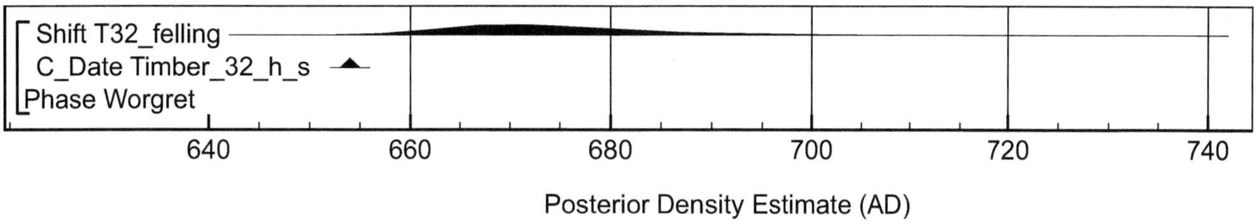

Figure 46. Probability distributions of dates from Worgret.

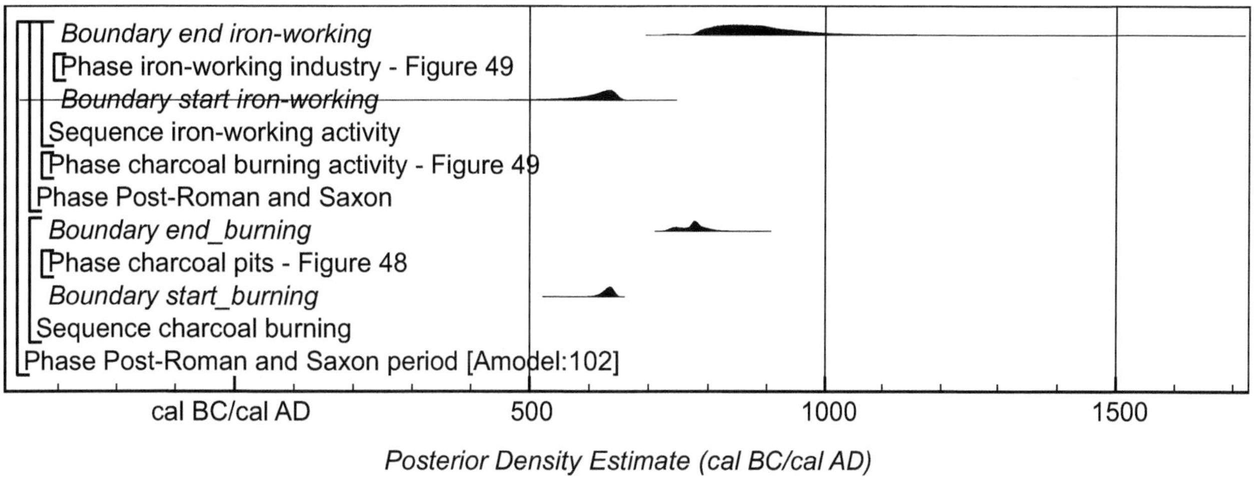

Figure 47. Overall structure for the model for the chronology of Bestwall Quarry. The component sections of this model are shown in detail in Figures 48 and 49.

Bestwall Quarry

A 13-year 'rescue' archaeology project uncovered a multi-period landscape with features dating from the early Mesolithic to the post-medieval period and comprise field systems, droveways, working areas, domestic structures, pit clusters, industrial activity, burials, and ritual deposits. A chronological model for the post-Roman and Saxon

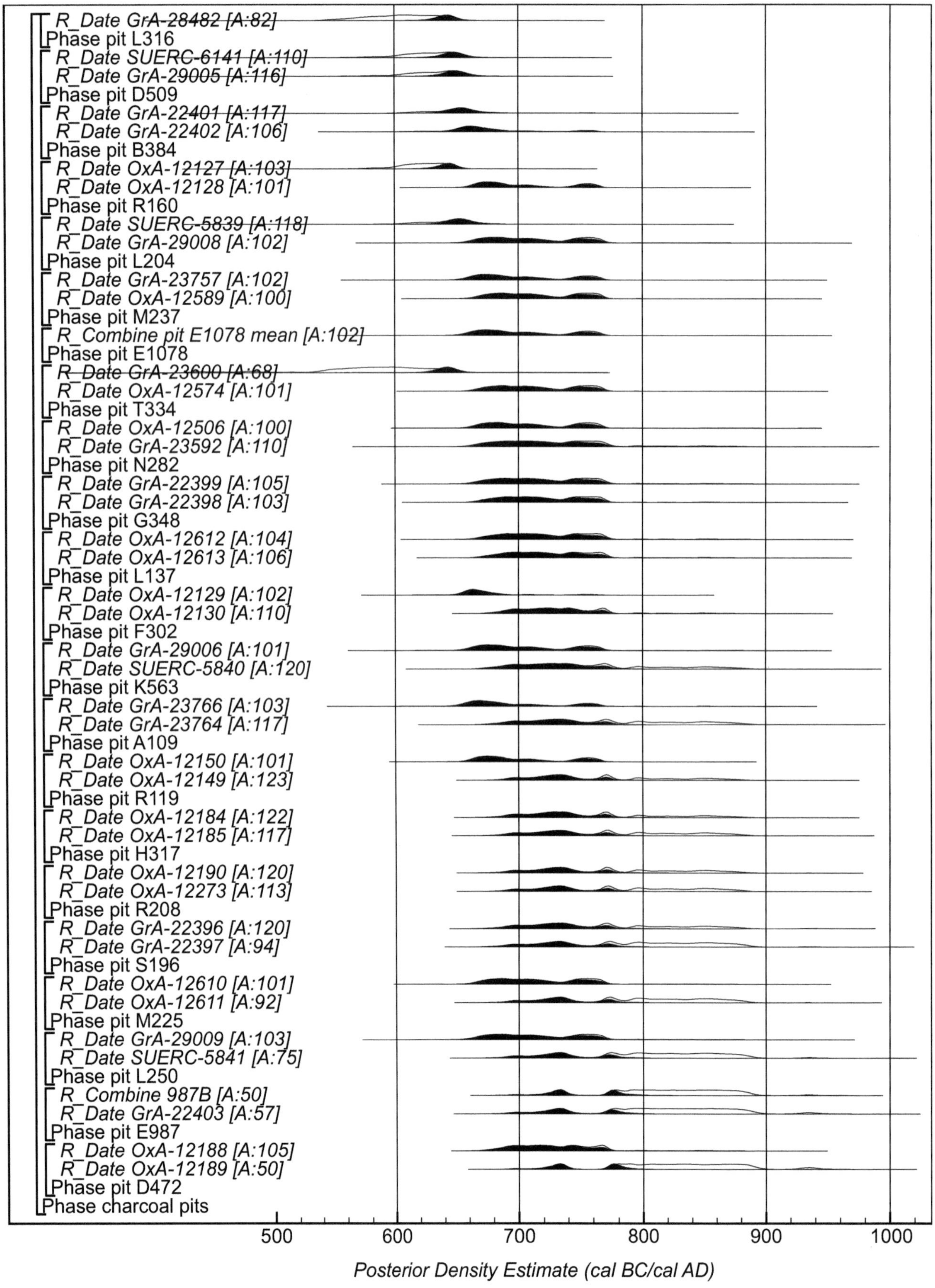

Figure 48. Probability distributions of dates from Bestwall Quarry. The overall format is identical to Figure 42.

elements of the site is presented in Ladle (2012, figs 108–9); re-running this model (Figures 47-49) but with OxA-12819 from spread treated as a *terminus post quem* given how significantly earlier it is than any other dated iron working activity provides estimates for ironworking activity on the site beginning in *cal* AD 490–665 (*95% probability*; *start iron working*; Figure 47), probably *cal* AD 590–650 (*68% probability)* and ending in *cal* AD 775–1055 (*95% probability*; *end iron working*; Figure 47), probably *cal* AD 795–925 (*68% probability).*

Ramsbury, Wiltshire

Excavations at the High Street Ramsbury in 1974 revealed an iron smelting and smithing site that consisted of at least three phases of bowl furnaces and associated features, including a timber-framed shelter (Haslam 1980).

Six radiocarbon measurements (Table 4) were obtained and the chronological model shown in Figure 50 that includes the dates as deriving from a single phase of activity, with stratigraphic relationships derived from Haslam (1980, fig 10) has good overall agreement (Amodel=92) and suggests iron working activity was taking place in the second half of the first millennium cal AD.

Rockingham Forest

Samples of slag, ore, roasted ore, fines, and charcoal were taken from slag patches and mounds as part of a survey of early iron smelting sites in Rockingham Forest, Northamptonshire (Bellamy *et al.* 2001). Thirteen radiocarbon determinations were obtained from five sites; Fineshade, Gretton, Bulwick, Oundle Wood, and Easton Hornstock Wood (Table 4). All 13 samples consisted of bulked unidentified charcoal and given the possibility for both significant age-at-death offsets and material of different ages being incorporated into the samples they only provide *termini post quos* for iron smelting activity.

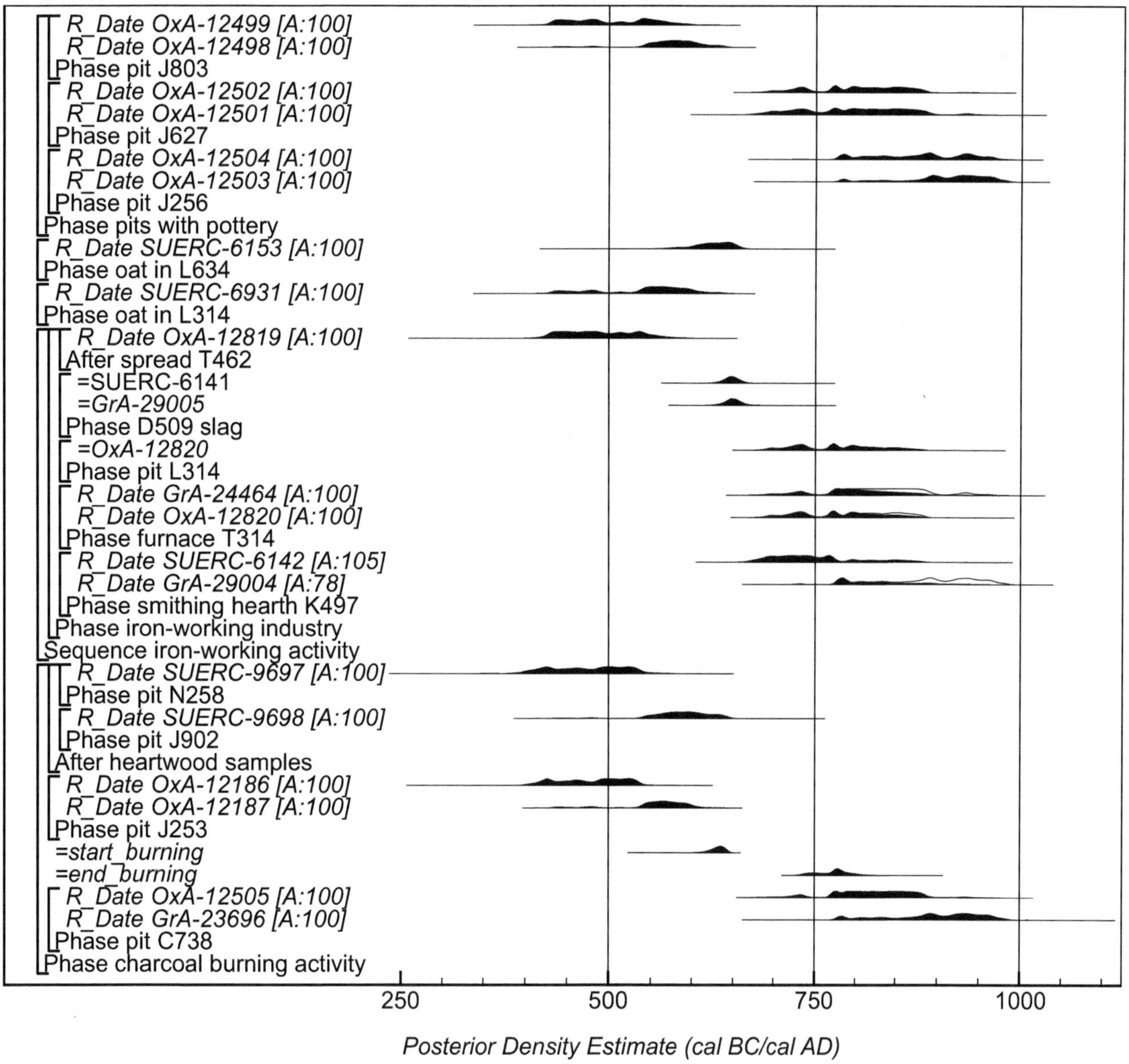

Figure 49. Probability distributions of dates from Bestwall Quarry. The overall format is identical to Figure 42.

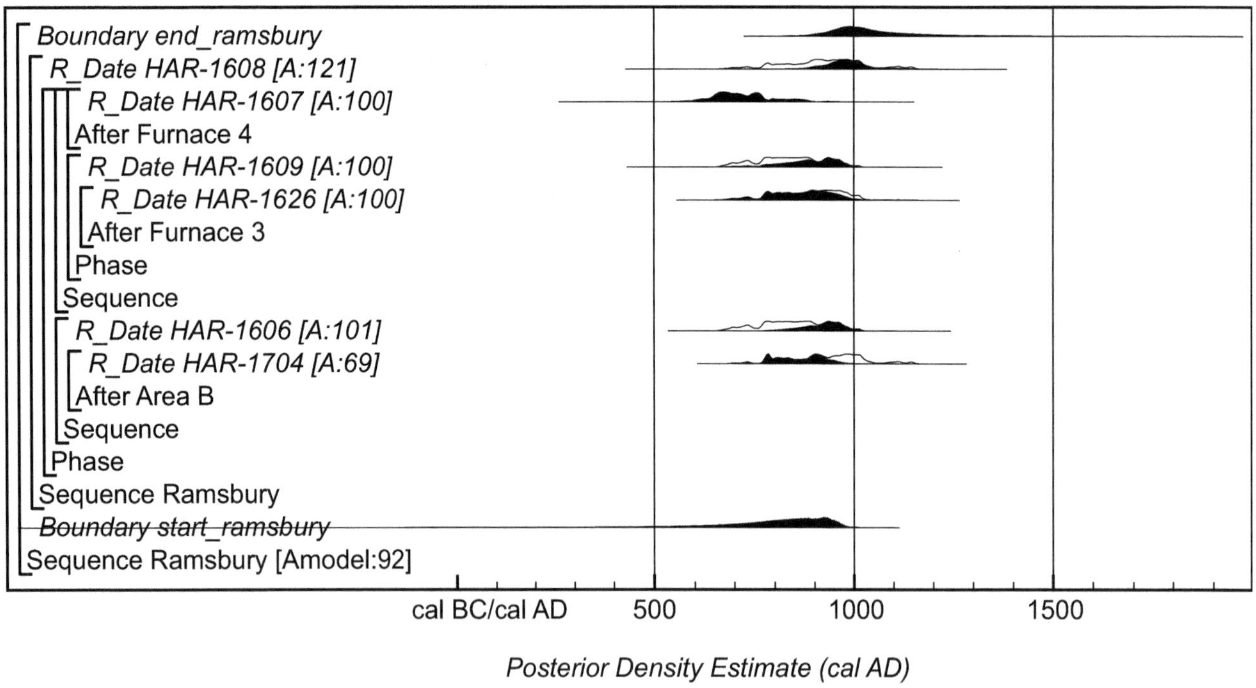

Figure 50. Probability distributions of dates from Ramsbury. The overall format is identical to Figure 42.

Wakerley, Northamptonshire

In 2005 Archaeological Services and Consultancy Ltd undertook a programme of archaeological trial trenching on land at Wakerley, Northamptonshire, following earlier phases of desk-based assessment, fieldwalking and geophysical survey, with 103 trenches excavated over an area of 122 hectares (Fell 2007).

A complex of late Iron Age or early Roman furnaces was identified in the north central part of the site. Evidence for Saxon iron smelting was also identified. This was more dispersed than the Roman features and included a substantial complex adjacent to Wakerley Great Wood. A number of features identified as possible ore roasting pits/ channel hearths and furnaces were present, sealed by a large deposit of slag. Further possible ore roasting pits were identified at the west end of the airfield and the northeast end of the site, adjacent to the wood.

Six radiocarbon measurements (Table 3) were obtained from the fills of furnaces and channel hearths, interpreted as possible ore-roasting pits. The chronological model shown in Figure 51 excludes the measurement (Beta-222897; Table 4) that relates to Iron Age activity and includes the dates on short-lived charcoal fragments relating to iron smelting as deriving from a single phase of activity. The model has good overall agreement (Amodel=86) and suggests iron working activity was taking place in the second half of the first millennium cal AD.

Fineshade Abbey, Northamptonshire

Archaeological excavations within the former kitchen garden of Fineshade Abbey in 1998 resulted in the excavation of a group of iron smelting furnaces and associated features, including hearts and ditches (Mudd 2006). A single radiocarbon determination on fragments of oak heartwood (Table 4) from furnace 46 provides a *terminus post quem* for its last use given an unknown age-at-death offset.

Wittering: Bonemills Farm, Cambridgeshire

An archaeological excaluation on the route of an Anglian Water pipeline in 1997 by Cambridgeshire County Council Field Archaeological Service revealed the remains of two iron-smelting furnaces and other metalworking features near Bonemills Farm, Wittering Wall (2011). Short-lived fragments of charcoal from furnace 1 and the possible bloomsmithing hearth provide dates for the last use of both features (Table 4).

Millbrook, Sussex

During 1979–80 a new water main was installed from Hosted Keynes to anew reservoir at Black Hill on Ashdown Forest by the Mid-Sussex Water Company. Rescue excavations undertaken by the Wealden Iron Research Group after the discovery of a bloomer furnace site revealed furnaces, hearths and a slag heap all associated with iron working (Tebbut 1982). A radiocarbon date from sample of soil together with a few fragments of oak charcoal probably from mature timbers (Keepax 1980) provides a *terminus post quem* for iron working (Table 4), while an archaeomagnetic date affords a better estimate for the date of the activity (Table 7).

Rook Hall, Site 2, Essex

Excavated from 1982 to 1988 by Pat Adkins in advance of gravel quarrying site 2 at Rook Hall uncovered Saxon

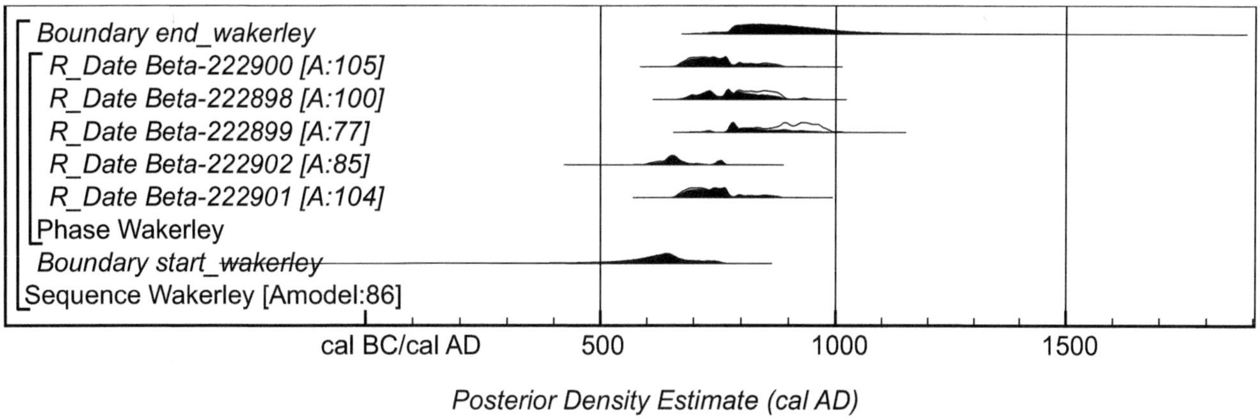

Figure 51. Probability distributions of dates from Wakerley. The overall format is identical to Figure 42.

Table 7. Archaeomagnetic date associated with iron smelting activity from Millbrook, Sussex

Sample	Material and Context	Date
	Southern part of furnace and south-eastern sector of hearth 1	AD 860±60

Table 8. TL date associated with iron smelting activity from Little Totham, Rook Hall, Essex

Sample	Material and Context	Date
TL-90	Fragment of tuyere from F1911 Site 2	AD 530±290

activity both domestic and industrial and included hearths, six sunken featured buildings and possibly at least one large post-built building as well as large quantities of metalworking debris concentrated in one area. The metalworking activity comprised slag, cinder, ore and tuyere fragments which was largely discarded in pits although one feature had *in-situ* tuyeres and vitrified furnace wall and is interpreted as a smelting furnace of the slag- tapping type. Thermoluminescence and radiocarbon dates (Tables 4 and 8) provide an indication of the age of the iron working activity.

Conclusions

Non-slag tapping furnaces occur in the pre-Roman Iron Age and were supplanted by slag tapping technology in most of Romanised Britain, but were reintroduced in the early medieval period, before being replaced by slag tapping again in the ninth/tenth centuries cal AD. The model shown in Figure 41 that includes the scientific dates listed in Table 3 from post-Roman metalworking sites in England, Wales, and Ireland with non-tapping and tapping technologies, together with associated dates from slag heaps and unrecorded furnace technologies has good overall agreement (Amodel=105) and suggests the beginning of post-Roman ironworking began in *cal* AD 465–640 (*95% probability*; *start_iron*; Figure 41), probably *cal* AD 540–625 (*68% probability*). The main flourit of iron working activity appears to have been in the seventh to tenth centuries cal AD, with Churchills Farm, Hemyock appearing to be relatively late.

The use of slag-pit and slag-tapping furnaces for the smelting of iron at Churchills Farm took place over a period of *1–70 years* (*95% probability*; *hemyock*; Figure 41) and probably *1–55 years* (*68% probability*) in the mid-ninth to mid-tenth centuries cal AD. These technologies used both split wood and cereal packing in the furnaces. The presence of Upper Greensand-Derived pottery in pit [556], which radiocarbon determination suggests belongs to a similar period to the production of iron at Churchills Farm, indicates that there was also a ceramic industry operating on the Blackdown Hills at this time but there spatial and economic relationship is not known.

Chapter 4

The Iron Industry

Tim Young

Introduction

The production of iron was achieved during the early medieval period by first smelting the iron ore in a shaft furnace and then working the raw iron to reduce and redistribute impurities and slag inclusions. The smelting furnace (often referred to as a bloomery) was a clay structure, fed with iron ore and charcoal at its top, which reduced the descending iron ore to metallic iron through reaction with ascending carbon monoxide (produced by combustion of the charcoal fuel). The combustion was produced in most cases by an air blast provided by bellows which entered the furnace through one or more blow-holes, at close to ground level. Some varieties of furnace employed tubular ceramic objects, tuyères, to carry the blast into the furnace, rather than using a simple blow-hole in the ceramic wall. The furnaces may have variously been cylindrical in shape, bottle-shaped, or domed.

The iron produced in the smelting reaction typically accumulated as a solid, if impure, block, known as a bloom, just below the level of the air blast. Not all the iron in the ore went into the bloom; the remainder, plus the impurities in the ore together with parts of the furnace structure that had melted, formed a liquid slag. The slag provided an environment within which the bloom could form, and its chemical composition was important for controlling that of the growing bloom. Excess slag would drain downwards past the bloom. There were two broad categories of management of the slag. In some furnaces, the excess slag was drained from the furnace, typically though an arched opening on one side of the base of the furnace, so that it cooled and solidified outside the furnace. This process is known as tapping the slag. An alternative approach was to let the slag drain downwards into a pit or chamber below the furnace. Furnaces employing this second approach may be referred-to as non-tapping, or slag pit furnaces. In order to support the initial furnace charge, but to allow space for the bloom to grow and the slag to drain, the basal pit or chamber of a non-tapping furnace was typically packed with a combustible material before the smelt commenced. This pit-packing was usually of round or split wood, but in some instances a packing of cereal stems (or even complete plants) or grass was used. Controlling the drainage of the slag was important, to ensure that there was room in the furnace for the bloom to grow, to permit removal of impurities such as phosphorus that might otherwise be taken-up by the metallic iron, and to control the ease with which the furnace could be prepared for its next use at the end of a smelt.

The raw bloom produced in the smelting furnace would be extracted (either through the top or through a basal arch) and then reworked by a smith to remove impurities and to control the distribution and form of the remaining slag inclusions. At Churchills Farm, evidence was found for both slag tapping and non-tapping furnaces, but there was extremely little evidence for the subsequent smithing of the blooms, which must have taken place elsewhere.

This chapter describes, in some detail, the evidence for the type of furnaces employed and for the nature of the smelting reaction, as indicated by the chemical and mineralogical composition and texture of the slags. The evidence is interpreted to permit comparison of the operation with that of other early medieval iron smelting, so that Churchills Farm may be placed into a historical and economic context.

The Nature of the Evidence

The evidence for the metallurgical activities on the site derives from consideration of both the metallurgical features, the truncated bases of bloomery iron smelting furnaces, and the residues that were recovered from both the associated metallurgical and non-metallurgical contexts. The furnaces included both five examples in which the slag was retained within a basal pit (the non-tapping, or slag pit, furnaces) and four examples in which the slag was tapped from furnace during the smelt, so that it solidified in an external pit or channel. There were also two cut features that were only dubiously identifiable as furnaces.

Approximately 1.1 tonnes of archaeometallurgical residues from iron production were collected from the site. Before coming into the hands of the University of Exeter the collection had undergone various changes of storage location whereby some storage sacks had split, and had been sub-sampled for a pilot assessment. Some of the material extracted from the collection for this early attempt at a technological classification was present at the time of assessment by this author, but none carried secure context information. As such, the quantifications offered here are given with the caveat that a small proportion of the excavated metallurgical residues are not represented.

Some of the largest individual assemblages came from late features (ditches, drains and clay extraction pits), in which the residues were reworked or residual. From an early stage in the post-excavation analysis, therefore, it was decided to focus on those slags securely associated with metallurgical features. This part of the collection was quantified, but for all contexts it must be borne in mind that material may have been removed from the assemblage prior to formal assessment (Table 9). This subsample of the overall collection had a total weight of approximately 226 kg, and formed the core material of the assessment (Young 2013), in which the materials were examined visually (with a low-powered hand lens or microscope when required).

General Description and Affinities of the Slag Pit Furnaces (see Figures 11-13 in Chapter 2)

The basal pits of the slag-pit furnaces form a morphologically-tight group:

- Furnace [756]: 0.45 m by 0.44 m and 0.25 m deep.
- Furnace [776]: 0.48 m by 0.52 m and 0.17 m deep.
- Furnace [787]: 0.39 m in diameter and 0.3 m deep.
- Furnace [794]: 0.5 m by 0.44 m and 0.45 m deep.
- Furnace [799]: 0.5 m by 0.46 m and 0.26 m deep.

Three of the furnaces contained large residue assemblages (furnace [756] 18 kg; furnace [794] 17 kg; furnace [799] 13.5 kg) which suggests that these furnaces may have undergone little clearance of waste after their last use; the others (furnaces [776] and [787]) only contained small residue assemblages and may therefore have been at least partially cleaned, perhaps to prepare them for a future smelt. The residues comprised fragments of porous slag cake of the form commonly termed 'furnace bottom' (which would have formed immediately below the bloom, not at the bottom of the pit), together with prilly flow slags and sometimes a dense basal 'puddle' where flows had penetrated low in the pit, perhaps early in the smelt. There was little significant preservation of furnace ceramic within the slag-pits (perhaps reflecting the lack of space for such material to accumulate in an uncleared pit). All the furnaces showed clear evidence for the use of a cereal pit-packing, and the residue assemblages are notable for their lack of burrs (the dense,

Table 9. Summary catalogue of residues from Churchills Farm. Items in italics are of less certain provenance

Context	Context notes	Context total (kg)	Bag note	Item weight (kg)	Item number	Item notes
(507)	fill of 'posthole' 506	18.87				Moderately large collection of non-tapped slags similar to those from (781) but less numerous. Some evidence for cereal packing.
(509)	upper fill of ditch 508					Much of this material seems to be tapped slag – with larger flow lobes and a hint of surficial reddening; worn surfaces on some pieces suggest a degree of reworking/residuality.
(513)	Fill of pit 512	0.28				
(529)	Fill of gully 528	4.27				
(531)	Fill of gully 530	3.17				
(539)	fill of tree hollow 538 (not shown on plans)	34.89	multiple sacks			collection of fresh-appearing slag from a pit. Most pieces (95%) are probably tapped, including some very large blocks reminiscent of the flows at Tisbury, with a few pieces of charcoal-rich material; no certain slagpit material
(529)	Fill of gully 528	2.98				
(557)	Fill of pit 556	150.56				
(560)	Fill of pit 559	27.31				
(583)	Fill of pit 582	15.1				
(570)	Fill of tree hollow 569 (not shown on plans)	0.82				
(571)	Fill of pit 589	41.62				
(505)	Fill of gully 504	11.53				
(579)	Fill of pit 572	25.93				
(580)	Fill of pit 572	9.59				
(583)	Fill of pit 582	14. 91				
(584)	Fill of pit 582	27.66				
(586)	Fill of gully 587	3.68				
(588)	Fill of pit 589	10.15				

Context	Context notes	Context total (kg)	Bag note	Item weight (kg)	Item number	Item notes
(505)	Fill of gully 504	1.81				
(593)	Fill of gully 592	2.36				
(677)	Fill of gully 667	26.48				
(601)	Fill of pit 589	10.23				
(616)	Fill of pit 715	70.16				contains good tapslag
(618)	Fill of pit 715	16.00				
(619)	Fill of pit 715	22.45				
(628)	Fill of pit 627	1.92				
(640)	Fill of pit 639	2.89				
(652)	Fill of pit 651	1.37				
(657)	Fill of gully 656	1.57				
(676)	Fill of pit 675	2.105		2.105	total	4 pieces, one obscured , but dense flow slags – at least one with coarsely crystalline quenched puddle
(677)	Fill of gully 667	4.87				
(678)	Fill of pit 675	0.632		0.502	6 + bits	oxidised fired ceramic, partly vitrified
				0.13	3	dense flow slags
(679)	Fill of elongated part of pit 675	1.475		1.475		rather scrappy assemblage of thin flow slags with some as slightly prill- or rod- like flows, fragments of oxidised fired lining
(681)	Fill of gully 680	69.93	multiple sacks			very large FB fragments, with very fine lobes on chilled margin
(685)	Fill of pit 684	4.02				
(688)	Fill of pit 684	0.76				
(696)	Fill of pit 694	9.52				
(707)	Fill of gully 705	28.36				most pieces appear dense, non-tapping slags, possibly some tapslag but not certain. Worn material, all rather weathered
(730)	Fill of root disturbance on edge of pit 729	2.14				
(718)	Fill of gully 717	0.38				
(722)	Fill of gully 721	1.44				
(726)	Fill of channel 725	1.85				
(728)	Fill of gully 727	5.68				
(730)	Fill of pit 729	41.50				small part of collection – rest discarded on site (*c*. 280 kg). Very good tapslag in moderately large blocks
	unmarked block from student colln		*730 in thesis*	*4.525*	*1*	*tap slag block labelled (2), very dense, similar in size to Tisbury blocks, base shows lobes in isolation except where on the upper margins there is a smooth non-wetted surface; top locally reddened and has a large iron clast in its proximal end*
(757)	Fill of furnace 756	17.91		17.11	1	large rounded mass representing most of a FB
				0.8	many	fragments of above
(759)	Fill of furnace 758	8.47		3.2	c80	small fragments of grey flow slag with grey resinous surface, forming good tapslag-like flows
				5.27	10	large pieces of flow slag including at least two foci of down wall flow
(760)	Fill of furnace 758	1.415		1.415		242 g of further furnace pit flow slag sheet/birdsfoot; remainder probably FB and wall fragments
(770)	Deposit	18.90				
(772)	Fill of furnace 771	13.645		0.796	22	oxidised lining – major pieces vitrified and slagged – others less so

Table 9 ***continued***

Context	Context notes	Context total (kg)	Bag note	Item weight (kg)	Item number	Item notes
				1.215	2	large blocks of vitrified oxidised lining, conjoin to form slab just below bowing hole with increasing oxidation to vivid red at point, possibly rests on reduced fired material quite abruptly but uncertain; blowhole itself is not seen
				4.485	6	major blocks of tap slag like material – including flows prilling down into charcoal bed
				2.95	200?	small fragments of flows
				3.715	60	smaller fragments of flows
				0.484	6	lining and burnt stone – all reduced-fired
(777)	Fill of furnace 776	3.375		0.374	5	small pieces
				0.786	1	very shiny basal non-wetted surface, dense slag passing up into less well-structured with probable cereals
				2.215	1	large block of porous FB
(781)	Fill of furnace 778	116.692	bag 1	1.6	c80	small pieces of grey fired clay, flow fragments and prills with other furnace floor debris
			bag 2	10.95	1	large unwashed FB
			bag 3	4.35	14	porous FB fragments
				3.96	3	pieces of flat-topped slag puddle with lobate margin and straw impressions on top.
				1.175	1	porous FB adhering to pit wall – mildly fused not full burr
			bag 4	8.38		mainly unwashed FB and wall material
				1.17		angle of wall pieces of sinter-like material
			bag 5	5.28	1	FB block
				2.015	1	rounded block, but possibly much adhering clay
				0.442	1	FB block
				1.13	1	FB block
			bag 6	16.11	9	large FB blocks, one piece shows more interesting texture, possibly showing flow fragments
			bag 7	4.925	1	large FB block
				2.955	1	large FB b block
				1.05		debris
			bag 9	19.17		mainly porous FB, but includes 4.1 kg (14 pieces) of dense puddle with cereal (and wood?) impressions
			bag 8	22.51		bag contained broken bag inside from context (793)
	unmarked block from student colln		*c(781) in thesis*	*9.52*	*1*	*large slag block, labelled (1), very dense lobate 'furnace bottom' with some brecciated, some non-wetted contacts, some hints of straw in the upper part*
(788)	Fill of furnace 787	15.435		1.095	c40	small fragments – wall slag interaction and thin on-wetted highly reflective sheets
				5.65	1	large block of finely prilly FB – shows hints of denser oblique basal flows, top planar, rough and rusty; piece can't be reassembled and appear to be missing at least one recently-broken fragment; just possibly a hint of cereal on one part of larger block
				0.92	1	similar to above
(790)	Fill of furnace 789	3.315		3.315		mostly thin pit bottom flow, but also fragment of ore and some wall-related material

Context	Context notes	Context total (kg)	Bag note	Item weight (kg)	Item number	Item notes
(793)	Fill of furnace 792	3.31		3.31		inner unmarked bag with wall or FB fragments; this material is probably (see above) muddled with a small amount of material from (781). The dominant material in the mixed group is a tapslag-like material – this is assumed to be from (793) since there is no similar material in (781).
(795)	Fill of furnace 794	20.63	bag 1	8.145	c50	small fragments
				3.56	3	large joining fragments, rather messy furnace floor material with some flows
			bag 2	5.88		unwashed material – some fb, but much appears mixed with wall material – needs washing
				3.045		(2.44 kg left after washing is mainly soil/burnt clay)
(798)	Fill of furnace 789	6.48				
(800)	Fill of furnace 799	13.55		5.915	1	very porous FB, small back has some material that is prilly around small charcoal but if this FB was *in situ* then there were no dense flows
				7.635	rest	
(808)	Fill of channel 807	27.13				Single large FB in archive
(810)	Fill of pit 809	2.14				
(505)	Fill of gully 504	0.09				
(814)	Fill of gully 813	3.06				
(820)	Fill of ditch 819	4.69				
(822)	Fill of pit/posthole 821	3.27				single large FB fragment in archive
(826)	Fill of pit/posthole 825	0.06				
(828)	Fill of pit/posthole 827	0.56				
(830)	Fill of 829	0.60				
(849)	Fill of ditch 848	9.01				
(856)	Fill of posthole 855	26.90				
(858)	Fill of posthole 857	2.55				
(866)	Fill of posthole 850	0.69				
(873)	Fill of gully 892	2.63				
(875)	Fill of gully 874	5.10				
(882)	fill of probable late feature					medium sized SHC and tapslag block

bulbous slag masses developed in the zone of interaction between the hot-zone and the furnace/pit wall just below the blowhole).

The most similar early medieval slag pit furnaces with evidence for cereal pit-packing to those of Churchills Farm are those from Yorkley and from Clearwell Quarry, both in the Forest of Dean, Gloucestershire and from Eckington in Derbyshire. At Yorkley, a single, unexcavated furnace was located in an evaluation trench (Young 2015d). At Clearwell Quarry the initial evaluation (OAU 2002) produced evidence for four furnaces ([5604] 0.3 m x 0.36 m x 0.06 m deep; [5605] 0.3 m x 0.36 m x0.06 m deep; [7004] 0.55 m x 0.42 m x 0.26 m deep; [7005] 0.4 m x 0.47 m x 0.31 m deep), with the furnaces yielding abundant cereal grains and slags with impressions of cereal stalks. The subsequent full excavation (Pine *et al.* 2010) provided evidence for a further 33 furnaces, all or most of slag pit type, but failed to identify any evidence for pit packing. The site at Eckington produced two furnaces, one with a mixed cereal/wood packing (furnace [52]) and a second (furnace [69]) containing only very limited residues. Both furnaces were 0.3 m in diameter and 0.3 m deep.

In contrast, the slag pit furnaces on the nearby sites of Culmstock Road, Hemyock (Rainbird and Young 2015), and Burlescombe (Reed *et al.* 2006), show reinforcement of the pit wall by almost planar clay walls/linings on the blowing-wall side, forming a chord to the pit outline in plan. Both those sites preserved examples of the clay walls extending as high as the blowhole, both show residue assemblages with significant burrs and both showed evidence for the use of a wood pit-packing.

The furnaces at Culmstock Road had moderate to large basal pits:

- F14: diameter of 0.45 m and 0.3 m deep.
- F17: diameter of 0.9 m and 0.24 m deep.
- F26: diameter of 0.84 m and 0.48 m deep.
- F27: diameter of 0.75 m and 0.4 m deep.

The pits at Burlescombe were similarly broad, transverse in plan, but even deeper:

- Furnace 525: 0.45 m by 0.8 m and 0.6 m deep.
- Furnace 529: 0.78 m by 1.1 m and 0.75 m deep.
- Furnace 539: 0.75 m by 0.84 m and 0.65 m deep.

The 'bowl furnaces' (so-called in the excavation report, which also describes the evidence for their superstructure) at Ramsbury (Haslam 1980) are broadly similar to those of Burlescombe and Culmstock Road, and similarly included planar-surfaced, chord-like clay walls on the blowing side of the furnaces:

- Furnace 1: 0.8 m by 0.6 m and 0.2 m deep.
- Furnace 2: 0.85 m by 0.9 m and 0.35 m deep.
- Furnace 3: 1.1 m by 1.0 m and 0.3 m deep.

Details and Sampling of the Slag-Pit Furnaces

Furnace [756] (undated)

An approximately 0.45 m by 0.44 m and 0.25 m bowl-shaped pit, containing a single large, presumably *in situ*, furnace bottom fragment, approximately 0.28 m in diameter and 0.2 m thick comprising much of the 'fill'. The main fragment weighed 17.1 kg and there was also 0.9 kg of debris, giving an overall weight of surviving furnace bottom as 18 kg. The furnace bottom contains much fairly fine-grained charcoal debris and shows cereal stem impressions (and carbonised cereal stems) on its base. The furnace bottom was sampled to provide investigated samples HCF1–4.

Furnace [776] (dated by charcoal samples OxA-27885 and SUERC-45861)

Originally interpreted as a posthole, 0.48 m by 0.52 m, the fill contained a 2.2 kg block of porous furnace bottom, 0.37 kg of small fragments and a 0.79 kg piece of basal dense slag with cereal stem impressions. The materials in this furnace were not sampled.

Furnace [787] (dated by charcoal samples UBA-22703 and OxA-27886)

A circular pit 0.35 m in diameter, filled by slag and fired clay, presumably collapsed superstructure. The two retrieved furnace bottom fragments weighed 5.65 kg and 0.92 kg with the smaller piece including some cross-floor flows. The larger piece showed some limited evidence for impressions of cereal stems. There was also a total of 1.095 kg of small fragments, mainly from interaction between the slag and wall. The recorded section of the pit shows a complex relationship of materials, probably suggesting that the furnace was partially cleared of slag before the superstructure debris entered the pit. The furnace bottom was sampled as HCF5 and the basal flow as HCF6.

Furnace [794] (dated by charcoal samples SUERC-45863 and UBA-22704, as well as cereal grains SUERC-56929 and UBA 27273)

The cut is 0.5 m by 0.44 m and 0.45 m deep. The pattern of slag distribution in the furnace suggests blowing may have been from the southeast. The recovered residues comprised a total of approximately 17 kg of furnace bottom and basal flow material, mixed with several kilograms of pit wall clay. The residues were sampled as HCF7 for a furnace bottom fragment, HCF8 for the margin of a basal puddle, HCF9 from a dense slag puddle and HCF10 from a basal flow slag. In addition, the furnace ceramic was sampled as HCF11.

Furnace [799] (dated by charcoal samples SUERC-56930 and UBA27274)

A bowl-shaped pit with steep sides, 0.5 m by 0.46 m and 0.26 m deep, contained 13.5 kg of porous furnace bottom and prilly flow slags, which appeared to be *in situ*. The residues were not sampled.

General description and affinities of the slag tapping furnaces (see Figures 14-17 in Chapter 2)

Four furnaces with extended tapping channels were recognised, together with a poorly-preserved possible fifth:

- Furnace [758]: trench 1.45 m by 0.4 m wide.
- Furnace [771]: trench 1.9 m by 0.5 m wide; furnace 0.31 m wide and 0.4 m long.
- Furnace [789]: trench 1.9 m long and 0.5 m wide and 0.22 m deep distally; furnace 0.36 m wide, 0.45 m long and 0.11 m deep.
- Furnace [792]: preserved trench is 1.5 m long and cannot have been more than 2.25 m originally, and up to 0.5 m wide; furnace c. 0.38 m long.
- 'Furnace' [805]: 0.27 m wide and preserved for 1.16 m, before being cut by [807].

The furnaces were each constructed over a trench, with the section below the furnace shaft somewhat narrower and shallower than the distal end of the trench. The preserved trenches were 1.45–1.90 m in length and 0.4–0.5 m in width. None of the furnaces preserved any *in situ* component of their superstructures, but three examples showed a variation in the fills at the proximal end, suggesting a length of the trench of 0.38 m to 0.45 m formed the section below the shaft. The lack of structural evidence of the furnace prevents determination of the location of the blowing hole/tuyère.

The associated residues provide little additional evidence for the mode of operation of the furnaces. None of the furnaces preserved *in situ* slag within the furnace base itself (at least none was recognised as such and none is visible on the site photographs). The tapping channels contained small amounts of tapped slag, some apparently *in situ*, including small bird's foot structures suggesting a fall from the tap arch into the tapping channel.

The morphology of the tapping furnaces resembles that of furnace [409] at Tisbury (author's unpublished data). This furnace is built over a trench 1.53 m long, a maximum of 0.60 m wide and 0.42 m wide below the furnace shaft. This furnace is currently undated, but is believed to be probably twelfth- to thirteenth-century in date. The Tisbury furnace, in common with most medieval furnaces, showed evidence for the blowing having been undertaken from a direction (the south) at right angles to the tapping arch (the east).

There are few sites with slag-tapping furnaces of the eighth to tenth centuries, but examples are known from South Hook (Crane and Murphy 2010), Ramsbury (Haslam 1980) and Emersons Green (Young and Young 2013).

At South Hook, two slag tapping furnaces were positioned apparently at one end of a bow-sided building (Complex 1). A single directly associated radiocarbon date gives a calibrated date of *cal* AD 720–1000 (Beta-222371;1150 ± 50 BP). Furnace 1081 was built over a trench 1.5 m long, 0.5 m wide and 0.5 m deep at its northern end where it was cut into the slope to lie beneath the superstructure. Furnace 1071 was built over a gully between 1.3 m and 2 m long, 0.4 m wide and also 0.5 m deep at its northern end. The basal chamber of the furnace was transverse in each case (*c*. 0.6 m long and up to 0.8 m wide), with the proximal wall strengthened with a stone slab, suggesting blowing from the proximal side of the furnace. The lateral sides of the chamber were splayed. Tapslag flows were in situ on the gully floor and had accreted in such a way as to give a distinct drop through the tapping passage.

At Ramsbury the late Furnace 4, apparently followed the use of the non-tapping furnaces described above. The excavation report implies an early ninth-century date, but recalibration and Bayesian modelling of the radiocarbon dates by Bayliss (quoted in Boyer and Keys 2013), suggested modelled dates for Furnace 4 of *cal AD 830–1020* at 95% probability, model not shown or *cal AD 890–990* at 68% probability and the modelling given in (Chapter 3, Table 5).) suggests Posterior Density Estimates of the of ironmaking in Furnace 4 as *cal AD 880–1195* (95% probability) or *935–1080* (68% probability). Furnace 4 has an unusual morphology, being built over a much larger pit than the other examples described here. This pit was approximately 2.3 m long, 0.6 m wide around the furnace base, widening out to about 1.2 m wide towards the distal end. The furnace shows the development of large furnace bottoms in the proximal end, and these are overlain by various flowed slag, which progressively built up a slag step, over which the slag formed a rapid drop towards the outside of the tap arch. The deepest section of the pit was close to the outer margin of the tap arch. The features of the furnace are unique in combination, but all can be paralleled on the other sites.

A suite of radiocarbon dates from the large iron smelting site at Emersons Green suggested a date for production of *c*. AD 850–950 according to the excavators (Young and Young 2013), and their modelling (Chapter 3) gives a Posterior Density Estimates for the first use of Furnace 1 of *cal AD 830–950* at 95% probability, for the TAQ for the first use of furnaces 2, 10 and 11 of *cal AD 815–970* at 95% probability, and for the TPQ for the first use of furnaces 3 and 9 of *cal AD 535–680* at 95% probability (Table 5). The furnaces are slightly problematic in their interpretation, for although all have been claimed as slag tapping, and some have clear evidence for this, others are less certainly so. The ceramic superstructure was relatively well-preserved in many cases and shows a strongly splayed profile, which recalls that of Ramsbury Furnace 4. The furnaces were constructed within large pits.

Details and Sampling of the Slag Tapping Furnaces

Furnace [758] (dated by charcoal sample OxA-27884)

The recorded evidence is very unclear for this feature; it may include a trench-built furnace, 1.45 m by 0.40 m, but the furnace end of the structure is poorly preserved. The middle part of the probable tapping channel contained tapped slags (including a bird's foot), sampled as HCF21–22.

Furnace [771] (dated by charcoal samples OxA-28004 and UBA-22707)

This appears to be a trench-built furnace that may merge southwards into an unrelated feature. The main trench appears to be 1.90 m long and 0.50 m wide, with the base of the furnace itself slightly narrower (0.31 m) and extending 0.40 m from the north end of the trench. A large tapslag flow weighing at least 5.7 kg was broken off near the mouth of the furnace, but extended almost 0.5 m along the trench. The distal end of the trench appears to have borne unrelated *ex situ* slags. The main slag flow was sampled as HCF19, with smaller pieces of tapslag sampled as HCF18 and HCF20.

Furnace [789] (dated by charcoal samples OxA-27977 and SUERC-45859 from the proximal section of the tapping channel)

This is apparently a trench-built furnace, with the trench 1.90 m long and 0.50 m wide and 0.22 m deep at its distal maximum. The furnace itself appears to have rested over the 0.45-m long end of the trench, with a maximum width of 0.36 m and a maximum preserved depth of about 0.11 m. The 0.4-m length of trench outside the furnace circle is 'rich in lining' (798). This proximal section of the trench yielded sampled materials HCF23, tapslag, and HCF24, ore.

Furnace [792] (dated by charcoal samples SUERC-56928 and UBA27270)

This furnace was badly damaged by later activity. The surviving trench is 1.50 m long and cannot have been more than 2.25 m originally, and is 0.5 m in maximum width. The trench contained tapslag, except for the northern 0.38 m that was probably the furnace base. The tapslag had been muddled after excavation with some slag from (781), but there appeared to be approximately 22 kg of tapped slag from this feature, together with 3.3 kg of slags probably from the furnace base and associated wall. Two samples of tapslag were analysed as samples HCF16-17.

Details and Sampling of the Possible Furnaces (see Figure 18 in Chapter 2)

'Furnace' [778] (dated by charcoal samples SUERC-45862 and UBA-22705, together with cereal grains SUERC-56927 and UBA27275)

Curious large pit with associated channel, basal puddle and furnace bottom slags sampled. Total of approximately 95 kg of slag recovered, almost all furnace bottom material, several pieces with straw impressions. Photographs of the pit appear to show a burnt floor, but its dimensions (1.25 m long by 0.64 m wide and 0.41 m deep) and shape (steep sides with a flat floor) are not similar to those of either class of the other furnaces. Initially, pit [778] was interpreted as a slag tapping furnace along with channel [807]. This seems unlikely give the residues contained within. Samples were analysed of two examples of furnace bottom (HCF12-13) and two examples of dense basal slag puddles (HCF14–15).

'Furnace' [805] (dated by charcoal samples SUERC-56931 and UBA27271)

This a poorly-preserved gully-like feature cut by [807]. Cut [807] has been associated with [778] as a furnace, but this is not certain. No residues were retained from this feature. The gully is very narrow, 0.2 m, at its upslope (southern) end, but is almost twice as wide in its presumed continuation north of the intersection with cut [807]. If this is a tapping channel, then it predates [807], associated with [778] which solely contains slag-pit furnace residues.

Details and Sampling of Other Slag-Bearing Features

Pit [675] (dated by charcoal samples UBA-22706 and SUERC-45860)

This pit yielded a sparse slag assemblage, of which a pale grey tapped slag was sampled as HCF25. Most of the residue assemblage appears to have been from the non-tapping process and the dating of the feature coincides with the dates from the early medieval furnaces.

Pit [556] (dated by charcoal samples SUERC-56923 and UBA 27272; Upper Greensand-Derived pottery also present)

The pit produced a large collection of residues. These residues were mainly of tapped slags, but some dense slag blocks were of more uncertain origin, perhaps having formed as slag blocks within the base of the furnaces. Tapped and dense slags were sampled from this feature as HCF26–HCF30.

The Organic Remains from the Furnace Deposits

The organic remains from the furnace deposits (see Chapter 6) also provide some useful insight into the technology. The principal wood charcoals were *Quercus* (oak), *Corylus* (hazel) and *Alnus* (alder). Some of the *Alnus* and *Corylus* fragments gave evidence for wood-boring beetles, suggesting that the wood may have been seasoned prior to charcoaling, or that some fallen wood was collected. The residue evidence from the non-slag-tapping furnaces (furnaces [756], [794] and [799] were sampled in detail) indicates the use of a cereal packing to the basal pit. The principle cereal recorded was *Avena* (oats), with much lesser quantities of *Hordeum* (barley), *Secale* (Rye) and *Triticum* (wheat). It is not clear whether the oats were wild or cultivated. Grass stems may have been present in addition to the crop remains. The only slag-tapping furnace investigated in detail was [805], one of the suspect 'furnaces', comprising a shallow gully with no archaeometallurgical residues collected. The significance of the results from [805] is therefore unclear.

Charcoal from *Cytisus*/*Ulex* (broom/gorse) was recovered from several furnaces, and provided material for the dating of [778], [792] and [794]. Spines from *Ulex* were recovered from contexts beyond Area D but not from the furnaces, making the distinction between broom and gorse in the latter difficult. *Cytisus*/*Ulex* was recorded in moderate quantities in the fill of slag tapping furnace [758] and problematic burnt pit [778], and in small quantities (1 or 2 fragments) in non-tapping furnaces [787] and [794], slag tapping furnaces [771] and [792], and possible slag tapping furnace [805]. There seems little correlation, therefore, between furnace type and the presence of *Cytisus*/*Ulex* though its use may have differed. Nonetheless, the presence of this material is slightly unexpected (although it was similarly recorded in the slag tapping furnaces at South Hook (Crane and Murphy 2010)). It may simply have been another charcoal fuel, or it may have been part of the pit packing the non-tapping furnaces, or it may be an indicator that highly combustible material was also used in the basal section of the early slag tapping furnaces. Further work on other sites is required, including some focussed sampling.

Potential Technological Influences

Setting the iron production technology at Churchills Farm into a wider context is no easy proposition. Recognition of variety within non-slag tapping furnaces in Britain and

Ireland has only been a feature of work of the last decade (see Figure 52 for the location of comparative sites). Older site reports rarely have sufficient detail to reconstruct smelting technology on the basis of the residues alone. The difference between flow slags in non-tapping furnaces and tapped slags was rarely, if ever, appreciated prior to the last decade.

Rapid advances in archaeometallurgical understanding, and an increased expectation regarding the detail of observations, have left many previous interpretations inadequate or worse. Furthermore, layers of academic synthesis have been built upon a corpus of poorly-identified, or misidentified older assemblages, leading to great deficiencies in many of the published overviews (McDonnell (1989), Birch (2011), Fleming (2012) and Harrington and Welch (2014)). Placing the technologies in their broader European context is complicated by the relevance of the archaeometallurgical literature of at least twelve European countries, each with its own terminology, furnace classification and archaeological processes. The following account has been created notwithstanding these issues, and within the limitations imposed by this project, as a starting point for a renewed analysis of early medieval ironmaking in Britain. The discussion challenges significant parts of the current received narrative on the development of iron smelting in early medieval Britain.

Three distinct iron smelting technologies can be identified in use within Wessex between the late ninth and early tenth centuries:

1. the large slag-pit furnaces of Burlescombe (Reed *et al.* 2006), Culmstock Road, Hemyock (Rainbird and Young 2015) and Ramsbury (Haslam 1980) (and probably also Millbrook (Tebbutt 1982), Romsey (McDonnell 1988) and Bywood Farm (Griffith and Weddell 1996)),
2. the smaller cereal-packed slag-pit furnaces of Churchills Farm, Hemyock,
3. the slag tapping furnaces of Ramsbury, Churchills Farm, Hemyock and Emersons Green (Young and Young 2013).

By the mid eleventh century, in complete contrast, there was a relatively homogeneous use of small slag tapping furnaces right across Britain, including the later phase of smelting at Churchills Farm, which then showed progressive evolution through the later Middle Ages. The potential technological influences on the three types of the ninth to tenth centuries, together with the nature of the furnaces of the preceding sixth to eighth centuries, are discussed in the following sections and placed with their broader European context.

Non-tapping Furnaces of the Sixth to Tenth Centuries in Britain and Their Origins

The most commonly-applied model for the development of iron smelting in the post-Roman period has been that non-tapping furnaces became prevalent, as influences from Central and Eastern Europe mostly replaced the Roman slag-tapping technology. McDonnell (1989), for instance, states that that slag blocks of the type he describes as '*Schlackenklotz*' have been 'found in eastern England from Lincolnshire in the north to Hampshire in the south, with a high concentration in East Anglia'. This term was employed apparently to emphasise similarity with the Scharmbeck- / Drengsted-type furnaces (which were single-use furnaces that formed very large slag blocks in cereal-packed slag pits) in, for instance, Denmark and Germany. The presence of some examples of the characteristic slag blocks of this furnace type in Britain appears indisputable (e.g. the slag block from Aylesham, Norfolk; Tylecote 1986, Fig 81). McDonnell (1989) provided, however, just three examples where such blocks are supposed to have been found on excavations: Romsey, Hampshire (McDonnell 1988), Mucking, Essex (MU Jones as a pers. comm.) and Rook Hall, Little Totham, Essex (Cranstone 1988). None of these occurrences actually provides a convincing example of a Scharmbeck- / Drengsted-type slag block. In Denmark, the cessation of the use of the large slag-pit furnaces (Scharmbeck- / Drengsted-type) is dated to the early seventh century (Rasmussen *et al.* 2006; Jouttijärvi and Voss 2013), so the few British examples, mostly surface finds from East Anglia, are likely also to be fifth to sixth century in date. The other claimed examples are likely to represent furnace bottoms from other classes of smaller non-tapping furnace.

Recognition of smaller non-tapping furnaces has been poor until recently. In part this is due to poor discrimination of slags that were tapped from the furnace and those which only flowed inside. Many of the smelting furnaces of the pre-Roman Iron Age across northern Europe, including Britain, were of this type, although their use in Southern Britain almost entirely ceased during the Roman period. The situation was different for areas outside the Roman Empire, where their use persisted, with various morphological varieties, from the early Iron Age through to the medieval period. There are some examples of small non-tapping furnaces from Roman Britain, at sites in North West Wales for example (Crew 1987, 1989, 1991, 1998, 2009), which all have an arch into the basal chamber of the furnace. It is usually assumed that a non-tapping technology was reintroduced into post-Roman Britain from outside, but technological *refugia* in perhaps Cornwall or Wales cannot be entirely excluded. Interestingly, North and West Wales have produced several early medieval sites with slag assemblages, characterised by small scale flow slags, rather than by large coherent furnace bottoms, which are somewhat similar to the earlier assemblages from the same area. These include unpublished assemblages from Cefn Graianog, Gwynedd (where different metalworking areas have produced multiple radiocarbon determinations with calibrated dates spanning the seventh to ninth centuries, although slag tapping may be represented in the as yet undated later phases; Young 2015b, Young 2015c), Borras Quarry, Wrexham (a single date from a smelting furnace

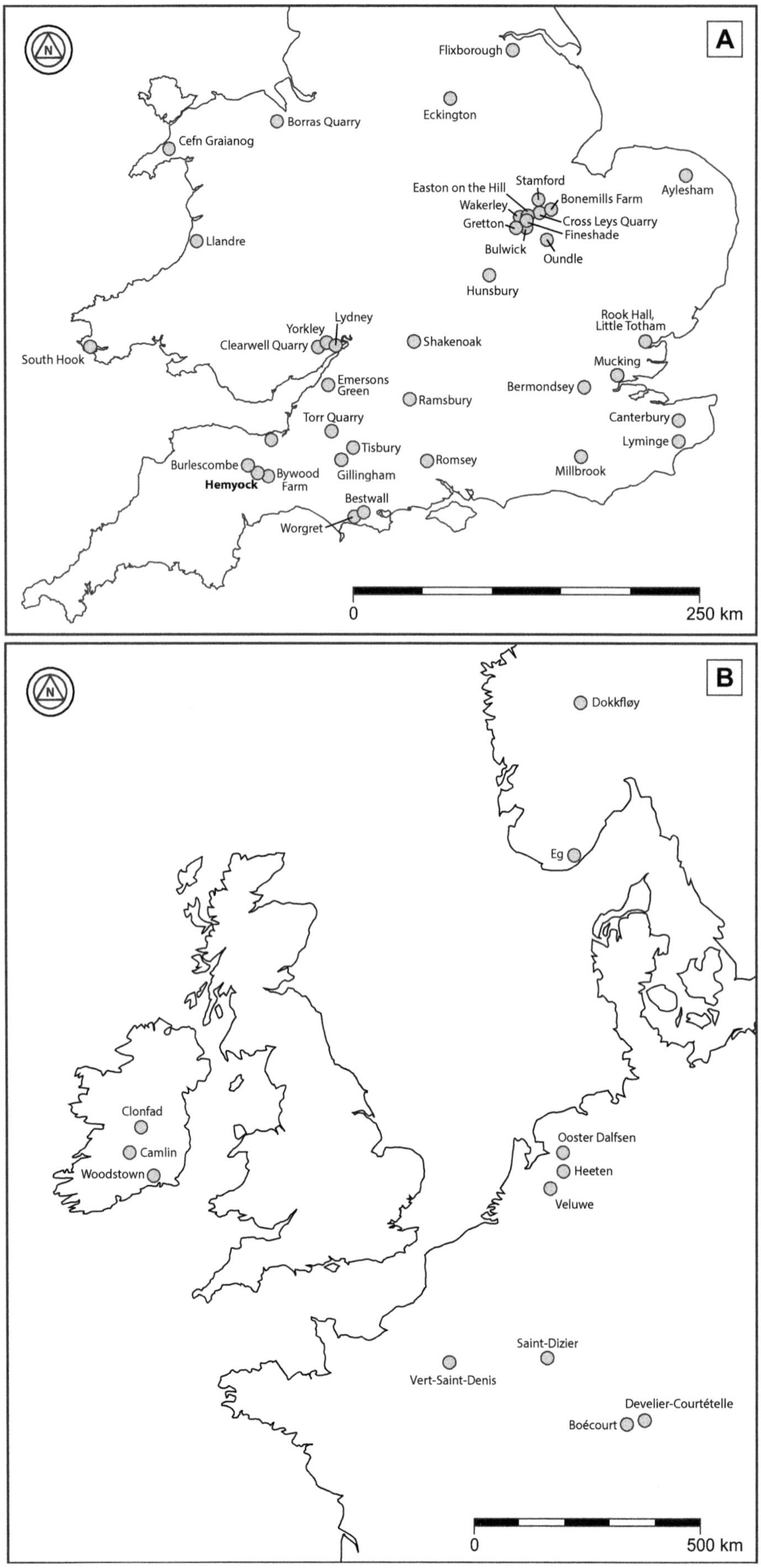

Figure 52. A: Map showing known early medieval iron production localities in England and Wales discussed in the text, and B: Map showing known iron production localities of similar date and/or technology in Ireland, France, Switzerland, Netherlands, and Norway discussed in the text.

suggests a seventh century date; work in progress) and Llandre, Ceredigion (a deposit containing smelting slag has produced a date of cal AD 680–890 (UBA-24080; 1221 ± 37 BP); Young 2016). Small slag pit furnaces were probably also represented by slag assemblages from Carhampton, Somerset (Hollinrake and Hollinrake 1998; probably sixth to seventh century).

The modestly-sized, cereal-packed slag-pit furnaces at Churchills Farm, are an interesting variant on the non-tapping tradition. Although the cereal packing of the single-use Scharmbeck- / Drengsted-type furnaces of the North European Plain is well known (Pleiner 2000), use of this type of furnace appears to have ceased by the early seventh century (Rasmussen *et al.* 2006). Cereal-packing of the slag pit in smaller, reusable, non-tapping furnaces is less well known (wood-packing is much more common), but has been recognised in a few examples in Britain and Ireland (although the technology is very likely to have been under-reported). A possible Iron Age (or early Roman) example has been recorded as a surface find at Hasholme, East Yorkshire (pers. obs.), and undated slags of this kind were recovered from a site at Folly Court, Wokingham, Berkshire (Young, in prep), a site for which an adjacent furnace has been dated to the Iron Age by both pottery and a date of 350–320 (4.1%) and 210–50 (91.3%) *cal* BC (SUERC-74032; 2122 ± 28 BP). An example from Leda Cottages, Kent (Paynter 2007, Fig. 4), may also be of latest Iron Age or early Roman date. Three early medieval examples, closer in age to those at Churchills Farm, are also known. What is probably the earliest is from Eckington, Derbyshire, where a partly cereal-packed slag-pit furnace is associated with a second furnace which produced a single date of cal AD 650–770 (SUERC-75177, 1315 ± 30 BP). Two sites are known from the Forest of Dean, Gloucestershire: Clearwell Quarry (Pine *et al.* 2009; Paynter *in* OAU 2002) produced multiple furnaces, which gave three closely clustered radiocarbon dates (*cal AD 765–895* (*95% probability*; *last_clearwell*); Chapter 3*)*, and Yorkley (Young 2015d), dated by a single determination of cal. AD 690–890 (SUERC-65353, 1225 ± 29 BP). There are two recorded occurrences of cereal packing from Ireland. At Camlin 3, Co. Tipperary (Young 2011) a cereal (or grass) packed slag-pit of probable sixth to seventh-century date contained an *in situ* cake, with other similar material found nearby *ex situ*. Similar, but fragmentary material, was recovered at the monastic site of Clonfad, Co. Westmeath, dated to between the sixth and ninth centuries (Young 2009a, 2012).

Non-tapping furnaces with a large (0.8 to 1.0 m diameter) slag-pit, and with a thick ceramic lining applied to the pit on the blowing wall, extending upwards into an almost planar wall containing the single blowhole, and generating a large porous furnace bottoms, are a common form of furnace in eighth to ninth century Wessex (seen at Ramsbury, Burlescombe and Culmstock Road, Hemyock; Haslam 1980, Reed *et al.* 2006, Rainbird and Young 2015). The residues from these furnaces are characterised by a strong interaction between the hot-zone and this wall, leading to the formation of large burrs on the proximal side of the furnace bottoms. The non-tapping furnace at Millbrook, Sussex (Tebbutt 1982) may be another example of this type, and the residues from Romsey (McDonnell 1988) may also derive from use of such furnaces as may the furnace bottom reported from Bywood Farm (Griffith and Weddell 1996).

The method of use of these furnaces has been much debated. The examples at Ramsbury (furnaces 1,2 and 3; Haslam 1980) were described by the excavator as 'bowl furnaces', but it was argued that stakeholes in their base were intended to support a domed superstructure until it had fired. So far as can be determined from the report, the Ramsbury furnaces showed evidence for a wood pit packing. With broadly similar structural evidence (except for the stakeholes), the furnaces at Burlescombe (Reed *et al.* 2006) were interpreted as open furnaces, solely with a ceramic wall on the blowing side. Taken at face value, the pits would have had an unusual shape when in use, with a planar blowing wall but apparently very openly-splayed sides. Revision of the dating evidence (see Chapter 3) provides a Posterior Density Estimate for the last dated event at Burlescombe of *cal AD 780–990* at 95% probability. Those at Culmstock Road, Hemyock (Rainbird and Young 2015) were apparently rather similar to the Burlescombe examples, with planar blowing walls and coarse wood pit packing, but with poorly-understood channels connecting the pits to gullies. These channels possibly facilitated drainage of the slag-pits on a poorly-drained site prone to flooding. Revision of the Culmstock Road dating (see Chapter 3) suggests a Posterior Density Estimate for the last dated event there of *cal AD 720–900 (92%) or 925–945 (3%).* A further example, probably, but not certainly allied to this group, is the large non-tapping furnace (1.0 m by 0.95 m overall) at Millbrook in the Sussex Weald (Tebbutt 1982). The records of this furnace are a little unclear, but it possessed clay linings which were upstanding on one side, and multiple stakeholes were also evident in the pit, suggesting supports for a superstructure (even if only during its construction). An associated radiocarbon date (unfortunately of mature oak) gives a calibrated date of cal AD 660–970 (with 52% probability of the range AD764–885; 1220 ± 70 BP).

Despite the strong similarities, there are also significant differences between these sites. One of the furnaces at each of the Culmstock Road and Burlescombe sites is small (approximately 0.5 m diameter, like the Churchills Farm slag-pit furnaces, rather than the approximately 1m diameter of the rest of this group) and the Burlescombe pits are twice as deep as those at Culmstock Road and Ramsbury.

A site (HER monument ref: MDV56368) at Bywood Farm (5 km SSE of Churchills Farm) has produced a single date of cal AD 680 – 880 (AA 17827;1260 ± 50 BP) from charcoal trapped in a large 'furnace bottom', which suggests the possible presence of another site employing this technology. The precise context of this material is unclear, however, with the major slag mounds at this locality (150 m and 680 m south of the findspot of the dated material) being of Roman age.

Archaeological work in Romsey has provided evidence for a major phase of ironmaking during the early medieval period, with thick deposits of residues having been located by several excavations (McDonnell 1988; Scott 1996). The nature of the slag remains uncertain, but it was dominated by furnace bottoms, with only a small quantity of tapslag being found on one site. The furnace bottoms were dense, typically comprising amalgamated flows, with a maximum weight of 40 kg for a complete example. McDonnell described the blocks as upward-narrowing blocks, implying the use of the Scharmbeck/ Drengsted type furnace, but this would appear extremely unlikely. The typical Scharmbeck/ Drengsted type furnace was not cleared after use, so the slag blocks do not typically occur on dumps; they have a typical weight of hundreds of kilograms. The description, however, resembles the descriptions and images of the non-tapped slag blocks from Clearwell Quarry, Gloucestershire (mentioned above as an example of cereal pit-packing). Although the Clearwell blocks were also described as upward-narrowing when examined in isolation, enhanced by the impression given by Figure 14 of Pine *et al.* 2009, but this is in contradiction to Figure 7, which shows the same block in situ in a narrowing-downwards orientation. The Clearwell blocks too often formed dense masses of amalgamated flows, but had a maximum weight of 10 kg. Clearly, the Romsey residues would benefit from reinvestigation; if the maximum furnace bottom size of 40 kg is correct, then it might imply that the furnaces employed also belong within this group. Their dating, too, is uncertain; although commonly attributed to the sixth/seventh century, the published radiocarbon dates are of uncertain relationship to the metalworking. In the area of the Abbey itself, a layer predating the thin ironworking deposits in that area has been dated to cal AD 550–870 (OxA-2314; 1355±80 BP) and a bone from the ironworking layer to cal AD 650–1000 (OxA-2313; 1215±80 BP). Stratigraphic evidence suggests that the activity is only reasonably certainly prior to the foundation of the nunnery *c.* AD 907.

Unfortunately, beyond this small group of sites, there are not extensive analogues for this style of furnace elsewhere in Britain, nor do they resemble contemporary furnaces in Ireland. Analogues for this furnace type might be found further afield; their large dimensions resemble some of the non-tapping furnaces of Southern Norway for example. Hodgkinson (2008) suggested, more plausibly, similarity of the slag pit furnace at Millbrook to the slag-pit furnaces of the Iron Age in the Vecht region (Heeten) of the Netherlands, with their 40-60 kg furnace bottoms (Groenewoudt and van Nie 1995). The excavated example at Heeten dates to the first half of the fourth century, but this furnace type does not appear to have been replaced by slag tapping technology until the seventh century, which would theoretically permit its transfer to Britain. An origin for the large non-tapping furnaces of Wessex within the earlier technology of the Low Countries seems the most likely potential explanation.

Slag Tapping Furnaces of the Sixth to Tenth Centuries in Britain and Their Origins

The slag tapping technologies of early medieval Britain were potentially the result of multiple influences: continuity of practice from the Roman period (probably including multiple varieties of furnace), technologies introduced from Merovingian/Frankish Europe and perhaps technology introduced from Scandinavia (including by Viking expansion). Although evidence for slag tapping furnaces is widespread across Southern Britain, there are issues both with both the quality of the recording of residue assemblages and of the dating evidence. Detailed interpretation of these records is commonly not possible.

A widespread use of slag tapping technology is indicated by a large number of sites across central and Southern Britain from which tapped slag has been claimed (although the potential for confusion between tapped slag and flow slag from non-tapping furnaces must be noted). These include:

1. Flixborough, Lincolnshire (bulk of the smelting evidence is from Period 4, the early to mid ninth century, but some is earlier; Starley and Loveluck 2009)
2. Stamford, Lincolnshire (late ninth to early eleventh centuries; Burchard 1982)
3. Bonemills Farm, Cambridgeshire (probably seventh to ninth century on the basis of radiocarbon dates; Wall 1999, 2011)
4. Cross Leys Quarry, Cambridgeshire (probably sixth to eighth century on the basis of radiocarbon dates; Fleming 2012);
5. Hunsbury, Northamptonshire (eighth to ninth centuries on the basis of pottery; Jackson 1993-4),
6. Fineshade Abbey, Northamptonshire (sixth to seventh century on the basis of radiocarbon dates, but with later working too; Mudd 2006).
7. Shakenoak, Oxfordshire (Brodribb *et al.* 1972), sixth to seventh centuries on the basis of artefact evidence.
8. Worgret, Dorset, where tapslags had been used to infill a timber structure (Maynard 1988; dated to after AD664 by dendrochronology; Hinton 1992)
9. Bestwall Farm, Dorset (Ladle 2012), where features containing slag range from late fifth or early sixth to eighth centuries.
10. Gillingham, Dorset (Heaton 1992).
11. possible mid eighth century slags from the Bermondsey Abbey area, Southwark (Bowyer and Keys 2013).
12. the slag assemblage from Lyminge (Keys 2011) is not yet fully investigated, but apparently includes tapped slag

These data suggest that slag tapping was widespread in Southern Britain in the seventh and eighth centuries, but the story in the fifth and sixth centuries is less clear (see the compilation of relevant dates in Table 4). The cited examples do not provide clear evidence for the morphology or evolution of slag tapping furnaces in Britain over this period. The model of slag tapping disappearing from Southern Britain after the Roman period, to be reintroduced two centuries or so later, certainly looks less convincing than it once did, but the lack of clear fifth-century sites precludes any certainty.

An example of the difficulties in establishing the particular style of slag tapping furnace, in the absence of the furnaces themselves, is provided by recent work in Canterbury (McDonnell and Young 2015), where a persistent proportion of slags present in contexts of the main smithing phase of *c.* AD 750–850 were possibly derived from a Roman-style smelting furnace (including the 'slag rods' that are characteristic of many Roman sites). No furnace was discovered, but the constant proportion of smelting slag in the assemblages argued against residuality. The strong similarity of the 'tapslags' and 'slag rods' from Canterbury with the local Roman smelting residues must be tempered by recognition of the presence of both apparent tapslags and slag rods in rather similar circumstances in an otherwise dominantly smithing assemblage from the Merovingian site of Develier-Courtételle in Switzerland (Eschenlohr *et al.* 2007). Given the potential for a strong Frankish influence in Canterbury, such an alternative interpretation must be considered.

More convincing Merovingian influence may be suggested by one of the earliest reasonably well-dated slag tapping furnaces from early medieval England, at Rook Hall, Little Totham, Essex (discussed earlier in this chapter). Charcoal from furnace F1911 gave an age of cal AD 550–770 (with an 87% probability of AD550–730; GU-2151, 1380 +/- 60 BP). A fragment of tuyère from F1911 also gave a thermoluminescence date of AD530 +/- 290. The illustrations of this furnace (e.g. Figure 8 at http://adsl06805.freespace.surfree.co.uk/ and those of the tuyères on the same page; accessed 4/12/15) show evidence for a furnace of very similar style to those of Merovingian age from central Europe. In particular, the use of 'D'-sectioned ceramic tuyères is a very unusual feature, not known to be paralleled at any other British site. Furnaces with this mode of ventilation (albeit in a very different thick-walled morphology) have been described as the Bellaire type, after the location of the first detailed excavation of examples in Switzerland (Pelet 1973; Pleiner 2000). They appear to be directly derived from Roman forms (Cabboi *et al.* 2007; Eschenlohr and Serneels 1991). Excavation at Boécourt, in the Swiss Jura (Eschenlohr and Serneels 1991) provides a very detailed picture of this type, and other examples are known from eastern France (Leroy 1997; Laurent *et al.* 1994). Radiocarbon determinations from the Boécourt furnaces provides dates of cal AD 420–640 (ARC 361, 1520+/-50 BP), cal AD 420–650 (ARC 363, 1500+/-50 BP) and cal AD 380–630 (ARC 368, 1560+/-60 BP) and palaeomagnetism a date of AD700+/-150, suggesting a date between mid-sixth and mid-seventh centuries. The Boécourt furnaces show re-use of Roman tile for the furnace interior, as did the later furnace at Ramsbury (Haslam 1980). They appear to have been blown via ceramic tuyères, both from one side of the tapping arch and from high in the furnace. This direction of blowing is also a feature of the Ramsbury furnace.

Furnaces of late Merovingian-Carolingian age are present in a remarkable series of iron smelting settlements at Saint-Dizier, France (Haut Marne; Leroy and Merluzzo 1998) ranging from the eighth to twelfth centuries. The oldest furnace (furnace 1000) is present in the first phase of the eastern settlement at Chêne Saint-Armand and produced a date of cal AD 650–880 (1280 +/-55 BP), with the excavators arguing for a date in the first half of the eighth century. The furnace had an unusual broad shape in plan with a ceramic block tuyère associated with its collapsed wall. The broad shape is formed by a circular furnace base approximately 1 m in diameter, overlapping a tapping pit of approximately 1.5 m in diameter. Furnace 56 at the nearby settlement at la Pièce de Fournées (with a radiocarbon age from extraction pits of cal AD 670–900 (92.7%) or AD 920–950 (2.7%); 1220 +/- 50 BP; and with pottery dating to *c.* AD 800) was of similar design to f1000 at Saint-Dizier. These furnaces are thinner-walled, as in the Rook Hall examples. The Rook Hall furnaces are overprinted by multiple rebuilds around a single tapping pit, but may have had a similar ground plan to the Saint-Dizier furnaces. In Carolingian France, slag tapping furnaces have been recorded on several sites. At Vert-Saint-Denis (Seine-et-Marne), for instance, smelting took place from the late seventh/early eighth to eleventh centuries (Goustard *et al.* 1998; Daveau *et al.* 2000). The furnaces were slag-tapping and built into one end of an elongate (but broad) pit.

Elsewhere in Northern Europe, there was a marked spread of slag tapping in the seventh to ninth centuries. In the Netherlands slag tapping furnaces were associated with the development of a substantial area of iron production in the Veluwe in this period (Joosten and van Nie 1995; Joosten *et al.* 1997). This area forms part of the hinterland of the emporium of Dorestad, and therefore a potential source of influence into other regions. The development of the 'rattlestone' ores of the Veluwe represented a marked break from the earlier tradition of bog iron ores smelted in slag-pit furnaces that had characterised the Iron Age. In Denmark, slag tapping furnaces have not been recognised so far in this period (Lyngstrøm 2013), with a dearth of evidence following the cessation of the large slag-pit furnaces (Drengsted- / Scharmbeck-type; Jouttijärvi and Voss 2013) in the early seventh century (Rasmussen *et al.* 2006).

In Norway, smaller slag tapping furnaces seem to have replaced the variety of non-tapping furnaces that were present in different areas until the seventh century. On the southern coastal fringes of Norway, the non-tapping Eg furnace appears related to some of the slag-pit furnaces of Denmark (Jensen 2013b). In the Dokkfløy region of Southern Norway, the early large non-tapping furnaces (Østland furnace; 0.9 m to 1.5 m internal diameter, with slag blocks of up to 450 kg; Larsen 2013b) were replaced by smaller slag-tapping furnaces in the late seventh to eighth centuries (Larsen 2013a). Details of the small slag-tapping furnaces of the area from *c.* AD 800–1400 were provided by Mjærum (2013). Further north in Norway the large early non-tapping furnaces were of the Trondelag furnace type, with large stone-built slag pits with a large lateral opening (Larsen 2013b) and the use of these too appears to have ceased around AD 600 (Espelund 2015), to be replaced by slag-tapping varieties.

In Sweden, slag tapping technology appeared with the Viking Age (from the ninth century), but Hjärthner-Holdar *et al.* (2013) suggested that in practice many slags were too viscous for true tapping because of the local ore composition. In general, the early slag tapping technologies of Scandinavia appear to show rather simple, possibly somewhat ephemeral, shaft furnaces adjacent to pits (i.e. they were not constructed over trenches).

In Ireland, the Viking *longphort* at Woodstown, Co. Waterford (Young 2009b; 2014b) provides an example nearer to Wessex of a slag tapping furnace of resumed Viking influence. This slag tapping furnace, quite unlike any known furnace of that period in Ireland, was constructed within the terminal of one of the enclosure ditches and is likely to date to around the mid ninth century. Whilst this suggests a date for slag tapping technology being introduced to Ireland, the detailed location of the furnace within an existing ditch does not provide an analogue for the morphology of any known British example.

The slag tapping furnaces of Wessex of the ninth to tenth centuries (as described above), do not form a neat, coherent group. The slag tapping furnace at Ramsbury (Furnace 4; Haslam 1980) has a very unusual form, with a steep rear wall, and strongly splayed sides and a very large size. The profile shows a marked step where the slag flowed out of the chamber through the tapping arch – largely caused by the build-up of slag, including quite large furnace bottoms, in the base of the furnace itself. Indeed, the form of the furnace chamber is not dissimilar to that of the large slag pit furnaces of Wessex; the excavator described it as a 'developed bowl furnace'. Some of these features may also be observed in some of the furnaces at Emersons Green (Young and Young 2013), particularly a strong 'splay' to the lower section of the shaft wall, the development of 'furnace bottoms (a 40 kg examples was present in the base of furnace F1) and the step (the 'slagfall' of Young and Young 2013). The overall morphology of the Emersons Green furnaces, with their broad pits, may have been influenced by their construction on a hard bedrock substrate. Although there were apparently no supporting residues, the similarity of Hearth 2 at Millbrook (Tebbutt 1982) to a poorly-preserved slag tapping furnace is striking, and it is possible that Millbrook, like Churchills Farm and Ramsbury, shows examples of furnaces of both technologies. Features previously claimed as a large slag-tapping smelting furnace with adjacent smithing hearths at *Hamwic* (Holdsworth 1976, 42), have subsequently been discounted as such (Morton 1992, 160-165).

Outside Wessex, an installation of slag tapping furnaces at South Hook, Pembrokeshire (Crane and Murphy 2010), of cal AD 720–1000 (Beta-222371; 1150 ± 50 BP), shows steep rear walls, a transverse plan with splayed sides, and a step in the floor of the tapping arches, at least partially created by uncleared slag, but were constructed over small trenches. They thus show characteristics intermediate between those of Furnace 4 at Ramsbury and those of Churchills Farm. The strong similarity of the South Hook furnaces to the forms in Wessex is important, for it shows that this style of furnace existed outside the immediate cultural setting of Wessex, even before the Norman conquest.

Although the construction of slag tapping furnaces in Wessex is variable (as discussed above), the form found at Churchills Farm, in which the furnace shaft was constructed over one end of a narrow trench, 1.45–1.90 m in length and 0.4–0.5 m in width, has a special significance in the development of the bloomery in Britain. This general form would appear close to the root of the development of bloomery furnaces in Southern Britain in the post-Norman conquest period. The same general form of furnace would be likely to have produced the tapped slags from the later medieval pits, ditches and gullies at Churchills Farm. Very similar residues were also characteristic of a site at Tisbury, Wiltshire, where two furnaces believed to be of between the eleventh and thirteenth centuries (although the associated pottery has a long chronology) were excavated (author's unpublished data). One furnace, with a broad tapping pit, lay in the corner of a post-built structure with an external drip gully that had been back-filled with closely packed tapslag blocks each weighing up to 14 kg. The second furnace had a trench-built construction similar to those at Churchills Farm. The lowest point of the tapping channel was below the outer margin of the tapping arch (a feature also seen at Ramsbury) and had a floor that sloped steeply upwards into the basal chamber of the furnace itself (another characteristic interpreted as being an indicator of an early structure). Broadly similar construction was observed in some of the slightly later furnaces at Torr Quarry, Leighton, Somerset (probably the twelfth to thirteenth centuries; Young 2014c) and Lydney (probably late thirteenth century; Young 2017). Within the broader Norman world, there are parallels to be found with the eleventh to mid-thirteenth century bloomery furnaces of the eastern and western settlements at Chêne Saint-Armand, Saint-Dizier, France (Leroy and Merluzzo 1998). These furnaces comprised a circular furnace base 0.35 m to 0.45 m in diameter, a narrow tapping channel 0.1 m to 0.25 m wide and 0.15 m to 0.8 m long, and a tapping pit 0.95 m to 1.2 m long and 0.5 m to 0.95 m wide.

The Furnaces of the Eighth to Tenth Century Wessex

By the eighth century there were, therefore, multiple styles of furnace in use in southern Britain. The evidence from Canterbury hints at survival of some larger Roman-style domed furnaces (although influence from Merovingian

Europe rather than Roman Britain is also possible). The most common form of furnace, however, in much of Southern Britain may have been a small slag-tapping furnace, most probably derived directly from Romano-British technology, although an influence and/or reintroduction from Merovingian Europe in the seventh century (as appears to have occurred in Scandinavia) cannot be excluded. Various non-tapping furnaces were also employed. Evidence from Derbyshire and the Forest of Dean shows that at least some of these employed a cereal pit-packing.

The replacement of non-tapping furnaces by slag tapping technology, as at Ramsbury, has long been taken as a marker of a technological shift within ironmaking in Britain. Importantly, and in part as a result of the analyses presented here, it is perhaps less clear now that this is the case, at least as a simple linear progression. On a broad scale, one form of slag tapping furnace did become entirely dominant in Southern Britain by the eleventh century, but it appears to have replaced multiple contemporaneous technologies, both tapping (which may have been the usual technology of much of central, eastern and southern Britain, from at least as early as the seventh century, and possibly without break since the Roman period) and non-tapping. Indeed, it might be argued that at least four distinct technologies either evolved within, or were introduced to, southern Britain, within the late eighth to early tenth centuries.

Firstly, there were the very large slag pit furnaces with a planar blowing wall (as seen at Burlescombe, Culmstock Road, Ramsbury and perhaps Millbrook, Romsey and Bywood Farm; all lying within Wessex), that are without any clear antecedent, but derivation from the Iron Age furnaces of the Low Countries is possible. Secondly, there were the cereal-packed small slag pit furnaces (as seen at Churchills Farm), for which the earlier examples (in Derbyshire and the Forest of Dean) lie, possibly coincidentally, within the area of Mercia.

The third technology is represented by the large and unusual Furnace 4 at Ramsbury, which has no clear precursor, but shows some similarities (blowing through the back wall, splayed sides) with Merovingian examples. Some aspects of this morphology are also visible in the Emersons Green slag tapping furnaces. Finally, there are the slag tapping furnaces of small size (as at Churchills Farm) constructed over narrow trenches, which appear to be close to the root of the most common medieval furnace type. The origin of these is unclear, but their likely evolution from the small Roman slag tapping furnace may have happened within Britain or outside. If the trench-built and pit-built slag tapping furnaces are regarded as variants of the same type, then the furnaces of Emersons Green may perhaps be included in this fourth group.

Instead of a single event involving replacement of the use of non-tapping by slag tapping furnaces, an alternative model may be proposed involving a more complex pattern of the contemporaneous use of multiple furnace types, out of which one type eventually became dominant (see Chapter 7). The origin of those various furnace types is speculative: the non-tapping furnaces may indicate influences from Ireland or from the Low Countries (not necessarily directly), the large slag tapping furnace might indicate a Western European influence and the smaller slag tapping furnaces might either reflect a Western European influence or an indigenous evolution. Many more examples will be needed before such patterns can be clarified and understood, but they must surely indicate a period of significant mobility of artisans.

The Residues

Distribution of the Residues

The collections included four broad types of assemblage classed by the nature of the producing context:

1. Those collected from sub-circular pits, which were recorded in the field either as furnaces (presumably where clearly 'burnt') or as postholes. These assemblages are entirely residues from iron smelting in a non-slag tapping iron smelting furnace. Many of these assemblages were likely to comprise in situ materials. Accordingly, five 'slag-pit' furnace assemblages are identified (from furnaces [756], [776], [787], [794] and [799]).
2. Those collected from elongate features, recorded as probable furnaces with tapping channels. The residue assemblages support the attribution to slag-tapping furnaces for most of these, although only a limited amount of residue was in situ; there were no large in situ tapslag flows (the largest being in context (772), a fill of furnace [771]). Three contexts involving elongate cuts containing slag are probably not slag tapping furnaces: the assemblage from context (781) (the fill of burnt pit [778]) comprises a large collection of 117 kg of residues from slag-pit iron furnaces, the assemblage from adjacent context (808) is smaller but also includes large furnace bottom fragments from slag-pit furnaces, and the assemblage from fill (676) of cut [675], originally interpreted as a furnace, but now reinterpreted as a pit containing a mixed slag assemblage. There are therefore four slag tapping furnaces (furnaces [758], [771], [789] and [792]) identified on the basis of morphology and residues (a further possible furnace [805] contained no residues).
3. Those collected from pits, including the pits rich in pottery (539, 616, 730). These assemblages are dominated by tapped slags, with a minor component of residues from the non-slag tapping process (at a level compatible with being residual material). Pit fill (730) appears to have been particularly slag-rich (although not all the slag was retained). These assemblages probably document a late phase of bloomery iron production that is not reflected in the metallurgical structures and was therefore presumably undertaken outside the excavated area.

4. Those collected from late ditches and drains (509, 676, 681, 707, 882). This material comprises a mixture of residues, typically in relatively low concentrations and many of the pieces are worn, indicating these materials were probably residual.

Description of the Residues

The iron smelting slags could be divided into several morphological classes:

Residues from Non-slag Tapping Furnaces

Furnace Bottoms

The part of the furnace immediately below the bloom generally accumulates a large mass of slag. This slag mass (known as a 'furnace bottom' although it does not typically form in the very bottom of the pit) generally has the form of amalgamated flow slags prills surrounding small remnant fragments of charcoal fuel and, lower in the pit, the pit packing. This may result in the furnace bottom being more or less dense. The lowest density furnace bottoms may be very friable; denser furnace bottoms have a higher potential for preservation in large blocks. The densest parts of the furnace bottom are usually below the blowhole, where the hot zone causes most reaction and the slag mass impinges on the ceramic of the pit/furnace wall. Where strong reaction occurs, a burr may form (a dense slag mass that corrodes a depression into the furnace wall to form a bulbous, rounded contact). Where the hot fluid top of the slag mass reacts more gently with the wall, a rounded raised lobe of slag may form along the contact of the furnace bottom and wall. Below this zone of reaction, the slag of the furnace bottom may accumulate against the pit wall, and may do so through the rapid chilling of descending slags to form an accumulation of flow-lobed slag, with a characteristic shiny, non-wetted surface against the wall. Preservation of flow lobes may just be in a thin skin against the wall, and their evidence may be destroyed by further slag flow internally. The most intact furnace bottom pieces (from Furnace [756]) weighed approximately 18 kg, probably close to the original weight of the cake.

Flow Slags

These are slags that exhibit signs of fluid flow, but which did not flow out of the furnace. They typically form low in the slag pit of a non-slag tapping furnace, where rapid slag flow (particularly down the blowing wall) may generate accumulation of flow-lobed slags against the wall and inflows across the pit floor. Flow slags may also flow around the pit-packing material. In many cases such material was split wood, and complex forms of flow slag around former pieces of wood may be present. Such slags may be very dense and may grade into more conventional furnace bottom material. Finer flow slag particles, including both individual flow prills and sub-spheroidal droplets may be more associated with vertical slag flow through the fuel and pit packing.

Slag 'Puddles'

Where sufficient slag flowed into the pit of a non-slag tapping furnace and accumulated rapidly, dense puddles of slag without clear flow features may occasionally form. As discussed below, these may particularly be a property of slag-pit slags when the pit packing was cereals (see below).

Residues from Slag Tapping Furnaces

Tapped Slags (Tapslags)

These were slags that exhibit signs of fluid flow (typically they comprise amalgamated flows of slag with a characteristic 'ropey' surface texture). For a slag to be able to be interpreted as having been tapped, there must be evidence that it flowed outside the furnace. Such evidence may include strong surficial reddening, where the hot slag surface has oxidised in the air during cooling. Some slags may be clearly identifiable as tapped slags from there is-situ location in a furnace tapping channel.

Furnace Slags

These residues are the slags remaining inside a slag tapping furnace after the tapping has taken place. In many ways they can be considered as the equivalent of the furnace bottom, but in a tapping furnace. No such slags were identified in this project, since certain discrimination of small fragments of charcoal-rich furnace slags from charcoal-rich furnace bottoms is possible. They are discussed here because they represent an unknown component of the Hemyock assemblage and therefore the overall slag composition produced by a slag-tapping is unknown. It is usually assumed that since most of the slag is tapped, that the tapped slag composition can be taken as representative of the slag produced by a smelt as a whole, but this is not strictly true.

For the non-slag tapping furnaces, the slag assemblage will be markedly modified by the form of the pit and by the nature of the pit packing. The packing is a combustible material that fills the pit before the smelt, but which is consumed once the slag starts to flow downwards, creating space for the slag and the growth of the bloom. For most examples of non-slag tapping furnaces in Britain (both during the pre-Roman Iron Age and the early medieval period) the pit packing was mainly split wood with some roundwood. For a small number of occurrences, the pit packing was formed of cereal or grass stalks – and this is the case at Churchills Farm. The pit packing is demonstrated by the moulds of stalks within and on the margins of furnace bottom fragments as well as particularly by impressions associated with slag puddles. The pit packing is also represented by fragments of carbonised stalks and grains. The relationship between the presence of slag puddles and a cereal pit packing may be significant, with such a puddle being much less likely to have space to form when the pit packing was of wood. The form of the pit also influences the nature of the slag assemblage. A shallow pit would tend to concentrate the slag and promote the generation of a denser furnace bottom, whereas a deeper pit does not constrain the slag and a large, porous furnace bottom may result.

Methods of Scientific Analysis

An analytical programme was developed to address various questions raised by the assessment, which had corroborated field evidence that the site included furnaces both with, and without, a slag tapping facility. A selection of materials was made to provide analytical data on the composition of residues from across the ranges of both furnace type and residue type (Table 10). The selected samples were slabbed on a diamond saw and subsamples used firstly for preparing a polished block for use on the Scanning Electron Microscope (SEM) and secondly for crushing for preparation of a whole-sample chemical analysis. Polished blocks for investigation on the SEM were prepared in the Earth Science Department, The Open University. Electron microscopy was undertaken on the LEO S360 analytical electron microscope in the School of Earth and Ocean Sciences, Cardiff University. Microanalysis was undertaken using the School's Oxford Instruments INCA ENERGY energy-dispersive x-ray analysis system (EDS).

The site code used for the samples is HCF. Locations of EDS analyses are presented as sample-area-analysis (e.g. HCF2 SOI2 #3). The area of the sample in a particular image is referred to as SOI (SOI = Site Of Interest in the terminology of the INCA microanalysis software) and individual analyses (points or areas) are labelled #m. The primary microanalytical data and images of all SOIs including, where appropriate, details of the analysed points/areas are held with the project archive. All EDS analyses were collected with all elements analysed (including oxygen, but not carbon; all samples were carbon-coated). Analytical totals were frequently far from 100%, because the analytical system is designed to provide totals of 100% from spot analyses in the centre of the field. The area analyses required for this project are not standardised in the same way and will diverge from a total of 100% (either above or below, depending on the location of the area with respect to the centre of the field). In order to make the microanalytical results easily comparable across materials (and also sites), no attempt has been made to adjust for the oxidation state of elements with variable valency. The figures employed here have therefore been constructed with elements expressed as oxides in weight% calculated stoichiometrically, except for mineral structure calculations, where the measured oxygen has been used.

Analyses of olivine have been quoted using the following convention: the proportions of iron and magnesium have been used to first define the relative proportions of forsterite (Fo; Mg_2SiO_4) and fayalite (Fa; Fe_2SiO_4) in the form FanFom, where n+m = 100. The proportions of calcium and manganese have then been taken to calculate percentage substitutions into the olivine. Finally, the substitution of phosphorus for silicon has been expressed as atoms per formula unit (APFU), where the formula unit ideally has a single silicon atom. Values of more than 0.03 APFU phosphorus (equivalent to approximately 1wt% P_2O_5) are defined as phosphoran fayalite (Boesenberg and Hewins 2010). Throughout this report standard mineral terminology is applied to both natural and anthropogenic materials – although artificial phases are no longer strictly considered to be minerals.

Bulk chemical analysis was undertaken using two techniques. The major elements (Si, Al, Fe, Mn, Mg, Ca, Na, K, Ti, and P) were determined by X-Ray Fluorescence using a fused bead on the Wavelength- Dispersive X-Ray Fluorescence (WD-XRF) system in the department of Geology, Leicester University (this also generated analyses for S, V, Cr, Sr, Zr, Ba, Ni, Cu, Zn, Pb and Hf). Whole-specimen chemical analysis for thirty six minor and trace elements (Sc, V, Cr, Co, Ni, Cu, Zn, Ga, Rb, Sr, Y, Zr, Nb, Mo, Sn, Cs, Ba, La, Ce, Pr, Nd, Sm, Eu, Gd, Tb, Dy, Ho, Er, Tm, Yb, Lu, Hf, Ta, Pb, Th, U) were undertaken using a sample in solution on the ThermoElemental X-series Inductively-Coupled Plasma Mass Spectrometer (ICP-MS) in the School of Earth and Ocean Sciences, Cardiff University (this also generates lower quality results for Fe, Mn, Ti, P that are used mainly for quality assurance purposes). Key data derived from the chemical analyses are presented in Tables 11–12.

Microstructure

The microstructure and mineralogy of the samples show broadly similar characteristics, irrespective of process, reflecting their narrow range of chemical composition (see below; Figure 53). For all the slags, the primary phase is wustite (although a few samples suggest that small particles of iron may locally have preceded the wustite). The wustite dendrites are overgrown in many instances by hercynite, forming euhedral or subhedral crystals (HCF2, HCF14, HCF19, HCF22, HCF23, HCF25; e.g. Figures 54e, 56f, and 58c). In some samples (HCF8, HCF16, HCF26; e.g. Figures 54d, 59c, and 59e), euhedral hercynite is only present adjacent to flow lobe boundaries. All the samples showed some hercynite in a cotectic with olivine (e.g. Figures 54a, 54c, 56b, 57c, 58c, and 59b), except for some samples where the olivine was of a particularly fine grainsize (e.g. HCF16).

Olivine is the dominant phase in most samples, except the most iron-rich, which are dominated by wustite. The olivine is mostly more iron-rich than Fa92 (except for sample HCF16) and all the other tapslags have olivine that is more iron-rich than Fa96. The olivine also shows mostly low levels of substitution by both calcium and manganese (Figures 60 and 61). The olivine also shows appreciable levels of substitution of phosphorus for silicon, such that all the olivine may be classified as phosphoran (Figure 62). In many samples the olivine bears small grains of apatite

Table 10. Sampled material

Sample number	Furnace feature number	Context	Date	Material		Technology	Chem	SEM
HCF1	756	757	Early medieval	large FB	#1	slagpit	y	y
HCF2	756	757	Early medieval	large FB	#2	slagpit	y	y
HCF3	756	757	Early medieval	large FB	#3	slagpit	y	
HCF4	756	757	Early medieval	large FB	#4	slagpit	y	
HCF5	788	787	Early medieval	FB – prilly	#1	slagpit	y	
HCF6	788	787	Early medieval	FB – lower flow	#2	slagpit	y	
HCF7	794	795	Early medieval	FB fragment		slagpit	y	y
HCF8	794	795	Early medieval	flow lobed margin		slagpit	y	y
HCF9	794	795	Early medieval	dense puddle		slagpit	y	y
HCF10	794	795	Early medieval	tapslag-like basal flow		slagpit	y	y
HCF11	794	795	Early medieval	lining		slagpit	y	
HCF12	778	781	Early medieval	FB	#1	slagpit	y	
HCF13	778	781	Early medieval	FB	#2	slagpit	y	
HCF14	778	781	Early medieval	dense puddle	#1	slagpit	y	y
HCF15	778	781	Early medieval	dense puddle	#2	slagpit	y	
HCF16	792	793	Early medieval	tapslag	#1	tapping	y	y
HCF17	792	793	Early medieval	tapslag	#2	tapping	y	
HCF18	771	772	Early medieval	tapslag	#1	tapping	y	
HCF19	771	772	Early medieval	tapslag	#2	tapping	y	y
HCF20	771	772	Early medieval	lining		tapping	y	
HCF21	758	759	Early medieval	tapslag (birdsfoot)	#1	tapping	y	
HCF22	758	759	Early medieval	tapslag	#2	tapping	y	y
HCF23	790	789	Early medieval	tapslag		tapping	y	y
HCF24	790	789	Early medieval	ore		tapping	y	
HCF25	675	676	Medieval	grey tap slag		tapping	y	y
HCF26		557	Medieval	tap slag	#1	tapping	y	y
HCF27		557	Medieval	tap slag	#2	tapping	y	
HCF28		557	Medieval	tap slag	#3	tapping	y	
HCF29		557	Medieval	dense flowed grey slag		tapping	y	y
HCF30		557	Medieval	dense massive grey slag		tapping?	y	y

in its outer rim (e.g. Figure 54c) and such apatite may also appear as elongate bodies, probably plates, within the interstitial areas.

The interstitial areas are mainly filled with a leucite-wustite cotectic (e.g. Figure 54b, 55d, 56f, 57c, 58c, and 59b), but late stage olivine (with cotectic apatite and hercynite) are also usually present (e.g. Figure 56e and 56f). Near vesicles and other discontinuities, the proportion of leucite in the slag typically rises, both as a component of the leucite-wustite cotectic (e.g. Figure 54b), but also as simple leucite, which may occur both as discrete grains and as discontinuous rims to the voids (e.g. Figure 54f).

Table 11. Major elements by XRF. < = below detection. All elements presented as wt% oxide

Sample number	SiO_2	Al_2O_3	Fe_2O_3	FeO	MnO	MgO	CaO	Na_2O	K_2O	TiO_2	P_2O_5	LOI	Total
Slags from slagpit furnaces													
HCF1	13.53	3.96	76.38	68.74	1.34	0.35	0.82	0.04	0.69	0.27	1.103	-5.81	98.69
HCF2	13.72	3.35	75.80	68.22	1.36	0.42	1.22	<0.010	0.39	0.25	1.227	0.99	98.96
HCF3	10.69	3.29	81.43	73.28	1.30	0.28	0.59	0.01	0.32	0.25	0.986	-4.95	99.35
HCF4	11.55	3.68	79.48	71.53	1.39	0.30	0.85	<0.010	0.31	0.25	1.256	-2.58	99.28
HCF5	17.75	5.75	70.34	63.31	1.54	0.57	0.38	0.27	1.10	0.38	1.260	-4.50	99.57
HCF6	11.70	5.43	76.04	68.43	1.59	0.30	0.53	0.15	0.95	0.31	1.749	-6.32	99.00
HCF7	16.29	3.95	73.28	65.95	1.29	0.50	1.11	0.08	0.73	0.29	1.256	-5.37	99.02
HCF8	11.61	4.69	77.61	69.85	0.88	0.42	1.02	0.11	1.27	0.25	0.872	-6.99	99.01
HCF9	11.51	3.92	79.86	71.87	0.80	0.44	0.97	0.06	0.59	0.23	0.731	-6.77	99.37
HCF10	9.00	4.29	83.36	75.03	0.76	0.27	0.58	0.05	0.69	0.21	0.796	-7.10	100.24
HCF12	19.11	4.67	70.65	63.59	0.98	0.41	0.97	0.13	0.73	0.31	1.108	-3.88	99.36
HCF13	21.47	4.38	69.19	62.27	1.36	0.58	1.05	0.06	0.92	0.30	1.148	-4.98	100.71
HCF14	18.35	6.26	67.81	61.03	1.93	0.55	0.99	0.07	1.07	0.45	1.184	-5.51	99.02
HCF15	15.13	4.27	75.33	67.80	0.95	0.37	1.01	0.07	0.87	0.27	1.052	-5.99	99.64
HCF29	13.79	4.40	73.79	66.41	2.82	0.29	1.29	0.07	1.32	0.26	0.999	-5.79	99.53
HCF30	12.02	3.58	75.92	68.33	3.18	0.47	1.10	0.06	1.03	0.25	1.109	-6.99	99.19
Lining													
HCF11	66.36	15.24	6.65	5.98	0.10	1.70	<0.003	0.25	4.83	0.94	0.181	1.39	97.80
HCF20	73.72	10.99	5.20	4.68	0.08	0.90	0.04	0.48	3.07	0.87	0.216	2.94	98.72
Slags from early slag tapping furnaces													
HCF16	9.03	3.41	82.42	74.18	0.93	0.32	1.13	0.02	0.55	0.23	1.400	-6.69	99.81
HCF17	15.01	5.86	70.82	63.74	0.58	0.63	1.57	0.10	1.57	0.37	1.702	-6.16	98.53
HCF18	12.52	3.06	77.72	69.95	1.62	0.35	1.43	0.05	0.94	0.21	1.332	-7.50	99.51
HCF19	14.65	3.34	74.79	67.31	1.72	0.37	1.37	0.04	0.96	0.22	1.340	-6.76	99.17
HCF21	14.17	3.52	76.33	68.70	1.38	0.30	0.77	0.09	0.99	0.29	0.719	-7.15	98.83
HCF22	7.81	3.92	81.15	73.03	1.74	0.37	1.52	0.02	0.67	0.25	1.148	-7.27	98.99
HCF23	17.42	5.79	68.55	61.69	1.89	0.44	0.65	0.12	0.78	0.44	1.358	-6.17	97.73
Slags from late slag tapping furnaces													
HCF25	13.54	4.34	73.88	66.50	2.49	0.34	1.10	0.04	0.96	0.30	1.431	-6.66	98.80
HCF26	17.33	6.15	69.75	62.77	1.11	0.48	0.81	0.08	1.20	0.41	1.238	-5.25	98.90
HCF27	17.37	6.02	70.66	63.60	1.00	0.31	0.83	0.07	0.67	0.40	1.241	-5.53	98.86
HCF28	21.30	6.62	63.92	57.53	1.22	0.41	1.15	0.17	1.97	0.46	0.708	-5.30	98.20
Ore													
HCF24	6.36	3.36	74.97	67.47	0.26	0.04	<0.003	<0.010	0.17	0.23	1.234	12.09	98.86

In the furnace bottom slags from the non-slag tapping furnaces, contacts between the slag and fuel particles are often marked by the development of a thin lamina of metallic iron, which may also occur in more granular form in the adjacent slag (e.g. Figure 54d and 54f). Within many of the slags the slag mass was built through agglomeration of flow lobes. Where adjacent lobes formed in quick succession in reducing conditions there may be no bounding crust to the lobes (e.g. Figure 55d, 58a, and 58d), but more commonly an oxide crust was developed. In most examples where this was formed inside the furnace, the crust appears to be of wustite, upon which hercynite may have nucleated (e.g. Figure 57a, 57b, and 57d). For some of tapped slag lobes, more complex, hammerscale-like crusts with magnetite and hematite may be found, often forming the sites for growth of complex spinels into the lobe interior (e.g. Figure 58e, 59c, 59d, and 59f). The most extreme example of crust formation under oxidising conditions (in sample HCF26) led to the widespread formation of iscorite in a zone up to 300 μm thick below the surface (Figure 59f).

Table 12a. Trace elements by ICP-MS. All elements presented as ppm

Sample number	Sc	V	Cr	Co	Ni	Ga	Rb	Sr	Y	Zr	Nb	Mo
Slags from slagpit furnaces												
HCF1	8.2	47.9	90.8	210.0	17.4	6.3	32.7	100.7	52.7	115.4	4.24	0.70
HCF2	8.8	37.6	61.9	52.8	80.1	5.0	16.4	101.8	45.0	193.0	4.93	0.42
HCF3	6.7	40.1	79.2	58.9	9.0	5.8	15.6	63.7	32.4	142.8	4.92	0.62
HCF4	6.5	32.4	49.2	22.0	32.7	5.8	14.5	80.6	45.1	122.0	2.87	0.42
HCF5	16.0	88.8	65.9	36.4	81.5	7.5	42.6	51.5	66.3	199.1	6.04	0.36
HCF6	14.6	65.2	31.3	18.4	41.3	7.1	30.3	74.3	90.6	127.5	5.56	0.34
HCF7	7.8	43.6	61.3	16.1	11.2	6.2	27.5	96.1	43.6	193.4	4.62	0.77
HCF8	12.8	63.3	70.3	20.2	6.2	4.6	27.1	80.0	68.6	112.7	3.32	0.22
HCF9	11.5	56.2	45.8	14.7	10.6	4.1	14.5	72.9	60.2	141.6	4.68	0.27
HCF10	12.8	55.9	51.6	18.9	16.4	4.5	16.9	58.5	66.4	123.8	3.78	0.29
HCF12	18.1	113.7	85.3	9.1	8.1	5.1	31.2	44.4	67.8	238.6	5.52	0.35
HCF13	15.8	94.0	68.4	18.9	5.7	5.4	33.8	53.6	63.1	249.0	5.96	0.49
HCF14	19.4	91.5	95.6	14.1	25.3	8.1	31.8	83.3	94.5	205.0	7.82	0.42
HCF15	15.1	82.6	61.6	10.1	60.9	6.7	27.0	56.0	46.4	255.3	5.87	0.37
HCF29	10.2	72.9	49.1	8.6	5.4	5.8	27.1	63.2	56.8	204.3	5.16	0.26
HCF30	11.6	88.4	99.2	17.8	22.6	6.3	27.6	64.9	51.8	181.6	4.98	0.51
Lining												
HCF11	10.1	86.6	99.6	18.7	55.4	19.2	165.6	63.7	31.0	494.9	17.82	0.55
HCF20	8.0	79.5	82.9	8.1	12.8	13.1	123.5	53.9	28.5	679.3	16.93	0.83
Slags from early slag tapping furnaces												
HCF16	11.2	70.3	41.9	11.6	4.2	5.9	12.3	51.5	49.4	149.8	5.41	0.31
HCF17	23.2	186.4	78.4	14.4	7.0	6.6	33.0	83.1	62.4	203.0	7.29	0.32
HCF18	9.2	55.7	54.5	20.3	4.1	5.3	21.1	63.7	58.2	131.1	3.32	0.36
HCF19	10.3	61.9	58.2	28.8	0.6	5.1	24.4	65.1	65.1	117.4	2.62	0.37
HCF21	6.4	42.3	48.5	20.1	5.2	6.2	32.4	102.8	42.0	192.4	5.68	0.40
HCF22	10.2	56.9	66.5	20.3	4.2	6.2	20.2	194.7	54.2	101.2	3.32	0.41
HCF23	9.6	56.9	52.9	23.7	4.1	8.6	36.0	86.9	62.2	228.8	9.53	0.32
Slags from late slag tapping furnaces												
HCF25	20.0	117.9	78.3	13.8	15.0	5.4	24.8	59.2	70.3	166.4	6.03	0.36
HCF26	25.8	149.9	103.2	13.0	7.7	6.5	44.5	58.7	83.0	191.8	8.15	0.40
HCF27	35.7	152.3	117.6	10.5	17.0	5.5	22.7	52.0	84.8	226.7	8.78	0.53
HCF28	24.3	91.9	89.8	18.5	26.2	5.9	68.1	76.2	90.4	220.7	8.86	0.24
Ore												
HCF24	6.5	42.1	39.4	91.3	23.9	5.0	19.0	15.2	39.3	117.5	4.25	0.54

Details of Sampled Materials: Materials from Non-tapping Processes

HCF1 to HCF4 ((757)/[756])

These four samples were taken from a single large block of 'furnace bottom' weighing 15.4 kg. Sample HCF1 was taken from dense slag that would have been adjacent to the pit wall, HCF2 from charcoal-rich slag distally at mid height, HCF3 from a sub-horizontal denser band just above HCF2 and HCF4 was taken from charcoal-rich slag just above the prilly base. Although all four samples were subjected to elemental analysis, just two (HCF1 and HCF2) were examined on the SEM.

Sample HCF1 (Figure 54a–d) showed a rather inhomogeneous texture. The primary wustite in the slag is overall very abundant, but varies markedly both in proportion and morphology, but is mainly present as rather stout dendrites with domains of >0.5mm. The wustite locally shows some relationship with the occurrence of hercynite, present in a cotectic with the dominant olivine. The main olivine phase shows rather little variation in composition, between Fo4Fa96 and Fa100, with up to 2% substitution by calcium and a constant 4% substitution by manganese. Some late olivine (see below) shows a composition of Fa100 with up to 11% calcium substitution. Phosphorus is present in the main olivine at levels of 0.02 atoms per formula unit (APFU) in the cores, rising 0.08

Table 12b. Trace elements by ICP-MS. All elements presented as ppm

Sample number	Sn	Cs	Ba	La	Ce	Pr	Nd	Sm	Eu	Gd	Tb
Slags from slagpit furnaces											
HCF1	0.78	2.61	208.6	30.90	40.65	6.09	22.79	5.03	1.09	4.96	0.82
HCF2	1.72	1.35	239.8	23.43	31.58	4.90	18.67	4.16	0.96	4.23	0.69
HCF3	1.77	1.40	192.7	21.31	27.82	4.20	15.79	3.55	0.78	3.59	0.57
HCF4	1.21	1.26	192.0	26.00	33.78	5.18	19.41	4.48	1.02	4.48	0.74
HCF5	1.25	3.12	218.5	44.16	60.08	9.20	34.46	7.35	1.64	7.42	1.14
HCF6	1.12	1.94	228.3	57.52	72.72	11.75	44.73	9.62	2.23	9.99	1.55
HCF7	1.15	2.43	188.4	26.27	38.47	5.55	20.72	4.68	1.14	5.18	0.83
HCF8	0.31	1.82	181.6	42.17	71.54	9.75	36.16	7.66	1.91	8.97	1.41
HCF9	0.69	1.22	170.5	33.66	57.38	7.83	29.11	6.25	1.44	7.19	1.13
HCF10	1.69	1.29	142.7	38.30	65.05	8.74	32.66	6.87	1.66	7.98	1.24
HCF12	1.42	2.35	146.6	31.35	54.24	7.52	28.16	6.11	1.46	7.08	1.08
HCF13	1.15	2.55	241.8	24.85	35.35	5.48	21.09	4.80	1.15	5.64	0.90
HCF14	1.16	2.70	310.8	57.11	80.37	11.40	43.91	9.20	2.15	10.36	1.57
HCF15	1.12	2.05	180.8	26.27	41.26	6.02	22.68	5.00	1.20	5.30	0.87
HCF29	1.41	1.25	386.3	29.54	43.19	6.58	25.56	5.87	1.36	6.16	0.96
HCF30	2.83	1.57	330.3	29.67	50.52	6.92	28.30	6.74	1.50	6.69	1.07
Lining											
HCF11	4.30	17.01	528.9	34.64	69.43	8.24	27.96	5.18	0.96	4.23	0.66
HCF20	2.33	11.58	406.5	28.07	57.53	6.65	22.93	4.37	0.79	3.91	0.65
Slags from early slag tapping furnaces											
HCF16	2.06	1.02	175.4	29.37	36.74	5.53	20.39	4.31	1.03	5.06	0.79
HCF17	0.83	2.54	194.6	39.52	50.01	7.72	28.40	5.88	1.39	6.52	1.03
HCF18	0.63	1.55	283.1	27.27	42.29	5.84	23.13	5.01	1.29	6.12	0.93
HCF19	0.33	1.83	305.6	29.85	46.92	6.35	25.86	5.64	1.36	6.59	1.02
HCF21	1.57	1.88	273.7	24.64	40.26	5.16	19.77	4.28	0.97	4.49	0.70
HCF22	0.92	0.92	348.2	32.31	49.63	6.67	25.37	5.66	1.38	6.21	0.93
HCF23	1.44	3.90	208.0	50.20	65.16	9.69	35.36	7.15	1.67	7.40	1.16
Slags from late slag tapping furnaces											
HCF25	2.27	1.79	229.0	39.53	49.26	7.43	27.60	5.76	1.19	5.67	0.88
HCF26	4.85	3.58	250.4	49.49	62.13	9.86	37.89	8.07	1.61	7.71	1.17
HCF27	1.58	1.71	184.0	46.81	57.62	9.41	35.26	7.70	1.59	7.76	1.21
HCF28	0.68	4.91	219.1	55.33	65.14	9.99	36.97	7.45	1.61	7.67	1.17
Ore											
HCF24	1.82	7.06	67.0	24.91	26.95	4.81	17.88	3.69	0.88	3.99	0.60

APFU on the margins. Thus, most of the external parts of the main phase olivine (and all of the late phase olivine) may be classified as phosphoran fayalitic olivine (phosphoran olivine was defined by Boesenberg and Hewins (2010) as having greater than 0.03 atoms per formula unit APFU, of phosphorus).

The areas interstitial to the main olivine show a complex structure with moss-like rounded growths of a leucite-wustite cotectic, locally euhedral apatite (a sodium-bearing apatite, with a little potassium and probably a small proportion of iron substitution for calcium) and thin films of late olivine. In some cases, there is apatite embedded in the outer rim of the main phase olivine. The normal microstructure described above changes near the site of embedded fuel fragments (and locations of former fuel fragments). These areas are marked by the development of small amounts of iron in blebs and films around charcoal particles. The contacts are also marked by the development of large crystals of leucite.

Sample HCF2 (Figure 54e–f) was similar to HCF1, but rather more heterogeneous. The primary wustite varied from very densely blebby dendrites in iron-rich areas to very spares, delicate, but very wide dendrites in iron poor areas. Some areas were wustite-free and may represent pore fills. Areas of coarse wustite also tended to be the areas with the coarsest hercynite crystals, which commonly

Table 12c. Trace elements by ICP-MS. All elements presented as ppm

Sample number	Dy	Ho	Er	Tm	Yb	Lu	Hf	Ta	Pb	Th	U
Slags from slagpit furnaces											
HCF1	4.74	0.96	2.82	0.43	2.87	0.44	2.50	2.20	1.47	2.77	1.95
HCF2	4.06	0.82	2.37	0.38	2.53	0.40	3.23	0.46	1.08	2.38	1.91
HCF3	3.30	0.66	1.99	0.30	2.16	0.36	2.89	0.37	2.05	2.27	1.47
HCF4	4.25	0.88	2.60	0.38	2.62	0.41	2.32	0.36	1.54	2.29	1.78
HCF5	6.38	1.30	3.73	0.54	3.70	0.58	3.77	0.61	2.49	3.98	4.33
HCF6	8.51	1.75	4.96	0.72	4.86	0.75	2.57	0.60	3.66	3.94	5.87
HCF7	4.82	0.98	2.87	0.44	3.06	0.48	3.83	0.47	2.59	3.12	1.88
HCF8	7.87	1.57	4.38	0.61	3.95	0.63	2.46	0.53	1.07	3.13	3.42
HCF9	6.25	1.28	3.49	0.51	3.28	0.52	2.71	0.47	1.85	2.60	2.93
HCF10	6.90	1.40	3.69	0.55	3.52	0.55	2.19	0.49	0.57	2.65	3.15
HCF12	6.28	1.26	3.64	0.54	3.60	0.58	4.40	0.59	1.43	3.93	8.24
HCF13	5.26	1.10	3.36	0.51	3.56	0.59	3.84	0.52	1.85	3.43	5.19
HCF14	8.99	1.81	5.07	0.75	4.93	0.81	3.78	0.74	3.65	4.39	5.56
HCF15	5.05	0.95	2.78	0.41	2.93	0.44	3.99	0.39	2.12	3.39	7.72
HCF29	5.40	1.13	3.27	0.49	3.61	0.55	3.34	0.55	1.21	3.42	5.08
HCF30	5.93	1.10	3.23	0.48	3.43	0.49	3.31	0.44	2.48	2.68	3.91
Lining											
HCF11	3.80	0.75	2.29	0.37	2.59	0.42	9.27	1.92	25.76	12.00	2.37
HCF20	3.55	0.78	2.31	0.36	2.83	0.45	12.74	1.45	20.07	10.52	2.51
Slags from early slag tapping furnaces											
HCF16	4.48	0.95	2.77	0.40	3.00	0.46	2.79	0.66	1.96	2.51	4.24
HCF17	5.82	1.22	3.54	0.53	3.76	0.57	3.61	0.66	1.58	4.40	5.95
HCF18	5.46	1.15	3.34	0.47	3.25	0.51	2.45	0.40	1.11	2.30	3.57
HCF19	5.82	1.27	3.69	0.54	3.62	0.58	2.39	0.43	1.82	2.55	3.72
HCF21	4.02	0.84	2.46	0.37	2.47	0.39	3.73	0.44	2.34	3.01	1.92
HCF22	5.27	1.08	3.13	0.47	3.22	0.52	2.10	0.46	1.55	2.54	2.29
HCF23	6.32	1.29	3.68	0.54	3.62	0.57	3.80	0.65	2.98	4.29	2.16
Slags from late slag tapping furnaces											
HCF25	5.04	1.05	3.14	0.45	3.17	0.50	2.75	0.43	0.94	2.77	5.27
HCF26	6.45	1.36	3.86	0.58	3.95	0.61	3.16	0.52	1.29	4.01	6.11
HCF27	6.65	1.39	4.05	0.60	4.17	0.64	3.68	0.64	1.73	4.59	10.19
HCF28	6.86	1.45	4.26	0.63	4.19	0.67	4.04	0.76	1.62	4.83	6.80
Ore											
HCF24	3.17	0.66	1.98	0.29	1.95	0.31	2.02	0.40	12.71	2.56	1.36

overgrew the wustite. Hercynite also occurred elsewhere more conventionally intergrown with the olivine. Olivine composition ranged (core to margin) from Fa94Fo6 with 4% calcium and 5% manganese substitution to Fa98Fo2 with 7% calcium and 5% manganese substitution. Phosphorus substitution in the olivine was 0.02–0.06 APFU, making the olivine mostly slightly phosphoran. As with sample HCF1, the rims of the olivine were commonly intergrown with apatite, and the two phases commonly co-occur in the interstitial areas, alternating with patches of leucite-wustite cotectic. Metallic iron was present in the areas around charcoal clasts and areas of void/weathering products hint that it may have been originally rather more abundant.

HCF5 and HCF6 ((787)/[788])

Sample HCF5 was taken from the typical texture of a 5.7 kg fragment of furnace bottom and *HCF6* from its dense basal flow. Neither of these samples was submitted for SEM investigation.

HCF7 to HCF11 ((795)/[794])

These samples were taken from a varied suite of pit floor materials. Sample HCF7 was taken from a 232 g fragment of typical furnace bottom. Sample HCF8 was from a fragment of flow-lobed slag from the very margin of the pit weighing 334 g. Sample HCF9 was taken from a 630 g

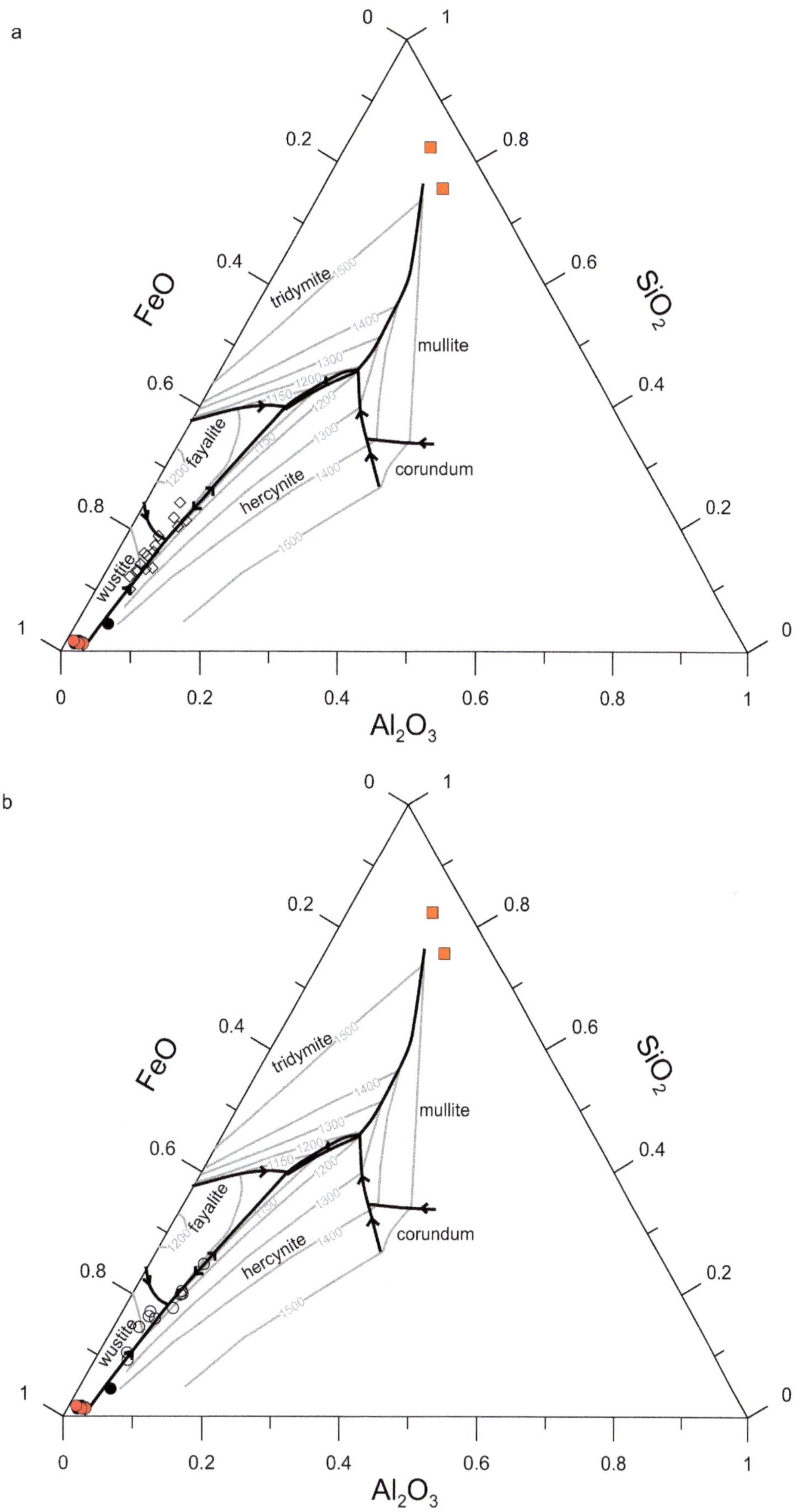

Figure 53. Major element composition of bulk analyses of residues plotted within the ternary system SiO_2-Al_2O_3-FeO (fields after Schairer and Yagi 1952, fig 6). (a) analyses of residues from non-tapping furnaces (open diamonds), with analyses of lining (orange squares), analysis of ore from Churchills Farm (black filled circle) and from Dunkeswell (red filled circle; after Young 2015a), and (b) analyses of residues from slag-tapping furnaces (open circles), with analyses of lining (orange squares), analysis of ore from Churchills Farm (black filled circle) and from Dunkeswell (red filled circle; after Young 2015a).

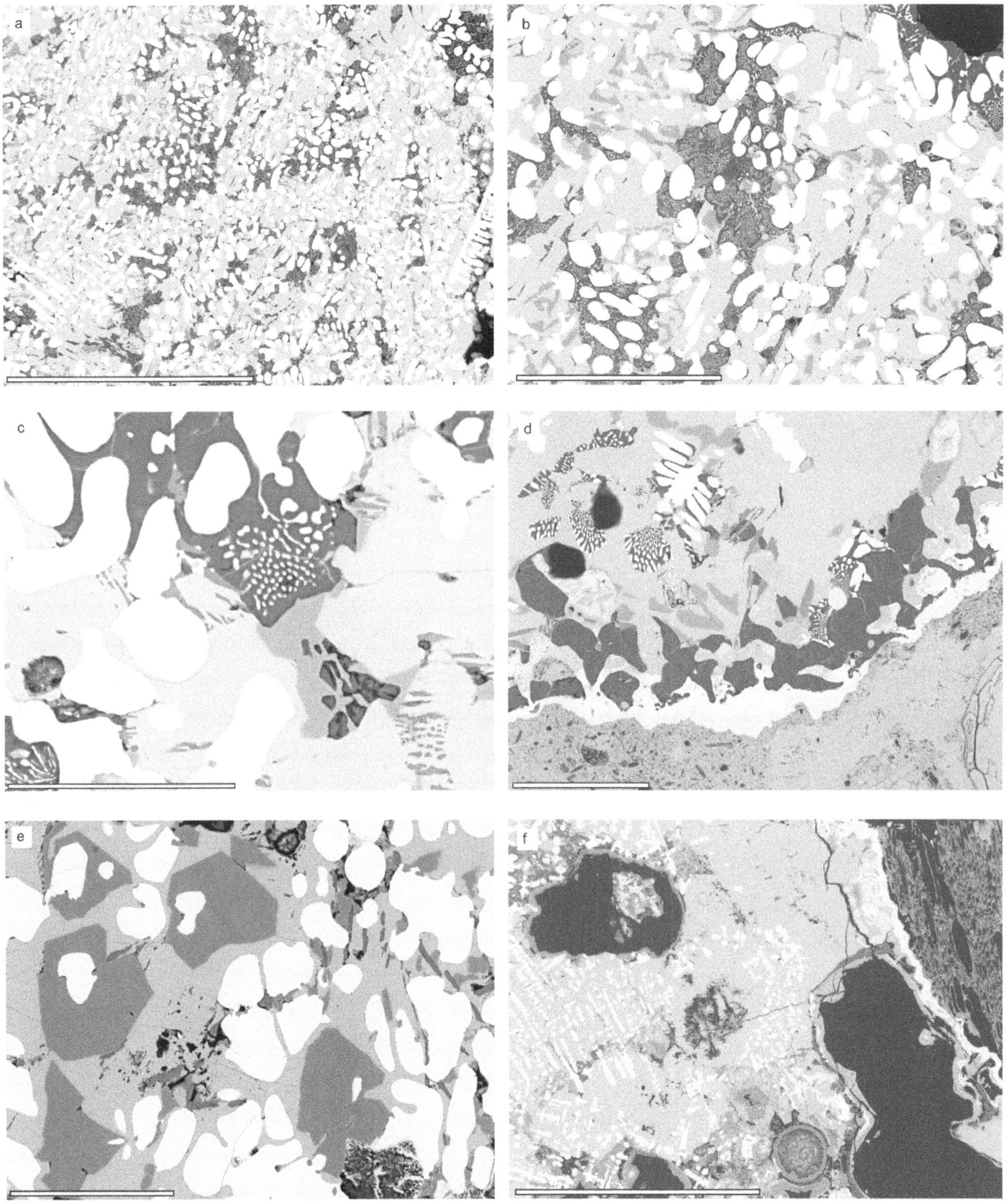

Figure 54. Backscattered electron photomicrographs of samples from 'furnace bottoms' from non-slag tapping furnaces. (a) Typical slag texture with substantial wustite dendrites (white), elongate fayalite (pale grey) and leucite-dominated interstitial areas (dark). HCF1, SOI1 (600 µm-scale). (b) Detail showing similar texture to (a), with early wustite (white), fayalite to cotectic hercynite (pale grey and mid-grey respectively) and interstitial areas mainly filled by a leucite-wustite cotectic. Leucite dominated material also surrounds the vesicle (black; upper right). HCF1, SOI2(200µm-scale). (c) Detail showing the leucite-wustite cotectic in an interstitial area. The primary wustite (white) is overlain by fayalite which bears cotectic hercynite (mid grey) and near the margins lamellae of apatite (mid grey, fractionally darker than the hercynite). The interstitial area is filled by leucite (dark grey) or a leucite-wustite cotectic, with a few grains of apatite. HCF1, SOI4 (70 µm-scale). (d) Contact area between the slag and a mineralised fuel clast (lower part of image). The boundary is marked by a thin zone of metallic iron (partially oxidised), in contact with a zone of irregularly shaped leucite (dark), which abuts a zone of very coarse-grained slag with a very low wustite content. HCF1, SOI8 (100 µm-scale). (e) A variant of the slag texture in which the hercynite (mid-grey) is euhedral or subhedral, overlying wustite (white) and followed by fayalite (pale grey). HCF2, SOI2 (600 µm-scale). (f) Broad view of contact between slag and fuel particle (right). The fayalite is very coarse-grained and follows large, but delicate, wustite dendrites, The contact with the fuel is marked by a thin zone of metallic iron. The large vesicle (lower right) shows formation of an incomplete rim of leucite-dominated slag. HCF2, SOI4 (600 µm-scale).

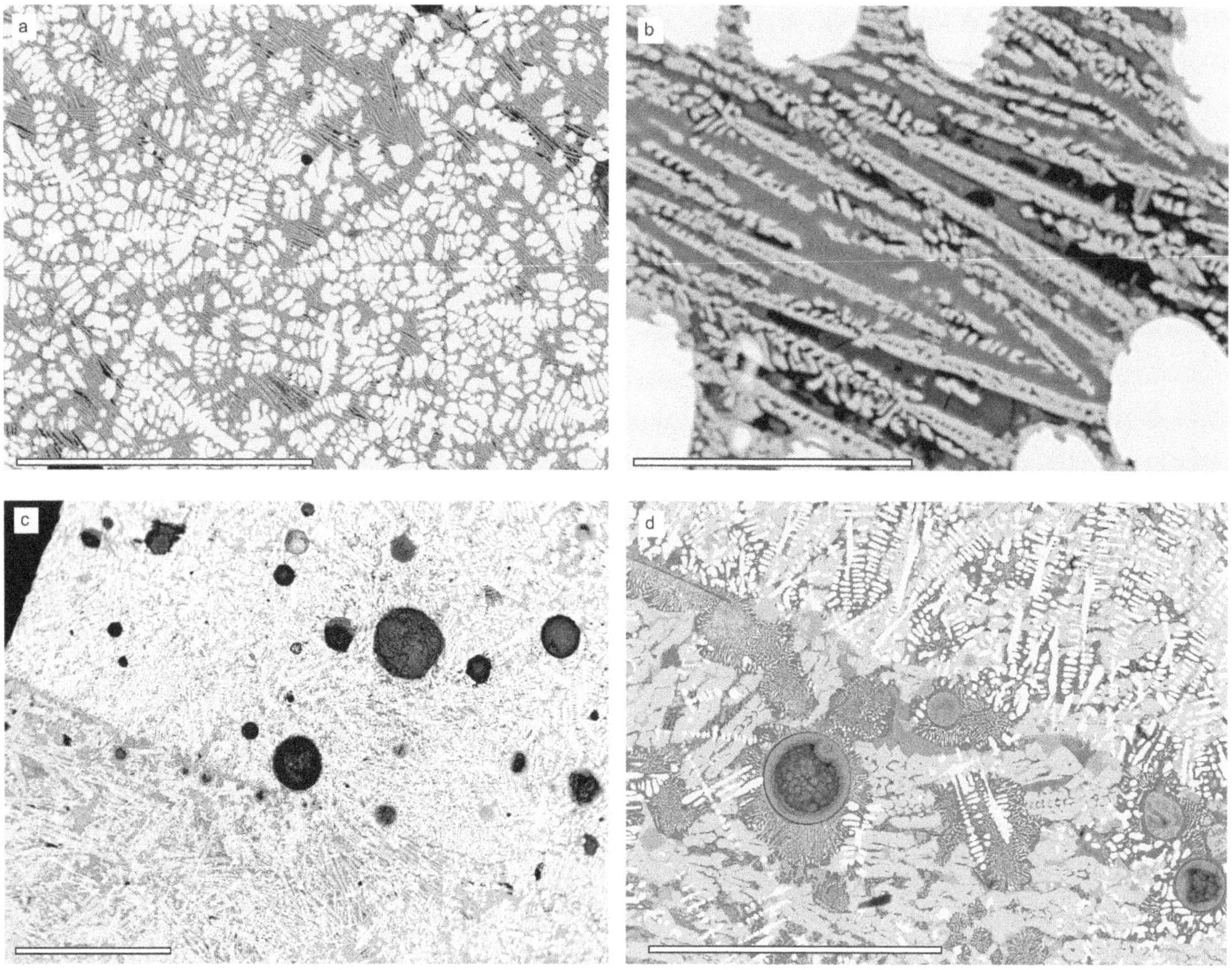

Figure 55. Backscattered electron photomicrographs of samples from the lobed margins of 'furnace bottoms' from non-slag tapping furnaces. (a) Typical 'quench-textured' slag with rounded wustite dendrites (pale) and a groundmass of parallel fayalite laths. HCF8, SOI1 (600 μm-scale). (b) Detail of (a) to show elongate fayalite crystals in glass. HCF8, SOI2 (40μm-scale). (c) Broad view of internal contact between slag lobes. HCF8, SOI7 (1 mm-scale). (d) Detail of (c) showing abundant leucite-wustite in lobe to lower left and the elongate wustite dendrites growing off the lobe contact towards the upper right. HCF8, SOI8 (300 μm-scale).

piece of dense slag 'puddle', interpreted as being from the pit floor. Sample HCF10 was also a dense basal slag, but having a 'tapslag-like' morphology and a weight of 272 g. The suite of slags is completed by a 78 g fragment of lining which provided sample HCF11. Of this suite, samples HCF7, HCF8, HCF9 and HCF10 were investigated using the SEM.

Sample HCF7 had a typical heterogeneous furnace bottom microstructure. The primary wustite (locally with inclusions of metallic iron) was typically of quite dense, stubby dendrites with domains typically of 0.2 mm, but variable. The dominant phase was olivine, with cores of approximately Fa96Fo4, with 1% calcium and 4% manganese substitution and margins of Fa99Fo1 with 2% calcium and 4% manganese substitution. Phosphorus substitution varied from 0.03 APFU internally to 0.09 APFU towards the margins of the olivine. Hercynite was present as a cotectic with the olivine. The olivine also had embedded apatite grains close to its rims. The interstitial areas show rounded masses of wustite-leucite cotectic, separated by thin films of fayalite, apatite and hercynite. Towards the larger voids, particularly those containing charcoal (present as iron oxide infills of the wood structure), the texture shows a more granular wustite (commonly with iron cores) followed by an olivine with little development of cotectic hercynite. Interstitial areas are dominated by leucite, with a higher proportion occurring on its own, rather than in a cotectic with wustite, particularly on the cavity margins which may show a leucite rim.

Sample HCF8 (Figure 55a–d) shows an entirely different microstructure, more typical of a flowed slag. The primary wustite comprises dendrites varying from stubby, irregular and curvilinear to much large (0.5 mm) and slightly more delicate. The subsequent olivine is in the form of extremely elongate, narrow skeletal crystals (up to 0.6 mm in length). The olivine showed compositions varying from Fa96Fo4, with 1% calcium and 3% manganese substitution to Fa97Fo3 with 2% calcium and 3% manganese substitution. The very fine scale of the crystals probably limited the ability of the EDS system to determine internal

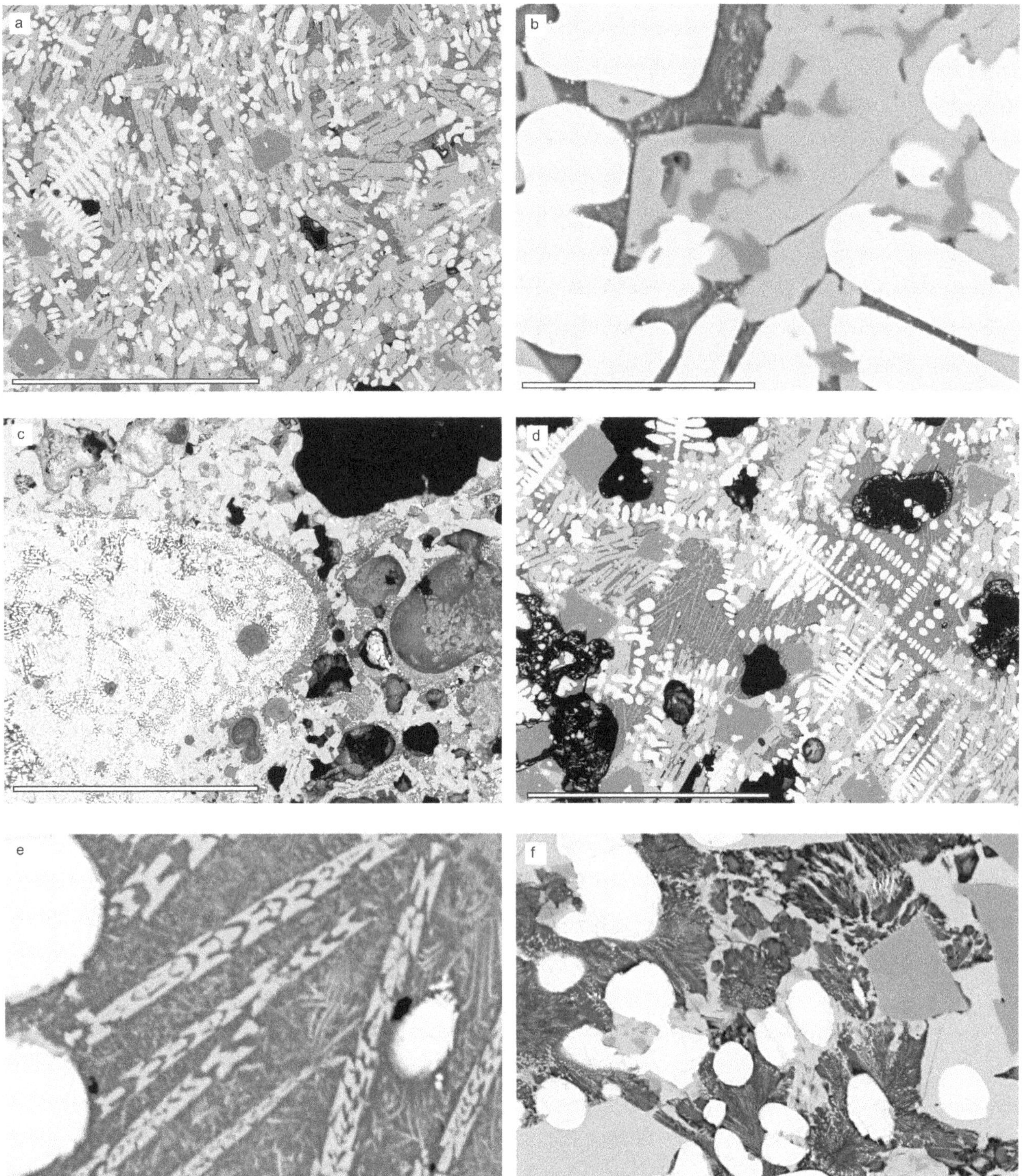

Figure 56. Backscattered electron photomicrographs of samples from 'basal slag puddles' from non-slag tapping furnaces. (a) Typical slag texture, with early wustite dendrites of moderately rounded outline, locally overlain by euhedral hercynite and elongate fayalite (mid grey). HCF14, SOI7 (600 µm-scale). (b) Detail showing early wustite (bright) overlain by fayalite (pale grey) with cotectic of hercynite (mid-grey), and with complex fine-grained interstitial areas. HCF9, SOI2 (40 µm-scale). (c) Inhomogeneous region with rounded wustite-rich bleb to left (probably an incompletely mixed melted ore droplet), bearing a leucite fringe (centre) and more typical slag to right. HCF9, SOI9 (600 µm-scale). (d) Slag variant with multiple generations of olivine, following the early wustite and euhedral hercynite. HCF14, SOI2 (600 µm-scale). (e) Detail of (d) showing fine olivine in interstitial area. HCF14, SOI3 (40 µm-scale). (f) Leucite-rich interstitial area in which the leucite (dark) is associated with a late-stage olivine, all overlying the main olivine (pale grey), euhedral hercynite (mid-grey) and dendritic wustite (white). HCF14, SOI5 (70µm-scale).

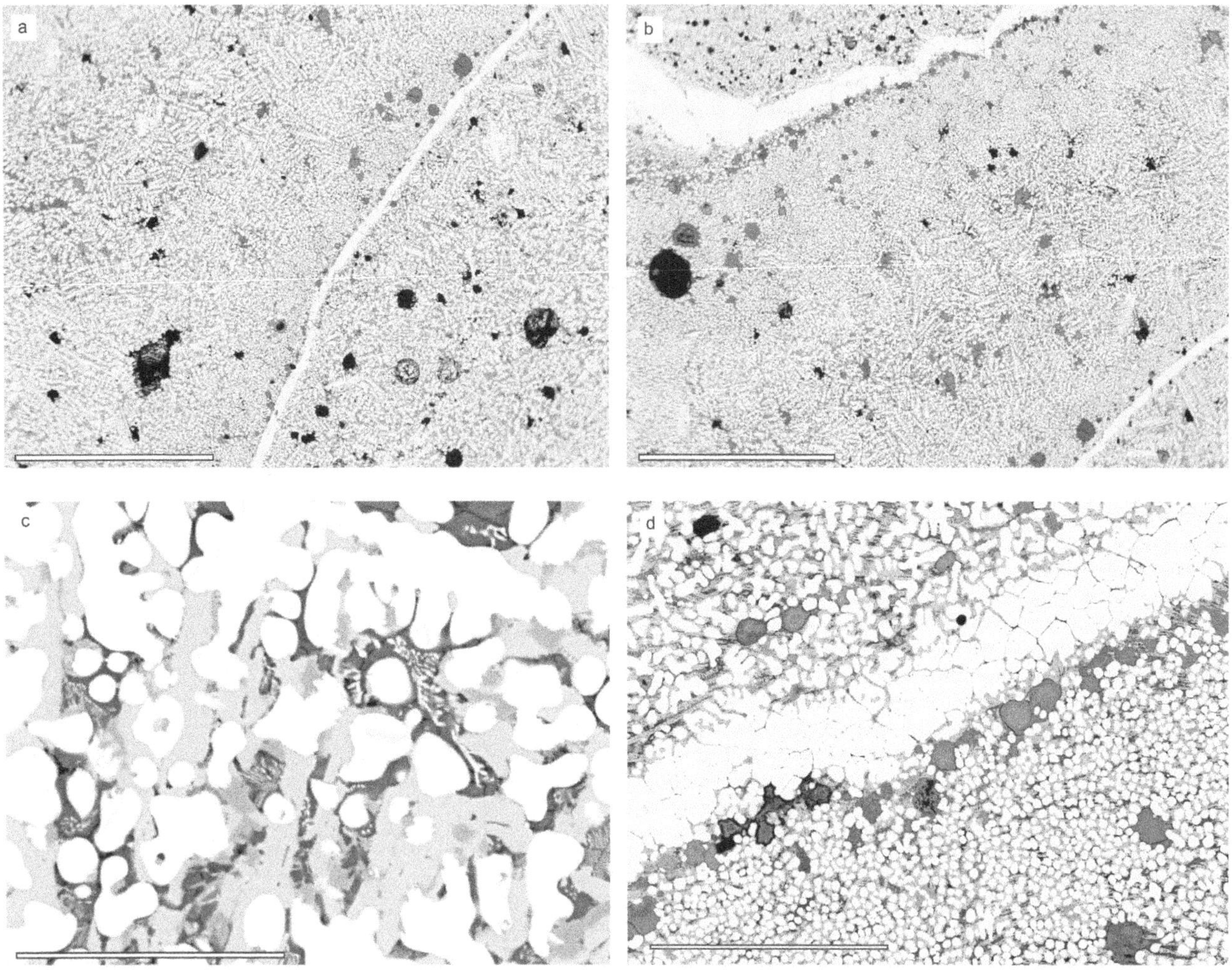

Figure 57. Backscattered electron photomicrographs of samples from flow slags from non-slag tapping furnaces. (a) Typical slag texture with flow lobes marked by iron oxide rim. HCF10, SOI1 (1 mm-scale). (b) As (a) ,but with one rim cut obliquely to appear very broad in the section. HCF10, SOI2 (1 mm-scale). (c) Typical slag texture detail, showing poorly-formed, rounded, wustite dendrites, followed by fayalite plus hercynite cotectic and with dark leucite-rich interstices. HCF10, SOI8 (60 µm-scale). (d) Lobe boundary, lower lobe has very fine wustite (locally overgrown by hercynite) rather similar to that in the droplet in Figure 56 (c). HCF10, SOI10 (300 µm-scale).

variation. The phosphorus substitution ranged from 0.04 to 0.08 APFU. The interstitial areas appeared glassy at the maximum resolution of the SEM. Within the body of the slag, the flow lobe margins were picked out by concentrations of leucite (mainly in thin plates, probably forming the location for nucleation of the subsequent cotectic) and of a leucite-wustite cotectic.

Sample HCF9 (Figure 56b–c) proved to be rather heterogeneous, with a dominant texture comprising stubby, irregular wustite dendrites with rounded elements, followed by an elongate olivine, followed in turn by the development of hercynite and apatite, with a very fine-grained crystalline groundmass. This typical texture occurs over most of the sample but in discrete areas – possibly indicating the presence of coalesced flow lobes. Between these areas there are regions that are more vesicular and more highly leucitic. There are also a few regions with a very coarse, angular olivine and at least one rounded area with a pervasive 'spongy' texture to the dominant wustite (suggesting an incompletely-reacted ore particle). The olivine ranged from Fa96Fo4 with 3% calcium and 2% manganese substitution to Fa98Fo2 with 5% calcium and 2% manganese substitution. In one case a late stage olivine apparently showed 20% calcium substitution. Phosphorus substitution varied from 0.02 to 0.07 APFU.

Sample HCF10 (Figure 57a–d) was a very wustite rich flow slag, with well-developed flow lobes bounded by well-developed, thick, oxide crusts. Where examined, the crusts appeared to be entirely of granular wustite, but the precision of the analyses would be compatible with the presence of a proportion of magnetite. The olivine is subordinate to the wustite and shows compositions of Fa97–98Fo3–2, with 1% of calcium and 3% of manganese substitution. Phosphorus substitution varied from 0.03 to 0.08 APFU.

HCF12 to HCF15 ((781)/[778])

Samples HCF12 and HCF13 were taken from typical furnace bottom fragments weighing 1085 g and 956 g respectively. Samples HCF14 and HCF15 were taken from examples of dense basal 'puddles' weighing 1160 g and

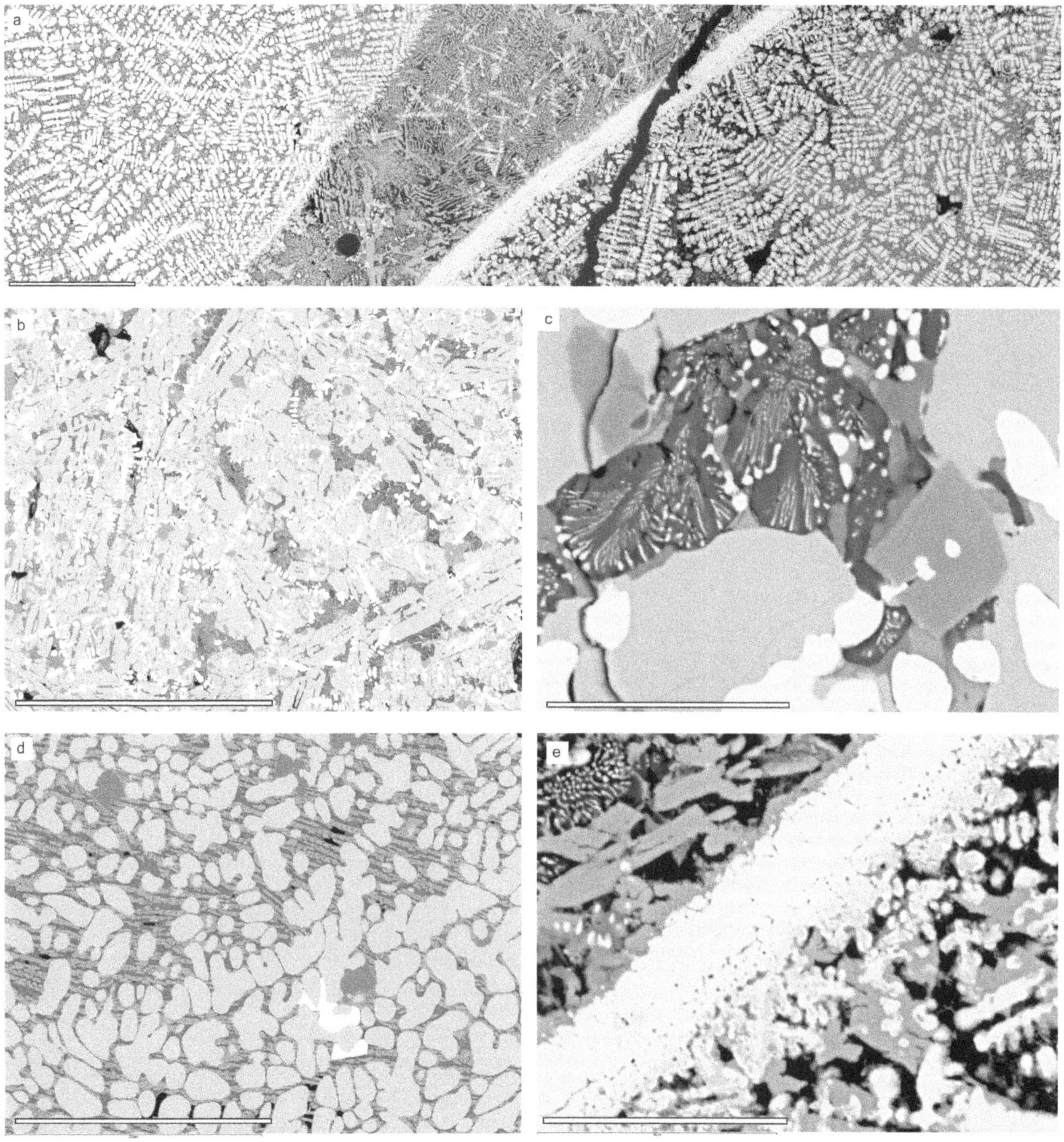

Figure 58. Backscattered electron photomicrographs of samples from tapped slags from early medieval slag-tapping furnaces. (a) Montage showing several flow lobes, all with quench-textured of elongate, delicate, complex wustite dendrites, followed by fine fayalite. One lobe boundary is marked by oxide rim (see also (e)), the other solely by a change in the slag texture (see also (d)). The quench textures of the right two lobes, with lamellar fayalite (centre) and fayalite closely coating the wustite dendrites (right), resemble those of the later tapslags (Figure 59), but in neither case is iscorite present. HCF16, SOI3-5 (100 µm-scale). (b) Typical slag texture in a coarser-grained area away from the lobe margins. The early wustite is sparse and locally overgrown by euhedral hercynite. The subsequent elongate olivine contains abundant hercynite cotectic. The interstitial areas (dark) are dominated by a leucite-wustite cotectic. HCF23, SOI4 (600 µm-scale). (c) Detail of (b) showing interstitial areas, with leucite, leucite-wustite cotectic, wustite and apatite. The primary wustite is overlain by euhedral hercynite and fayalite-hercynite cotectic, with the outer parts of the fayalite also containing apatite. HCF23, SOI2 (40 µm-scale). (d) Cryptic lobe boundary demarked by change in the proportion of wustie (mid grey). The white overgrowth to the wustite in the lower lobe is iron. Both lobes show some large subhedral hercynite. HCF22, SOI2 (200 µm-scale). (e) Oxide boundary between lobes. First-formed lobe (lower right), shows inward –growing oxide dendrites from the rim (probably mainly wustite), the outlines of which suggest they were originally a spinel (they are now multiphase with wustite, bright, and duller spinel, probably magnetite). On both sides of the boundary the later-formed slag has fine, but elongate olivine with leucite-wustite eutectic. HCF16, SOI6 (40 µm-scale).

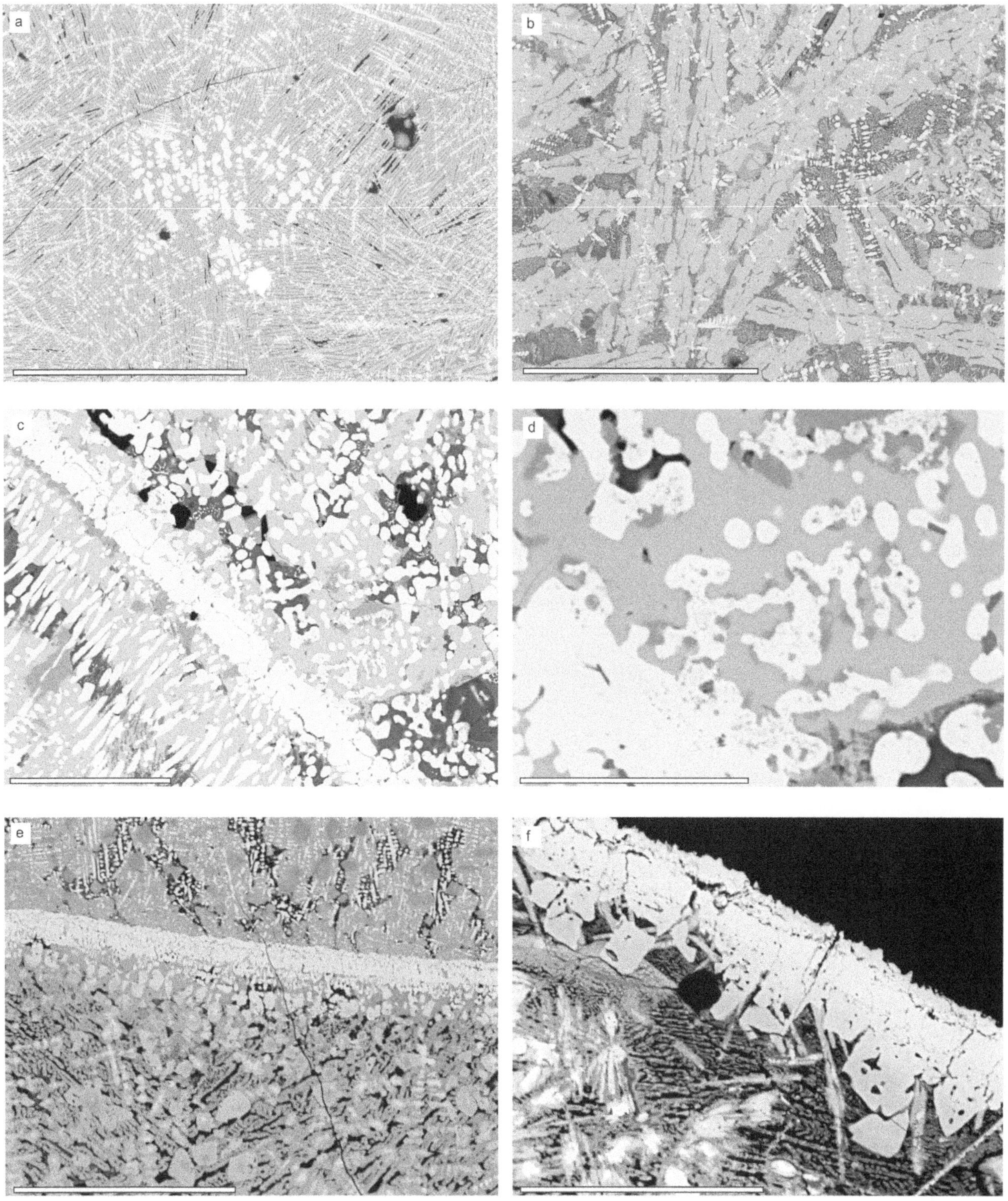

Figure 59. Backscattered electron photomicrographs of samples from tapped slags from medieval contexts. (a) Typical quenched tapslag, with variable, but mostly very delicate and long wustite dendritic arrays, followed by sheaves of elongate fayalite. HCF29, SOI2 (100 µm-scale). (b) Detail of coarser slag texture, showing the elongate fayalite to be rich in hercynite cotectic, with some hercynite also present as small early euhedral grains. The interstitial areas are filled by leucite-wustite cotectic. HCF29, SOI6 (40 µm-scale). (c) Detail of a flow lobe rim. The rim becomes more porous (and probably richer in magnetite inclusions), into the lobe towards the upper right (presumably the earlier), with the dendritic wustite of the lobe showing relationship with protrusions from the rim. The later coarse-grained lobe (now to lower left) shows nucleation of wustite dendrites onto the planar outer face of the rim, which is also coated in tiny euhedral hercynite. HCF25, SOI3 (100 µm-scale). (d) Detail of (c) showing protrusions from the (originally lower) face of the rim, which bear pores and act as nucleation sites for the subhedral hercynite. HCF25, SOI4 (40 µm-scale). (e) Example of a lobe boundary (in correct orientation) showing similar features to those of (c) and (d). The quenching of the lower lobe has produced thin fayalite coats on the wustite and hercynite dendrites. The upper lobe has abundant euhedral hercynite. HCF26, SOI8 (90 µm-scale). (f) Example of a lobe boundary in which the inner face of the rim has developed euhedral magnetite-rich spinels. The quench textured lamellae comprise fayalite and iscorite coating the wustite dendrites. HCF26, SOI4 (60 µm-scale).

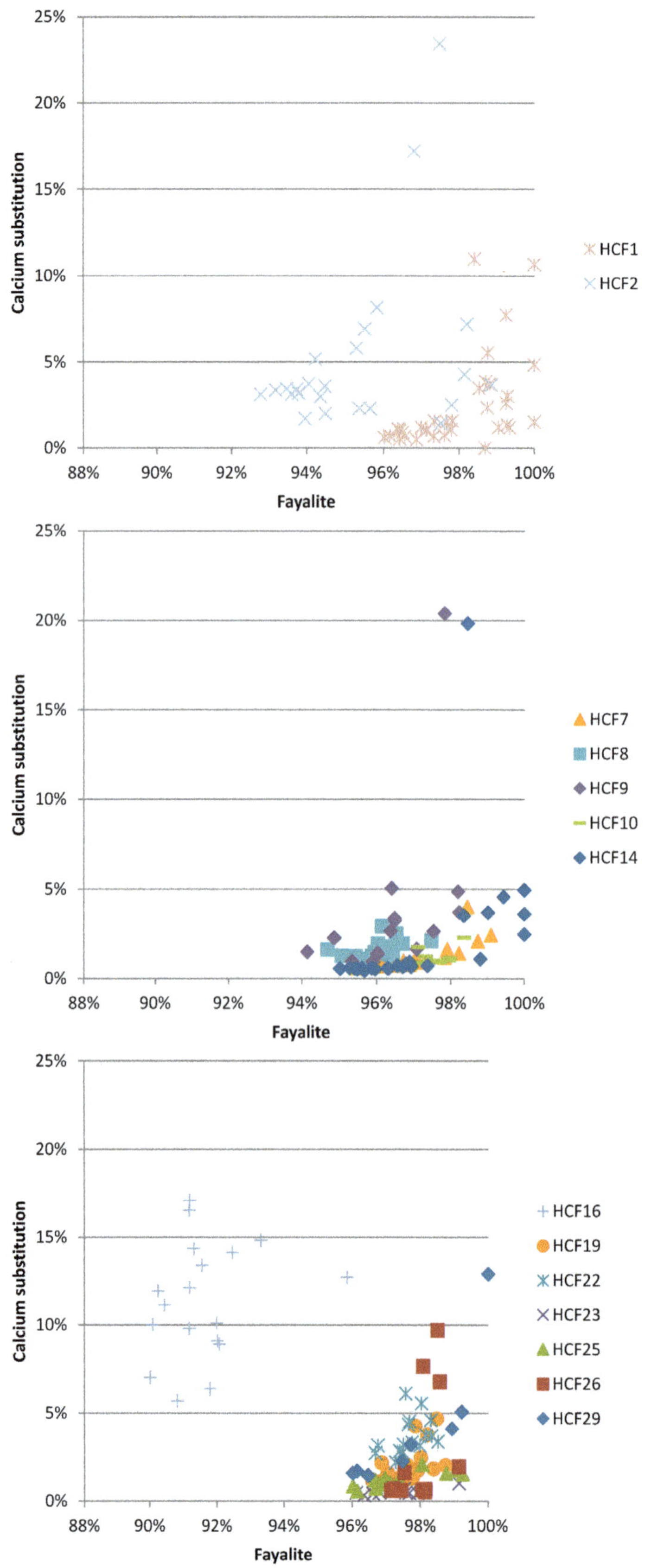

Figure 60. EDS microanalyses of olivines, showing % calcium substitution against the % fayalite (where the olivine is expressed on the forsterite-fayalite solid solution). Calcium is preferentially taken up late in the development of the olivine. The upper diagram demonstrates the high levels of calcium substitution in a large furnace bottom from context (757), the fill of furnace [756]. HCF1 was a sample of dense slag from close to the pit wall, HCF2 was a low density, charcoal-rich slag from the distal part of the block. The middle diagram shows analyses from other non-tapping materials, including FB slag (HCF7, 8) and basal flowed slags (HCF9, 10, 14). The lower diagram shows analyses from tapped slags, showing (with the exception of unusual sample HCF16 from furnace [792]) a much lower degree of variation than for the non-tapped slag samples.

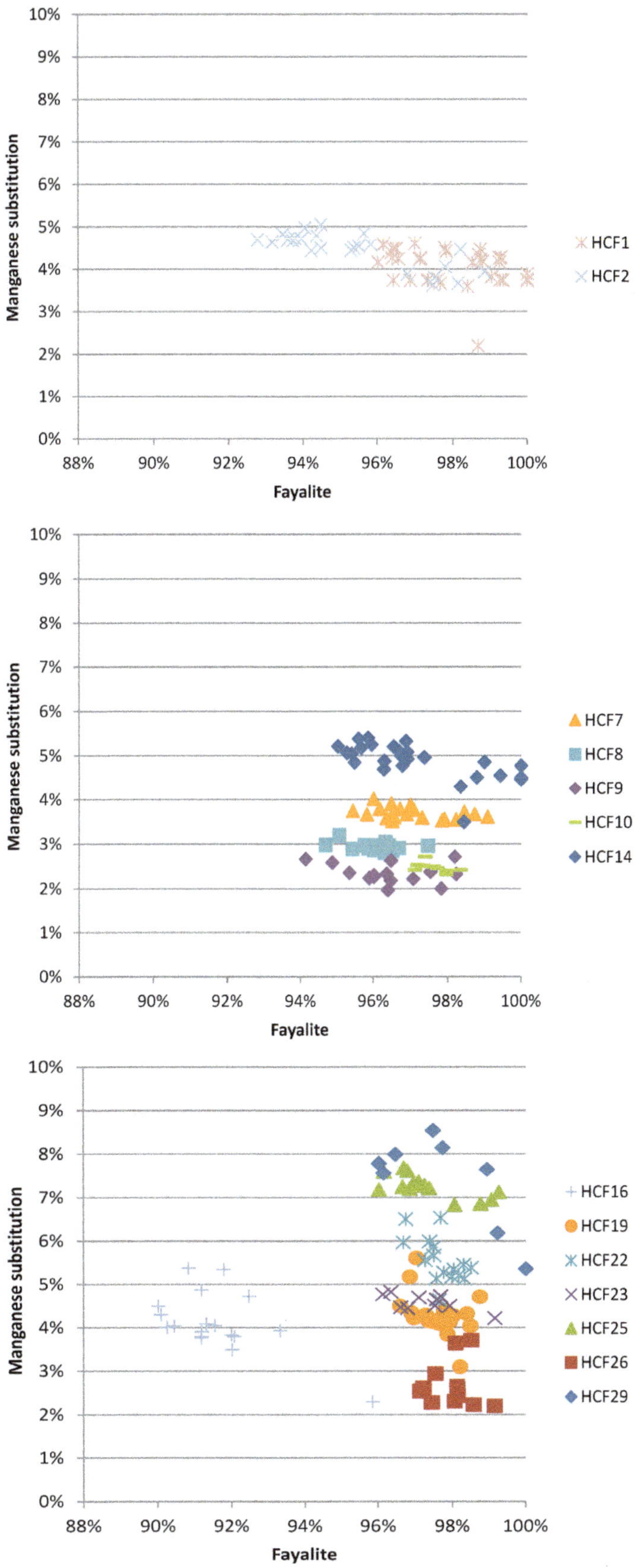

Figure 61. EDS microanalyses of olivines, showing % manganese substitution against the % fayalite (where the olivine is expressed on the forsterite-fayalite solid solution). Manganese uptake by the olivine declines slightly as it forms. The upper diagram demonstrates the continuity on manganese substitution in a large FB from context (757), the fill of furnace [756]. HCF1 was a sample of dense slag from close to the pit wall, HCF2 was a low density, charcoal-rich slag from the distal part of the block. The middle diagram shows analyses from other non-tapping materials, including FB slag (HCF7, 8) and basal flowed slags (HCF9, 10, 14). The lower diagram shows analyses from tapped slags, showing (with the exception of unusual sample HCF16 from furnace [792]) a much lower degree of variation in magnesium than for the non-tapped slag samples, but a greater variation in manganese.

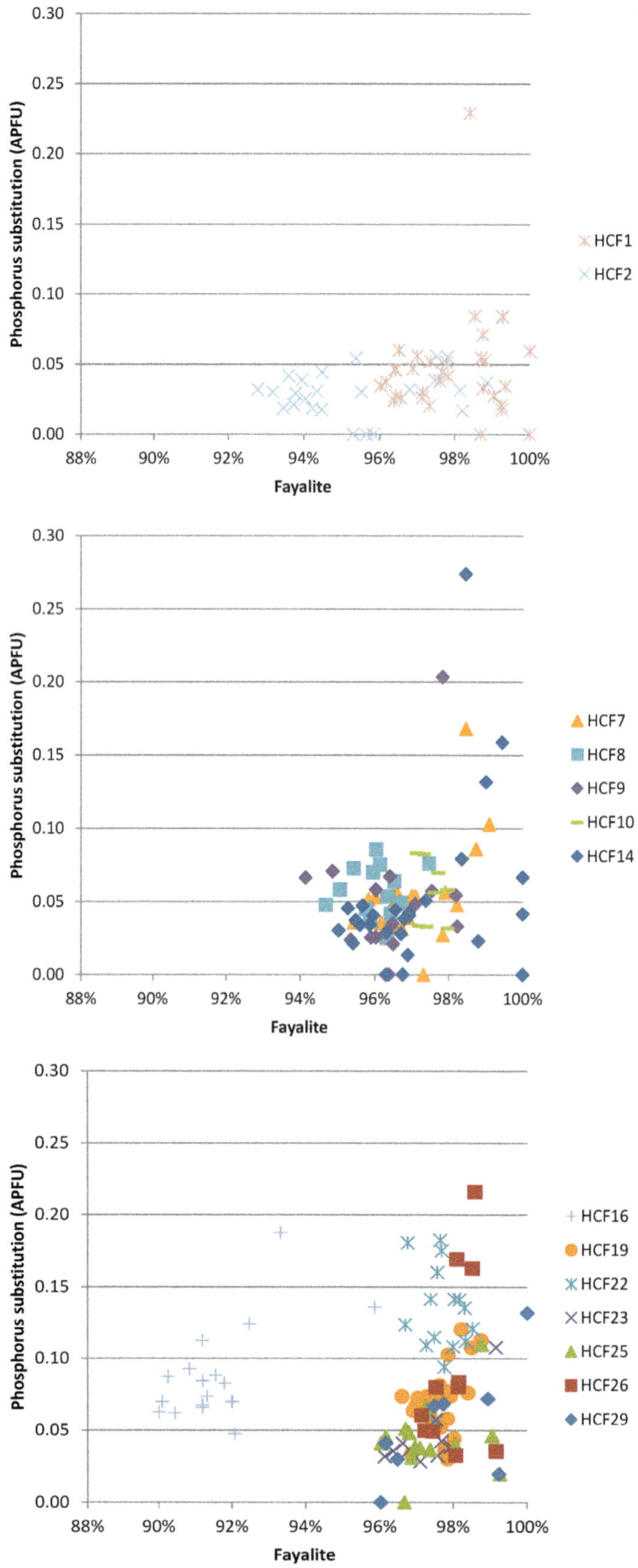

Figure 62. EDS microanalyses of olivines, showing phosphorus substitution (in atoms per formula unit) against the % fayalite (where the olivine is expressed on the forsterite-fayalite solid solution). Manganese uptake by the olivine declines slightly as it forms. The upper diagram demonstrates the continuity on phosphorus substitution in a large FB from context (757), the fill of furnace [756]. HCF1 was a sample of dense slag from close to the pit wall, HCF2 was a low density, charcoal-rich slag from the distal part of the block. The middle diagram shows analyses from other non-tapping materials, including FB slag (HCF7, 8) and basal flowed slags (HCF9, 10, 14). The lower diagram shows analyses from tapped slags.

634 g respectively. Only sample HCF14 was taken for examination on the SEM; this was from the upper-middle section of the puddle, well away from the pit wall.

Sample HCF14 (Figure 56a, d–f) shows a very coarse-grained microstructure. The primary wustite shows well-developed dendrites with domains in excess of 1 mm. In places, the wustite is overgrown by euhedral hercynite with grains commonly of 50 μm and locally of up to 200 μm. The subsequent olivine is large (individual elongate crystals are probably of several millimetres, but each crystal is broken down into block sub-units. The interstitial areas are commonly large and dominated by moss-like growths of leucite and leucite-wustite cotectic. In places the leucite contains parallel sheets of apatite. Olivine composition is typically variable between Fa96–98Fo4–2, with 1% calcium and 5% manganese substitution. The rims and overgrowths of late olivine show analyses suggesting up to 20% calcium substitution in small areas (though some olivine may contain apatite inclusions, see below). Phosphorus substitution varies from 0.01 to 0.08 APFU, but with some analyses of the late-stage interstitial olivine showing up to 0.13 APFU (although these high values may reflect fine-scale intermixing with apatite)

Details of Sampled Materials: Materials from Early Tapping Processes

HCF16 to HCF17 ((793)/[792])

The two samples were taken from 622 g and 794 g blocks of slag respectively. Only one of these two tapslag samples from furnace [792] was taken forward for SEM investigation (sample HCF16).

Sample HCF16 (Figure 58a, e) showed a series of slightly unusual quenched microstructures with a succession of flow lobes of differing composition. Area analyses show a range of iron content from 50 to 66% FeO – the broadest range of internal variation exhibited by any of the examined material and a relatively low iron content. The typical texture within the core of the lobes shows a primary delicate dendritic wustite (in some areas quite coarse wustite) followed by fine, elongate fayalitic olivine with a very fine crystalline interstitial groundmass. The flow lobe boundaries show thick upper oxide crusts 20–25 μm thick. The oxide ratios suggest the outer parts of the crust are rich in magnetite (and possibly even hematite), but that the lower, inner parts are richer in wustite. However, the crusts show altered relicts of inward growing spinel dendrites of typical angular outline. The dendrites probably have included components of both hercynite and magnetite. They are overgrown by an olivine with composition varying from Fa90Fo10 with 7% calcium and 4% manganese substitution and with phosphorus substitution of 0.06 APFU, to Fa93Fo7 with 15% calcium and 4% manganese substitution with phosphorus substitution of 0.19 APFU. The high levels in the analyses of both calcium and phosphorus might be associated with mixing with apatite and/or glass, but equally may genuinely reflect an unusual composition for this quenched material. Immediately below some of the boundaries a further unusual quench texture is exhibited by the olivine forming an overgrowth to the wustite with interstitial voids.

HCF18 to HCF20 ((772)/[771])

These samples include two samples of tapslag (samples HCF18 and HCF19) and one sample of lining (HCF20) from furnace [771]. HCF19 was taken from the tip of an *in situ* flow with a total weight of 5.7 kg. Of these samples, only HCF19 was examined with the SEM.

Sample HCF19 showed a flow lobed structure with lobes of relatively similar compositions and with a rather iron-rich composition. The primary wustite shows well developed dendrites with arrays of approximately 0.5 mm, followed by localised equant hercynite growing directly on the wustite and elongate fine olivine with lengths of 0.6 mm and possibly as much as 1 mm. The olivine varies only a little in composition from Fa97Fo3 with 1% calcium and 4% manganese substitution to Fa98 with 5% calcium substitution and 1% manganese substitution. Phosphorus substitution varies from 0.7 to 0.11 APFU, so the olivine is moderately phosphoran. The lobe boundaries are marked by incomplete oxide crusts formed largely of wustite with rounded cavities. The slag adjacent to the boundaries is commonly vesicular, and on one side of the boundary the wustite extends into the adjacent wustite dendrites. The interstitial areas are very small and are probably mainly crystalline and rich in leucite.

HCF21 to HCF22 ((759)/[758])

Samples HCF21 and HCF22 were from two separate pieces of tapped slag from furnace [758]. HCF22 was from a conventional tapslag flow, but HCF21 was from a well-developed ‘birdsfoot’ structure showing flow downwards from a single point into a hollow where the flows diverged. Of the two, only HCF22 was investigated on the SEM.

Sample HCF22 (Figure 58d) was iron-rich, resulting in high proportion of wustite in the slag. Discontinuities within the slag, marked by variations in the proportion and morphology of the wustite, probably marked transient flow boundaries. In areas where the wustite was most dense, the development of dendrites became masked by the overall blebby microstructure. The wustite blebs were locally overgrown by euhedral hercynite of up to approximately 30 μm. The wustite was followed by very delicate elongate olivine up to 200 μm in length. The olivine was of Fa97–98Fo3–2 with 2–6% calcium and 5–6% manganese substitution. Phosphorus substitution varied from 0.06 to 0.18 APFU, but with almost all measurements above 0.11 APFU. The olivine was amongst the more manganoan and certainly the most phosphoran of the analysed examples. One small area of the sample showed metallic iron between the wustite blebs. The outer margin of the flow lobe locally showed an unusual structure in which a variable oxide crust supported very fine inward-growing olivine dendrites with no surviving interstitial material.

HCF23 to HCF24 ((790)/[789])

These samples represent a tapslag (HCF23) and an ore fragment (HCF24) from the same context. Only the tapslag was investigated under the SEM.

Sample HCF23 (Figure 58b–c) was rather coarse-grained for a tapped slag. The primary phase was wustite in small, sparse but stout, dendrites. The wustite was spatially associated with large euhedral hercynite. These was followed by large olivine crystals (with elongate crystals well in excess of 1 mm in length and 100 μm in width, but divided into smaller blocky subunits. The olivine possessed a hercynite cotectic and the growth of the olivine often appears influenced by the form of the preceding wustite dendrites. The olivine compositional range was restricted, ranging from Fa96Fo4 with no calcium and 5% manganese substitution to Fa99Fo1 with 1% of calcium and 4–5% of manganese substitution. Phosphorus substitution was typically approximately 0.03 APFU, but locally reached 0.11 APFU. The interstitial areas commonly bore crystals of apatite overlying either the fayalite or hercynite and were largely filled with a leucite-wustite cotectic.

Details of Sampled Materials: Materials from Late Tapping Processes

HCF25 ((676)/[675])

Sample HCF25 (Figure 59c–d) was the single sampled tapslag specimen from pit [675]. The sample was taken from a 252 g fragment of pale grey slag with slight reddening of the surface. The typical slag texture has primary wustite in well-developed dendrites which appear to have an elongate form with slightly stubby, rounded lateral branches, with overall arrays of up to 0.5 mm. In some areas (most noticeably at the bases of flow lobes) the wustite is followed by euhedral hercynite, but mostly the hercynite occurs as an irregularly shaped cotectic within the olivine. The olivine is elongate and large, with crystal lengths of up to 1.5 mm. The olivine shows compositions of Fa96Fo4 with 1% of calcium and 7% of manganese substitution to Fa98Fo2 with 2% of calcium and 8% of manganese substitution. This is some of the most manganoan fayalite recorded in the project. The highly manganoan composition may be the cause of the very pale grey bulk appearance. Levels of phosphorus substitution are typical around 0.04 to 0.05 APFU, making the olivine mildly phosphoran.

The sequence of textures across the lobe boundaries appears consistent. The boundaries themselves are of wustite, which becomes cavernous into the underlying lobe. The wustite in these inner protrusions may carry small inclusions, possibly of magnetite. The crust may be laminated parallel to its surface, and bears a striking resemblance to hammerscale. The outer surface of the crust is smooth, with dense wustite. The overlying lobe may show fine scale wustite nucleating on the underlying crust, but often the base of a lobe has vesicles, often shows large areas of fayalite relatively free of wustite and may show large interstitial areas rich in leucite.

HCF26 to HCF28 ((557))

Samples HCF26 to HCF28 were samples of large tapslag blocks recovered from mixed dump deposit (557) within pit [556]. Of these, only HCF26 was investigated under the SEM.

Sample HCF26 (Figure 59e–f) showed an unusual microstructure for a tapslag, with evidence for an abnormally high degree of superficial oxidation. The typical internal texture of the lobes was of very finely dendritic wustite followed by local euhedral hercynite and then by finely dendritic or elongate olivine. The olivine mostly shows restricted range of composition of Fa96–98Fo4–2 with 1% calcium and 3% manganese substitution. Phosphorus substitution was measured as 0.08 APFU. Occasionally higher calcium and phosphorus substitutions were recorded (up to 10% calcium substitution and 0.17 APFU phosphorus), but it is unclear if these are genuinely substitutions into fayalite or inclusions of apatite.

Internal flow lobe crusts show dense crusts (in which the oxide ratio suggests a high proportion of magnetite) that pass inwards into a zone of euhedral spinels (mainly of hercynite cored on small magnetite grains). The spinels are followed by very fine olivine. In some olivine (the earliest phase?) the olivine appears to coat the iron oxide dendrites (similar structures were seen in sample HCF16).

External lobe crusts show the development of a substantial external zone for which the oxide ratio suggests that hematite is the dominant phase. The core of the crust is probably of magnetite and this passes internally into a zone dominated by euhedral (albeit sometimes skeletal) spinels, with both magnetite and hercynite present. The euhedral spinels contain small inclusions of uncertain origin, with similar inclusion present in the cores of iron oxide (probably mainly wustite) dendrites growing into the interior of the lobe. These dendrites are overlain and encased by iscorite within a zone up to 300 μm thick below the surface.

This texture is unusual in tapslags, but closely resembles those seen in spheroidal hammerscale (Young 2012) where the influence of a strongly oxidising environment during cooling allows a progression from wustite to more oxidised phases, particularly iscorite as cooling progresses (but within a very short timescale during quenching).

HCF29 to HCF30 ((557))

The two samples HCF29 and HCF30 were each taken from large blocks of dense slag, weighing 2.3 kg and 1.7

kg respectively. Sample HCF29 showed ceramic adhering to the upper surface, suggesting it may have accumulated beneath the tapping arch of a furnace. Sample HCF30 was tentatively interpreted as a dense slag formed internally to the furnace on the basis of its morphology.

Sample HCF29 (Figure 59a, b) showed a typical microstructure of very delicate wustite dendrites (with arrays of up to 700 µm) followed by delicate elongate fayalite of at least 1 mm length. The olivine showed compositions of Fa96–100Fo4–0 with rather variable levels of calcium substitution of 1% to 5% and typically with 8% manganese substitution. Phosphorus substitution varied from 0 up to 0.07 APFU. This composition is similar to that of the olivine in sample HCF25. The internal lobe boundaries with the sample showed asymmetric oxide crusts, with one sharp edge (external) and one with a more gradational edge (internal). The gradational side faced a fine texture with elongate olivine separated by leucite-rich interstitial areas. The sharp external face was overlain by a coarser texture of primary sparse wustite dendrites overlain by large olivine with lengths of more than 0.5 mm and widths of 50 µm. The olivine bears large cotectic areas of hercynite. The interstitial areas are large dominated by leucite-wustite cotectic, but also characterised by increased size of the primary wustite. To some extent a similar odd patchy texture can be observed in the finer-grained material below the lobe contact too.

Sample HCF30 showed a heterogeneous texture with primary wustite that was generally abundant, typically in stout dendrites, but occasionally in more granular textures. The subsequent olivine carried hercynite cotectic and was in large elongate crystals. The interstitial areas showed complex mixtures of leucite-wustite cotectic, with late-stage fayalite and plates of apatite. In one area there was a detached fragment of oxide lobe crust, that showed typical cavernous oxides, but which appeared to have undergone some degree of reaction with the encasing slag, possibly including some resorption.

Chemical Composition of Sampled Materials

Bulk Composition

The elemental compositions of the residues are provided in Tables 11–12. The major element composition of the residues may conveniently be considered within the system SiO_2-Al_2O_3-FeO (see Figures 53a and 53b for non-tapping and tapping furnaces respectively; after Schairer and Yagi 1952, fig 6). The fields of both bulk analyses and areal micro-analyses (see below) lie close to the divide between hercynite and wustite/fayalite. The diagrams suggest that the samples will all have evolved close to the fayalite-wustite-hercynite common point – a feature borne-out by the complex relationships between these three mineral phases in the microstructures.

The ternary diagram can be used to model system development during smelting. As a first approximation (Thomas and Young 1999a; 1999b) the ore supplied to the furnace reacts with the hearth lining to produce a 'smelting mixture' (which will therefore lie on a line between the lining composition (orange dots) and the composition of the ore (black dot is ore from this project; red dots are analyses of similar ore from Dunkeswell (Young 2015a)). Production of the bloom involves removal of iron from this mixture, driving the slag composition in a direction directly away from the FeO pole, producing the characteristic linear array of observed compositions. In practice, the system is not at equilibrium, so different 'smelting mixtures' and different degrees of iron extraction may exist in different parts of the furnace and at different times during a smelt. It should also be remembered that the analyses represent multiple smelts, undertaken under differing conditions with different batches of raw material.

The ternary diagrams show the rather limited range of iron contents present in the slags, and that the residues from the two processes show broadly the same range. In both cases the most iron-rich residues lie very close to the composition of the potential smelting mixture and reflect compositions from which relatively little iron has been extracted. The aluminous composition of most of the residues restricts the ability of the system to extract a very high proportion of iron, because the resultant slags would be driven well into the hercynite field on the ternary, within which the liquidus temperature and slag viscosity rise markedly. Of the other major elements, most are present in variable, but typically low concentrations, except for manganese and phosphorus, present as key components of the iron ore. The behaviour of these two elements is discussed in detail below.

The trace elements are generally present in low concentrations, reflecting their low abundance in the high-grade ore. The ICP-MS analyses show elevated levels of copper, and to a lesser extent of zinc. The levels of copper were not borne-out by the XRF analyses and it is believed there was some minor contamination of the ICP-MS samples, probably by a copper alloy (potentially during sample preparation from a damaged saw blade or similar). The trace elements are otherwise fairly unremarkable. The concentrations of uranium are moderately elevated in some of the residues, commensurate with levels in the ore.

The rare earth elements (REE) show upper crust-normalised profiles (Figure 63) in which those of the residues are approximately parallel to that of the ore sample. The profiles show slight relative depletion of many of the light REE, with a marked negative cerium anomaly. The middle REE are only very gently humped and there is slight relative enrichment of the heavy REE (probably particularly influenced by the contribution from the furnace lining which shows this feature).

The profiles of the tapped slags are much more tightly bunched than those of the non-tapped slags, which include examples that are both more enriched and more depleted

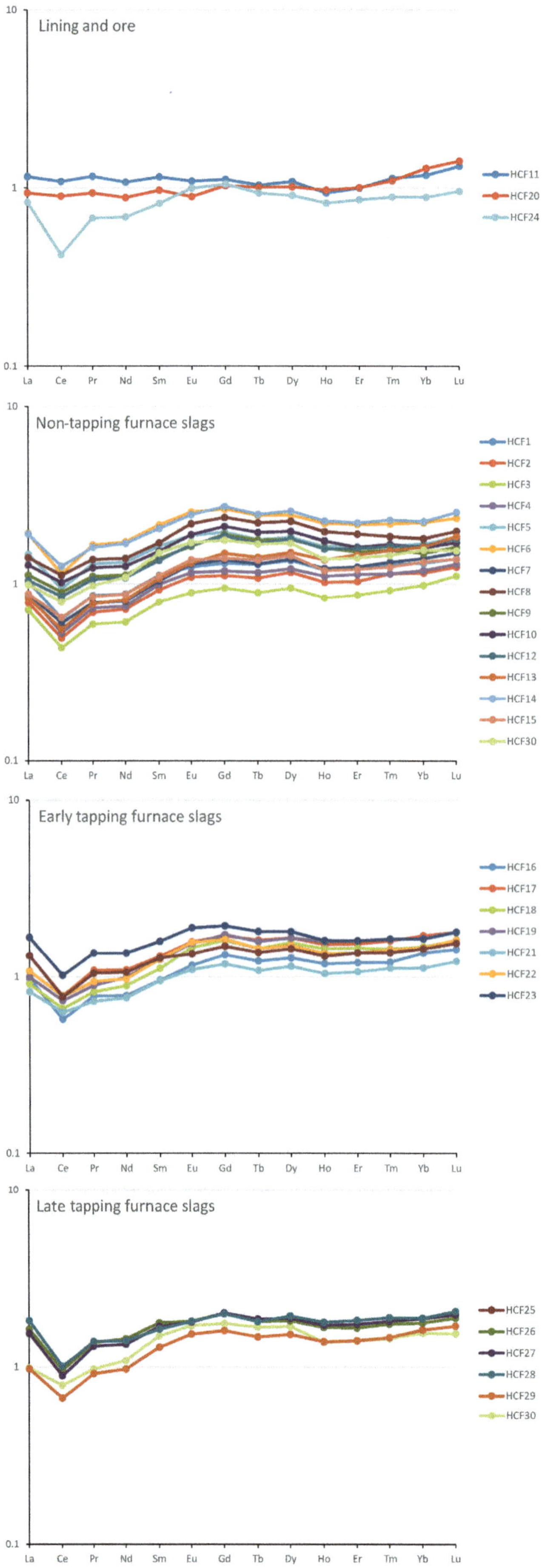

Figure 63. (REE) upper crust-normalised rare earth element profiles (normalisation after Taylor and McLennan 1981.) for analyses of residue samples from Churchills Farm, Hemyock.

than the tapped slags. This feature is even more prominent if the compositions are recalculated on an iron-free basis (Figure 64). In this model the tapped slags are extremely tightly clustered (except for HCF16), which is both lower and flatter. One interesting feature of these diagrams is that they illustrate that the REE content of the non-tapped slags is commonly higher than for the tapped slags. The elevation of the profiles on an iron free basis shows that they are not being concentrated by higher degree of iron extraction, but they must reflect either a higher REE content of the ore, a higher REE content of the lining, or a 'smelting mixture' with a higher contribution from the ceramic compared with the tapped slags.

Micro-variation in Composition

Measurement of small areas of the samples by EDS provides an estimate of the bulk composition of small volumes of the samples – much smaller than for the bulk analysis by ICP-MS/XRF that is intended to provide an overall elemental composition for a sample. The variation on a small scale is illustrated by the binary plots of Figure 65. These mostly use compositions normalised against silica to reduce the influence of the variable iron content of the samples. The data are also presented on the SiO_2-Al_2O_3-FeO ternary (Figure 66). In general the measurements are slightly more aluminous than bulk estimates – possibly due, in part at least, to an avoidance of analysing 'rusty' areas.

The ternary diagrams emphasise the iron-rich nature of the samples, although they also demonstrate that some small areas show fractionation to significantly lower iron contents than the average for the sample. Nonetheless, the analyses are limited in their extent into iron-poor compositions. The diagrams presented in Figure 65 demonstrate the greater degree of internal variability within the materials from the non-slag tapping furnaces (left hand column of figures) than the slag tapping furnaces (right hand column of figures). The Al_2O_3/SiO_2 ratio reflects variation in the 'smelting mixture', as well as some fractionation process occurring inside the furnace (by free-flowing Si-rich slag flowing away from initial Fe-Al rich precipitates). The MnO/SiO_2 ratio may reflect the original Mn content of the ore, but will also be increased by increased iron extraction into the bloom. The P_2O_5/SiO_2 will have similar controls, with the added complication that a variable amount of the phosphorus may be absorbed by the metallic iron in the bloom. The K_2O/SiO_2 ratio will be influenced both by the addition of potassium from clay minerals (in the furnace lining and ore), but also largely by the potassium present in the fuel ash. Potassium capture from the ash may be largely through the vapour phase, and is hence both very variable and very local in its concentration. The CaO/SiO_2 will also be largely influenced by the fuel ash. It is possible that those samples with rather extreme calcium concentrations may have (accidentally) been fed with a more lime-rich ore, or smelted in a lime-rich clay furnace, rather than having unexpectedly high uptakes from the ash.

Variation in Olivine Composition

The olivine chemistry could to large degree be predicted from the bulk chemistry of the samples, but nonetheless the variations do provide an insight into the nature of the samples, their inhomogeneity, and their evolution during cooling and their ability to fix phosphorus. The variations are presented in Figures 60–62.

Calcium (Figure 65) is largely concentrated in late-stage olivine (i.e. olivine which will have a higher proportion of fayalite compared to forsterite – and so plot towards the right of the diagrams). Most of the flowed slags show rather restricted ranges of composition, but the furnace bottom samples (HCF1 and HCF2) show a much wider range, illustrating the inhomogeneity of the furnace bottom slag. Sample HCF16 is at variance with other tapped slags (as it was in some of the plots on Figure 65). The magnesium- and calcium- rich nature of this sample suggests it was derived from the use of an unusual charge in the furnace (perhaps containing some dolomite or an ankeritic iron ore?). Occasional analyses of late-stage olivine show very high calcium contents and also of phosphorus. Rather than being particularly phosphoran and calcian olivine, it is possible these olivines contained inclusions of apatite that fell within the analysed volume.

The variation on the manganese content of the olivine (Figure 61) is much more regular. Although there is a slight decline in manganese content as the olivine becomes less forsteritic, that decline is moderate. The variation in HCF1 and HCF2 is much more regular than for calcium. The more magnesian composition of the olivine in HCF1 than in HCF2 would be compatible with HCF1 having formed at a higher temperature and/or earlier than HCF2 – a possibility itself compatible with the origin of HCF1 in the dense slag nearer to the pit wall, where early and hot slag was likely to have flowed, rather than HCF2 which was in the possibly later and more progressively-generated core of the charcoal-rich slag mass.

The variation in phosphorus is less tightly clustered than for calcium or manganese, probably reflecting the low concentrations (so greater potential analytical error) and the possibility of interference from inclusions of apatite or phosphorus rich glass, as well as true variation in the degree to which the olivines are phosphoran.

The diagrams do suggest, however, that the olivine is almost entirely phosphoran and that large amounts of phosphorus have been fixed in the olivine. In general, the phosphorus capture by the olivine in the flowed slags (whether tapped or not) appears higher than that of the furnace bottom, possibly because of their more rapid cooling. Further consideration of the behaviour of phosphorus in terms of the bulk composition if the slags is given below.

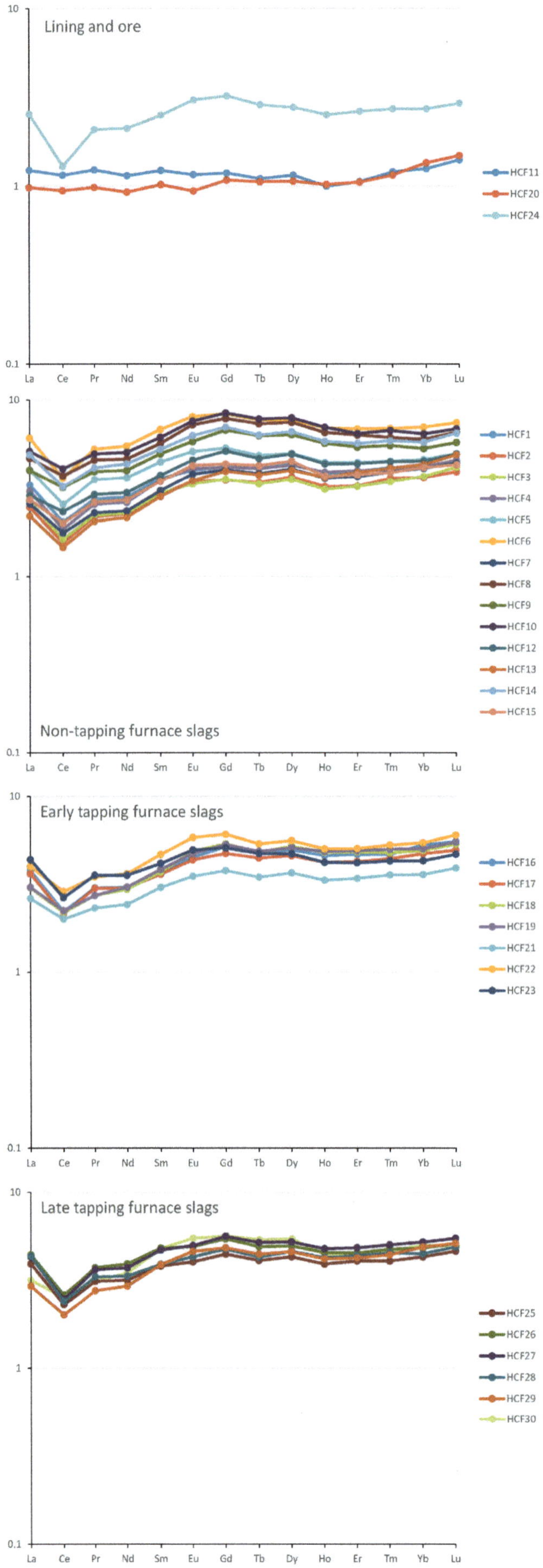

Figure 64. (REE) upper crust-normalised rare earth element profiles (normalisation after Taylor and McLennan 1981.) for analyses of residue samples from Churchills Farm, Hemyock, recast on an iron-free basis.

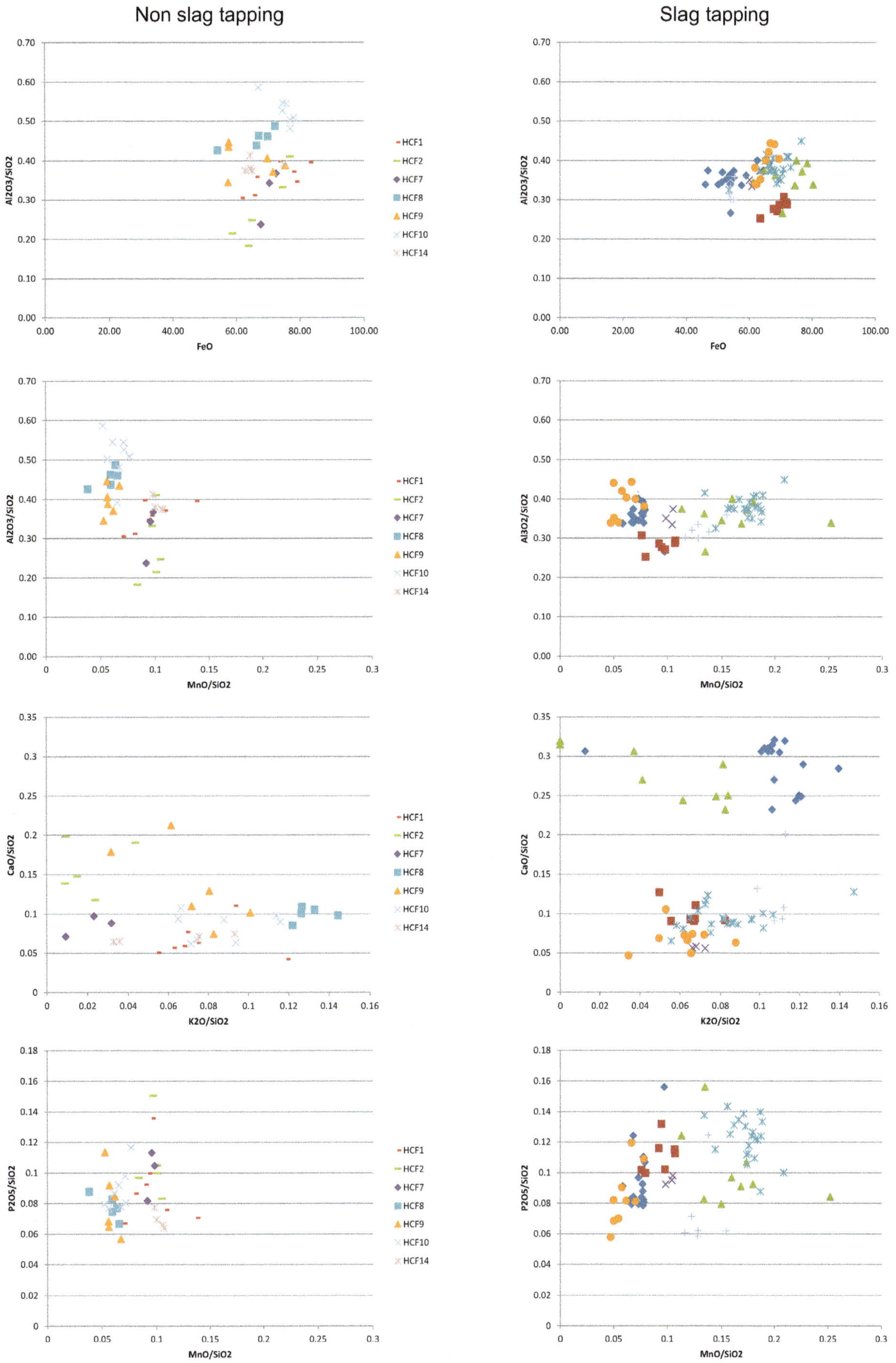

Figure 65. Binary plots of elemental ratios and elemental concentrations (in wt%) for EDS area analyses of samples from Churchills Farm, Hemyock.

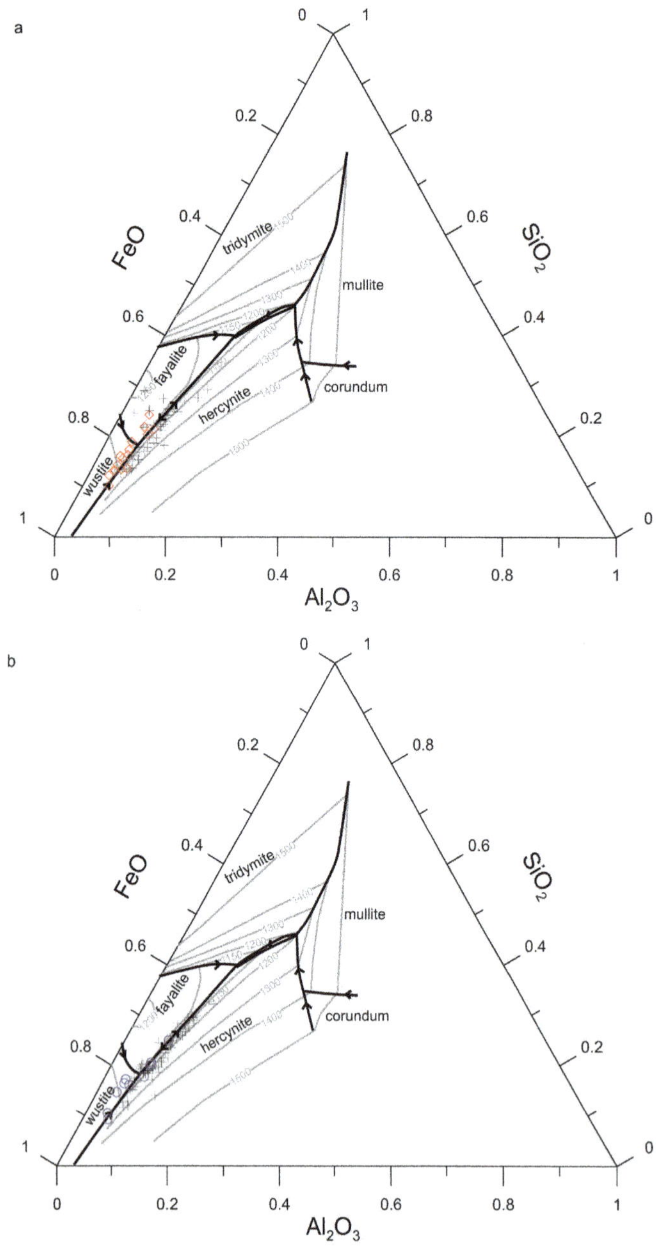

Figure 66. Major element composition of micro-area analyses by EDS of residues plotted within the ternary system SiO_2-Al_2O_3-FeO (fields after Schairer and Yagi 1952, fig 6). (a): analyses of residues from non-tapping furnaces showing analyse of basal flowed slag as red diamonds and of furnace bottoms as crosses, and (b): analyses of residues from tapping furnaces showing tapped slags of early medieval age as crosses and those probably of later medieval age as blue circles.

Interpretation of the Residues

Furnace Mass Balance and Yield

It is very difficult to model a robust mass balance for the smelting reaction, because small variations in the composition of high-grade ores make large differences in the calculation. The following discussion is only able to give an approximation to likely values.

The most likely ore composition is close to that of the analysed ores from Dunkeswell (Young 2015a), but these show significant inter-sample variability (Figures 67 and 68). A substantial degree of variability in the analysed residues probably reflects this ore heterogeneity. A further problem is that mass balance calculations would be affected strongly by the degree of matrix attached to the goethite concretions and the precise physical state of the ore feed to furnaces is unknown. Nonetheless, when the residue analyses are presented on an iron free basis (Figure 67), they show a reasonable fit to the tie-line between the Dunkeswell ores and the observed furnace lining from Churchills Farm. Some elements are particularly variable in the ore, with uranium being markedly so (the recast analyses vary from 41 to 54ppm, with the analysed ore fragment from Churchills Farm (HCF24) having only 11ppm). However, it is remarkable that the analysed tapslag fragment (HCF23) from the same furnace (furnace [789]) as the ore fragment shows a similarly low uranium content (Figure 67), suggesting that the slag was indeed derived from the smelting of a low-uranium ore.

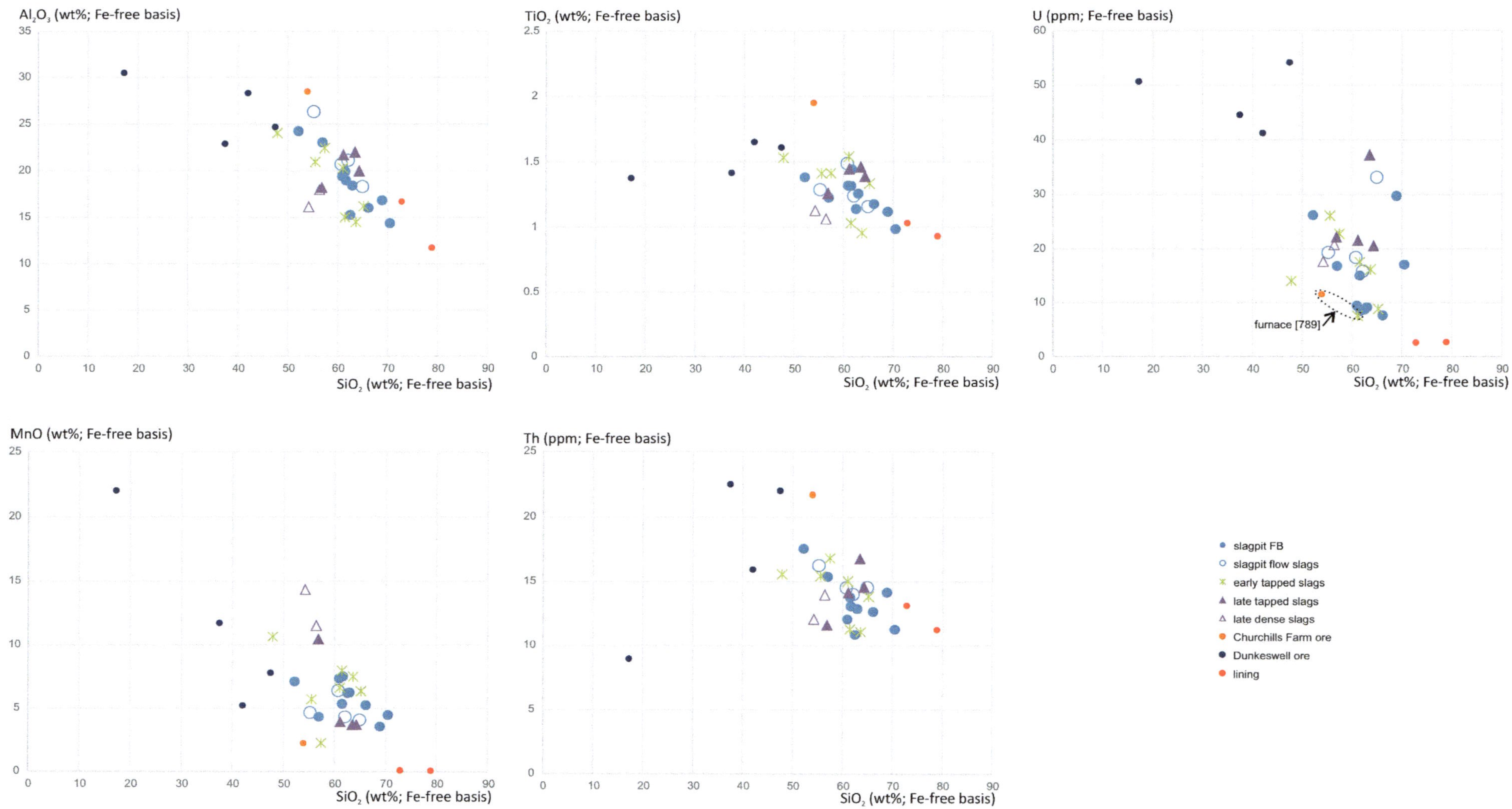

Figure 67. Bivariate plots of data from bulk chemical analyses, recast on an iron-free basis, plotted against silica (also recast on an iron-free basis). For many components (Al_2O_3, MnO, TiO_2, Th) the data plot close to the join between the average composition of furnace lining and the average composition of ore from Dunkeswell (Young 2015a). This shows the various blends of lining and ore involved in the smelting reaction.

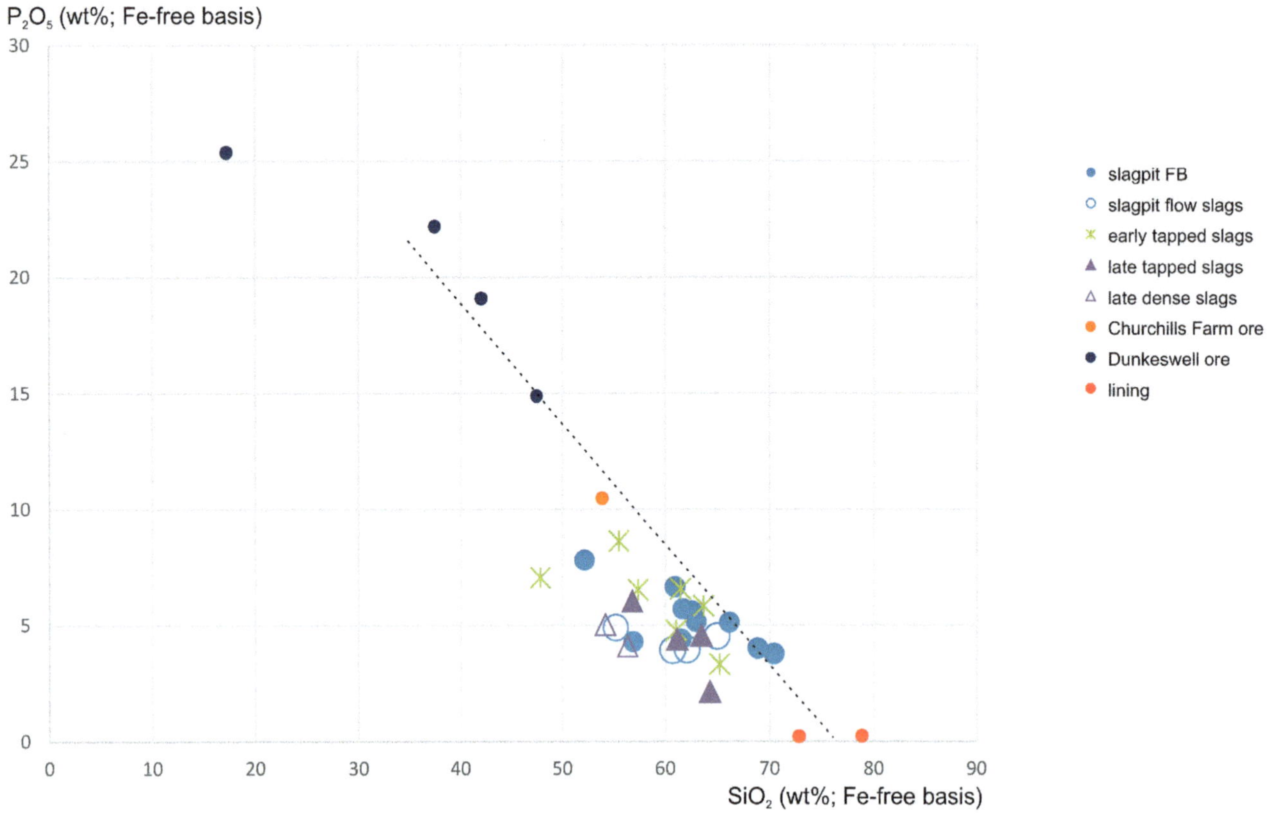

Figure 68. Binary plot of P_2O_5 (wt%) against SiO_2 (wt%) for residues from Churchills Farm and for iron ore samples from Dunkeswell Airfield (after Young 2015a), with the analyses recalculated on an iron-free basis. The data for phosphorus show that the residues contain less phosphorus they would be expected to have for simple mixing with conservation of this element (represented by the dashed tie line between average Dunkeswell ore and average lining). Up to half of the available phosphorus has been lost from the system – much of this may be to the metal.

Phosphorus (Figure 68) shows a systematic deviation from the tie-line when plotted in the same way. The residues show a strong tendency to be depleted in phosphorus with respect to the tie-line. This indicates either that the ore analyses were unrepresentative of the smelting feedstock in containing more phosphorus, or, far more likely, that the system was not closed with respect to phosphorus, which was lost either to the vapour or to the metal. This is discussed further below.

The graphical method outlined below (and in Figure 69) for establishing the mass balance parameters employs means of the various groups of residues. Since the numbers of analyses in each group are restricted then there will have been considerable potential error on the mean. Since the discussion above has established that, for most elements, a tie-line between the lining and Dunkeswell ore provides a good approximation to the smelting mixture, a graphical approach to modelling the mass balance is adopted here (Figure 69). This approximation to the mass balance employs a two-stage approach:

1. the 'smelting mixture' must lie on the tie-line between the ore and lining compositions (excluding the input of the fuel ash, the major elemental components of which would be CaO and K_2O).
2. the bulk slag composition of the system will evolve from this mixture on a trajectory directly away from the FeO pole on the FeO-SiO_2-Al_2O_3 system (Figure 53) or from the origin on Figure 69, as iron is extracted from the 'smelting mixture' as metal.

For the model, the ore composition is taken as the mean of a group of ores from Dunkeswell Airfield analysed previously (DUNK1-3; Young 2015a). The lining composition is taken as the mean of analyses HCF11 and HCF20.

When the values for the mean compositions of the three groups of residues are plotted, it can be seen (Figure 69, right column) that the two early technologies have values that plot very close to together. The following discussion treats the early technologies as a single process, and uses a composition midway between the two means. The values derived from the graphs of Figure 69 are presented in Table 13. The means of the solutions for the two periods of ironmaking have been employed to derive output and extractive efficiency figures as below.

For the late slag tapping technology, the 'smelting mixture' lies on the ore-lining tie-line at approximately 93% ore. The trajectory away from the origin demonstrates average enrichment of approximately 234%. When this solution is modelled numerically, with the addition of 0.6% of fuel ash to provide sufficient calcium for the observed residue composition, then the following approximate figures may be derived:

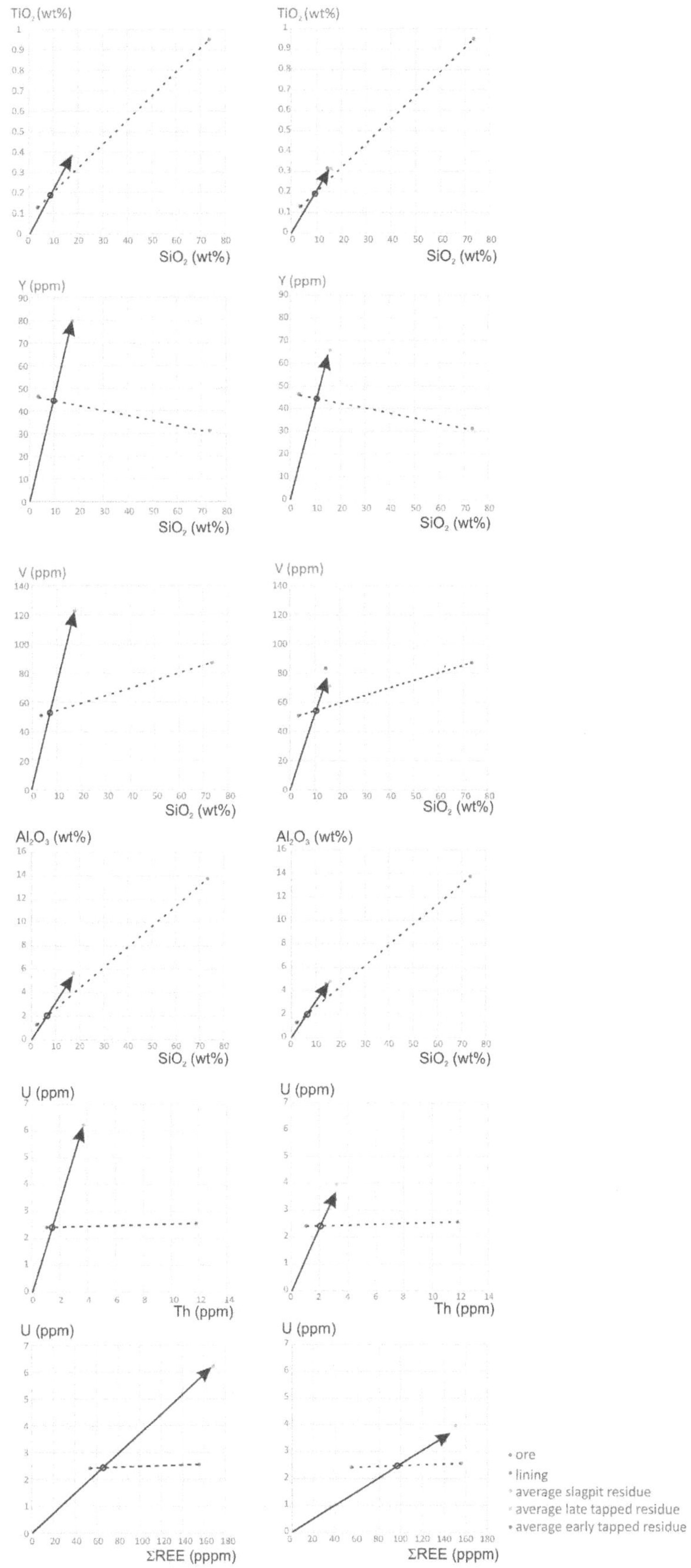

Figure 69. Graphical estimates for mass smelting mass balance. For each diagram the dashed line connects the ore and lining compositions. If the contribution of the fuel ash is excluded, these lines define the possible 'smelting mixtures' (for the elements employed in these plots, their content in the fuel ash is very low). The elements will then be concentrated from the 'smelting mixture', as a first approximation, by the removal of iron from the mixture as metal. The course of the concentration is marked by the arrow, which connects the initial smelting mixture composition and that of the smelting residues. The left hand column of figures illustrates the later (eleventh/twelfth-century) smelting slags from the slag-tapping furnaces, the right column show the same plots for the ninth/tenth-century smelting.

Table 13. Mass balance parameters derived from the plots in Figure 70. Values in parentheses excluded from average calculation

System	Early medieval		Medieval	
	% ore	Concentration (%)	% ore	Concentration (%)
TiO_2 v SiO_2	92	161	92	200
Y v SiO_2	90	143	91	178
V v SiO_2	90	143	95	234
Al_2O_3 v SiO_2	94	230	95	279
U v Th	91	154	96	259
U v REE	*(58)*	*(149)*	90	256
Average	**91**	**166**	**93**	**234**

1. 924 g of reduced anhydrous ore, plus 70 g of lining and 6 g of fuel ash produce 445 g of iron and 427 g of slag.
2. This corresponds to an extractive efficiency of 65% (the proportion of iron in the ore extracted as metal). This is a very high figure, with typical bloomery extractive efficiencies in the 45-65% range, with only one site considered by Thomas (2000) producing a higher figure (medieval bloomery slags from Mwyndy, S Wales).
3. The modelled slag would contain 0.76% additional P_2O_5 compared with the observed average slag composition.

For the early phase of ironmaking, the graphical solution suggests a 'smelting mixture' on the ore-lining tie-line at approximately 91% ore. In this case, however, the average enrichment was only 166%. The model is not a good fit for the REE data, so the ore must be only imperfectly modelled. When this solution is modelled (similarly with the addition of 0.6% of fuel ash), then the following figures may be derived:

1. 906 g of reduced anhydrous ore, plus 90 g of lining and 6 g of fuel ash produce 309 g of iron and 602 g of slag.
2. This corresponds to an extractive efficiency of 46%, a value at the lower end of the range for early bloomeries.
3. The modelled slag would contain 0.10% additional P_2O_5 compared with the observed average slag composition.

The raw ore contains on average 20.9% by weight of oxygen and water that would be lost to create the theoretical anhydrous reduced ore. So, normalising to 1 kg of raw ore gives the following approximate values:

1. the early medieval processes yielded 270 g of iron and 530 g of slag
2. the post-Conquest slag tapping process yielded 380 g of iron and 370 g of slag.

Although there is no direct evidence for the phosphorus content of the iron produced, the mass balance models show an excess of phosphorus in the residues, which must either have entered the iron or been lost from the system. The precise values for phosphorus indicated are probably of little significance given the approximate nature of the model.

These calculations are extremely tentative and the observed mismatch, for instance in the predicted and actual content of the REE in the slag, shows that the modelling is poor for some elements. Nonetheless, the illustrations in Figure 69 show that enrichment (and therefore yield) was certainly significantly less for the early processes compared with the later one, and that (as the line of concentration during iron removal for the early processes always lies to the right of that for the later process) the early processes had a smelting mixture involving a slightly higher proportion of melted furnace lining (assuming the ore and lining were actually the same in both cases).

Ore Source

The Churchills Farm excavation produced direct ore-provenancing evidence in the form of both analyses of the slags and of a single ore fragment. Other recent investigations of early medieval metalworking in the Blackdown Hills area at Culmstock Road, Hemyock (Young 2014a; Rainbird and Young 2015) and of iron ores at Dunkeswell (Young 2015a) have provided opportunities for additional lines of evidence. Unfortunately, there were no analytical data for the Burlescombe site (Reed *et al.* 2006), which also lies in close proximity.

Analysis of ores and slags from all three sites has shown many similarities between them, but has also produced evidence for the differences. These Blackdown Hills sites were not quite as homogeneous as might have initially been expected. Although various lines of evidence exist, the genetic relationships are particularly well demonstrated by the patterns of distribution of the rare earth elements (REE), summarised by Figure 70.

The composition of the ore exploited at Churchills Farm has been discussed in the previous section. A reasonable quality of mass balance solution has been achieved by utilising a composition for ore corresponding to the mean of the three analyses DUNK1–3, the three analyses of laminated goethitic boxstone from Dunkeswell (Young 2015a). For the earlier phase the fit is slightly less good, but is similar.

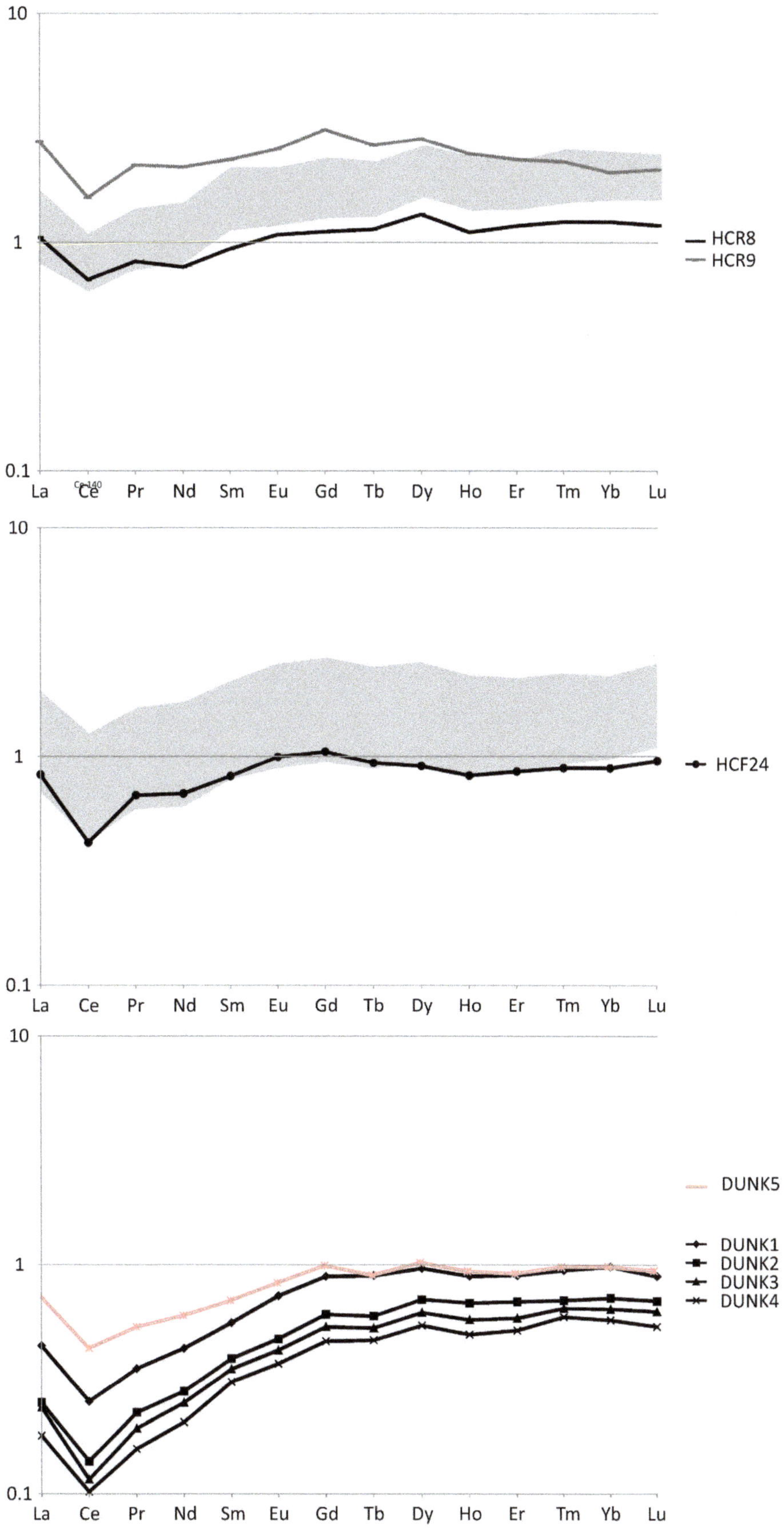

Figure 70. (REE) upper crust-normalised rare earth element profiles (normalisation after Taylor and McLennan 1981.) for analyses of residue samples from Churchills Farm, Hemyock and comparative sites. Upper figure: analyses of samples from the early medieval iron smelting site at Culmstock Road, Hemyock (data from Young 2014a). Shaded area shows field occupied by profiles of slag samples; lines indicate the profiles of ore samples. Middle figure: analyses of samples from Churchills Farm, Hemyock. Shaded area shows field occupied by profiles of slag samples; line indicates the profile of the ore sample. Lower figure: analyses of samples from Dunkeswell (data from Young 2015a). Red line shows the profile of the slag sample; black lines indicates the profiles of the ore samples.

The analyses of residues from the smelting site in Culmstock Road showed a more inclined upper crust-normalised REE profile for elements heavier than cerium than do the analyses of residues from Churchills Farm. This more inclined profile was also demonstrated by one of the two ores sampled from the Culmstock Road site (sample HCR8). This sample was a fresh 166 g block of a low-density yellow/brown goethitic or limonitic pelletal iron ore. It has voids coated in a yellow hydrated iron oxide (Young 2014, 4). This was representative of a number of fragments of ore from the site, all compatible with an origin with the Upper Greensand. The analysed samples (HCR8 and HCR9) are, however, problematic in being too impure (having too high silica and alumina contents) to have generated the observed slags. This may be an illustration of the common issue in which ore from smelting sites may not necessarily be from casual loss, but from positive discard of reject material.

The ore used at Culmstock Road may also be modelled by using the reverse process to the calculation of yield. The same 'smelting mixture' (94% ore) and a similar extractive efficiency (60%) have been applied to the Culmstock Road data, to produce model ore compositions (Figure 71). These model data suggest that the ore smelted at Culmstock Road was more similar to the Dunkeswell material than had been previously appreciated (*contra* Rainbird and Young 2015). The model ore shows a composition (Figure 71) that is similar in most respects to those of the Dunkeswell ores. It differs in having a much higher manganese content, estimated as equivalent to 1.5 to 1.6wt% MnO. The manganese content is similar, however, to the ore fragment HCR8 from Culmstock Road (although the model ore differs from HCR8 in many other parameters).

Archaeological excavation of undated ore pits at Dunkeswell (Cotswold Archaeology 2015; Young 2015a) produced rather similar field evidence to that previously obtained at Broadhembury (Reed 1997) – with large goethite boxstone concretions present within the Clay with Flints (Gallois 2004, 2009; Isaac 1981). The REE profiles of samples (DUNK1-4) of these ores were more markedly depleted in many of the light REE and had a more prominent negative cerium anomaly than seen in the analyses form Churchills Farm, but are otherwise very similar. The Dunkeswell ores showed phosphorus contents equivalent to 0.6 to 1.1wt% P_2O_5 and manganese contents of 0.2 to 1.0wt% MnO. These values are compatible with the ore composition required to produce the Churchills Farm residues and their variability might explain the range of compositions seen in the Churchills Farm residues, particularly of manganese.

Thus, it appears that although iron oxide ores found as nodules in the Clay with Flints may have been the ore source for the smelting both at Culmstock Road and Churchills Farm, the two sites employed slightly different ore sources. Churchills Farm employed ores of essentially similar type to those from Dunkeswell. The earlier Culmstock Road site utilised ores that were more intimately associated with weathered greensand lithologies (although the presence of those materials on site may have been due to discard of the lowest grade ores) and that had a slightly elevated manganese content. All the ore types are strongly phosphoric and manganoan, with their similarities due largely to the geological origin of the ores within the Clay with Flints from the deep ancient weathering of the Upper Greensand below the sub-Clay with Flints unconformity.

Alloys and the Significance of Phosphorus

Given the highly phosphoric nature of the ores and residues, it is worth considering whether the different smelting technologies employed at Churchills Farm reflect an attempt to control the proportion of phosphorus entering the iron.

Phosphoric iron was a major product of areas where iron was produced from high phosphorus ores (which includes many sedimentary iron ores, particularly most bog iron ores). Phosphoric iron is harder than pure iron and so was able to be employed for uses where hardness was a desirable property (such as the cutting edges of tools and weapons). Phosphoric iron appears extensively in this role in the pre-Roman Iron Age, but increasingly through time the use of steel became more important. Steel is an alloy of iron containing carbon. Because of its complex phase relationships, the physical properties of steel may be modified not only by its carbon content, but by its heat treatment – enabling steel to be used for a variety of uses where particular combinations of hardness and toughness may be required.

In addition to these two alloys, the use of iron with very low concentrations of both phosphorus and carbon was also desirable. Low-C and low-P iron is soft and ductile, thus making it an ideal material for use where the iron needs to be worked without becoming brittle (e.g. for nails) or for use where its softness enabled the formation of energy absorbing materials (e.g. for the backs of axes away from the cutting edge). Low-P iron is also the desirable starting material for the generation of carbon steels.

By the ninth century the use of these three distinct materials – phosphoric iron, steel, and low-carbon/phosphorus iron – had become highly specialised. Their differential use in the fabrication of knives, for instance, demonstrating how nuanced the creation of even apparently simple, every day, objects had become. The production of these three materials was therefore an important part of ninth-century industry. To some extent, the smelting of low-P ores to generate low-P iron suitable for use both as soft iron and as a base for steelmaking, would have been a preferred route. The large-scale smelting at Emersons Green (Young and Young 2013), exploiting the low-P goethite ores of the southern part of the Worcester Graben (Young and Thomas 1998) would have been one source of low-P iron in the late ninth to early tenth centuries, and a source closer to the heart of Wessex than the main outcrop of such ores in the Forest of Dean.

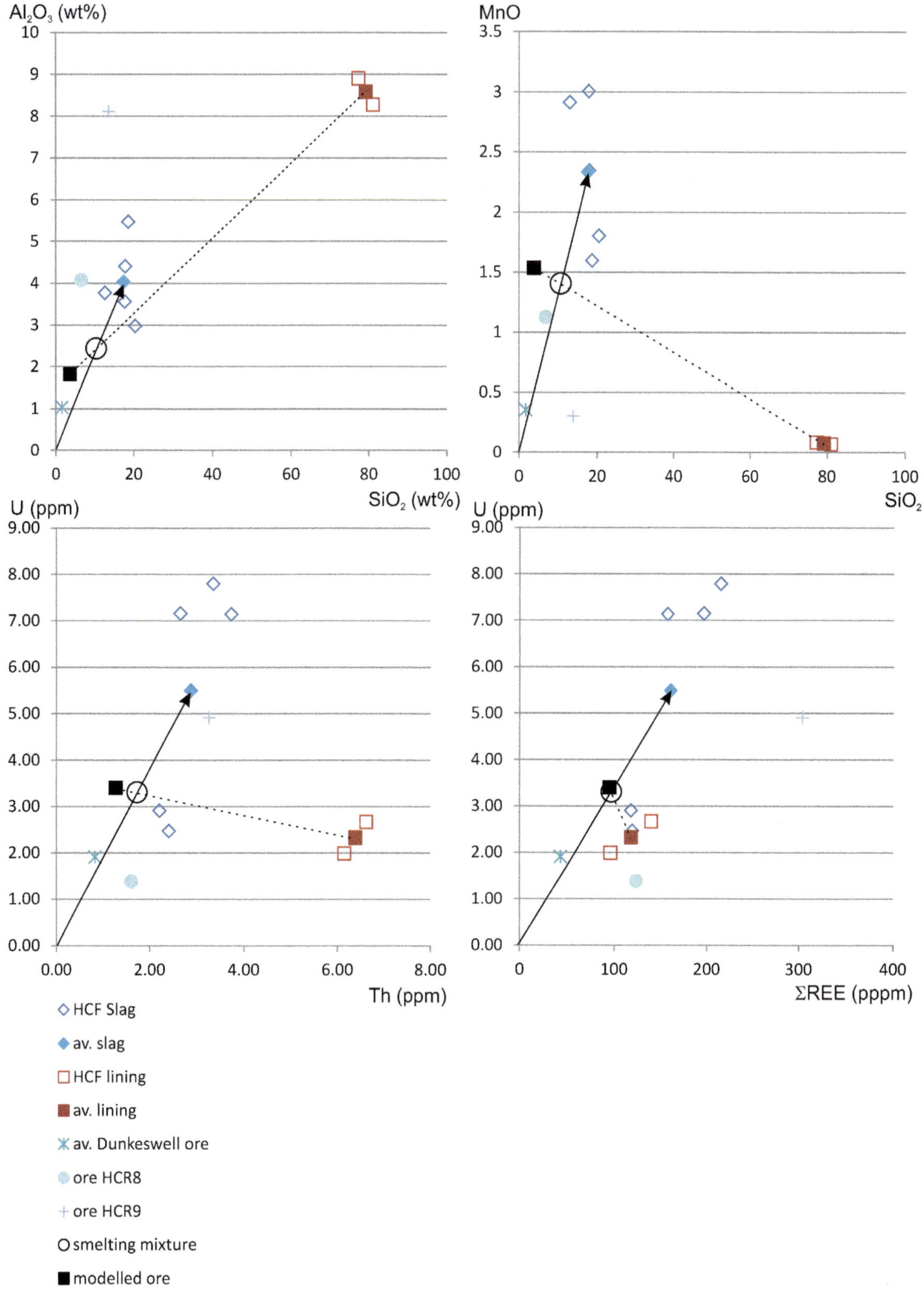

Figure 71. Graphs showing modelling of the ore composition for the Culmstock Road using the yield and smelting mixture derived for the early medieval smelting at Churchills Farm. Contrary to the evidence from the ore present on the site (Rainbird and Young 2015), the smelted ore was probably rather similar to that exploited for Churchills Farm.

It is also possible, however, to control the amount of phosphorus entering the metal during smelting of phosphoric ores. This can be achieved both by controlling the precise degree of reduction occurring in the furnace (overly reducing conditions will reduce more of the phosphorus into the iron) and probably through careful slag management (ensuring that that phosphorus held in the slag is moved away from contact with the bloom before it can revert). The mass balance calculations for the three processes at Churchills Farm, as described above, all resulted in model slags with an excess of phosphorus over that actually observed in the residues. Although some of that phosphorus may have been lost to gas, it would seem very likely that all three processes produced phosphoric iron, probably with little difference between them.

It should also be noted that phosphoric iron may be able to have its phosphorus content reduced by secondary 'hearth remelting' techniques, such as those described by Ole Evenstad in Norway in the late eighteenth century (Jensen 1968; Wagner 1990). The first stage of the 'Evenstad process' entails the remelting of iron under slightly different hearth conditions (but with a strong horizontal air-blast into a very hot hearth of variable depth). The production of steel may also be achieved by different routes. A useful distinction can be made between low carbon steels, which may form in the bloomery furnace under appropriate circumstances, and high carbon steels that may be required to be formed by a distinct and specialised process. Simple carburation of iron (for instance by heat treating the artefact or raw iron and 'soaking' the iron in charcoal at temperature for a long period) may be used to 'steel' the edge of an iron implement, or to create a small piece of stock steel. This simple carburation will not, however, alter the slag content of the iron, so both this approach and simple bloomery steel will be as rich in slag inclusions as is 'normal' bloomery iron.

In contrast, where high-carbon steels have been observed from early medieval contexts, they are commonly almost entirely lacking slag inclusions. This suggests that high-carbon steels were produced by a mechanism in which the steel had been liquid, allowing slag separation. Three separate mechanisms have been proposed for the occurrence of such steels in early medieval Britain. Firstly, some steel in early medieval Europe may have been imported from outside. External trade involving the import of crucible steel from the east has been discussed particularly in the context of the famed '*Ulfberht*' swords (e.g. Williams 2009). Secondly, a process of remelting cast iron to decarburise it (rather as in the finery process of the post-medieval period) has been suggested by Mack *et al.* (2000) on the basis of finds from *Hamwic*, dating to the eighth and ninth centuries. Finally, there is much current interest in the use of remelting techniques to adjust the carbon content of bloomery iron. There was a second stage to the process described by Eventstad (and discussed above); this remelted the iron for a second time (which had had its phosphorus content reduced in a first remelting) to increase its carbon content. Such a remelting process achieves the opposite of the finery process (see above). A small-scale steel-making process described by Aristotle (in *Meteorologica*) involving the remelting of a low carbon bloomery iron to produce a high carbon steel, was long assumed to be fanciful, but has been rehabilitated, first, theoretically, by Wagner (1990) and later, practically, by Sauder (2013). This process has been shown to produce steel with controllable carbon content and a low proportion of slag inclusions.

In view of the above discussion, with its multiplicity of proven and potential early medieval metallurgical techniques, a key point is that the extreme similarity of the chemical composition of the residues from the two early medieval furnace technologies at Churchills Farm precludes any possibility that the furnaces were undertaking significantly different metallurgical tasks. Rather, they were both undertaking the primary smelting of iron ore, employing the same ore, with a very similar efficiency of production. It is possible, however, that different furnace types might have been employed in the production of different qualities of iron and, in particular, the production of iron with different phosphorus contents. Indeed, the analysis of the Churchills Farm slag provides some tantalising glimpses of subtle differences between the performance of the tapping and non-tapping furnaces.

This, and other potential differences, was investigated through consideration of the composition of residues when re-cast on iron free basis (Figure 67). For many components (Al_2O_3, MnO, TiO_2, Th) the data plot close to the join between the average composition of furnace lining and the average composition of ore from Dunkeswell (Young 2015a). This illustrates the various blends of lining and ore involved in the smelting reaction. Data for uranium are scattered because the ore is extremely heterogeneous with respect to uranium (recast analyses vary from 41 to 54ppm, with the analysed fragment from Churchills Farm having only 11ppm). The data for calcium show that neither ore nor lining contained significant enough amounts of it to provide the concentration observed in most of the slags, and it was therefore almost entirely derived from the fuel ash. Some samples (notably HCF16 and HCF22, but also other examples of the group of early medieval tapped slags) show more elevated calcium, and it is possible that these indicate incorporation of a more lime-rich ore in the charge.

The data for phosphorus (Figure 68) show that the Churchills Farm residues contain a reduced level of phosphorus compared with the tie-line – in some samples as little as approximately half of the level of phosphorus they would be expected to have for simple mixing with conservation of this element. Up to half of the available phosphorus has been lost from the system – much of this may be to the metal. There is, however, little difference in the phosphorus contents in residues from the slag tapping and non-tapping processes, so it is difficult to propose differential use of the furnace types according to their control of phosphorus.

Despite the identification of some differences between the slags of the tapping and non-tapping furnaces, none of the evidence appears to indicate a difference in yield or likely chemistry. Extremely subtle differences (but nonetheless ones which might be important to the practitioner) might not be discernible from the small dataset of analyses, but it must be considered whether the choice of technologies employed at Churchills Farm has roots elsewhere.

Chapter 5

The Pottery Industry

John Allan, David Dawson and Graham Langman

with contributions from Jens C.Ø. Andersen, A.G. Collings, M.J. Hughes, Laurence Keen, Oliver Kent, Sarah Newstead, Gavyn K. Rollinson, Roger T. Taylor and Matt Tompkins

Introduction

The unexpected recovery of 1.4 tonnes of pottery waste at Churchills Farm, Hemyock, in 2008 was one of the most dramatic finds of medieval and later ceramics ever made in South-West England. About 53,000 sherds filling 197 large sacks were recovered; their discovery appeared all the more remarkable because they represented the output of a previously unknown production centre. With the exception of a small series of Saxo-Norman pottery and a few other sherds, all the collection is of the same date: *c.* 1500–50. It is of great interest in showing on a grand scale the transition from medieval production (mainly jugs with only a few examples of other forms) to the much wider range of vessels typical of the sixteenth century.

Hemyock was one of a number of kilns scattered across South and West Somerset and the neighbouring part of East Devon, sometimes described as the South Somerset and West Somerset pottery industries, whose best-known and most extensively explored centre was Donyatt in south Somerset (Coleman-Smith and Pearson 1988; Coleman-Smith 2002). New chemical and petrological analyses arising from the Hemyock project have allowed us to build up our understanding of the fabrics of this group of kilns and their neighbours; study of the Hemyock finds has also allowed us to identify features which distinguish this pottery from that made in the same period at Donyatt.

The find has also allowed some progress to be made in the field of pottery technology. These include a reinterpretation of the purpose of cylindrical kiln props, and new evidence for the way in which oven tiles were employed. Among the other specialist products represented, the floor-tiles are also very significant finds; Keen describes them below as 'without any doubt the most important evidence for the manufacture of floor-tiles in Devon'.

Methodology

The entire collection was initially quantified in the near-standard manner used in post-Roman pottery studies: by visual inspection, followed by sherd count, weighing, minimum vessel counts and calculations of EVE (Estimated Vessel Equivalent) for each vessel form, and for each category of material in each context. The last index is particularly valuable in quantifying kiln waste, where it is normally impossible to distinguish individual vessels, rendering minimum vessel counts almost meaningless for the more common vessel types (although sometimes useful, e.g. in showing that several vessels of a rare type are present even though there are no rim sherds and therefore no entry in the EVEs). The detailed results of this quantification are deposited in the site archive.

In designing the post-excavation strategy we have placed great emphasis on developing the scientific analysis of the fabrics of Hemyock and neighbouring kilns. The background to our work may briefly be described. From the late 1970s, our reports on medieval and later ceramics from South-West England commonly included petrological reports based on thin-sectioning. From the late 1990s, three of the authors of the present publication (JA, MH and RT) have collaborated in developing this form of pottery study, publishing reports which combine formal analysis with very detailed petrological investigation, and with analyses of the chemical composition of pottery (Allan 1998; *idem* and Langman 2002; Allan 2003; *idem* and Blaylock 2005; Allan *et al.* 2011; *idem* 2014; Allan *et al.* 2015). Alongside the examination of a sherd in thin-section, Dr Taylor has examined much wider areas of the surfaces and broken edges of sherds, allowing the identification of rare inclusions which will not necessarily appear in a thin-section, and making observations about the surfaces of inclusions which are not visible when thin-sectioned. Dr Hughes' series of reports using ICP and its successor ICP–MS are steadily building up a map of the chemical composition of the local potteries of South-West England. Analyses of pottery from 12 kiln sites and more than 40 consumption sites in South-West England have now been published – but often with limited resources, restricting the numbers of samples which can be commissioned. We seek to enlarge the number of samples from each site to improve the database of comparative material.

In a quite separate initiative, three other contributors to the present report (JCØA, DD and GKR) have recently begun to explore the application of the very powerful tool of QEMSCAN analysis to the ceramics of South-West

England. This automated technique maps and identifies the minerals present in a specimen with a much higher level of definition than is customary in pottery studies; typically the analysis of a single sample will entail the mapping of up to five million sample points. A pilot project in 2012, carried out on 12 sherds from Taunton Castle and eight from production sites in Somerset, illustrated the power of the technique (Andersen *et al.* 2016a; 2016b). When used in conjunction with traditional photographs and micrographs, this approach has the potential to form the basis of a guide to the characteristics of particular fabric types – a development of the *On-line Fabric Type Series* published for *Worcestershire, for example* (<http://www.worcestershireceramics.org>). The technique has the great merit of offering a means of distinguishing the mineral composition of the clay matrix of a vessel from that of the inclusions added as filler to the body. It therefore offers a means of interpreting the chemical signature of a sample arising from ICP-MS, in which these two components cannot be differentiated. The technique also has other potential to inform understanding of other aspects of pottery – for example the changes in chemistry which arise during firing.

Here we have sought to combine these two different approaches. This requires certainty that the same vessels are being analysed by the different techniques. To achieve this we have selected 20 large sherds of kiln waste from Hemyock and production sites in Somerset, then have broken each one into three pieces, submitting one for Dr Taylor's petrological study, another for Dr Hughes' work on ICP–MS and the third for QEMSCAN analysis.

This chapter will first outline the documentary background for pottery production in the area, then describe the context and composition of the kiln waste, with a catalogue of the illustrated material. A small collection of Saxo-Norman sherds, and the later Portuguese coarsewares are also described. A series of detailed accounts are then given on the paving-tiles, the evidence for the operation of the kiln, and the three forms of scientific analysis described above. The chapter will conclude with a comparison of the results from each of the scientific analyses, and a general discussion.

Medieval Documentary Evidence

Matt Tompkins

It is not easy to find documentary evidence for a medieval pottery industry in Hemyock, due to the small number of records relating to the village which have survived. In particular, there are disappointingly few manorial records – accounts, rentals and court rolls – which are normally very useful in this context. However a few scraps of information have been found, and much can be extrapolated from the more plentiful evidence available from the adjacent parish of Clayhidon.

At the end of the Middle Ages Hemyock was a parish of small hamlets and scattered farms centred on the small village at Hemyock itself, where stood the parish church and, from the 1380s, Hemyock castle. It has even been suggested that the village owes its existence to the castle (Ryder 2013, 40), but that seems improbable given the late date of the castle's construction; its licence to crenellate was obtained in 1380. The population of the entire parish was probably under 400 in 1524 (based a population of 89 taxpayers: Stoate 1979, 36–7). In 1566 the village contained at least 14 dwellings, probably not many more, with a population unlikely to have exceeded 100 (DHC Z17/3/19, ff. xi-xxi). The surrounding landscape was a complex one of many small irregularly-shaped fields, some arable but mostly pasture, and plentiful woods and heaths. What common fields there were had all been enclosed by 1566, and probably a century or two earlier, and the farming inhabitants would have made their living principally by stock-rearing and dairying, with some arable farming (Rippon 2012, 121–37; Fox 1991, 156, 173, 318; Campbell 2000, 442, table 4.08, figs 4.04, 6.05). It is likely that there would have been a sizeable class of small-holding cottagers and landless labourers who could have provided a workforce for a pottery industry, but the sources which would confirm this do not exist.

The village was the administrative centre of the manor of Hemyock, which was coterminous with the parish. In the early thirteenth century the manor came into the ownership of the Hidon family, who took their name from their adjoining manor of Clayhidon. For the next three centuries the two manors were held together, first by the Hidons and then, after Margaret de Hidon married Joce de Dinham in 1292, by the Dinhams of Hartland, a wealthy and influential family with large landholdings in the South West and the south Midlands. From 1362 until 1400 they were held by Sir William Asthorp, husband of Margaret de Dinham, but reverted to the Dinhams after his death. The Hidons had probably lived in Hemyock or Clayhidon, and William Asthorp may have made his home there – he held only one other manor and it was he who built Hemyock castle – but the Dinhams had several residences, principally Hartland, and are unlikely to have spent much time in either manor (Fox and Padel 2000, xxvii–xxxi; *CIPM 1399–1405*, no. 105).

In 1501 Sir John Dinham died, leaving his four daughters as his co-heirs. His estates, comprising some 15 manors and a number of other properties in six counties, were not divided among them and their husbands, as was normally done; instead they continued to be managed as an undivided estate, called the 'Dinham Lands', the yearly income from which was divided between the four co-heirs and in due course their own descendants and heirs. This arrangement seems to have continued until at least 1590, as annual accounts of the profits survive up to that date (Fox and Padel 2000). However some of the constituent manors may have been sold off at some earlier point; Sir John Popham, chief justice of the King's Bench, seems to have acquired Clayhidon and part of Hemyock during the reign of Queen Elizabeth. The Popham family retained them until the middle of the eighteentheighteenth century. The remaining quarter of Hemyock passed to the Every family (Lysons 1822, 267).

Few records survive from the medieval manor of Hemyock. Those that do are mostly to be found in the Arundell of Lanherne archive, now at the Cornwall County Record Office. The Arundells had inherited a quarter share in the Dinham lands in 1501, Sir Thomas Arundell having married one of the four Dinham co-heiresses. Some of the Dinham muniments consequently came into the Arundells' possession, though unfortunately not those relating to the manor of Hemyock, whose fate is now unknown. All that is available for Hemyock are various estate-wide summaries, including many of the post-1501 yearly accounts of the Dinham Lands which were presumably produced in quadruplicate for the four co-heirs; these are brief and provide little detail of each individual manor. The Arundells did, however, get the records of the sister manor of Clayhidon, which we will return to.

In the late Middle Ages the pottery industry in England was predominantly small-scale and dispersed, often carried on part-time by cottagers and small farmers. Rural potters sometimes gathered in small marginal settlements dedicated to the industry, but were also found scattered in ones and twos among the general agricultural population. Full-time potting seems often to have been an occupation of necessity rather than choice, easily abandoned if an agricultural holding could be acquired. After the Black Death, when land became more available, the part-time farmer-cum-potter became more prominent, but large specialist manufactories also developed (Le Patourel 1968, 101–26; McCarthy and Brooks 1988, 70–81; Dyer 1982, 37; Astill 1983, 226–8; Dyer 2005, 141–3).

The generally low status and economic obscurity of the industry and many of its practitioners meant that it often passed unnoticed in contemporary sources. The available evidence for its presence in a locality is frequently limited to minor place- and field-names, to occupational surnames such as Potter or Crocker (of most significance before about the mid thirteenth century, since after that time most surnames were hereditary), and in fortunate cases to references in manorial records to rents paid for digging clay. In many manors potters had to pay the lord for licence to dig clay, usually less than 1s. a year, whether they dug on their own holding or in the manorial waste and commons. Clay from the potter's own holding might be dug from pits in his closes or crofts, but also in his strips in common fields (Le Patourel 1968).

The only direct documentary evidence for potters in medieval Hemyock is two surnames recorded in lay subsidy returns of the 1330s. A Ralph le Crokker was listed in 1330, and in 1332 a John Pottere was assessed for 8d. tax – the lowest rate, paid by one third of the 32 taxpayers in Hemyock (Gover *et al.* 1932, 617, where a connection between these two taxpayers and the present-day Potters Farm and Crockers Farm is suggested; Erskine 1969, 37). It cannot be certain that their surnames reflected their occupations, as by this date a large proportion of the population had acquired hereditary surnames and it may have been their ancestors who had been potters (as was most likely the case with three men surnamed Potter who appear in Hemyock subsidy returns of 1524, 1544 and 1581 (Stoate 1979, 36; 1986, 13; 1988, 85) – but it is a possibility. If they were indeed potters, then John Pottere's low assessment may suggest he was a cottager engaged full-time in pottery.

Some indirect evidence for late medieval potters in Hemyock may also be provided by field names in a 1566 survey of the manor of Hemyock (DHC Z17/3/19, ff. xi–xxi). It lists 48 tenants and describes the landholdings of 45 of them in some detail, naming every close, croft and parcel of meadow or woodland. Of these 45 holdings, fully one third, scattered across the parish, included one or more closes called *Pitland* (or in one case *Pitfurlong*, perhaps indicating enclosure from a former open field). The same 15 holdings also contained a close called *Cleyland*, a croft and meadow called *Puttescroft*, and a close called *Newecroft* with a *pitt* in it. A sixteenth holding included a *pitt* in a close called *Honyhilles* – 'honey' in minor place-names is sometimes a reference to particularly sticky clayey soil (Field 1993, 42). Other holdings may well have included pits, but in fields known by other names. Again, it cannot be certain that all of these Pitlands contained current or former claypits; some may have been marlpits, or possibly even stone quarries (see Collings' discussion of the nineteenth-century evidence below; a recent study of the ancient landscape of the Blackdown Hills describes numerous old pits in nearby Luppitt and Yarcombe parishes as only 'a few sand and clay pits and large numbers of marl pits' (Rippon *et al.* 2006a); but if even a few of them were claypits it would constitute evidence for a late medieval pottery industry in the manor.

The survey seldom states the location of these fields, but does sometimes give that of the tenement to which they belonged. Three of the 16 holdings were centred on dwellings in Hemyock village, two of them cottages and the third comprising two half-tenements held together. The latter holding, belonging to a Henry Walronde, contained a four-acre close called Pitland and a meadow and a croft, each of one acre and both called Puttescroft. One of these holdings may later have become Churchills Farm.

The same 1566 survey presents a similar picture of numerous field names referencing pits in the adjacent manor of Clayhidon; here they are found in more than a third of the 36 customary and conventionary holdings (DHC Z17/3/19, ff. i–ix). In four cases it is stated explicitly that the holding includes a *pitt* (one of them planted with *appultrees*) and a further 11 include closes, crofts or meadows with names referencing pits, usually Pitland and in one case Cleypitland. Where the location of the tenement to which these fields belonged can be identified, it is always in the northern half of the parish – mainly north of the river Culm, but in two cases immediately south of it.

Particularly interesting is a statement that Thomas Acourt, tenant of Heazle Farm in the far north-west of the parish (which included a close called Pitland and two pieces called Pittes), also held '*lez cleypittes* anciently taken within the manor and in the past ought to have paid 73s. 4d. and now pays only 20s.'

The fortunate accident of the preservation of Clayhidon manorial accounts and court rolls running from 1331 until 1500 in the Arundell of Lanherne archive enables us to discover more about the late medieval history of these ancient claypits, and gives an idea of what might have been possible if the equivalent Hemyock records also survived. The earliest rolls have not been read in their entirety, but sampling has not revealed any references to potters, claypits or clay rents before 1378, when a Ralph Pottere was brought before the manor court and fined 6d. for brawling and drawing blood with a cudgel. Then in 1381 a court roll records that a tenant was fined for making many pits (*fodias*) in his tenement without licence and the following year's annual account records a new, additional, rent of 13s. 4d. for *la cleypyttys* (CRO AR/2/495, court held on All Saints, 5 Ric II (11 Nov 1381) and account for the year ended Michaelmas 6 Ric II (1382)). A 1397 rental (CRO AR2/495 m. 74) includes a payment of 53s. 4d. for *Cleyputte* and this incremental rent continues to appear in the accounts until they end in 1500.

Throughout that period the identity of the person paying the 53s. 4d. incremental rent changed several times, as did the precise description of what it was paid for, but the amount always remained the same:

- 1397: William Clyverdene 'for *Cleyputte*'
- 1411–13: Walter Pyle for 'digging clay in 8 acres of land in Heazle Field' or 'Heazle furlong' (among other parcels Pyle rented a close of demesne land called Heazle Furlong for 7s. per annum)
- 1420–1: John Pyle and William Garland for 'digging clay in their tenement(s)'
- 1427: late John Pyle and William Garland for 'digging clay in the lord's tenement'
- 1471–84: 'from a lease of the clay pit granted to William Coute and Geoffrey Peke
- 1499–1500: 'from a lease of the clay pit granted to William Hoigge' (CRO AR/2/496 mm. 27–8; AR/2/497 m. 5; AR/2/500; AR/2/501; AR/2/502 mm. 7–9, 18–21; AR/2/503, mm. 1–3).

In 1472 the rent was increased by 20s. – perhaps because the clayfields had been extended beyond the original 8 acres – but always continued to appear in the accounts as 53s. 4d. plus an increment of 20s. The accounts end in 1500, but as we have seen, the 1566 survey noted that Thomas Acourt of Heazle paid 20s. for *lez cleypittes* but ought to have paid an additional 53s. 4d. (perhaps by that date the original 8-acre site had been exhausted).

It seems clear that these claypits must have been in Heazle – as in the 1566 survey, the references to them did not specify their location, save in 1411–13 when they were said to be in 8 acres of land in Heazle field or furlong. In 1566 Acourt's holding in Heazle included an 8-acre close called Pitland and two pieces called Pittes, while in the 1842 tithe award Heazle Farm included two fields called Hither and Yonder Pitland, which together comprised almost 7 acres.

The size of the payment for the Heazle claypits suggests that it was for something rather unusual, possibly extraction on a hitherto unseen scale. Jean Le Patourel's survey of references to medieval potters and clay rents found none paying more than 1s. per tenant per year and most considerably less; against this 53s. 4d., more than 50 times the highest rent found by her, implies a truly industrial level of extraction. The Heazle pottery may have been one of the new large-scale production centres which emerged in England at this time.

It is by no means certain that the 1381 entries mark the start of clay extraction in Clayhidon; it may well have been going on for many years previously but for some reason did not attract extra rent, or simply was not mentioned in the manorial records (the date 1381 may be significant – just when Sir William Asthorp had begun building Hemyock castle, and perhaps needed new revenues to fund the work). On the other hand the place-name Clayhidon may itself give a clue as to the timing of the emergence of pottery as a significant economic activity in the parish. Throughout most of the Middle Ages and well into the early modern period the name was simply Hidon. The earliest occurrence of the Clay- prefix listed in *Place-Names of Devon* is from 1485. It had no doubt been in occasional use for some time before that year, but it seems unlikely that it first began to be used more than a century previously – which hints that its adoption might have been influenced by the emergence of the large Heazle operation.

The accounts do not record any other clay rents than the Heazle one, but the numerous pit references in the 1566 survey suggest that other tenants may have been digging clay without paying an extra rent, perhaps because they were digging in their own holdings (the *cleypyttys* seem to have been located on the lord's demesne land), perhaps because they were only doing it on a small scale.

Without more evidence, it is impossible to say whether other smaller potteries were operating elsewhere. For a start, it would be useful to know whether the numerous pits and Pitland fields mentioned in the 1566 survey were claypits or marlpits. Some at least must have been claypits supplying potteries. We have certain archaeological evidence of a pottery at Churchills Farm in Hemyock. Another may have been at Garlandhayes in Clayhidon, not far from Heazle and in a similar position on the side of a high valley. One of the tenants exploiting the Heazle claypits in the 1420s was William Garland, no doubt from the family who gave their name to Garlandhayes, possibly even himself the tenant there. In 1566 the two holdings at Garlandhayes included two closes called Pitland and Pitclose and a meadow called Pitmead. The larger tenement was held by Roger Pyke, no doubt from the same family as the Geoffrey Peke who had been one of the lessees of the Heazle claypits in the 1470s and 1480s. In the 1524 lay subsidy a William Peke paid 12d., the second largest assessment in a parish where 80% paid 4d. or less, and only 10% paid more than 7d. (Stoate 1979, 39). Could his wealth have been derived from pottery?

By 1500 Hemyock was probably specialising in pastoral farming, a fairly seasonal business, and its farmers would have had the spare capacity to operate a pottery in the off-seasons). Was there another 'super-pottery' in Hemyock to match that in Clayhidon, or was the industry there a matter of several small operations, perhaps carried on full-time by cottagers or part-time by agricultural tenants? Again it is impossible to say without more evidence, but we can be confident that at least one of the Pitland fields recorded in 1566 must have been a claypit supplying a pottery, as we have the archaeological evidence from Churchills Farm.

Later Documentary and Cartographic Evidence for Pottery Production around Hemyock

A.G. Collings

The detailed picture of land-use in Hemyock parish which can be gathered from nineteenth-century records is relevant to the study of the medieval pottery industry in this area because it provides evidence of the location of places where clay was worked in earlier times. The tithe survey of 1841–3 recorded 67 field names containing the word 'Pit'. Only three gave any indication of their function – a flax pit, a marl pit and a saw pit. The first large-scale Ordnance Survey map of 1887 recorded 31 pits in the modern parish, 13 of which were identified as clay pits, the others being for gravel (12) or sand (6). The absence of any marl pits does suggest that their identification, particularly for earlier pits, may not be totally reliable. Seven of the claypits were within 600 m of Churchills Farm. Some may have been used for cob wall construction or brick-making; a short-lived brick-works, the Culm Davy Brick Company with its two pits, also lay 1.1 km north-west of the village centre, in Culm Pyne, which was a detached part of Clayhidon parish prior to 1882. The works probably closed soon afterwards; the maps of 1887 and 1904–5 show it as disused. All the claypits shown on these maps lie on the Mercia Mudstones.

Pits of the sort mapped in nineteenth-century Hemyock are surprisingly common and widespread features of the parishes of the Blackdown Hills; Figure 72 shows their location in relation to the geology of the area. Many are recognisable as landscape features nowadays; they are commonly both large and deep. It is unlikely that so many features spread over many parishes represent the activities of potters, and probable that most represent pits dug for marling fields. Nevertheless their distribution offers a guide to the areas in the local landscape where clay resources were exploited traditionally.

Context of the Assemblage

Most of the collection was recovered from two large pits, 715 and 589; both were almost certainly former claypits. The sequences of deposits in them, and other pits of this date and probable function, are shown in Figure 25.

Fill 616 of pit 715 yielded the greatest concentration of sherds from the site (20,055 – 99% of the sherds recovered from this pit). Some 18,192 sherds were recovered from pit [589]; the main concentration was in layer 588, where 14,081 sherds were found (77% of the total from the pit). Two other pits also contained kiln waste but in smaller amounts: Pit [686] with an upper fill, 687 over a lower primary fill 693; and Pit [694] with layers 695 (top red material), 696 (middle black layer) and 697 (lower black deposit).

The pottery from each of the two main pit groups is presented separately in the Catalogue, followed by items from miscellaneous contexts. We have not found meaningful distinctions in the composition of the two main assemblages, however; we have therefore discussed them together.

Composition of the Assemblage

There are three components in the assemblage: imported pottery, local pottery showing signs of use, and kiln waste. The first two components are very minor ones. One Raeren cup/mug and three Portuguese coarsewares (the latter discussed below by Sarah Newstead) are present. Imported ceramics are not unusual finds on English kiln sites of this period; for example, at least three Raeren stoneware cups and one Cologne/Frechen vessel were found among the early sixteenth-century kiln waste at Donyatt site 3 (Coleman-Smith and Pearson 1988, 81, 339–40), and similar finds were recovered among the Goldsmith Street kiln waste from Exeter (Allan 1984a, 198, Nos 1696–7). Instances of higher-quality imported wares found at pottery kilns and glasshouses are described by Hurst and Gaimster (2005, 270) in their study of Werra slipware.

Two bowls from context 616 display external soot-marks, showing that not all the English pottery is kiln waste. It is of course possible that further sherds among this material represent domestic pottery which has left no obvious use-marks, but we suspect that their number is low. Sooting is very commonly seen on bowl sherds in household rubbish of this date, but in this collection the two sooted sherds may be compared with over 1000 which were not sooted, including hundreds of definite waster sherds. The near-absence/absence of animal bone, small finds or other sorts of domestic rubbish, and the marked concentration of sherds in single contexts, suggest to us that the proportion

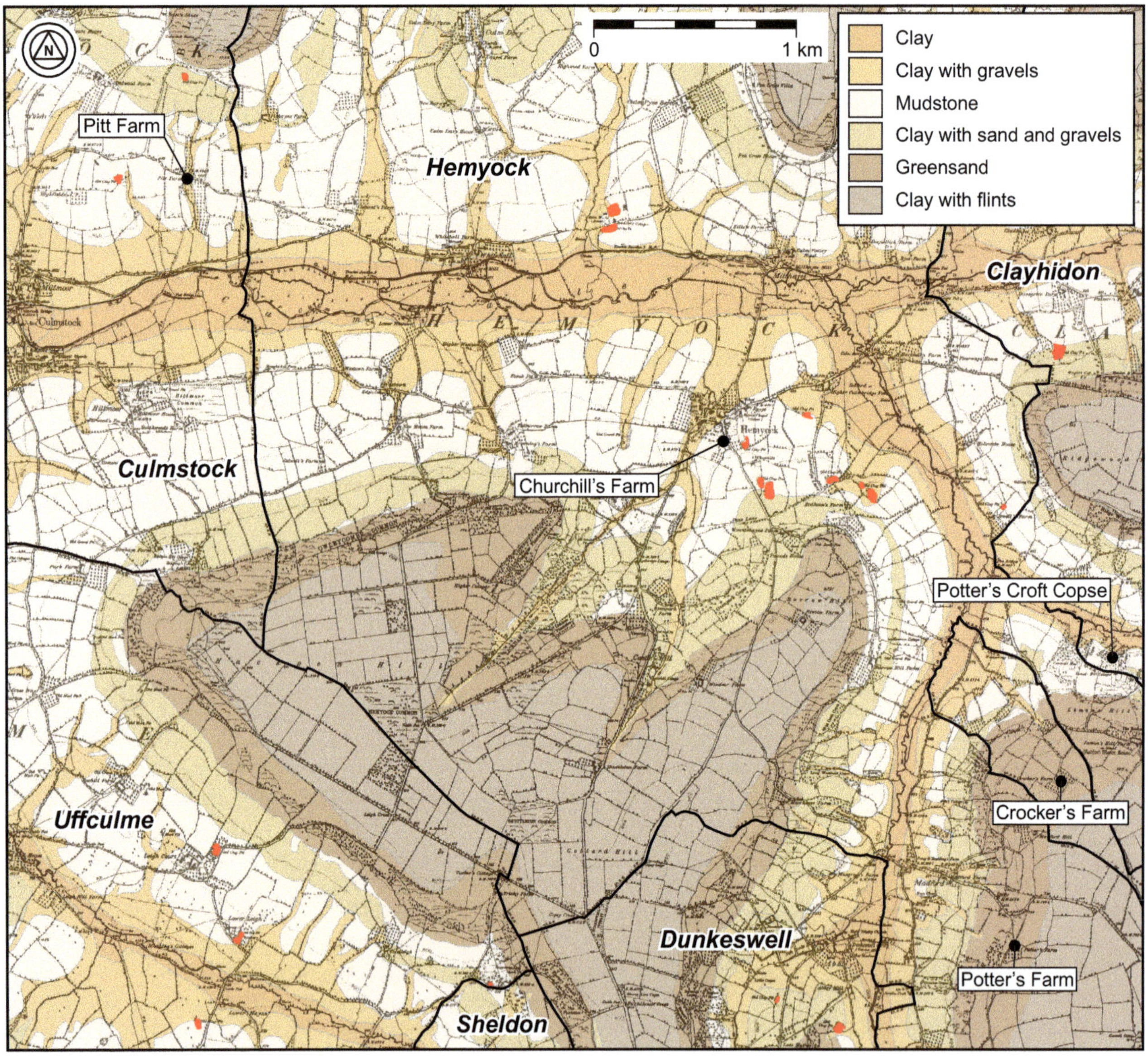

Figure 72. The location of clay-pits around Hemyock in 1841 and 1887, with underlying geology (based on the Hemyock Tithe Apportionment 1841 (*courtesy of the Devon Heritage Centre*), late nineteenth-century Ordnance Survey First Edition 25 inches to 1 mile and British Geological Survey soil parent material dataset, sheet ew311 (© Crown Copyright and Landmark Information Group Limited (2016). All rights reserved. (1889)).

of domestic ceramics in the collection is probably low or very low.

Broad Categories of Ceramics

The overall breakdown of the collection from all contexts (excluding the imports) is shown in Table 14. The biases of each index used to quantify the collection will be evident: the sherd count exaggerates the proportion of the more fragile domestic pottery, whilst the measures of weight emphasise the proportions of the heavier tiles and kiln furniture.

Domestic Wares

Table 15 shows the proportion of the total of kiln waste made up by the different vessel forms, expressed as a proportion of the number and weight of vessels, the Estimated Vessel Equivalent and the Minimum Number of Vessels. The most useful index is the Estimated Vessel Equivalent, calculated from the rims rather than the bases. Minimum Vessel counts understate the proportion of the total represented by the most common forms (where no additional vessels can be distinguished after the Estimated Vessel Equivalent has been calculated) and exaggerate the output of the most distinctive and uncommon types, but bring out the presence of a few rare forms which do not feature in the EVE count (e.g. rectangular baking dishes).

The assemblage is dominated by jugs, which make up fully 63% of all vessels by EVE (although it should be noted that this figure is exaggerated slightly by the inclusion of cisterns, which have the same rim form and are recognisable only from their bung-holes). Bowls form the second most common category, with 23% of the total by the same index. Jars are the third common vessel type (10% by EVE); cisterns (not recognised in the EVE but

Table 14. Sum total of Hemyock kiln waste, divided by broad classes of ceramic output. EVE estimated vessel equivalents, MNV = minimum number of vessels

Form/Type	Sherds	Weight (kg)	EVE	MNV
Domestic vessels	44,535 (84%)	871.890 (62%)	302.47	264
Oven and floor tile	3064 (6%)	225.407 (16%)	-	-
Ridge tiles and louvers	3026 (6%)	170.151 (12%)	-	-
Cylindrical kiln props	2277 (4%)	149.868 (11%)	50.4	-
Sum total	**52,902**	**1417.316**	**352.87**	264

Table 15. Sum totals of vessel types (all Hemyock kiln waste). EVE = estimated vessel equivalents, MNV = minimum number of vessels

Form/Type	Sherds	Weight (kg)	EVE	MNV
Sgraffito yellow-glazed slip and line decorated	19	0.337	1.2 (0.4%)	9 (1.6%)
Plain yellow-glazed slipware	3	0.188	0.1 (0.03%)	2 (0.4%)
Jug: plain rim	235	4.970	36.7 (12%)	37 (6.9%)
Jug: thumbed rim	842	38.046	154.2 (51%)	155 (29%)
Jug: flat handle	648	39.692	-	-
Jug: twisted handle	351	25.608	-	-
Jug: rod handle	16	0.890	-	-
Cup	37	1.029	0.6 (0.2%)	25 (4.7%)
Beaker	5	0.263	0.6 (0.2%)	1 (0.2%)
Tankard	59	0.871	1.4 (0.5%)	12 (2.2%)
Chafing dish	20	0.397	-	8 (1.5%)
Bowl: hammer-head rim	848	48.371	50.4 (17%)	51 (9.5%)
Bowl: plain rim	257	11.586	19.7 (6.5%)	20 (3.7%)
Jar	343	6.959	29.4 (10%)	125 (23%)
Storage jar	32	1.054	1.25 (0.4%)	13 (2.4%)
Cistern	183	8.370	-	10 (1.9%)
Bucket-handled pot	60	2.502	2.6 (0.9%)	20 (3.8%)
Pipkin/skillet	4	0.312	-	3 (0.6%)
Baking pan/apple roaster	44	2.866	-	17 (4.8%)
Lid	15	0.379	0.35 (0.1%)	4 (0.8%)
Candle holders	2	0.067	-	1 (0.2%)
Chamber pot? (plain glazed)	4	0.263	0.5 (0.17%)	3 (0.6%)
Standing costrel	15	0.624	3.5 (1.16%)	6 (1.2%)
Watering pot	4	0.228	-	3 (0.6%)
Unclassified forms	20	0.574	-	12 (2.2%)
Decorated body: slip, sgraffito and incised lines (mostly jugs)	4449	71.789	-	-
Decorated body: metallic stripes	34	0.867	-	-
Plain body/base sherds	35,986	602.788	-	-
Sum total	**44,535**	**871.890**	**302.5**	**537**

listed in the sherd count) were probably the next most common (4.5% of the sherds which could be attributed to a specific vessel type). The small proportion of cups and other small drinking vessels (jointly making up less than 1% of the total) is especially notable. All the other forms are uncommon, but the presence of some uncommon vessel forms such as apple roasters and candle holders may be noted.

Catalogue

Pit [715] (Figures 73–78)

Unless stated otherwise, illustrated sherds are from 616. Nos 1, 4–6, 21, 36, 43–4 and are definite wasters with glaze over edges or gross distortion; others are under-fired (e.g. 2, 7–8, ?16, 35?, 46) or over-fired (9–12, 27, 29).

1–8. Sgraffito-decorated slipwares. The slip on most sherds is pitted; sherd backs are mainly oxidised and unglazed but No. 4 is reduced grey. Internal brown to olive-green glaze. 1–5 dishes, 1–2 and 4–5 with compass-scribed arcs; 2 low-fired with no sign of glaze over the slip (even in the sgraffito lines); uncertain whether the glaze did not mature and has been stripped or this vessel was unglazed; 3 the triangles on the rim edge pared away; 4 with impressed five-point combing and compass-drawn arcs; 5 with compass points visible close to the rim; 6 closed form, warped and almost flat, with compass-drawn sgraffito daisy wheel (apotropaic?); 7 shallow bowl or jug, under-fired, no visible glaze, the slip (shown black) almost stripped from the interior and exterior; 8a form uncertain (a jug?), with external slip (shown black) and yellow glaze; 8b lower body sherd, possibly from the same vessel.

9–12. Cups, 9–10 with reduced green internal and external glaze, each possibly formerly with second handle; 11 cup with dark purple-brown glaze, single- or double-handled? 12 cup with reduced green internal and external glaze; fired upright, with blobs of slip spilled onto rim top (shown black in drawing), single- or double-handled. (9–10 from 716).

13–20. Jugs, 13–16 with flat-topped rims and bands of slip decoration on neck and mid green, dark green and pale orange-brown glazes, 13 with pinched spout,

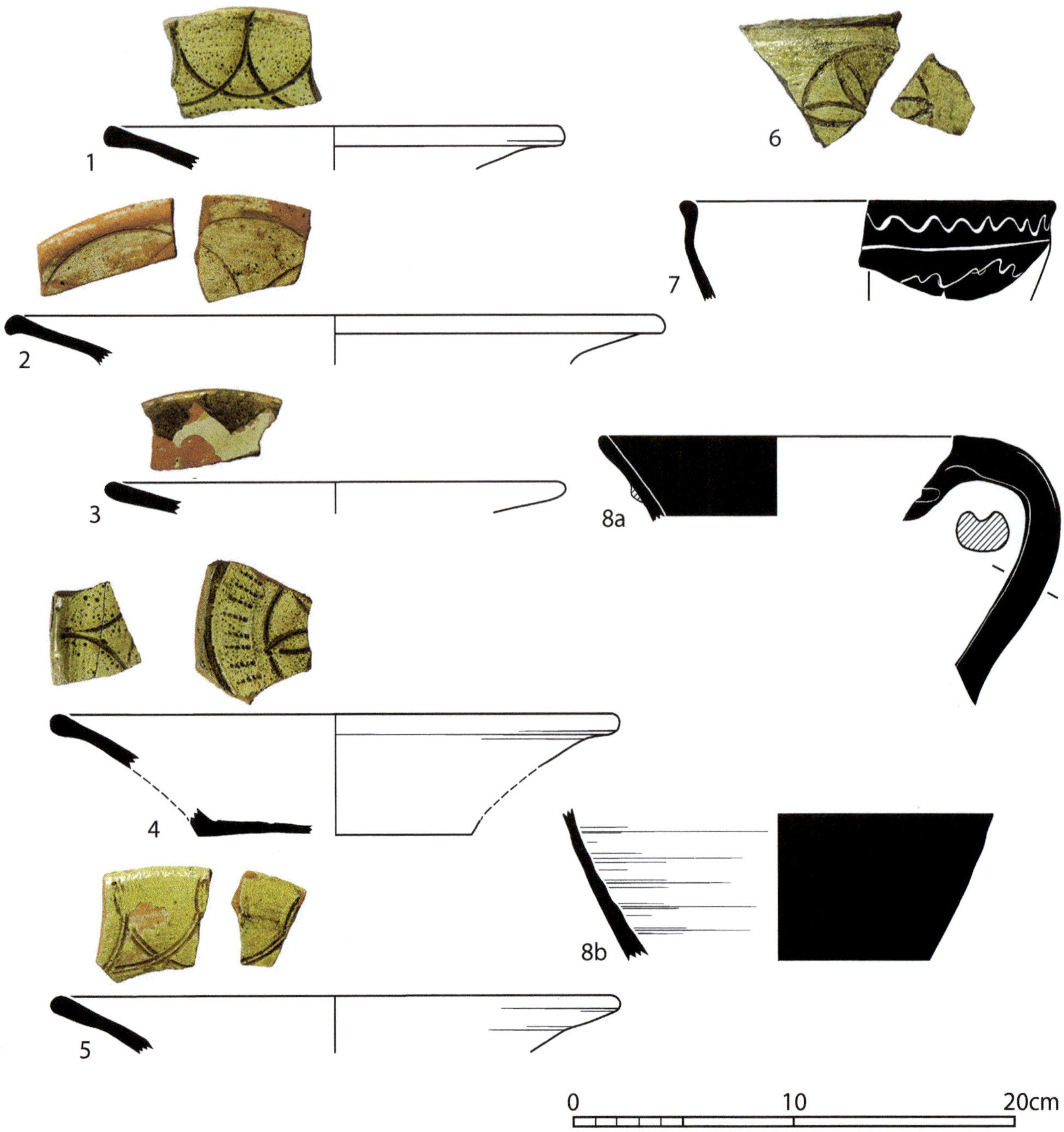

Figure 73. Early sixteenth-century kiln waste from pit [715]: sgraffito-decorated slipwares. Scale 1:4 *(drawn by S. Goddard).*

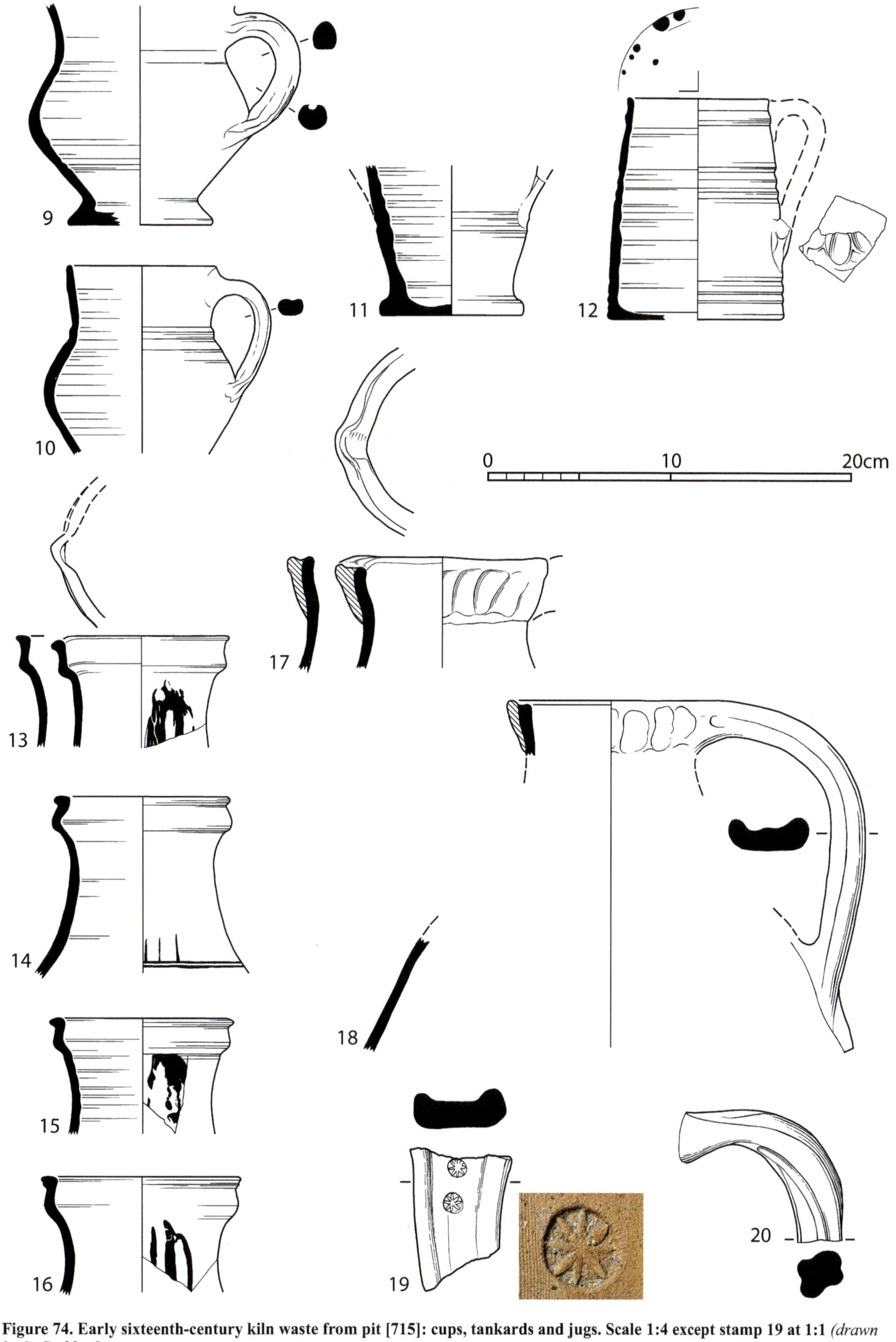

Figure 74. Early sixteenth-century kiln waste from pit [715]: cups, tankards and jugs. Scale 1:4 except stamp 19 at 1:1 *(drawn by S. Goddard).*

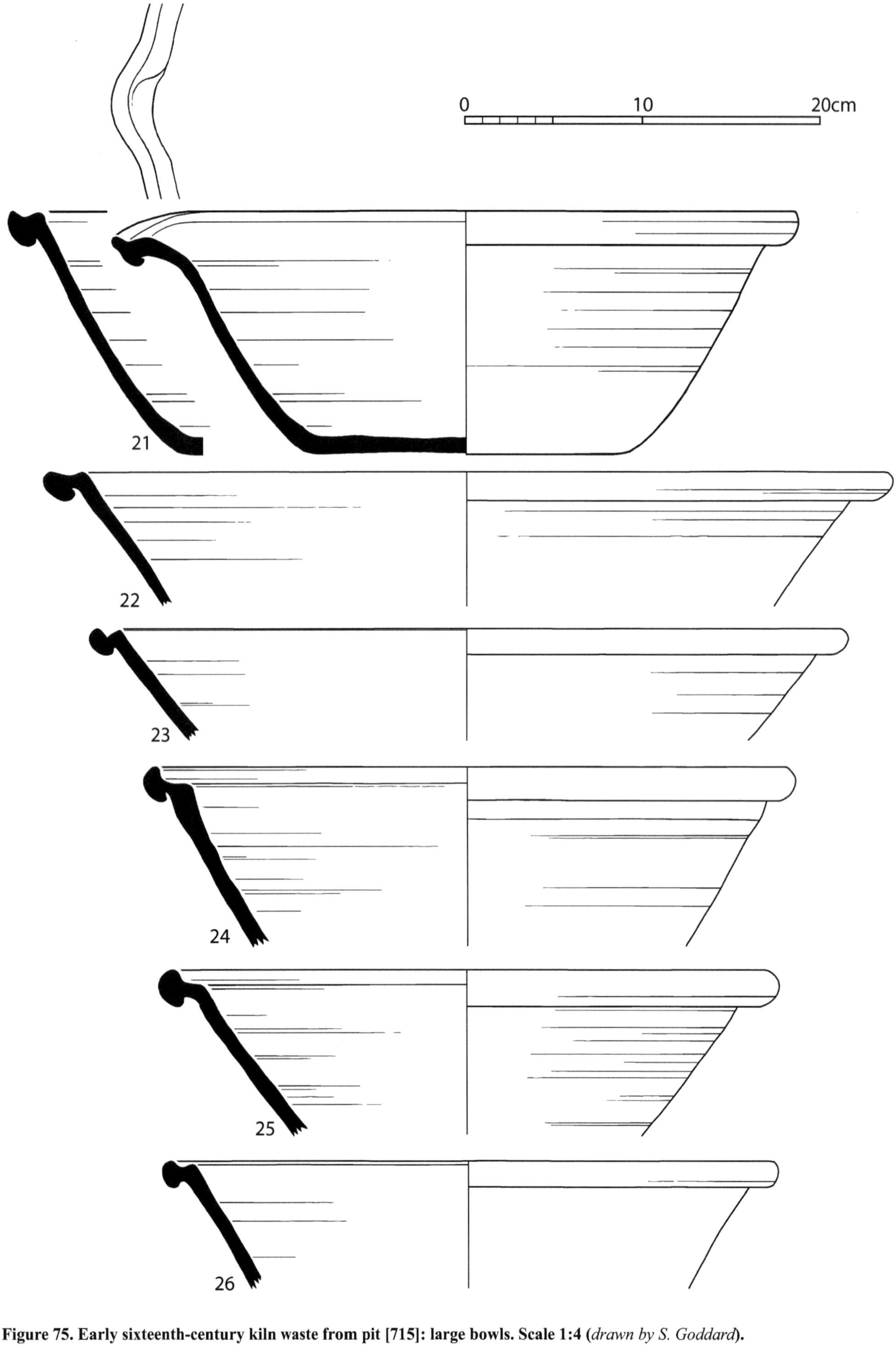

Figure 75. Early sixteenth-century kiln waste from pit [715]: large bowls. Scale 1:4 (*drawn by S. Goddard*).

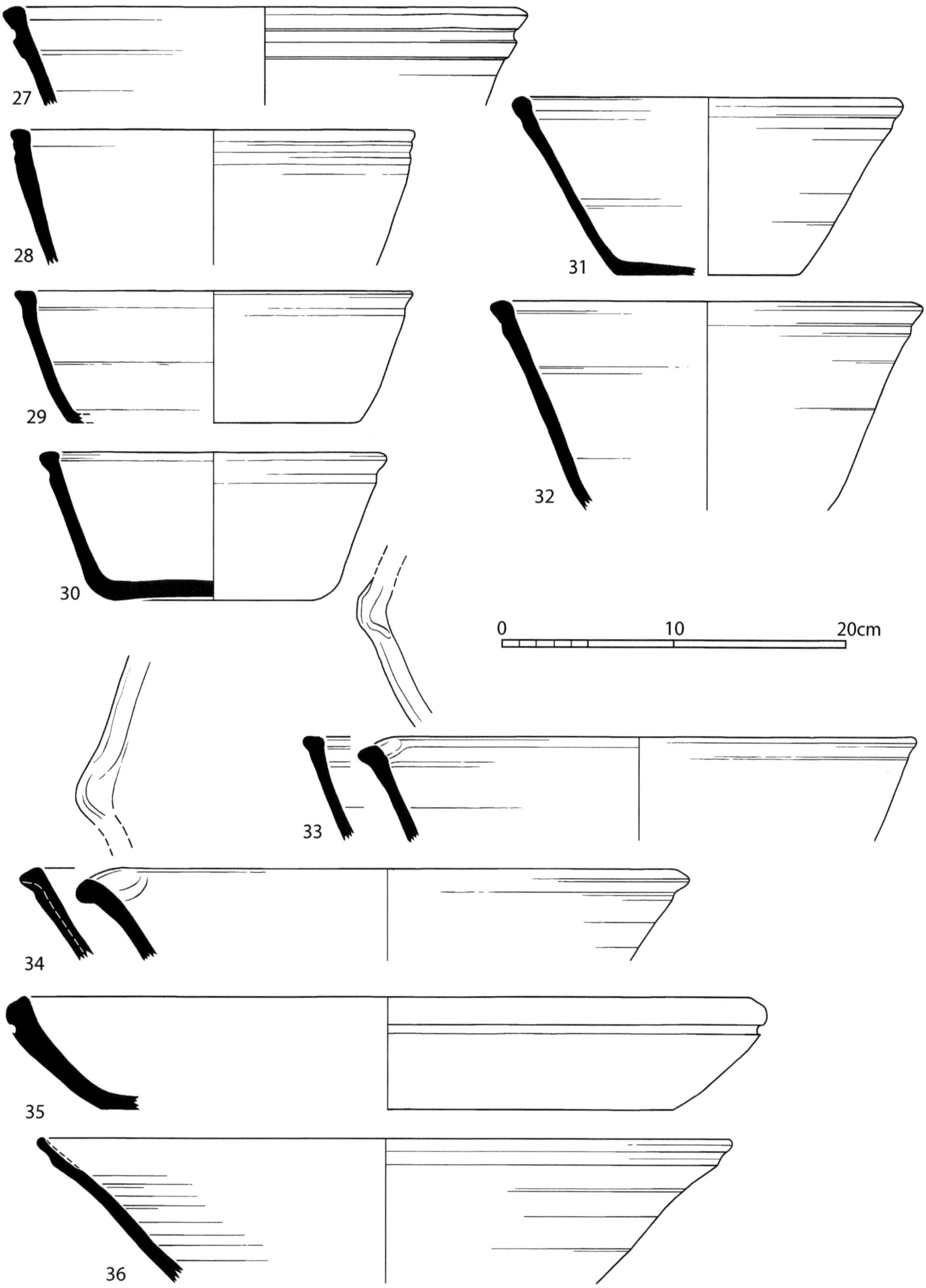

Figure 76. Early sixteenth-century kiln waste from pit [715]: small bowls. Scale 1:4 (*drawn by S. Goddard*).

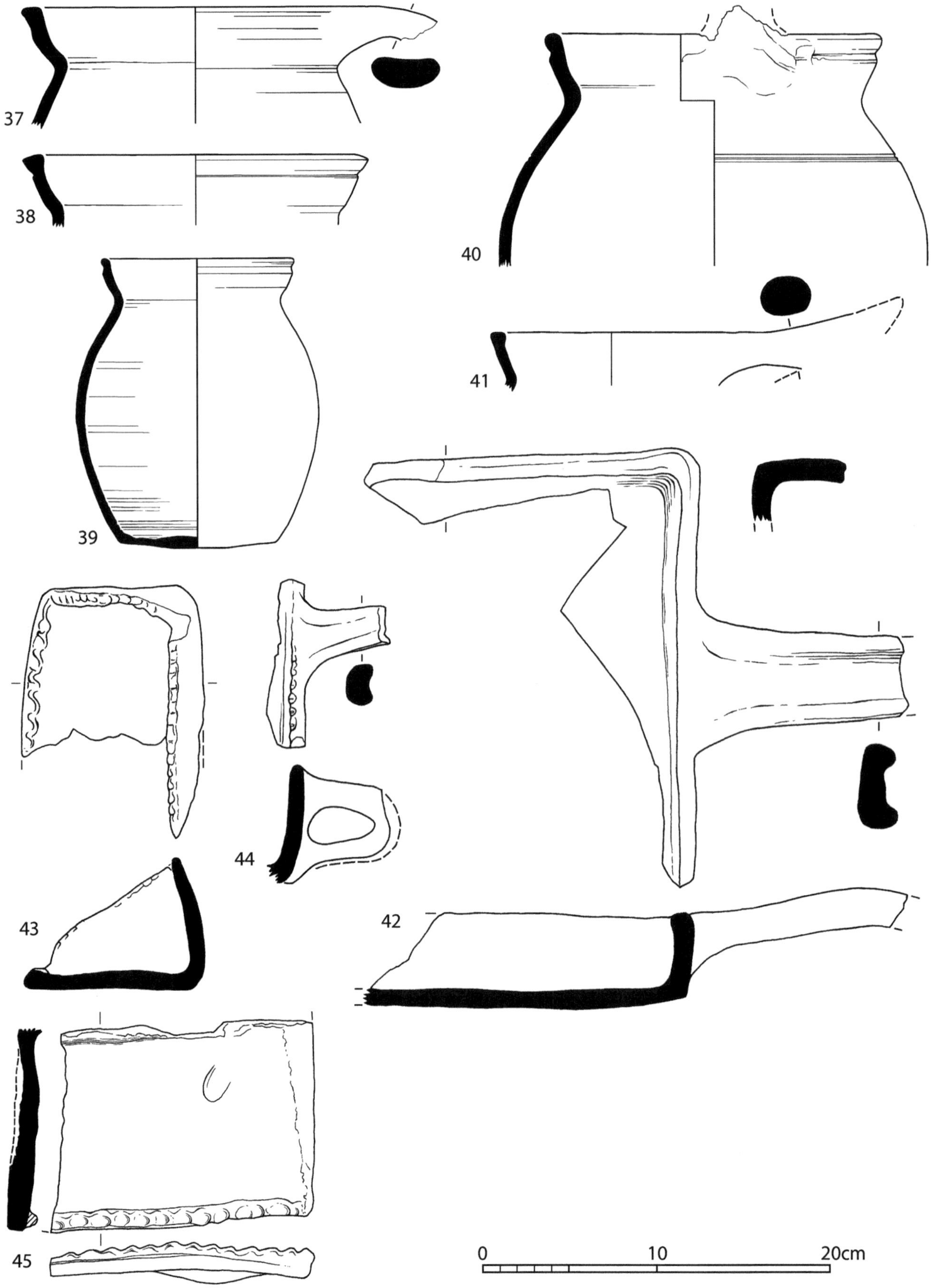

Figure 77. Early sixteenth-century kiln waste from pit [715]: miscellaneous forms. Scale 1:4 (*drawn by S. Goddard*).

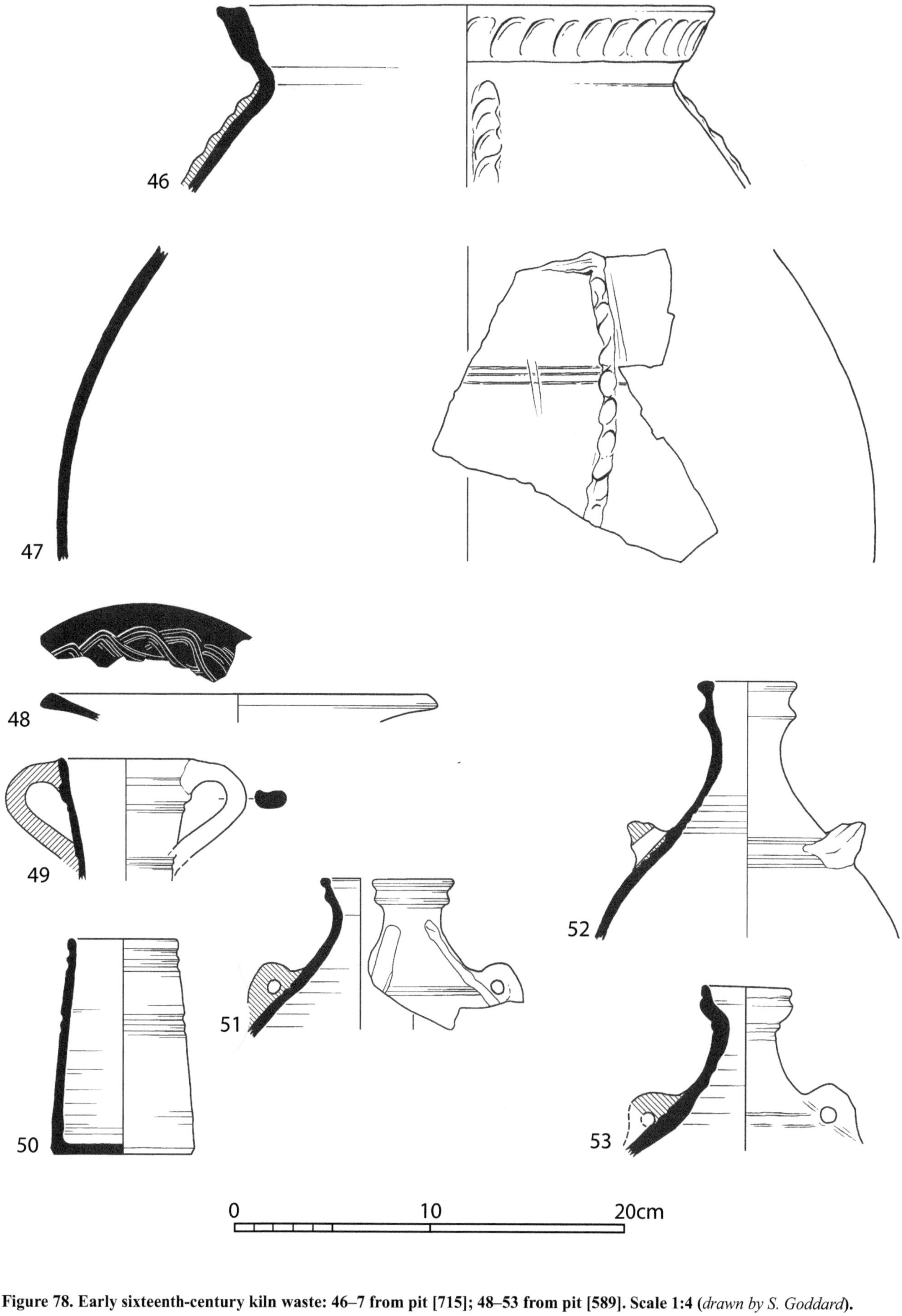

Figure 78. Early sixteenth-century kiln waste: 46–7 from pit [715]; 48–53 from pit [589]. Scale 1:4 (*drawn by S. Goddard*).

17–18 with applied thumbed strips round necks, 18 with four knife stabs in lower handle attachment. 19–20 handles, 19 with impressed rosette stamps, 20 with edge of thumbed strip on rim.

21–6. Large bowls (pancheons), 21 with broad pulled lip (probably present on all such bowls), all with internal mid green, reduced green, orange-brown and mid brown glazes.

27–36. Small bowls with internal glazes – over-fired dark grey to black (27, 36), oxidised light green (28), reduced olive green (29, 33), light green-brown, thinning on walls (30), orange-brown (31, 35, ?under-fired), reduced and blackened; 33–4 with pinched spouts. 31 has been sooted from domestic use.

37–41. Closed forms with internal oxidised green-brown (37, 40) or mid green (39, 41) glaze – jars (37–9), bucket-handled pot (40) and skillet (41).

42. Slab-built rectangular dripping tray with knife-trimmed exterior, under-fired internal glaze.

43–5. Rectangular apple roasters (?) with pie-crusted rims and oxidised pale green (43) or mid brown (45) internal glaze. No. 43 has an open front, a sloping side and a high back. These vessels presumably had two loop handles.

46–7. Jar(s)? – or perhaps large globular jugs (cf. an example from Exeter: Allan 1984a, No. 1700, which has a pulled lip and a handle scar), with applied thumbed strips and internal glaze – under-fired and yellow-green (46) and traces only (47).

Pit [589] (Figures 79–80)

Nos 48, 50, 55, 69, 71 and 78 are definite wasters with glaze over broken edges, or blistered glaze or grossly distorted bodies; other vessels are over-fired (49) or probably under-fired (52, 80). All vessels are from 588 unless stated otherwise.

48. Sgraffito-decorated slipware dish, the slip brushed over the incised combed scrolls; extremely thin (?laminated) towards the centre, the back unglazed (588, 599).

49. Two-handled cup, high-fired with reduced body and reduced dark green-black glaze.

50. Cylindrical vessel without handle (lower half of vessel complete). The inverted rim of a jug, placed over the central girth of the vessel, has adhered to the glaze (588, 712).

51–3. Standing costrels with paired applied lug handles over wheel-thrown grooves, 51 with vertical applied strips in iron-rich clay. External glaze, not matured and almost lost from 52, green-brown on 53.

54–68. Jugs, unglazed internally with external green-brown glaze, all except 57 with a sgraffito-decorated slip band on the shoulder, 54–5 with applied thumbed strips, 54 and 56 with flat handles, 55 and 58 twisted, 54–5 with slash-marks in handles near junction with rim.

69–72. Cisterns, unglazed internally, with splashes of external glaze, 69–71 heavily over-fired, the glaze reduced to dark grey (69–71 from 571).

73–5. Jars with internal mid green to reduced olive green glaze.

76. Small shallow bowl with internal dark green-brown glaze; pulled lip.

77–9. Bucket-handles pots with external glaze, 78 with pulled lip, 79 reduced in final phase of firing.

80. Slab-built rectangular dripping pan with pouring lip (top right) and knife-pared unglazed exterior.

Miscellaneous contexts and forms (Figure 81)

1. 81. Chafing dish with mid green internal and external glaze (693, pit [686]).
2. 82–3. Lids, or 82 the base of a chafing dish stand, with external light green glaze; 83 a delicate wide-mouthed bowl, unglazed (693 as above; 644).
3. 84–5. Large unglazed horizontal handles (rather than feet), formerly applied to a gently curving vessel wall (both 616; 85 a definite waster).

Architectural Ceramics

Architectural ceramics are represented by more than 6000 sherds. If the kiln furniture is excluded, they make up 12% of the assemblage by sherd count but 25% by weight (Tables 14 and 16). Ridge tiles, which can almost always be distinguished from the other architectural ceramics, form almost half this total (49.7% by sherd count, 42% by weight). The remainder consist of floor-tiles and oven tiles, which are often indistinguishable in a fragmented state. Oven tiles are the more common of the two types among the recognisable fragments (61% of the total).

These figures probably do not represent well the relative quantities of these products made at Hemyock. On the one hand, flat tiles are far less prone to damage in the kiln than hollow wares, especially open forms, so the proportion of tiles produced may have been much higher than their proportion among the wasted sherds. On the other hand, oven tiles and floor-tiles were commonly reused in kiln structures, causing their retention on-site.

Ridge Tiles (Figure 82, Nos 86–93)

The ridge tiles seem to have been of a single uniform type with quite high and close-set moulded peaks (one pierced: No. 92), slightly thickened sides where they abutted their neighbours, and well-glazed slopes, sometimes with a trace of white slip (No. 86); no examples of applied plastic decoration (quite common in medieval Somerset) or brushed slip decoration were noted. One sherd from the bottom edge of a tile was pierced (No. 93). The backs are sanded.

Louvers

Single fragments of probable louver were present in contexts 696 and 716. Both consisted of part of a domed

Figure 79. Early sixteenth-century kiln waste from pit [589]: jugs. Scale 1:4 (*photo: S. Goddard*).

vessel with a small circular vent hole, with glaze dribbles and glaze spots.

Oven Tiles (Figure 83, Nos 96–7)

A distinctive feature of the Hemyock kiln waste is the presence of numerous flat moulded slabs of coarse unglazed tile, sometimes with additional chert inclusions in the fabric. Some 2625 fragments of this type were recovered: some 5% of the total collection by sherd count but 22% by weight. A high proportion of this material (74% by sherd count) was not firmly attributable to a specific type of tile, but 685 pieces were identified as examples of a specific form, consistent both in thickness and shape; they are identified here as oven tiles (see discussion below). The two intact examples of these products are wedge-shaped, like the voussoirs of an arch, and examination of the fragments showed repeatedly that in many instances the corners were not quite at 90 degrees, nor the sides parallel. Some 685 fragments of

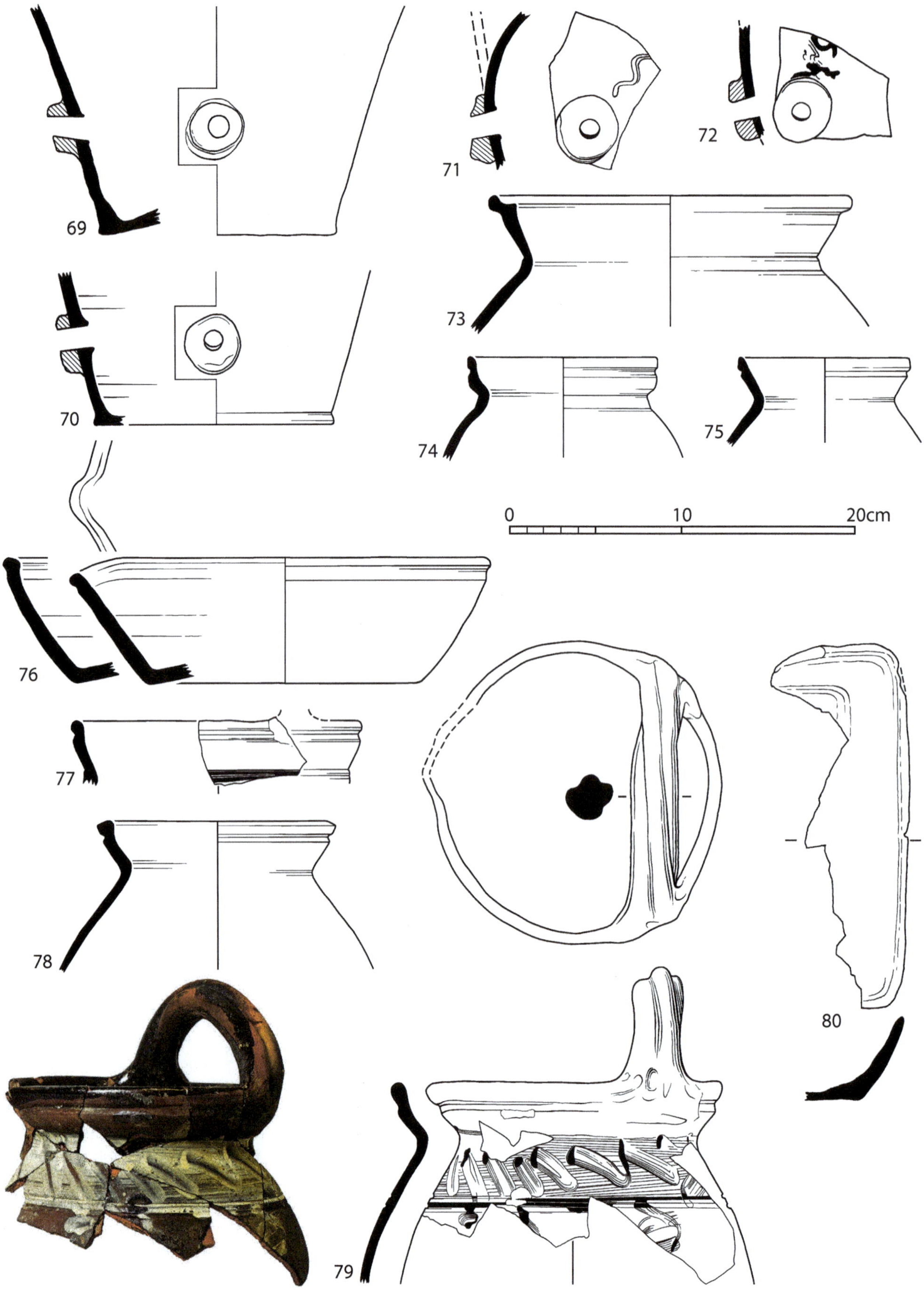

Figure 80. Early sixteenth-century kiln waste from pit [589]: cisterns, jars, etc. Scale 1:4 (*photo: S. Goddard*).

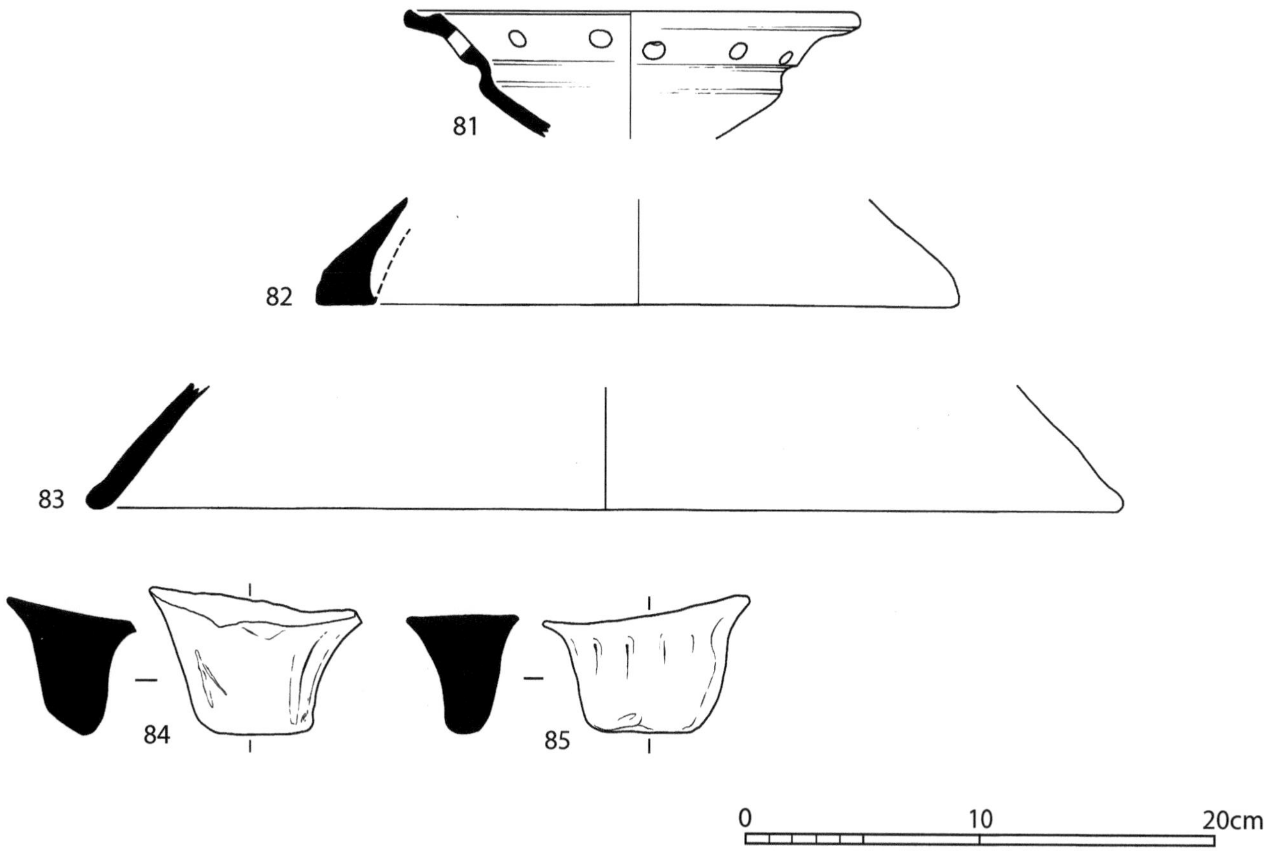

Figure 81. Early sixteenth-century kiln waste from other contexts. Scale 1:4 (*photo: S. Goddard*).

Table 16. Total quantities of architectural ceramics from all contexts

Form/Type	*No. sherds*	*Weight (kg)*
Ridge tile	3024	169.691
Louver	2	0.460
Two-colour floor-tile	38	3.682
Plain glazed floor-tile	123	15.569
Unglazed floor-tile	265	15.082
Oven tile	685	71.431
Oven or floor tile	1940	118.230
Total	**6090**	**395.558**

this type weighing 71.431 kg were firmly identified. Since a complete example 20 mm thick weighs 550 g, they represent the equivalent of about 130 complete tiles by weight. Some have slightly chamfered edges but others do not. The backs of most specimens are pierced with tapering rectangular holes, almost certainly achieved with a nail or a group of nails mounted in a block.

The dimensions of a sample of 95 examples from context 616 were recorded. They proved to be highly standardised products, the lengths of their bottom edges all in the range 99–104 mm, with top edges of 117–25 mm and their sides between 145–7 mm (details in archive). Initially their consistent thickness (Table 17) suggested to the writers that they might have been formed by rolling a slab of clay between two boards of fixed height. The potter John Hudson informs us, however, that it is unlikely, and that these tiles were probably made in moulds.

Table 17. Thicknesses of oven tiles (95 examples)

Thickness (mm)	**18**	**19**	**20**	**21**	**22**	**23**	**24**	**25**
No. of examples	3	2	52	7	13	9	7	2

Function of the 'Oven Tiles'

Hemyock is the third place where substantial collections of these tiles have been recovered, the others being at Donyatt (Coleman-Smith and Pearson 1988, 332–3) and Pitt Farm, Culmstock, in the neighbouring parish to Hemyock (Adams and Garrett 2015, section 3). At Pitt Farm the excavators made the interesting (and we think correct) observation that the impressions in the backs of some of the tiles found there were formed by impressing fossil crinoids into the tile (*ibid.*). A few wedge-shaped tiles of this type have also been recovered from farm and village sites in East Devon; they are present in small numbers, for example in the Nan Pearce fieldwalking collection from Membury and Stockland (finds at the RAM Museum, Exeter). Hitherto they have been classified as 'kiln tiles' or as tiles suitable for flooring an oven; in the latter case tiles of differing radius and curvature would have been needed to form the concentric rings in an oven floor. The samples

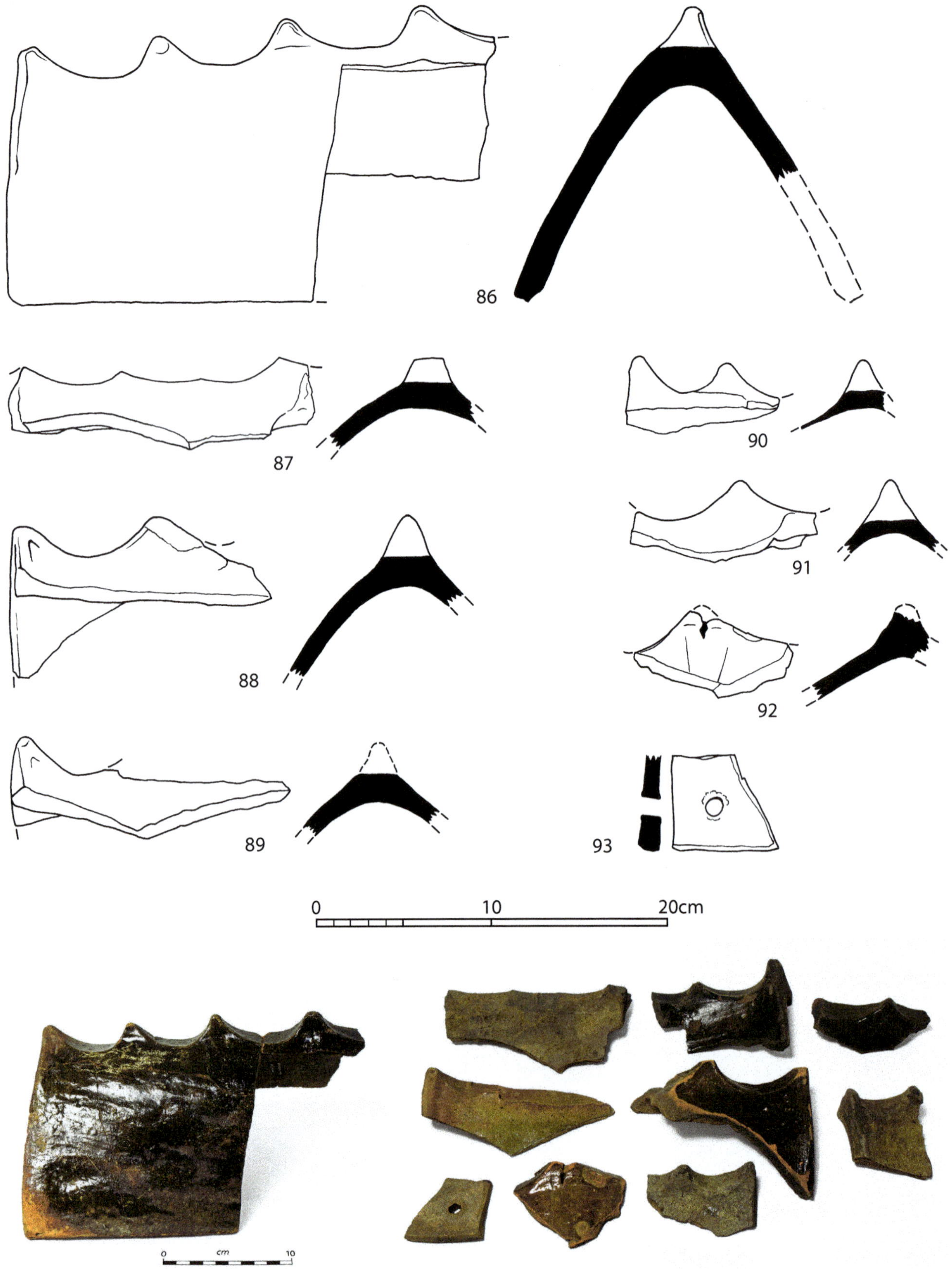

Figure 82. Early sixteenth-century kiln waste: ridge tiles. Scale 1:4 (*photo: S. Goddard*).

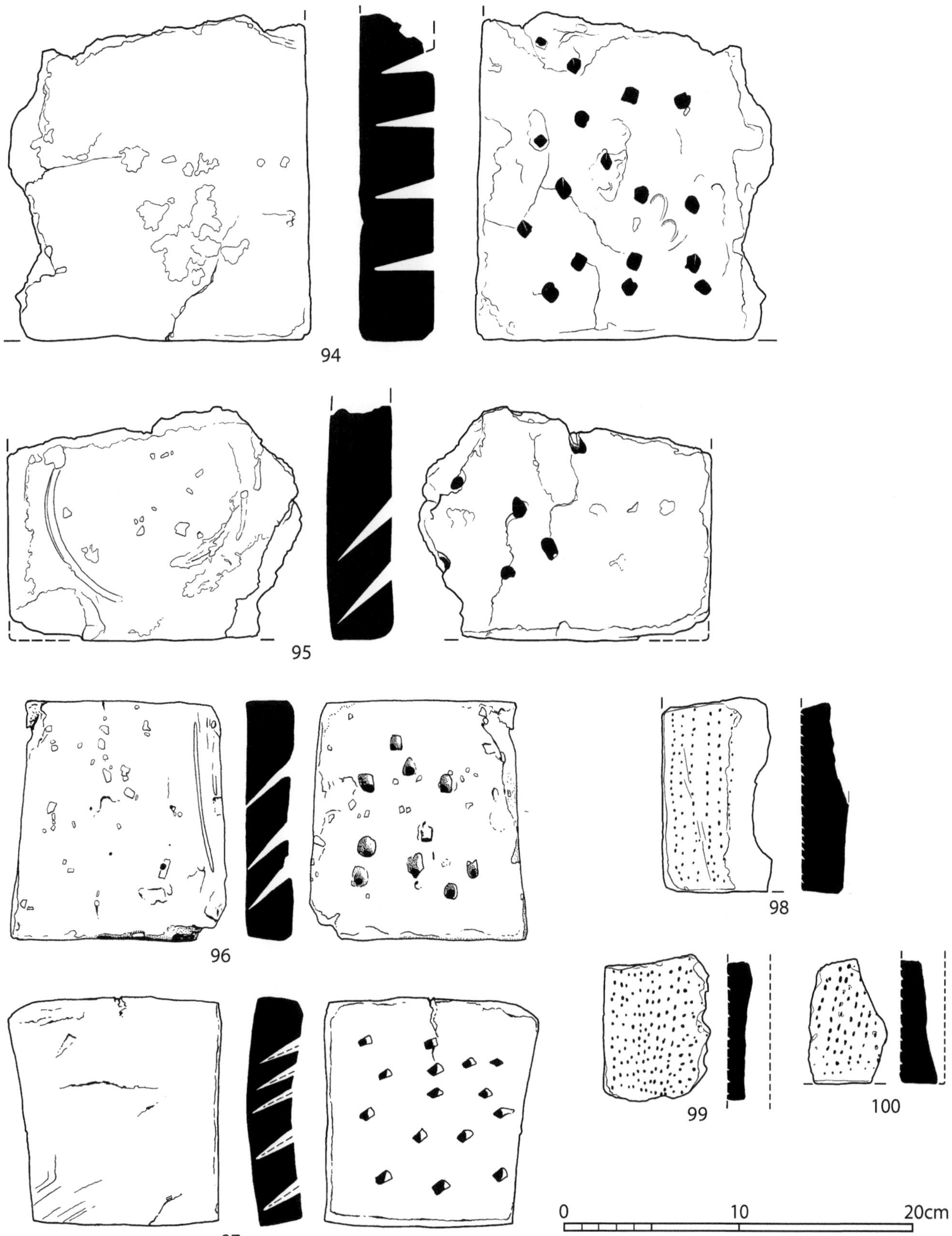

Figure 83. Early sixteenth-century kiln waste: floor-tiles (94–5) oven tiles (96–7) and tiles with fine stab-marks (98–100). Scale 1:4 (*photo: S. Goddard*).

from Hemyock and Pitt Farm are however of uniform dimensions.

We have asked a number of specialists in the vernacular buildings of East Devon and South Somerset whether they had seen tiles of this type in standing buildings (We are grateful to John Thorp, Stuart Blaylock and Nat Alcock for their comments). Peter Child was able to offer us one possible parallel: the oven of the ground-floor kitchen of the east wing of Netherton Hall, Farway, East Devon (SX 1845 9586). The walls of the oven consist of courses of small thin tiles, comparable in size to the Hemyock finds.

Floor-Tiles

At Hemyock, as at other kilns in the South West including Donyatt, Bideford, Great Torrington and Barnstaple, wasted floor-tile fragments have been found intermixed with domestic pottery (Coleman-Smith and Pearson 1988, 325, 327, 330; Allan *et al.* 2005, 173–4; Allan *et al.* 2007, 146; unpublished finds from South West Archaeology's excavation at the Exeter Inn, Barnstaple). Separate tile kilns are not known in the region in the late Middle Ages or early modern period. It therefore appears that tiles were fired in these kilns alongside domestic earthenware. Even in the case of the North Devon kilns which were major producers of relief-decorated paving-tiles, the tile waste forms a surprisingly low proportion of the total waste: a fraction of 1% (references cited above). This low figure may result from the fact that flat tiles are far less prone to damage in the kiln than hollow wares, especially open forms; the proportion of flat wares produced may have been much higher that their proportion of the wasted sherds.

The paving-tiles are discussed in full by Laurence Keen, below.

The Paving-Tiles

Laurence Keen

A total of 73 decorated tile fragments were recovered. They may be divided into four distinct groups, on the basis of the presence of two-colour decoration, sizes and other types of decoration. Group 1 tiles (25 examples) have shallow stamped decoration with most inlaid with white slip, others stamped but with a minimal amount of inlay. The majority are fragmentary and generally over fired. Tiles of Group 2 (nine examples) have a brushed slip on the upper surface, decorated with free-hand additions. Group 3 tiles (nine examples) have a brushed slip on the top surface, one with *sgraffito* decoration. Tiles of Group 4 (30 examples) are all plain with glaze over white slip, or with only an iron-rich glaze.

The Tile Groups

Group 1

This is the largest group, with 25 examples (context 571:3; 591:1; 616:18; 644; 1; 674:1; 712:1). When the designs are sufficiently discernible they are illustrated here (Figure 84, 1–7). Most are over-fired, reduced and warped wasters. Thicknesses are usually between 18 and 20mm, with four shallow scoops on the complete examples. Where the design has not been properly filled with slip, the stamp is only 0.55mm deep (Figure 84, 4). Only one tile has no signs of being a waster (Figure 84, 8).

Group 2

Nine fragments (context 571:2; 616:4; 696:2; 697:1) have slipped decoration with an iron-rich glaze, and a steep bevelled edge and sideways cut shallow scoops on the backs. The shallow designs (Figure 84, 9–12) all appear to have been applied free hand.

Group 3

Nine examples (context 619:7; 697:2) have brushed-slip top surfaces. None allows the complete size to be determined. Only one shows a thickness of 24 mm, and one has minimal *sgraffito* decoration (Figure 84, 13).

Group 4

The plain white-slipped examples, nineteen in total (context 616:17; 693:2) are from tiles either a maximum of 120, 173 or 197 mm square, when one edge is complete. The average thickness is 23 mm, with almost vertical edges. The unsanded backs all have remains of vertically cut circular keying scoops about 15 mm deep and 25 mm in diameter. The majority have the impressions of holes, 6–10 mm square and up to 14 mm deep, added after the scoops had been cut. One tile has small nail holes rather than square impressions: these, too, added after the scoops had been cut. No example is large enough for the number of scoops on complete tiles to be determined.

Eleven tiles have no white slip, only an iron-rich glaze on the upper surface (context 601:1; 616:6; 4 with no marked context). With unsanded backs, these, too, have circular scoops, 25 to 30 mm in diameter and the same impressions, a maximum of 6 mm square and up to 13 mm deep. One tile from 616 has a diagonal side of 194mm, not from a scored and broken half tile from a complete quarry, but formed from the start as a triangular tile. Another has a diagonal side, but this has been broken from a complete square tile, scored in half before firing.

Discussion

The discovery of this assemblage is extremely important for the study of medieval tiles, not only in Devon, but for the South West generally. For, no other kiln sites producing

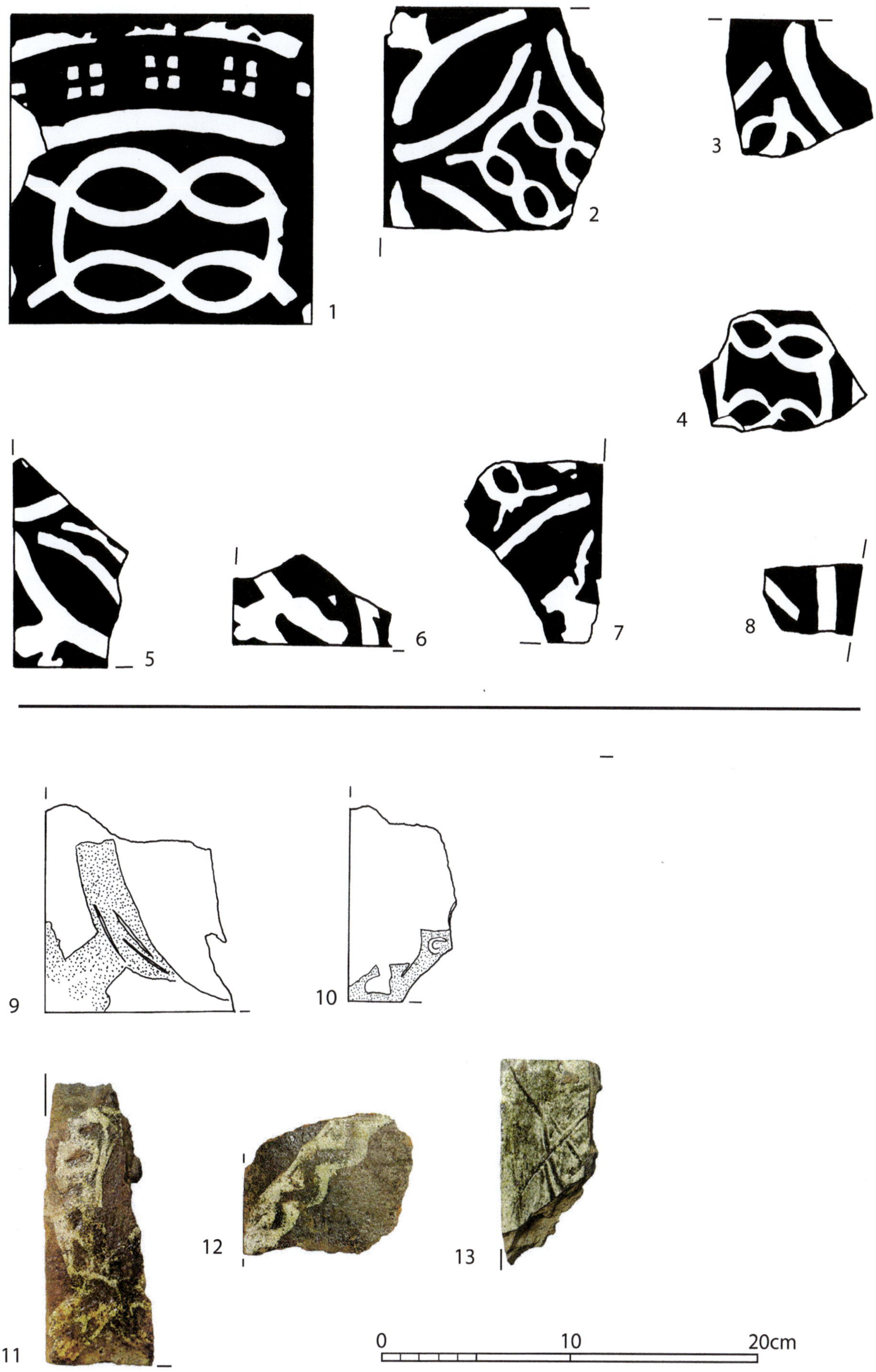

Figure 84. 1–8, Hemyock, Group 1. Scale 1:3. *Drawn by Laurence Keen.* **9–12, Hemyock, Group 2. Scale 1:4.13, Hemyock, Group 3. Scale 1:4.**

paving-tiles are known in Devon: the nearest production site is at Donyatt, Somerset, where the evidence is limited, but this, nevertheless, with the Hemyock material, helps us to understand the dynamics of floor-tile production and distribution in the region.

Group 1

The tiles are easily identifiable with the same designs found in several churches in East Devon, which, before the Hemyock excavations enabled the author to propose that the tiles belong to the *East Devon Group.* For the Hemyock designs (Figure 84, 1–8), 1 used the same stamp as design 6 (Figure 85), and fragments 2–7 all belong to design 10: the design from which fragment 8 comes is uncertain. The design parallels for the rest of the group in Devon and Somerset are detailed in the Gazetteer below, and the considerations of dating and design influence are discussed later in this section.

Techniques of Manufacture and Laying of Pavements

The designs are usually inlaid with white slip, but this is no more than a maximum of 1mm deep. Some have crisp edges to the designs, with the slip at a slightly lower level than the surrounding fields. This suggests that 'slip-over-stamp' was sometimes used, but not consistently. The loose tiles from Hemyock and from the excavations at Woodbury, show that the tiles were made with steep, knife-cut sides. The backs, always unsanded, usually have five shallow, knife-cut scoops. For the layout of the pavements, it should be noted that the evidence suggests that all of the tiles in this group were laid at ninety degrees to the walls of the churches, since no diagonally cut tiles have been found. Furthermore, there are no plain tiles, so the decorated tiles were laid without any plain tiles surrounding the decorated panels.

Inscriptions

The repertoire of designs (Figures 85, 1-15 and 86, 16-17) includes inscriptions, the letters left on the quarry with their backgrounds stamped and filled with slip, so appearing, after the glazing, in black or brown. The letter-forms are simple, but there are mistakes. Designs 1 and 2 have *confido in dno* (*in domino confido* – Psalm 11.1) but the extensions over *o* and *i* are not needed. Designs 3 and 17 are not found together and are of different sizes, but would have produced *Ave maria iesus.* Design 15, from Cadeleigh, *ARIA*, must surely have been part of another inscription with *AVE MARIA*. Design 16, found only at Woodbury, has *AVE M*, dark against a white background. It was obviously part of another four-tile *AVE MARIA* inscription, but the second tile has not been found. The quarter of a Tudor rose in the corner demonstrates that the tiles were intended to be used in groups of four, arranged so that the rose was completed in the adjacent sets of four. Design 4 was also designed to be laid in groups of four. Designs 5, 6 and 7 were obviously intended to be laid as a set of nine tiles. In Devon this is a unique occurrence.

The Devon inscriptions should be considered in more general contexts. It may be noted that none is found in the earlier repertoire of designs in Exeter Cathedral, that at Buckfastleigh there is one tile with *Iesus*, dark against a slip background (Exeter Archaeology project 6393), and that at Stoke Rivers a tile of the *North Devon Inlaid Group*, belongs to a four-tile design in a circle containing an inscription which defies deciphering (it starts with *o v*). At Weare Gifford there is another tile belonging to the later relief group, the design stamped on a larger quarry, but without inlay: it appears to belong to the same four-tile set with another part of the inscription, which is not sensible (Cramp 2012, 138, Fig. 3, 16). These demonstrate that, not only were the carvers of the wooden stamps literate enough to comprehend the texts, but they had the skill to produce a coherent text, bearing in mind that the letters had to be carved in reverse.

Tiles with devotional texts to the Virgin Mary, are not unexpected but are somewhat rare. One from Pitstone, Buckinghamshire, probably made at Penn, has the inscription *AVE MARIA GRATIA PLENA* (Hohler 1942, P3, 29, 105). In the Cistercian abbey of Rievaulx, Yorkshire, there are tiles with *AVE MARIA,* and from Rievaulx and Byland *AVE MARIA G* (Eames 1980, designs 1434, 1435). From Whalley Abbey, Lancashire, and Meaux, Yorkshire, are tiles with *AVE MARIA* (Beaulah 1929, Fig. 41; 1933, Fig. 14).

The finest set of tiles with devotional texts to the Virgin was made by the Malvern tilers for the Lady Chapel in Gloucester Cathedral in about 1480. The pavement includes four-tile sets with the inscription *Ave maria gratia plena*, and sixteen-tile sets with the text *Ave maria gratia plena Dominus tecum*, the texts all inlaid.The inscription *In Domino confido* is rare. Hohler collected designs from the Little Brickhill kilns in Buckinghamshire and published one (Hohler 1942, 27 and 127, LB 11) with the poorly executed inscription *In Domino confido*, contained on one tile and to be viewed from the outside not the centre (Figure 87). Mynard's re-excavation of the kiln site and reassessment of the tiles published all of the designs with new drawings (Mynard 1975). His designs 10 and 10a (*ibid.,* 69) are reproduced here, though, despite Hohler's convincing reading of the inscription, he wrote that it 'bears an illegible inscription' (*ibid.,* 61–2). Eames, too, ignored Hohler's reading, noting that her design 1444 (catalogue nos 1356, 3269 and 3270) 'includes a circular band decorated with a series of strokes, circles and squiggles that looks like an illiterate copy of an inscription' (Eames 1980, 267).

Mynard considered the tiles to be 'of late medieval date' and 'could have been made at any time during the fifteenth century' (Mynard 1975, 74). Eames's further consideration of the material placed the tiles in the 16th century, 'perhaps within the first three decades' (*ibid.,* 268).

Figure 85. *East Devon Group* **designs 1-15. Scale 1:4.** *Drawn by Laurence Keen.*

Figure 86. *East Devon Group* **designs 16-17. Scale 1:3.** *Drawn by Laurence Keen.* **18, Westleigh, North Devon. 19 design in Abbot Sebrok's pavement, Gloucester Cathedral, dated 1455. Scale 1:4.** *Drawn by Laurence Keen.*

Figure 87. Tile from Little Brickhill, Buckinghamshire. Scale 1:3. Courtesy of the Trustees of the British Museum.

The Devon tiles are of special interest since the inscriptions all appear as dark letters against a background of white slip. The letter forms are well cut, somewhat naive, but nevertheless readable. In general terms the tiles may be compared with tiles in northern England, where, as Stopford has noted 'the lettering appeared dark against a light background on the finished tiles' (Stopford 2005, 82).

Dating

The pottery, discussed above, suggests a date of *c.* 1500–50 for its production. This date provides a possible date for the manufacture of the floor-tiles. For Devon, as for other regions, the dating of tiles is often speculative. Exceptionally, documentary evidence or a sequence for the design development allows a chronology to be suggested. In Devon, it is fortunate that the Exeter Cathedral fabric accounts provide, not only secure dates of 1279–80 and at least 1325–6 for the tiles laid in the cathedral, but for the introduction of well-made designs deriving from tiles in Wessex, produced in the late 1240s and 1250s (Allan and Keen 1984, 234–6). But this dating provides only a *terminus post quem* for the rest of the tiles made in Devon.

Whatever date may be suggested for the floruit of tile production in the county, it has been shown that in North Devon, stamps for the production of a group of inlaid tiles, made in the Barnstable-Bideford area, were used on larger, gravel-tempered relief tiles produced in the seventeenth and eighteenth centuries in the same area (Keen 1969, 150), suggesting that Ward Perkins's pertinent observation that 'These printed [*sic*] tiles belong probably to the early sixteenth century, or at the earliest to the close of the fifteenth century, and they were thus contemporary with the earliest of the post-medieval relief-tiles characteristic of this area, by which they were in turn eventually supplanted' was not far off the mark (1941, 44).

Tiles from this *North Devon Inlaid Group* are particularly well represented in the churches of Westleigh and Stoke Rivers. They are all two-colour, not only well designed but technically competent. Despite Ward Perkins's comment suggesting a late-fifteenth or early sixteenth-century date, they are not yet fully published, although it is this writer's intention that they should form part of a census of tiles from Devon and Cornwall. However, their dating needs to be addressed here in the context of a suggested date for the *East Devon Group*. One design (19 here), a quarter circle enclosing the arms of Clare, should be considered for the first time. It is very similar to one tile in Abbot Sebrok's pavement in Gloucester Cathedral. This pavement has a splendid sixteen-tile design which incorporates a tile with the date 1455 (design 18 here). The conclusion, therefore, is that, first, not only was the Gloucester design translated to North Devon from Malvern, where the Gloucester tiles were made, perhaps by one of the tilers with a pattern book, but, secondly, that tiler may have been responsible for establishing the *North Devon Inlaid Group*, at some time after 1455, most probably in the closing years of the fifteenth century. Such a date might fit well for the *East Devon Group*, since the tiles from Hemyock were associated with pottery of *c*. 1500. Unfortunately, there is no secure architectural dating for any of the tiles in the *East Devon Group*, but it is not beyond the bounds of possibility that the tiles from Woodbury may belong to the building of the new north aisle of the church, completed in the 1530s (Cherry and Pevsner 1989, 917).

It may be suggested that the *East Devon Group* carries on the traditions of the *North Devon Inlaid Group* and was contemporary with, or heralded the arrival of a later group made for Newenham Abbey, Axminster. This group has inlaid tiles bearing the arms of Hugh Oldham, bishop of Exeter, 1505-19, and those of Abbot John Ellys (1512-24). It was thought that these tiles were made and laid between 1512 and 1519, but a later date is feasible (Allan and Silvester 1981, 166 and fig. 4, 12–17). These may be compared with tiles for Hailes Abbey, Gloucestershire, designed during the abbacy of Stephen Sagar between 1527 and 1539, with single, four- and sixteen-tile patterns, which are 'some of the most beautifully drawn tile designs known' (Eames 1980, I, 257–63).

All of this material demonstrates that paving-tiles were being made right up to the Dissolution, and that some tilers survived to produce the eclectic Renaissance tiles for Sir William Sharington Lacock Abbey, Wiltshire, in about 1550 (Gotch 1901, 30 and pl. IX; Tait 1970; Eames 1980, 266).

Floor-Tiles and the Reformation

Devotional inscriptions addressed to the Virgin Mary, and two with a quote from a psalm, may be considered in the context of the Reformation's affect on old liturgical and religious practices and observances, when rood-screens, paintings, images of saints, stained glass windows, relics and altars were swept away. For Devon the process has been brilliantly described by Orme (2013, 151-90): his review supersedes any previous account in its details and references. In Exeter, the churchwarden's accounts for the church of St Petrock provide dramatic details of the demolition of the rood, the washing away of images and overpainting with lime wash, removing the pulpit and a side altar, and then the sale of images and the high altar, between 1547 and 1550 (Dymond 1882, 453–4, quoted by MacCaffrey 1975, 190–1).

With windows deprived of their saints, niches without statues, altars demolished and rood-screens with the saints defaced, the survival of floor-tiles with religious texts seems somewhat curious. Was this because the officials did not understand the Latin, or that, for the churches in out-of-the-way locations, the officials had too little time for an extensive purge on what had to be removed? Or, was it simply that the removal of large areas of flooring would have caused too much disruption?

Groups 2 and 3

Tiles with free-hand decoration (Group 2) have no known parallels in Devon, but may provide a link with tiles from Donyatt, Somerset, as does the single example of Group 3.

Tiles with designs applied in white slip exist in the collections from Launceston Priory, Cornwall (Peter 1896, Figs 6–9), and Frithelstock, Devon (Radford 1935, Pls XLVII, 1–2 and XLVIII, 1–4). This technique is unusual and was first recognised at Campsea Ash Priory, Suffolk (Keen 1971, 147 and Fig. 40, 16–19). For the tilers this technique obviated the necessity of producing a design produced by a carved stamp and allowed free-hand individual expression. It is clear that this freedom allowed some tilers to produce tiles with only simple slip decoration, brushed, and/or with simple free-hand incised *sgraffito* additions. The brushed-slip decoration found at Hemyock may be paralleled with tiles made at Donyatt, Somerset, with examples found at Sherborne and Shaftesbury Abbeys, Dorset (Emden 1977, designs 245–9; Keen 2005, 127). It may be significant that the treatment of the backs, with scoops and impressed small keys, seems to be the usual technique for these tiles.

The evidence from the excavations at Donyatt provides, not only interesting parallels, but raises crucial questions. Slip-decorated and tiles with *sgraffito,* dated by the excavator to 1500-50, have nail holes and scoops on the backs (Coleman-Smith and Pearson 1988, 323, and fig.169, 34/2 – 34/9, 34/12; Coleman-Smith 2002, fig. 22, 34/2-34/4, fig. 23, 34/5-34/10, with dating changed to 1500-75). Additionally, the excavations yielded tiles with inlaid decoration (*idem* 1988, Figs 34/1, 34/14, 34/10, 34/15, 34/17-34/20; 2002, 34/12). It is noteworthy, that one inlaid design is used on a larger quarry than intended for the stamp, and that the same design is used without any inlay.

It is clear that the Donyatt potteries were producing inlaid tiles in the medieval period. Seven designs from Sherborne

Abbey (Group 4, Keen 2005, 125, 127) have a fabric similar to that found at Donyatt, as well as the same designs, but David Williams' analysis of samples from Sherborne and Donyatt does not provide conclusive evidence that the Sherborne group was made in Donyatt, but such a conclusion is very likely (*ibid.*, 127), in which case, Donyatt would provide an example of medieval stamps being used in a post-medieval industry, to be paralleled in the pottery centres of North Devon (Keen 1969, 150).

A possible link with Donyatt is provided by Group 12 inlaid tiles at Cleeve Abbey, Somerset (Harcourt 2000, 61–2, Fig. 25, 167–9).

While it can be established that the Donyatt kilns were producing inlaid tiles and that some of the stamps were used in the post-medieval industry, there is no reason to suggest that this had any affect on the production of tiles for Devon. This is probably not the case for the slip-decorated and *sgraffito* tiles found at Hemyock. The question as to whether the Hemyock tiles influenced the Donyatt production, or if the motivation was the other way, must remain open, but there is clearly a connection.

Group 4

Undecorated tiles must always have been a common production, so those in Group 4 are not exceptional. Their significance here is their size and the treatment of the bottom surfaces, not only with circular scoops, but with square impressions, from a small square wooden tool or metal implement, or nails: all to aid, not only the firing process, but to facilitate an easy keying on the mortar base bed on which they were laid. Without analyses of the fabric, it is presently impossible to place these within the wide range of plain tiles in Devon. It should be noted that fabric analyses of plain tiles, so frequently ignored or discarded, may produce interesting results, as shown at Ottery St Mary (Allan and Keen 2006).

Conclusion

The material from Hemyock is, without any doubt, the most important evidence for the manufacture of floor-tiles in Devon. Although it was not directly associated archaeologically with a kiln, the fragments and wasters demonstrate that it was.

Despite the fact that the assemblage is somewhat small, its analysis, with four identifiable groups, is extremely important for its contribution to the study of paving-tiles in the West Country, and in Devon in particular.

The Group 1 tiles are of special interest since they confirm an East Devon production, previously recognised only by designs in several churches and their general appearance (Figure 88).

It should be noted that a nine-tile design, as seen at Buckland-in-the-Moor (Figure 85, 5–7), is unusual. Such an arrangement is not found anywhere else in the South West. Multiple tile arrangements of nine and sixteen are closely paralleled in the Midlands. In Worcester Cathedral there are nine- and sixteen-tile designs, datable to 1377–80 (Keen 1978, 157, Figs 6, 9). They exist especially in Gloucester Cathedral, in Abbot Sebrok's pavement, dated internally and designed in 1455, and in the Lady Chapel for a splendid series of four- and sixteen-tile designs, datable to the completion of the chapel in the 1480s. As Eames (1951, 37) noted, the Canynges pavement from Bristol 'bears a striking resemblance in general layout and design' to Abbot Sebrok's pavement. The Canynges pavement, now datable to between 1481 and 1515, contains nine different sets of sixteen-tile designs (*ibid.*, Pl. XXIV) and, like the Gloucester pavements, was no doubt made in the same tilery at Malvern. The decorated panels in these pavements are all surrounded by plain, dark tiles: a feature not indicated for the Group 1 tiles.

These sets must have required considerable expertise, not only in cutting the design stamps, but in their laying. This may be the reason why such arrangements are not found frequently.

Might it be suggested that the nine-tile arrangement at Buckland-in-the-Moor resulted from a connection between Devon and Midlands tilers? Such a link is not altogether impossible, since one tile design in Abbot Sebrok's pavement (Figure 86, 19) is remarkably similar to one design in the *North Devon Inlaid Group* at Westleigh (Figure 86, 18). Tiles in this group are well made and designed, so with this design link, must have been made after 1455, providing a *terminus post quem* for the somewhat inferior designs and technique for the *East Devon Group*.

In addition to the nine-tile design at Buckland-in-the-Moor, the devotional inscriptions in the group are exceptional in the corpus of tiles in the South West. Again, it may be suggested that there might have been some workshop connection between Devon and the Midlands, where inscriptions were a familiar feature in pavements.

The distribution of the Group 1 tiles (Figure 88) may pose questions if the production site is correct for all of the sites, since they are rather dispersed. Without documentary evidence the dynamics of distribution are rarely understood: the example of Windsor Castle, with copious accounts for the purchase, transport and laying of tile from Penn between 1351 and 1365 is exceptional (Keen 2002).

Inspired by E.M. Jope's distribution maps of pottery (Jope and Threlfall 1959, Figs 10, 13), this author attempted to provide a distribution map of tiles from the late fourteenth-century kiln at Bawsey, King's Lynn (Keen 1971, fig. 41; 1980, fig. 28: 2002, n. 40). It was noted that the majority of the tiles came from sites within a 20-mile radius, with five sites between 20 and 30 miles and four between 30 and 40 miles (Keen 1980, 218). The distribution of Penn tiles, with over 150 sites, is extensive

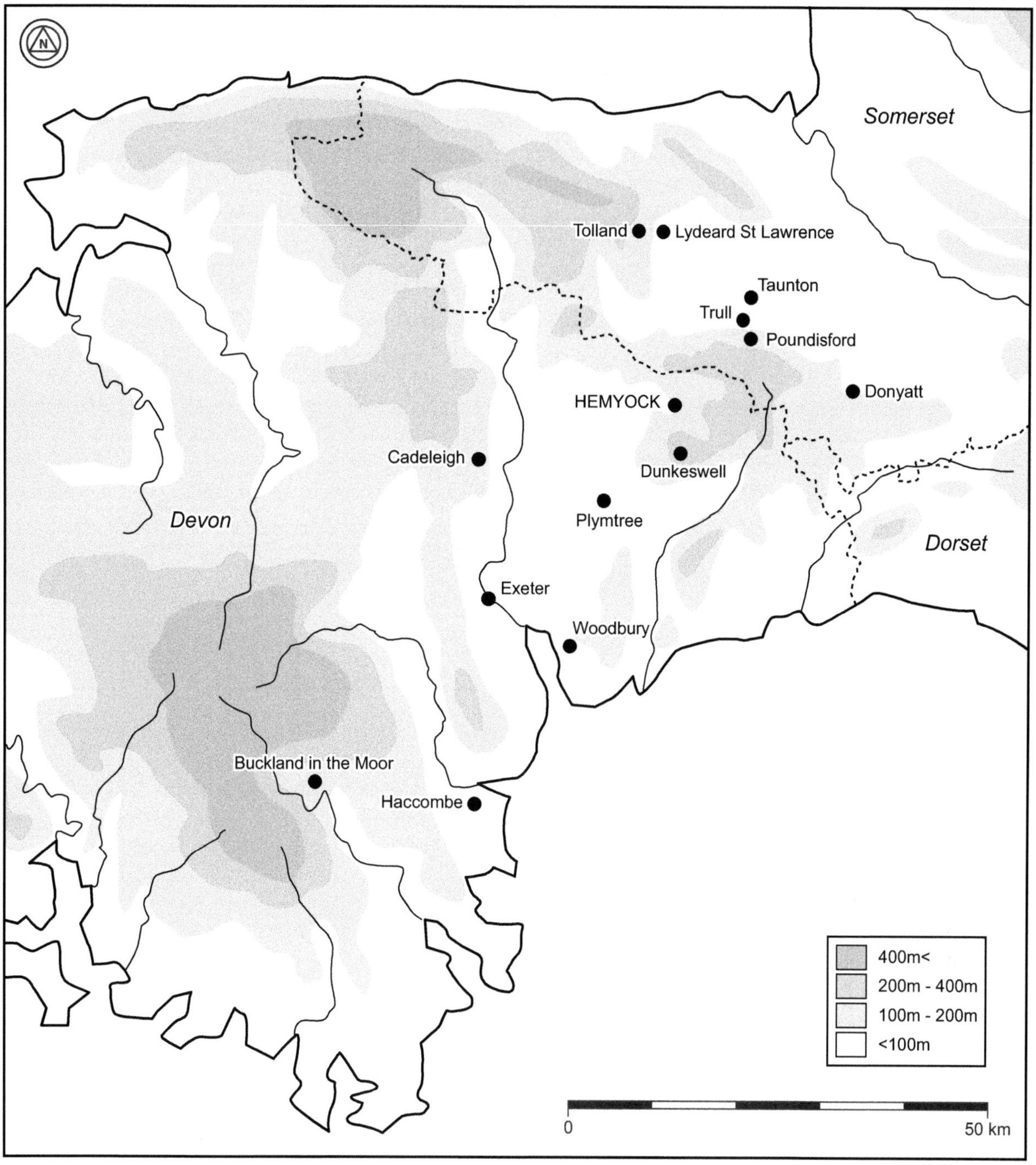

Figure 88. Distribution map of Group 1 sites.

but a very large number lie within 20 miles of Penn (Keen 2002, 228, fig. 9).

For the Group 1 tiles from Hemyock, the Devon distribution is not extensive. However, the distances, perhaps, are more than might be expected, and there is no cluster of sites close by: the furthest site is Buckland-in-the-Moor, at 35 miles (56 km). Ecclesiastical or family connections might have been responsible for such a wide-ranging distribution. But it should be suggested that the tilers were unlikely to have been itinerant, unless chemical analysis produces other evidence.

The discussion above for Groups 2 and 3 had to include reference to the Donyatt potteries as regards brushed slip- and *sgraffito*-decorated tiles. Additionally, the evidence that Donyatt produced inlaid tiles needed comment, since all the techniques used had to be considered, not only with regard to material from Sherborne and Shaftesbury Abbeys, but for their possible relevance for manufacture at Hemyock. Without any comparable material in Devon, the brushed slip and *sgraffito* tiles at Donyatt may, possibly, indicate a manufacturing contact between Donyatt and Hemyock: this is clearly not the case for the two-colour tiles of Group 1. The medieval inlaid and the later slip and *sgraffito* tiles at Donyatt indicate an unbroken sequence of production. Whether or not there was any influence from Donyatt on the Hemyock production must remain unclear, unless the analysis of the pottery from Hemyock and the discussion of stylistic and technical links between the two sites provides an answer to the question.

If the dating of the groups from Hemyock may be assigned correctly to the early sixteenth century, this must surely indicate that the East Devon tile-makers were totally aware of, and followed the floor-tile tradition of the centres that produced the fourteenth-century tiles for Exeter Cathedral and the later fifteenth/early sixteenth-century examples in North Devon. If floor-tile production was continuous or was interrupted in the later fourteenth century by the Black Death, in the present state of knowledge, this remains uncertain. However, the Hemyock material indicates an artisan production, which takes its place as part of the requirements for a place of worship, showing that, for the rebuilding of churches in the early sixteenth century, as suggested by Group 1 tiles at Woodbury, where the tiles might have been associated with the north aisle of the 1530s, older traditions were still accessible. It is a significant addition to the study of paving-tiles in Devon and important for the understanding of tile production in the South West generally.

Gazetteer of Tiles of Group 1, Other Than Hemyock

Distribution of Designs (Figures 85 and 86)

1. Buckland-in-the-Moor
2. Buckland-in-the-Moor; Cadeleigh; Haccombe
3. Buckland-in-the-Moor; Cadeleigh; Dunkeswell; Trull; Woodbury
4. Buckland-in-the-Moor; Woodbury
5. Buckland-in-the-Moor
6. Buckland-in-the-Moor; Cadeleigh; Woodbury
7. Buckland-in-the-Moor; Haccombe
8. Buckland-in-the-Moor
9. Buckland-in-the-Moor
10. Buckland-in-the-Moor; Cadeleigh; Haccombe; Woodbury
11. Buckland-in-the-Moor; Cadeleigh; Haccombe; Woodbury
12. Cadeleigh
13. Plymtree; Taunton
14. Plymtree
15. Cadeleigh
16. Woodbury
17. Lydeard St Lawrence; Poundisford Park; Tolland

Buckland-in-the-Moor, Devon, St Peter, Parish Church

Here is the largest collection of tiles in the group. The church guide book (St Peter's District Church Council, April 2011) notes that 'From 1850 the tiles were recorded as being scattered around the floor of the nave, but were collected and moved to their current position during the restoration which was completed in 1907.' They are now at the west end of the nave, underneath the tower arch. The sensitive relaying consists of six rows, east to west, and twenty, north to south, with a row of about one-third tiles along the northern edge (Figure 89). The designs are:

1 (1); **2** (23); **3** (17); **4** (2); **5** (5); **6** (3); **7** (8); **8** (2); **9** (1); **10** (2); **11** (4).

Some of the tiles are illustrated in http://www.legendarydartmoor.co.uk/images/Buckland10.gif.

Cadeleigh, Devon, St Bartholomew, Parish Church

The tiles have been relaid, randomly, in the Leach chapel in the north chancel aisle, with some at the west end of the nave. The designs present are:

2 (3); **3** (6); **6** (2 and a fragment); **10** (27); **11** (24 and two halves); **12** (1); **15** (1, bottom worn).

Dunkeswell, Devon, Abbey

An extensive collection of decorated tiles has been relaid in the sanctuary of the present church. A large number of tiles from the abbey was collected and relaid in Wolford Chapel nearby. Mitchell (1995) records one small fragment of his

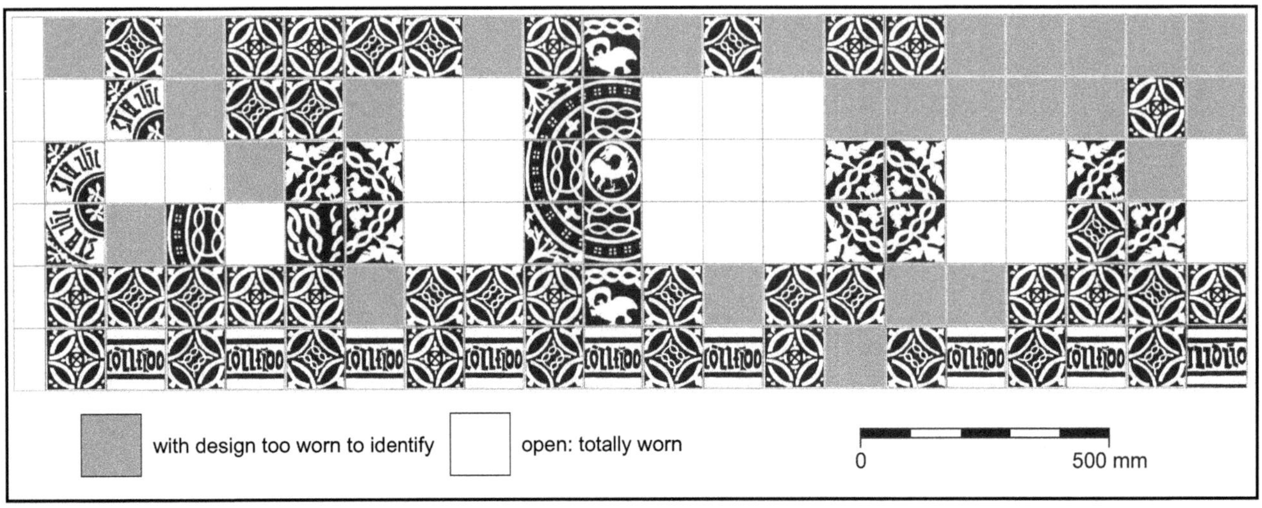

Figure 89. Buckland-in-the-Moor, tiles as presently laid. *Redrawn by J. Bird after an original by Laurence Keen.*

design 25, which seems to be part of design 3. No other pieces of this group are recorded.

Haccombe, Devon, St Blaise, Parish Church

The tiles here are of special interest, since they were recorded, with plans, by Augustus Wollaston Franks, on his visit to Devon, when he also recorded the pavements in Exeter Cathedral. Devon is not listed in Cherry's list of Franks's tours (1997, 186–7). His drawings were passed to Lord Alwyne Compton, who published a paper on them in 1846 (Compton 1846). The tiles are among the first to be published in any detail from England: the article includes a plan (opp. 152), but with no individual designs. The tiles also received the attention of Albert Way during 1841–51 (National Library of Wales) and a plan was published by Parker in 1850 (pl. 208). Twenty-seven designs were discussed again in 1921 by Searley, who published two plates of designs (pls I and II): pl. I design 11 is design 10 here. Among the designs not illustrated is '(c) A nondescript animal (?horse) within a circle' (*ibid.*, 195) – undoubtedly design 7. He also refers to a fragment, with 'some lettering in relief' (*ibid.*, 197), presumably design 2. Among the tiles, which are surely relaid, are:

2 (2); **7** (2); **10** (12); **11** (5).

The tiles are laid in the north aisle, mainly to the south of the monuments to Sir Hugh Courtney, d. 1425 and his wife, It is in this part of the church that there are plain Normandy tiles and polychrome tiles from Spain, with three designs.

Lydeard St Lawrence, Somerset, Parish Church

Design 17 (Lowe 2003, design 41).

Plymtree, Devon, St John, Parish Church

Around the ledger for Richard Harward, 1685, in the south aisle, are rows of single tiles of designs 13 or 14: nine in good condition and nine worn or fragmentary: two are over fired. The designs are not consistent: there is only one of design 13. Hallam 1951, 66, 71.

Poundisford Park, Somerset

In 1940 Ward Perkins published a set of tiles 'laid in the floor of the passage which connects the spiral staircase with the chamber believed formerly to have been the muniment room'. The house dates to *c.* 1546, but Ward Perkins, because medieval carved masonry was found there in 1929, considered that this, and the tiles were likely to have come from Taunton Priory (125, 127). A not wholly implausible alternative, he suggested, is that the tiles 'were made for the house when it was built'. One tile (pl. XI, 6) a quarter circle, has the inscription *Ave ma* (Lowe 2003, design 41). This is part of an inscription not found in Devon, but illustrated here are design 17. It is the beginning of an inscription found at Buckland-in-the-moor (design 3 here), *ria iesus*, paralleled at Trull (Ward Perkins 1940, pl. XI, 7; Lowe 2003, design 42) and found on a smaller tile from Lydeard St Lawrence and on a similar larger tile from Tolland, Somerset. A very debased version of the design 17 is found at Wootton Courtney, Somerset (Lowe 2003, design 562 For dating, Ward Perkins (1940, 128) thought that the tiles 'illustrate clearly the crudity into which local traditional craftmanship had fallen before it finally gave way to the new fancies of the Renaissance'.

Taunton, Somerset, St James's Churchyard

Design 13 (Lowe 2003, no. 217). It was published by Hallam (1951, 71 and Pl. VI, 24), who suggested that it was 'an importation', noting its occurrence at Plymtree.

Tolland, Somerset, St John the Baptist, Parish Church

Design 17 (Lowe 2003, design 41)

Trull, Somerset, All Saints, Parish Church

Design 3 (Ward Perkins 1940, design 7; Lowe 2003, design 42).

Woodbury, Devon, St Swithin, Parish Church

Sixty-six tile fragments, with thirteen complete tiles, were recovered from excavations in 2009–10 by AC Archaeology under the tower for kitchen facilities and lavatories (Wakeham and Firth 2012, Pls 6–8). The excavators concluded that the 'medieval tiles were from the main body of the church and predate 1409' when the tower was built (*ibid.*, 8); this dating cannot be sustained. Those belonging to this group are **3** (1); **4** (1); **6** (2 fragments, one complete); **10** (7); **11** (4); **16** (2). All of the tiles have shallow inlay of 0.5–1 mm and are 23–24 mm thick, all with steep bevels and four or five scoops on the back. One tile of design 11 shows that the stamp had a small crack. Here it may be suggested that the tiles could belong to the building of the north aisle in *c.* 1530.

Evidence of Kiln Furniture, Setting and Structure

David Dawson and Oliver Kent

Kiln Furniture (Figures 90 and 91, Nos 101–14)

Pierced Cylindrical Vessels

These are roughly thrown unglazed vessels with simple thickened upright rims, cylindrical or slightly tapered bodies and flat bases. Many sherds display a hole cut in the side just above the base, and this was probably a feature of every vessel. In all 2,277 sherds weighing 159.58 kg were recovered. The greatest concentrations were from contexts 616 in pit [715] (1,250 sherds weighing 80.56 kg)

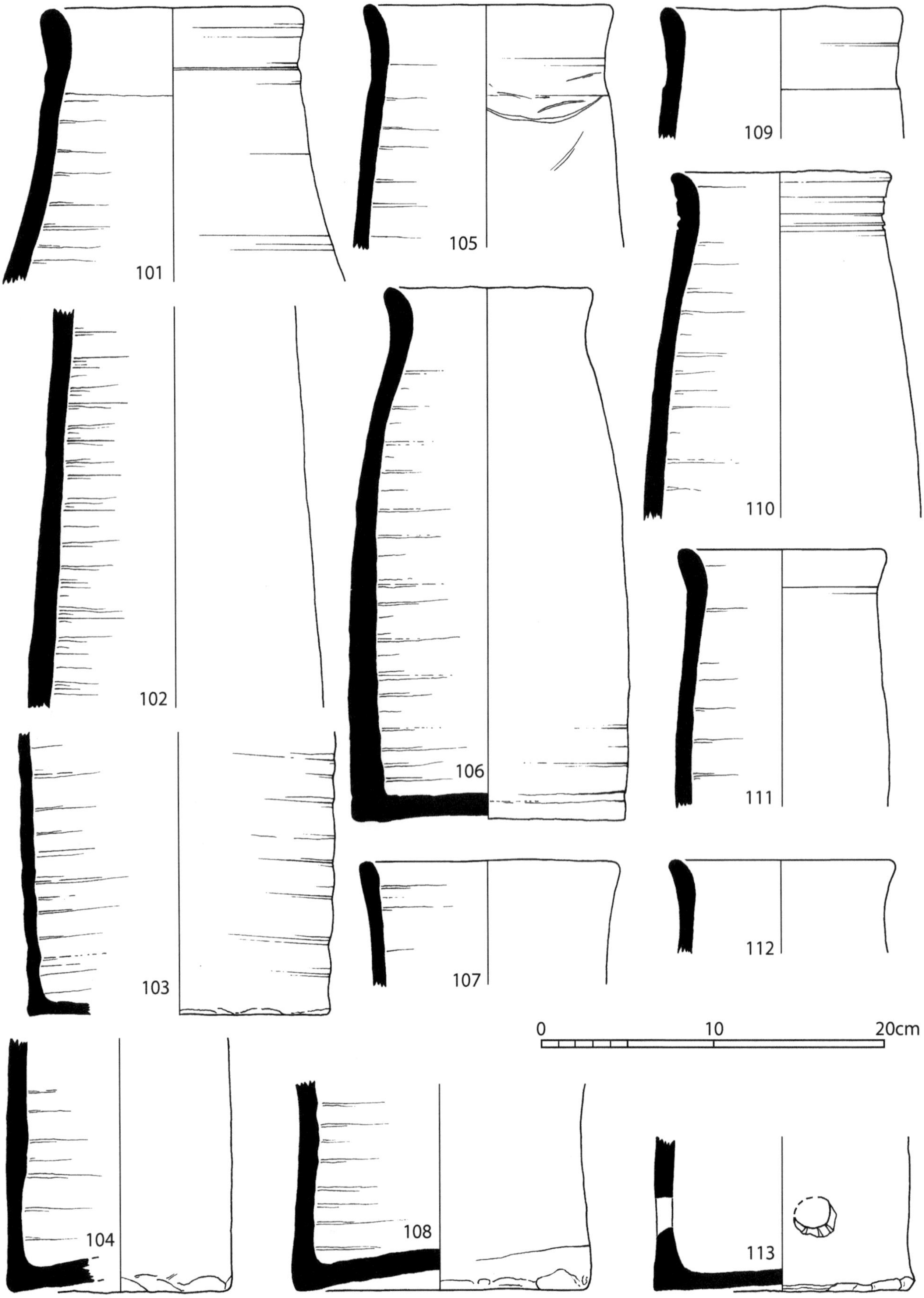

Figure 90. Cylindrical kiln furniture from context 588 (*drawn by S. Goddard*).

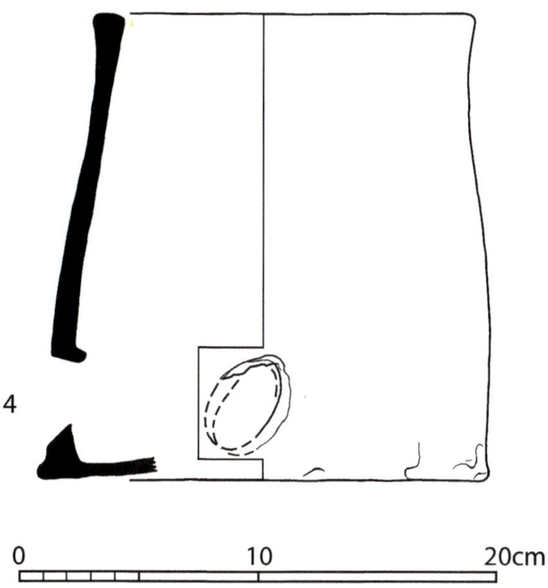

Figure 91. Complete profile of a cylindrical kiln prop from context 628 (*drawn by S. Goddard*).

Table 18. Measurements of base diameters of cylindrical props in context 588 (sample of 86 rims)

Rim diameter (cm)	**6**	**6.5**	**7**	**7.5**	**8**	**8.5**	**9**	**9.5**	**10**	**??**
No. of vessels	2	2	3	8	13	49	5	–	5	1

and 588 in pit [589] (462 sherds weighing 42.87 kg). Many were reduction-fired and showed signs of being fired repeatedly. With a single exception, there were no signs of glaze splashes or even patches of vaporized glaze on any of them. The slightly tapering shape would allow practical stacking despite the variations in dimensions. The rims range from 60 mm to 110 mm wide, the average rim being 82 mm. Base diameters are similar. The few complete or near-complete profiles suggest a height range of 200–300 mm (Table 18).

The precise function of these vessels cannot at present be deduced, either from evidence from Hemyock or from similar examples elsewhere. Although such vessels are often published as saggars, i.e. vessels that contain and protect small glazed vessels during firing, the key problem is that they are very small – too small to contain any of the forms occurring with them archaeologically.

Saggars are also commonly marked with areas of glaze. The only strong evidence for the use of saggars before the introduction of such technology with the tin-glaze industry in the late sixteenth century is from a relatively small number of sites, notably those associated with the production of Cistercian ware cups at Wrenthorpe (Yorks) *c.* 1500–50 (Brears 1967, 34–5; Moorhouse and Roberts 1992, 104–5, 136–7) and black-glazed cups as at Harlow (Essex) *c.* 1620–50 (Davey and Walker 2009, 152–5). Here the cup is placed on the base of the inverted saggar and a second saggar placed over the top. Evidence of small pierced vessels untouched by glazes, such as those at Hemyock, is more common, and ranges from the medieval 'cooling tower' shapes at Colstoun, East Lothian, and Stenhousemuir, Falkirk (Hall 2004, 56, 61, 62; *idem* 2008, 18–19) to late seventeenth-century cylindrical vessels at the Stella Maris Convent site at Bideford and at Great Torrington, both North Devon (Allan *et al.* 2005, 172, 186, 188; *idem* 2007, 142). Perhaps the nearest broadly contemporary parallels are the examples from the unpublished excavations by South West Archaeology at the Exeter Inn, Barnstaple, Devon (pers. obs. the authors).

It is suggested here that the probable function of these vessels was as props in loading the ware. One possible piece of evidence is provided by two collapsed bowls. By the form of the galleried rims of the bowls it is clear that the galleries were designed to bear the weight of an inverted stack of identical vessels. The centre of the inside of what would have been the bottom vessel of the stack is unglazed and bears the circular mark of a cylindrical support (Figure 92). It is probable that one of the shorter vessels such as 14 illustrated could have provided the support required to help prevent the rim tearing and spreading under the weight during firing. Although there is no other evidence for similar use of cylindrical vessels from Britain, it was common practice in the Eastern Mediterranean (see evidence from Mikro Pisto and Veria in Papazotou 1999 and Zikos 1999). There is scope for further research on sites producing vessels with this type of rim to see if other instances can be found. Another way in which such props function is illustrated by the potters of Bahla in Oman where to achieve the tightest possible pack water jars are stacked inverted alternating with stacks of jars with the rim upward. Each stack of inverted jars is raised on a similar prop so that the neck of a vessel is paired with the belly of its neighbours (Gibson 2005, 47). However it should be emphasised that there is no evidence that jugs for example were stacked this way at Hemyock.

Conical Supports

Only one example from context 588 was sufficiently complete to be described fully:

Figure 92. Possible 'shadow' of a cylindrical support on the inside of a waste stack of pans.

Figure 93. Conical support.

Diameter 172 mm, surviving height 113 mm. Fabric coarse with large fragments of chert (?). Vertical finger-marks from fashioning the piece (Figure 93).

Another more fragmentary example was found in context 616, and probable parts of others occur in contexts 518 and 599, but once crushed these objects rapidly become unidentifiable amongst the other fired debris.

There are no precise parallels for such pieces from Britain. They may be a one-off solution to a specific packing problem. They may have served a similar function to the thrown mushroom props used in making Cistercian wares recorded at the Potovens/Wrenthorpe potteries near Wakefield, Yorkshire (Brears 1967, 34–5; Moorhouse and Roberts 1992, 105, 138) but this is unlikely as the Hemyock example has no signs of glaze scarring on the base. Indeed from the firing patterns seems to have been placed in contact with the floor with the missing top upward. A more likely function, as cited above, would be to support the centre of the base of a stack of inverted pans, as was common earlier practice in the Eastern Mediterranean (as at Mikro Pitro and Veria) but there is no direct evidence for this (Papazotou 1999; Zikos 1999).

'Oven' Tiles as Separators

These tiles are described above. Irrespective of their primary designed purpose, comparison with other sites such as Donyatt site 13 (Coleman-Smith 2002, 124–32) suggests that we may expect to see evidence of these tiles being used secondarily as supports and separators within the kiln pack. Evidence for this typically takes the form of glaze runs and adhesion marks from stacked vessels. There is no evidence that these were used in this way as kiln furniture at Hemyock but see the discussion below under evidence of kiln structure.

Kiln Setting

The range of evidence for the packing of the kilns is in the form of possible kiln furniture and both negative and positive evidence for the contact of vessels in the kiln. It would appear likely that pan forms were fired inverted resting on the backs of their rims using an unglazed pan at the bottom, placed on an unglazed cylindrical support. The galleried rim forms facilitate this method and occur on other production sites such as the early seventeenth-century site 2 at Donyatt (Coleman-Smith and Pearson 1988, 236–7). Hollow-ware forms appear to have been stacked inverted. The paucity of sherds of pottery and tile carrying evidence of being used to separate ware and the lack of glaze drips on the kiln furniture are unusual and may relate to the sparse nature of the glazing of the ware and the preponderance of forms glazed only internally.

Evidence of Kiln Structure

The two main pit groups (588 and 616) appear to contain debris representing the clearance of and demolition of one or more small pottery kilns built of tile and or clay. Evidence for the specific form of the kiln is lacking although the tapered form of the tiles would suggest a circular structure. Parallels for this kind of construction can be found in the local area particularly at Donyatt site 13 and probably took a form similar to the double-firebox open-topped structure as reconstructed in the Bickley experiments (Dawson and Kent 1999, 167–71).

Fired Clay Fragments

Substantial amounts of fired clay fragments were recovered from contexts 588 in pit [589] (191 fragments weighing 1.32 kg), 616 in pit [715] (619 fragments weighing 15.84 kg) and 687 in pit [686] (300 fragments weighing 3.88 kg). All tended to be hard-fired on the surface and of rapidly diminishing hardness behind, and some show signs of being tempered with grass or straw. Some also showed marks of being roughly smoothed with the hand and with some kind of tool. A small proportion of these fragments may have

Figure 94. The reconstruction of kiln 2 at site 13 Donyatt (courtesy of Nicholas Dawson and the Bickley Ceramics Project).

formed parts of conical supports similar to those described above but were too small to offer a definite interpretation. The majority probably formed part of one or more clay-built kiln structures, in particular the inner surface of the ware chamber or parts of the floor and substructure which, as observed in the Bickley experiments of 1981–2010, tend to be fired in this way (Dawson and Kent 1999, 167–71; Figures 94 and 95). Substantial fragments of comparable material have been recovered from excavations at the Exeter Inn, Barnstaple (pers. obs. the writers). Repeated firings produce a hard inner surface on a structure that remains essentially raw clay (pers. obs. the authors). Once demolished, much of the wall returns to its natural state, leaving only the characteristic fired surface graduated from hard to soft through its thickness. Only one fragment (context 567) was encrusted with lead glaze; otherwise there were no signs of glaze dribbles or vapour marks. It should be noted that these fragments display none of the characteristics of burnt cob or daub: wattle impressions, charcoal inclusions, or uneven firing.

A further 311 fragments weighing 11.30 kg were recovered from elsewhere on the site. As two of these from 557 and seven from 676 were associated with pottery waste, it is probable that the fired clay fragments from the rest of the site are evidence of a range of different activities. As the fragment from 567 suggests, some would have been fragments of kiln structure.

'Oven' Tiles

These have been described above. Whilst there is evidence such as glaze-scars that similar tiles from other sites were used as separators or kiln shelves, their commonest purpose may have been in the construction of the kiln. Certainly the surviving substructure (the fireboxes and underpart of the ware-chamber) at the early seventeenth-century kiln 2 at Donyatt, was made almost entirely of such tiles laid in courses (Coleman-Smith and Pearson 1988, 125–32). A large number of these, many with glaze-scars, were donated to Chard and District Museum for the purposes of reconstructing a kiln and were examined in 2012 by Roger Carter, David Dawson and Peter Wood. Some of these were rubbed to form a circular edge of approximately 1.5m in diameter but there were only 39 complete examples from Hemyock and none displayed this feature.

Figure 95. Part of the eroded kiln wall of the reconstruction of kiln 2 at site 13 Donyatt (courtesy of the Bickley Ceramics Project).

Similar tiles have been illustrated and published from the Donyatt production sites 2 (fourteenth-century), sites 3, 5 and 16 (all sixteenth-century), another site 2 (seventeenth/eighteenth-century) and site 4 (eighteenth-century) (Coleman-Smith and Pearson 1988, 327–33). Similar tiles have also been noted from Wrangway (seventeenth-century) only 7 km away over the Somerset border, and with glaze-scars as stray finds during fieldwalking at Wambrook and Chardstock on the other side of the Blackdown Hills (Pearson *et al.* 2015).

A Note on the Saxo-Norman Sherds

John Allan

A small collection of 61 Saxo-Norman sherds of Upper Greensand-Derived ware was recovered from (557); it was associated with roundwood which has been subjected to radiocarbon dating. 7 further sherds of the same type were present in the overlying context (558), and 11 from (730), including a tubular fragment (whether spout or lamp stem) in the latter deposit; small quantities within other features and residual finds from other deposits brings the total to 180 sherds. As the medieval pottery industry of South-West England is currently understood, these finds could be dated on typological grounds alone anywhere in the period *c.* 950–1200, although a date at the earlier end of this range would be favoured, since they show a mix of oxidised and reduced sherds; by *c.* 1200 such wares are uniformly reduction-fired. However, when modelled, the two radiocarbon dates from 557 give a date range of AD 900–30. This is the earliest evidence for the use of such wares, and is indeed at odds with the other piece of dating evidence from early tenth-century Somerset on which the dating of the emergence of pottery use has been based: Rahtz's evidence from Cheddar Palace. At Cheddar the upper fill of a large boundary ditch (Ditch A) contained a coin of *c.* 930 alongside many animal bones but no pottery (Rahtz 1979, 53). This has seemed good evidence that pottery was not in use at the palace *c.* 930, and thus that the use of ceramics began at a later date. Rahtz's sequence has been challenged by John Blair; with regard to this ditch he does not take issue with the closing date, but suggests that the lower deposits in the feature are also of tenth-century date, the ninth-century coins in them being residual (Blair 1996, 114–16). If this argument is accepted, it simply increases the quantity of domestic waste present in the early tenth century and underlines the lack of associated pottery.

Portuguese Coarsewares

Sarah Newstead

There are four sherds of Portuguese coarseware in the Hemyock assemblage, all of which probably originated from the region of Aveiro, Portugal, a coastal city known for its salt trade from the sixteenth to eighteenth centuries (Newstead 2015). All the sherds exhibit characteristics of this zone of production; they have a red-orange colour, with the sherds from context 616 exhibiting a darker strip of colour at the fabric core. All of the sherds are highly micaceous, with ill-sorted muscovite mica present on both the surface and throughout the fabric. They also contain small to medium white and rose quartz grains, with some grains visible on the surfaces of the sherds; typical for Aveiro productions (Newstead 2013). Three of them have rough, external burnish lines, which is normally associated with Aveiro productions from the sixteenth and seventeenth centuries, particularly when combined with a highly micaceous fabric. All of the sherds likely represent either bottle (*bilha*) or standing costrel (*cântaro*) vessels, which were common forms exported from Aveiro in the early sixteenth century and were used as tableware and liquid storage in English contexts. The sherds from context 616 probably come from a single vessel. Aveiro kilns produced large amounts of ceramics during the latter part of the fifteenth to the early eighteenth century, and products from these kilns represent the most commonly-encountered Portuguese earthenware on English sites from this period (Newstead 2014). Ceramics from Aveiro have been found regularly along coastal sites in South-West England, such as at Exeter and Plymouth, but the Hemyock sherds represent the first time Aveiro-type ceramics have been firmly identified from an inland context in England (Newstead 2015). The presence of these Portuguese sherds on a major inland pottery production site at Hemyock signifies the overall trade and social connections between South-West England and Central/Northern coastal Portugal in the sixteenth century, with Aveiro ceramics regularly included as auxiliary cargo on English ships trading salt out of Aveiro and other goods from Porto, a major transshipment point for Aveiro products. It is also possible that these Portuguese vessels arrived via the English trade around the Bay of Biscay, as there is evidence that Aveiro-produced ceramics where being transshipped in quantity to this region during the sixteenth century (Newstead 2015). Despite a potentially varied arrival to England, the Portuguese sherds at Hemyock suggest that there was a greater presence of Portuguese goods in inland communities in the South West in the sixteenth century than was previously appreciated.

Scientific Analyses: The Value of the Combined Approach

John Allan

The object in subjecting three parts of individual sherds of pottery to three different forms of scientific analysis was to explore how these three techniques complemented each other; how together they would help achieve the vision expressed by David Peacock by correlating scientific and visual data so that findings can be extrapolated on a larger scale (Peacock 1977, 25) and lastly to postulate a strategy for sampling in the future. The full data sets from each analysis together with those of the pottery specialists

Table 19. Samples from production sites selected for analysis by visual petrology, ICP-MS and QEMSCAN

Sample number	Description (context number)
Hemyock: kiln waste	
1/1	Unglazed jug base, reduced and reoxidised (571)
1/2–3	Oven tiles, reduced and reoxidized (571, 588).
1/4	Bowl rim, heavily reduced dark grey fabric, internal reduced dark green lead glaze (571).
1/5	Kiln prop rim, reduced grey fabric (571).
1/6	Bowl rim, reduced and re-oxidised fabric, internal brown lead glaze (588).
Hemyock: Upper Greensand-Derived wares, 10–12C	
1/7–9	Unglazed body sherds, reduced surfaces (all 557).
Bridgwater Chandos Glass Cone, 19C (Boore and Pearson 2010)	
1/10	Bowl rim, heavily reduced dark grey fabric, reoxidised red external surface with dark green reduced internal lead glaze.
1/11	Basal angle of a pancheon, oxidised red sandy fabric with occasional particles of lime, plain oxidised brown lead glaze with black speckles, trailed white slip decoration.
Wrangway kiln waste, 17C (Pearson *et al.* 2015)	
1/12	Knife-trimmed basal angle of a pancheon, sandy red fabric, internal raw lead glaze.
1/13	Body and basal angle of a jar, red reoxidised sandy fabric, internal reduced black lead glaze with areas of iridescence and with reduced green splash runs on the exterior. The internal glaze has occasional embedded white ?quartz crystals.
Hole Common, Lyme Regis: Samples 1/14–15 not supplied for analysis.	
Donyatt site 2, Whitney Bottom (Coleman-Smith and Pearson 1988)	
1/16	Everted rim of a jar, oxidised red fabric with particles of lime and ?glauconite, internal brown lead glaze on rim with patches of iridescence.
1/17	Rim of a bowl, red fabric with traces of internal lead glaze and splashes of white slip inside and out.
Donyatt site 3, Whitney Bottom (Coleman-Smith and Pearson 1988)	
1/18	Basal angle of a jar, buff reoxidised fabric with iron-rich inclusions <2mm, internal patchy reduced green glaze, partially burnt off.
1/19	Basal angle of a jar, reoxidised red fabric with particles of lime and ?glauconite, internal reduced black lead glaze with areas of iridescence.
Crowcombe, 17C? (Unpublished). The site lies on the south flank of the Quantocks.	
1/20	Body sherd, reoxidised red sandy fabric, internal possible burnt off slip or glaze.
Nether Stowey, 17C (Coleman-Smith and Pearson 1970). The site is now under the village bypass.	
1/21	Rim sherd of a pancheon, red fabric and traces of an internal brown oxidised lead glaze.
Hemyock: clay samples	
1/22	Brown clay from Churchills Farm, Hemyock.
1/23	Orange clay from Churchills Farm, Hemyock.

are published here so that the reader can make their own judgements.

Selection of Samples for Petrological and Chemical Analyses

Six samples of kiln waste from Hemyock, three examples of Saxo-Norman pottery from the same site and ten samples from other kiln sites in Somerset were subjected to mineralogical analysis (Roger Taylor), chemical analysis by ICP-MS (Mike Hughes), and automated scanning electron microscopy (SEMS-EDS QEMSCAN – Jens Andersen, Gavyn Rollinson and David Dawson) (Table 19). In addition, seventeen samples of domestic pottery and three floor-tiles from consumption sites were submitted for analysis by ICP-MS alone (Table 20). Where feasible, we have tried to select published vessels. Results are discussed by Hughes, below.

Petrological Analysis

Roger T. Taylor

Introduction

The 19 kiln samples listed in Table 19 were examined under the binocular microscope at magnifications of X20 and X40, followed by examination of thin-sections under the binocular microscope at X50 and X100. Inclusions are described in descending order of frequency. Examination

Table 20. Additional samples from consumer sites selected for analysis by ICP-MS only

Sample number	Place	Site and context number	Description	Publication
2/1	Exeter	Goldsmith Street 264/290	Tripod cauldron	Allan 1984, No. 1704
2/2	Exeter	Goldsmith Street 201	Tripod cauldron	Allan 1984, No. 1725
2/3	Exeter	Goldsmith Street 228	Jug neck	Allan 1984, No. 1757
2/4	Exeter	Goldsmith Street 228	Bowl rim	Allan 1984, No. 1768
2/5	Exeter	Goldsmith Street 228	Bowl rim	Allan 1984, No. 1778
2/6	Exeter	Goldsmith Street 228	Alembic spout	Allan 1984, No. 1782
2/7	Taunton	Kennedy's Yard TK1	Jug sherd	Bennett and Pearson 1984, 87
2/8	Taunton	Kennedy's Yard TK (1) [2]	Jug sherd	Bennett and Pearson 1984, 87
2/9	Taunton	Kennedy's Yard TK (1) [2]	Cup sherd	Bennett and Pearson 1984, 87
2/10	Taunton	Kennedy's Yard TKA1 27K (1)(2)	Bodysherd	Bennett and Pearson 1984, 87
2/11	Taunton	Kennedy's Yard III (1)	Jar rim	Bennett and Pearson 1984, 87
2/12	Taunton	Kennedy's Yard R3/S/7AP	Storage jar rim	Bennett and Pearson 1984, 87
2/13	Bridgwater	George Street 277	Jug rim	Allan forthcoming
2/14	Bridgwater	George Street 310		Allan forthcoming
2/15	Bridgwater	George Street 499	Jug handle	Allan forthcoming
2/16	Bridgwater	George Street 315	Cup bodysherd	Allan forthcoming
2/17	Bridgwater	George Street 461	Jug rim	Allan forthcoming
2/18	Cadeleigh	Church floor	Complete floor-tile	Unpublished
2/19	Woodbury church	AC Archaeology excavation	Floor-tile fragment	Unpublished
2/20	Woodbury church	AC Archaeology excavation	Floor-tile fragment	Unpublished

of the thin-sections confirms the general mineralogy and provenance determined from examination by binocular microscope. It is apparent that some of the physical and mineralogical features seen in the sherds are not seen in the thin-sections, while some details of the matrix and finer-grained components are more apparent at the higher magnifications of the thin-sections. As is usually the case, the petrology of ceramic coarse wares closely reflects the local geology of the pottery sites, both in respect of the clay and the tempering material used.

A Note on the Preparation of Thin-Sections

The metallic coating applied to the surface of these sections substantially reduces the light transmission for optical polarised light microscopy and reduces some of the finer detail visible in the matrix clay. For future projects of this type, a separate set of thin-sections for optical microscopy would be advisable.

Samples 1–6: Hemyock Kiln Waste

Sample 1

A uniform smooth finely micaceous clay fabric with muscovite flakes up to about 0.05 mm.

- Quartz: two sub-rounded polished grains seen, 0.6 mm.
- Muscovite flakes: up to *c.* 0.05 mm.

Mineralogical Detail from Thin-Section

- Quartz: *c.* 20%. Predominantly angular uniformly distributed up to 0.1 mm, rarely 0.2 mm; very fine quartz in the matrix, probably less than 30 μ.
- Mica: Muscovite as slender laths, mainly orientated with the fabric, up to 0.1 mm, rarely 0.2 mm.
- Limonite: Very dark brown almost opaque mainly small grains less than 0.1 mm scattered throughout, rarely 0.3 mm.
- Grog-like inclusions or clay pellets: Rounded pellets usually containing fine quartz but less than in the surrounding matrix, 0.3–2 mm.
- Zircon(?): Rare, one grain with crystal form, high relief and birefringence, *c.* 0.1 mm long.

Comment: A uniform smooth finely micaceous clay fabric.

Sample 2

Temper *c.* 15%.

- Chert: White, light grey and white and grey-mottled angular fragments, 0.2–0.6 mm.
- Quartz: transparent to translucent to white opaque, angular to well-rounded, 0.2 mm.
- Ferruginous/manganiferous pan: Sparse black angular fragments, 0.8–2 mm.
- Matrix: Silty/finely sandy clay with grains of quartz, less than 0.05 mm.

Mineralogical Detail from Thin-Section

- Quartz: Angular to well-rounded grains, 0.05–1 mm
- Chert: Brownish cryptocrystalline, angular to sub-rounded fragments, 0.2 –2.2 mm.
- Ferruginous pellets: Reddish brown by reflected light, dark brown to black opaque particles, rounded some containing quartz silt finer than the surrounding matrix.
- Matrix: Much of the matrix is light to dark brownish in plane polarised light and isotropic between crossed polarisers suggesting the presence of glass.it contains fine quartz less than 0.05 mm.

Sample 3

Oven tile. Temper: the larger grains less than 5%.

- Quartz: Sparse transparent to translucent, sub-angular to well-rounded and polished grains, 0.8 mm. Single sub-rounded white grain, 6 mm.
- Chert: Rare grey and white mottled sub-angular fragments, 0.5–2.5 mm and white irregular fragments, 2.5 mm.
- Mica: Muscovite as a scatter of cleavage flakes, 0.05–0.1 mm, occasionally 0.3 mm.
- Matrix: Smooth finely micaceous clay with fine ferruginous mottling.

Mineralogical Detail from Thin-Section

- Quartz: Common uniformly distributed angular to sub-angular grains 0.05–0.15 mm, *c.* 15%. One broken well-rounded grain 0.5 mm, original length *c.* 1 mm. Composite rounded quartz grains: 0.3 and 0.5 mm.
- Mica: Sparse muscovite laths up to 1.25 mm long.
- Matrix: Both oxidised and reduced sections optically active between crossed polarisers.
- Ferruginous grains: Opaque grains and steaks some translucent brown throughout the section.

Comment: Mineral components derived from the Upper Greensand.

Sample 4

Bowl rim sherd. Temper % not determined. Fabric originally uniformly and abundantly finely sandy/silty with quartz grains less than 0.05–0.1 mm; comparable with Sample 5. Fabric originally uniformly and abundantly finely sandy/silty with quartz grains less than 0.05–0.1 mm and, again, comparable to Sample 5.

Mineralogical Detail from Thin-Section

- Quartz: Angular grains common, up to 1.5 mm.
- Chert: Single angular fragment on the margin of the section, 1.5 mm.
- Mica: A scatter of slender laths aligned parallel to the surfaces of the sherd, up to 0.15 mm.
- Zircon(?): A single rounded grain with high relief and birefringence, 0.03 mm.
- Matrix: The matrix is isotropic with crossed polarisers indicating the glassy nature.

Sample 5

Cylindrical kiln furniture, the core becoming vitrified, porous and bubbly. Temper: % not determined.

- Quartz: A scatter of transparent colourless to white opaque angular to rounded grains, some showing surface polish, some showing internal 'crackled' fracturing, 0.2–1.5 mm.
- Chert: A scatter of white and mottled angular fragments, 0.2–1.1 mm, rarely 4 mm.
- Mica: Muscovite as sparse cleavage flakes, up to about 0.05 mm, rarely 0.15 mm.
- Matrix: Appears to have been mainly composed of uniform fine quartz sand up to about 0.1 mm. The nature of matrix clay cannot be distinguished.

Mineralogical Detail from Thin-Section

- Quartz: finer angular to sub-angular grains 0.05–0.15 mm, *c.* 20%. Larger rounded grains, 0.3–1.3 mm, a broken rounded grain 3.1mm largest dimension, a metaquartzite grain rounded, 2.0 mm with sutured internal quartz grains, less than 5%.
- Mica: Sparse muscovite laths up to 0.1 mm.
- Chert: Sparse sub-angular fragments 0.5–2 mm. Some fragments have corroded/embayed margins where reacting with the matrix/glass.
- Matrix: Dark with some very fine quartz silt, isotropic between crossed polarisers, probably glassy.

Comment: The mineral content is derived from the Upper Greensand.

Sample 6

Wasted bowl rim. Temper *c.* 15%.

- Quartz: Transparent to translucent colourless angular to well-rounded with some polished grains, 0.2–0.6 mm, rarely 1 mm.
- Tourmaline: Sparse black vitreous rounded grains, 0.1–0.3 mm.
- Matrix: Smooth finely micaceous clay.

Mineralogical Detail from Thin-Section

- Quartz: Angular to sub-angular with rare rounded grains, 0.05–0.3 mm but mainly larger than 0.1 mm, *c.* 15%.
- Mica: Sparse muscovite laths up to 0.1 mm.
- Chert: Sub-angular fragments (x 2), 0.4 mm.
- Sandstone: An irregular silicified fragment with sand grains similar to those in the body of the pottery, 1.5 mm.

- Ferruginous pellets: Dark reddish brown to opaque, sub-rounded, evenly distributed up to 0.1 mm, rarely 0.2 mm. Many appear to have shrunk during firing.
- Matrix: Uniform, optically active clay with some very fine quartz silt and mica.

General Comment on the Hemyock Pottery

Most of the samples show some evidence of mineral content derived from the Upper Greensand; in some cases the small quantities represented suggest incidental inclusion in the clay.

The Cretaceous Upper Greensand was laid down during a transgressive rise in sea level; it contains a suite of minerals believed to have been derived from the Dartmoor granite. Tourmaline var. schorl is one of the most common, and zircon has been noted in the present study. Rutile and topaz have also been noted from the Upper Greensand (Hancock 1969). Plagioclase and microcline feldspar have been noted in thin-sections of Upper Greensand-Derived pottery from Sherborne Old Castle, Dorset (Taylor 2003).

Two characteristic features of coarse wares from the area of the western outcrop of the Upper Greensand are evident in these samples: well-rounded quartz grains with polished surfaces, and fragments of chert. This combination has been found in pottery of Bronze Age, Iron Age and medieval date in East Devon. At this site the clay is most probably derived from the weathering of the Triassic Marls underlying the Upper Greensand around Hemyock.

It is most likely that the tempering sand has been obtained from streams draining from the Upper Greensand, rather than being directly quarried from the outcrop. This would account for the small size and in some cases partial rounding of the chert which occurs at a specific horizon in the Upper Greensand. Periglacial solifluction may also have played a part in the distribution of superficial clay deposits.

Considering the site location and geology, it is likely that the clay was obtained from the weathering profile of the Permian marls or their related Head deposits.

Samples 7–9: Saxo-Norman Sherds from Hemyock

Sample 7 (Samples 8–9 are very similar and not described in detail)

Bodysherd. Temper *c.* 10%, rather unevenly distributed, with higher concentrations on surfaces.

- Quartz: Transparent colourless to opaque white and grey angular to well-rounded and polished grains, 0.05–2 mm, rarely 3.35 mm.
- Chert: A scatter of white angular to sub-angular fragments, 1–3 mm.
- Tourmaline: Sparse black vitreous polished grains, 0.2–0.4 mm.

Mineralogical Detail from Thin-Section

- Quartz: Angular to well-rounded grains 0.05–1.6 mm; includes some composite quartzitic grains, *c.* 25%, some with sutured margins to internal quartz grains.
- Chert: A scatter of angular to rounded fragments 0.3–0.8 mm.
- Sandstone: A silicified (chert-cemented) angular fragment, 1.4 mm.
- Tourmaline (schorl): Two rounded grains, 0.1mm, and mica laths less than 0.05 mm.
- Matrix: Optically active with some fine quartz silt.

Comment: Upper Greensand-Derived fabrics, predominantly quartz, the chert relatively sparse.

Samples 10–11: Bridgwater: Chandos Glass Cone

Sample 10

Bodysherds, high-fired verging on stoneware. Temper: % not determined.

- Quartz: Possible remnant angular grains and rare rounded grains seen on the outer surface, 0.1 mm.
- Matrix: Smooth clay. The core has an unusual finely speckled (*c.* 0.02 mm) white texture suggestive of post-firing recrystallisation. This texture can also be seen on the outer surface but is less conspicuous there.

Mineralogical Detail from Thin-Section

- Quartz: A scatter of angular grains, some of them composite, 0.05–0.2 mm, 1–2%.
- Feldspar: One plagioclase (probably sodic) grain identified, *c.* 0.05 mm.
- Matrix: Dark in plain and polarised light and in extinction between crossed polarisers with much very fine quartz silt, some less than 30 μ. There is weak optical activity in the oxidised outer surface. There are some irregular patches which may be calcium carbonate, 0.1–0.3 mm. It is possible that the matrix is more or less glassy although it would be unlikely that the free calcium content would have survived such temperatures without reaction.

Comment: Spalls occur on the outer surface over soft white calcareous inclusions, 1–3 mm. These are recarbonated, previously calcined, calcium carbonate, perhaps originally shell fragments. Similar inclusions can be seen on the inner surface where they cause slight bulging of the glaze. The clay could come from an estuarine source; the very fine-grained silty nature of much of the quartz content would support this conclusion.

Sample 11

Temper *c.* 20%.

- Quartz: Translucent to opaque angular to sub-rounded grains, 0.1–0.2 mm.
- Soft white grains: Sparse, some showing tabular form perhaps originally shell, slightly calcareous, 0.2–0.5 mm.
- Matrix: Smooth clay, slightly calcareous in places.

Mineralogical Detail from Thin-Section

- Quartz: Angular grains, unevenly distributed, 0.5 mm.
- Shell and calcareous fragments: Elongated fragments up to 1.0 mm and sub-rounded more equidimensional calcareous fragments with a possible bryozoan fragment, *c.* 2%. A circular area of calcium carbonate *c.* 5 mm in diameter and enclosing a sub-angular 2 mm quartz grain may also be of sedimentary origin.
- Mica: Muscovite, sparse laths mainly in the matrix up to, 0.1 mm.
- Matrix: Optically active with some fine mica and fine silty quartz. There are some irregular areas and streaks with a much higher content of silty quartz less than 0.05 mm.

Comment: The shell content indicates clay deposited an intertidal estuarine intercalation within the alluvial deposits of the Bridgwater area.

General Comment on Bridgwater Sherds

The fine silty nature of the quartz in the matrix together with the calcium carbonate and shell content of these sherds indicates that the clay was being sourced from the Quaternary alluvial deposits of the Bridgwater area.

Samples 12–13: Wrangway

Sample 12

Wasted pancheon, the interior slipped. Temper *c.* 20%.

- Quartz: Transparent to translucent white and occasional opaque angular to well-rounded grains, 0.1–0.8 mm, rarely 1.3 mm.
- Feldspar: White cleaved sub-angular grains, 0.1–0.6 mm.
- Mica: Muscovite as sparse cleavage flakes, 0.05–0.2 mm.
- Chert: Rare white mottled angular fragment, 0.5 mm.
- Matrix: Finely micaceous clay.

Mineralogical Detail from Thin-Section

- Quartz: Angular to sub angular grains 0.05–0.3 mm, sparse well-rounded grains, 0.4–0.6 mm, *c.* 20%.
- Chert: Sparse sub-angular to sub-rounded fragments 0.3–0.5 mm.
- Mica: A scatter of muscovite laths up to 0.1 mm.
- Matrix: Optically active with some very fine quartz silt and mica less than 0.05mm and some less than 30 μ.

Comment: An Upper Greensand-Derived fabric. Feldspar, a normal constituent of the Upper Greensand, is particularly common in this vessel.

Sample 13

Wrangway Fabric B (jar sherd). Temper *c.* 20%.

- Quartz: Transparent colourless to translucent and white opaque, angular to well-rounded and occasional polished grains, 0.1–0.8 mm, rarely 2.1 mm.
- Feldspar: Sparse white cleaved grains, 0.2–0.4 mm.
- Matrix: Silty/finely sandy clay.

Mineralogical Detail from Thin-Section

- Quartz: Angular to sub angular rarely rounded grains, some composite, 0.05-0.4 mm, one well-rounded grain, and 1.3 mm.
- Chert: A scatter of angular to sub-rounded fragments, 0.1–0.5 mm and 2 mm.
- Mica: Sparse laths up to 0.1 mm.
- Ferruginous pellets: One opaque pellet 1.7 mm.
- Matrix: Weak optical activity in the oxidised parts, fine silty quartz less than 0.05 mm common.

General Comment on the Wrangway Pottery

As at Hemyock, the Triassic Mercia Mudstone is the source of the clay, with the small coarser hard mineral content being derived from the Upper Greensand, either from local streams running off the escarpment or from Pleistocene periglacial solifluction incorporating sand in the near-surface levels of the Mercia Mudstone. However, the content of readily definable Upper Greensand components is lower in Wrangway sherds than in those from Hemyock. See also comment on Hemyock sherds.

Samples 14–15: Lyme Regis

Samples not supplied for analysis.

Samples 16–17: Donyatt site 2

Sample 16

Temper: the larger quartz grains *c.* 10% of the body.

- Quartz: Transparent to translucent colourless, sub-angular to sub- rounded grains, 0.05–0.5 mm.
- ?Tourmaline: A scatter of black hard rounded and some polished grains, 0.05–0.15 mm.
- Ferruginous inclusions: Sparse soft brownish red sub-rounded equidimensional, 0.05–3 mm.
- Matrix: Silty clay with fine white mica common.

Mineralogical Detail from Thin-Section

- Quartz: Angular to sub-angular grains, 0.05–0.2 mm, *c.* 10%, unevenly distributed.

- Ferruginous pellets: A scatter of opaque rounded pellets, 0.05–0.15 mm.
- Matrix: Moderately optically active; quartz silt and muscovite flakes common, generally less than 0.05 mm.

Comment: The detail from the section does not altogether reflect that derived from examination of the large surface area of the sherd. It is probable that the sand content is derived from the Upper Greensand, particularly if the identification of tourmaline is correct. The ware is quite porous with many more or less irregular air cavities.

Sample 17

Temper: *c.* 10%.

- Quartz: Transparent to translucent colourless grains sub-angular to rounded, some polished, 0.05–0.2 mm.
- Ferruginous inclusions: Soft reddish-brown, sub-rounded and equidimensional, some elongated parallel to the foliation structure of the sherd, 0.05–1.5 mm.
- Matrix: Silty clay with fine white mica common, rarely mica flakes reach 0.15 mm.

Mineralogical Detail from Thin-Section

- Quartz: Angular to sub angular rarely rounded grains, 0.05–0.2 mm.
- Mica: Muscovite, a scatter of laths 0.05–1 mm.
- Tourmaline (schorl): One angular grain, pleochroic light blue to neutral with high relief and birefringence, 0.06 mm.
- Ferruginous pellets: Rounded dark brown to opaque, some containing quartz silt, 0.05–0.2 mm. Common translucent brownish-orange pellets are common – generally rounded and some weakly optically active, 0.05–0.1 mm.
- Matrix: Moderately optically active, quartz silt and mica laths common less than 0.05 mm.

Comment: The ware is quite porous with many small more or less irregular air cavities. The unusual orange-brown pellets have only been seen in this thin-section; their nature is uncertain. They may be ferruginous, possibly haematitic.

General Comment on the Sherds from Donyatt Site 2

The location of the Donyatt kilns on the Jurassic Lower Lias indicates that this was the source of the clay used. Both these sherds have distinctly more sandy fabrics than those from site 3, described below. Although the kilns were some distance from the Upper Greensand outcrop, the sand content probably derived from there, particularly if the identification of tourmaline is correct. It cannot be determined whether it was used as a deliberate tempering addition or as an incidental inclusion in the local clay as a result of periglacial effects.

Samples 18–19: Donyatt Site 3

Sample 18

Jar. Temper % not determined.

- Quartz: Rare transparent grains sub-angular to rounded grains, 0.05–0.2 mm, two sub-rounded grains, 1.5 and 2 mm seen.
- Ferruginous inclusions: Soft reddish brown common, sub-rounded equidimensional and some elongated parallel to the foliation structure of the sherd, 0.05–1.5 mm.
- White inclusion: Soft not carbonate, possibly dehydrated gypsum ($CaSO_4$), 1 mm.
- Matrix: Silty clay with fine white mica common.

Mineralogical Detail from Thin-Section

- Quartz: Rare angular grains, 0.1–0.12 mm.
- Ferruginous pellets: Common, dark brown, mainly rounded, 0.05–1 mm, usually less than 0.2 mm.
- Matrix: Common uniform fine quartz silt and mica laths less than 0.05 mm, much probably less than 30 μ.

Comment: Based on the site geology, the clay is from the Jurassic Lower Lias, with incidental quartz inclusions. The ferruginous content suggests digging from within the weathering profile. The body has some air cavities but not to such a degree as Nos 16 and 17.

Sample 19

Temper: % not determined.

- Quartz: Rare transparent sub-rounded rounded, 0.05-0.2 mm, one greyish sub-rounded 1mm grain seen.
- White inclusions: Sparse soft, possibly dehydrated gypsum ($CaSO_4$), approximately square section, 0.3–2.5 mm.
- Ferruginous inclusions: Soft reddish brown, sub-rounded to angular, 0.05–1.5 mm.
- Matrix – Silty clay, finely micaceous with muscovite flakes up to 0.05 mm.

Mineralogical Detail from Thin-Section

- Quartz: Sparse angular grains, 0.05–0.1 mm.
- Ferruginous pellets: Common dark brown generally rounded, some containing quartz silt, 0.05–1.7 mm, generally less than 0.4 mm.
- Mica: A scatter of muscovite laths, 0.05–1 mm.
- Matrix: Weakly optically active, quartz silt and mica laths less than 0.05 mm common, much probably less than 30 μ.

Comment: As for Sample 18, above.

Comment on Donyatt Site 3

Probably Liassic clay, based on the site geology, with incidental quartz inclusions. Ferruginous content suggests digging from within the weathering profile. The body has some air cavities but not to such a degree as Samples 16 and 17.

Sample 20: Crowcombe

Bodysherd, oxidised earthenware. Temper *c.* 15%.

- Quartz: Colourless transparent to translucent sub-angular to sub-rounded grains, 0.05–0.5 mm, rarely 1 mm.
- Matrix: Smooth, finely micaceous clay.

Mineralogical Detail from Thin-Section

- Quartz: Angular to rounded grains, 0.05–0.3 mm, rather unevenly distributed, *c.* 10% including sandstone.
- Rock fragments: Sandstone, a scatter of fine-grained generally rounded fragments with quartz and mica, 0.1–1.2 mm. The largest fragment shows some degree of foliation.
- Matrix: Quite strongly optically active with some quartz silt less than 0.05 mm.

Comment: The clay may possibly be derived from the Triassic Mercia Mudstone Group; the sandstone content could reflect the proximity of the Devonian sandstones of the Quantocks, either directly or indirectly from the Otter Sandstone. The low hard mineral content suggests that the clay was used as dug from the Triassic Mercia Mudstone Formation. Incidental inclusions of quartz and sandstone may derive from the local hard rock formations of the Quantocks.

Sample 21: Nether Stowey

Rim sherd of a pancheon. Oxidised earthenware fabric, hard fired. Temper: % N/D

- Quartz: Rare grains, up to 0.1 mm.
- Mica: A scatter of muscovite flakes, up to 0.1mm.
- Ferruginous pellets: Light brown rounded larger examples with much quartz silt, bordering on pellets of poorly incorporated clay, 0.2–1.2 mm.
- Matrix: Smooth finely micaceous clay with some quartz silt, grains size less than 0.05 mm.

Mineralogical detail from thin section

- Quartz: Sparse angular to sub-rounded grains 0.05–0.15 mm
- Matrix: Moderately optically active, quartz silt and some mica laths common less than 0.05 mm.

Comment: The section shows pale brownish mottled rounded 'pellets' which are isotropic and could be phosphatic. The overall fine grain size of the quartz in the section suggests that it is entirely derived from the indigenous quartz content of the Mercia Mudstone. Any phosphate content is likely to be of organic origin. The clay used as dug without any other additions.

Plasma Spectrometry Analysis

M.J. Hughes

Introduction

Chemical analysis using inductively coupled plasma spectrometry (ICPS) was applied to a selection of the pottery from Hemyock and associated sites to see whether there were different chemical patterns among this material. It also examined the chemical relationship between this pottery and previously-analysed examples of South-West English pottery including Upper Greensand-Derived wares found at a range of sites in Somerset, Devon and Dorset; petrological study and ICP had both confirmed the distinctive nature of this fabric (Hughes 2002; 2003; 2005; Allan *et al.* 2011; Hughes 2014).

Chemical analysis of the fabric of pottery provides a means of identifying ceramics which were made from the same clays, and probably at the same location, by looking for very similar patterns of chemical composition of the clay fabric. The selection of ceramics for analysis included the 19 kiln samples also analysed by petrography and QEMSCAN for this project (Table 19), supplemented by a further 20 possible Hemyock products from local consumer sites, including pottery from Exeter, Taunton, and Bridgwater, and floor-tiles from churches at Cadeleigh and Woodbury, a total of 39 samples (Table 20; the sample numbers are prefixed with 2/ so to distinguish them in the text from the primary Hemyock samples analysed by QEMSCAN, petrography and ICP and listed in Table 19).

Inductively-coupled plasma spectrometry (ICPS) was applied, using both the atomic emission and mass spectrometry versions; the technique and subsequent statistical processing were the same as those previously described for earlier investigations of pottery of the region (Hughes 1998; 2002; 2003; 2010; 2014). The samples were analysed at the Department of Earth Sciences, Royal Holloway, University of London, and at the University of Durham, Department of Earth Sciences using their standard techniques for ICP-AES and ICP-MS for a total of 40 elements; their results were shown to be compatible with minor adjustments for some major elements. Full ICP results are given in Table 21.

Interpretation of the ICP Analyses Using Principal Components Analysis

Detailed interpretation of the analyses was carried out with multivariate statistics, namely Principal Components

Table 21. Full list of analyses of samples by inductively coupled plasma spectrometry (ICPS), including those also analysed by petrography and QEMSCAN (Sample nos. 1/1-21) and consumer sites (2/1-20)

Sample number	Laboratory number	Al_2O_3	Fe_2O_3	MgO	CaO	Na_2O	K_2O	TiO_2	P_2O_5	MnO	Co	Cr	Cu	Ni	Sc	Sr	V	Y	Zn	Ba	Rb
Hemyock																					
1/1	RS 1	16.9	7.82	4.22	0.37	0.19	5.16	0.84	0.17	0.07	22.0	98	14.5	42	15.3	50	99	23.9	144	465	140
1/2	RS 2	11.8	7.60	3.82	0.30	0.16	3.42	0.57	0.11	0.09	18.4	74	17.2	32	11.6	35	68	23.3	142	343	96
1/3	RS 3	15.1	6.77	5.51	0.49	0.18	4.47	0.75	0.23	0.07	17.5	90	18.1	39	14.3	44	84	25.9	158	431	122
1/4	RS 4	15.4	6.73	4.68	0.27	0.18	4.91	0.74	0.04	0.07	25.4	98	11.5	38	15.6	40	96	27.6	164	450	152
1/5	RS 5	13.0	8.44	2.69	0.33	0.14	3.96	0.60	0.14	0.07	21.2	88	10.9	38	12.5	39	92	20.2	171	385	126
1/6	RS 6	15.1	6.63	4.12	0.22	0.20	5.04	0.64	0.11	0.07	18.4	94	14.8	45	14.5	43	87	32.4	222	436	149
1/7	RS 7	12.8	5.39	1.20	0.51	0.10	1.87	0.63	0.27	0.16	19.7	111	18.5	45	13.1	39	97	24.9	113	296	70
1/8	RS 8	13.8	4.77	1.21	0.91	0.12	1.97	0.67	0.43	0.04	15.6	106	17.0	41	14.4	55	108	23.0	65	302	86
1/9	RS 9	12.1	4.89	1.15	0.82	0.12	2.03	0.54	1.11	0.07	20.7	93	20.1	40	13.2	65	92	19.3	65	300	75
Bridgwater Chandos																					
1/10	RS 10	13.4	5.56	2.40	8.79	0.70	2.85	0.73	0.14	0.11	37.6	94	12.9	38	13.7	291	110	28.9	107	386	137
1/11	RS 11	13.9	5.71	2.69	9.27	0.60	3.04	0.71	0.15	0.12	17.3	81	11.4	39	13.4	296	84	22.3	108	374	130
Wrangway																					
1/12	RS 12	15.6	6.43	3.58	0.54	0.17	6.02	0.69	0.16	0.15	21.6	101	18.9	63	15.6	48	81	22.8	177	527	166
1/13	RS 13	15.1	6.23	4.22	1.11	0.19	5.65	0.68	0.12	0.12	24.0	109	23.5	59	14.9	51	84	22.3	200	496	175
Donyatt Site 2																					
1/16	RS 14	16.9	6.81	1.27	0.26	0.68	2.53	0.85	0.06	0.02	15.7	128	13.9	39	16.7	76	119	24.1	108	428	104
1/17	RS 15	16.5	5.85	1.22	0.35	0.44	2.36	0.83	0.04	0.02	15.6	111	30.5	41	17.6	63	130	26.6	86	350	103
Donyatt site 3																					
1/18	RS 16	20.6	4.85	1.04	0.53	0.28	2.72	1.07	0.07	0.02	18.5	132	24.4	32	22.0	81	151	26.2	78	429	116
1/19	RS 17	21.3	6.51	1.01	0.33	0.25	2.65	1.11	0.05	0.02	19.5	136	25.7	32	20.4	68	144	32.0	76	412	114
Crowcombe																					
1/20	RS 18	16.1	6.43	6.92	0.48	0.32	4.98	0.73	0.11	0.14	21.5	96	17.8	49	15.0	48	75	28.5	276	533	157
Nether Stowey																					
1/21	RS 19	17.2	6.76	3.45	0.46	0.31	6.12	0.79	0.44	0.11	23.1	108	18.2	56	16.0	78	89	28.0	452	736	191
Exeter																					
2/1	DA1	16.4	7.43	1.55	0.39	0.25	2.64	0.70	0.08	0.02	17.7	122	28.6	55	16.4	111	148	22.1	85	280	123
2/2	DA2	17.8	8.18	1.59	0.59	0.21	2.43	0.74	0.33	0.02	24.3	129	50.6	72	17.7	116	193	34.0	109	305	126
2/3	DA4	18.2	9.47	1.33	0.40	0.55	2.52	0.84	0.16	0.02	9.5	140	30.2	42	17.7	142	194	18.0	76	352	112
2/4	DA5	16.2	7.10	1.47	0.72	0.53	2.42	0.75	0.41	0.03	11.1	124	32.7	47	15.0	181	128	15.0	108	378	104
2/5	DA6	17.4	7.77	1.55	0.41	0.35	2.47	0.72	0.14	0.02	17.1	129	35.1	49	18.0	123	183	21.9	79	310	117
2/6	DA7	19.4	6.37	1.57	0.42	0.76	2.75	0.86	0.12	0.03	14.1	139	18.0	46	18.4	158	135	20.8	99	410	113
Taunton																					
2/7	DA9	17.6	6.10	1.46	1.03	0.86	2.73	0.85	0.94	0.03	10.4	131	25.3	42	17.1	221	136	18.3	77	616	101
2/8	DA10	17.4	7.01	1.49	0.60	0.75	2.62	0.82	0.15	0.04	17.6	133	27.9	65	17.5	182	170	27.2	115	441	103
2/9	DA11	16.0	6.49	3.78	0.21	0.34	5.57	0.66	0.09	0.10	23.5	109	24.6	62	13.8	100	103	33.0	354	635	166
2/10	DA12	19.5	5.76	1.16	0.42	0.42	2.89	1.11	0.04	0.03	23.6	141	26.0	42	19.3	134	146	32.2	93	431	117
2/11	DA13	20.8	6.30	1.14	0.62	0.39	2.78	1.04	0.18	0.01	8.7	153	28.5	32	18.3	177	180	21.4	68	435	127
2/12	DA15	16.4	7.83	1.29	0.93	0.58	2.47	0.92	0.36	0.04	16.5	136	30.8	60	16.6	244	143	26.2	109	434	104
Bridgwater																					
2/13	DA17	18.0	5.95	1.69	0.71	0.40	2.71	0.84	0.26	0.06	32.6	132	37.6	119	19.1	179	173	43.3	157	447	117
2/14	DA18	18.2	6.55	1.72	1.20	0.36	2.63	0.76	0.38	0.05	28.6	140	29.9	116	19.6	178	176	33.2	144	430	122
2/15	DA19	17.4	6.26	1.64	0.85	0.36	2.64	0.83	0.47	0.06	34.78	137	47.8	140	19.3	193	166	46.0	177	437	113
2/16	DA21	14.9	5.96	3.51	0.46	0.35	4.99	0.62	0.82	0.05	13.8	83	47.4	50	11.6	172	93	20.1	364	377	127
2/17	DA16	18.4	5.61	1.68	0.92	0.44	2.79	0.86	0.60	0.05	39.4	137	38.6	115	19.3	239	175	44.4	180	480	115
Cadeleigh																					
2/18	DA22	16.7	7.38	3.99	1.63	0.20	6.00	0.74	0.16	0.09	387.7	155	27.2	838	15.9	117	127	36.5	170	496	167
Woodbury church																					
2/19	DA23	17.6	7.84	3.64	0.25	0.24	5.74	0.73	0.10	0.09	26.4	108	24.4	56	15.7	91	113	37.6	183	483	160
2/20	DA24	12.2	5.59	2.27	0.13	0.15	3.97	0.77	0.06	0.06	16.7	89	18.5	35	12.5	71	91	26.7	113	382	130

Table 21 *continued*

Sample number	Laboratory number	Zr*	Nb	Cs	Pb	Th	U	La	Ce	Pr	Nd	Sm	Eu	Gd	Tb	Dy	Ho	Er	Tm	Yb	Lu
Hemyock																					
1/1	RS 1	166	19.4	20.6	107	13.7	2.69	38.9	81.9	9.0	35.2	6.4	1.24	5.35	0.90	3.72	0.71	2.12	0.37	2.05	0.29
1/2	RS 2	102	9.1	14.8	324	10.0	2.34	34.8	71.9	8.2	32.3	6.0	1.14	5.09	0.88	3.59	0.69	2.01	0.33	1.85	0.24
1/3	RS 3	160	18.7	17.7	81	13.2	2.63	39.7	73.9	9.6	37.6	7.0	1.36	5.94	1.06	4.39	0.86	2.51	0.43	2.47	0.34
1/4	RS 4	221	14.8	22.6	63	13.9	3.23	38.7	80.7	9.6	38.1	7.1	1.40	6.10	1.09	4.71	0.97	2.79	0.56	2.93	0.38
1/5	RS 5	99	9.7	23.3	394	10.3	2.41	33.3	63.6	7.7	30.2	5.6	1.05	4.71	0.81	3.37	0.68	1.80	0.31	1.82	0.24
1/6	RS 6	111	16.1	31.3	751	12.0	2.42	41.4	79.2	10.2	41.0	7.8	1.59	7.00	1.22	5.02	0.99	2.83	0.47	2.43	0.34
1/7	RS 7	170	13.9	4.9	25	9.6	2.09	32.1	62.7	7.9	31.2	5.8	1.16	4.96	0.92	3.91	0.81	2.41	0.45	2.51	0.36
1/8	RS 8	183	17.7	6.7	21	10.8	2.09	37.0	62.1	8.7	34.2	6.1	1.19	5.09	0.91	3.65	0.76	2.28	0.43	3.73	0.34
1/9	RS 9	164	11.5	4.7	21	9.5	2.02	33.1	70.2	7.9	31.2	5.7	1.10	4.60	0.81	3.37	0.68	2.19	0.38	2.13	0.39
Bridgwater Chandos																					
1/10	RS 10	200	11.1	10.2	4542	11.5	2.41	40.0	77.7	9.6	38.6	7.5	1.55	6.50	1.21	5.11	1.06	3.06	0.55	3.09	0.43
1/11	RS 11	114	18.8	9.7	356	10.4	1.85	39.1	76.0	9.3	37.6	7.2	1.45	5.77	0.99	3.88	0.77	2.60	0.37	1.97	0.28
Wrangway																					
1/12	RS 12	166	18.9	32.1	3722	13.6	2.48	40.7	88.4	9.8	39.1	7.2	1.44	5.99	1.03	4.20	0.83	2.34	0.40	2.95	0.33
1/13	RS 13	121	14.9	40.3	1538	12.7	2.54	41.6	78.4	9.8	39.4	7.2	1.40	5.88	1.03	3.88	0.75	2.12	0.39	1.96	0.28
Donyatt Site 2																					
1/16	RS 14	131	20.3	6.7	309	12.0	1.99	39.2	80.4	9.1	35.9	6.3	1.30	5.40	0.93	3.59	0.72	2.08	0.35	1.77	0.25
1/17	RS 15	189	21.7	7.7	1137	13.6	3.17	38.6	79.1	9.5	38.8	7.2	1.44	5.77	1.01	4.09	0.87	2.52	0.45	2.54	0.37
Donyatt site 3																					
1/18	RS 16	192	26.2	8.5	408	14.9	3.23	41.4	139.6	9.1	34.8	5.7	1.22	5.43	0.91	3.69	0.77	2.22	0.38	2.15	0.28
1/19	RS 17	189	26.7	8.9	400	14.7	3.02	44.8	98.7	10.9	43.4	7.5	1.56	6.56	1.16	5.05	1.00	2.98	0.48	2.62	0.36
Crowcombe																					
1/20	RS 18	180	20.7	26.8	233	14.3	2.56	48.8	89.5	11.6	46.3	8.6	1.71	7.21	1.29	5.08	1.06	2.98	0.51	2.92	0.43
Nether Stowey																					
1/21	RS 19	151	22.4	36.6	212	15.9	3.32	50.2	98.8	12.3	49.7	9.2	1.91	7.63	1.35	5.35	1.04	2.85	0.48	2.69	0.37
Exeter																					
2/1	DA1	98	17.2	9.1	107	11.5	2.76	32.5	69.9	8.5	31.6	6.1	1.25	4.84	0.76	4.18	0.81	2.18	0.37	2.22	0.35
2/2	DA2	90	17.5	9.9	95	12.2	3.49	39.3	80.5	10.9	41.5	7.8	1.63	6.97	1.04	5.70	1.12	2.92	0.48	2.83	0.44
2/3	DA4	114	17.8	7.9	81	12.3	2.83	30.4	57.7	6.8	24.1	4.2	0.85	3.34	0.52	2.98	0.61	1.71	0.30	1.89	0.31
2/4	DA5	102	16.0	6.6	417	11.0	2.52	27.0	50.8	5.9	20.7	3.6	0.70	2.76	0.43	2.47	0.51	1.47	0.27	1.66	0.27
2/5	DA6	98	17.3	8.5	478	12.4	3.81	34.1	66.3	8.3	30.5	5.4	1.08	4.30	0.66	3.70	0.75	2.04	0.35	2.12	0.33
2/6	DA7	106	18.4	7.5	450	13.1	2.30	33.8	65.6	8.1	29.9	5.4	1.08	4.30	0.65	3.65	0.73	1.99	0.34	2.09	0.33
Taunton																					
2/7	DA9	112	17.5	6.3	346	12.1	2.89	35.7	67.8	8.2	29.1	5.1	1.01	3.81	0.58	3.25	0.66	1.84	0.33	2.06	0.33
2/8	DA10	84	16.9	6.9	136	12.0	2.37	41.8	81.2	11.1	41.6	7.9	1.60	6.53	0.96	5.14	0.98	2.53	0.41	2.41	0.38
2/9	DA11	97	15.8	28.4	473	14.3	2.78	43.2	80.4	11.4	43.3	8.3	1.64	7.35	1.07	5.77	1.12	2.91	0.47	2.76	0.43
2/10	DA12	113	20.5	7.5	42	13.4	2.73	43.9	96.9	11.6	43.5	8.0	1.67	6.66	1.01	5.53	1.09	2.85	0.47	2.76	0.44
2/11	DA13	132	19.8	8.5	473	13.6	2.82	40.8	74.9	8.6	29.5	4.9	0.98	3.92	0.62	3.55	0.72	2.02	0.35	2.17	0.35
2/12	DA15	121	17.4	7.4	428	11.8	3.08	35.5	72.3	9.1	33.4	6.2	1.26	5.15	0.78	4.39	0.88	2.38	0.40	2.44	0.39
Bridgwater																					
2/13	DA17	115	16.6	8.7	217	12.3	3.36	48.3	99.7	13.6	52.1	10.1	2.17	9.03	1.37	7.51	1.47	3.81	0.61	3.58	0.57
2/14	DA18	115	17.2	9.2	121	12.9	3.29	44.2	88.1	11.1	41.2	7.6	1.60	6.53	1.00	5.49	1.08	2.88	0.47	2.80	0.45
2/15	DA19	110	16.2	8.00	642	11.9	3.3	50.9	97.4	13.4	50.9	9.5	2.0	8.87	1.33	7.31	1.46	3.8	0.61	3.46	0.56
2/16	DA21	75	15.6	25.7	360	9.0	2.18	30.5	63.5	7.9	29.5	5.4	1.05	4.41	0.64	3.45	0.69	1.76	0.29	1.75	0.27
2/17	DA16	123	16.5	8.5	148	12.6	3.44	48.2	95.7	13.4	51.6	9.9	2.13	9.08	1.36	7.44	1.47	3.81	0.62	3.56	0.57
Cadeleigh																					
2/18	DA22	147	17.5	28.5	1154	14.8	3.34	43.7	84.7	11.1	41.6	7.8	1.51	6.77	1.04	5.73	1.14	3.02	0.50	2.96	0.46
Woodbury church																					
2/19	DA23	100	18.1	30.1	839	14.2	3.03	48.4	90.4	12.1	45.4	8.6	1.69	7.71	1.15	6.32	1.24	3.21	0.52	3.01	0.46
2/20	DA24	94	16.7	20.8	548	11.6	2.56	39.0	81.7	9.7	35.7	6.3	1.21	5.37	0.82	4.55	0.89	2.36	0.39	2.29	0.36

Table 21 footnote

The elements Al_2O_3 to MnO are in weight percent; all the rest are in parts per million (ppm). Chemical element symbols: Al_2O_3 aluminium; Fe_2O_3 iron; MgO magnesium; CaO calcium; Na_2O sodium; K_2O potassium; TiO_2 titanium; P_2O_5 phosphorus; MnO manganese; Co cobalt; Cr chromium; Cu copper; Ni nickel; Sc scandium; Sr strontium; V vanadium; Y yttrium; Zn zinc; Ba barium; Rb rubidium; Zr zirconium; Nb niobium; Cs caesium; Th thorium; U uranium; Rare earth elements: La lanthanum; Ce cerium; Pr praesodimium; Nd neodymium; Sm samarium; Eu europium; Gd gadolinium; Tb terbium; Dy dysprosium; Ho holmium; Er erbium; Tm thulium; Yb ytterbium; Lu lutetium. *The zirconium figure is unreliable due to incomplete dissolution of minerals containing this element (principally zircon).

Analysis (PCA) which simultaneously considers the concentrations of many elements in each sample (Tabachnick and Fidell 2007; Baxter 1994 and 2003; Shennan 1997). The MINITAB version 16 statistical package was used.

All 39 samples were included in an initial principal components analysis, in which the majority of the ICP atomic emission and mass spectrometry elements could be included (34 in all); samarium and erbium were omitted because of high correlations with other rare earth elements. Cumulatively 73% of the total variation in the chemistry of all samples was contained within the first three principal components (39%, 24% and 10% respectively). The first principal component was correlated positively with the concentrations of many elements, effectively showing the clay matrix to temper ratio within the fabric of the pottery – temper inclusions usually act as a simple 'diluent', lowering the concentrations of elements in the overall fabric. Discriminating features between production centres are found in elements present in the clay minerals and others such as mica and feldspars. The second and third components bring out the chemistry of these minerals, and so are more useful to plot, as in Figure 96, which divided the samples along the horizontal axis (second component) into two broad groups, with those in the right-hand group containing all the samples from Hemyock, Wrangway, Bridgwater Chandos, Crowcombe, Nether Stowey, Cadeleigh and Woodbury Church, and the Bridgwater George Street cup sherd Sample 2/16. The left-hand group contained all the samples from Exeter, Taunton, Donyatt and three sherds from George Street, Bridgwater (Samples 2/13, 2/15, and 2/17) which formed a separate sub-group (upper left of Figure 96), and are practically identical in chemistry, probably indicating the same firing. A fourth sherd from Bridgwater (Sample 2/14) was very close to some Taunton sherds.

The second principal component was strongly associated with higher concentrations towards the right of Figure 96 of the alkalis potassium, rubidium and caesium; manganese; magnesium; and zinc (in descending order of

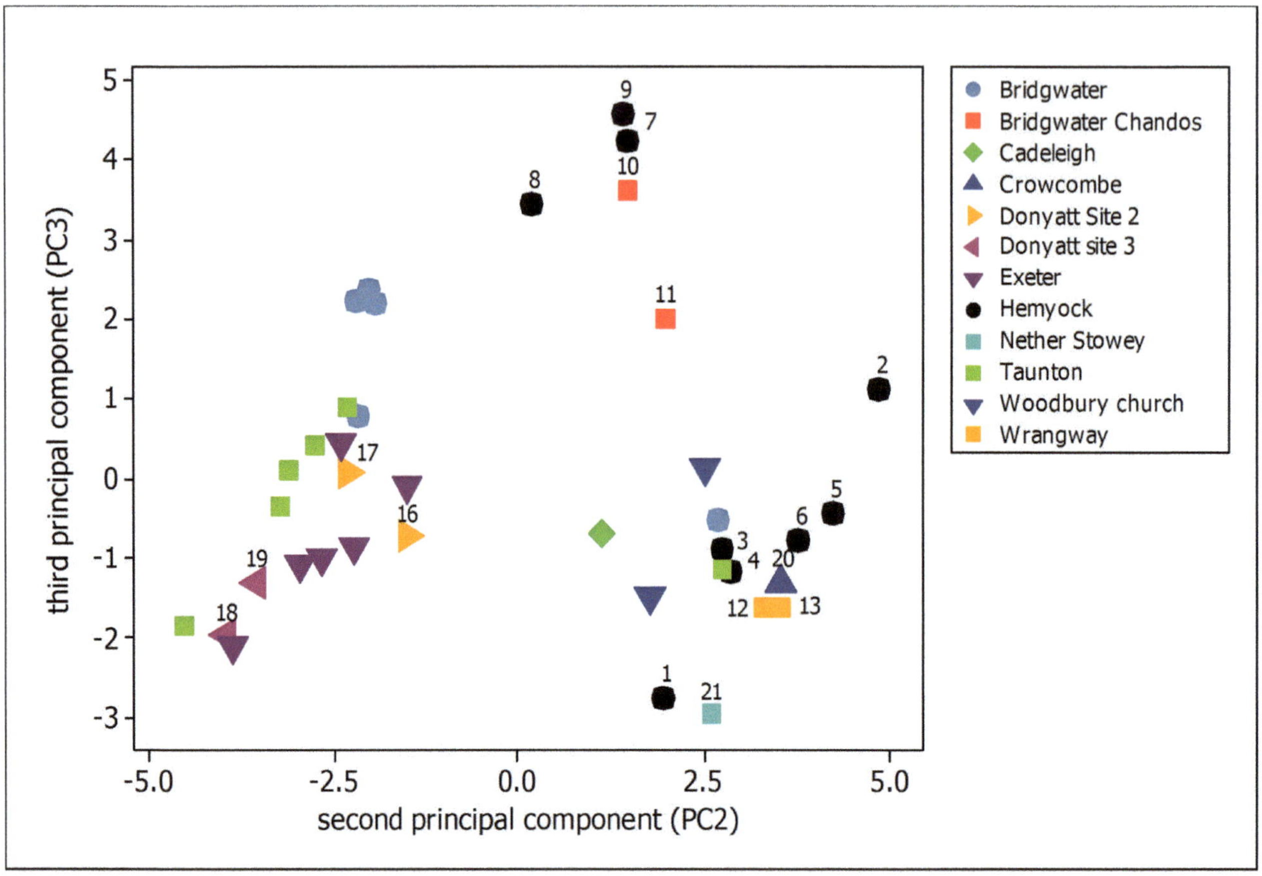

Figure 96. Plot of the second and third principal components of all samples analysed by ICP atomic spectrometry and mass spectrometry in this project; sample numbers opposite a symbol correspond to those of Table 20.

contribution to the component), but lower concentrations of chromium, scandium, vanadium, aluminium, titanium, sodium, strontium and copper. This combination of element concentrations is associated with the right-hand group and is a characteristic chemistry of the pottery of Hemyock and associated sites which used Upper Greensand-Derived clay, identified by petrological analysis as containing significant proportions of feldspars (Taylor, above). Pottery associated with the production at Donyatt contains the reverse combinations of these elements. Petrological analysis has shown that feldspars are absent from these Jurassic Lower Lias clays (*ibid.*). Donyatt kiln sites 2 and 3 are similar but not identical in chemistry (as previously noted for this production centre – Hughes 1998). Previous ICP analyses of Donyatt products showed very similar chemical compositions (*ibid.*; Hughes 2002) and replicated the differences in clay chemistry between the kilns at the site (Hughes 1998, 66). Two earlier ICP-atomic emission analyses of Crowcombe pottery have practically identical analyses to Sample 20 analysed here, apart from slightly lower rare earth element concentrations (Hughes 1998, 64–5). Crowcombe differs from Hemyock pottery in having significantly higher magnesium and zinc and higher aluminium, thorium and rare earth elements. Petrological analysis has shown that feldspars are absent from these Jurassic Lower Lias clays.

Notably the rare earth elements and thorium and uranium were not distinguishing features between the two groups of samples in Figure 96 as a whole. However, the third component showed higher concentrations of calcium and some of the heavy rare earths towards the top of Figure 96 (lutetium, ytterbium and terbium), but lower concentrations of the alkalis potassium, rubidium and caesium; iron, aluminium, thorium and magnesium. The Hemyock sherds split into two groups, with the three Saxo-Norman Upper Greensand-Derived sherds (Samples 7–9) at the top centre; one of the Bridgwater sherds (Sample 10) was close to this group on this plot. The left-hand group is compact, suggesting production of all these at Donyatt, whose kiln sherds it contained. The Taunton sherds formed a compact sub-group suggesting a single kiln's products. The Exeter sherds showed a wider chemical spread but still within the Donyatt pattern. Only three Bridgwater George Street sherds (Samples 2/13, 2/15, and 2/17) differed from the main group, forming a very close cluster above them, which suggests they were from the same clay/kiln firing, though their separation from the Donyatt sherds may imply production elsewhere.

To better understand the samples contained within the Hemyock group in Figure 96, they were compared to previous ICP analyses of pottery of the region with similar chemical features (especially those with high potassium).

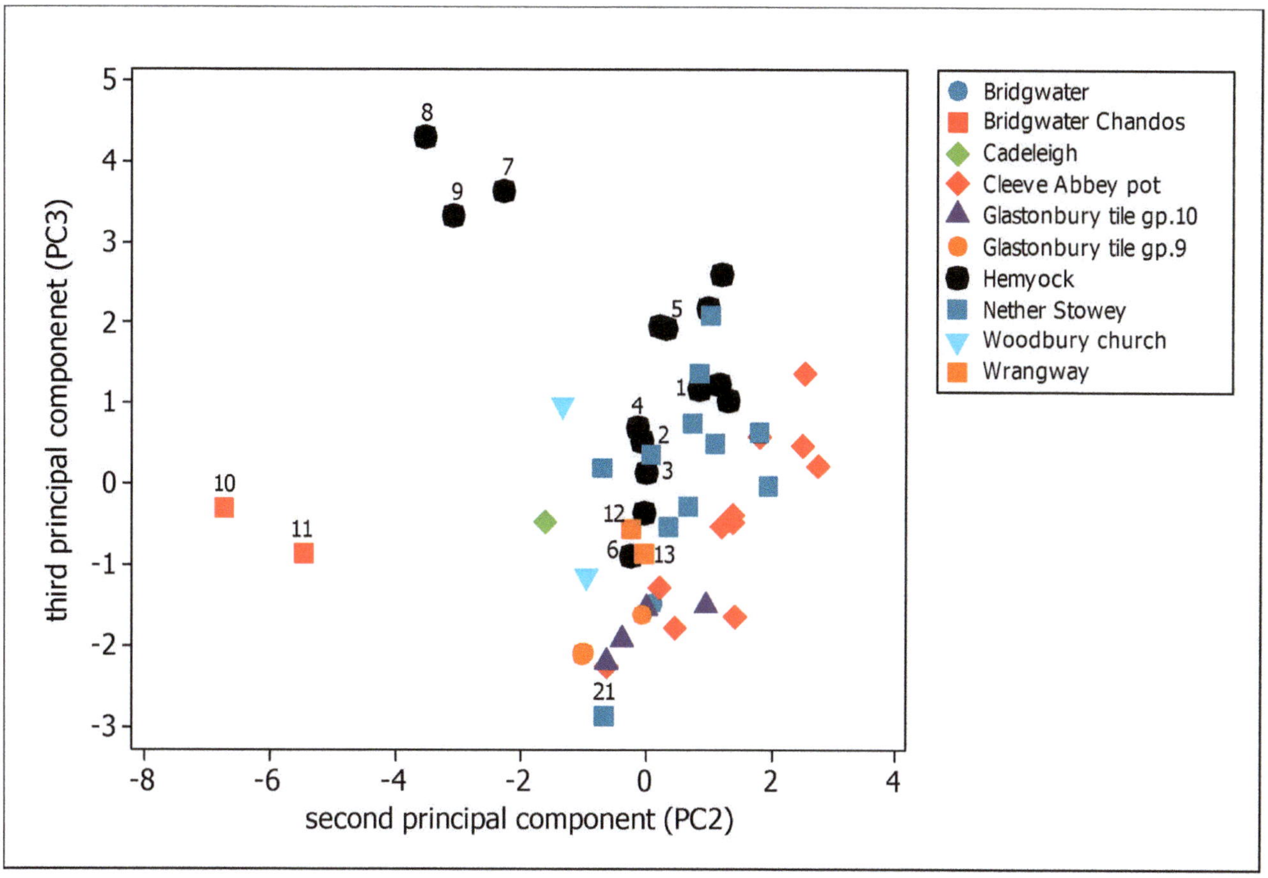

Figure 97. Plot of the second (horizontal axis) and third (vertical axis) principal components arising from all the samples analysed recently, combined with previous analyses of comparison material from other sites sharing a similar high potassium concentration to that found among Hemyock material. The comparison material was all analysed by ICP-atomic spectroscopy only, so fewer elements could be used than Figure 96 to generate the principal components.

These were present at only a minority of sites subjected to ICP analysis, including ten sherds from Hemyock used to compare against coarse pottery from Glastonbury Abbey (Hughes 2015, 265) and Calstock, Cornwall and found to be clearly distinguishable from either, and from similar South Somerset pottery (Hughes 2014). Other high potassium pottery was found at Nether Stowey, and some from Cleeve Abbey (Hughes in Allan 1998). Although most of the decorated floor tiles analysed from Glastonbury Abbey were locally produced, tile groups 9 and 10 had very similar chemistry to each other, suggesting a common origin, which contained high potassium and manganese (Hughes in Harcourt 2015, 292). This was close to the pattern for Nether Stowey, while pottery from Crowcombe and floor-tiles from Cleeve Abbey appeared to be associated (suggesting production to the west of the Quantocks) but were distinguishable from Nether Stowey on the east (Harcourt 2015; Hughes 2015). Although the few sherds of pottery previously analysed from Barnstaple had high potassium percentages, they differed in having higher calcium and magnesium and were not included in the comparison (Allan 1998). These analyses were combined with those of Figure 96 and principal components re-run. However, since all the comparative analyses were by ICP-atomic emission alone, lacking the mass spectrometry elements, the elements on which the statistics was based were reduced to 23. As a general rule, the larger the number of elements considered, the more reliable and perhaps clearer the interpretation of the results. As in the previous test, the first component reflected percentage of temper so the second and third components were plotted for data interpretation (Figure 97). The Hemyock samples split into the same two groups as before, but this time the three Upper Greensand-Derived sherds (Samples 7–9) are clearly separated from the Bridgwater Chandos sherds (Samples 10 and 11) whose clay chemistry is not found among any of the comparison analyses. Reassuringly, the Hemyock sherds analysed on the two different occasions intermingled despite analysis by two different laboratories. There was considerable overlap between the main Hemyock group and sherds from Nether Stowey, but separation from the Glastonbury tile and Cleeve Abbey pottery groups.

To explore the relationship between the cluster of samples on the right of Figure 97, a further re-run of the principal components was made after excluding the Hemyock Upper Greensand-Derived and Bridgwater Chandos sherds. This re-run (Figure 98) still showed overlapping of the Hemyock and Nether Stowey sherds, a degree of overlap with some of the Cleeve pottery sherds but clear separation of both from the Glastonbury tiles and the Wrangway sherds which overlapped with other examples of the Cleeve pottery. The two Woodbury church tiles showed different chemistry from each other; one (in the bottom centre of Figure 98) is close to some Nether

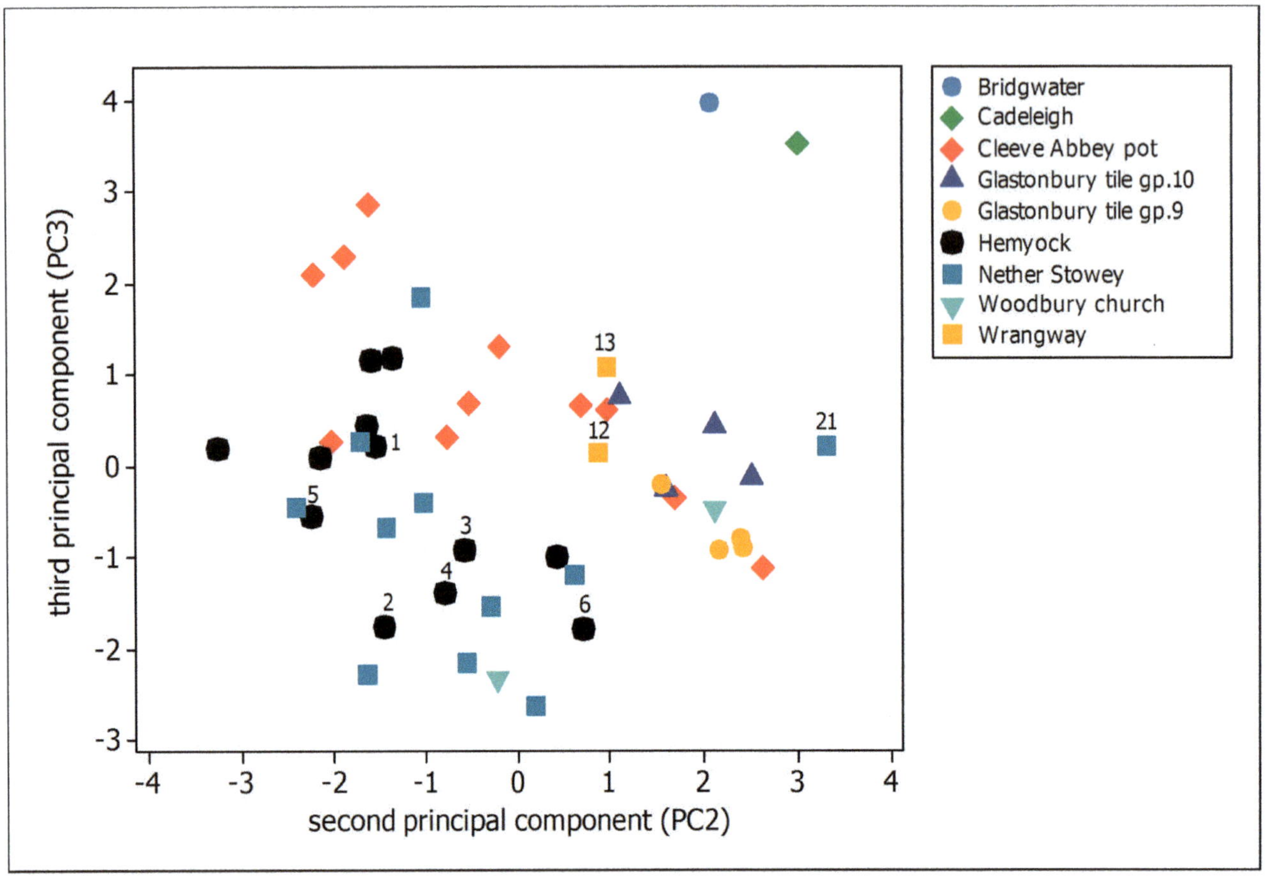

Figure 98. Plot of the second (horizontal axis) and third (vertical axis) principal components arising from a further statistical test of a subset of the samples of Figure 97, namely excluding the Upper Greensand-Derived ware from Hemyock (Samples 7–9) and Bridgwater Chandos sherds (Samples 10 and 11).

Stowey sherds, while the other is closely associated with tile group 9 from Glastonbury (lower right). Given the short geographic distance between Hemyock and Wrangway, the finding of different clay chemistry is useful. However, the similar clay chemistry for Hemyock and Nether Stowey pottery is troubling, since it was expected to show greater chemical difference, given the greater geographic distance than Wrangway (for example). The previous analyses of ten Nether Stowey sherds were by ICP-atomic spectrometry only, lacking the mass spectrometry elements of the present investigation. It is possible that if these mass spectrometry results were available for the Nether Stowey material, a separation might be discovered, although this is speculation. However the single Nether Stowey sherd analysed here (Sample 21) was significantly different from the earlier ICP analyses (well separated in Figure 98), and its petrological description was also different to the previous Nether Stowey kiln sherds which had a coarse fabric containing inclusions of red mudstone, quartz, micaceous slate and micaceous silty slate (Hughes 1998), whereas petrologically the matrix of Sample 21 is a silty clay with fine white mica and ferruginous inclusions. Chemically, Sample 21 contained significantly more alkalis (sodium, potassium rubidium, caesium), calcium, strontium, thorium and rare earth elements than either the Hemyock or other Nether Stowey sherds analysed. The chemical difference could derive from two clay types being used by the Nether Stowey potters. A single sherd from Bridgwater, George Street (Sample 2/16) was chemically similar to the tile from Cadeleigh, but neither were like samples from any other sites.

Integration with Other Investigations on the Samples

All the waster sherds from Hemyock, regardless of the type of product or the specific context (contexts 571 and 588) have very similar mineralogical features and ICP analyses. In contrast, the Saxo-Norman Hemyock Upper Greensand-Derived wares (Samples 7–9) contain significant kaolinite (QEMSCAN), a relatively pure aluminium silicate, which would explain the relatively low percentages of potassium, iron and magnesium compared to the other Hemyock sherds. QEMSCAN shows a high percentage of inclusions of potassium feldspar in the Wrangway (Samples 12 and 13) and Nether Stowey (Sample 21) sherds compared with low amounts in Hemyock kiln waste sherds (Samples 1–6), and this explains the higher potassium, rubidium and caesium ICP results for Wrangway and Nether Stowey than Hemyock. The Nether Stowey sherd contained significant calcium phosphate (QEMSCAN), and the phosphorus figure for this sample (0.44%) is significantly higher than the range for most other sherds (0.05–0.2%). QEMSCAN indicated a significant percentage of calcite in the Bridgwater Chandos sherds (Samples 10 and 11) and the pair had much higher lime than any other sherds (8.8/9.3%). They also contained substantial percentages of plagioclase feldspar (sodium, calcium silicates) and the sherds' higher sodium (0.71/0.73%) figures were much above, for example, the Hemyock sherds (Samples 1–6) (0.14–0.19%); some of the additional lime may also be present as calcium feldspars. More generally, QEMSCAN indicated that the inclusions across all the sherds were predominantly quartz, of which a significant percentage was also present in the matrix. This confirms the assumption that the first principal component in the statistical tests on these ICP results principally reflects the percentage of a relatively pure silica temper (inclusions and matrix) in each fabric.

Discussion and Conclusions

ICP analysis of the Hemyock pottery and comparison groups showed the following:

1. The Hemyock kiln waste, Samples 1–6, showed a consistent high-potassium chemical pattern, clearly different chemically from the three Saxo-Norman Upper Greensand-Derived wares from the same site (Samples 7–9).
2. The high-potassium Hemyock pottery could be clearly distinguished chemically from the other kiln samples from Bridgwater (Samples 10 and 11), Wrangway (Samples 12 and 13), Donyatt sites 2 (Samples 16 and 17) and 3 (Samples 18 and 19), and the single sherds from Crowcombe (Samplel 20) and Nether Stowey (Sample 21), although earlier analyses of medieval pottery from Nether Stowey by ICP-AES alone could not be distinguished chemically from Hemyock samples (1–6).
3. The high-potassium Hemyock pottery could also be distinguished from earlier analyses of two tile groups in similar clays from Glastonbury Abbey. Of other material analysed, the tiles from Cadeleigh and Woodbury church also showed chemical differences from the Hemyock samples.
4. Comparison with late medieval pottery previously analysed from Cleeve Abbey showed that some of the high-potassium pottery from the abbey overlapped chemically with the Hemyock kiln waste, but other sherds were closer to Wrangway and some to Glastonbury tiles.
5. Good concordance was found between the ICP and petrological and QEMSCAN data on the same sherds analysed.

Mineralogical Analysis Using Automated SEMS-EDS (QEMSCAN)

Jens C.Ø. Andersen, David Dawson and Gavyn K. Rollinson

Introduction

The analysis described here explores the mineralogical variations in ceramic samples from the excavations at Hemyock and comparative material from other sites. The work follows on from an investigation carried out in 2012 into the mineralogical composition of Somerset ceramics

Table 22. Mineralogical types previously identified from Taunton Castle and Somerset localities (Andersen et al. 2016a; 2016b; Dawson and Dawson 2016)

Type	Description
Type A	The clay composition of the matrix is dominated by Fe-Al-K silicates with some muscovite/illite. This type has no or little kaolinite. Inclusions are predominantly quartz and K-feldspar. Plagioclase feldspar and calcite are absent from both inclusions and matrix. Glauconite is locally significant. Type A appears to be consistent with post-medieval West Somerset wares from Crowcombe, Langford Budville, Nether Stowey and Wrangway and Taunton Castle fabric types 74, 83 and 89 (Dawson pers. obsv; Coleman-Smith and Pearson 1970; Pearson *et al.* 2015).
Type B	The clay composition of the matrix is a mixture of Fe-Al-K silicates and kaolinite (between 1:1 and 2:1) with significant (although less) muscovite/illite. The matrix has significant Fe-Al silicates and plagioclase feldspar. Two subtypes are defined by differences in the inclusions
Type B1	Inclusions of quartz and K-feldspar. Glauconite is locally significant but calcite is absent. This subtype includes late medieval production at Donyatt Site 4 and the two post-medieval samples from production waste from near Wanstrow as well as two medieval sherds from Taunton Castle (unclassified and type 14 = Ilchester B) (Coleman-Smith and Pearson 1988; Vranch 1988)
Type B2	Inclusions of quartz and calcite with minor K-feldspar. This subtype includes four medieval sherds from Taunton Castle (types 3, 7B, 8 and 15).
Type C	The matrix clay composition of type C is closely similar to type B except the content of kaolinite appears to be slightly less. Inclusions are 60-70 percent calcite with the remaining being quartz and minor alkali feldspar. This group includes two medieval sherds from Taunton Castle types 7A and 23.
Type D	The clay composition of the matrix is predominantly kaolinite and muscovite/illite with only minor Fe-Al-K silicates. Quartz is below 20 percent and plagioclase dominates over alkali feldspar. The inclusion population is much more diverse than in all other types. Around 70 percent is quartz but the remaining 30 percent include alkali feldspar, muscovite/illite, kaolinite, and Fe-Al silicates. The group includes production at Donyatt Site 13 and a single sherd from Taunton Castle type 62, both of which are post-medieval (Coleman-Smith 2002).

that will form part of a report on the pottery from Taunton Castle (Andersen *et al.* 2016b). Here, samples from Hemyock have been compared with samples from known late medieval and post-medieval pottery production sites across Somerset. The aim in 2012 was to explore how variable ceramic samples are across the county, and to establish whether any of the sherds found at Taunton Castle could be identified to particular production sites. That study encompassed post-medieval ceramics from Crowcombe, Donyatt sites 4 and 13, Langford Budville, Nether Stowey, Wanstrow and Wrangway. It identified distinct groupings in the ceramic types, based on the mineralogical assemblage of the matrix and inclusion populations, some of which could also be recognised in materials from Taunton Castle.

Whilst the geographical and geological setting of Hemyock has already been outlined in Chapter 1, it is useful to remind the reader of the situation here. Hemyock is situated toward the western end of the Blackdown Hills. The geological bedrock formation is the Mercia Mudstone Group of Triassic age, which in the surrounding hills are succeeded by the Upper Greensand Formation of Cretaceous age. The Jurassic Lias Group which dominates the time interval between the Triassic and Cretaceous is absent in this area. The current catchment area of the River Culm that runs through Hemyock only drains the Triassic and Cretaceous rocks. Our previous study in Somerset identified strong links between the bedrock formations and the ceramics produced; in particular the distinct West Somerset types from sites on Triassic bedrock yielded products with very similar mineralogical characteristics (Table 22, type A). Based on the geology, it would be expected that ceramics produced at Hemyock would have similar characteristics.

Methodology

The mineralogical composition of the samples was explored using the technique described by Andersen *et al.* (2016a). Polished thin-sections of each sherd were produced, where possible, to provide sections across the sherds. Individual specimens were photographed and then carbon-coated for analysis by QEMSCAN 4300 at Camborne School of Mines, University of Exeter. The QEMSCAN is an automated scanning electron microscope that uses a focused electron-beam to generate characteristic X-ray spectra in points on the thin-section surface. Automated beam control, movement of the sample holder below the beam and the collection of spectra allow for the collection of information on more than 50,000 points per hour. These spectra are then classified into mineralogical groups by comparison with a spectral database (a species identification protocol, SIP); neighbouring analyses that are similar are interpreted to be part of the same particle, and the results include not only information on the amount of each mineral, but also characteristic two-particle size distributions for each mineral, particle shape information and statistics on the relations between minerals.

The Fieldscan analytical mode allows for the collection of compositional data in a pre-defined grid across the sample surface, yielding visual representations of the distribution of minerals as well as quantitative data. A customised discriminator was introduced to distinguish the sample matrix defined as particles less than 63 µm (in geological terms this is the discrimination between sand and silt), which is used as a proxy for the clay material used in the ceramic, and inclusions (particles greater than 63 µm) which are used as an approximation of the material used

Table 23. Mineral groups used in the QEMSCAN analysis

Mineral group	Constituents
Fe sulphides	pyrite, marcasite, pyrrhotite (and possibly jarosite)
Pb glaze	lead-bearing silicates, oxides and sulphides/sulphates
Barite	barite
Chrome	spinel chromite, chrome spinel
FeO_x/CO_3	siderite, hematite, magnetite, goethite, ochre and limonite.
Mn phases	all manganese bearing minerals including pyrolusite, rhodonite, rhodocrosite and umber
Rutile	rutile, anatase, brookite
Ilmenite	ilmenite
Zircon	zircon
REE phases	monazite, xenotime, allanite
Quartz	quartz, opal, chert, flint, chalcedony
Plagioclase feldspar	plagioclase feldspar
K-Feldspar	orthoclase, sanidine, microcline
Muscovite/illite	muscovite, illite
Fe Al K silicates	iron-bearing (ferruginous) clays (smectite, montmorillonite, nontronite), biotite mica
Glauconite	any phase with Fe, Al, K, Mg,Si,O
Kaolinite	kaolinite, halloysite, dickite, kyanite, sillimanite, andalusite
Tourmaline	tourmaline
Fe Al silicates	chlorite/clinochlore, nontronite, vermiculite
Mg Al silicates	palygorskite, magnesiochloritoid
Mg silicates	asbestos, talc, serpentine minerals
Ca Fe Al silicates	epidote, zoisite, clinozoisite
Calcite calcite, chalk, limestone, lime, ankerite, dolomite	calcite, chalk, limestone, lime, ankerite, dolomite
Ca phosphates	apatite, tooth and bone material
Others	any other mineral

to temper the clay. A further modifier takes into account that many small matrix particles may touch and generate an interconnected framework in the samples. As this material would enclose many particles of other minerals, it will appear to have a very high surface area to a given volume. It must be noted, however, that although this method appears to be robust, some cross-over can be expected between the groups. It is particularly noticeable that inclusions composed of fine-grained mixtures of minerals (such as recycled ceramic fragments and consolidated mudstone inclusions) are expected to report to the matrix.

As X-ray spectra are characteristic for the chemical elements rather than minerals, a combination of element signals is used to identify the minerals. This however means that minerals with similar elements may appear in the same mineral group. Table 23 lists the mineral groupings used in this report.

Results

The samples from Hemyock display significant variability both in their matrix and inclusion assemblages (Figures 99 and 100; full analyses in Figures 101-121). For clarity, the Pb-glaze has been excluded from the mineralogical comparisons, and minerals appearing at less than 0.25 vol% are considered to be (near) absent.

The samples from the two deposits at Hemyock (contexts 571 and 588) are indistinguishable in terms of their mineralogy. The matrix is dominated by Fe-Al-K silicates with 10–15% quartz, around 5% K-feldspar and 5–10% muscovite/illite. They have no plagioclase feldspar and very little kaolinite in the matrix. The inclusion assemblage has more than 90% quartz and only minor K-feldspar (less than 6%). Curiously, Samples 2 and 5 have substantial Fe-oxides (5% and 2.5% respectively), which are much higher than the amounts we have encountered elsewhere (a sample from Taunton Castle had 0.5%). As for the matrix, the complete absence of plagioclase feldspar is noticeable.

The three Saxo-Norman Upper Greensand-Derived sherds from context 557 (Samples 7–9) are substantially different from Hemyock kiln samples 1–6 with respect to their matrix, as well as their inclusion assemblages. These three samples are mineralogically similar, with a matrix mixture of 30–40% Fe-Al-K silicates with 25–30% kaolinite and

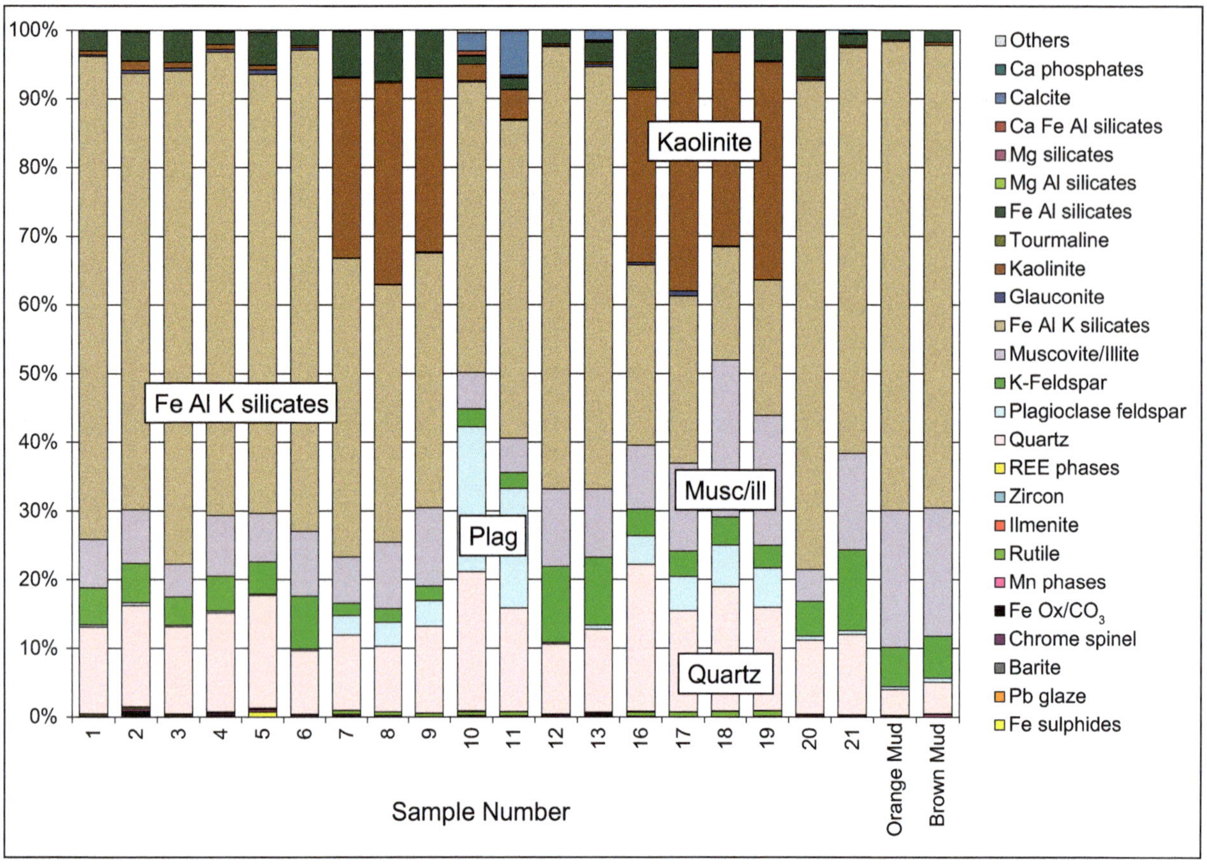

Figure 99. Comparison of matrix components of the samples.

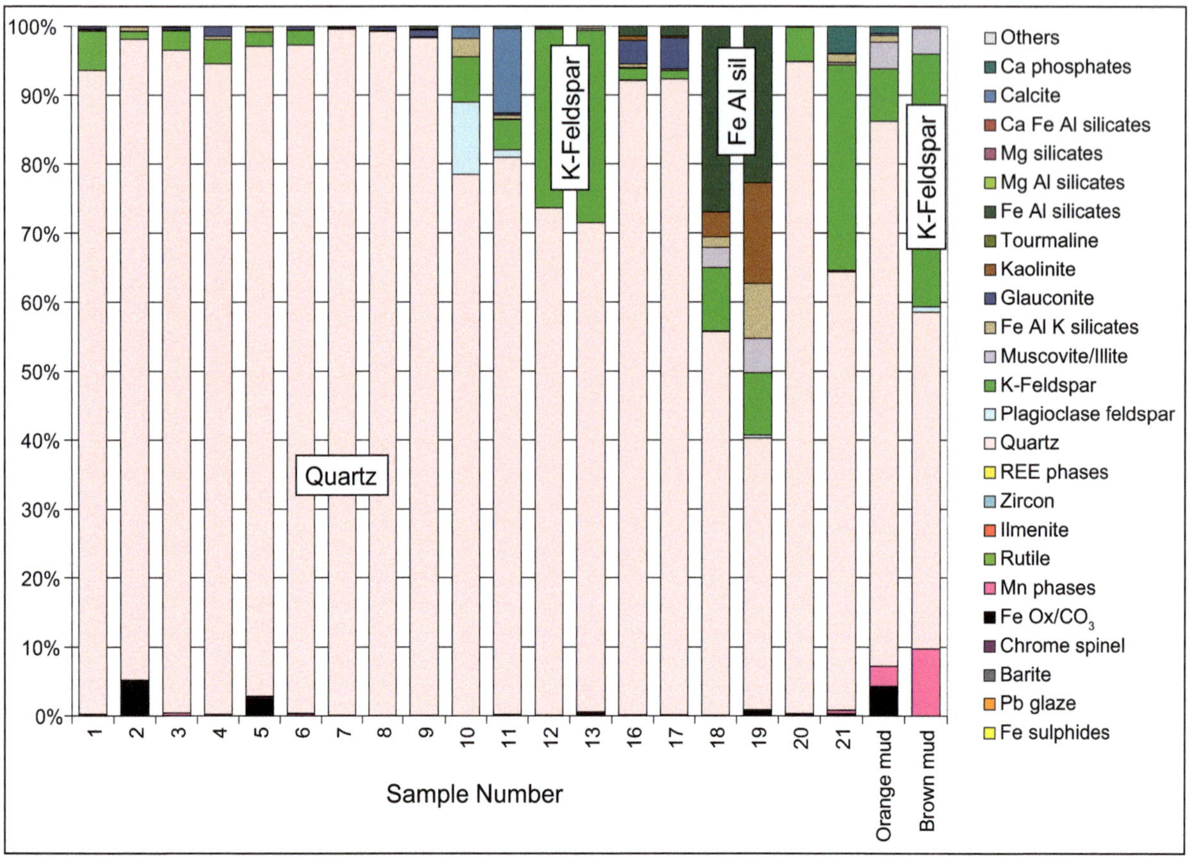

Figure 100. Comparison of inclusion populations in the samples.

around 10% muscovite/illite, 10% quartz and 5–10% Fe-Al silicates. The matrix carries a couple of percent of plagioclase feldspar, which dominates over K-feldspar. The inclusions are very pure quartz with only traces of glauconite.

The samples from Bridgwater Chandos Glass Cone (Samples 10 and 11) are very distinctive in their composition. The matrix is dominated by 40–50% Fe-Al-K silicates and has minor (5%) muscovite/illite and kaolinite. However, the samples have substantial amounts of plagioclase feldspar (15–20%) and significant (3–6%) calcite. Approximately 80% of the inclusions consist of quartz, with variable amounts of K-feldspar, plagioclase feldspar and calcite. Traces of Ca-Fe-Al silicates are also unique to these samples.

The samples from Wrangway (Samples 12 and 13), Crowcombe (Sample 20) and Nether Stowey (Sample 21) have matrix compositions that are dominated by 60–70% Fe-Al-K silicates, with 3–15% muscovite/illite, 10–12% quartz and minor Fe-Al silicates. The inclusion assemblages are somewhat variable. Both samples from Wrangway have 70–75% quartz and 25– 30% K-feldspar with virtually no other minerals. The sample from Crowcombe has a similarly simple assemblage of 95% quartz and 5% K-feldspar. The sample from Nether Stowey, in contrast, has a more varied inclusion assemblage with 65% quartz, 30% K-feldspar and unexpectedly 4% Ca-phosphates.

Mineralogical Types Previously Identified from Taunton Castle and Other Somerset Localities (Andersen *et al.* 2016a; Dawson and Dawson 2016)

Type A

The clay composition of the matrix is dominated by Fe-Al-K silicates with some muscovite/illite. This type has no or little kaolinite. Inclusions are predominantly quartz and K-feldspar. Plagioclase feldspar and calcite are absent from both inclusions and matrix. Glauconite is locally significant.

This type appears to be consistent with the post-medieval West Somerset wares from Crowcombe, Langford Budville, Nether Stowey and Wrangway and Taunton Castle fabric types 74, 83 and 89 (Dawson pers. obsv; Coleman-Smith and Pearson 1970; Pearson *et al.* 2015).

Type B

The clay composition of the matrix is a mixture of Fe-Al-K silicates and kaolinite (between 1:1 and 2:1) with significant (although less) muscovite/illite. The matrix has significant Fe-Al silicates and plagioclase feldspar. Two subtypes are defined by differences in the inclusions:

- Type B1: Inclusions of quartz and K-feldspar. Glauconite is locally significant but calcite is absent. This subtype includes late medieval production at Donyatt Site 4 and the two post-medieval samples from production waste from near Wanstrow, as well as two medieval sherds from Taunton Castle (unclassified and type 14 = Ilchester B) (Coleman-Smith and Pearson 1988; Vranch 1988).
- Type B2: Inclusions of quartz and calcite with minor K-feldspar. This subtype includes four medieval sherds from Taunton Castle (types 3, 7B, 8 and 15).

Type C

The matrix clay composition of type C is closely similar to type B, except that the content of kaolinite appears to be slightly less. Inclusions are 60–70% calcite, the remainder being quartz and minor alkali feldspar. This group includes two medieval sherds from Taunton Castle types 7A and 23.

Type D

The clay composition of the matrix is predominantly kaolinite and muscovite/illite with only minor Fe-Al-K silicates. Quartz is below 20% and plagioclase dominates over alkali feldspar. The inclusion population is much more diverse than in all other types. Around 70% is quartz but the remaining 30% include alkali feldspar, muscovite/illite, kaolinite, and Fe-Al silicates

The group includes products from Donyatt Site 13 and a single sherd from Taunton Castle type 62, both of which are post-medieval (Coleman-Smith 2002).

Discussion and Interpretation

The samples from Hemyock contexts 571 and 588, as well as samples from Crowcombe, Wrangway and Nether Stowey, are closely similar to Somerset mineralogical type A. This is consistent with our previous observation of the link to the Triassic bedrock, and the matrix compositions are also consistent with the two samples of natural clay from the site that were also investigated (Samples 22 and 23). However, there are a few variations which have not been previously observed in this type. Most notably Samples 2 and 5 from Hemyock carry significant inclusions of FeO_x/CO_3, Sample 13 from Wrangway has minor amounts of calcite in the matrix, and the sample from Nether Stowey has significant amounts (4%) of Ca-phosphates (possibly bone material) in the inclusion assemblage. Although these differences from the type description are distinctive, our sampling does not allow us to identify clearly new sub-types at this stage. We note however that the absence of kaolinite and plagioclase feldspar appear to be the most distinctive characteristics of type A.

The matrix of the samples from context 557 most closely matches type B_1. This is unexpected and suggests a clay composition that is not derived from the Triassic bedrock. The matrix is somewhat similar to samples from areas with Liassic bedrock (Donyatt and Wanstow). The closest exposures of the Lias are approximately 6 km to the east-

Sample number: 1	Context number: 571	CSM lab. code: C03150016

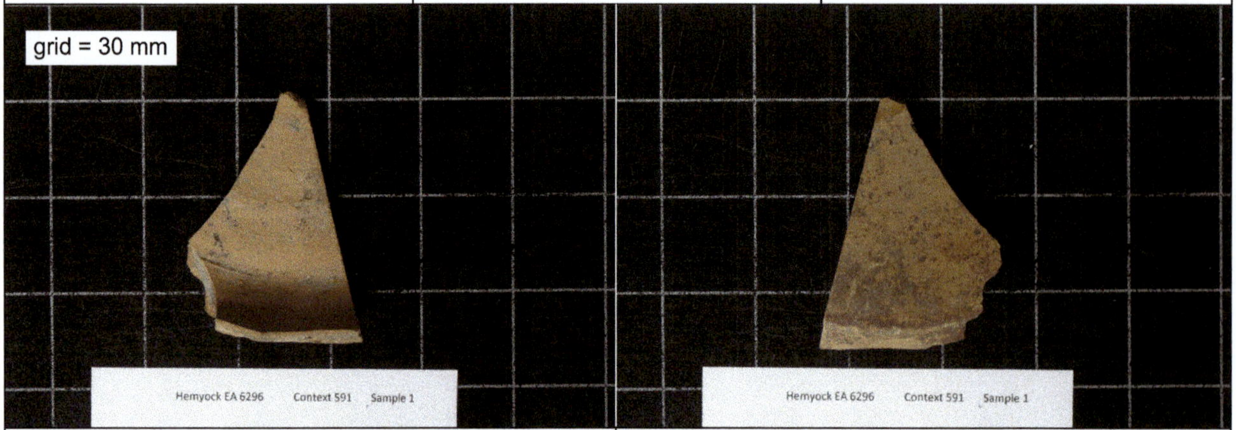

Fabric description	**Mineralogical description**
Reduced and reoxidised fabric, unglazed.	The sherd has 95 vol% matrix and 5 vol% inclusions. The inclusion population is composed of fairly pure quartz (~93 vol%) with some K-feldspar (6 vol%). The matrix is composed of Fe-Al-K silicates (70 vol%) and quartz (13 vol%), with minor muscovite/illite (7 vol%), K-feldspar (5 vol%) and Fe-Al silicates (3 vol%). Kaolinite and plagioclase are nearly absent. Traces of glauconite are found as inclusions and as part of the matrix.
Form	**Mineralogical type**
Basal angle of a jug.	A
Analogues	**Notes**
West Somerset type	None

Visual appearance of thin section (transmitted light)	**Mineralogical map**	**Key to mineral map** (mineral groups listed in Table 23)
		Fe sulphides Pb glaze Barite Chrome spinel Fe Ox / CO_3 Mn phases Rutile Ilmenite Zircon REE phases Quartz Plagioclase feldspar K-feldspar Muscovite / Illite Fe Al K silicates Glauconite Kaolinite Tourmaline Fe Al silicates Mg Al silicates Mg silicates Ca Fe Al silicates Calcite Ca phosphates Others

Figure 101. Analysis of Sample 1: Hemyock, jug base.

Sample number: 1	Context number: 571	CSM lab. code: C03150016

Mineralogical composition

	Matrix	Inclusions	Bulk
Fe sulphides	0.002	0.000	0.001
Pb glaze	0.014	0.000	0.014
Barite	0.000	0.000	0.000
Chrome spinel	0.003	0.000	0.003
Fe Ox/CO_3	0.035	0.000	0.035
Mn phases	0.305	9.753	0.360
Rutile	0.128	0.000	0.128
Ilmenite	0.017	0.000	0.017
Zircon	0.006	0.000	0.006
REE phases	0.000	0.000	0.000
Quartz	4.621	48.765	4.881
Plagioclase feldspar	0.596	0.802	0.597
K-Feldspar	6.068	36.669	6.249
Muscovite/Illite	18.705	3.694	18.616
Fe Al K silicates	67.305	0.211	66.908
Glauconite	0.016	0.000	0.015
Kaolinite	0.386	0.106	0.384
Tourmaline	0.018	0.000	0.018
Fe Al silicates	1.728	0.000	1.718
Mg Al silicates	0.002	0.000	0.002
Mg silicates	0.006	0.000	0.006
Ca Fe Al silicates	0.006	0.000	0.006
Calcite	0.021	0.000	0.021
Ca phosphates	0.003	0.000	0.002
Others	0.011	0.000	0.011

Particle size distribution

Matrix (< 63 µm) = 95.2 vol%
Inclusions (> 63 µm) = 4.8 vol%

Mineralogical type

Total measurement points = 2952730
Measurement spacing = 10 µm

Visual representation of mineralogy
(Pb-glaze has been excluded in these diagrams; FO = Fe-Ox/CO_3, qz = quartz, pl = plagioclase, ksp = K-feldspar, ms/ill = muscovite/illite, FAKS = Fe-Al-K silicates, glt = glauconite, kln = kaolinite, FAS = Fe-Al silicates, cc = calcite)

Matrix

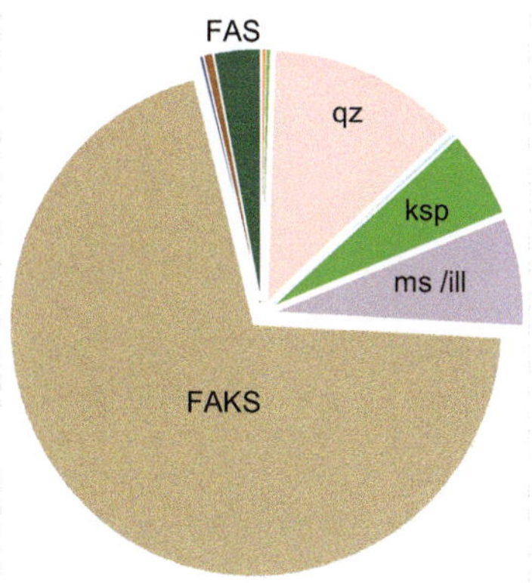

Inclusions

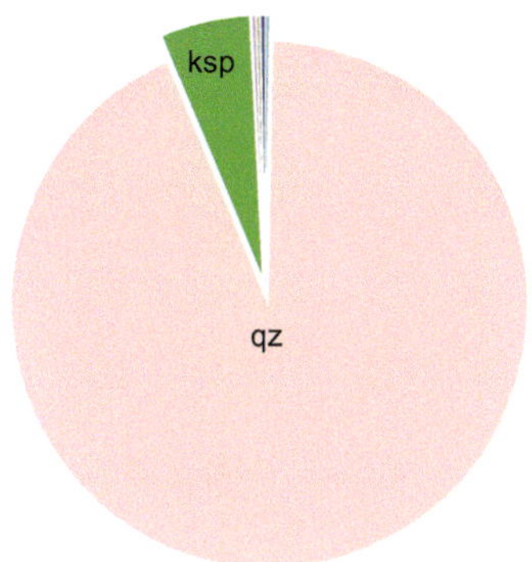

Bulk

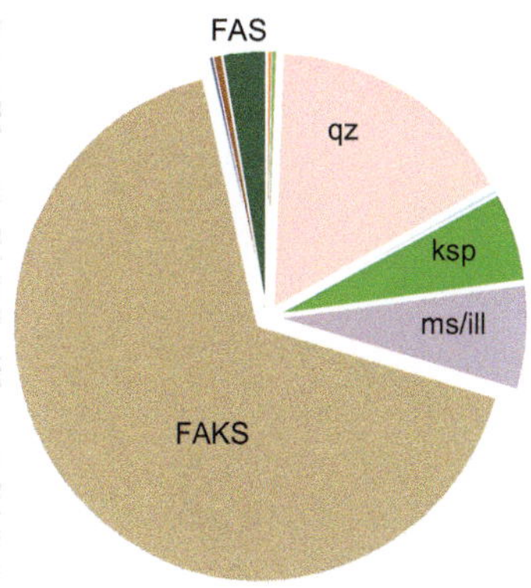

Figure 101 *continued.*

Sample number: 2	Context number: 571	CSM lab. code: C03150032

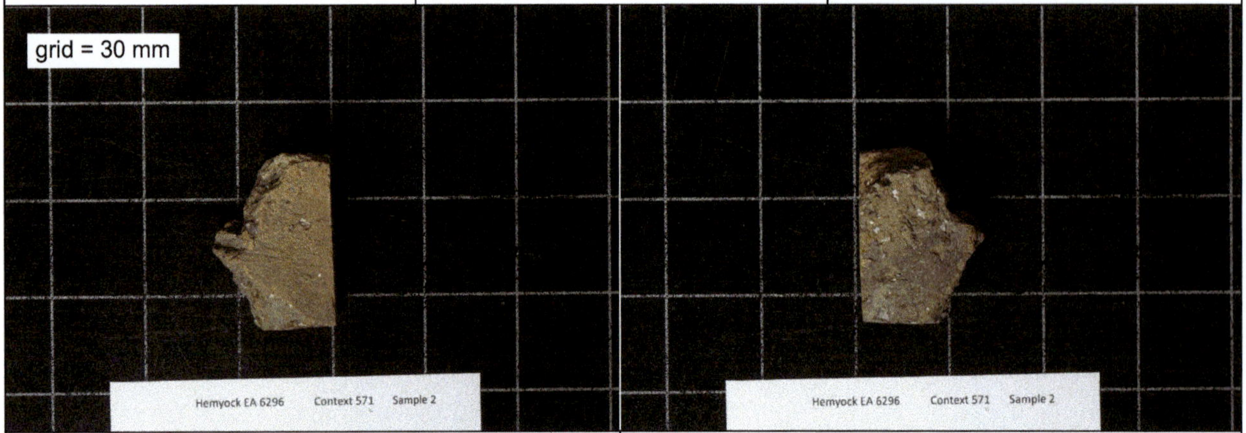

Fabric description

Reduced and reoxidised fabric,chert (?) inclusions.

Mineralogical description

The sherd has 78 vol% matrix and 22 vol% inclusions. The inclusion population is composed of fairly pure quartz (93 vol%) with significant Fe-Ox/CO_3 (5 vol%) and only trace K-feldspar (1 vol%).The matrix is composed of Fe-Al-K silicates (63 vol%) with quartz (15 vol%), K-feldspar (6 vol%), muscovite/illite (8 vol%) and Fe-Al silicates (4 vol%). Minor kaolinite (1.3 vol%) is present but only traces of plagioclase. The matrix also carries traces of glauconite.

Form

Sherd of oven tile, reduced and reoxidised fabric, ?chert inclusions.

Mineralogical type

A

Analogues

Notes

A large, rounded, fine-grained inclusion reports to the matrix.

Visual appearance of thin section (transmitted light)

Mineralogical map

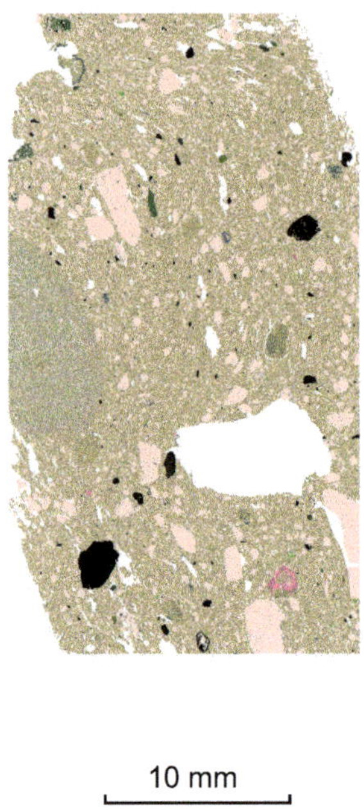

Key to mineral map
(mineral groups listed in Table 23)

- Fe sulphides
- Pb glaze
- Barite
- Chrome spinel
- Fe Ox / CO_3
- Mn phases
- Rutile
- Ilmenite
- Zircon
- REE phases
- Quartz
- Plagioclase feldspar
- K-feldspar
- Muscovite / Illite
- Fe Al K silicates
- Glauconite
- Kaolinite
- Tourmaline
- Fe Al silicates
- Mg Al silicates
- Mg silicates
- Ca Fe Al silicates
- Calcite
- Ca phosphates
- Others

Figure 102. Analysis of Sample 2: Hemyock, oven tile.

Sample number: 2	Context number: 571	CSM lab. code: C03150032

Mineralogical composition

	Matrix	Inclusions	Bulk
Fe sulphides	0.061	0.000	0.047
Pb glaze	0.071	0.000	0.055
Barite	0.000	0.000	0.000
Chrome spinel	0.003	0.000	0.002
Fe Ox/CO_3	0.788	5.060	1.747
Mn phases	0.286	0.082	0.240
Rutile	0.227	0.020	0.180
Ilmenite	0.088	0.008	0.070
Zircon	0.024	0.009	0.021
REE phases	0.004	0.000	0.003
Quartz	14.741	92.909	32.295
Plagioclase feldspar	0.418	0.000	0.324
K-Feldspar	5.687	1.118	4.661
Muscovite/Illite	7.844	0.054	6.095
Fe Al K silicates	63.468	0.605	49.352
Glauconite	0.461	0.018	0.361
Kaolinite	1.337	0.000	1.037
Tourmaline	0.061	0.009	0.049
Fe Al silicates	4.157	0.107	3.247
Mg Al silicates	0.028	0.000	0.021
Mg silicates	0.129	0.000	0.100
Ca Fe Al silicates	0.007	0.000	0.005
Calcite	0.039	0.000	0.030
Ca phosphates	0.016	0.000	0.012
Others	0.055	0.001	0.043

Particle size distribution

Matrix (< 63 μm) = 77.5 vol%
Inclusions (> 63 μm) = 22.4 vol%

Mineralogical type

Total measurement points = 5163171
Measurement spacing = 10 μm

Visual representation of mineralogy
(Pb-glaze has been excluded in these diagrams; FO = Fe-Ox/CO_3, qz = quartz, pl = plagioclase, ksp = K-feldspar, ms/ill = muscovite/illite, FAKS = Fe-Al-K silicates, glt = glauconite, kln = kaolinite, FAS = Fe-Al silicates, cc = calcite)

Matrix	Inclusions	Bulk

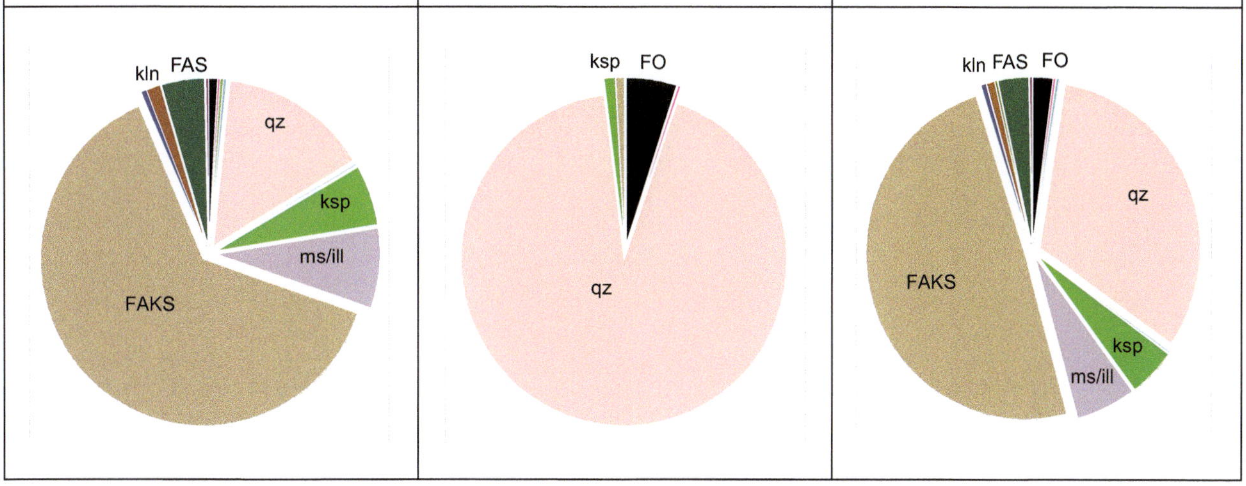

Figure 102 *continued.*

Sample number: 3	Context number: 588	CSM lab. code: C03150017

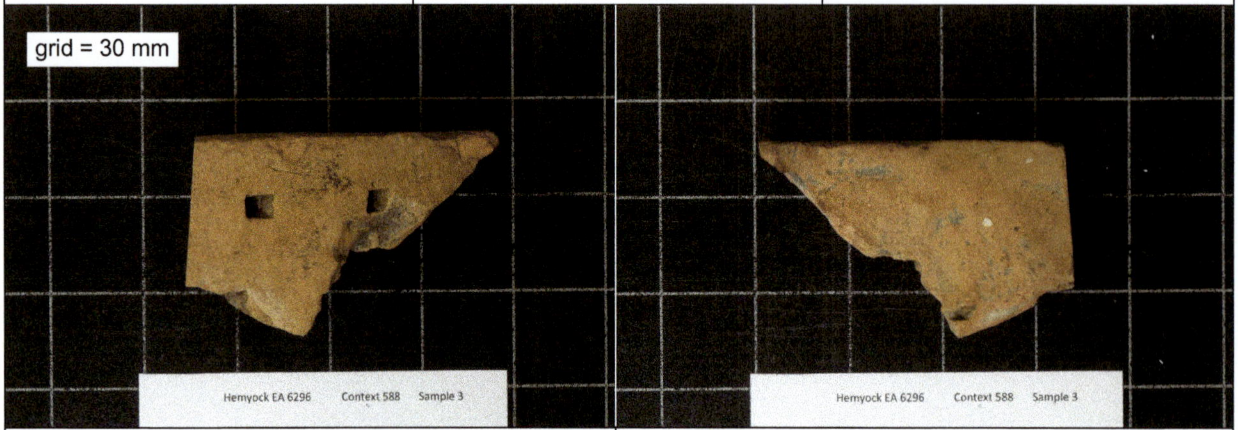

Fabric description	Mineralogical description
Reduced and reoxidised fabric, ?chert inclusions.	The sherd has 92 vol% matrix and 8 vol% inclusions. The inclusion population is composed of nearly pure quartz (96 vol%) with only minor K-feldspar (3 vol%). The matrix is composed of Fe-Al-K silicates (72 vol%) with quartz (13 vol%), Fe-Al silicates (4 vol%), K-feldspar (4 vol%), and muscovite/illite (5 vol%). Kaolinite and plagioclase are nearly absent. Traces of glauconite are found as inclusions and as part of the matrix.
Form	**Mineralogical type**
Sherd of oven tile, stabbed on underside.	A
Analogues	**Notes**
West Somerset type.	None.

Visual appearance of thin section (transmitted light)	Mineralogical map	Key to mineral map (mineral groups listed in Table 23)

Key to mineral map:
- Fe sulphides
- Pb glaze
- Barite
- Chrome spinel
- Fe Ox / CO_3
- Mn phases
- Rutile
- Ilmenite
- Zircon
- REE phases
- Quartz
- Plagioclase feldspar
- K-feldspar
- Muscovite / Illite
- Fe Al K silicates
- Glauconite
- Kaolinite
- Tourmaline
- Fe Al silicates
- Mg Al silicates
- Mg silicates
- Ca Fe Al silicates
- Calcite
- Ca phosphates
- Others

Figure 103. Analysis of Sample 3: Hemyock, oven tile.

Sample number: 3	**Context number: 588**	**CSM lab. code: C03150017**

Mineralogical composition

	Matrix	Inclusions	Bulk
Fe sulphides	0.001	0.000	0.001
Pb glaze	0.001	0.000	0.001
Barite	0.000	0.000	0.000
Chrome spinel	0.003	0.000	0.003
Fe Ox/CO_3	0.070	0.042	0.068
Mn phases	0.042	0.365	0.066
Rutile	0.214	0.014	0.199
Ilmenite	0.073	0.000	0.068
Zircon	0.022	0.000	0.020
REE phases	0.003	0.000	0.003
Quartz	12.718	96.103	19.047
Plagioclase feldspar	0.231	0.000	0.214
K-Feldspar	4.091	2.773	3.991
Muscovite/Illite	4.815	0.036	4.452
Fe Al K silicates	71.740	0.140	66.305
Glauconite	0.470	0.321	0.459
Kaolinite	0.851	0.000	0.786
Tourmaline	0.024	0.000	0.022
Fe Al silicates	4.467	0.205	4.143
Mg Al silicates	0.027	0.000	0.025
Mg silicates	0.060	0.000	0.055
Ca Fe Al silicates	0.002	0.000	0.002
Calcite	0.032	0.000	0.030
Ca phosphates	0.030	0.002	0.028
Others	0.012	0.000	0.011

Particle size distribution

Matrix (< 63 μm) = 92.4 vol%
Inclusions (> 63 μm) = 7.6 vol%

Mineralogical type

Total measurement points = 5845212
Measurement spacing = 10 μm

Visual representation of mineralogy
(Pb-glaze has been excluded in these diagrams; FO = Fe-Ox/CO_3, qz = quartz, pl = plagioclase, ksp = K-feldspar, ms/ill = muscovite/illite, FAKS = Fe-Al-K silicates, glt = glauconite, kln = kaolinite, FAS = Fe-Al silicates, cc = calcite)

Matrix

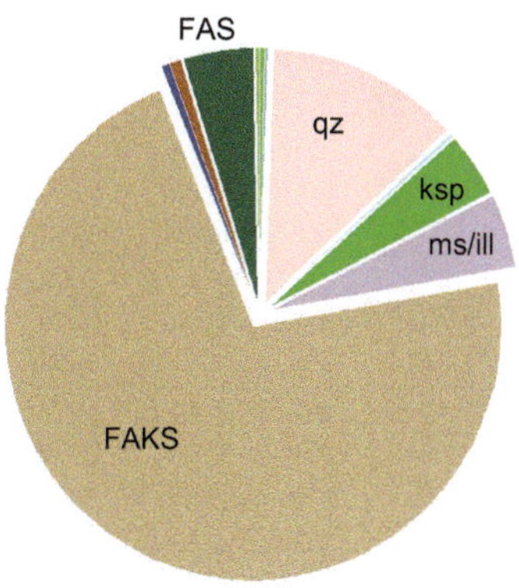

Inclusions

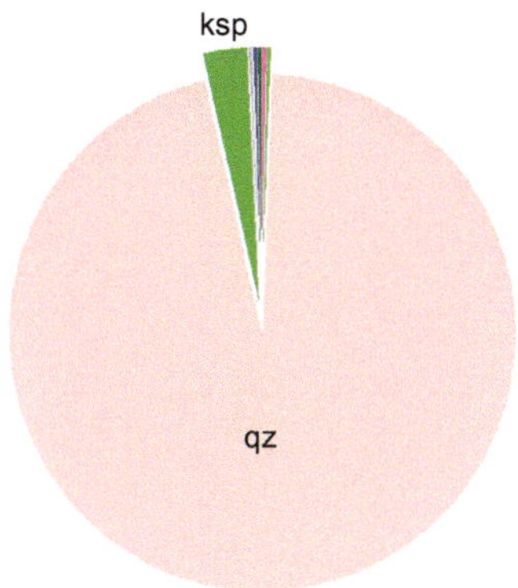

Bulk

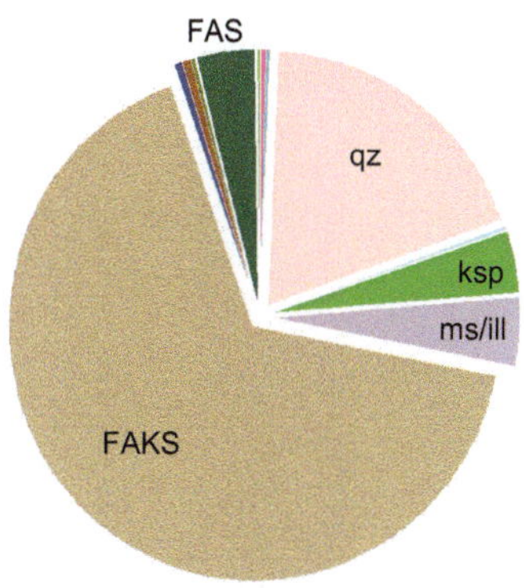

Figure 103 *continued.*

Sample number: 4	Context number: 571	CSM lab. code: C03150018

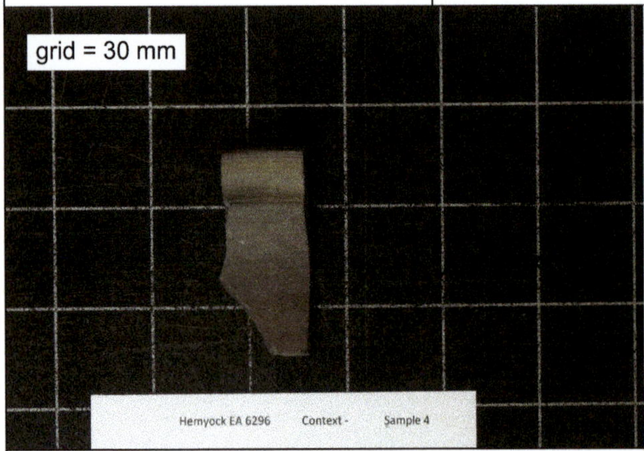

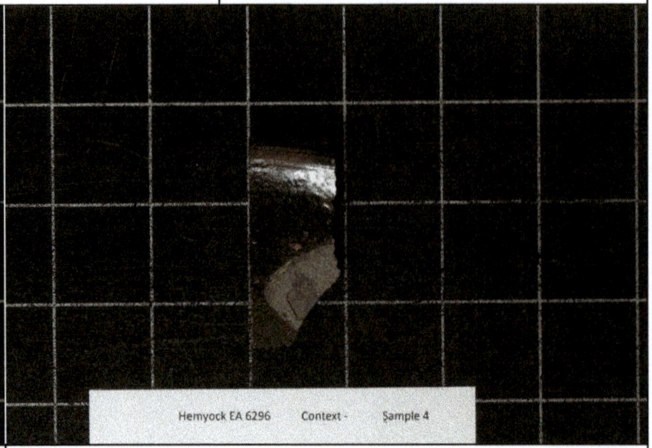

Fabric description	Mineralogical description
Heavily reduced dark grey fabric, internal reduced dark green lead glaze.	The sherd has 92 vol% matrix and 8 vol% inclusions. Apart from the 5 vol% Pb-glaze, the inclusion population is composed of fairly pure quartz (~94 vol%) with minor K-feldspar (3 vol%) and glauconite (1.5 vol%). The matrix is a mixture of Fe-Al-K silicates (67 vol%), quartz (14 vol%) and muscovite/illite (9 vol%) with minor K-feldspar (5 vol%), and Fe-Al silicates (2 vol%). Kaolinite and plagioclase are nearly absent, but the matrix also carries traces of glauconite.
Form	**Mineralogical type**
Rim sherd of a bowl.	A
Analogues	**Notes**
West Somerset type.	Lead glazed on one side, possibly with a thin kaolinite-slip underneath.

Visual appearance of thin section (transmitted light)	Mineralogical map	Key to mineral map (mineral groups listed in Table 23)

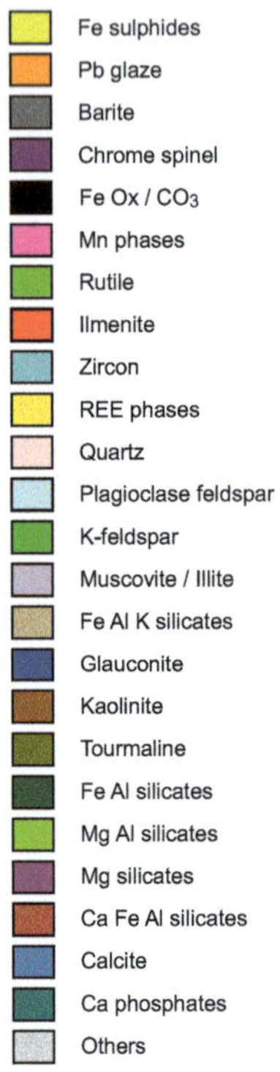

Figure 104. Analysis of Sample 4: Hemyock, bowl rim.

Sample number: 4	Context number: 571	CSM lab. code: C03150018

Mineralogical composition

	Matrix	Inclusions	Bulk
Fe sulphides	0.008	0.000	0.007
Pb glaze	0.720	5.242	1.093
Barite	0.000	0.000	0.000
Chrome spinel	0.012	0.012	0.012
Fe Ox/CO_3	0.236	0.018	0.218
Mn phases	0.181	0.146	0.178
Rutile	0.156	0.022	0.145
Ilmenite	0.102	0.008	0.095
Zircon	0.025	0.000	0.023
REE phases	0.005	0.000	0.004
Quartz	14.299	89.419	20.499
Plagioclase feldspar	0.308	0.000	0.283
K-Feldspar	4.989	3.292	4.849
Muscovite/Illite	8.842	0.016	8.114
Fe Al K silicates	66.917	0.441	61.430
Glauconite	0.419	1.384	0.499
Kaolinite	0.700	0.000	0.643
Tourmaline	0.005	0.000	0.005
Fe Al silicates	1.798	0.000	1.649
Mg Al silicates	0.009	0.000	0.009
Mg silicates	0.089	0.000	0.082
Ca Fe Al silicates	0.002	0.000	0.002
Calcite	0.031	0.000	0.028
Ca phosphates	0.009	0.000	0.008
Others	0.136	0.000	0.125

Particle size distribution

Matrix (< 63 μm) = 91.7 vol%
Inclusions (> 63 μm) = 8.3 vol%

Mineralogical type

Total measurement points = 2297582
Measurement spacing = 10 μm

Visual representation of mineralogy
(Pb-glaze has been excluded in these diagrams; FO = Fe-Ox/CO_3, qz = quartz, pl = plagioclase, ksp = K-feldspar, ms/ill = muscovite/illite, FAKS = Fe-Al-K silicates, glt = glauconite, kln = kaolinite, FAS = Fe-Al silicates, cc = calcite)

Matrix

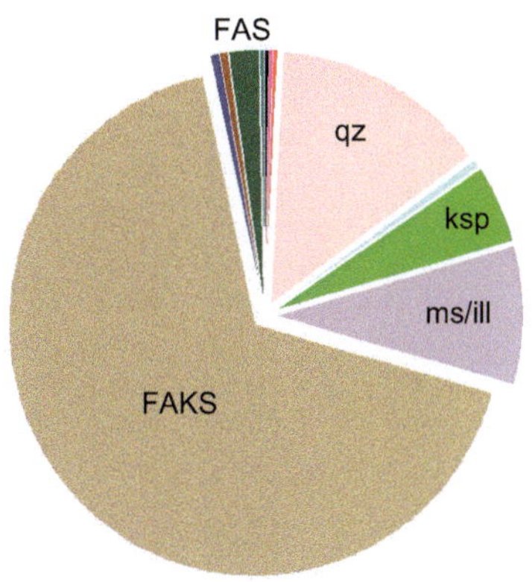

Inclusions

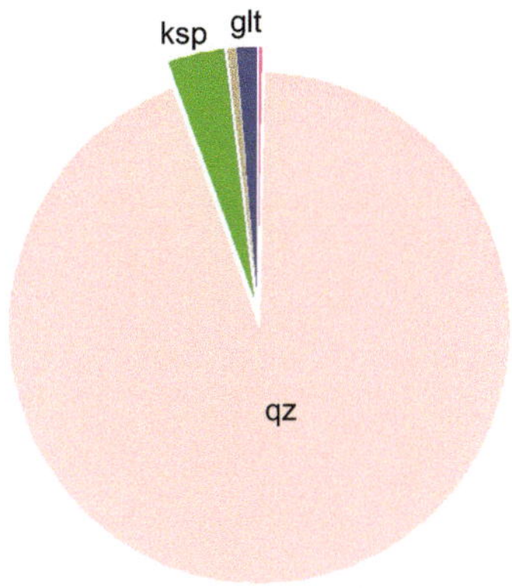

Bulk

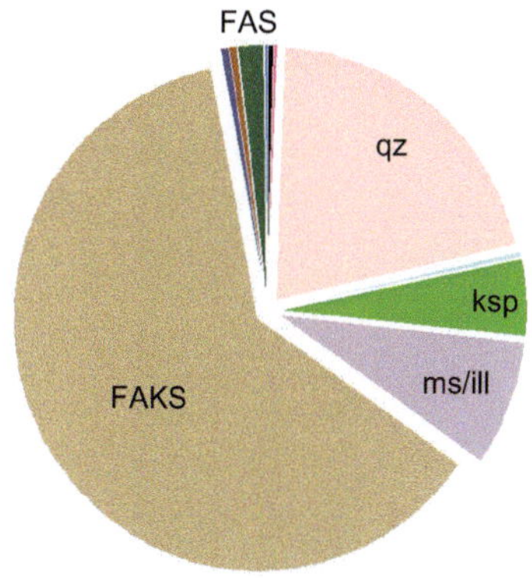

Figure 104 *continued.*

Sample number: 5	Context number: 571	CSM lab. code: C03150019

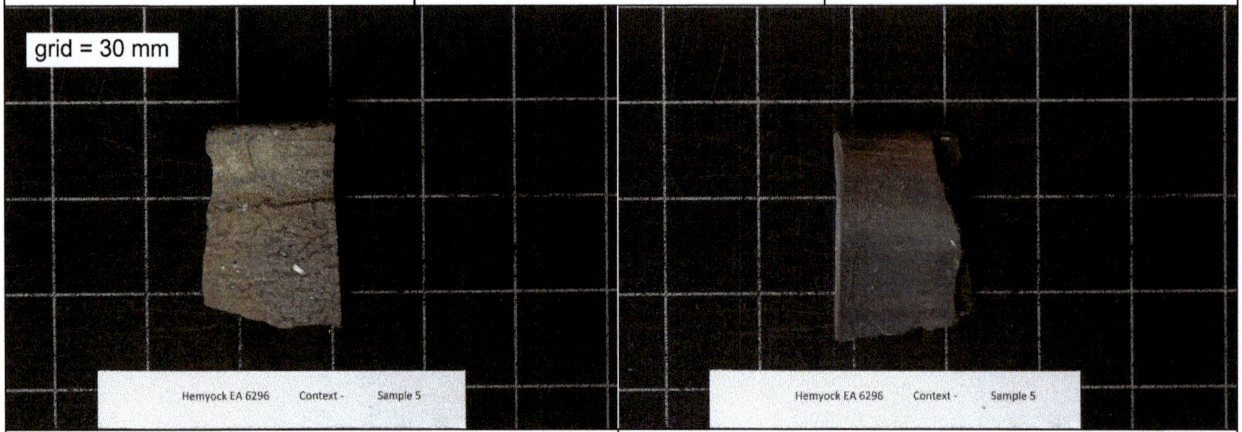

Fabric description	**Mineralogical description**
Reduced grey fabric with chert inclusions, unglazed.	The sherd has 86 vol% matrix and 14 vol% inclusions. The inclusion population is composed of fairly pure quartz (94 vol%) with minor K-feldspar (2 vol%) and has significant Fe-Ox/CO_3 (2.5 vol%) which all relate to one inclusion particle. The matrix is composed of Fe-Al-K silicates (64 vol%) and quartz (16 vol%), with minor muscovite/illite (7 vol%), K-feldspar (5 vol%) and Fe-Al silicates (5 vol%). Kaolinite and plagioclase are nearly absent, but the matrix carries traces of glauconite.
Form	**Mineralogical type**
Rim sherd of cylindrical vessel.	A
Analogues	**Notes**
	None.

Visual appearance of thin section (transmitted light)	**Mineralogical map**	**Key to mineral map** (mineral groups listed in Table 23)
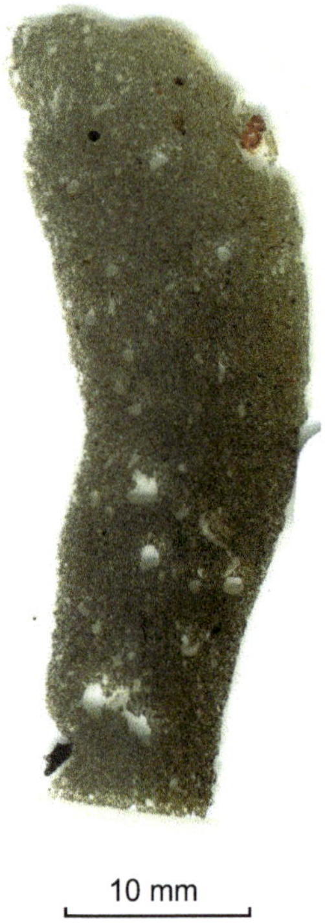	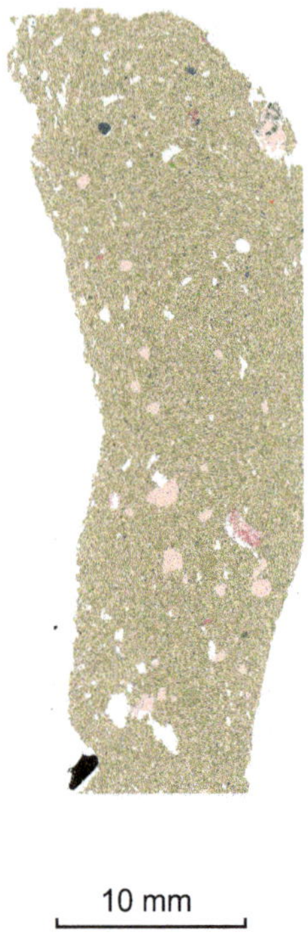	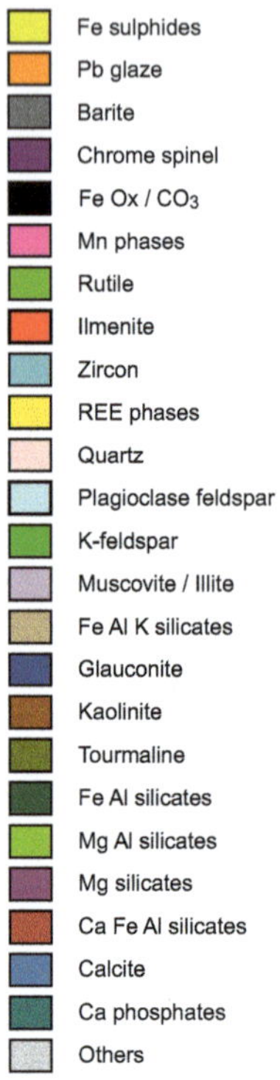

Figure 105. Analysis of Sample 5: Hemyock, cylindrical vessel rim.

Sample number: 5	Context number: 571	CSM lab. code: C03150019

Mineralogical composition

	Matrix	Inclusions	Bulk
Fe sulphides	0.712	0.000	0.612
Pb glaze	0.272	0.000	0.233
Barite	0.000	0.000	0.000
Chrome spinel	0.003	0.000	0.003
Fe Ox/CO_3	0.058	2.489	0.400
Mn phases	0.293	0.208	0.281
Rutile	0.113	0.039	0.103
Ilmenite	0.112	0.047	0.102
Zircon	0.024	0.016	0.023
REE phases	0.004	0.000	0.003
Quartz	16.330	94.258	27.306
Plagioclase feldspar	0.242	0.000	0.208
K-Feldspar	4.640	2.097	4.282
Muscovite/Illite	7.076	0.033	6.084
Fe Al K silicates	63.724	0.574	54.830
Glauconite	0.630	0.133	0.560
Kaolinite	0.669	0.000	0.575
Tourmaline	0.016	0.000	0.013
Fe Al silicates	4.727	0.083	4.072
Mg Al silicates	0.004	0.000	0.003
Mg silicates	0.066	0.000	0.057
Ca Fe Al silicates	0.005	0.000	0.004
Calcite	0.013	0.000	0.011
Ca phosphates	0.013	0.021	0.014
Others	0.254	0.001	0.219

Particle size distribution

Matrix (< 63 μm) = 85.9 vol%
Inclusions (> 63 μm) = 14.1 vol%

Mineralogical type

Total measurement points = 3922594
Measurement spacing = 10 μm

Visual representation of mineralogy

(Pb-glaze has been excluded in these diagrams; FO = Fe-Ox/CO_3, qz = quartz, pl = plagioclase, ksp = K-feldspar, ms/ill = muscovite/illite, FAKS = Fe-Al-K silicates, glt = glauconite, kln = kaolinite, FAS = Fe-Al silicates, cc = calcite)

Matrix

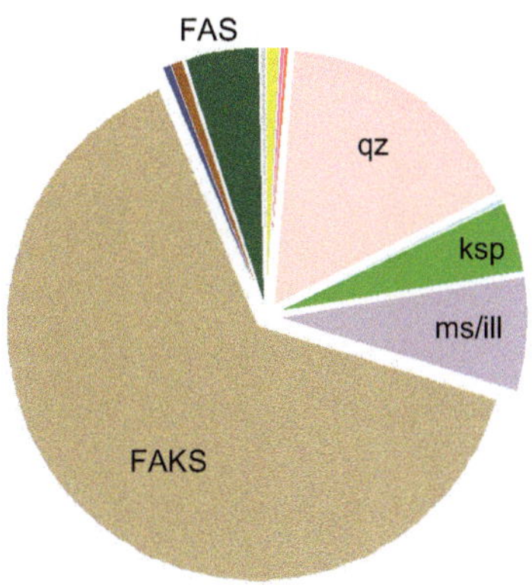

Inclusions

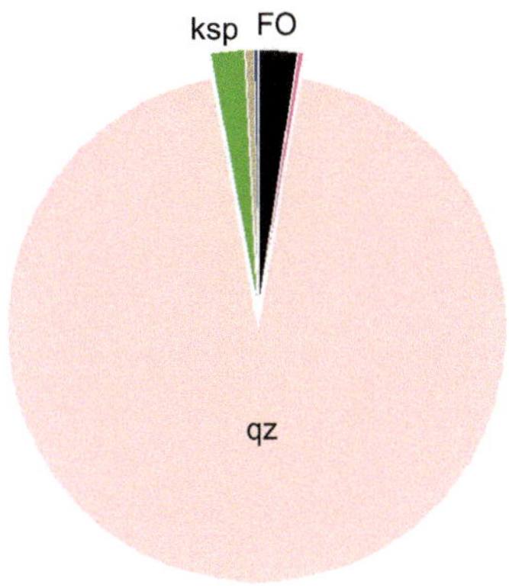

Bulk

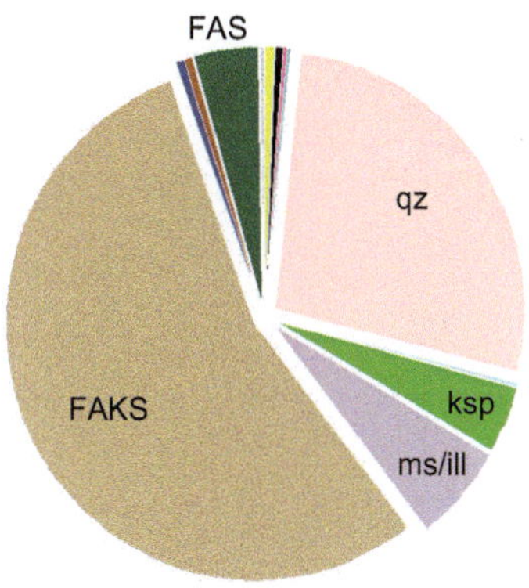

Figure 105 *continued.*

Sample number: 6	Context number: 588	CSM lab. code: C03150020

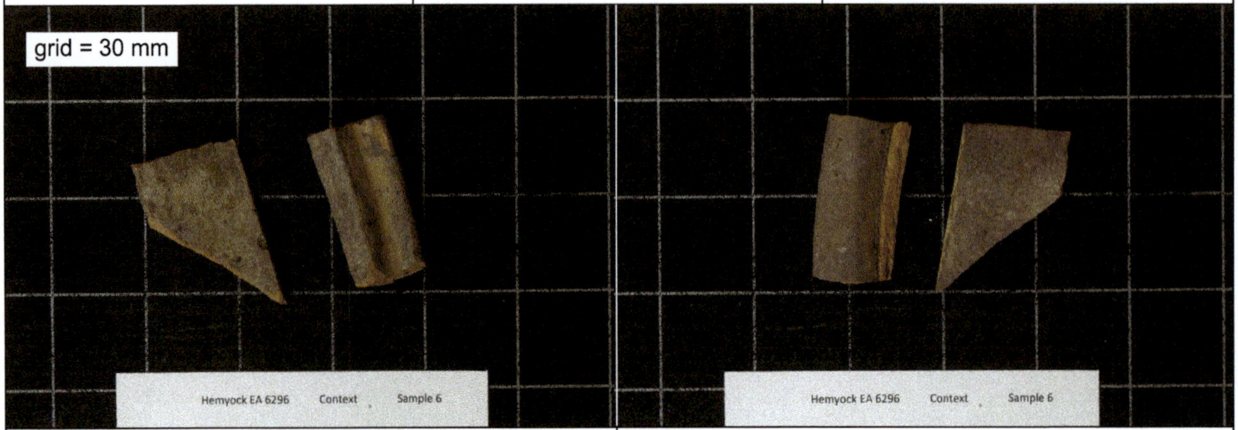

Fabric description	Mineralogical description
Reduced and reoxidised fabric; plain internal lead glaze.	The sherd has 87 vol% matrix and 13 vol% inclusions. The inclusion population is composed of nearly pure quartz (97 vol%) with only minor K-feldspar (2 vol%). The matrix is composed of Fe-Al-K silicates (70 vol%) with quartz (9 vol%), K-feldspar (8 vol%), muscovite/illite (10 vol%) and Fe-Al silicates (2 vol%). Kaolinite and plagioclase are nearly absent. Traces of glauconite are found both as inclusions and in the matrix.
Form	**Mineralogical type**
Rim sherd of a bowl.	A
Analogues	**Notes**
	The sherd carries significant amounts of Pb-glaze in matrix within the interior.

Visual appearance of thin section (transmitted light)	Mineralogical map	Key to mineral map (mineral groups listed in Table 23)
 10 mm	 10 mm	Fe sulphides Pb glaze Barite Chrome spinel Fe Ox / CO_3 Mn phases Rutile Ilmenite Zircon REE phases Quartz Plagioclase feldspar K-feldspar Muscovite / Illite Fe Al K silicates Glauconite Kaolinite Tourmaline Fe Al silicates Mg Al silicates Mg silicates Ca Fe Al silicates Calcite Ca phosphates Others

Figure 106. Analysis of Sample 6: Hemyock, bowl rim.

Sample number: 6	Context number: 588	CSM lab. code: C03150020

Mineralogical composition

	Matrix	Inclusions	Bulk
Fe sulphides	0.010	0.000	0.009
Pb glaze	0.209	0.037	0.186
Barite	0.000	0.000	0.000
Chrome spinel	0.001	0.000	0.001
Fe Ox/CO_3	0.020	0.006	0.019
Mn phases	0.167	0.191	0.170
Rutile	0.130	0.050	0.120
Ilmenite	0.040	0.056	0.042
Zircon	0.014	0.041	0.017
REE phases	0.003	0.000	0.002
Quartz	9.277	96.872	20.704
Plagioclase feldspar	0.266	0.000	0.231
K-Feldspar	7.589	2.116	6.875
Muscovite/Illite	9.502	0.013	8.264
Fe Al K silicates	69.846	0.069	60.743
Glauconite	0.397	0.454	0.404
Kaolinite	0.275	0.032	0.243
Tourmaline	0.005	0.000	0.004
Fe Al silicates	2.155	0.045	1.880
Mg Al silicates	0.007	0.000	0.006
Mg silicates	0.020	0.000	0.017
Ca Fe Al silicates	0.002	0.011	0.003
Calcite	0.018	0.000	0.016
Ca phosphates	0.028	0.006	0.025
Others	0.019	0.000	0.017

Particle size distribution

Matrix (< 63 μm) = 87.0 vol%
Inclusions (> 63 μm) = 13.0 vol%

Mineralogical type

Total measurement points = 5163171
Measurement spacing = 10 μm

Visual representation of mineralogy
(Pb-glaze has been excluded in these diagrams; FO = Fe-Ox/CO_3, qz = quartz, pl = plagioclase, ksp = K-feldspar, ms/ill = muscovite/illite, FAKS = Fe-Al-K silicates, glt = glauconite, kln = kaolinite, FAS = Fe-Al silicates, cc = calcite)

Matrix

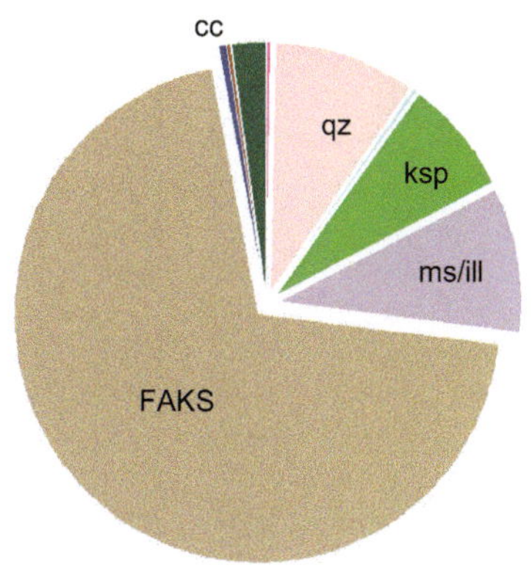

Inclusions

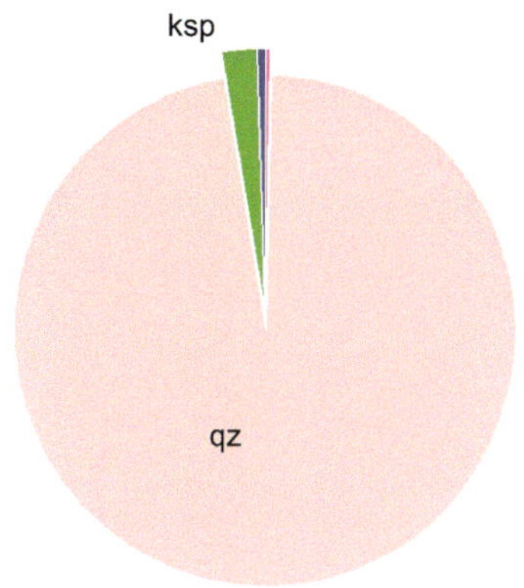

Bulk

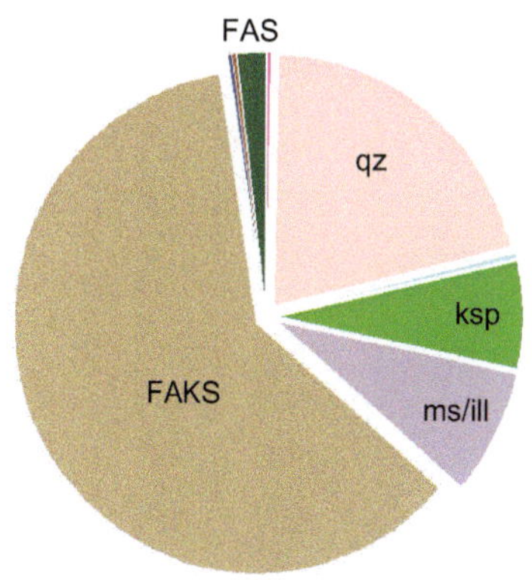

Figure 106 *continued.*

Sample number: 7	**Context number: 557**	**CSM lab. code: C03150021**

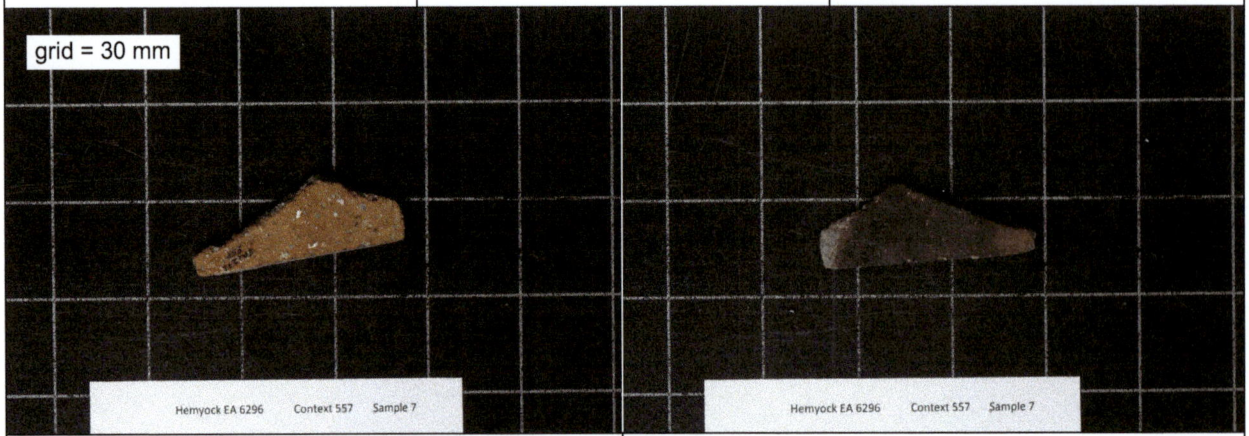

Fabric description	**Mineralogical description**
Reduced chert-tempered fabric with one reoxidised surface, unglazed.	The sherd has 71 vol% matrix and 29 vol% inclusions. The inclusion population is made of extremely pure quartz (99 vol%) with virtually no other minerals. The matrix is composed of Fe-Al-K silicates (43 vol%) and kaolinite (26 vol%) with muscovite/illite (7 vol%), quartz (10 vol%) and Fe-Al silicates (7 vol%). Plagioclase (3 vol%) dominates over K-feldspar (2 vol%). No glauconite was found.
Form	**Mineralogical type**
Body sherd.	B_1
Analogues	**Notes**
	None.

Visual appearance of thin section (transmitted light)	**Mineralogical map**	**Key to mineral map** (mineral groups listed in Table 23)
 10 mm	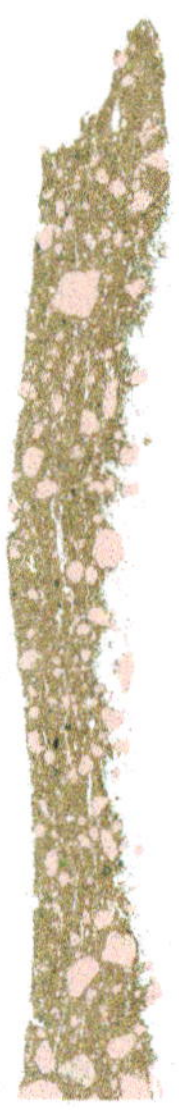 10 mm	Fe sulphides Pb glaze Barite Chrome spinel Fe Ox / CO_3 Mn phases Rutile Ilmenite Zircon REE phases Quartz Plagioclase feldspar K-feldspar Muscovite / Illite Fe Al K silicates Glauconite Kaolinite Tourmaline Fe Al silicates Mg Al silicates Mg silicates Ca Fe Al silicates Calcite Ca phosphates Others

Figure 107. Analysis of Sample 7: Hemyock, body sherd.

Sample number: 7	Context number: 557	CSM lab. code: C03150021

Mineralogical composition

	Matrix	Inclusions	Bulk
Fe sulphides	0.120	0.000	0.085
Pb glaze	0.052	0.000	0.037
Barite	0.000	0.000	0.000
Chrome spinel	0.003	0.000	0.002
Fe Ox/CO_3	0.100	0.000	0.072
Mn phases	0.192	0.039	0.148
Rutile	0.499	0.000	0.356
Ilmenite	0.029	0.000	0.021
Zircon	0.014	0.051	0.025
REE phases	0.002	0.000	0.001
Quartz	10.943	99.480	36.271
Plagioclase feldspar	2.893	0.008	2.067
K-Feldspar	1.746	0.129	1.284
Muscovite/Illite	6.796	0.022	4.858
Fe Al K silicates	43.425	0.039	31.014
Glauconite	0.073	0.000	0.052
Kaolinite	26.130	0.059	18.672
Tourmaline	0.209	0.058	0.166
Fe Al silicates	6.516	0.117	4.686
Mg Al silicates	0.005	0.000	0.003
Mg silicates	0.051	0.000	0.037
Ca Fe Al silicates	0.004	0.000	0.003
Calcite	0.037	0.000	0.026
Ca phosphates	0.028	0.000	0.020
Others	0.132	0.000	0.094

Particle size distribution

Matrix (< 63 μm) = 71.4 vol%
Inclusions (> 63 μm) = 28.6 vol%

Mineralogical type

Total measurement points = 1134251
Measurement spacing = 10 μm

Visual representation of mineralogy
(Pb-glaze has been excluded in these diagrams; FO = Fe-Ox/CO_3, qz = quartz, pl = plagioclase, ksp = K-feldspar, ms/ill = muscovite/illite, FAKS = Fe-Al-K silicates, glt = glauconite, kln = kaolinite, FAS = Fe-Al silicates, cc = calcite)

Matrix

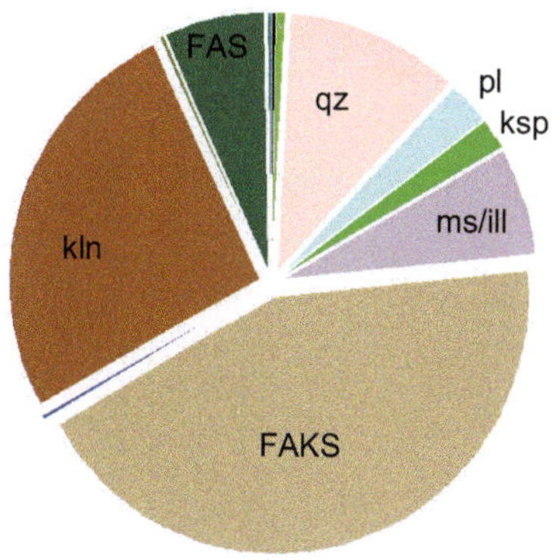

Inclusions

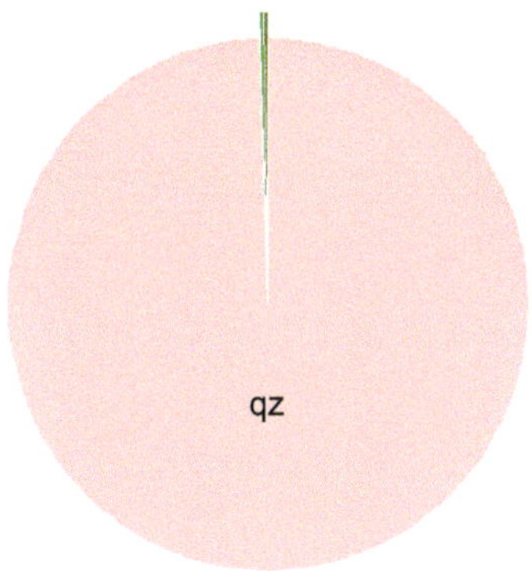

Bulk

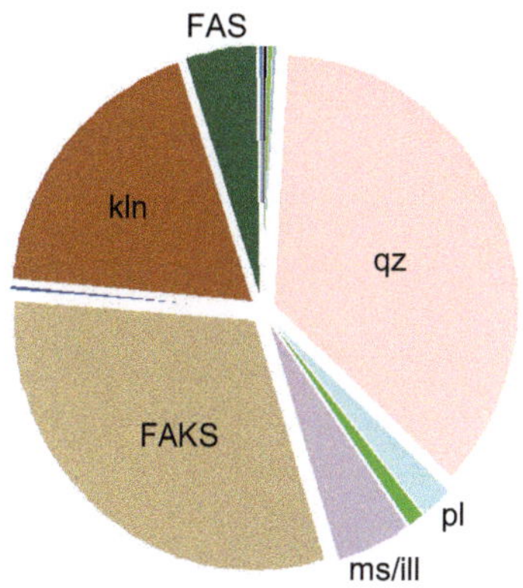

Figure 107 *continued.*

Sample number: 8	Context number: 557	CSM lab. code: C03150022

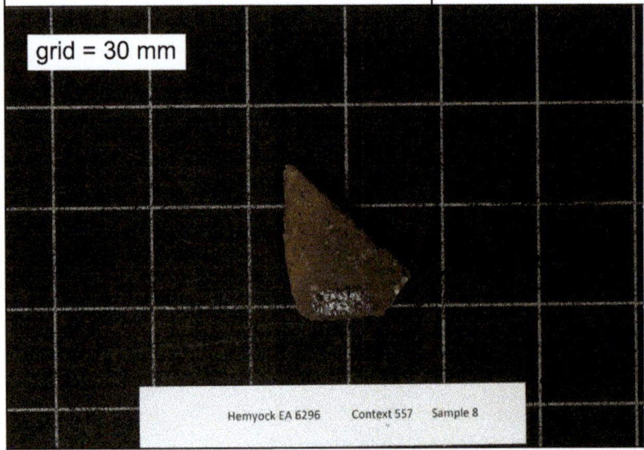

Fabric description	**Mineralogical description**
Reduced chert-tempered fabric, unglazed.	The sherd has 74 vol% matrix and 26 vol% inclusions. The inclusion population is made of extremely pure quartz (99 vol%) with only traces of glauconite. The matrix is composed of Fe-Al-K silicates (37 vol%) and kaolinites (29 vol%) with muscovite/illite (10 vol%), quartz (10 vol%) and Fe-Al silicates (7 vol%). Plagioclase (4 vol%) dominates over K-feldspar (2 vol%). No glauconite was found in the matrix.
Form	**Mineralogical type**
Body sherd.	B_1
Analogues	**Notes**
	None.

Visual appearance of thin section (transmitted light)	**Mineralogical map**	**Key to mineral map** (mineral groups listed in Table 23)
		Fe sulphides Pb glaze Barite Chrome spinel Fe Ox / CO_3 Mn phases Rutile Ilmenite Zircon REE phases Quartz Plagioclase feldspar K-feldspar Muscovite / Illite Fe Al K silicates Glauconite Kaolinite Tourmaline Fe Al silicates Mg Al silicates Mg silicates Ca Fe Al silicates Calcite Ca phosphates Others

Figure 108. Analysis of Sample 8: Hemyock, body sherd.

Sample number: 8	Context number: 557	CSM lab. code: C03150022

Mineralogical composition

	Matrix	Inclusions	Bulk
Fe sulphides	0.038	0.000	0.028
Pb glaze	0.027	0.000	0.020
Barite	0.001	0.000	0.000
Chrome spinel	0.003	0.000	0.002
Fe Ox/CO_3	0.110	0.000	0.081
Mn phases	0.063	0.000	0.047
Rutile	0.493	0.000	0.363
Ilmenite	0.017	0.000	0.013
Zircon	0.016	0.022	0.017
REE phases	0.001	0.000	0.001
Quartz	9.540	99.201	33.185
Plagioclase feldspar	3.507	0.000	2.582
K-Feldspar	1.998	0.135	1.506
Muscovite/Illite	9.704	0.016	7.149
Fe Al K silicates	37.445	0.042	27.581
Glauconite	0.069	0.444	0.168
Kaolinite	29.297	0.077	21.591
Tourmaline	0.210	0.000	0.154
Fe Al silicates	7.080	0.063	5.229
Mg Al silicates	0.032	0.000	0.024
Mg silicates	0.056	0.000	0.042
Ca Fe Al silicates	0.008	0.000	0.006
Calcite	0.054	0.000	0.040
Ca phosphates	0.012	0.000	0.009
Others	0.222	0.000	0.163

Particle size distribution

Matrix (< 63 μm) = 73.6 vol%
Inclusions (> 63 μm) = 26.4 vol%

Mineralogical type

Total measurement points = 699901
Measurement spacing = 10 μm

Visual representation of mineralogy
(Pb-glaze has been excluded in these diagrams; FO = Fe-Ox/CO_3, qz = quartz, pl = plagioclase, ksp = K-feldspar, ms/ill = muscovite/illite, FAKS = Fe-Al-K silicates, glt = glauconite, kln = kaolinite, FAS = Fe-Al silicates, cc = calcite)

Matrix

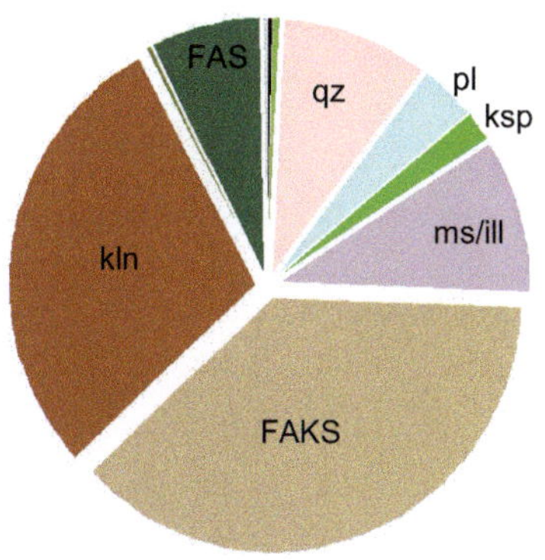

Inclusions

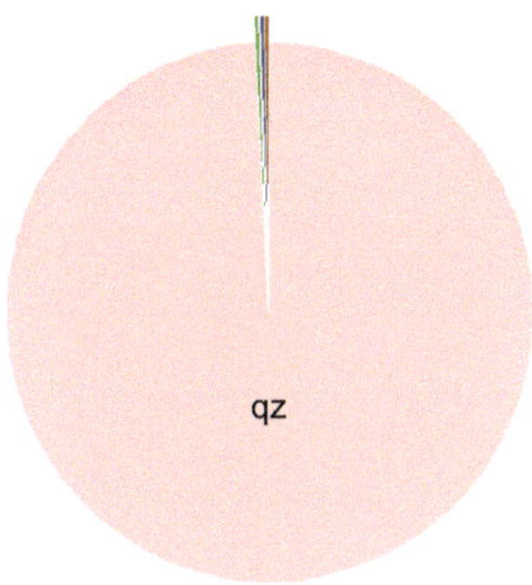

Bulk

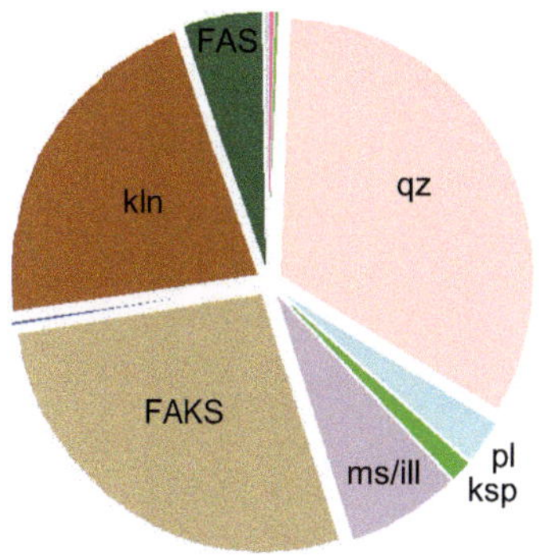

Figure 108 *continued.*

Sample number: 9	Context number: 557	CSM lab. code: C03150023

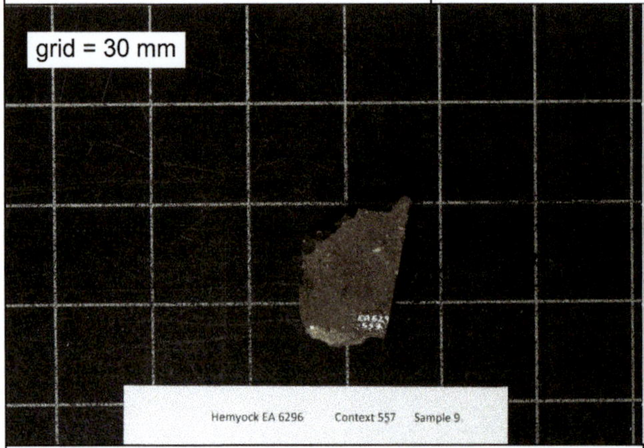

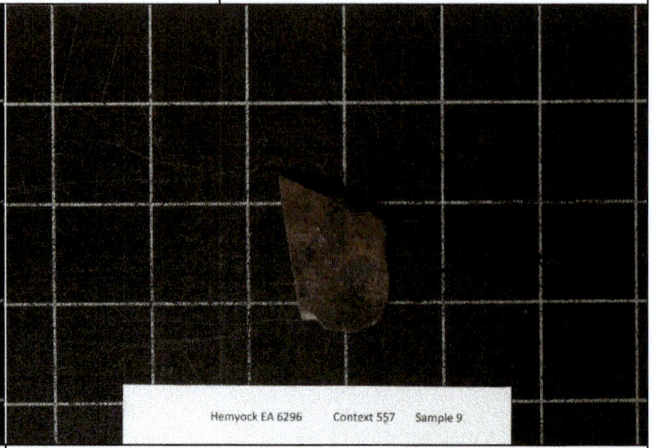

Fabric description	Mineralogical description
Reduced chert-tempered fabric, unglazed.	The sherd has 75 vol% matrix and 25 vol% inclusions. The inclusion population is composed of nearly pure quartz (98 vol%) with around 1 vol% glauconite. The matrix is composed of Fe-Al-K silicates (37 vol%) and kaolinite (25 vol%) with some muscovite/illite (11 vol%). It carries significant quartz (13 vol%) and Fe-Al silicates (7 vol%). Plagioclase (4 vol%) dominates over K-feldspar (2 vol%). Traces of glauconite are also found in the matrix.
Form	**Mineralogical type**
Body sherd.	B_1
Analogues	**Notes**
	None.

Visual appearance of thin section (transmitted light)	Mineralogical map	Key to mineral map (mineral groups listed in Table 23)

10 mm

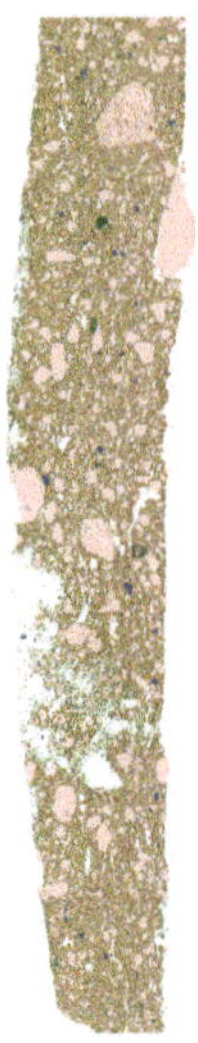

10 mm

Key to mineral map:

- Fe sulphides
- Pb glaze
- Barite
- Chrome spinel
- Fe Ox / CO_3
- Mn phases
- Rutile
- Ilmenite
- Zircon
- REE phases
- Quartz
- Plagioclase feldspar
- K-feldspar
- Muscovite / Illite
- Fe Al K silicates
- Glauconite
- Kaolinite
- Tourmaline
- Fe Al silicates
- Mg Al silicates
- Mg silicates
- Ca Fe Al silicates
- Calcite
- Ca phosphates
- Others

Figure 109. Analysis of Sample 9: Hemyock, body sherd.

Sample number: 9	Context number: 557	CSM lab. code: C03150023

Mineralogical composition

	Matrix	Inclusions	Bulk
Fe sulphides	0.001	0.000	0.001
Pb glaze	0.001	0.000	0.001
Barite	0.000	0.000	0.000
Chrome spinel	0.001	0.000	0.001
Fe Ox/CO_3	0.014	0.000	0.011
Mn phases	0.036	0.000	0.027
Rutile	0.436	0.014	0.332
Ilmenite	0.022	0.023	0.022
Zircon	0.011	0.000	0.008
REE phases	0.002	0.000	0.002
Quartz	12.657	98.246	33.845
Plagioclase feldspar	3.768	0.000	2.835
K-Feldspar	2.095	0.016	1.580
Muscovite/Illite	11.416	0.051	8.602
Fe Al K silicates	37.073	0.079	27.915
Glauconite	0.248	0.990	0.431
Kaolinite	25.211	0.092	18.993
Tourmaline	0.105	0.050	0.091
Fe Al silicates	6.783	0.440	5.213
Mg Al silicates	0.013	0.000	0.010
Mg silicates	0.025	0.000	0.019
Ca Fe Al silicates	0.005	0.000	0.003
Calcite	0.031	0.000	0.024
Ca phosphates	0.016	0.000	0.012
Others	0.031	0.000	0.023

Particle size distribution

Matrix (< 63 µm) = 75.2 vol%
Inclusions (> 63 µm) = 24.8 vol%

Mineralogical type

Total measurement points = 1349784
Measurement spacing = 10 µm

Visual representation of mineralogy
(Pb-glaze has been excluded in these diagrams; FO = Fe-Ox/CO_3, qz = quartz, pl = plagioclase, ksp = K-feldspar, ms/ill = muscovite/illite, FAKS = Fe-Al-K silicates, glt = glauconite, kln = kaolinite, FAS = Fe-Al silicates, cc = calcite)

Matrix

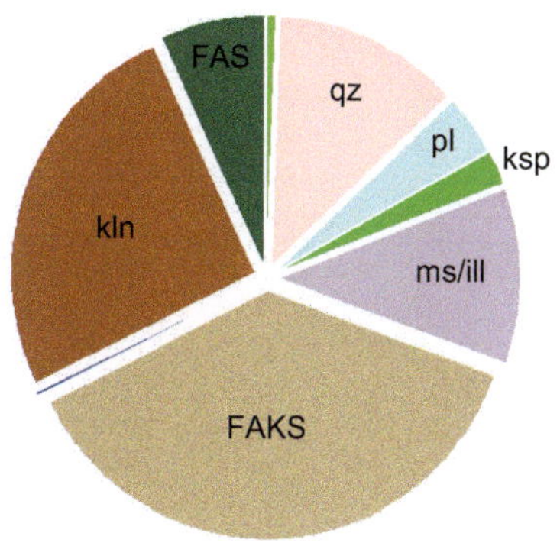

Inclusions

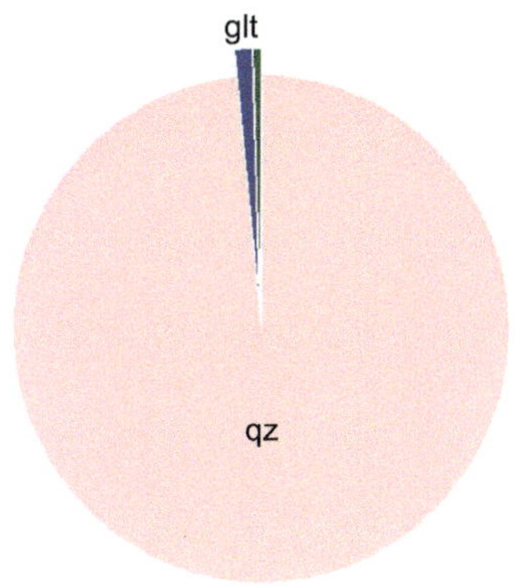

Bulk

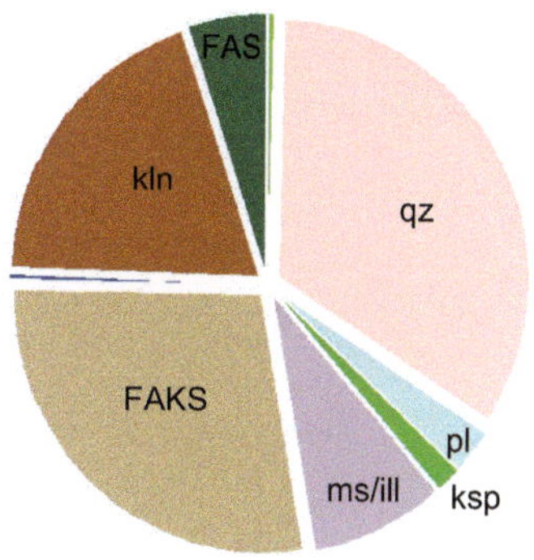

Figure 109 *continued.*

Sample number: 10	Bridgewater Chandos Glass Cone	CSM lab. code: C03150024

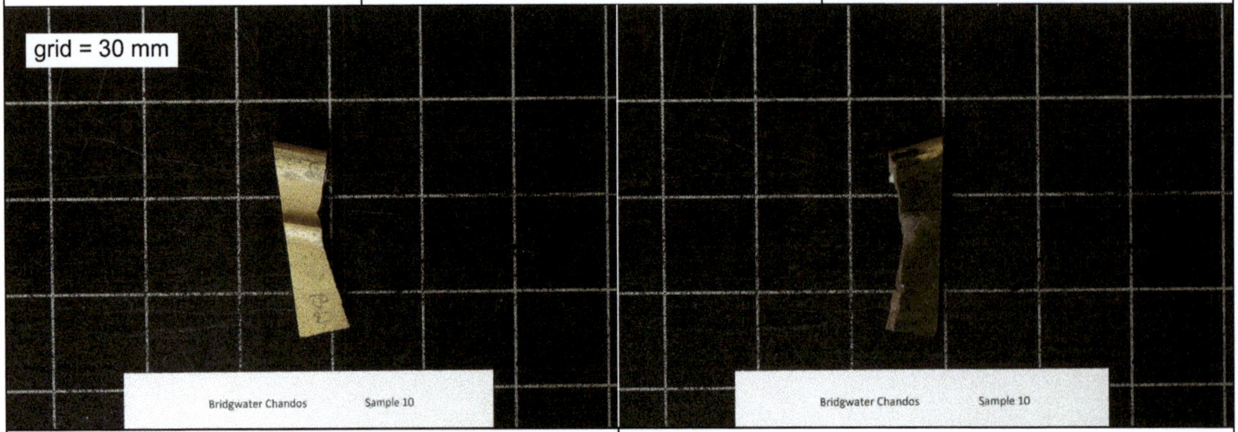

Fabric description	Mineralogical description
Heavily reduced dark grey fabric, reoxidised red external surfaces with dark green internal glaze.	The sherd has 99 vol% matrix and 1 vol% inclusions. Apart from 12 vol% Pb-glaze, the inclusion population is made of quartz (69 vol%) with plagioclase (9 vol%), K-feldspar (6 vol%), some Fe-Al-K silicates (2 vol%) and minor calcite (1.5 vol%). The matrix is composed of Fe-Al-K silicates (42 vol%) with substantial amounts of quartz (20 vol%) and plagioclase (21 vol%), minor muscovite/ illite (5 vol%), kaolinite (2 vol%), calcite (3 vol%), K-feldspar (3 vol%) and Fe-Al silicates (1 vol%). The matrix carries traces of rutile, Ca-Fe-Al silicates and glauconite.
Form	**Mineralogical type**
Rim sherd of a bowl.	C
Analogues	**Notes**
	No glaze in the interior of the specimen.

Visual appearance of thin section (transmitted light)	Mineralogical map	Key to mineral map (mineral groups listed in Table 23)
 10 mm	 10 mm	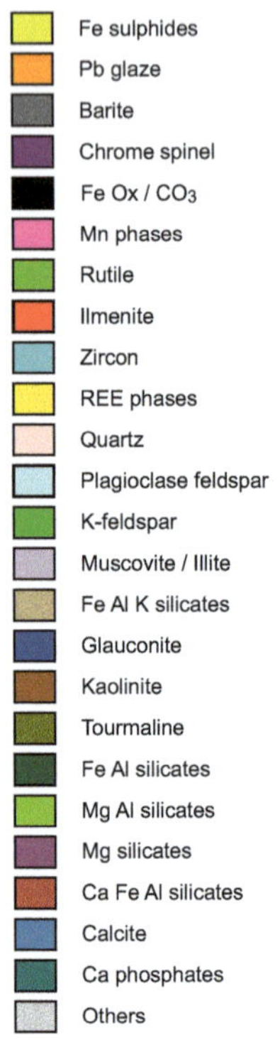

Figure 110. Analysis of Sample 10: Bridgwater Chandos Glass Cone, bowl rim.

Sample number: 10	Bridgwater Chandos Glass Cone	CSM lab. code: C03150024

Mineralogical composition

	Matrix	Inclusions	Bulk
Fe sulphides	0.103	0.012	0.10
Pb glaze	0.061	11.808	0.23
Barite	0.000	0.000	0.00
Chrome spinel	0.003	0.000	0.00
Fe Ox/CO_3	0.082	0.000	0.08
Mn phases	0.017	0.000	0.02
Rutile	0.539	0.000	0.53
Ilmenite	0.135	0.000	0.13
Zircon	0.019	0.000	0.02
REE phases	0.002	0.000	0.00
Quartz	20.216	69.229	20.92
Plagioclase feldspar	21.115	9.258	20.94
K-Feldspar	2.591	5.769	2.64
Muscovite/Illite	5.276	0.024	5.20
Fe Al K silicates	42.259	2.298	41.68
Glauconite	0.205	0.000	0.20
Kaolinite	2.412	0.000	2.38
Tourmaline	0.007	0.000	0.01
Fe Al silicates	1.176	0.012	1.16
Mg Al silicates	0.072	0.000	0.07
Mg silicates	0.045	0.000	0.04
Ca Fe Al silicates	0.614	0.000	0.61
Calcite	2.596	1.481	2.58
Ca phosphates	0.045	0.077	0.05
Others	0.411	0.031	0.41

Particle size distribution

Matrix (< 63 µm) = 98.6 vol%
Inclusions (> 63 µm) = 1.4 vol%

Mineralogical type

Total measurement points = 2870569
Measurement spacing = 10 µm

Visual representation of mineralogy
(Pb-glaze has been excluded in these diagrams; FO = Fe-Ox/CO_3, qz = quartz, pl = plagioclase, ksp = K-feldspar, ms/ill = muscovite/illite, FAKS = Fe-Al-K silicates, glt = glauconite, kln = kaolinite, FAS = Fe-Al silicates, cc = calcite)

Matrix

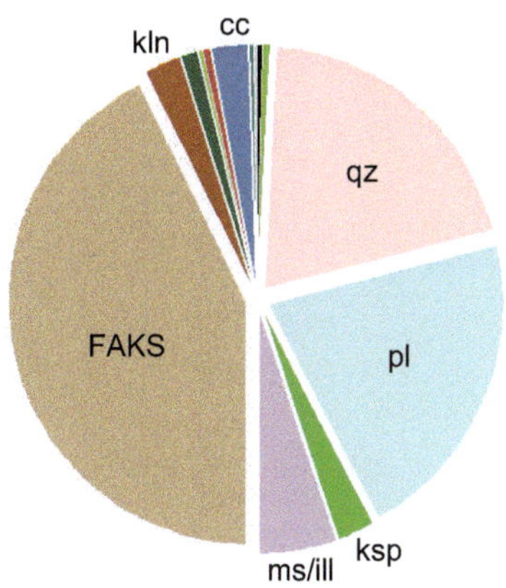

Inclusions

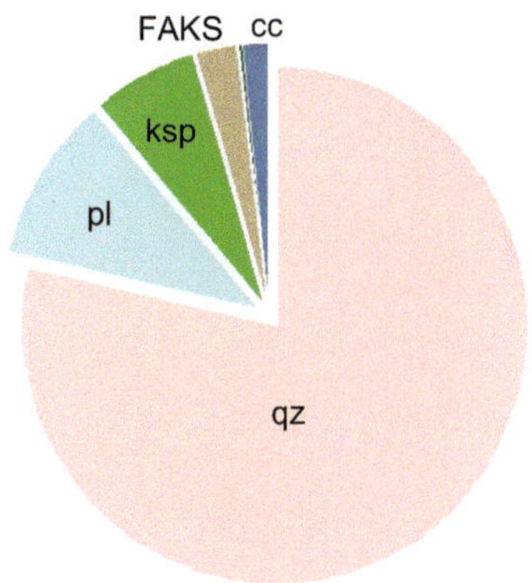

Bulk

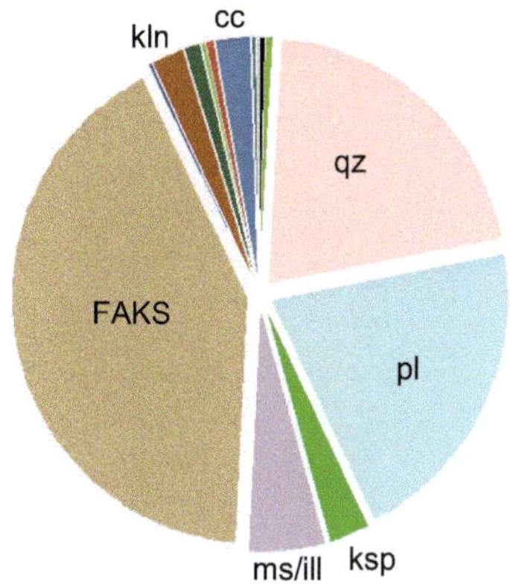

Figure 110 *continued.*

Sample number: 11	Bridgewater Chandos Glass Cone	CSM lab. code: C03150025

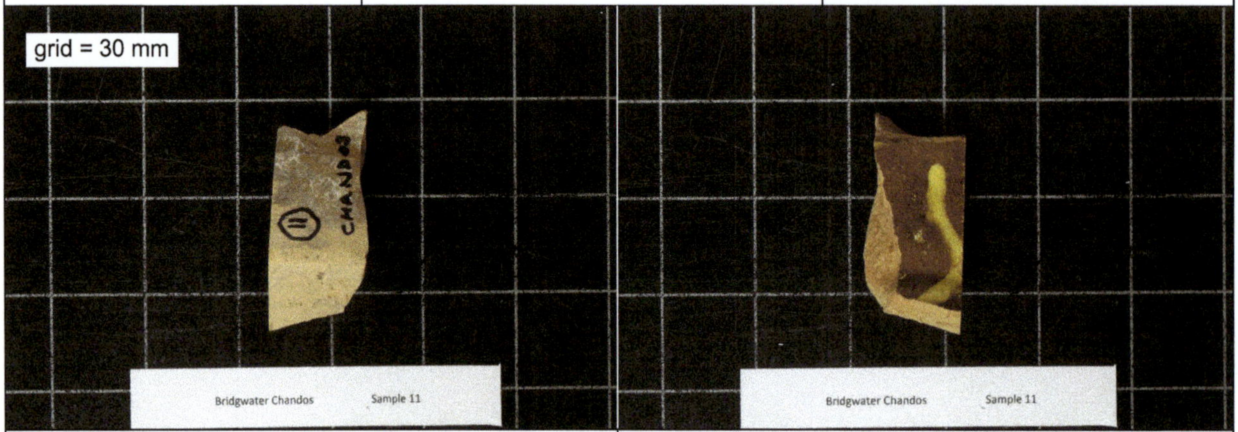

Fabric description	Mineralogical description
Oxidised red sandy fabric with occasional particles of lime, plain oxidised brown lead glaze with black speckles, trailed white slip decoration.	The sherd has 93 vol% matrix and 7 vol% inclusions. Apart from 6 vol% Pb-glaze, the inclusions are quartz (76 vol%) with calcite (11 vol%), K-feldspar (4 vol%), and traces of plagioclase (1 vol%), Ca-phosphates and glauconite. The matrix is Fe-Al-K silicates (46 vol%) with quartz (15 vol%), plagioclase (17 vol%), minor muscovite/ illite (5 vol%), kaolinite (4 vol%), calcite (6 vol%), K-feldspar (2 vol%) and Fe-Al silicates (2 vol%). The matrix c arries trace rutile, Ca-Fe-Al silicates and glauconite.
Form	**Mineralogical type**
Sherd of basal angle of a pancheon.	C
Analogues	**Notes**
	Specks of Pb-glaze in the matrix of the sherd.

Visual appearance of thin section (transmitted light)	Mineralogical map	Key to mineral map (mineral groups listed in Table 23)

Fe sulphides
Pb glaze
Barite
Chrome spinel
Fe Ox / CO_3
Mn phases
Rutile
Ilmenite
Zircon
REE phases
Quartz
Plagioclase feldspar
K-feldspar
Muscovite / Illite
Fe Al K silicates
Glauconite
Kaolinite
Tourmaline
Fe Al silicates
Mg Al silicates
Mg silicates
Ca Fe Al silicates
Calcite
Ca phosphates
Others

Figure 111. Analysis of Sample 11: Bridgwater Chandos Glass Cone, pancheon base.

Sample number: 11	Bridgwater Chandos Glass Cone	CSM lab. code: C03150025

Mineralogical composition

	Matrix	Inclusions	Bulk
Fe sulphides	0.030	0.000	0.028
Pb glaze	0.046	5.922	0.450
Barite	0.000	0.000	0.000
Chrome spinel	0.002	0.000	0.002
Fe Ox/CO_3	0.019	0.081	0.023
Mn phases	0.094	0.013	0.088
Rutile	0.605	0.036	0.565
Ilmenite	0.021	0.031	0.022
Zircon	0.010	0.010	0.010
REE phases	0.001	0.000	0.001
Quartz	15.060	75.979	19.251
Plagioclase feldspar	17.424	0.997	16.294
K-Feldspar	2.293	4.106	2.418
Muscovite/Illite	4.992	0.108	4.656
Fe Al K silicates	46.272	0.548	43.126
Glauconite	0.177	0.256	0.182
Kaolinite	4.273	0.000	3.979
Tourmaline	0.009	0.000	0.008
Fe Al silicates	1.705	0.006	1.588
Mg Al silicates	0.097	0.005	0.091
Mg silicates	0.081	0.000	0.075
Ca Fe Al silicates	0.228	0.077	0.218
Calcite	6.387	11.487	6.737
Ca phosphates	0.034	0.336	0.055
Others	0.142	0.002	0.132

Particle size distribution

Matrix (< 63 µm) = 93.1 vol%
Inclusions (> 63 µm) = 6.9 vol%

Mineralogical type

Total measurement points = 4746333
Measurement spacing = 10 µm

Visual representation of mineralogy
(Pb-glaze has been excluded in these diagrams; FO = Fe-Ox/CO_3, qz = quartz, pl = plagioclase, ksp = K-feldspar, ms/ill = muscovite/illite, FAKS = Fe-Al-K silicates, glt = glauconite, kln = kaolinite, FAS = Fe-Al silicates, cc = calcite)

Matrix

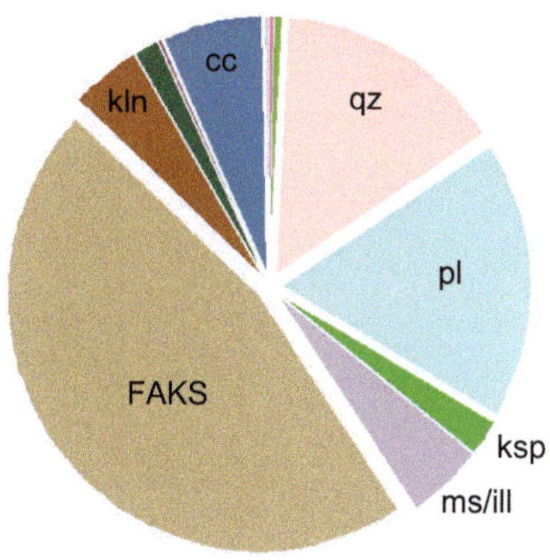

Inclusions

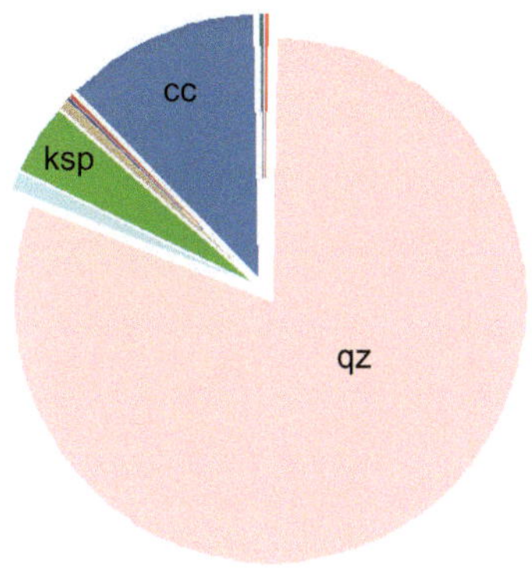

Bulk

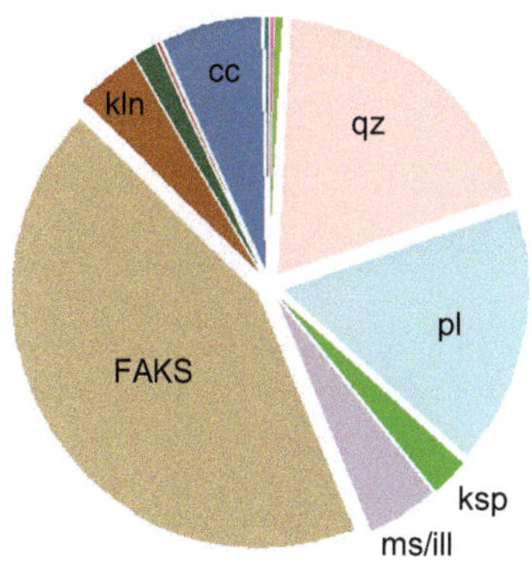

Figure 111 *continued.*

Sample number: 12	Wrangway	CSM lab. code: C03150026

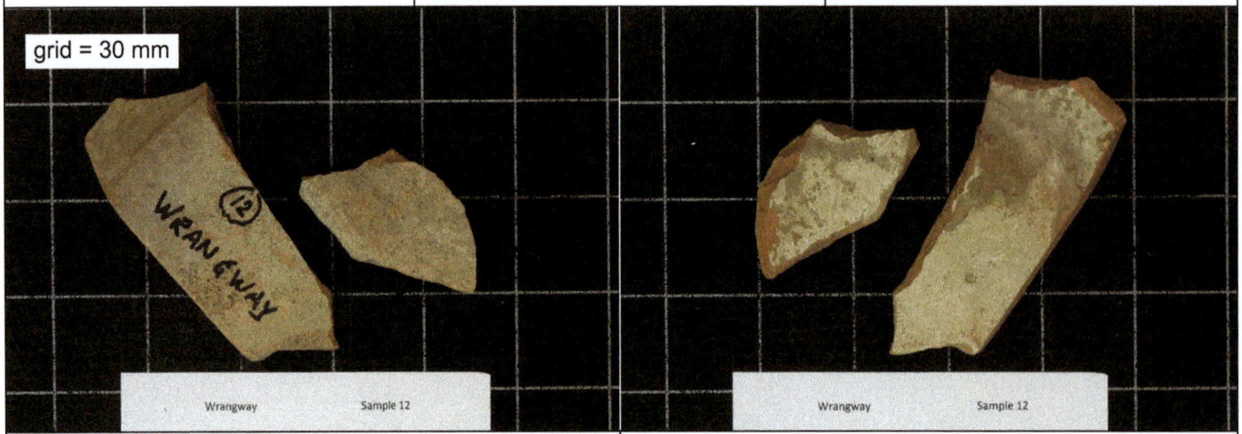

Fabric description	Mineralogical description
Sandy red fabric, internal raw lead glaze.	The sherd has 89 vol% matrix and 11 vol% inclusions. The inclusion population is a very clean mixture of quartz (74 vol%) and K-feldspar (26 vol%). The matrix is a mixture of Fe-Al-K silicates (64 vol%), quartz (10 vol%) and muscovite/illite (11 vol%) and K-feldspar (11 vol%) with minor Fe-Al silicates (2 vol%). Kaolinite, plagioclase and glauconite are nearly absent.
Form	**Mineralogical type**
Knife-trimmed basal angle of a pancheon.	A
Analogues	**Notes**
West Somerset type.	Lead glazed on one side carries abundant inclusions of K-feldspar and quartz. Some specs of glaze in the interior.

Visual appearance of thin section (transmitted light)	Mineralogical map	Key to mineral map (mineral groups listed in Table 23)
		Fe sulphides Pb glaze Barite Chrome spinel Fe Ox / CO_3 Mn phases Rutile Ilmenite Zircon REE phases Quartz Plagioclase feldspar K-feldspar Muscovite / Illite Fe Al K silicates Glauconite Kaolinite Tourmaline Fe Al silicates Mg Al silicates Mg silicates Ca Fe Al silicates Calcite Ca phosphates Others

Figure 112. Analysis of Sample 12: Wrangway, pancheon base.

Sample number: 12	Wrangway	CSM lab. code: C03150026

Mineralogical composition

	Matrix	Inclusions	Bulk
Fe sulphides	0.027	0.000	0.024
Pb glaze	1.070	0.048	0.959
Barite	0.001	0.000	0.001
Chrome spinel	0.002	0.000	0.002
Fe Ox/CO_3	0.015	0.025	0.016
Mn phases	0.166	0.042	0.152
Rutile	0.137	0.020	0.125
Ilmenite	0.034	0.000	0.030
Zircon	0.013	0.000	0.012
REE phaseWrangways	0.003	0.000	0.002
Quartz	10.109	73.530	17.025
Plagioclase feldspar	0.243	0.000	0.216
K-Feldspar	10.960	25.889	12.588
Muscovite/Illite	11.107	0.186	9.916
Fe Al K silicates	63.687	0.193	56.762
Glauconite	0.161	0.063	0.150
Kaolinite	0.242	0.000	0.216
Tourmaline	0.012	0.000	0.011
Fe Al silicates	1.907	0.004	1.699
Mg Al silicates	0.008	0.000	0.007
Mg silicates	0.027	0.000	0.024
Ca Fe Al silicates	0.002	0.000	0.001
Calcite	0.031	0.000	0.028
Ca phosphates	0.031	0.000	0.027
Others	0.005	0.000	0.004

Particle size distribution

Matrix (< 63 µm) = 89.1 vol%
Inclusions (> 63 µm) = 10.9 vol%

Mineralogical type

Total measurement points = 3738789
Measurement spacing = 10 µm

Visual representation of mineralogy

(Pb-glaze has been excluded in these diagrams; FO = Fe-Ox/CO_3, qz = quartz, pl = plagioclase, ksp = K-feldspar, ms/ill = muscovite/illite, FAKS = Fe-Al-K silicates, glt = glauconite, kln = kaolinite, FAS = Fe-Al silicates, cc = calcite)

Matrix

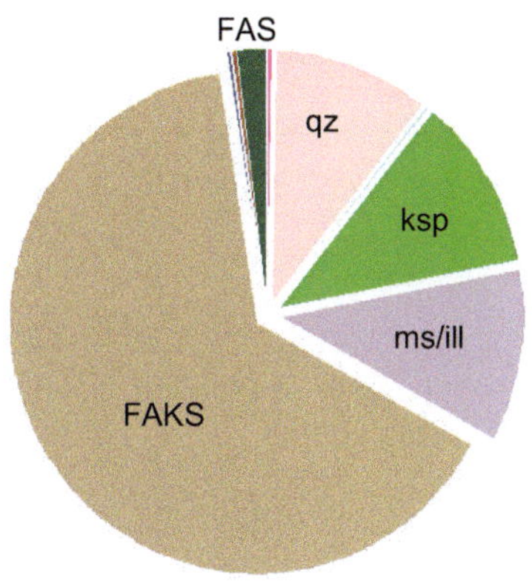

Inclusions

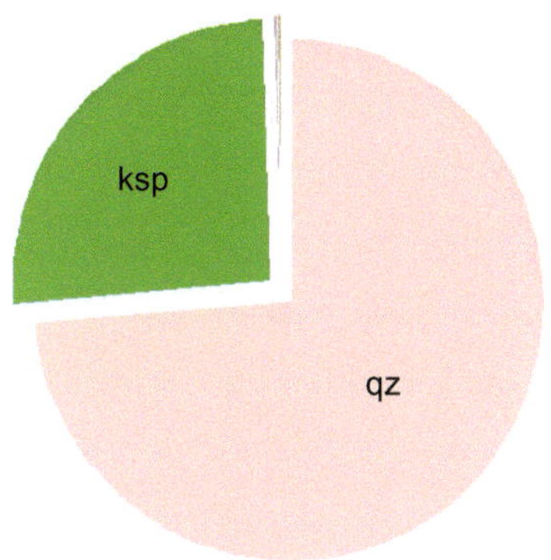

Bulk

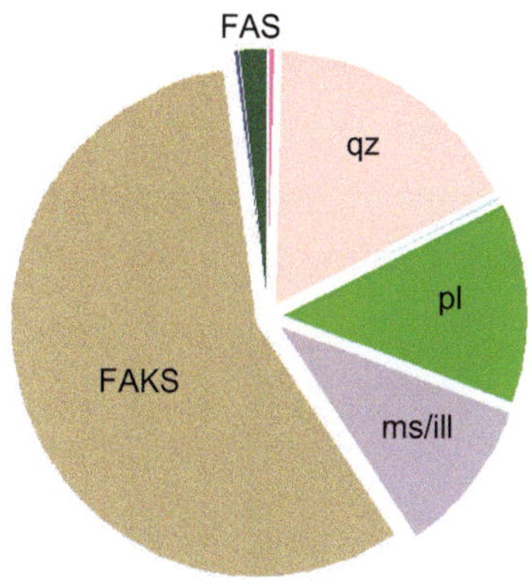

Figure 112 *continued.*

Sample number: 13	Wrangway	CSM lab. code: C03150027

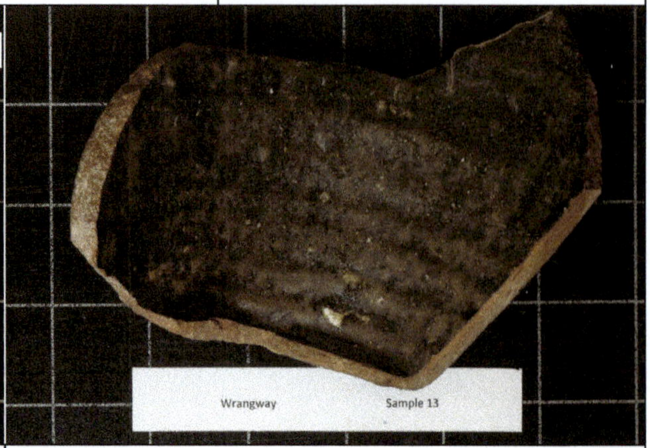

Fabric description	Mineralogical description
Red reoxidised sandy fabric, internal reduced black lead glaze with areas of iridescence and with reduced green splash runs on the exterior. The internal glaze has occasional embedded white quartz crystals.	The sherd has 89 vol% matrix and 11 vol% inclusions. Apart from minor Pb-glaze, the inclusion population is a very clean mixture of quartz (70 vol%) and K-feldspar (28 vol%). The matrix is composed of Fe-Al-K silicates (61 vol%) and quartz (12 vol%), with muscovite/illite (10 vol%), K-feldspar (10 vol%), Fe-Al silicates (3 vol%) and calcite (1 vol%). Only traces of kaolinite and plagioclase are present. Small traces of glauconite reported in the matrix relates to a large inclusion with Fe-Ox/CO_3.
Form	**Mineralogical type**
Body and basal angle of a jar.	A
Analogues	**Notes**
West Somerset type.	Glazed on one side, but with no specs of glaze inside the sherd. Fe-Ox/CO_3 all in one inclusion with glauconite.

Visual appearance of thin section (transmitted light)	Mineralogical map	Key to mineral map (mineral groups listed in Table 23)
 10 mm	 10 mm	Fe sulphides Pb glaze Barite Chrome spinel Fe Ox / CO_3 Mn phases Rutile Ilmenite Zircon REE phases Quartz Plagioclase feldspar K-feldspar Muscovite / Illite Fe Al K silicates Glauconite Kaolinite Tourmaline Fe Al silicates Mg Al silicates Mg silicates Ca Fe Al silicates Calcite Ca phosphates Others

Figure 113. Analysis of Sample 13: Wrangway, jar base.

Sample number: 13	**Wrangway**	**CSM lab. code: C03150027**

Mineralogical composition

	Matrix	Inclusions	Bulk
Fe sulphides	0.023	0.000	0.020
Pb glaze	0.569	0.612	0.574
Barite	0.000	0.000	0.000
Chrome spinel	0.003	0.000	0.003
Fe Ox/CO_3	0.345	0.363	0.347
Mn phases	0.090	0.170	0.099
Rutile	0.123	0.000	0.109
Ilmenite	0.069	0.013	0.062
Zircon	0.020	0.000	0.018
REE phases	0.004	0.000	0.004
Quartz	12.017	70.553	18.611
Plagioclase feldspar	0.627	0.000	0.556
K-Feldspar	9.827	27.669	11.837
Muscovite/Illite	9.829	0.249	8.749
Fe Al K silicates	61.113	0.322	54.264
Glauconite	0.366	0.013	0.327
Kaolinite	0.311	0.000	0.276
Tourmaline	0.003	0.000	0.003
Fe Al silicates	2.858	0.016	2.537
Mg Al silicates	0.095	0.000	0.084
Mg silicates	0.221	0.000	0.196
Ca Fe Al silicates	0.010	0.000	0.009
Calcite	1.427	0.000	1.266
Ca phosphates	0.035	0.020	0.033
Others	0.014	0.000	0.013

Particle size distribution

Matrix (< 63 μm) = 88.7 vol%
Inclusions (> 63 μm) = 11.3 vol%

Mineralogical type

Total measurement points = 3239300
Measurement spacing = 10 μm

Visual representation of mineralogy

(Pb-glaze has been excluded in these diagrams; FO = Fe-Ox/CO_3, qz = quartz, pl = plagioclase, ksp = K-feldspar, ms/ill = muscovite/illite, FAKS = Fe-Al-K silicates, glt = glauconite, kln = kaolinite, FAS = Fe-Al silicates, cc = calcite)

Matrix

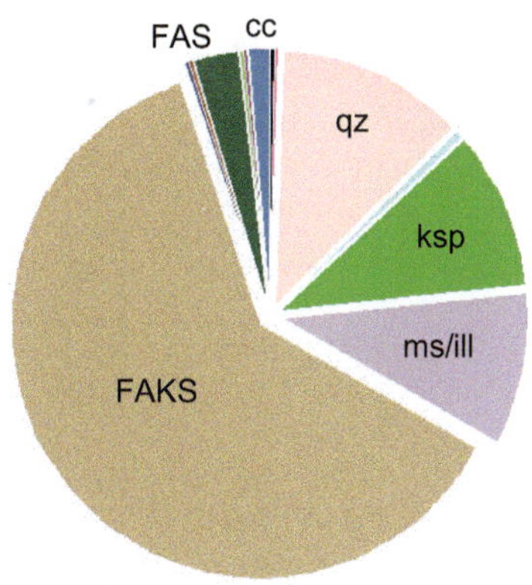

Inclusions

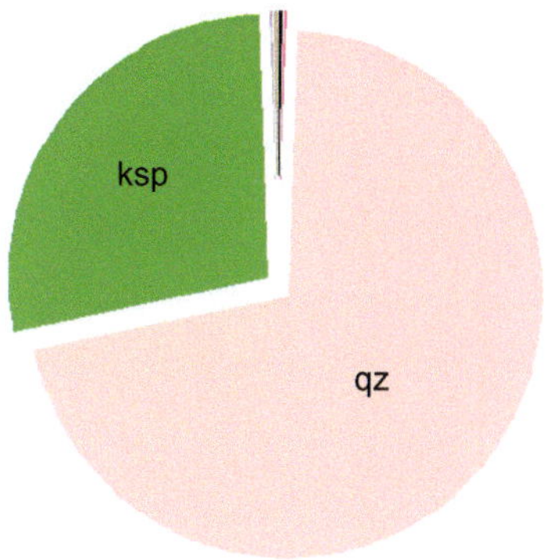

Bulk

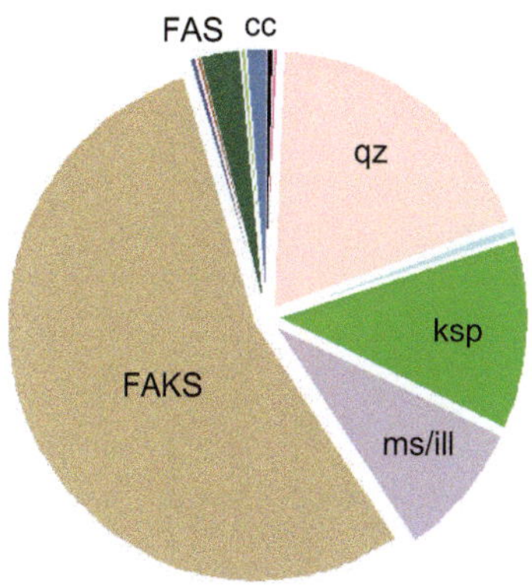

Figure 113 *continued.*

Sample number: 16	Donyatt site 2	CSM lab. code: C03150028

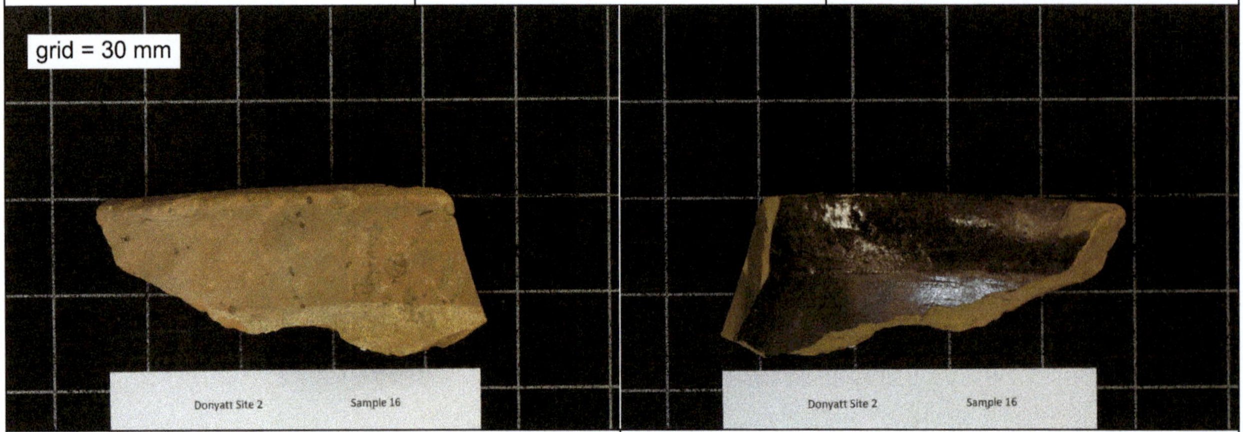

Fabric description	Mineralogical description
Oxidised red fabric with particles of lime and glauconite (?). Internal brown lead glaze on rim with patches of iridescence.	The sherd has 96 vol% matrix and 4 vol% inclusions. Apart from the Pb-glaze (7 vol%), the inclusion population is composed of quartz (86 vol%) with glauconite (3 vol%), K-feldspar (2 vol%) and Fe-Al silicates (1 vol%). The matrix is composed of roughly equal amounts of Fe-Al-K silicates (26 vol%), kaolinite (25 vol%) and quartz (21 vol%) with some muscovite/illite (9 vol%) and Fe-Al silicates (8 vol%). The matrix has equal amounts of plagioclase and K-feldspar (4 vol%), and traces of rutile, glauconite and tourmaline.
Form	**Mineralogical type**
Everted rim of a jar.	B_1 or D
Analogues	**Notes**
South Somerset type.	Pb-glaze on one side, no traces of glaze in the interior.

Visual appearance of thin section (transmitted light)	Mineralogical map	Key to mineral map (mineral groups listed in Table 23)
 10 mm	 10 mm	Fe sulphides Pb glaze Barite Chrome spinel Fe Ox / CO_3 Mn phases Rutile Ilmenite Zircon REE phases Quartz Plagioclase feldspar K-feldspar Muscovite / Illite Fe Al K silicates Glauconite Kaolinite Tourmaline Fe Al silicates Mg Al silicates Mg silicates Ca Fe Al silicates Calcite Ca phosphates Others

Figure 114. Analysis of Sample 16: Donyatt Site 2, jar rim.

Sample number: 16	Donyatt site 2	CSM lab. code: C03150028

Mineralogical composition

	Matrix	Inclusions	Bulk
Fe sulphides	0.007	0.000	0.006
Pb glaze	0.122	6.963	0.411
Barite	0.000	0.000	0.000
Chrome spinel	0.015	0.000	0.014
Fe Ox/CO_3	0.068	0.062	0.068
Mn phases	0.003	0.002	0.003
Rutile	0.572	0.039	0.549
Ilmenite	0.131	0.006	0.126
Zircon	0.015	0.022	0.016
REE phases	0.002	0.000	0.002
Quartz	21.398	85.552	24.114
Plagioclase feldspar	4.180	0.100	4.007
K-Feldspar	3.819	1.549	3.723
Muscovite/Illite	9.300	0.130	8.912
Fe Al K silicates	26.248	0.493	25.158
Glauconite	0.347	3.143	0.465
Kaolinite	25.094	0.561	24.055
Tourmaline	0.313	0.000	0.299
Fe Al silicates	8.300	1.376	8.007
Mg Al silicates	0.017	0.000	0.017
Mg silicates	0.020	0.000	0.020
Ca Fe Al silicates	0.002	0.000	0.002
Calcite	0.012	0.002	0.011
Ca phosphates	0.000	0.000	0.000
Others	0.014	0.000	0.014

Particle size distribution

Matrix (< 63 μm) = 95.8 vol%
Inclusions (> 63 μm) = 4.2 vol%

Mineralogical type

Total measurement points = 4922104
Measurement spacing = 10 μm

Visual representation of mineralogy
(Pb-glaze has been excluded in these diagrams; FO = Fe-Ox/CO_3, qz = quartz, pl = plagioclase, ksp = K-feldspar, ms/ill = muscovite/illite, FAKS = Fe-Al-K silicates, glt = glauconite, kln = kaolinite, FAS = Fe-Al silicates, cc = calcite)

Matrix

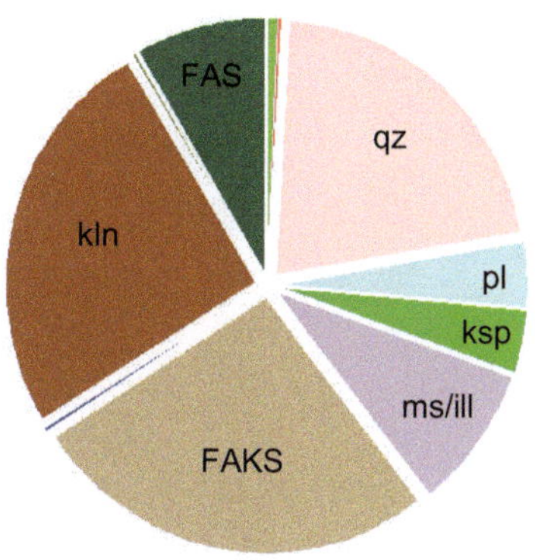

Inclusions

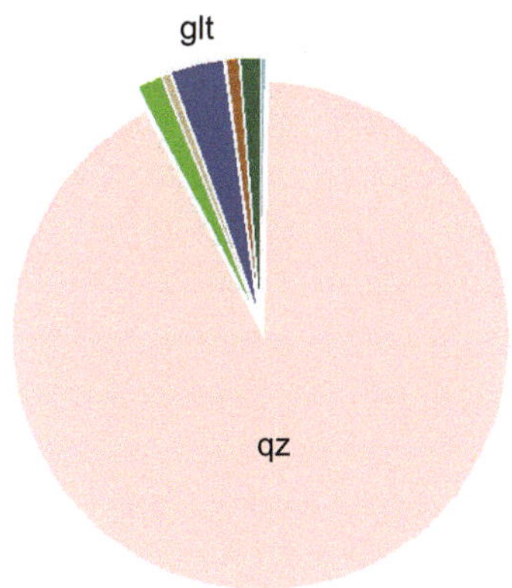

Bulk

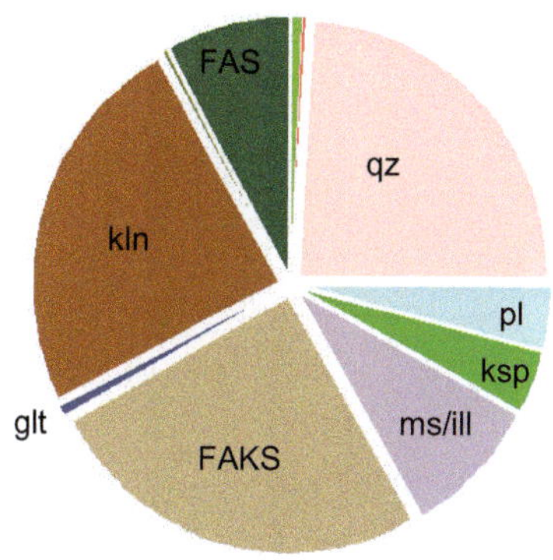

Figure 114 *continued.*

Sample number: 17	Donyatt site 2	CSM lab. code: C03150029

Fabric description	Mineralogical description
Red fabric with traces of internal lead glaze and splashes of white slip inside and out.	The sherd has 88 vol% matrix and 12 vol% inclusions. The inclusions are made of fairly pure quartz (92 vol%) with significant glauconite (5 vol%) and minor K-feldspar (1 vol%) and Fe-Al silicates (1 vol%). The matrix has more kaolinite (32 vol%) than Fe-Al-K silicates (24 vol%) and significant muscovite/illite (13 vol%) and quartz (15 vol%) and minor Fe-Al silicates (5 vol%). Plagioclase (5 vol%) dominates over K-feldspar (4 vol%), and the matrix carries traces of glauconite and rutile.
Form	**Mineralogical type**
Rim of a bowl.	B_1 or D
Analogues	**Notes**
South Somerset type.	Pb-glaze on one side, no traces of glaze in the interior.

Visual appearance of thin section (transmitted light)	Mineralogical map	Key to mineral map (mineral groups listed in Table 23)
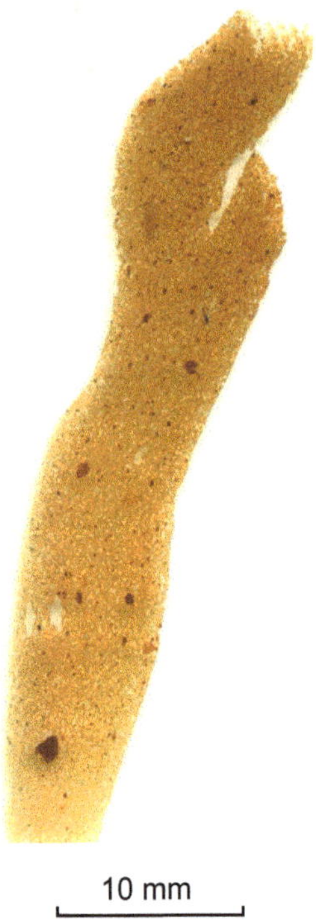	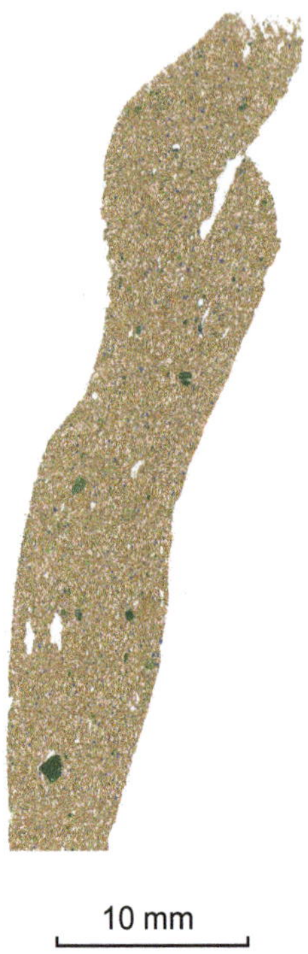	Fe sulphides Pb glaze Barite Chrome spinel Fe Ox / CO_3 Mn phases Rutile Ilmenite Zircon REE phases Quartz Plagioclase feldspar K-feldspar Muscovite / Illite Fe Al K silicates Glauconite Kaolinite Tourmaline Fe Al silicates Mg Al silicates Mg silicates Ca Fe Al silicates Calcite Ca phosphates Others

Figure 115. Analysis of Sample 17: Donyatt Site 2, bowl rim.

Sample number: 17	Donyatt site 2	CSM lab. code: C03150029

Mineralogical composition

	Matrix	Inclusions	Bulk
Fe sulphides	0.003	0.000	0.003
Pb glaze	0.195	0.044	0.177
Barite	0.000	0.000	0.000
Chrome spinel	0.006	0.000	0.005
Fe Ox/CO_3	0.030	0.000	0.026
Mn phases	0.004	0.000	0.003
Rutile	0.609	0.063	0.544
Ilmenite	0.048	0.032	0.046
Zircon	0.015	0.009	0.014
REE phases	0.002	0.000	0.002
Quartz	14.683	92.171	23.828
Plagioclase feldspar	4.971	0.020	4.387
K-Feldspar	3.752	1.200	3.451
Muscovite/Illite	12.735	0.040	11.237
Fe Al K silicates	24.301	0.202	21.457
Glauconite	0.769	4.518	1.211
Kaolinite	32.293	0.216	28.507
Tourmaline	0.136	0.006	0.120
Fe Al silicates	5.367	1.471	4.907
Mg Al silicates	0.011	0.007	0.010
Mg silicates	0.048	0.000	0.042
Ca Fe Al silicates	0.002	0.000	0.002
Calcite	0.016	0.000	0.015
Ca phosphates	0.000	0.000	0.000
Others	0.005	0.000	0.005

Particle size distribution

Matrix (< 63 μm) = 88.2 vol%
Inclusions (> 63 μm) = 11.8 vol%

Mineralogical type

Total measurement points = 2937950
Measurement spacing = 10 μm

Visual representation of mineralogy
(Pb-glaze has been excluded in these diagrams; FO = Fe-Ox/CO_3, qz = quartz, pl = plagioclase, ksp = K-feldspar, ms/ill = muscovite/illite, FAKS = Fe-Al-K silicates, glt = glauconite, kln = kaolinite, FAS = Fe-Al silicates, cc = calcite)

Matrix

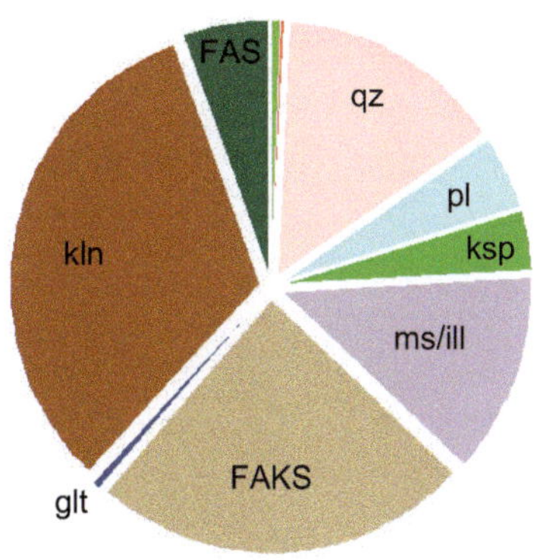

Inclusions

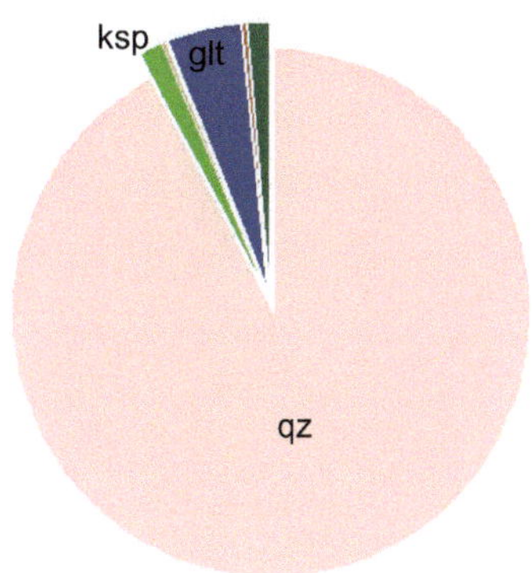

Bulk

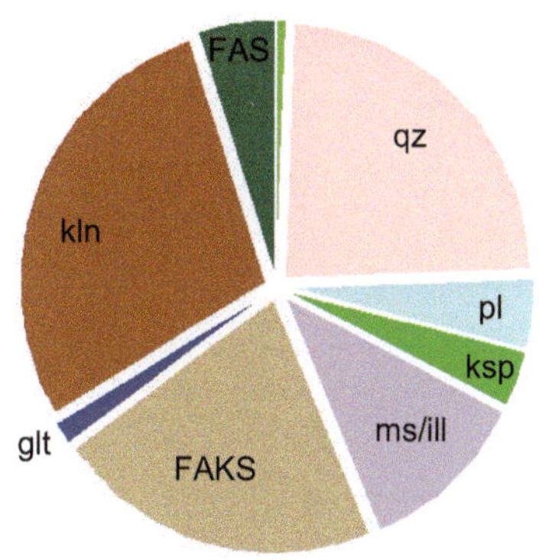

Figure 115 *continued.*

Sample number: 18	Donyatt site 3	CSM lab. code: C03150031

Fabric description	Mineralogical description
Buff reoxidised fabric with iron rich inclusions <2 mm, internal patchy reduced green glaze, partially burnt off.	The sherd has 99 vol% matrix and 1 vol% inclusions. Apart from substantial Pb-glaze (25 vol%), the inclusion population is composed of quartz (42 vol% and Fe-Al silicates (20 vol%) with significant K-feldspar (7 vol%) and some kaolinite (3 vol%), muscovite/illite (2 vol%), and Fe-Al-K silicates (1 vol%). The matrix has more kaolinite (28 vol%) and muscovite/illite (23 vol%) than Fe-Al-K silicates (16 vol%). Quartz occupies 18 vol% and Fe-Al silicates 3 vol%. Plagioclase (6 vol%) dominates over K-feldspar (4 vol%). The matrix traces of rutile but no glauconite.
Form	**Mineralogical type**
Basal angle of a jar.	D
Analogues	**Notes**
South Somerset type.	Pb-glaze on one side, no traces of glaze in the interior.

Visual appearance of thin section (transmitted light)	Mineralogical map	Key to mineral map (mineral groups listed in Table 23)
 10 mm	 10 mm	Fe sulphides Pb glaze Barite Chrome spinel Fe Ox / CO_3 Mn phases Rutile Ilmenite Zircon REE phases Quartz Plagioclase feldspar K-feldspar Muscovite / Illite Fe Al K silicates Glauconite Kaolinite Tourmaline Fe Al silicates Mg Al silicates Mg silicates Ca Fe Al silicates Calcite Ca phosphates Others

Figure 116. Analysis of Sample 18: Donyatt Site 3, jar base.

Sample number: 18	Donyatt site 3	CSM lab. code: C03150031

Mineralogical composition

	Matrix	Inclusions	Bulk
Fe sulphides	0.002	0.000	0.002
Pb glaze	0.045	24.769	0.253
Barite	0.000	0.000	0.000
Chrome spinel	0.007	0.000	0.007
Fe Ox/CO_3	0.020	0.000	0.020
Mn phases	0.003	0.000	0.003
Rutile	0.743	0.066	0.737
Ilmenite	0.066	0.000	0.065
Zircon	0.013	0.000	0.013
REE phases	0.002	0.000	0.002
Quartz	18.083	41.829	18.283
Plagioclase feldspar	6.093	0.080	6.043
K-Feldspar	4.064	6.891	4.088
Muscovite/Illite	22.837	2.252	22.664
Fe Al K silicates	16.488	1.128	16.359
Glauconite	0.130	0.000	0.129
Kaolinite	28.116	2.697	27.902
Tourmaline	0.093	0.000	0.092
Fe Al silicates	3.115	20.286	3.259
Mg Al silicates	0.010	0.000	0.010
Mg silicates	0.025	0.000	0.025
Ca Fe Al silicates	0.005	0.000	0.005
Calcite	0.016	0.000	0.016
Ca phosphates	0.017	0.000	0.017
Others	0.008	0.000	0.008

Particle size distribution

Matrix (< 63 µm) = 99.2 vol%
Inclusions (> 63 µm) = 0.8 vol%

Mineralogical type

Total measurement points = 5036282
Measurement spacing = 10 µm

Visual representation of mineralogy

(Pb-glaze has been excluded in these diagrams; FO = Fe-Ox/CO_3, qz = quartz, pl = plagioclase, ksp = K-feldspar, ms/ill = muscovite/illite, FAKS = Fe-Al-K silicates, glt = glauconite, kln = kaolinite, FAS = Fe-Al silicates, cc = calcite)

Matrix

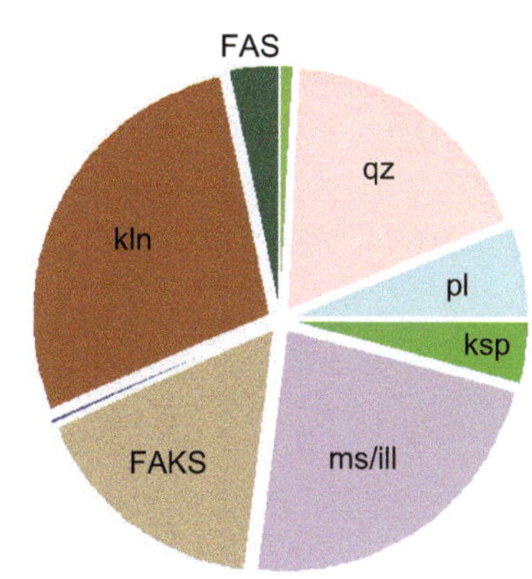

Inclusions

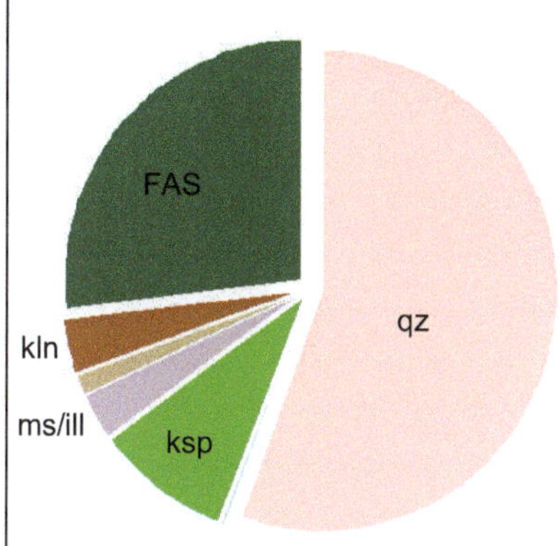

Bulk

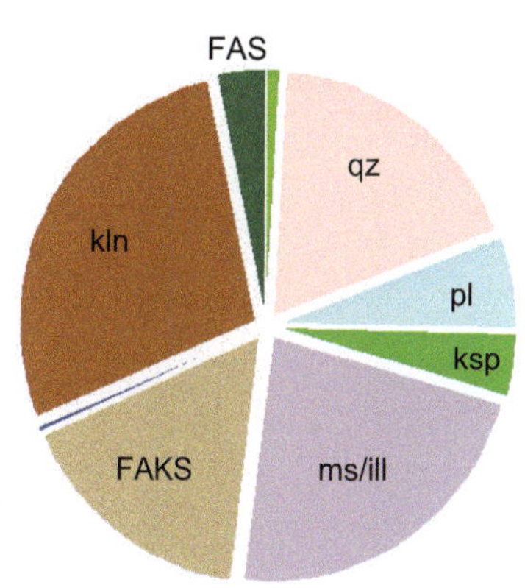

Figure 116 *continued.*

Sample number: 19	Donyatt site 3	CSM lab. code: C03150030

Fabric description	Mineralogical description
Reoxidised red fabric with particles of lime and glauconite (?), internal reduced black lead glaze with areas of iridescence.	The sherd has 99 vol% matrix and 1 vol% inclusions. Apart from substantial Pb-glaze (65 vol%), the inclusion population is composed of quartz (14 vol%), Fe-Al silicates (3 vol%) and K-feldspar (3 vol%) with kaolinite (5 vol%), muscovite/illite (2 vol%), and Fe-Al-K silicates (3 vol%). The matrix has more kaolinite (31 vol%) than muscovite/illite (19 vol%) and Fe-Al-K silicates (20 vol%). Quartz (15 vol%) and plagioclase (6 vol%) dominate over K-feldspar (3 vol%). The matrix carries Fe-Al silicates (4 vol%) and traces of rutile. No glauconite was found.
Form	**Mineralogical type**
Basal angle of a jar.	D
Analogues	**Notes**
South Somerset type.	Pb-glaze on one side, no traces of glaze in the interior.

Visual appearance of thin section (transmitted light)	Mineralogical map	Key to mineral map (mineral groups listed in Table 23)

Key to mineral map:

- Fe sulphides
- Pb glaze
- Barite
- Chrome spinel
- Fe Ox / CO_3
- Mn phases
- Rutile
- Ilmenite
- Zircon
- REE phases
- Quartz
- Plagioclase feldspar
- K-feldspar
- Muscovite / Illite
- Fe Al K silicates
- Glauconite
- Kaolinite
- Tourmaline
- Fe Al silicates
- Mg Al silicates
- Mg silicates
- Ca Fe Al silicates
- Calcite
- Ca phosphates
- Others

Figure 117. Analysis of Sample 19: Donyatt Site 3, jar base.

Sample number: 19	Donyatt site 3	CSM lab. code: C03150030

Mineralogical composition

	Matrix	Inclusions	Bulk
Fe sulphides	0.006	0.000	0.006
Pb glaze	0.032	64.633	0.361
Barite	0.000	0.000	0.000
Chrome spinel	0.006	0.000	0.006
Fe Ox/CO_3	0.073	0.236	0.074
Mn phases	0.002	0.000	0.002
Rutile	0.801	0.082	0.802
Ilmenite	0.054	0.000	0.054
Zircon	0.011	0.000	0.011
REE phases	0.001	0.000	0.001
Quartz	14.921	13.929	14.992
Plagioclase feldspar	5.736	0.129	5.736
K-Feldspar	3.268	3.216	3.284
Muscovite/Illite	18.825	1.760	18.834
Fe Al K silicates	19.575	2.812	19.589
Glauconite	0.066	0.000	0.066
Kaolinite	31.465	5.170	31.491
Tourmaline	0.194	0.000	0.194
Fe Al silicates	4.408	8.033	4.449
Mg Al silicates	0.005	0.000	0.005
Mg silicates	0.022	0.000	0.022
Ca Fe Al silicates	0.000	0.000	0.000
Calcite	0.013	0.000	0.013
Ca phosphates	0.004	0.000	0.004
Others	0.003	0.000	0.003

Particle size distribution

Matrix (< 63 µm) = 99.5 vol%
Inclusions (> 63 µm) = 0.5 vol%

Mineralogical type

Total measurement points = 4574943
Measurement spacing = 10 µm

Visual representation of mineralogy
(Pb-glaze has been excluded in these diagrams; FO = Fe-Ox/CO_3, qz = quartz, pl = plagioclase, ksp = K-feldspar, ms/ill = muscovite/illite, FAKS = Fe-Al-K silicates, glt = glauconite, kln = kaolinite, FAS = Fe-Al silicates, cc = calcite)

Matrix

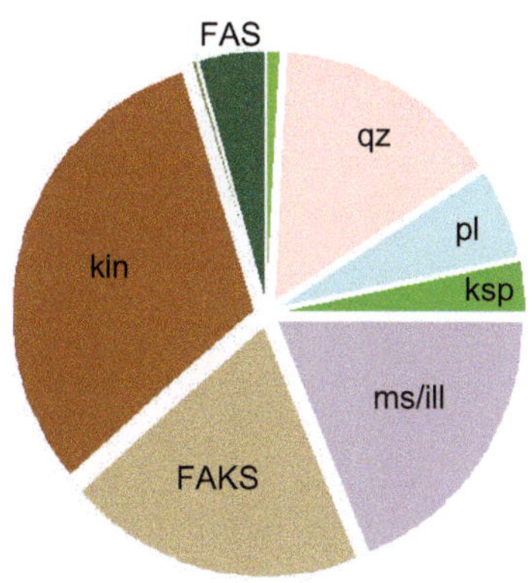

Inclusions

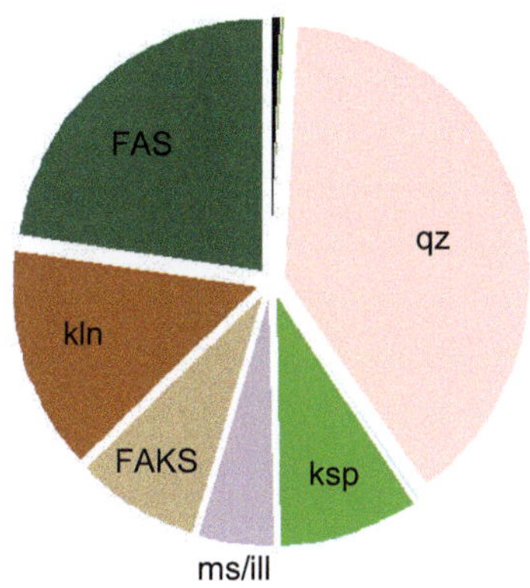

Bulk

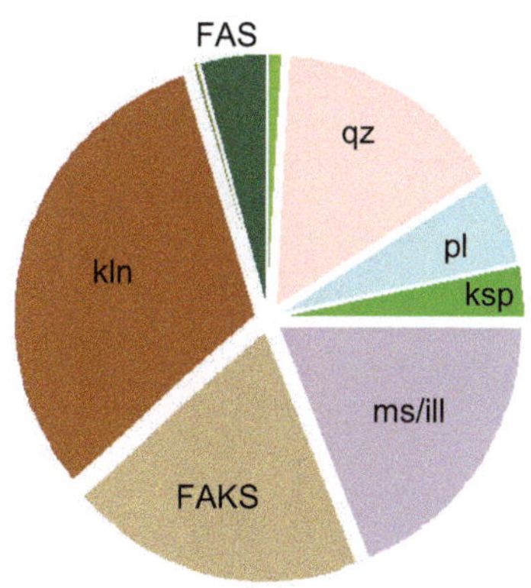

Figure 117 *continued.*

Sample number: 20	Crowcombe	CSM lab. code: C03150033

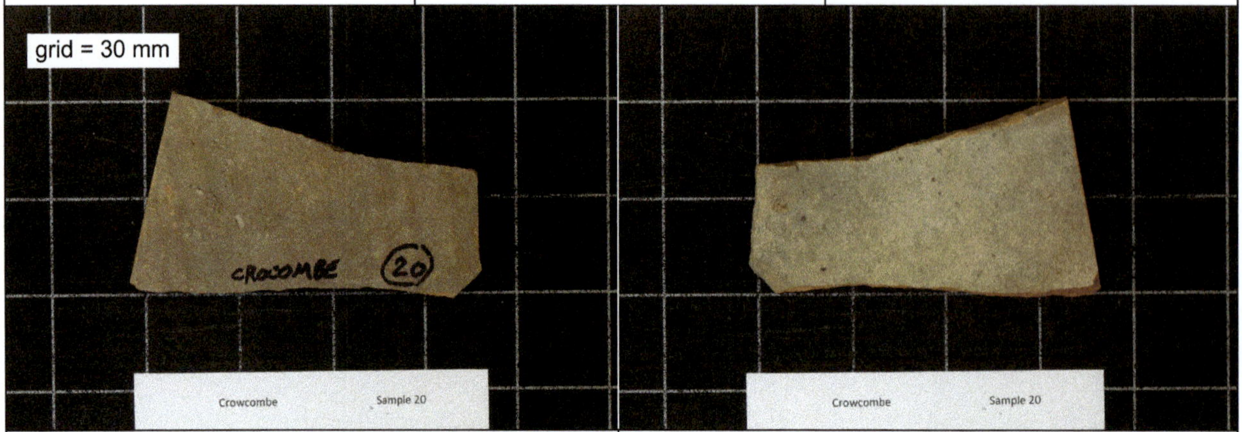

Fabric description	**Mineralogical description**
Reoxidised red sandy fabric, internal possible burnt off slip or glaze.	The sherd has 94 vol% matrix and 6 vol% inclusions. The inclusion population is a very pure mixture of quartz (94 vol%) and K-feldspar (5 vol%).The matrix is dominated by Fe-Al-K silicates (71 vol%) with quartz (11 vol%) and minor K-feldspar (5 vol%), muscovite/illite (5 vol%) and Fe-Al silicates (7 vol%). Kaolinite, plagioclase and glauconite are nearly absent.
Form	**Mineralogical type**
Body sherd.	A
Analogues	**Notes**
West Somerset type.	Thin specks of glaze on one side, a couple of specks of Pb-glaze also in the matrix of the sherd.

Visual appearance of thin section (transmitted light)	**Mineralogical map**	**Key to mineral map** (mineral groups listed in Table 23)
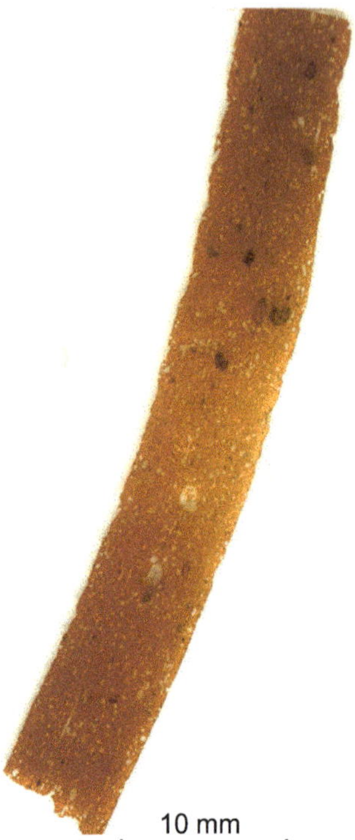		Fe sulphides Pb glaze Barite Chrome spinel Fe Ox / CO_3 Mn phases Rutile Ilmenite Zircon REE phases Quartz Plagioclase feldspar K-feldspar Muscovite / Illite Fe Al K silicates Glauconite Kaolinite Tourmaline Fe Al silicates Mg Al silicates Mg silicates Ca Fe Al silicates Calcite Ca phosphates Others

Figure 118. Analysis of Sample 20: Crowcombe, body sherd.

Sample number: 20	Crowcombe	CSM lab. code: C03150033

Mineralogical composition

	Matrix	Inclusions	Bulk
Fe sulphides	0.006	0.000	0.005
Pb glaze	0.149	0.000	0.140
Barite	0.000	0.000	0.000
Chrome spinel	0.002	0.000	0.001
Fe Ox/CO_3	0.020	0.177	0.030
Mn phases	0.192	0.105	0.186
Rutile	0.132	0.029	0.125
Ilmenite	0.030	0.000	0.028
Zircon	0.012	0.007	0.012
REE phases	0.003	0.000	0.002
Quartz	10.788	94.568	16.073
Plagioclase feldspar	0.580	0.026	0.545
K-Feldspar	5.039	4.903	5.030
Muscovite/Illite	4.670	0.037	4.378
Fe Al K silicates	71.054	0.058	66.576
Glauconite	0.216	0.025	0.204
Kaolinite	0.275	0.003	0.258
Tourmaline	0.009	0.000	0.009
Fe Al silicates	6.530	0.041	6.120
Mg Al silicates	0.064	0.000	0.060
Mg silicates	0.139	0.000	0.130
Ca Fe Al silicates	0.002	0.000	0.002
Calcite	0.048	0.000	0.045
Ca phosphates	0.034	0.021	0.033
Others	0.006	0.000	0.005

Particle size distribution

Matrix (< 63 μm) = 93.7 vol%
Inclusions (> 63 μm) = 6.3 vol%

Mineralogical type

Total measurement points = 3069032
Measurement spacing = 10 μm

Visual representation of mineralogy
(Pb-glaze has been excluded in these diagrams; FO = Fe-Ox/CO_3, qz = quartz, pl = plagioclase, ksp = K-feldspar, ms/ill = muscovite/illite, FAKS = Fe-Al-K silicates, glt = glauconite, kln = kaolinite, FAS = Fe-Al silicates, cc = calcite)

Matrix

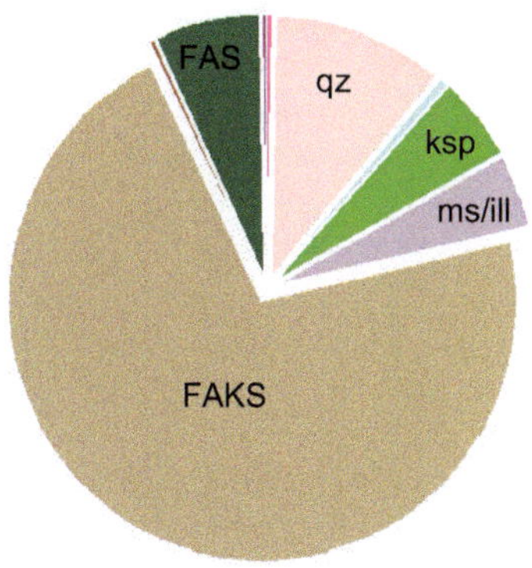

Inclusions

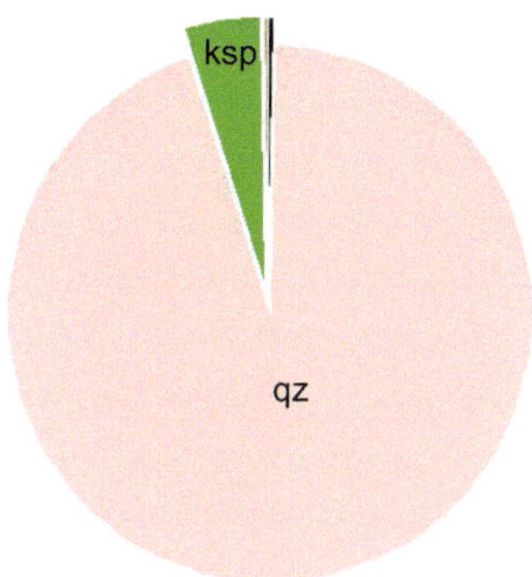

Bulk

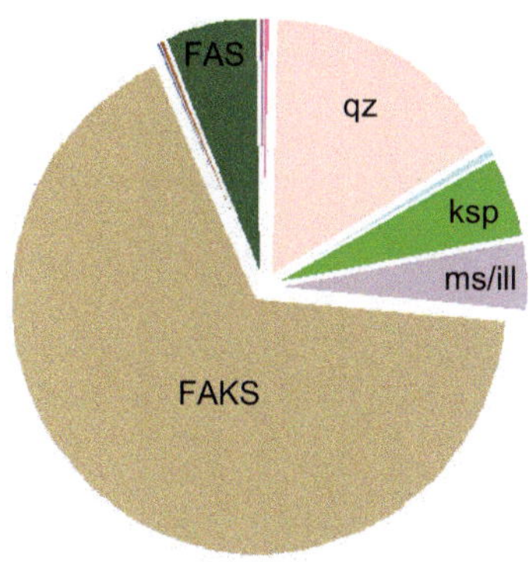

Figure 118 *continued.*

Sample number: 21	Nether Stowey	CSM lab. code: C03150034

Fabric description	Mineralogical description
Red fabric with traces of an internal brown oxidised lead glaze.	The sherd has 99 vol% matrix and 1 vol% inclusions. The inclusion population is a mixture of quartz (64 vol%) and K-feldspar (30 vol%) that carries minor Fe-Al-K silicates (1 vol%) and unusual amounts of Ca-phosphates (4 vol%). The matrix is composed of Fe-Al-K silicates (59 vol%) with quartz (12 vol%), muscovite/illite (14 vol%) and K-feldspar (12 vol%), and minor Fe-Al silicates (2 vol%). Traces include plagioclase and Ca-phosphates, but kaolinite and glauconite are nearly absent.
Form	**Mineralogical type**
Rim sherd of a pancheon.	A
Analogues	**Notes**
West Somerset type.	Traces of Pb-glaze in the matrix of the sherd.

Visual appearance of thin section (transmitted light)

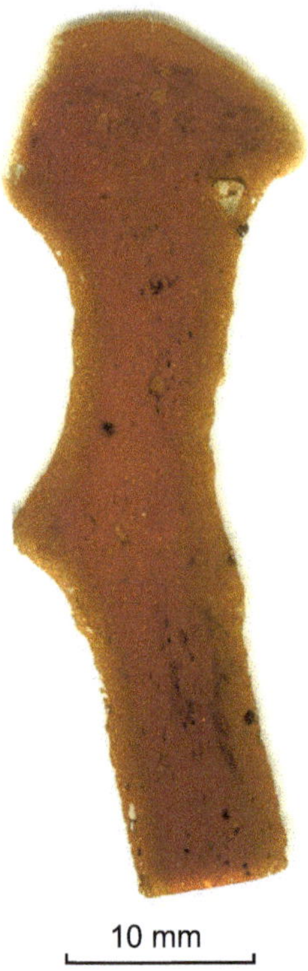

Mineralogical map

Key to mineral map
(mineral groups listed in Table 23)

- Fe sulphides
- Pb glaze
- Barite
- Chrome spinel
- Fe Ox / CO_3
- Mn phases
- Rutile
- Ilmenite
- Zircon
- REE phases
- Quartz
- Plagioclase feldspar
- K-feldspar
- Muscovite / Illite
- Fe Al K silicates
- Glauconite
- Kaolinite
- Tourmaline
- Fe Al silicates
- Mg Al silicates
- Mg silicates
- Ca Fe Al silicates
- Calcite
- Ca phosphates
- Others

Figure 119. Analysis of Sample 21: Nether Stowey, pancheon rim.

Sample number: 21	Nether Stowey	CSM lab. code: C03150034

Mineralogical composition

	Matrix	Inclusions	Bulk
Fe sulphides	0.001	0.000	0.001
Pb glaze	0.018	0.000	0.017
Barite	0.000	0.000	0.000
Chrome spinel	0.002	0.000	0.002
Fe Ox/CO_3	0.024	0.306	0.028
Mn phases	0.116	0.471	0.120
Rutile	0.144	0.000	0.143
Ilmenite	0.028	0.031	0.028
Zircon	0.018	0.000	0.018
REE phases	0.003	0.000	0.003
Quartz	11.694	63.541	12.314
Plagioclase feldspar	0.579	0.190	0.574
K-Feldspar	11.728	29.830	11.945
Muscovite/Illite	14.008	0.380	13.845
Fe Al K silicates	59.034	1.220	58.343
Glauconite	0.160	0.010	0.158
Kaolinite	0.221	0.000	0.219
Tourmaline	0.020	0.063	0.020
Fe Al silicates	1.556	0.010	1.538
Mg Al silicates	0.003	0.000	0.003
Mg silicates	0.025	0.000	0.025
Ca Fe Al silicates	0.005	0.000	0.005
Calcite	0.161	0.000	0.159
Ca phosphates	0.378	3.948	0.421
Others	0.072	0.000	0.071

Particle size distribution

Matrix (< 63 μm) = 98.8 vol%
Inclusions (> 63 μm) = 1.2 vol%

Mineralogical type

Total measurement points = 4097104
Measurement spacing = 10 μm

Visual representation of mineralogy
(Pb-glaze has been excluded in these diagrams; FO = Fe-Ox/CO_3, qz = quartz, pl = plagioclase, ksp = K-feldspar, ms/ill = muscovite/illite, FAKS = Fe-Al-K silicates, glt = glauconite, kln = kaolinite, FAS = Fe-Al silicates, cc = calcite)

Matrix

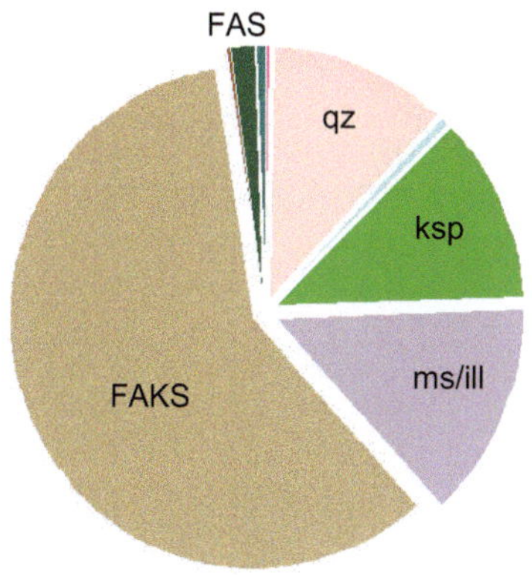

Inclusions

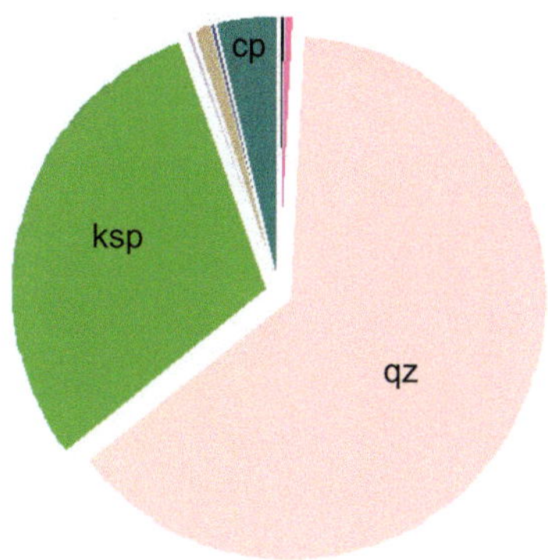

Bulk

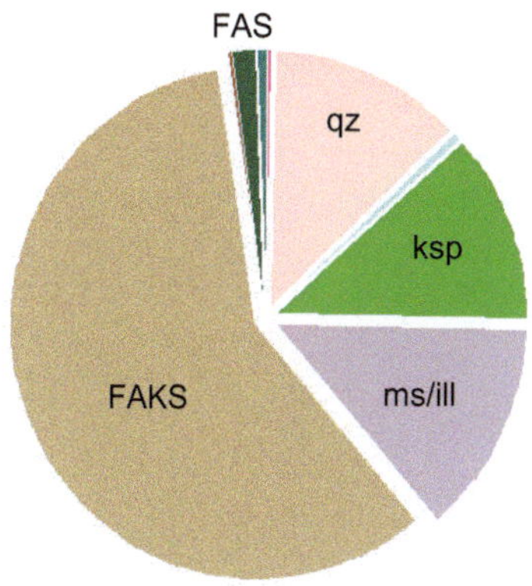

Figure 119 *continued.*

Sample number: 22	Brown mud	CSM lab. code: n/a

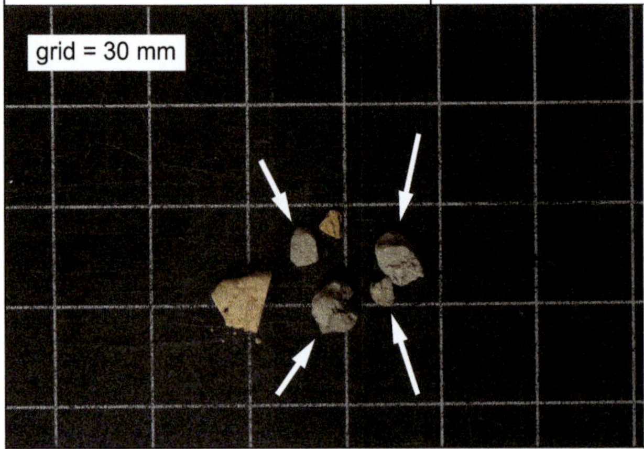

block diameter = 30 mm

Fabric description	Mineralogical description
	The mud has 99.95 vol% matrix and 0.05 vol% inclusions. The inclusion population is a mixture of quartz (49 vol%) and K-feldspar (37 vol%) that carries significant Mn-phases (10 vol%), muscovite/illite (4 vol%) and traces of plagioclase (1 vol%). The matrix is composed of Fe-Al-K silicates (67 vol%) with quartz (5 vol%), muscovite/illite (19 vol%) and K-feldspar (6 vol%), and minor Fe-Al silicates (2 vol%). Traces include plagioclase (0.6 vol%), kaolinite (0.4 vol%) and Mn-phases (0.3 vol%), but glauconite is nearly absent.
Form	**Mineralogical type**
	A
Analogues	**Notes**
	Mud sample collected on excavation site.

Mineralogical map	Key to mineral map (mineral groups listed in Table 23)

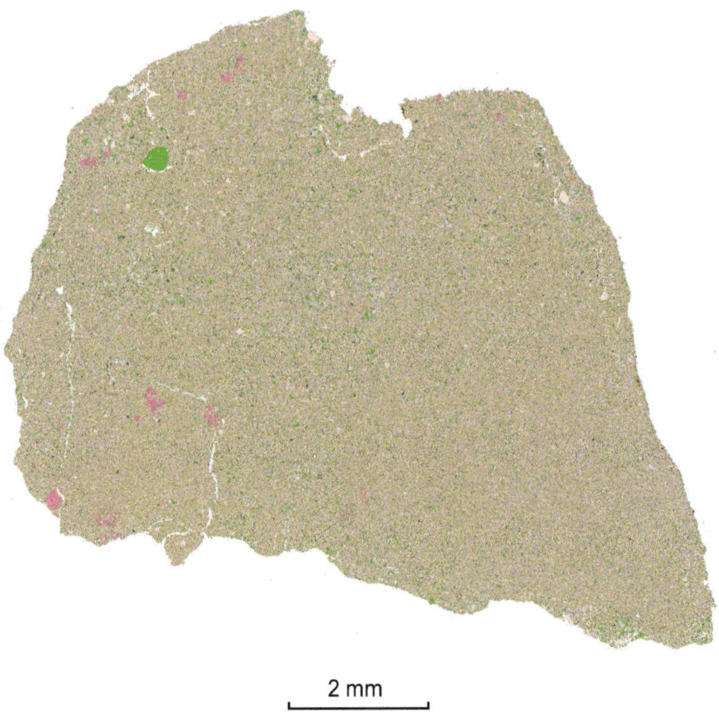

- Fe sulphides
- Pb glaze
- Barite
- Chrome spinel
- Fe Ox / CO_3
- Mn phases
- Rutile
- Ilmenite
- Zircon
- REE phases
- Quartz
- Plagioclase feldspar
- K-feldspar
- Muscovite / Illite
- Fe Al K silicates
- Glauconite
- Kaolinite
- Tourmaline
- Fe Al silicates
- Mg Al silicates
- Mg silicates
- Ca Fe Al silicates
- Calcite
- Ca phosphates
- Others

Figure 120. Analysis of Sample 22: brown mud.

Sample number: 22	**Brown mud**	**CSM lab. code: n/a**

Mineralogical composition

	Matrix	Inclusions	Bulk
Fe sulphides	0.002	0.000	0.001
Pb glaze	0.014	0.000	0.014
Barite	0.000	0.000	0.000
Chrome spinel	0.003	0.000	0.003
Fe Ox/CO_3	0.035	0.000	0.035
Mn phases	0.305	9.753	0.360
Rutile	0.128	0.000	0.128
Ilmenite	0.017	0.000	0.017
Zircon	0.006	0.000	0.006
REE phases	0.000	0.000	0.000
Quartz	4.621	48.765	4.881
Plagioclase feldspar	0.596	0.802	0.597
K-Feldspar	6.068	36.669	6.249
Muscovite/Illite	18.705	3.694	18.616
Fe Al K silicates	67.305	0.211	66.908
Glauconite	0.016	0.000	0.015
Kaolinite	0.386	0.106	0.384
Tourmaline	0.018	0.000	0.018
Fe Al silicates	1.728	0.000	1.718
Mg Al silicates	0.002	0.000	0.002
Mg silicates	0.006	0.000	0.006
Ca Fe Al silicates	0.006	0.000	0.006
Calcite	0.021	0.000	0.021
Ca phosphates	0.003	0.000	0.002
Others	0.011	0.000	0.011

Particle size distribution

Matrix (< 63 μm) = 99.95 vol%
Inclusions (> 63 μm) = 0.05 vol%

Mineralogical type

Total measurement points = 149804
Measurement spacing = 10 μm

Visual representation of mineralogy

(Pb-glaze has been excluded in these diagrams; FO = Fe-Ox/CO_3, qz = quartz, pl = plagioclase, ksp = K-feldspar, ms/ill = muscovite/illite, FAKS = Fe-Al-K silicates, glt = glauconite, kln = kaolinite, FAS = Fe-Al silicates, cc = calcite)

Matrix	Inclusions	Bulk

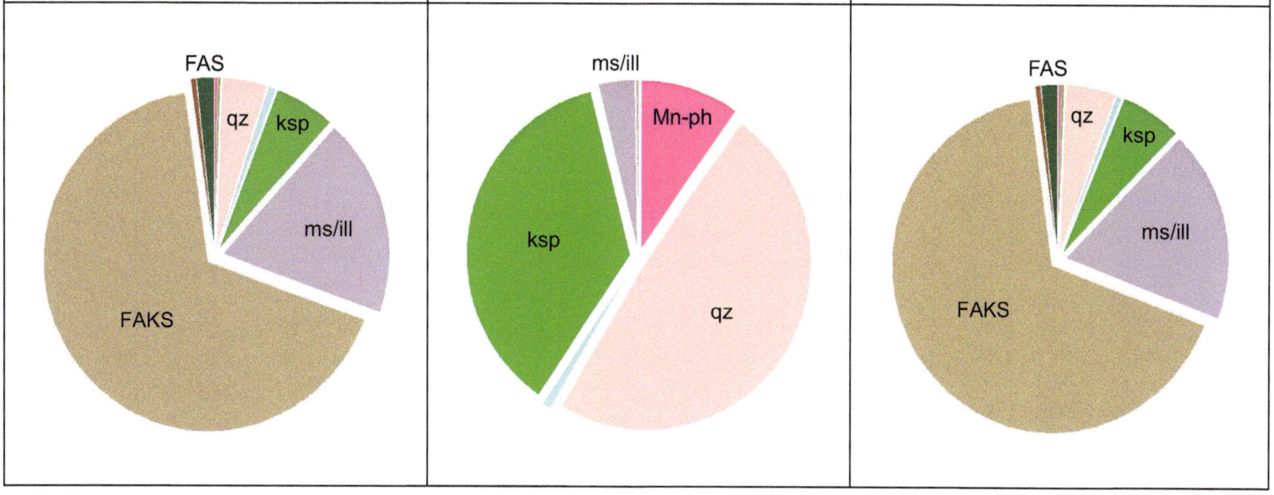

Figure 120 *continued.*

Sample number: 23	Orange mud	CSM lab. code: n/a

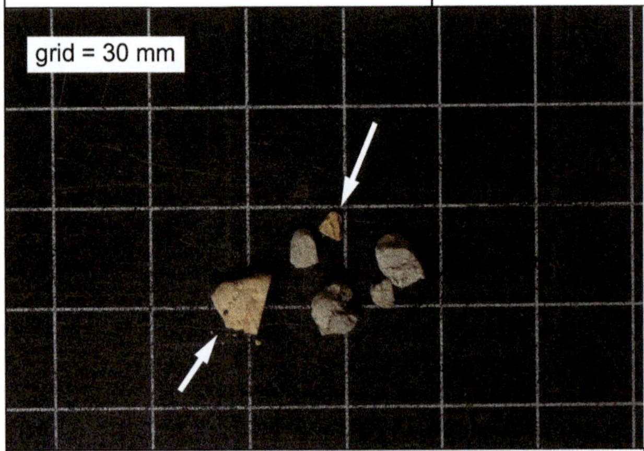

block diameter
= 30 mm

Fabric description	Mineralogical description
	The mud has 99.7 vol% matrix and 0.3 vol% inclusions. The inclusions are a mixture of quartz (79 vol%) and K-feldspar (8 vol%) with minor muscovite/illite (4 vol%), Fe-Ox/CO3 (4 vol%), Fe-Al-K silicates (1 vol%), Mn-phases (1 vol%) and Ca-phosphates (1 vol%) and traces of calcite. The matrix is composed of Fe-Al-K silicates (68 vol%) with quartz (4 vol%), muscovite/illite (20 vol%) and K-feldspar (6 vol%), and minor Fe-Al silicates (1 vol%). Traces include plagioclase (0.4 vol%), but kaolinite and glauconite are nearly absent.
Form	**Mineralogical type**
	A
Analogues	**Notes**
	Mud sample collected on excavation site.

Mineralogical map	Key to mineral map (mineral groups listed in Table 23)

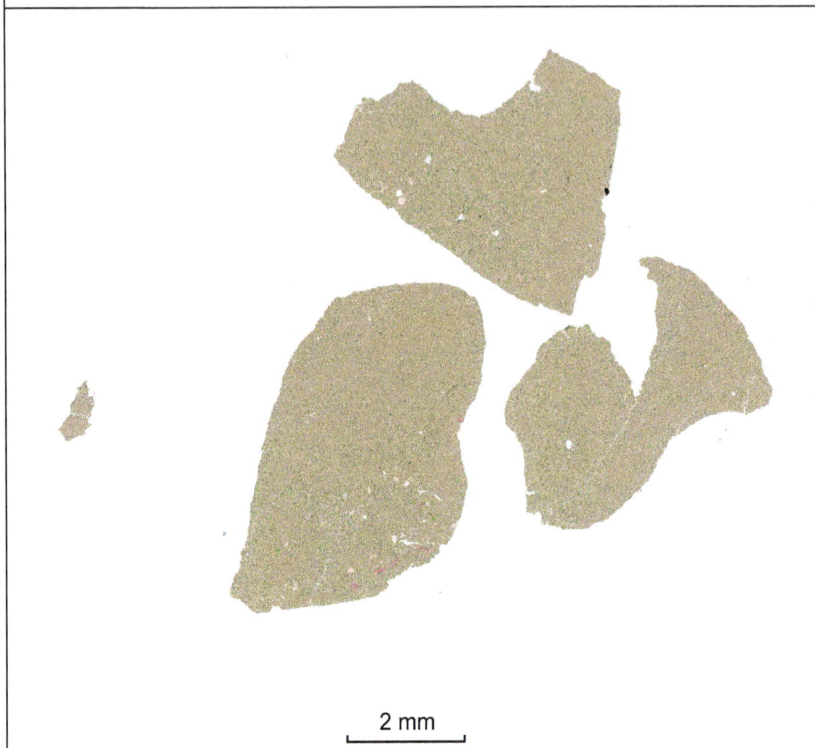

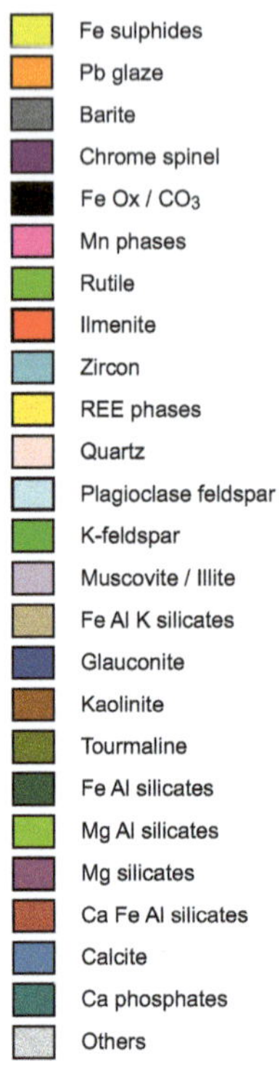

Figure 121. Analysis of Sample 23: orange mud.

Sample number: 23	**Orange mud**	**CSM lab. code: n/a**

Mineralogical composition

	Matrix	Inclusions	Bulk
Fe sulphides	0.003	0.000	0.003
Pb glaze	0.018	0.000	0.018
Barite	0.000	0.000	0.000
Chrome spinel	0.003	0.000	0.003
Fe Ox/CO_3	0.033	4.248	0.048
Mn phases	0.094	2.967	0.104
Rutile	0.098	0.000	0.098
Ilmenite	0.012	0.000	0.012
Zircon	0.005	0.000	0.005
REE phases	0.000	0.000	0.000
Quartz	3.795	79.018	4.061
Plagioclase feldspar	0.373	0.000	0.372
K-Feldspar	5.737	7.577	5.744
Muscovite/Illite	19.921	3.863	19.865
Fe Al K silicates	68.272	0.982	68.035
Glauconite	0.023	0.000	0.023
Kaolinite	0.183	0.000	0.182
Tourmaline	0.009	0.000	0.008
Fe Al silicates	1.365	0.000	1.361
Mg Al silicates	0.001	0.000	0.001
Mg silicates	0.004	0.000	0.004
Ca Fe Al silicates	0.007	0.000	0.007
Calcite	0.018	0.299	0.019
Ca phosphates	0.006	1.046	0.009
Others	0.020	0.000	0.020

Particle size distribution

Matrix (< 63 µm) = 99.7 vol%
Inclusions (> 63 µm) = 0.3 vol%

Mineralogical type

Total measurement points = 1329528
Measurement spacing = 10 µm

Visual representation of mineralogy
(Pb-glaze has been excluded in these diagrams; FO = Fe-Ox/CO_3, qz = quartz, pl = plagioclase, ksp = K-feldspar, ms/ill = muscovite/illite, FAKS = Fe-Al-K silicates, glt = glauconite, kln = kaolinite, FAS = Fe-Al silicates, cc = calcite)

Matrix

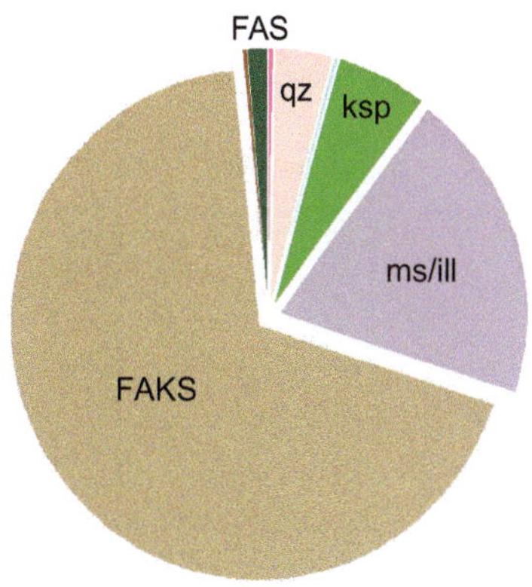

Inclusions

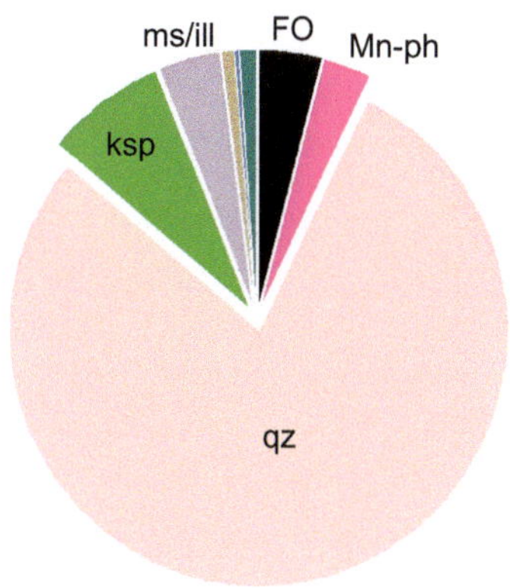

Bulk

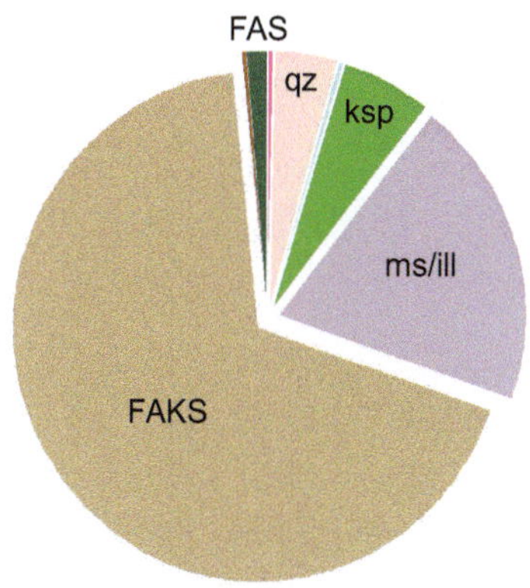

Figure 121 *continued.*

north-east from Hemyock and beyond the watershed at Culmhead. This suggests that either the sherds were produced and traded from a Liassic area or that they were produced with clay traded from a source in the Lias. With 98% quartz the inclusion assemblages are the purest of all the sherds we have investigated.

The samples from the Bridgwater Chandos Glass Cone are distinguished by their very high content of plagioclase feldspar in the matrix and the presence of calcite in the inclusions. The closest match is mineralogical type C, which has similarly high plagioclase, calcite and traces of Ca-Fe-Al silicates. This type was previously found only at Taunton Castle. Although the bedrock at Bridgwater is the Mercia Mudstone formation, it is overlain by more than 10 m of superficial (marine and river-deposited) sediments that include clays, marls, silts and sands and these are likely to have been the source of production materials.

The samples from Donyatt sites 2 and 3 appear to be somewhat intermediate in composition to the samples from Donyatt that have been investigated previously. And this may indicate that groups B_1 (Donyatt site 4) and D (Donyatt site 13) are not entirely separate but simply reflect a wider mineralogical spectrum.

The two samples from Donyatt site 3 have matrix compositions that are intermediate to types B_1 and D, although most similar to type D (which includes samples from Donyatt site 13, see Andersen *et al.* 2016a) in their relatively high content of muscovite/illite. It is noticeable that these samples also have a very diverse inclusion assemblage with 45-60% of K-feldspar, muscovite/illite, Fe-Al-K silicates kaolinite and Fe-Al silicates. The sample previously studied from Donyatt site 13 closely matches their matrix compositions and has a very similar 'dirty' inclusion assemblage. Apart from the K-feldspar, in other samples these components report almost exclusively to the matrix. This variable inclusion assemblage suggests either a less refined selection of inclusion materials or that grog, crushed fragments of previously fired clay, was used as part of the temper. We consequently consider these samples to belong to type D.

The samples from Donyatt site 2 also appear somewhat intermediate between types B_1 and D. However these samples are closer in composition to type B_1. The very 'clean' inclusion assemblage with more than 90% quartz is another similarity to samples from Donyatt site 4. We consider these samples to belong to type B_1.

The variability that is starting to emerge in the Donyatt samples suggests that perhaps the distinction of several types of matrix represents variability in the sources of clay rather than distinct sources of different composition. The diversity in inclusion assemblages would more likely represent differences in technique, including recycling grog or less refined criteria for the choice of inclusion materials.

Glauconite is a commonly used indicator mineral for material sourced from the Upper Greensand Formation. Traces of glauconite are found in most of the sample studied here. However as we have previously published, the mineralogical transformations of glauconite (as a low temperature mineral) undergoes during firing of the pottery are unknown (Andersen *et al.* 2016b, 286-288).

Summary

1. The samples from Hemyock contexts 571 and 588 are mineralogically similar to type (West Somerset Type wares). The bedrock geology and clay samples confirm they were probably produced locally.
2. The three Saxo-Norman sherds (Samples 7-9) from Hemyock context 557 (type B_1) appear to represent materials not produced locally but in an area of Liassic-derived materials similar to Donyatt and brought in.
3. The Bridgwater area as exemplified by the Chandos Glass Cone pottery is a potential production source for previously unprovenanced type C.
4. The variability of the Donyatt samples indicates significant differences in source materials and technique over time and between sites 2, 3, 4 and 13.

Comparison of Petrography, ICP-MS and QEMSCAN Data

Jens C.Ø. Andersen with comments by M.J. Hughes

Introduction

The use of petrography and chemical analysis (by XRF, ICP-OES or ICP-MS) is widespread in archaeology to determine compositional and structural differences between artefacts, and these techniques have been widely applied in South-West England as several previous publications show (Hughes 2002; 2005; 2010a). Petrography allows a skilled observer to make observations of the distinctive textures and properties of materials. This technique is essential to explore the properties and structure of artefacts, which can aid in the determination of production methods. It is also possible for the skilled observer to identify geological sources on the basis of particle shapes, trace fossils, and mineral assemblages. Observations can commonly be linked directly to the structure of the artefacts providing a necessary background for any interpretations of chemistry. The human intuition and skill is unrivalled for pattern recognition and to identify similarities and differences in the materials and manufacturing techniques involved in pottery production. However, observations are difficult to quantify and strongly dependent on the skill and expertise of the observer. The technique is also limited by the resolution of the optical microscope, and commonly it is impossible to identify components within the fine-grained matrix.

Chemical analysis by XRF, ICP-OES and ICP-MS are powerful tools to gain insight into the detailed composition of the materials, especially because very low abundances of trace metals can be determined. These allow for the identification of chemical signatures that may be diagnostic to individual material sources. The unrivalled precision of analysis enables the determination of many potential variables that can be used in isolation or combination to ascertain similarities or differences between materials. However, as these are bulk techniques, they suffer from the lack of differentiation between the material components within the artefacts. Most pottery would have been derived from a mixture of sources; notably the clay and the temper. The ICP analyses are dominated by the clay mineral components while the mineral inclusions contribute rather less to the overall chemistry with the very common exception that the total percentage of inclusions act as a diluetant, often, as when quartz is the principal inclusion, reducing the overall percentage of aluminium and associated elements. As a consequence, the chemistry can be difficult to relate to specific minerals unless such are visible in the fabric under magnification. The chemical results need to be presented using statistical methods in order to be understood in the context of the artefacts.

Automated analysis of mineralogy (in this study by QEMSCAN, but alternative methods are available) provides a relatively novel way to obtain quantitative mineralogical data. The results will obviously reflect the bulk composition to some extent, but the method has advantages in the ability for the analyst to differentiate components of the analysis; in our work, the separation of data for matrix, inclusions and the glaze. The drawback of the method is the limited amount of material that can be explored by this relatively time-consuming technique, which yields less coverage of a population of artefacts than what can be achieved by the comparatively inexpensive chemical techniques. Although the spatial resolution is great, the spectral precision is much lower than the ICP-MS, leading to the poor identification of chemical elements present in low concentrations within the constituent minerals.

Comparison of Results

The optical examination establishes that many of the examined materials from Hemyock have inclusion assemblages that can be correlated to sources in the Upper Greensand Formation, in contradistinction for example with the materials from the Bridgwater Chandos Glass Cone, which appear to have assemblages sourced from a carbonate-bearing source. The Upper Greensand-Derived assemblages are relatively pure quartz with minor K-feldspar. Glauconite is a diagnostic mineral that can be identified optically, but, when analysed by automated mineralogy, it becomes apparent that the mineral is variably preserved during the firing. While the Hemyock Samples 3-6 are described as Upper Greensand-Derived materials, Hemyock Samples 1-2 are not attributed to this source. The automated mineralogy shows that all of these samples are similar in their matrix and inclusion assemblages. Hemyock Sample 7 is also described as Upper Greensand-Derived, but along with the other materials from context 557 (Hemyock Samples 8-9), it is noticeable that they have a markedly different matrix composition to Hemyock Samples 1-6. While the inclusion assemblages would be consistent with Upper Greensand-Derived materials, the matrix confirms that the clay sources must have been different. The matrix of these materials is similar to compositions recorded from Donyatt (Samples 16-19).

When comparing the major components of the ICP-MS analysis with the QEMSCAN data, it is immediately apparent that there is no unique correspondence between most of the data. For example, Al_2O_3 is expected to be a major component of the clays, but is also hosted by plagioclase and K-feldspar. Fe_2O_3 is hosted by a wide range of minerals including Fe sulphides, Chrome spinel, FeO_x/CO_3, Ilmenite, Fe Al K silicates, Glauconite, Tourmaline, Fe Al silicates and Ca Fe Al silicates. TiO_2 is hosted by ilmenite and rutile, and may also be present in Fe-oxides.

Some correlations are very clear and correspond to expectations on the geochemical behaviour of the elements (Figure 122). It should come as no surprise, that the concentration of Pb displays good overall correlation with the amount of Pb-glaze (Figure 122a). Strontium (Sr) expectedly correlates well with the content of plagioclase feldspar (Figure 122b), consistent with the feldspar being the principal Sr host. The K_2O and Rb concentrations correlate strongly with the abundance of K-feldspar (Figure 122c-d).

The P_2O_5 correlates reasonably well with the abundance of Ca-phosphates for the majority of samples (Figure 123a), except for the reduced Saxo-Norman sherds (Samples 7, 8 and 9) from context 557 which have too little Ca-phosphate to account for the P_2O_5.

Other correlations are less clear and would require further study to fully understand. For example, the content of MnO appears to correlate poorly with the abundance of discrete Mn-phases (Figure 123b). There is no apparent correlation between the Ba and barite (Figure 123c), Zr and zircon (Figure 123d), or the rare earth elements (Y, La, Ce, Pr, Nd, Sm, Eu, Gd, Tb, Dy, Ho, Er, Tm, Yb, and Lu) and the content of REE phases (not illustrated).

Some correlations are unexpected. Notably, the ICP-MS data displays a strong positive correlation between Al_2O_3 and TiO_2 (Figure 124a) that defines a clear trend without discrimination between the samples from all of the different locations. While the chemical data do not differentiate the materials, the mineralogical data reveals differences in the TiO_2 host between rutile and ilmenite that are systematic with the archaeological context (Figure 124b). A group of materials that includes the reduced chert-tempered ware from Hemyock context 557 (Samples 7-9) as well as the samples from Donyatt display a strong correlation between Al_2O_3 and the content of rutile. The remaining materials

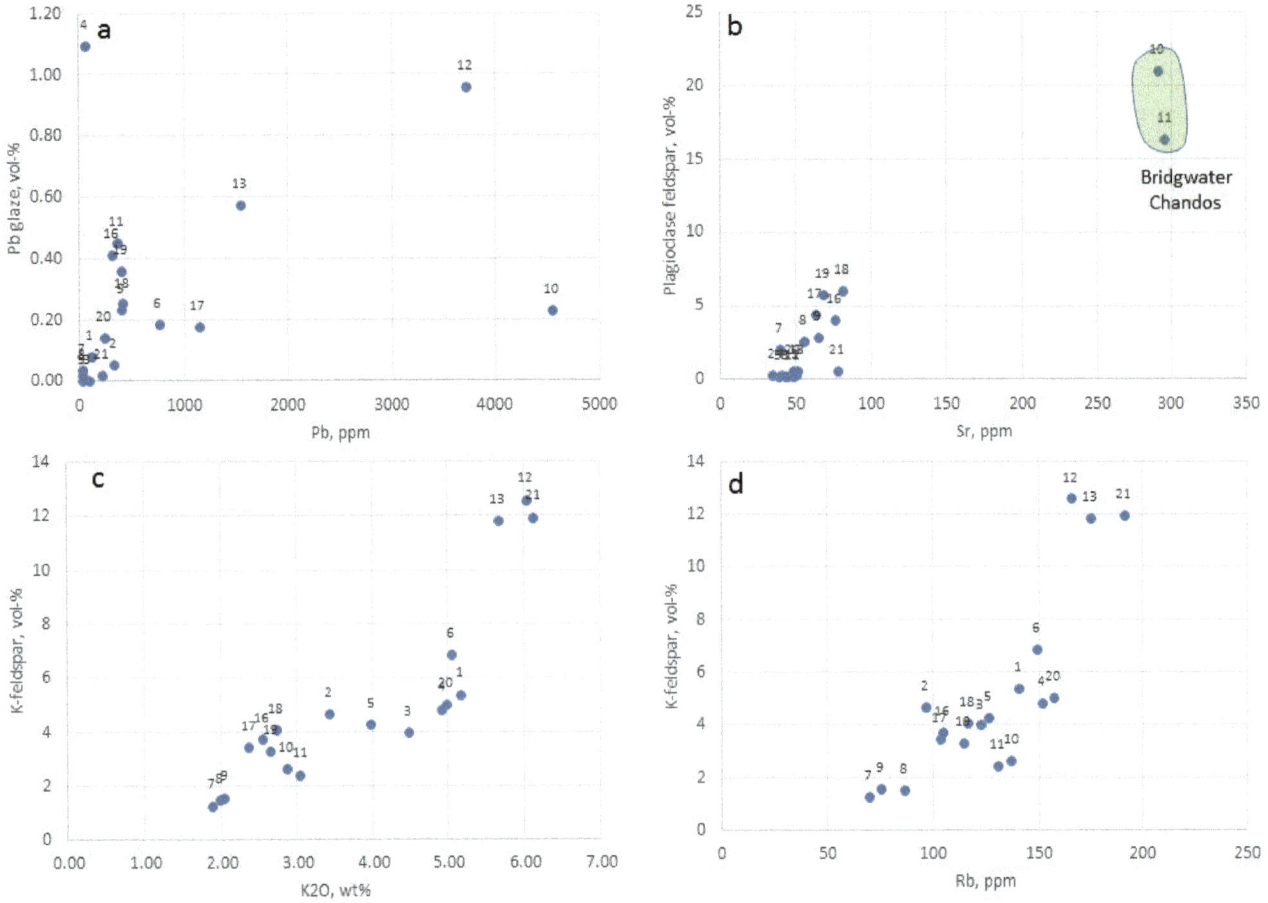

Figure 122. Elements that display good correlations between ICP-MS data and the expected mineral hosts (by QEMSCAN). a. Lead (Pb) and lead glaze. b. Strontium (Sr) and plagioclase feldspar. c. Potassium (K_2O) and K-feldspar. d. Rubidium (Rb) and K-feldspar.

have lower concentrations of rutile (Figure 124b) along with slightly higher ilmenite (not illustrated), but appear to display no systematic correlation with Al_2O_3. Further TiO_2 could also be hosted in magnetite, which is in the FeO_x/CO_3 group.

Discussion

The optical petrography and automated mineralogy confirm the characteristic inclusion assemblages associated with the Upper Greensand Formation. However, while the matrix cannot be differentiated by optical petrography alone, the automated mineralogy identifies distinct compositions between Samples 1-6 and 7-9. Samples 7-9 are comparable to materials from Donyatt (Samples 16-19), of which also Samples 16-17 have Upper Greensand-Derived inclusion assemblages. So while the optical petrography is consistent for the inclusion populations, the technique is unable to distinguish the very widely different matrix compositions.

The clear correlations between certain chemical elements (Pb, Rb, Sr, K_2O) and the mineralogical data confirm the general considerations about their likely host minerals. However, the lack of correspondence between elements such as Ba, Cr, MnO, Zr and to some extent P_2O_5 indicates that the mineralogical distribution of these elements is more complex. The scatter for elements that otherwise display good correlations is likely to reflect variability within the sample set. For example, despite great care being taken to extract samples for chemical analysis without glaze, the QEMSCAN analysis reveals lead glaze as a component within the interior of certain materials, possibly reflecting recycling or the generally dusty environment of a potter's workshop.

The variability in correlations between other elements with their expected principal mineral hosts suggests that other minerals may also be significant. For example, manganese commonly substitutes for iron, and consequently the amount of Mn-phases may only partially account for the total MnO content. The P_2O_5 is particularly interesting, as the correlations with the amount of Ca-phosphates appear to be reflecting the archaeological context. The reduced Saxo-Norman wares (Samples 7, 8 and 9) from context 557, in particular appear to have high P_2O_5 without significant amounts of detectable Ca-phosphates. While monazite, a cerium phosphate, is a potential alternative mineral host, it is not generally abundant in nature. It is more likely that phosphorous may have been added as bone ash, that the P_2O_5 adsorbed to clay minerals and when fired, yielded nano-scale mineral intergrowths that are below the spatial resolution of the QEMSCAN. Many other metals, such as Cu, Co, Ni, Th, U, V and Zn are able to adsorb to clay minerals, so it is unlikely that they will correlate well with any particular mineralogical components. They are likely to be controlled by the specific source environments,

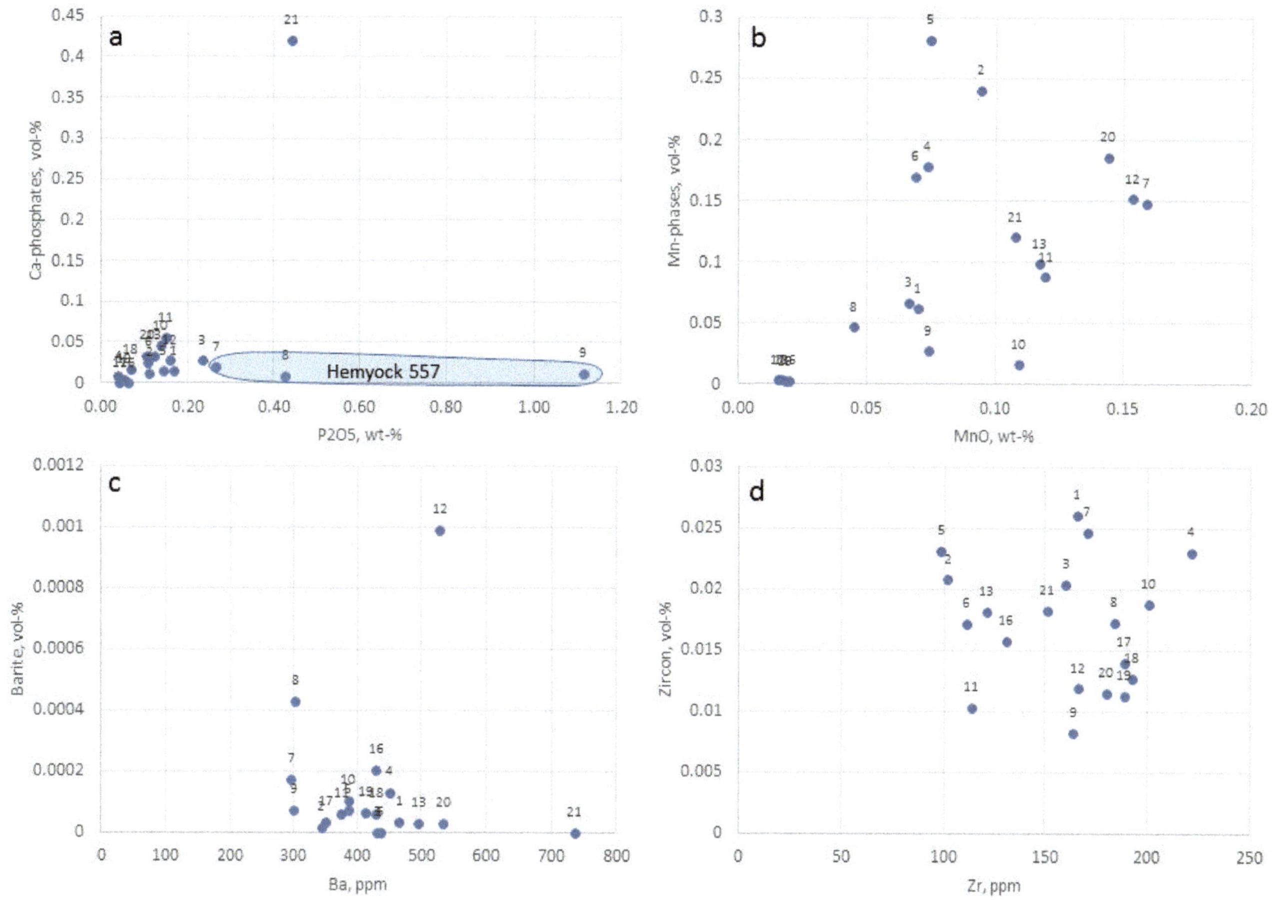

Figure 123. Elements that display poor correlations between ICP-MS data and the expected mineral hosts (by QEMSCAN). a. Phosphorus (P_2O_5) and Ca-phosphates. b. Manganese (Mn) and Mn-phases. c. Barium (Ba) and barite. d. Zirconium (Zr) and zircon.

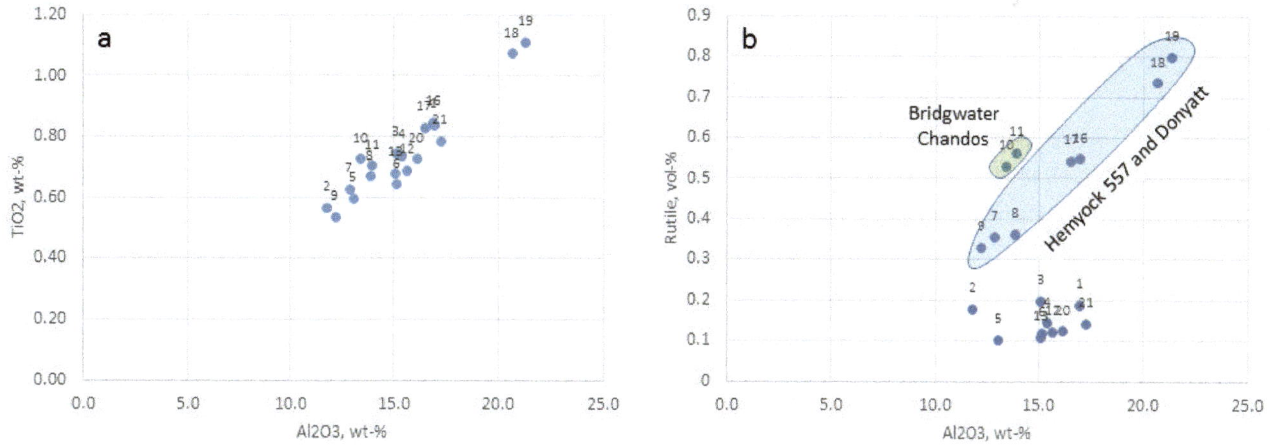

Figure 124. Correlation between Al_2O_3 and TiO_2 in the chemical data. b. Differences in rutile contents between samples defining the clear group of Hemyock context 557 with Donyatt.

where the metals may have been particularly available (for example, Cu, Co, Ni, Th and Zn, the granite-related terrains of Dartmoor; U and V perhaps from the concretion-bearing Littleham mudstone of East Devon).

The correlations between Al_2O_3 and TiO_2 are particularly intriguing and difficult to explain. Such a strong correlation would usually be inferred to indicate a common mineral host. However, no commonly occurring minerals contain both Al_2O_3 and TiO_2, and consequently the reason for this correlation must reflect the source materials. A possibility may lie in the co-deposition of the elements from a granite-derived source material during the deposition of the original clay, so that their abundances reflect the contribution from this granite-related source. It is notable, that ilmenite (and also titanomagnetite, measured as part of the FeO_x/CO_3 group) are highly affected by oxidation and reduction reactions, and in this capacity may be sensitive to the firing process of the pottery. While further studies would be required, this could to some extent explain why the correlation appears to be insensitive to the TiO_2 host mineral. Although we are currently unable to assess the specific reason for this correlation, it is not uncommonly observed in pottery ICP projects, especially where it seems that the same clay type has been used for pottery from different sources, for example London Clay used at kiln sites in North London and South Hertfordshire (Hughes 2010b).

It is fair to say that each analytical technique has strengths and weaknesses. Optical petrography is intuitive and inexpensive and adds valuable information on material properties, textures, and inclusion assemblages that directly can be correlated with the artefacts. The human intuition and flair for pattern recognition is unrivalled by quantitative techniques, but the method is subjective, limited by the optical resolution and lacks quantification. Observations on the matrix are limited by the resolution of the microscope and masked by the strong colourations that are typically related to oxidation-reduction reactions during the manufacturing process. The ICP-MS analysis adds a wealth of data on the bulk materials that are precise and statistically reliable. However, the method may suffer from incomplete dissolution (which clearly affects elements such as Nb and in particular Zr and for this reason Zr is never used in the ICP statistical studies) and a lack of differentiation between components in mixed materials. The results are typically not visually easy to correlate with the artefacts themselves. The automated mineralogy adds substantial novel information by the spatially resolved mineralogical data, which can be differentiated to the matrix, inclusions and other specific components in the materials. The results are statistically reliable, except for trace components and can be reproduced in visually attractive manners that can be directly compared with the artefacts. However, while the spatial resolution is very high, the spectral resolution is low, leading to the poor detection of element in low concentrations within host minerals.

The lack of correlation between data can have many reasons; notably that mineral components may not be representatively sampled during preparation of the materials, chemical elements may have several mineral hosts, and trace metals or minerals may be close to the lower limit of detection of each method leading to variability in the results. However, each method adds information that the other methods cannot provide.

A Strategy for Future Sampling

John Allan, David Dawson, Jens C.Ø. Andersen and M.J. Hughes

Clearly there is much work to be done to understand how the analyses fully correlate as there is in defining the chemical and mineralogical changes that pottery undergoes as exemplified by the breakdown of glauconite during the succession of oxidation, reduction and reoxidation in the firing process (Dawson and Kent 1999, 165-7; Andersen *et al.* 2016b, 286-8). Here is a significant additional consideration to the processes set out by Orton and Hughes involved in the transformation from clay to compositional analysis (Orton and Hughes 1993, 172).

The main analysis of any pottery assemblage has to depend on the skills of the archaeological pottery specialist and the resources available to them particularly of properly curated pottery type series and their accompanying documentation. These people will define the broader characteristic of a particular ware based on an assessment of skill and technique in making, in decoration, in the forms of vessel employed and in firing. This is done by assessing the intrinsic qualities of the ware and by comparison with pottery. They will also draw conclusions from the wares in relation to their context and their associated finds on the wider significance of the use and disposal of that particular ware. Information derived from optical microscopy will always form an important part in this process, especially if the services can be recruited of a geologist who is familiar with the mineralogy of the area concerned.

Scientific analysis, as further demonstrated here, makes a significant contribution to characterisation of the fabric of wares. The Medieval Pottery Research Group has envisaged and is working towards an on-line atlas of pottery fabric types from known production sites as a fundamental way of communicating such definitions to both specialist and non-specialist audiences (Irving 2011, 22). It is proposed that QEMSCAN be deployed to provide the essential visual reference for each broad fabric type. Its unique characteristics make it ideally suited to such a purpose. Geochemical analysis will remain an essential tool for characterising fabric types and should be more widely deployed to identify the range of fabrics and materials being used within single production centres and as well as exploring as yet uncategorised wares. In the longer term, the continuing interaction between these four specialisms and joint-decisions on where to best deploy techniques and resources will provide a more secure and more broadly understood basis for pottery studies.

General Discussion

John Allan

The Hemyock pottery collection is one of three major finds of early modern kiln waste recovered in Devon in recent years, the others being from the Exeter Inn, Barnstaple (where about 50,000 sherds were examined: Morris forthcoming) and from Hillside, Plympton (where about 30,000 sherds weighing about half a tonne were recorded: Ryan *et al.* forthcoming). They offer samples from the three main groupings of potteries known in the county: first those centred on the towns North Devon; second the coarseware industry making granite-derived pottery ('South-West micaceous' wares) along the coasts of south Devon and Cornwall, and third the dispersed rural industry around the Blackdowns of East Devon/South Somerset border, extending to Donyatt in South-East Somerset. When fully assembled, the data from these sites should add greatly to our understanding of pottery production in the county. At this stage, comparisons can be made between the material from Hemyock and that already published from Donyatt and North Devon.

Dating

Pottery of the type represented at Hemyock is now well known in Somerset, Devon and beyond in contexts of the late fifteenth and early and mid sixteenth centuries; comparable assemblages include pit groups containing imported pottery and other datable objects of this period from Taunton (Bennett and Pearson 1984, 87; Pearson 1984, MF 100–19), Bridgwater (unpublished groups from George Street) and Exeter (Allan 1984a, 150–72); they are also known in Dissolution deposits, probably of the late 1530s – for example at Cleeve Abbey (Allan 1998, 43–5, 50–1). The best-dated material comes from the fine sequence of stratified pit groups and other deposits at Exeter. The characteristic wide-bodied jugs with sgraffito bands and twisted or flat slashed handles were already in circulation there in a number of very late medieval groups for which a mid to late fifteenth century date seems probable; they came into use after a period (?early fifteenth century) when tall baluster jugs were the main product on the Exeter market (for the former: Allan 1984a, 65.818–19 and Fig. 49; for the latter Figs 47–8). The large bowls or pancheons represented in the Hemyock kiln waste are not present in a group of at least 120 late medieval vessels from Polsloe Priory, which contained imported pottery (Italo-Netherlandish maiolica, Raeren stonewares, Beauvais earthenwares, etc) broadly datable to the last quarter of the fifteenth century or the early sixteenth (*ibid.*, 91–2). On current evidence, then, the earliest possible start date for the kiln waste is *c.* 1500.

The latest datable contexts which contain pottery of this style belong to the mid sixteenth century or slightly later – probably the third quarter of the century. Again Exeter offers the most tightly dated material. Jugs and bowls in this style were found in the backfilling of a chapel which was demolished *c.* 1550 whose stonewares were mainly Raeren wares with two Frechen-Cologne vessels, and in a series of cultivation trenches containing a coin of 1556–65, a tile dated 1556 and mid sixteenth-century stonewares (*ibid.*, 168–71). The other group which has seemed to offer late dating for pottery of this type was found at Exeter Cathedral (*ibid.*, Fig. 79.1810–17). It was said to have been found in the 1950s in the backfill of the tomb of Bishop Grandisson, and thus datable between 1556 (when the tomb was intact) and 1586 (when its desecration is first recorded). We now know that the information about the provenance of the group was wrong: photographic evidence shows that most of these pots were displayed at the cathedral Chapter House in the 1930s. Later in the sixteenth century new forms of vessel including jugs imitating German stonewares came into circulation (*ibid.*, 172–3), and by 1600 a completely different range of forms was in use (*ibid.*, 174–8). The kiln material could belong to the mid sixteenth century, but a later date is unlikely.

Within the broad range of *c.* 1500–1560, one feature suggests an early date: the proportion of vessel types. This shows a strikingly high percentage of jugs, a significant presence of jars, and a relatively low showing for bowls (respectively 63%, 10% and 23% by EVE). Jugs had made up almost all the market in the fifteenth century. Although they remained the most common vessel form of the sixteenth century, their share declined: to 37% of local vessels in sixteenth-century Exeter, where the figure was down sharply to *c.* 10–13% after 1600 (by MNV: *ibid.*, 100, Fig. 54). Jars too tended to become less common in the course of the century; they made up 20% of the early sixteenth-century vessels at Donyatt but were no longer produced there by the early seventeenth century (Coleman-Smith and Pearson 1988, 98, Table 42 and 99, Table 43, cf the equivalent Exeter figures: 15% in the early sixteenth century, 9% in the latter part of the century, still less later: Allan 1984a, 100, Fig. 54). A pronounced growth in the use of bowls is a noticeable feature of the same century; at Exeter for example they form 16% of local vessels in deposits of 1500–50 but 27% of those of 1550–1600 (by MNV: *ibid.*, 100). In the seventeenth century this trend continued in some parts at least of the South West: in rural Devon, for example, bowls form about half or almost half the ceramic output (e.g. Allan *et al.* 2007, 159; 42% of 72 vessels at Hennard Jefford, Roadford: Allan and Langman in press). All these features of the Hemyock finds, then, may indicate a date towards the early end of the date-range – probably nearer 1500 than 1550.

There is however an alternative explanation of this evidence: that the Hemyock potters specialised in the production of jugs. The huge collection of broadly sixteenth-century ceramics from Glastonbury Abbey may be used to illustrate this possibility (Allan *et al.* 2015). The largest component among that material consists of coarseware from the Wanstrow potteries and their neighbours in North-East Somerset; the South Somerset potteries, principally Donyatt, however, supplied all or almost all the jugs in these assemblages (or at least all those which were sampled for ICP analysis: Hughes 2015). Specialist production in the production of cups is a familiar feature elsewhere in Britain (e.g. Brears 1971, 14).

Decoration

The most common form of decoration represented in the kiln waste consists of bands of slip decoration brushed onto the shoulders of jugs, through which combs, fingers or blunt-ended tools have been drawn whilst the slip was wet; over 4400 sherds with this type of decoration were counted, probably representing far more than the minimum vessel count of about 200 pots (Figure 79). This general style of sgraffito is well known from the early sixteenth-century Donyatt kilns (e.g. Coleman-Smith and Pearson 1988, 131–43, Nos 4/71, 4/90, 4/122–4, etc) and from consumer sites of the same period in the region (e.g. Cleeve Abbey: Allan 1998, 43, Nos 34–6; Exeter: *idem* 1984a, Nos 1802, 1876); it may be presumed to be a direct successor to the late medieval jugs with bands of slip, sometimes sgraffito-decorated, which were common in the region in the fifteenth century (e.g. Allan 1984a, Nos 1516–27 and the huge recent find of this type of jug from the Princesshay excavations in Exeter).

A much more specialist aspect of the assemblage is represented by a series of vessels with all-over slip and precise sgraffito decoration, most of it drawn with a compass (Figure 73, Nos 1–8; Figure 78, No. 48). They form a tiny proportion of the total collection (0.05% of the domestic pottery): a total of 18 sherds from nine vessels, six of them small dishes. They may perhaps have served some specialist function at table, such as presenting sauces or sweetmeats.

If the early sixteenth-century date of these finds is accepted, the latter are of particular interest on account of their early date. Hitherto, the earliest vessels decorated with true all-over slip known in South-West England have been the early sixteenth-century kiln wasters from Goldsmith Street, Exeter (Allan 1984a, Nos 1646, 1654, 1657, 1659). These, however, are not typical South-West English products: they appear to represent the output of a kiln operated by a potter or potters trained in the traditions of the Low Countries – probably an immigrant or immigrants (*ibid.*, 136–8). With that exception, the earliest true post-medieval slipwares in the region have been those the from Narrow Quay, Bristol,; Fore Street, Totnes, and Queen Street, Exeter, all datable to the very end of the sixteenth century or *c.* 1600 (Good 1987, 46–8; Allan 1984a, Nos 1999–2000; *idem* 1984b, Nos 38–9). These, however, are different in character: larger dishes and bowls with coarser sgraffito. For an earlier discussion of the origins of post-medieval sgraffito pottery in South-West England see Hurst 1964, 363–4. The Hemyock finds therefore appear to be the earliest known examples of all-over slip decoration made by the local potters of South-West England.

Hemyock and Donyatt

The Range of Vessel Forms

The overall range of products represented is very similar to that in Coleman-Smith and Pearson's Group 3 at Donyatt, but there are notable differences in the proportions represented (Table 24).

Distinguishing Products of the Two Centres

An initial research aim in this programme was to see whether pottery made at Hemyock, which on first viewing looked very similar to Donyatt ware, could be distinguished from it in hand specimen. With this aim, three of the writers (JA, DD, GL) re-examined the pottery from Donyatt site 3 held at the Somerset Heritage Centre, Taunton, alongside a substantial sample of Hemyock pottery. We noted the following differences:

1. The fabric of Hemyock pottery is smoother, with fewer incidental inclusions, and is less open-textured. Thus vessel walls tend to be thrown slightly thinner (around 4 mm for jug necks, for example, compared with *c.* 6 mm at Donyatt) and the general standard of potting is higher. Fine white mica inclusions are very rarely seen at Donyatt and are more plentiful at Hemyock. The higher quality of the fabric may explain the pronounced concentration of Hemyock on tablewares, especially jugs.
2. The glazes of Hemyock pottery share a characteristic with other West Somerset wares in that the abundant quartz in the body imparts a golden speckling in their normally reduced dark olive green colour. In contrast the glazes of Donyatt site 3 tend to be dark honey coloured to dark brownish-green and are flecked with

Table 24. Proportions of principal products in the kiln waste at Hemyock and Donyatt Group 3, excluding unidentified bodysherds (figures for Donyatt approximate, from Coleman-Smith and Pearson 1988, 98, Group 3)

Vessel type	**Donyatt: estimated no. vessels**	**Donyatt: no. of identified sherds**	**Hemyock: EVEs**
Jugs	23%	27%	63%
Jars/cooking pots	15%	20%	23%
Bowls	27%	22%	10%
Cisterns	11%	14%	?
Cups	8%	8%	2%
Pipkins	2.3%	0.4%	
Ridge tiles	10%	4%	[6%]
Floor- and oven-tiles	3%	1%	[6%]
Others	1%	2%	
Sample size	**785**	**3287**	

dark brown/black from abundant iron particles in the body.
3. Simple upright rims, thickened at the top, are typical of Donyatt jugs of this period. They contrast with jug rims at Hemyock, whose most common form rises from a waisted neck, splays out sharply, and rises almost vertically to a flat top (Figure 74, Nos 13–16, etc). Both potteries, however, produced jugs with applied thumbed strips reinforcing the rim. Jug handles in both places are a mix of flat examples with knife-slashing at top and bottom, and twisted ones were used at both centres.
4. Although the Hemyock potters occasionally used applied iron-rich clay strips e.g. in decorating costrels, all the jugs recovered there so far display surprisingly uniform decoration: a band of slip brushed onto the neck, through which broad lines or combing have been drawn when the slip was wet. By contrast, the Donyatt potters' most typical forms of decoration are the thin looped wavy line drawn through the slip band, and the use of knife-slashing, applied strips and stamps – sometimes using iron-rich clays (Coleman-Smith and Pearson 1988, 132–45).
5. There are no parallels at Hemyock to the wheel-thrown jars/cooking pots of Donyatt group 3 (Coleman-Smith and Pearson 1988, 80, Nos 108, 110, 111, etc).
6. The Hemyock pancheons are a standardised product with a hammer-headed rim (Figure 75, Nos 21–6). Although this form is recorded at Donyatt (*ibid.*, 232, 12/4–12/5), pancheons with applied thumbed reinforcing strips on the rim are far more common there (*ibid.*, 232–5, Nos 12/8–26).

These differences should often allow fieldworkers to distinguish between products from the two centres. Nevertheless, when sorting by hand, we concluded that it would be difficult to attribute body sherds specifically to one or other of the two centres.

Marketing Patterns

Pottery in the South Somerset tradition is by far the most common local ware on sites in South and Central Somerset and in much of South-East Devon. In the past this was sometimes attributed specifically to Donyatt; for example, Pearson concluded that fully 90% of the pottery used at Taunton in the sixteenth century was made there (Pearson 1984, MF and pers. comm. to the writers). In the 1990s Hughes undertook ICP analysis of 13 vessels from Cleeve Abbey which had been attributed on visual grounds to the Donyatt kilns. Four proved to match the Donyatt kiln samples but the other nine did not; they showed much closer matches to kiln waste from West Somerset (Hughes 1998). In a second exercise Hughes sampled six jugs from Glastonbury Abbey; all showed good matches to Donyatt (*idem* 2015). In order to extend this work, and as discussed in full above, here we have chosen samples from three major markets for sampling by ICPS: Exeter, Taunton and five from Bridgwater (six vessels each the first two, five from the last). When combined with the results of previous analyses from Cleeve Abbey and Glastonbury Abbey, this gives 30 specimens. Samples of floor-tiles from Cadeleigh and Woodbury which appeared to be from the same stamps as those represented in the Hemyock kiln waste were also examined.

Broadly, Donyatt emerges as a significantly more important supplier than Hemyock in the regional pottery market. The analyses confirmed that Donyatt was the dominant pottery at Taunton in the sixteenth century; it was the sole source of the range of vessels of that date sampled in this project. The conclusion is of considerable interest because Hemyock, Clayhydon and Wrangway are only between 13 km and 17 km from the town – slightly closer than Donyatt (20 km). Judging by the sample examined in this project, the South Somerset pottery found at Exeter, some 53 km away, also appears to come largely from Donyatt (although the analyses raise the possibility of a slightly wider range of suppliers there, and there is still a need to resolve the origins of Coarse Sandy Ware found at Exeter, not analysed here). At Glastonbury, Donyatt was the predominant source of jugs, but the pans came from East Somerset (Wanstrow). Hemyock seems to have marketed its wares westwards; its products are present at Cleeve Abbey and possibly also at Bridgwater, although our work has shown the need for further work in distinguishing Hemyock wares from the products of Nether Stowey. This exercise has shown the need for much further work to build up a fuller picture; in view of the evidence for specialist supply of specific vessel forms to some markets, the analyses illustrate the need to sample a wide range of pottery forms on each consumer site in order to understand the marketing pattern there.

Chapter 6

The Environment

Introduction

Environmental sampling from pits, ditches, hearths and furnaces was undertaken during the fieldwork stage. Samples were processed by Exeter Archaeology, with material washed through 1mm fabric mesh and 500 μ and 300 μ sieves. The sample residues and floats were oven-dried. Bulk samples were taken from 34 contexts which were initially scanned and assessed for their potential for further analysis of charred plant remains and wood charcoal, prior to developing a strategy for detailed analysis – the results of which are presented below.

Charred Plant Remains

Julie Jones

Methodology

Following assessment of the entire collection seven samples were highlighted for detailed analysis; four from iron furnaces and three from infilled clay extraction pits associated with the pottery kilns. These produced the greatest concentrations of oat grains (50+) plus other cereal remains with the addition of cereal/grass stems, arable weeds and evidence of heathland and woodland plants. These were examined under illuminated low-powered magnification with a stereo-binocular microscope with magnifications between x10 and x45. The charred cereals were identified with reference to Jacomet (2006), with seeds and fruits using Cappers *et al.* (2006) and Bertsch (1941), plus the aid of modern reference material. The results are recorded in Table 25. Nomenclature and habitat information follows Stace (1991). All remains were preserved by charring. Preservation of much of the cereal grain was variable, with some complete grains, but others showing degrees of fragmentation, some grains also showing pitting characteristic of exposure to high temperatures (Boardman and Jones 1990). Other grains showed a fine coating of sediment and occasional adhesion of orange-coloured possible metalworking debris (which is an observation also made in relation to the wood charcoal, see Challinor, below). Many of the smaller chaff items, such as awns and tiny floret fragments from oats, gorse spines and heather leaf fragments, as well as smaller weed seeds, were very well preserved.

The Charred Plant Remains

Oats (Avena)

Oats were the primary grain found at Hemyock, occurring in both furnace and pit contexts. Much of the grain was poorly preserved with many incomplete and showing degrees of fragmentation and/or distortion from the charring process, with much surface erosion.

In contrast to wheat and barley, oat has its spikelets in panicles with three grains in each spikelet enclosed in a floret. Oat grains are slender with the widest point in the middle. In general terms, in cultivated oats (*Avena sativa*) the first grains are large, with the second grains smaller, whilst wild oat (*Avena fatua*) is similar, if possibly more slender (Jacomet 2006). Measurements of complete grains were made from two of the furnace fills, with most kernels varying in length between 4 and 5 mm, with a maximum of 6.2 mm and minimum of 3.7 mm, although with a fairly consistent width of 1.4-2 mm, this smaller size perhaps more indicative of wild oat.

The diagnostic features necessary to determine between species are that the floret base of wild oat has a horseshoe-shaped 'sucker mouth' scar where the base has disarticulated from the rachis, whilst that of cultivated oat has a rounder, more irregular break (Moffett 1988). However, although examples were preserved in several contexts, some with florets still enclosing the grain, none preserved these necessary characteristics. If these were wild oats then, as it is an aggressive weed often found amongst other arable weed flora, it is always possible that they occurred as crop contaminants.

Wheat (Triticum), Rye (Secale cereale) and Barley (Hordeum)

Evidence from other cereals was fairly limited, with only occasional grain and chaff. Free-threshing wheat grains were the second most common, although there was no chaff. Barley was indicated by tiny fragments of rachis internode base found in all four furnace contexts, but with no grain present. There were also occasional rye grain and rachis internode fragments in three furnace contexts.

In addition, stem fragments occurred in one pit fill and all furnace contexts, but notably furnace 794 where 63 fragments were counted from fill 795. These were all Poaceae (Grass family) stems, cylindrical, hollow and

Table 25. Charred plant remains

		Area D furnaces				Area A pits			Habitat
	Feature	756	794	799	805	572	572	627	
	Context	757	795	800	806	580	581	638	
	Sample	312	322	322	329	302	303	305	
	Flot size (ml)	41	370	240	300	100	135	365	
Charred cereals									
Avena sp. (grain)	Oat	86	66	16	21	33	46	7	#
Avena sp. (frags)	Oat						36		#
c.f. *Avena* sp. (grain)	Oat					19			#
Avena sp. (grain with partial floret)	Oat	4	4						#
Avena sp. (floret frags)	Oat	10	3			1			#
Avena sp. (awns)	Oat	55	9			8	2		#
Hordeum sp. (rachis internode base)	Barley	2	4	2	2				#
Secale cereale (grain)	Rye			3	2				#
Secale cereale (rachis internode)	Rye		2	1					#
Triticum sp. (grain)	Free-threshing wheat		7	3			2		#
Cereal indet. (grain)	Cereal				2				#
Cereal indet. (stem and culm nodes)	Cereal	19	63	9	1	7			#
Charred weeds									
DENNSTAEDTIACEAE									
Pteridium aquilinum (L.)Kuhn (pinnules)	Bracken	1		1					WEad
RANUNCULACEAE									
Ranunculus acris/repens/bulbosus	Meadow/Creeping/ Bulbous Buttercup	1	3	2					DG
Ranunculus flammula L.	Lesser Spearwort		1						MPRw
FAGACEAE									
Quercus sp (bud)	Oak				1	4	1	11	HSW
BETULACEAE									
Alnus glutinosa (L.)Gaertner (bud)	Alder					1			RWw
Corylus avellana L. (nut frags)	Hazel		5		3	8	1		HSW
CHENOPODIACEAE									
Atriplex spp	Orache		3			5	1		CDn
Chenopodium album L.	Fat-hen		1						CDn
CARYOPHYLLACEAE									
Spergula arvensis L.	Corn Spurrey					1			sandy C
POLYGONACEAE									
Fallopia convolvulus (L.)A.Love	Black-bindweed		3			1			CD
Polygonum aviculare L.	Knotgrass		1						CD
Rumex acetosella L.	Sheep's Sorrel					1			Ho, CG, a
Rumex spp.	Dock		7	34	20	3			DG
BRASSICACEAE									
Raphanus raphanistrum ssp *raphanistrum* (capsule)	Wild Radish		1						CD
ERICACEAE									
Erica cinerea L. (leaf frag)	Bell Heather	1				2			Ed

		Area D furnaces				Area A pits			Habitat
ROSACEAE									
Rosaceae indet. (thorn)		2						1	HSW
Rubus sect. *Glandulosus* Wimmer and Grab	Bramble		4						DHSW
FABACEAE									
Lathyrus/Vicia spp.	Pea/Vetch				2	2	22		DG
Trifolium.Medicago spp.	Clover/Medick					1			DG
Ulex sp. (spine)	Gorse					10		18	EGWo
Ulex sp. (stem frags)	Gorse							9	EGWo
LAMIACEAE									
Prunella vulgaris L.	Selfheal		1						DG
PLANTAGINACEAE									
Plantago lanceolata L.	Ribwort Plantain		4	4		2			G
RUBIACEAE									
Galium aparine L.	Cleavers		70				1		CHSo
ASTERACEAE									
Anthemis cotula L.	Stinking Chamomile	1		4	1	7	10		CDh
Chrysanthemum segetum L.	Corn marigold					8	4		Ca
Tripleurospermum inodorum (L.) Schultz-Bip	Scentless mayweed					1			CD
CYPERACEAE									
Carex spp.	Sedge	3	5	4	1				GMPRW
POACEAE									
Bromus sp.	Brome					1	1		CD
Cynosurus cristatus L.	Crested Dog's -tail		1						G
Danthonia decumbens (L.)DC	Heath-grass	2	1			1	1	2	Ew sandy/peaty
Poaceae indet.	Grass					1	2		
Poaceae indet (stem frags)	Grass	5							
Moss (stem frags)		4							

Habitats
C: Cultivated/Arable. D: Disturbed. E: Heath/Moor. G: Grassland. H: Hedgerow. M: Marsh. P: Ponds, ditches – stagnant/slow flowing water. R: Rivers, streams. S: Scrub. W: Woodland.
a: acidic. d: dry soils. h: heavy soils. n: nitrogen rich soils. o: open habitats. w: wet/damp soils…
cultivated plant/of economic importance.

with a ridged surface, most showing the culm node – the area of thickening on the stem from which the leaf arises. Measurements from the collection from furnace 794 suggested two groups. The first showed stem width at the culm node between 2-3 mm and lengths varying from 2.5-6 mm, with the second slighter group <2 mm at the culm area and lengths <3 mm. This that indicate both cereal and wild grass stems occurred.

Arable Weeds

A small suite of arable weeds commonly found with cereal remains occurred in both pit and furnace contexts. These include black bindweed (*Fallopia convolvulus*) and cleavers (*Galium aparine*), both of which have a twining nature, that may have used the cereal stems as support, indicating that the straw was gathered with the crop, which may have been cut near the base or uprooted (although no roots were found) rather than by harvesting of individual ears by plucking. Black bindweed and scentless mayweed (*Tripleurospermum inodorum*) are weeds of both spring and autumn crops, while wild radish (*Raphanus raphanistrum* ssp *raphanistrum*) is typically associated with crops such as wheat that germinate in the autumn (Grime *et al.* 1988). Scentless mayweed prefers non-calcareous, free-draining soils which is consistent with the local geology.

Grassland Taxa

There is also a small suite of grassland taxa including ribwort plantain (*Plantago lanceolata*), selfheal (*Prunella vulgaris*), grasses (Poaceae) and docks (*Rumex*), the latter is also a persistent weed in cleared ground. Rodwell (1998, 32) cites a community of coarse-leaved tussock grasses with other grasses that includes *Plantago*, *Prunella* and several *Rumex* species in a habitat of ungrazed grassland or neglected agricultural land, so their presence at Churchills Farm may result from the ploughing of grassland followed by cultivation.

Heathland Taxa

The assemblage also includes heathland taxa, with gorse (*Ulex*) spines and stem fragments in fills of pits 572 and 627, with the latter containing the greatest amounts of *Ulex/Cytisus* charcoal roundwood (see Challinor, below and Table 27). In addition to the gorse spines the plant remains from pit 572 also included two bell heather (*Erica cinerea*) leaf fragments. A single example of the latter was also found within bulk flotation sample from furnace 756. There were also bracken (*Pteridium aquilinum*) pinnule fragments in two furnace contexts, with heath-grass (*Danthonia decumbens*) caryopses in all pit and two furnace contexts. The occasional moss stem fragments in furnace 756 could also have originated from heathland or woodland habitats.

Detailed Results

Furnaces

Following broad assessment the charred plant remains from four furnaces, 756, 794, 799 and 805, were analysed in detail. The first three of these are slag-pit types, with the last being a 'possible' furnace. These contained broadly similar assemblages, although furnace 794, with a larger sample float, included a more varied weed assemblage. Remains of oat were dominant in furnace 794, largely grain, including a few examples still retained in their floret, with other floret fragments and oat awns. Evidence for other cereals comes from barley rachis internodes, but no grain, occasional examples of rye grain and rachis internode, plus a few free-threshing wheat grains. In addition are the preserved remains of cereal stems, many with culm nodes. It is not possible to determine which cereal these relate to but it does suggest, together with the other chaff remains that whole unprocessed cereal ears were charred. Many of the weed seeds recovered are also those found growing amongst crops, including cleavers (particularly dominant in furnace 794) and black bindweed (which entangle themselves up cereal stems so would have been harvested with the crop). There is also evidence of woody taxa including oak (*Quercus*) bud, hazelnut (*Corylus avellana*) fragments and bramble (*Rubus* subg. *Glandulosus*) fruits, with oak and hazel charcoal in all contexts, all likely to reflect wood collected for the furnace.

Plant remains from the other eight furnaces (slag-pit: 776, 787; slag-tapping: 758, 771, 789, 792; and possible: 778) were all assessed in the initial stages of the project but produced very small assemblages and were not fully analysed. The collections from these were of similar composition to those analysed in full, with oat and wheat grain, cereal stem fragments and evidence of hazel and oak.

Pits and Ditches

Sampling of several medieval and early post-medieval pits and ditches yielded charred plant remains of sufficient quality and interest to warrant analysis.

The middle fill (580) of pit [572] contained abundant chert, iron slag and Upper Greensand-Derived pottery and appeared to derive from deliberate backfilling of the claypit. The pottery has broad currency *c.* AD 950-1200, but dating from pit 556 suggests that some forms were in use in Hemyock *c.* AD 900-930, suggesting that the charred cereals might be indicative of local vegetation as early as the tenth century. Charred cereal inclusions were largely oat grains, mostly in very poor condition, with occasional floret base and awns, two free-threshing wheat grains, plus a small suite of arable weeds including black-bindweed, stinking chamomile (*Anthemis cotula*), corn marigold (*Chrysanthemum segetum*) and corn spurrey (*Spergula arvensis*). Oak and alder (*Alnus glutinosa*) buds, hazelnut fragments and gorse spines are all reflected in the charcoal record. *Erica* leaf fragments also suggest the inclusion of heathland taxa as fuel. The upper fill (581) of this pit yielded thirteenth/fourteenth-century pottery, which may suggest gradual in-wash of a surviving depression at a later date. The charred plant remains are, however, broadly similar to the lower fill with oat grain and hulled and free-threshing wheat grains. Although the weed assemblage is less extensive, several of the same taxa occur.

Of the later clay extraction pits, dated to *c.* AD 1500-50 based on the quantities of Hemyock pottery within, only one of these pits [627] included charred plant remains, which included occasional oat grain, gorse stem fragments and spines, oak buds and a Rosaceae thorn.

Discussion

Sampling of the furnaces for environmental remains has provided clear evidence for the use of cereals, particularly oats, but also wheat, barley and rye in the iron-making process. The presence of cereal and/or grass stems, cereal chaff and common arable weed seeds indicates that whole ears of unprocessed cereal crops in addition to woodland and heathland taxa were used in these furnaces.

As was described by Tim Young in Chapter 4, the operation of a slag-pit furnace relied on a basal pit or chamber packed with a combustible material at the start of a smelt. This packing would have provided initial support to the overlying charge of ore, but once this basal area starts to heat up, the pit packing combusts, or partially combusts, to create space for the descending slag. We have seen that in early medieval Britain wood packing appears to be the primary material used, and in that sense the furnaces from Churchills farm are unusual. Henriksen (2003) describes evidence for the use of rye and barley in iron-smelting furnaces from southern Jutland in the Danish Iron Age (*c.* AD 400) and we might turn to these for comparative archaeobotanical evidence. The archaeobotanical samples from a number of sites yielded compacted cereal straw with ears attached which, as it was feared that flotation would cause fragmentation of root and stem, were examined unprocessed. Samples from Hvidhøjgård were almost exclusively rye straw with whole ears and roots intact indicating that these plants had been uprooted. Indeed some roots still had soil attached which was taken to show these cereals were brought direct from the fields rather than being stored. This observation has implications for the time of year during which smelting took place; at Hvidhøjgård it was suggested that it occurred in August when the rye was ready to harvest. The weed seeds, which vary in the two samples examined at Hvidhøjgård, were also taken to indicate that the rye was cultivated as a winter cereal. Further agricultural information was gleaned – the well-preserved roots were also used to calculate crop yield and point to a shallow depth of sowing resulting from broadcasting of the seed followed by light harrowing.

Mikkelsen, whose doctoral research analysed first to eighth-century smelting sites in Denmark (Mikkelsen 1998), has also undertaken experiments on how cereal packing is affected during the smelting cycle (Mikkelsen 1997). To begin, however, he calculated that the size of furnace witnessed archaeologically would require two square metres of rye to be harvested as packing material. It was shown that for the first eight to nine hours temperatures within the pit rose gradually, allowing slow drying of the grains. This resulted in low water content in the grains when actual charring took place, meaning the degree of 'popping', so typical of grains recovered from domestic hearths was reduced. Temperatures reached 185°C after nine hours, reaching a maximum of 313°C after 15¾ hours. Mikkelsen's experiment was not a complete success – in some parts of the furnace the straw remained un-charred – but it does show the potential, with the gradual rise in temperature, for cereal grains and stem fragments as well as those more fragile items such as fine chaff and weed seeds to slip to the bottom of the slag pit and escape complete destruction.

The volume of material and preservation of charred cereal remains from Churchills Farm were far less than in many of the Danish sites analysed by either Henriksen or Mikkelsen (see table 1 of Henriksen 2003 for quantification of the flots from six furnaces at Hvidhøjgård and Lerdal, for example), but despite this it is interesting to speculate that a similar process occurred here in Devon as part of iron production during the late ninth/early tenth centuries. The presence of gorse charcoal in some assemblages (see Challinor, below) is also thought likely to derive from packing in contrast to other charcoal more likely to have been from wood used as fuel.

The charred remains from the furnaces indicate that these are crop residues that include free threshing wheat, barley and rye, but are mostly oat. These may have come from a maslin crop – a practise of sowing different cereals together. It has been suggested that wheat and rye were a common maslin in Western Europe during the medieval period, although other mixes were known including barley and oat (Slicher van Bath 1963). They were a means of 'hedging one's bets' (Halstead and Jones 1989), a way of reducing the risk of crop failure, with for example rye being more frost resistant than bread wheat. However, the presence of scrub and heathland taxa indicates a range of sources for the material in the furnace and apart from the oats the cereal remains could simply be accumulated processing waste, simply used as tinder.

The identification of charred cereal stems suggests the whole ear was collected, with lack of evidence for roots and presence of twining taxa like cleavers and black-bindweed, perhaps indicating cereal stems were cut low at harvest, with all components used. The choice of cereals used to pack the charge of ore is unlikely to have been important and is a reflection of available crops from local farms. Evidence for the use of heathland plants like bracken, bell heather and moss (and gorse in the charcoal record) would have provided additional, relatively combustible packing material.

Mikkelsen (1997) suggested that unlike charred assemblages from features such as pits, ditches and floor layers normally investigated on archaeological excavations, which might be heavily mixed, that cereal remains in slag-pit furnaces are more representative of a single point in time. Employing data from well-preserved assemblages he suggested that the furnace assemblages provide a snapshot of one process, in a single season, with the cereals originating from one field, and can give a detailed representation of crop husbandry local to the site in question. The well-dated furnaces at Churchills Farm allow us to do the same; telling us what crops were grown, and what weeds, grasses and shrubby plants, grew locally in the late ninth and early tenth centuries.

In contrast the accumulation of material within the medieval and early post-medieval pits at Hemyock might have come from multiple primary sources and relate to different activities. Like the furnace collections, the charred cereal assemblages from these contexts are again dominated by oats, with rare free-threshing wheat grain, but we have little idea of provenance, or whether they are significantly older that the date of infilling.

An interesting assemblage of oats was recovered from a medieval tin 'blowing house' (for smelting tin) at Brownie Cross, close to Plympton, on the edge of Dartmoor. The date for the production of tin here, where structures from a tin smelter and tinners' shelter have been dated to 1190-1392 cal AD, is later than that of iron production at Churchills Farm, but it is useful to look at the suggested function in this context. Oak charcoal was abundant and appears to have been the dominant source of fuel for the blowing house; most plant remains were recovered from a large hollow (feature 1376) associated with a tinners' shelter (Challinor 2011). The hollow [1376], from which the grains and a large ceramic assemblage were recovered is likely to have been a rubbish pit associated with activities around the furnace, that is the preparation (warming if not cooking) of food and drink and its consumption. There were an estimated 9000+ oat grains from the entire hollow fill, plus awns and lemma bases together with more limited evidence of barley and a large arable weed assemblage, but no cereal stem fragments. It is likely to have been an unprocessed or partially processed crop, with such a substantial quantity of oats suggesting that these were deposited in a single event. It may be that the oats were destined for human consumption, especially as the ceramic assemblage from the hollow fill largely contained vessels associated with food and drink storage and consumption. Many showed signs of sooting likely to have resulted from contact with fire, implying the import of pre-prepared meals that were then re-heated within the tinners' shelter during mealtimes. Alternatively, the oats may have been fodder for horses, which may have been stabled close to the smelting site to assist with transportation of materials associated with tin smelting. Like processing for food consumption this would have required kiln drying to avoid spoilage for bulk storage, but either may have resulted in accidental charring of the crop. However, in view of the evidence from Hemyock it may be possible to speculate that the oats at Brownie Cross might have been utilised directly in the industrial process.

The cereal crop remains at Churchills Farm, in addition to gorse, may have provided combustible material for the late medieval pottery industry. The spines and stem fragments of gorse were only present in these later features associated with pottery wasters and, whilst it is reasonable to suggest that it was in some way used in this industry, it could also be of domestic origin; gorse was commonly favoured in bread ovens in the past due to the intense heat it provides (Grieve 1971).

Wood Charcoal

Dana Challinor

Introduction

Collections of wood charcoal were selected for detailed analysis following an initial assessment of all 31 bulk samples collected during the excavation. Analysis sought to be representative of the early medieval, Saxo-Norman and late medieval/early post-medieval phases of site activity, as well as the various uses to which the site had been put (iron production, pottery industry, agricultural). The selected samples also offered an important opportunity to examine and compare fuel use in different iron production technologies.

Methodology

Charcoal which was over 2 mm in transverse section was considered for identification and a sub-sample of 20-100 fragments (depending upon diversity and condition) was identified. The fragments were randomly selected, but where, after 30 fragments, diversity was very limited, the remaining material was scanned at low magnification for the presence of additional taxa. The charcoal was fractured and sorted into groups based on the anatomical features observed in transverse section at X7 to X45 magnifications. Representative fragments from each group were then selected for further examination using a Meiji incident-light microscope at up to X400 magnification. A total of 995 fragments were examined from 18 contexts. Identifications were made with reference to Schweingruber (1990), Hather (2000) and modern reference material. Classification and nomenclature follow Stace (1997).

Results

The samples selected for analysis had all produced abundant quantities of charcoal, but the preservation was variable, both in the degree of fragmentation and the condition. Much of the material exhibited strong orange-coloured inclusions, which inhibited the visibility of anatomical features. Iron staining is commonly produced in charcoal as a result of deposition in wet soils, which would be consistent with the 'seasonally waterlogged' soils of the site (see Chapter 1). As an alternative explanation, however, iron oxide resulting from the smelting process could also have led to the ferric deposits visible in the Hemyock fragments (Figure 125).

Eleven taxa were positively identified, with several to species level. In some cases, this was ascertained through anatomical characteristics, but in many it has been assumed that the native species is represented. No exotic taxa were positively identified in the assemblage and the following list provides some information on the likely genera/species.

Fagaceae:

Quercus spp., oak, large tree, two native species, not distinguishable anatomically.

Betulaceae:

Betula spp., birch, trees/shrubs, two native species, not distinguishable anatomically.

Alnus glutinosa, Gaertn., alder, tree, sole native species.

Corylus avellana L., hazel, shrub or small tree, only native species.

Figure 125. Fragment of oak from sample 309 showing orange deposits in vessels.

Salicaceae:

Populus spp. (poplar) and *Salix* spp. (willow), trees, are rarely possible to separate and not in the poor material from Hemyock.

Rosaceae:

Prunus spp., trees or shrubs, including *P. spinosa* L. (blackthorn), *P. avium* L. (wild cherry) and *P. padus* L. (bird cherry), all native, which can sometimes be separated on the basis of ray width. The material at Hemyock was not positively differentiated.

Maloideae, subfamily of various shrubs/small trees including several genera, *Pyrus* (pear), *Malus* (apple), *Sorbus* (rowan/service/whitebeam) and *Crataegus* (hawthorn), which are rarely distinguishable by anatomical characteristics.

Fabaceae:

Cytisus/Ulex, broom/gorse, shrubs, several native species, not distinguishable anatomically. The presence of *Ulex* spines in some of the samples (Jones, this report), suggests that this is the more likely taxon.

Aquifoliaceae:

Ilex aquifolium L., holly, evergreen tree or shrub, native.

Aceraceae:

Acer campestre L. field maple, tree, sole native species. The small ray width observed in the charcoal from Hemyock confirms that the native species (rather than the introduced *A. pseudoplatanus)* was present.

Oleaceae:

Fraxinus excelsior L. ash, tree, sole native species.

The friability and poor condition of the charcoal inhibited the accuracy of any growth ring analysis, but some general observations were made. Fragments with moderate or strong ring curvature were regularly observed in the Hemyock charcoal, with some whole stems including pith and bark (or cambial layer). Stem ages ranged between 5 and 15 years, with some younger, 3 year old twigs of *Cytisus/Ulex*. Few fragments were more than 10 mm in size, with the majority falling into the 8-4 mm sieve, or <4 mm. Growth rates were variable, but a commonly-observed pattern in stems was the presence of wide, early rings close to the pith; which is consistent with fast growth on coppicing. The occurrence of more mature trunk wood was evidenced by the presence of tyloses in oak, indicating heartwood.

Some degree of vitrification and radial cracking was frequently recorded. These are thought to be pre-depositional characteristics relating to the nature of the wood prior to charring (Marguerie and Hunot 2007, 1421), but their presence may vary according to the taxon (*Ulex* is prone to radial cracking, for instance) and it is currently unclear whether/how these features may be altered by the re-charring of charcoal fuel. Of greater interest is the presence of insect tunnels in some *Alnus* and *Corylus* fragments in samples 318, 327 and 329. Wood-boring beetles, which produce these tunnels, usually inhabit dead or dying wood, suggesting that the wood may have been intentionally seasoned prior to charring, or that fallen timber was collected and used.

Fuelling the Furnaces

Charcoal from nine iron-smelting furnaces was examined (slag-pit: 787, 794, 799; slag-tapping: 758, 771, 789, 792; possible: 778, 805) as well as material from associated pit 805. The assemblages produced quite a wide range of taxa (Table 26), with an average of six species per feature. There was some variation in the taxonomic composition of the individual assemblages (Figure 126), but it is clear that three particular taxa dominate all of the furnaces, representing more than 80% of the whole: *Quercus* (oak), *Corylus* (hazel) and *Alnus* (alder). It should be noted that for the purposes of the graph, 73 undifferentiated fragments of *Alnus/Corylus* were excluded which, if included, would have decreased the proportion of oak from 56% to 49%. The charcoal assemblage from slag-tapping furnace 771 was dominated by oak (83%), but its overall composition was similar to those from slag-pit furnace 789 and pit 805, so there does not appear to be any significant differences between the fuels used in each technology.

It is generally assumed that charcoal fuel would have been necessary to achieve the high temperatures and sufficiently reducing atmosphere required for iron smelting (Cleere and Crossley 1985; Goffer 2007, 174; Paynter 2011,

Table 26. Charcoal from early medieval iron smelting furnaces in Area D

Feature number		787	794		799	758	771	789	792	778	805	801
Context number		788	796	795	800	760	772	790	793	781	806	803
Sample number		320	321	322	323	314	327	324	319	318	329	328
Quercus sp.	oak	24 (r)	26 (rh)	7	32 (hsr)	37 (rh)	30 (rh)	28 (r)	27 (rh)	35 (r)	36 (sr)	12 (rs)
Betula sp.	birch	1				3 (r)					1	
Alnus glutinosa Gaertn.	alder	2	4r	7r	5 (r)	17 (r)				16r	2	7r
Corylus avellana L.	hazel	13r	5r	23r	3	1r	1	1	8 (r)	15r	1	19 (r)
Alnus/Corylus	alder/hazel	4	6	9r	4	16 (r)	7	3	9	11 (r)		4
Populus/Salix	poplar/willow	4r					(1)					
Prunus sp.	cherry type									1r		
Maloideae	hawthorn group	1r	3 (r)		1	10 (r)			3r	2r		2 (r)
Cytisus/Ulex	broom/gorse	1r	2r	2r		6r	1r			8r	2	
Ilex aquifolium L.	holly								1			
Acer campestre L.	field maple				3	1r	4			5	8	
Fraxinus excelsior L.	ash		1					1		1r		3 (r)
Indeterminate	diffuse porous						1	1				
Indeterminate			3 (b)	2b	2	9 (b)	5 (b)	1	2 (b)	6 (b)		3b
Total		**50**	**50**	**50**	**50**	**100**	**50**	**35**	**50**	**100**	**50**	**50**

r = roundwood; h = heartwood; s = sapwood; (brackets) denotes presence in some fragments only.

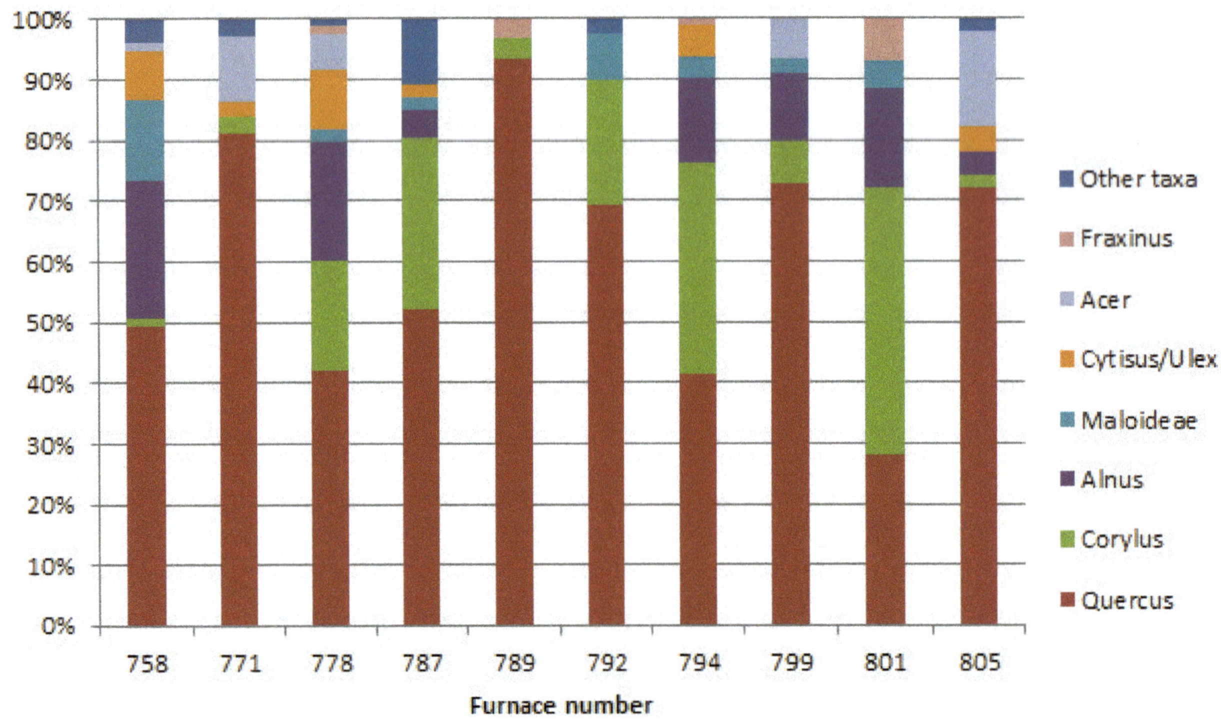

Figure 126. Taxonomic composition of the furnaces based upon fragment count (N=527, excluding indeterminate and undifferentiated Alnus/Corylus). 'Other taxa' includes species representing <1% of the whole assemblage.

2), although experimental evidence in slag-pit furnaces suggests that wood fuel performs the same function, albeit at a slower rate (Norbach 1997). As we are unable to determine from the archaeological charcoal whether it derived from wood or charcoal fuel, it is impossible to differentiate reliably. Whilst it is typical for the charge of ore in a slag-pit furnace to be packed with wood (Paynter 2011, 4), the charred plant remains suggests that cereals were used at Hemyock for this purpose (Jones, above) and so we can conclude that the wood charcoal derived from fuel. However, the presence of gorse charcoal in the assemblages is better accounted for by its use as packing (in combination with the cereals) than its use as charcoal fuel in the main furnace shaft.

Traditionally, charcoal was made from roundwood of 60 mm to 250mm in diameter, sawn into lengths of about a metre, which were then seasoned, prior to burning in a domed stack covered over with turf (Bond 2007, 280-290). The wood was usually sourced from coppiced stems, or perhaps the off-cuts from trees managed for timber (*ibid.*). Much of the charcoal from the furnaces at Hemyock, although fragmented, exhibited the fast growth and/or wide early rings consistent with growth ring patterns produced by coppicing. Coppicing cycles varied according to region and requirement but stands or underwood harvested for charcoal production were usually allowed *c.* 12 years growth (Rackham 2006, 205). Some of the Hemyock charcoal would fit with that model, although the frequent presence of oak heartwood indicates some more mature wood was also utilised (usually more than 20 years in age, though occasionally as young as 12 years; Gale 2006,114). Interestingly, this accords with the range of charcoal from the late eighth tolate tenth-century smelting furnaces at Burlescombe, Devon, which included both oak heartwood and narrow roundwood, along with a range of additional taxa (Gale 2006, 116).

Other Features

All of the other features from which charcoal was examined were initially presumed to be later in date than the furnaces, either as they contained Upper Greensand-Derived (*c.* 900-1200) or later 'Hemyock' pottery (*c.* 1500-1550). However, radiocarbon dating of charcoal from pit 556 suggests that some of the Upper Greensand-Derived pottery was produced and used *c.* 900-930 and thus was broadly contemporary with iron production. It must be reiterated, though, that this ceramic type found in other contexts may be as late as twelfth century in date. Some features, such as pit 572 which contained Upper Greensand-Derived sherds, also yielded slag. Consequently, some of the charcoal from such features may have derived from contemporary smelting, and it is noteworthy that the assemblages were not dissimilar, with the same range of taxa as the earlier samples (Table 27). Certainly, much of the charcoal came from narrow roundwood, and exhibited features consistent with coppicing.

Charcoal (or at least some of it) from the later clay extraction pits, dated to *c.* 1500-1550, which also contained large volumes of pottery wasters, probably originated from the pottery industry. Kilns would have used wood, rather than charcoal for fuel. It was suggested that the fuel for the Donyatt potteries was provided from trees growing in hedges, rather than local woodland (Rackham 1988), but there is little evidence to be conclusive either way at Churchills Farm, Hemyock. Figure 127 shows that there

Table 27. Charcoal from medieval and post-medieval features in Areas A and D: pits, ditches and clay extraction pits

Area		A						D
Feature type		pit		ditch	quarry pit			ditch
Feature number		572		680	715	589	627	872
Context number		580	581	681	616	588	638	873
Sample number		302	303	309	310	304	305	333
Quercus sp.	oak	35r	17 (r)	9 (r)	29 (rh)	18 (rh)	33 (r)	5 (r)
Betula sp.	birch			3r	1			1r
Alnus glutinosa Gaertn.	alder	4r		13 (r)	6 (r)	14 (r)	17 (r)	2
Corylus avellana L.	hazel	8r		4r	1	2 (r)	8r	1
Alnus/Corylus	alder/hazel	5r	2	7	5	3	10 (r)	11 (r)
Populus/Salix	poplar/willow			1		2r		3r
Prunus sp.	cherry type	4r						
Maloideae	hawthorn group			1		3r	3 (r)	
Cytisus/Ulex	broom/gorse		1r		4r	6r	16r	
Ilex aquifolium L.	holly				1			
Acer campestre L.	field maple							1
Fraxinus excelsior L.	ash			10 (r)			9r	
Indeterminate	diffuse porous	4			3 (r)			3
Indeterminate				2b		2b	4 (b)	3 (b)
Total		**60**	**20**	**50**	**50**	**50**	**100**	**30**

r = roundwood; h = heartwood; s = sapwood; (brackets) denotes presence in some fragments only.

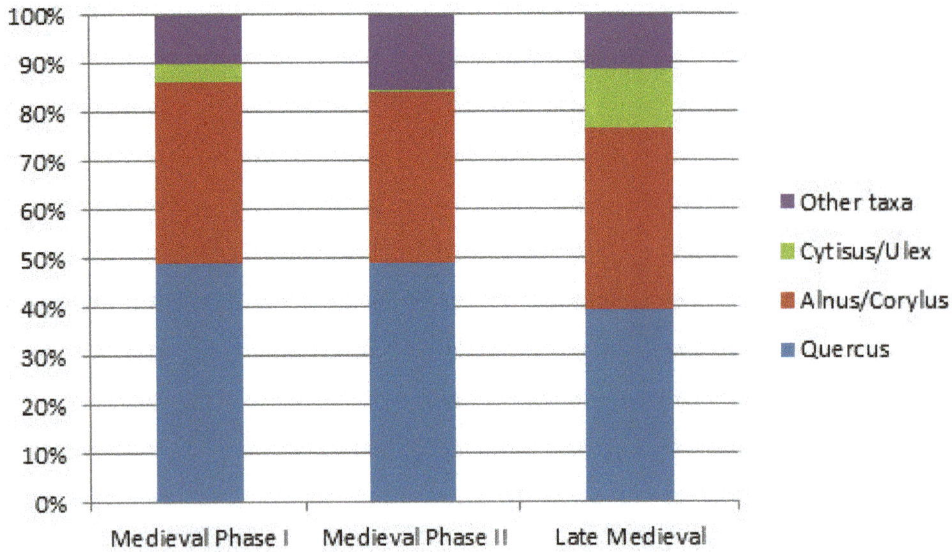

Figure 127. Taxonomic composition of charcoal by phase, based upon fragment count (N=939).

is remarkable consistency in the charcoal assemblages from the radiocarbon-dated ninth/tenth-century furnaces (Figure 127 Medieval Phase I) and the pits and ditches dated to between the tenth and thirteenth century based on the associated Upper Greensand-derived ceramics (Figure 127 Medieval Phase II), and the sixteenth-century clay extraction pits and ditches (Figure 127 Late Medieval). The remarkable similarity between the taxa quantities in Medieval Phase I and Medieval Phase II, and the fact that there is secure evidence for the currency of Upper Greensand-Derived pottery in the first half of the tenth century, might point us to conclude that much of Medieval Phase II is actually contemporary with Phase I and that material in the fills of these pits and ditches is related to the production of iron from the excavated furnaces.

A significant point of difference with the Late Medieval, however, is that there is *c*. 10% less oak, and a proportionate increase in the presence of heathland taxa (*Cytisus/Ulex*), in the latest features, and this must point towards the use of gorse as a fuel, perhaps as tinder, in the pottery kilns.

Conclusions

In conclusion, the early medieval iron smelting furnaces at Churchills Farm were fuelled by a range of wood types, with significant quantities of oak, hazel and alder. Whether wood or charcoal fuel was used, the character of the wood was largely consistent with the use of coppiced stems, and some supplementary use of mature oak. Analysis of the Churchills Farm charcoal assemblage broadly replicates the picture gained from charcoal recovered from iron smelting furnaces of similar date at Burlescombe (Gale 2006).

The general pattern of fuel use (oak, alder and hazel coppice) continued with Hemyock's early sixteenth-century pottery industry, with some evidence for the exploitation, increasing with time, of heathland resources. That the charcoal record suggests woodland management in this landscape from the late ninth century onwards is not surprising, especially when the heavy fuel requirements for iron smelting, and later, for the pottery industry, is taken into account. One estimate suggests that the production of a tonne of iron would have required the cutting of 0.8 ha of woodland to produce enough charcoal (Bond 2007, 292). Indeed, the success of the early sixteenth-century pottery industry, apparently using the same woodland resources centuries later, may be considered a testament to the skills of early medieval woodland management.

Chapter 7

Discussion

So far this book has outlined in detail the excavated evidence for both early medieval iron production and late medieval pottery production at Churchills Farm, and the great body of detailed scientific analysis that has been applied to illuminate the character of these industries. This final chapter collects together a series of discussions of broader themes related to these activities in Hemyock past, and their social and geographical contexts.

Historic Landscape Character

Chris Smart

The historic landscape is a valuable record that can offer an important contextualization of both the medieval settlement pattern, and iron and pottery industries at Hemyock, as well as across the broader Blackdown Hills region. A number of projects have sought to analyse and represent the historic character of this landscape, including a county-wide Historic Landscape Characterisation undertaken by Devon County Council (Turner 2007; also viewable online at: http://gis.devon.gov.uk/basedata/viewer.asp?DCCService=hlc), an historic landscape analysis of the Blackdown Hills AONB, the *Living Past* project, by Stephen Rippon, Chris Smart and Adam Wainwright at the University of Exeter (Rippon *et al.* 2006a; also available online at: http://hdl.handle.net/10036/4033 and http://hdl.handle.net/10036/4032), and a broader but extremely detailed study of regional landscape variation between Devon, Somerset and Dorset (Rippon 2012). For the purposes of this discussion the historic character types identified as part of the *Living Past* project will be used as these reflect one of the present author's (Chris Smart) stance on landscape development in this region, disputing the extent of former common field in certain parts of the Blackdown Hills (see Rippon *et al.* 2006a, figs 5.1 and 5.2, for example).

The character of the landscape surrounding Hemyock (Figure 128) reflects the development of a medieval settlement and field pattern, encroachment upon the more steeply-sloping valley sides, as well as the later medieval and post-medieval enclosure of the upland plateaux, which were previously unenclosed. The village at Hemyock sits within a patchwork of semi-irregular fields that are neither highly irregular nor particularly regular in outline, and fields of this type are found across the Blackdown Hills covering much of the land between the valley-bottom floodplains and the steeply-sloping valley sides. Analysis of the wider region indicates that field patterns of the same morphology are found over a much larger area and are often little changed from at least the seventeenth century (Rippon 2012, 128-9). The precise origins of this landscape type cannot be discerned but a recent study has shown that there is little Roman or early medieval inheritance in the historic field pattern in the South West (Rippon *et al.* 2015; see also Rippon 2012, 129).

Palaeoenvironmental evidence from the region (Fyfe *et al.* 2004; Rippon 2012, chapter 11) and specifically from the Blackdown Hills (Brown *et al.* 2014) suggests that open areas of this landscape had been so since late Prehistory, with the emergence of a regionally-distinct form of agriculture from about the eighth century AD. Analysis of pollen cores taken at Bywood Farm, Hemyock and Greenway Farm, Luppitt suggest that there was increased woodland clearance between the sixth and eighth centuries AD (*ibid.* 17) and whilst this is explicably linked with the process of settlement nucleation and agricultural development (Rippon 2010), we must also recognise the significant evidence for iron production – which would have demanded wood for fuel – at the same point in time. Taking into account both archaeological and palaeoenvironmental evidence it is reasonable to suggest that the farmed landscape of semi-irregular fields that surrounded the historic village of Hemyock, or at least parts of it, might have been familiar to those smelting iron here in the ninth and tenth centuries.

The ground rises to the south of the village, with the rolling countryside of the lower slopes rising steeply to the broad plateaux of Hackpen and Collard Hills which, even in the late nineteenth century, retained discrete areas of common. In the late nineteenth century the steepest slopes retained some woodland, though elsewhere open commons prevailed (e.g. Owleycombe Common to the southwest of Hemyock). It is probable that much larger tracts of the steeply-sloping valley sides and escarpments were once wooded, though increasing demands from at least the sixth century would have led to gradual deforestation unless managed. The historic character of some parts of the steeper slopes are characterised by irregularly-shaped fields that most likely derive from the piecemeal assarting of woodland or open common, and such fields can be seen to the south of Hemyock on the rising ground towards Castle Hill.

Many of the Blackdown Hills plateaux are characterised by regular, geometric fields with dead-straight boundaries, which derive from enclosure of open ground during the eighteenth and nineteenth centuries, and have been

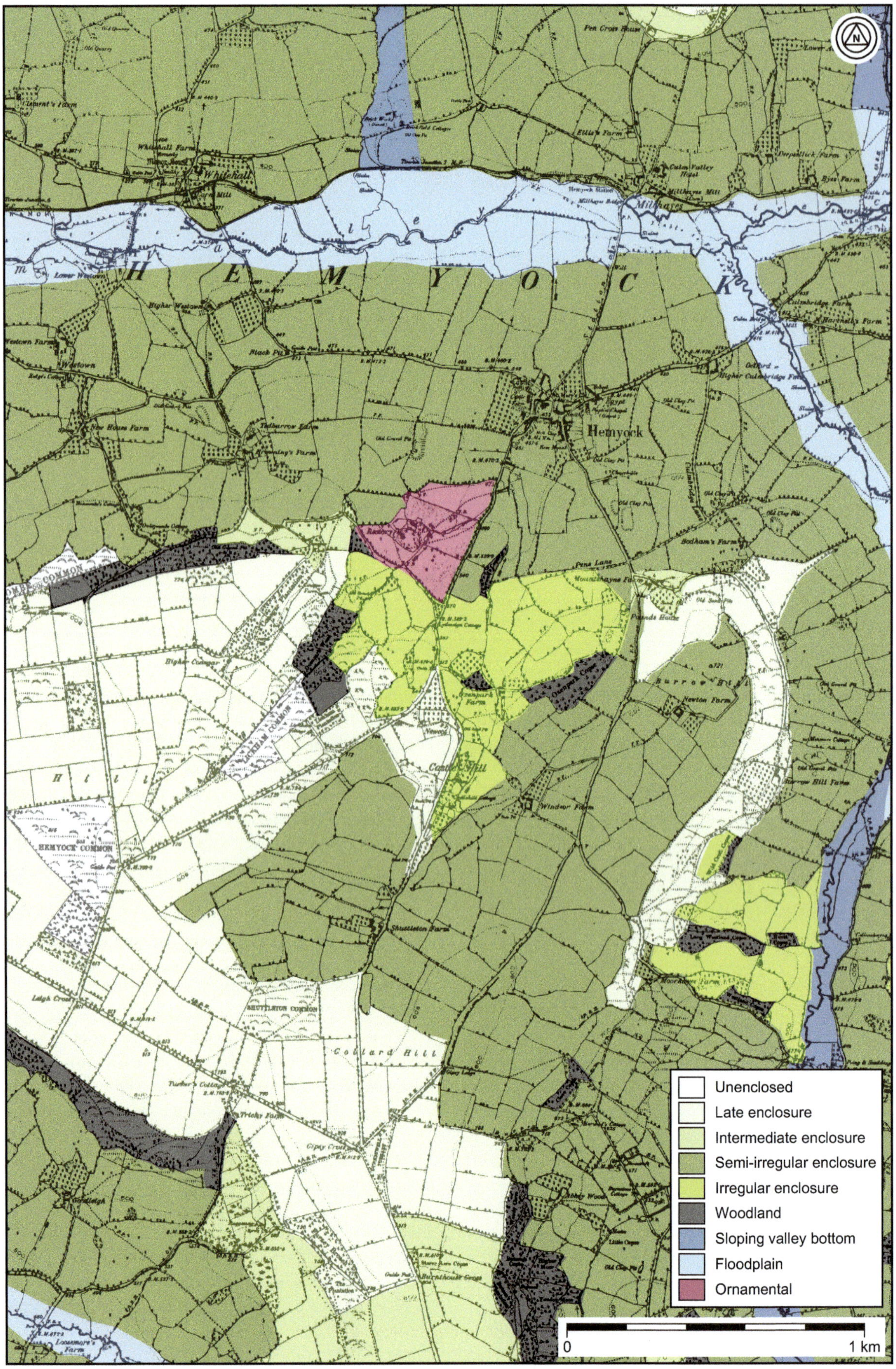

Figure 128. Detail of Historic Landscape Characterisation undertaken by the University of Exeter project 'Blackdown Hills Living Past' (Rippon *et al.* 2006a) showing the landscape character types of the countryside around Hemyock. Background mapping is late nineteenth century Ordnance Survey First Edition six inches to one mile (© Crown Copyright and Landmark Information Group Limited (2016). All rights reserved. (1889)).

described as 'Late Enclosure' (Rippon *et al.* 2006a, 19-23). Late nineteenth-century Ordnance Survey maps show that much of the plateaux had been brought under agricultural use – presumably improved grassland and some cultivation – though in some areas common and rough ground persisted. There are also large parts of the plateau margins – the land between the areas of Late Enclosure and the irregular/semi-irregular fields on the lower valley sides – that have been enclosed in a planned manner but probably at an earlier date. These 'Intermediate' fields have a regular form, often being broadly rectangular, but do not have dead-straight sides and, whilst their origins are yet unknown, they probably derive from the differential enclosure of former common and open field furlongs. That some of the earliest documented places – such as Gorwell, Hemyock parish, recorded in Domesday as *Gerwille*, and Sheldon, Sheldon parish, recorded in Domesday as *Sildene* – sit in areas of Intermediate fields implies that there could be relatively early underpinnings to field systems of the type.

Whilst there is evidently a link between the character of historic field patterns and the development of the medieval settlement pattern – situated on the lower valley sides and off of the floodplain – the exploitation of resources is not linked in such a straight-forward way. Whilst, for example, most of the known locations of iron ore extraction occur within areas of Late Enclosure (i.e. they were agriculturally unfavourable and unenclosed until the early modern era) this was not a choice based on the use of land of otherwise poor economic value but was determined by the suitability of mineralisation within the clay-with-flints. Likewise, the extent of clay extraction discussed above predominantly coincided with the Triassic mudstones, and occurred within areas mainly characterised by semi-irregular field patterns (i.e. those which might have origins from the eighth/ninth centuries onwards). To extract clay suitable for potting, or marling (for soil improving), it was necessary to dig extraction pits within the farmed parts of the countryside. As will be seen below, the associated production industries were not necessarily located for such pragmatic reasons.

A recent study of the Blackdown Hills, and its wider hinterland, has proposed a series of 'great estates' and 'early folk territories' (Rippon 2012). The proposed extent of these has been reconstructed using a combination of historic landscape analysis, charter and documentary evidence and one such 'great estate' has been named 'Greater Hemyock', which was part of a much larger Blackdown Hills 'early folk territory' (*ibid.* 176-7). Chapter 1 of this book set out the broad historical evidence for Hemyock – it was a royal estate in 1066 and by the time of Domesday was a hundredal centre – and it has also been suggested that a minster church was likely here (*ibid.*). The significance of Hemyock being a royal holding in relation to industry will be made apparent below. The hundred of Hemyock also encompassed Awliscombe, Buckerell, Clayhidon, Churchstanton and Dunkeswell, and Rippon's observation that the parish boundaries of these interlock, forming a larger unit (*ibid.* 177) is relevant to our consideration of access to mineral resources both pre- and post-Conquest. In the same vein, it is suggested that Culmstock and Uffculme were originally one – the boundary between the two parishes being long, straight and relatively recent – and part of a 'Greater Cullompton' estate, and this should be considered when thinking about the resources attached to the Burlescombe iron and later Culmstock pottery industries. A key point here is that these estates are of at least early medieval origin, becoming fragmented with successive land grants made to the church and secular elites (*ibid.* 193-5) such that charters suggest, for example, that Uffculme and Culmstock had become a separate estate from 'Greater Cullompton' by the eighth or ninth century (*ibid.* 172). Whilst there are no charters for Hemyock, it is reasonable to assume that this territorial structure was familiar to those engaged in the production of iron at Hemyock during the ninth and early tenth centuries.

Iron Production in Early Medieval Britain: Possible Cultural Influences on Technological Change

Tim Young

Modelling of the radiocarbon dates by Peter Marshall *et al.* (see Chapter 3) suggests that the two types of early medieval iron smelting furnace on the Churchills Farm site were broadly contemporary, or at least overlapping in age. The similarity in the chemical composition of their residues leaves no doubt that both performed the same task, namely the primary smelting of iron. Detailed analysis of the residues found no strong evidence to suggest that the iron was of significantly different composition, although there are very slight variances in the uptake of phosphorus by the slag, nor did it find evidence for a significant difference in the overall yield of the two processes. The analyses are, of course, not able to inform about the quality of the blooms created in terms of their carbon content or texture and thus potential ease of processing.

It is possible that an alternative explanation should be sought for the presence of two technologies apparently in use at the same time. In particular, the political and economic context of ironmaking needs consideration.

Current evidence for ironmaking in late ninth- to tenth-century Wessex is concentrated in three areas: at Ramsbury in Wiltshire, the Devon/Somerset Blackdown Hills, and Pucklechurch in South Gloucestershire. It is possible that the large iron smelting site at Romsey, Hampshire also dates, at least partially, to this period. For much of the ninth century the iron-bearing districts of Pucklechurch and the Forest of Dean would have been within Mercian territory, but by the time smelting began at Emersons Green, near Pucklechurch, the area would have been within the realm of Wessex (if the proposed dates of *c.* AD 875-950; Young and Young 2013, Section 8, are accepted; the modelling presented in Chapter 3 suggests a longer potential interval of *cal* AD 770–915 (*95% probability*) for Furnace 1 and a *TPQ* of AD 770–945 (*95% probability*) for Furnace 2). Pucklechurch was a royal estate, certainly gifted to the church by the mid tenth century, possibly by a grant from King Eadred to Bishop Wulfhelm of Wells, sometime between AD 923 and AD 926, but eventually held by Glastonbury Abbey with a render of 90 *massae* of iron at Domesday. Ramsbury has also been argued to have been a royal estate (Haslam 1980, 61-64), and it too passed to the church with the creation of a Bishopric of Ramsbury in *c.* AD 909. Romsey may have had an earlier ecclesiastical centre, but the nunnery probably dates from foundation in *c.* AD 907, again by royal gift. The pre-Conquest history of Hemyock is poorly documented, but it was a royal manor at the time of Domesday. It is also known that at least part of Burlescombe was in the pre-Conquest royal demesne, with a mid tenth century land grant from King Eadwigheld of land at Ashford (Finberg 1953; Hooke 1994). The history of iron smelting on these key sites may, therefore, need not so much be viewed as reflecting the background evolution in ideas and technology during this period, but perhaps more as the outcome of a deliberate royal policy.

With the desire to increase the output of iron, particularly on the royal estates, it may well have been appropriate to look for improved production techniques and technological ideas across the broader world within which Wessex existed. Maybe this is the framework within which to view the use of multiple new technologies?

It would appear likely that the Blackdown Hills had been incorporated into Wessex prior to the start of the iron-making activity at the site of Churchills Farm (probably by King Ine at the beginning of the eighth century). Maddicott (1989) has presented an interesting discussion on the significance of the South West for economic development under Alfred in the second half of the ninth century. He argued that Alfred significantly reoriented Wessex towards the South West, rather than the South East, with a growing importance placed on tin from Devon and Cornwall, as well as silver from Mendip (although the potential significance of Devon silver might now be emphasised as well; see Rippon *et al.* 2009 for a study of the significance of Devon silver from the thirteenth century onwards). Expansion of iron production in the South West might also have been associated with broader economic developments, in addition to the direct demand from major construction projects and the equipping of Alfred's army cited by Young and Young (2013) as well as the more mundane needs of regional agricultural communities.

The new evidence presented by Marshall *et al.* in Chapter 3 (Figure 38) suggests that ironworking at Churchills Farm commenced cal AD 850–935 (95% probability) and probably cal AD 870–910 (68% probability), and ended cal AD 900–980 (95% probability) and probably cal AD 905–950 (68% probability). These dates are indeed compatible with an origin under Alfred (r. 871–899) or Edward the Elder (r. 899–924) and suggest a very short lifespan for activity on the site (1–65 years (95% probability) and probably 1–35 years (68% probability)).

The dating of the other iron production sites in Wessex is less precise, but indicates an extended history of ironworking. Nearby sites in the Blackdown Hills employing wood-packed non-tapping furnaces at Bywood Farm (where a single date gave cal AD 660–880; AA 17827; Griffith and Weddell 1996) and Culmstock Road (where modelling of the two dates, Chapter 3, suggests *cal* AD 725–900 (*93% probability*) or *cal* AD 795–885 (*68% probability*)) have provided dates that are somewhat earlier than those for Churchills Farm. The two dates obtained at Burlescombe are less precise (their modelling suggests a date range of *cal* AD 785–970 (*95% probability*) or *cal* AD 840–945 (*68% probability*); Chapter 3), so the dating of that site as older than that at Churchills Farm is likely, but less certain. Further afield, the large non-tapping furnaces at Ramsbury are poorly dated, but predate the large slag tapping furnace which appears likely to be of ninth-century age.

The known British examples that display a similar technology to that of the non-tapping furnaces at Churchills Farm appear to predate the activity at Churchills Farm: Clearwell Quarry has produced a group of tightly clustered dates during full excavation (*cal* AD 765–895 (*95% probability*; *last_clearwell*); Chapter 3), and a site at Yorkley a single very similar date (cal AD 690–890; SUERC-65353, 1225 ± 29 BP); Eckington in Derbyshire is apparently rather older (a single date of cal AD 650–770; SUERC-75177, 1315 ± 30 BP).

The slag tapping furnaces at Ramsbury and Emersons Green differ in form to the early examples at Churchills Farm, but bear some similarities with each other. In both cases the furnaces are large, commonly have a widely-splayed profile to the lower shaft and show evidence for retention of slag within the base of the furnace (Furnace F1 at Emersons Green contained a 40 kg 'furnace bottom') leading to the development of a step in the slag-tapping channel. It should be noted, however, that the illustrations of the Emersons Green furnaces (Young and Young 2013) suggest that they may embrace a range of morphologies not highlighted by the accompanying descriptions. The furnaces at both sites are similarly poorly dated, but that at Ramsbury has been argued to be of ninth- or tenth-century date (Bayliss, quoted by Boyer and Keys 2013), whereas dates from Emersons Green and their modelling gives a potential span during the late eighth to tenth centuries (for Furnace 1 *cal* AD 770–915 (*95% probability*) and for Furnace 2 a *TPQ* of AD 770–945 (*95% probability*). The morphology of the Ramsbury and Emersons Green furnaces might suggest a type more evolutionarily-remote from those of the later medieval period than those at Churchills Farm (notwithstanding the lack of evidence at Churchills Farm for the furnace superstructure).

There has been considerable interest in the timing of the replacement of non-tapping furnaces by the slag tapping process in Wessex. The onset of slag tapping is frequently hailed as a marker in the development of iron making in England. Haslam (1980), for instance, commented:

'The larger furnaces, 2, 3, and 4, clearly represent two stages in a line of technological advancement ... Since Ramsbury is the first site to produce evidence of any early 9th-century developed tradition of iron smelting in England, it might even be that this was a new discovery at the time, worked out by an intelligent appreciation of new possibilities always inherent in basic techniques. The furnace complex at Ramsbury is therefore important both in its own right, and as an indicator of the possible significance of Ramsbury in the 9th century'.

The discussion presented in Chapter 4, however, provides an alternative view of the history of slag tapping. Traditions both of slag tapping and non-tapping furnaces may have been present in Wessex from a much earlier period, but the details remain obscure. The evidence from the Wareham area, Dorset (Bestwall, Worgret), indicates that even within the area of Wessex, slag tapping appears to have been in use well before the ninth century, perhaps as early as the seventh century (and potentially continuously since the Roman period). That means there are plenty of sources from which slag tapping may been introduced into Devon/Wiltshire – including other areas of Wessex, Frankish areas of France (and Frankish influenced areas of Britain, such as Kent), areas in the English Midlands, and the external Viking world. Furnace 4 at Ramsbury may well show an attempt to integrate imported ideas with aspects of the construction of the existing non-tapping furnaces. It might, potentially, represent an evolution from the non-tapping furnaces (as suggested by Hallam), but a derivation from either a local or distant influence is at least as likely. The temporal relationship between Ramsbury furnace 4 and the furnaces of Emersons Green is unclear. Emersons Green lies in an area that would have fallen within Mercia until after the death of Ceolwulf II, in AD 879. It is equally unclear whether there was continual development of the Ramsbury/Emersons Green into the type of slag tapping furnace employed at Churchills Farm, or whether that was a separate introduction or development. The Churchills Farm tapping furnaces are poorly characterised, but their narrow trench suggests a close relationship with subsequent furnaces of the twelfth and thirteenth centuries found across southern Britain (and northern France).

A tentative synthesis of the available information therefore suggests that during the eighth to ninth centuries a series of large smelting centres at Romsey, Ramsbury and in the Blackdown Hills area (including Hemyock) were developed on royal estates. These all employed a form of large slagpit furnace, perhaps ultimately derived from earlier forms used in the Netherlands, which had splayed sides and planar blowing wall. At some point, possibly in the ninth century, a slag tapping furnace, of large size, with splayed lower shaft walls came into use. Such furnaces are seen at Ramsbury and Emersons Green (within another royal estate). The origins of this type are unclear, but it may represent a fusion of slag-tapping technology with the earlier non-tapping furnace morphology. By the period of the early medieval smelting at Churchills Farm, probably in the late ninth or earliest tenth centuries, a smaller form of slag tapping furnace, built over a simple narrow trench, had either developed or been introduced. At the same (or possibly very slightly later) a style of non-tapping furnace that employed cereal packing also came into use at Churchills Farm. The known antecedents for this type of furnace are from Mercia and, in particular, had been in use in the Forest of Dean (which had fallen under the overlordship of Wessex by the period of the Churchills Farm ironmaking) within the period of late eighth to late ninth centuries.

The history of the technological evolution of iron smelting in Wessex is thus complex, and not simply a linear replacement of non-tapping by slag tapping furnaces. Instead, a picture of technologies that were both evolving *in situ* and being introduced from outside the immediate area is starting to emerge. It seems likely that behind this picture are craftspeople carrying their technology from one area to another. That the major smelting sites were apparently on royal estates, may suggest a deliberate policy to develop ironmaking capacity, not just by Alfred (who has received much acclaim for his acquisition of skilled people from outside Wessex), but also by other members of the house of Wessex. Does the appearance of the cereal-packed furnaces at Churchills Farm indicate the movement of smelters from Mercia to Wessex after a larger Kingdom of the Anglo-Saxons emerged in the 880s? Although much later, and within a very different economic and political context, one is reminded of the employment of Welsh ironworkers by Dunkeswell Abbey in the thirteenth century (Summerson 1985). Further work, involving both additional sites and improved dating, will be required to tease out the whole story.

Although there is a hiatus in iron production at Churchills Farm between the early tenth and eleventh centuries, we should not necessarily conclude that iron smelting at Hemyock stopped altogether. It is perfectly plausible that the focus of smelting shifted elsewhere in the vicinity, and this might be supported by the discovery of unprovenanced slags from across the village (discussed below), with smelting only returning to the location of Churchills Farm at later date, probably in the eleventh century.

This late phase of smelting at Churchills Farm is, unfortunately, not represented by direct structural evidence, but merely by slags dumped into pits. Analysis of these slags suggests a marked increase in the yield of iron from the ore, demonstrating that the similar physical appearance of these tapped slags and those of the early tenth century operation masks a significant technological development. One further difference of the Saxo-Norman slag assemblage is that it contains examples of large smithing hearth cakes (SHCs), probably produced during the working of the raw blooms into processed iron. These are few in number and, as with the remainder of the Saxo-Norman assemblage, were not associated with metallurgical features so they have not been investigated in detail as part of this project. Nonetheless, they provide a contrast with the earlier periods at Churchills Farm (together with the sites Culmstock Road and Burlescombe), which did not produce any residues from the secondary processes. This may suggest a change in the organisation of the industry, with some co-location of primary smelting and bloomsmithing operations in the later period. In contrast to the complex dynamics of iron smelting in the ninth and tenth centuries, the evidence from the site for the eleventh-century episode of iron smelting appears to show an activity entirely in keeping with what is known from other iron smelting sites of the period across southern Britain, and probably across northern France as well, suggesting rather homogenous technology by that period.

Sourcing of Raw Materials: Iron Ore and Clay

Chris Smart

When considering the distribution and availability of raw materials – whether iron ore, clay for furnace-building or, later, for potting – landholding and territorial structure are fundamental. It is known from post-Conquest accounts that the extraction of raw materials, even from common land, gave rise to disputes and was so bound by a complex system of rights (see Rippon *et al.* 2009 for an overview of mineral rights in the medieval period). Whilst there is no documentary evidence to illuminate how access to minerals was controlled in the early medieval period, at least some level of formality must be envisaged, with the exercise of royal and ecclesiastical powers being most likely. In view of the historical context outlined in Chapter 1, and the possible socio-political influences discussed above, it might be envisaged that early medieval iron production in and around Hemyock was a royal interest, even if indirectly.

Analysis of a fragment of iron ore from Churchills Farm, described earlier, concluded that there is a strong similarity between it and material excavated by Cotswold Archaeology at Dunkeswell Airfield (Cotswold Archaeology 2015); both are nodular iron oxide ores from the clay-with-flints. The ridgetop upon which Dunkeswell Airfield sits is known for an extensive area of iron ore extraction pits, which are visible on aerial photographs and witnessed through a series of excavations. The airfield was opened in 1943 as RAF Dunkeswell and it is believed that significant levelling occurred in 1941 during groundworks by contractor George Wimpey (Jarrett and Stevens 2010), such that we might presume that the type of pits surviving as earthworks on North Hill Common, Broadhembury (Griffith and Weddell 1996, 31-2, pl. 3), three kilometres to the southwest were upstanding across the area into the early twentieth century. A preliminary survey of the evidence for iron production on the Blackdown Hills, undertaken by Exeter Museums Archaeological Field Unit during the 1990s, recognised and excavated a sample of iron extraction pits 2.5-3.7m in diameter and up to 0.25 m deep (Figure 129) that were visible on a 1947 Royal Air Force aerial photograph (RAF/CPE/UK/1974/4299/(11/4/1947)) around the northern and western periphery of the airfield.

An archaeological evaluation in 2010 at Dunkeswell Parachute Club revealed ten intercutting pits, measuring between 1.5 m and 2.25 m in diameter and up to 1.75 m deep. The pits were sealed by 0.4 m of topsoil (Milby 2010). Whilst we must accept that truncation through levelling occurred at Dunkeswell when the airfield was built this might have been variable; the proximity and size of the intercutting pits suggests that either truncation here was limited, or that the pits are of different ages (if the pits were originally *much* deeper and extended *outwards* towards the top, then the later pits would have been largely removing backfill from earlier ones). Unfortunately, none of the pits could be dated. On the north side of the airfield, a watching brief revealed eight undated circular pits, measuring between 0.4 m and 1m in diameter and up to 0.25 m deep, sealed beneath shallow topsoil (Kerr-Peterson 2014), and here truncation appears to have been more severe. A strip, map and sample exercise, undertaken by Cotswold Archaeology ahead of the construction of a solar farm at the northeast edge of the airfield revealed sixteen undated ore extraction pits, measuring up to 1.2 m across and 0.95 m deep (Cotswold Archaeology 2015). These excavations took place during preparation of this volume and, as such, it was possible for Tim Young to correspond analyses of the ore samples recovered by Cotswold Archaeology at Dunkeswell with the fragments recovered from Churchills Farm and Culmstock Road, Hemyock, much to the benefit of our understanding. It is worth noting that whilst a single dense block of tapslag cake weighing 8.7 kg was recovered from the fill of pit 104 at the solar farm site, there is no other evidence for smelting at the point of extraction. A magnetic geophysical survey of a large proportion of the disused

Figure 129. Photograph showing the archaeological excavation of iron ore extraction pits at North Hill Common by Exeter Museums Archaeological Field Unit during the early 1990s. Note the significant depth surviving, as shown in section. Others excavated by commercial archaeological field units at Dunkeswell Airfield are much shallower and therefore likely to be heavily truncated (photo courtesy of Devon County Council Historic Environment Service).

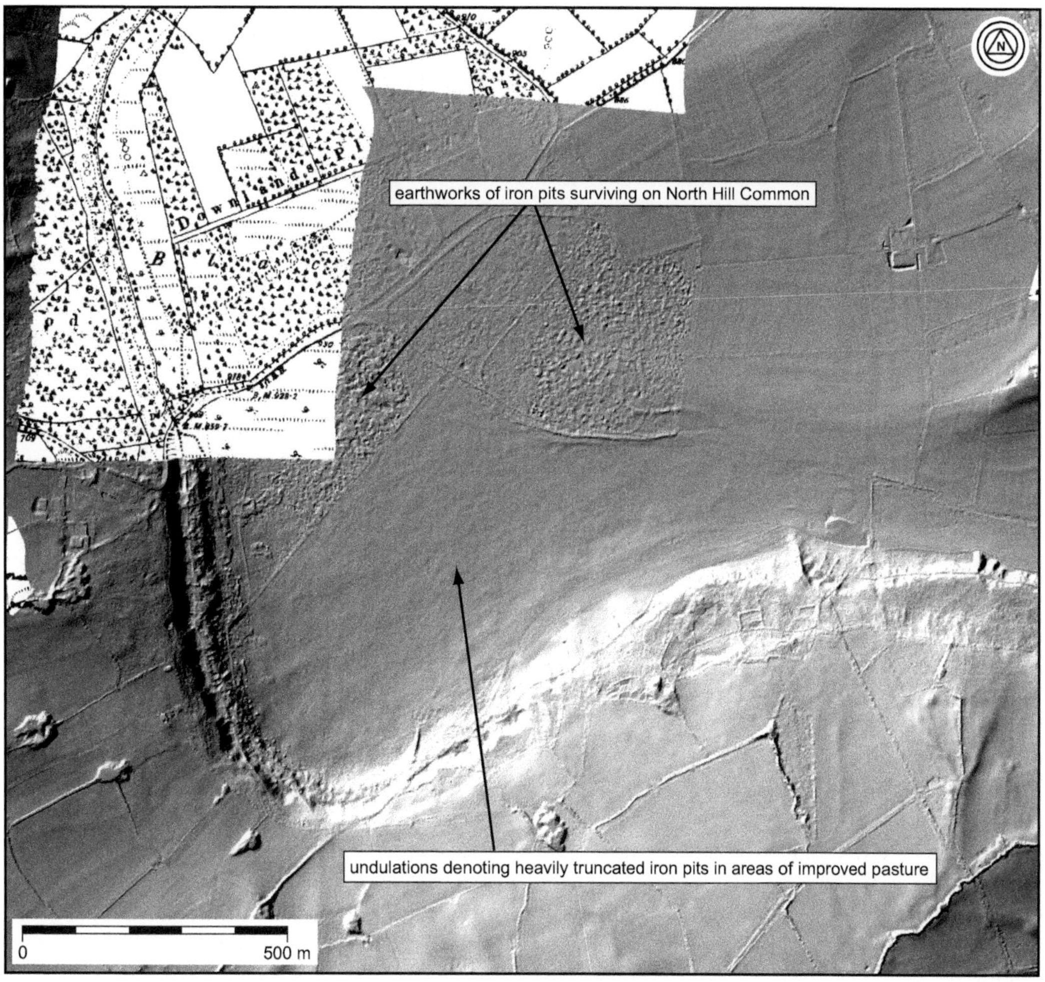

Figure 130. Hillshade model of 1m resolution Environment Agency LiDAR data covering part of North Hill Common, Broadhembury. The rough ground to the north side of the common has upstanding earthworks of iron ore extraction pits (visible on aerial photographs and sample excavated by EMAFU (Figure 129)). LiDAR data shows slight undulations across adjacent improved grassland, indicating a greater extent of iron ore extraction pits than can be seen on aerial photographs or on the ground.

northeast end of the airfield identified many hundreds of possible extraction pits, as well as former land divisions (Archaeological Surveys Ltd 2013) but none of the tell-tale signatures of *in situ* furnaces, though there remains the issue of early twentieth-century truncation.

In the thirteenth century it is known that the Abbot of Dunkeswell Abbey had metal founders under his employ and it surely a certainty that a proportion of the extraction pits on the nearby plateau belong to this period. This Cistercian house was not founded until 1201 so it has no bearing on the context of early medieval production at Churchills Farm, and it seems wholly unlikely that the same resources were not exploited in earlier times.

Taking the historic road south out of Hemyock it is five kilometres (three miles) to the plateau now occupied by Dunkeswell Airfield, which seems an entirely reasonable distance to transport a load of ore by packhorse or cart. It is possible, nonetheless, that other sources within the clay-with-flints might bear a similar chemical signature, but without a wider database of sources we cannot be sure. Certainly, there are other known areas of ore extraction in the countryside around Hemyock, including Hackpen Hill, 1.6 km (1 mile) southwest of the village, where aerial photographic evidence shows pits in an area now under heavily-improved pasture (Griffith and Weddell 1996, 32). Hackpen Hill is bisected by the parish boundary between Hemyock, and Uffculme/Culmstock and, as such, would have been divided between the two associated early medieval great estates suggested by Rippon, whereas Dunkeswell would have fallen wholly within Greater Hemyock.

If we then consider the broader availability of ores, and the evidence for smelting (often stray finds of slag or slag dumps), then we witness a pattern that supports the idea that on-site smelting at Dunkeswell was unlikely. The land at Dunkeswell Airfield aside, the largest concentration of iron ore extraction pits recognised to date is at North Hill Common, Broadhembury, where aerial photographic evidence shows pits over an area of *c.* 30 ha, with the present author having manipulated LiDAR data to show traces of their former extent beneath adjacent areas of improved pasture (Figure 130). It might be more appropriate to consider Dunkeswell and North Hill Common not as two separate areas of extraction but, given their physical contiguity, a single zone of ore

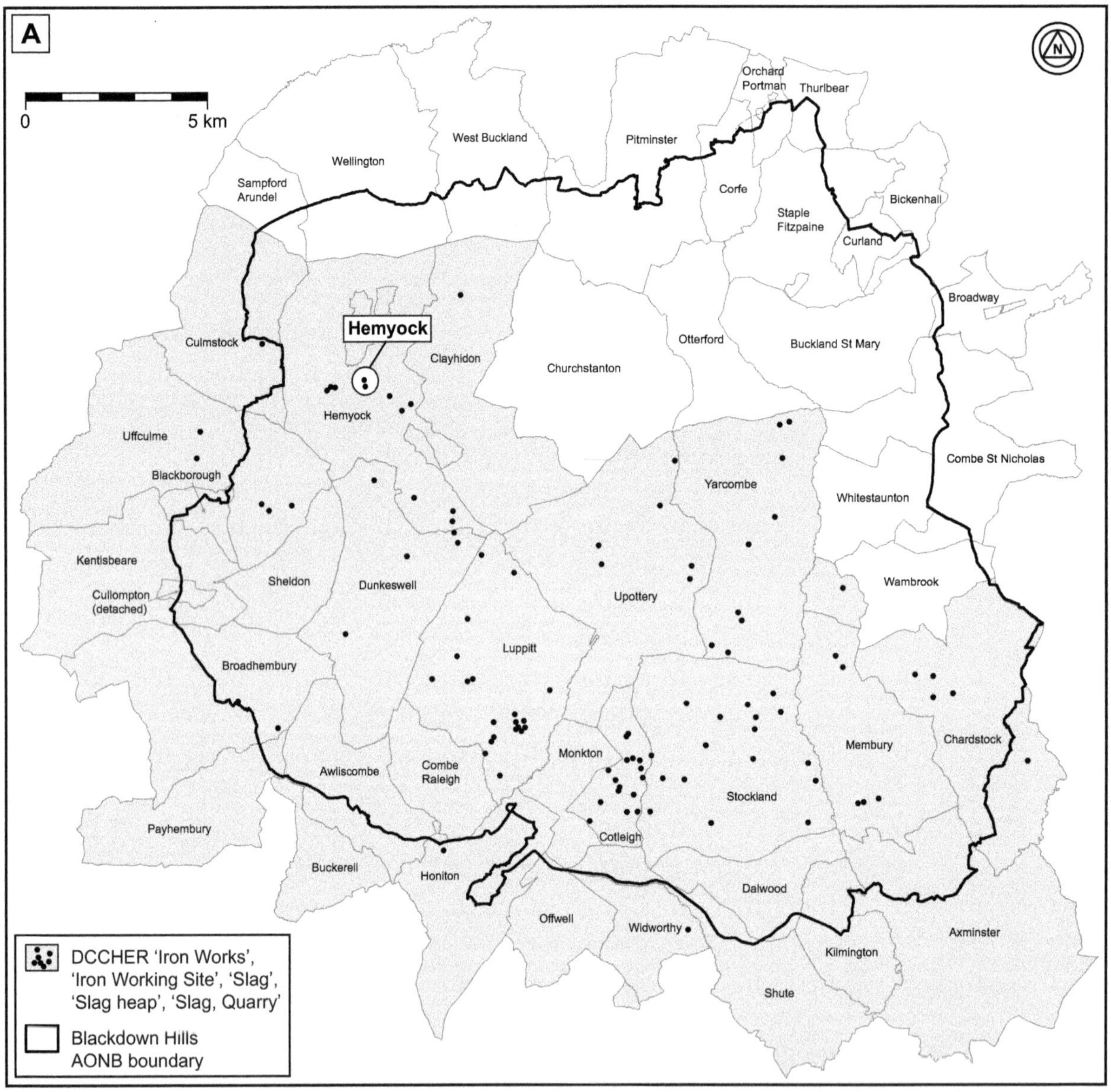

Figure 131 [left]. The extent of records for 'slag', 'slag heap', 'slag, quarry', 'ironworks' and 'iron working site' in the Devon County Council Historic Environment Record as of May 2016 in relation to historic parishes and the boundary of the Blackdown Hills Area of Outstanding Natural Beauty. This is taken to provide a starting point for future investigation of the iron production industry on the Blackdown Hills. The same data could not as easily be extracted from the Somerset Historic Environment Record but it is known that slag finds have been made in Somerset parishes also.

extraction stretching almost five kilometres along the same ridge. The only reason to divide the two may be linked to the medieval estate structure; Dunkeswell was part of Hemyock Hundred whereas Broadhembury parish (and therefore North Hill Common) lay in Hayridge Hundred – access to these resources may have been subject to these jurisdictions.

The picture is clear, however: extraction of nodular ores was focussed on the ridges and plateaux of Upper Greensand, and we should assume that this was the case throughout the known date range – Roman to medieval – of iron smelting on the Blackdown Hills. Conversely, the available data for the sites of smelting – the handful of excavated sites (e.g. Churchills Farm and Culmstock Road, Hemyock; Burlescombe) and the wider distribution of slag and slag dumps – shows a distinct trend towards the valley sides and bottoms (Figure 131). Two observations are worth making – it is the same valley sides and floors that were settled and farmed historically, and it is in these areas that access to the other essential raw materials – wood for fuel and clay for furnace construction – would have been easier. When the distribution of production evidence is considered against the character of the historic landscape there is a trend towards slag and slag dumps occurring in areas of irregular and semi-irregular fields, considered to be earliest in the sequence of enclosure. This, like the early medieval evidence from Hemyock, suggests that the iron industry was an integral part of the rural landscape and not a liminal activity. The exception to this general pattern is in Cotleigh parish where numerous slag finds have been made in areas of Intermediate enclosure – land possibly enclosed late in the medieval period. Most of the slag dumps and finds are, unfortunately, undated. It is impossible to estimate age

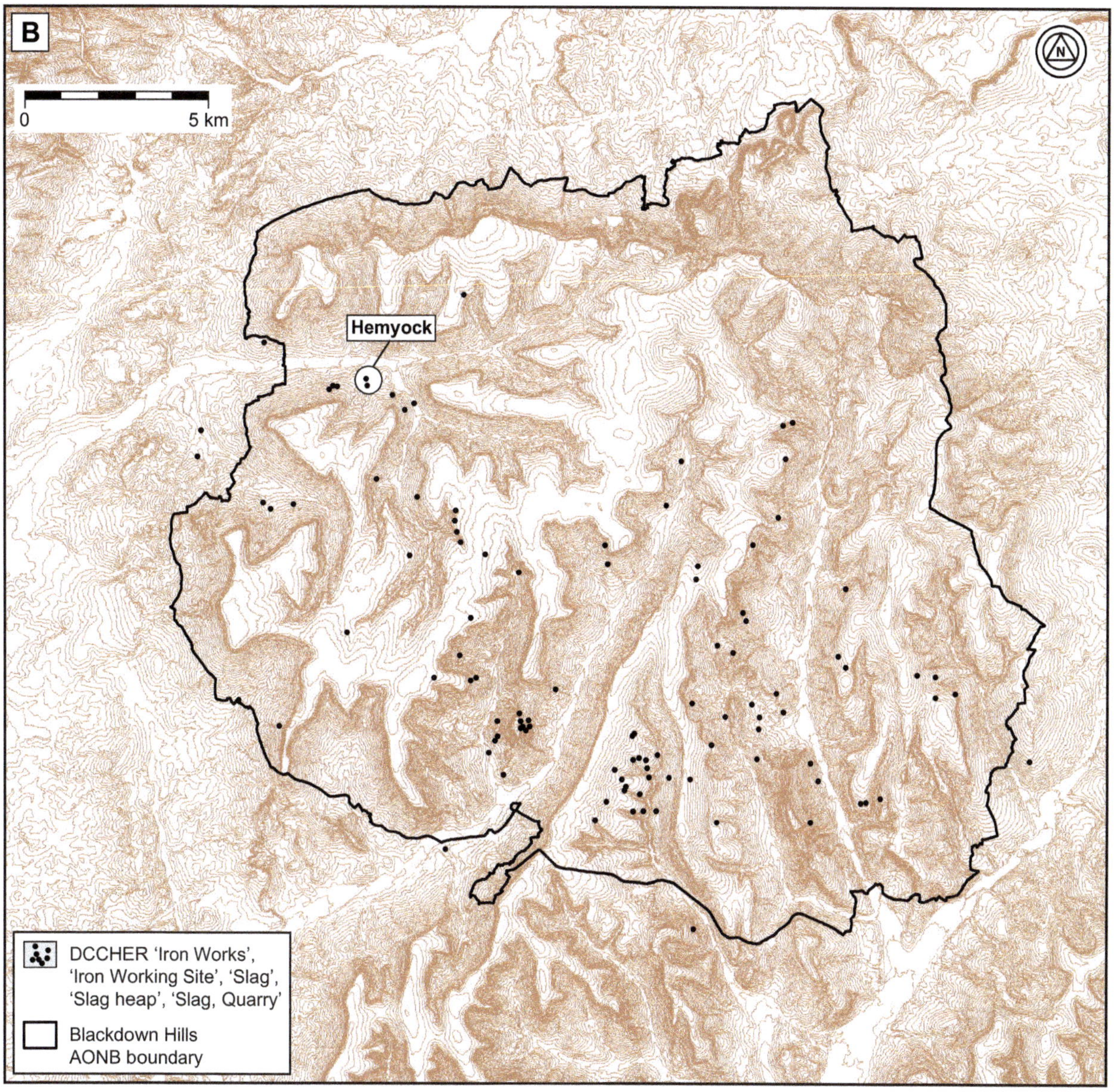

Figure 131 [right]. The extent of records for 'slag', 'slag heap', 'slag, quarry', 'ironworks' and 'iron working site' in the Devon County Council Historic Environment Record as of May 2016 in relation to the topography of the Blackdown Hills. It is noteworthy that the vast majority of findspots occur on the valley sides or lower slopes, rather than on the plateaux.

based on location within the historic landscape; slag from the core areas of medieval farmland is just as likely to be of Roman date than of early medieval or post-Conquest. For example, slag from Tedburrow Farm, Hemyock, one kilometre west of Churchills Farm, was dated using entrapped charcoal to 1815 +/- 65 BP (72-395 cal AD), whilst slag from Bywood Farm was dated 1260 +/- 50 BP (664-889 cal AD) (information from Devon County Council Historic Environment Service).

If we turn our attention to the extraction of clay, we can identify local demand at Hemyock in both the ninth/tenth centuries and the fifteenth/sixteenth centuries. The early medieval iron production evidenced at Churchills Farm would not only have required the extraction of iron ore – which appears to have come from the higher plateaux – there would also have been a need for clay from which to construct the associated furnaces. There is no precise answer as to the volume or weight of clay that each of the Hemyock furnaces would have required – either for the initial construction, for repair of internal wall material lost during the smelt, or for the re-blocking of the basal arch – but Tim Young has made some reasoned estimates. A modern recipe used by metallurgist Lee Sauder, employing dried powdered clay, would require an equivalent of about 350 kg of freshly dug clay for a furnace of the size evidenced at Churchills Farm. Alternatively, working on the basis of a volume calculation (assume a furnace shaft 1.3 m high, with internal diameter of 400 mm and external diameter of 560 mm) there would be 0.15 m^3 of clay needed, with a weight of about 300 kg (based on density of 2000 kg/m^3). Furthermore, chemical analysis of the slag from Churchills Farm suggests that about 15% of the slag derives from the furnace lining, so that for each smelt producing 20 kg of slag (an estimate based on furnace size and the recorded furnace bottoms) about 3 kg of clay would be needed to replace that lost in the reaction. If approximately 5 kg of clay was required to block the basal arch during each operation and, for example, there were 120 smelts per year, then ongoing requirements would account for almost one tonne of clay annually (Young pers.comm). What we do not know, of course, is how many times each of the Churchills Farm furnaces was used – though the scale of the undated waste from around Hemyock hints at a significant industry. It has been suggested, based on the weight of the slag taken from a 6% sample of the dump at Culmstock Road, that this dump alone might have contained 22 tonnes of smelting slag – and this does not account for any material taken away or truncated since deposition.

It can be assumed that the clay used for furnace construction would have been dug from the nearest suitable source; as Triassic mudstone underlies all of the village clay might actually have been dug onsite, or close by. The characteristics of the pits at Churchills Farm were described in Section 2, and most of the closely-dated examples were filled in the fifteenth/sixteenth century, but three might be contemporary with the production of iron (based on the presence of Upper Greensand-Derived pottery). If we take, for example, Pit 556, with maximum dimensions of 2.7 by 2.15 by 0.85 m, the volume of clay that could be extracted from it would be between approximately 2 m^3, and so could have provided about 4 tonnes of clay. Pit 729 was of broadly similar dimensions and had been back-filled with slag – about 800 kg it is estimated – and contained Upper Greensand-Derived pottery within its fill. There is no unequivocal evidence to link the digging of these pits with the construction of the furnaces at Churchills Farm – clay would also have been needed for potting, building, and for agricultural improvement – but the close relative dating and proximity certainly makes this possibility. Pits of such size would have provided sufficient clay for the construction of several furnaces, as well as allowed for much of their repair under intense use.

Evidence for the extraction of clay in the valleys of the River Culm and its tributary is extensive. There are various strands of evidence that point towards places where clay was dug historically – field-names of the early nineteenth-century tithe surveys, old pits marked on the First Edition

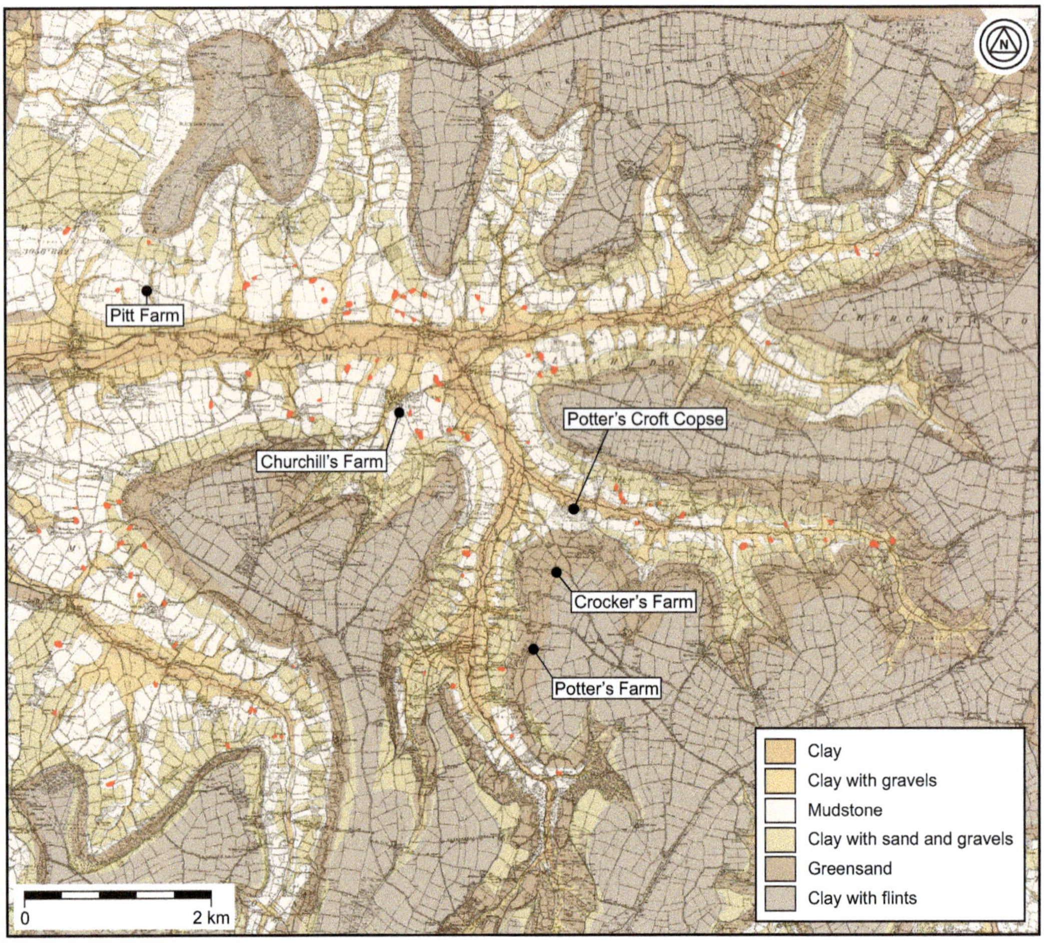

Figure 132. Map of pits shown on either the Ordnance Survey First Edition 25 inches to 1 mile (late nineteenth century) as claypit, marl pit, and/or those visible on Environment Agency 1 m resolution LiDAR data viewed as a hillshade model. The background mapping comprises late nineteenth-century Ordnance Survey First Edition 6 inches to 1 mile and British Geological Survey soil parent material dataset, sheet ew311 (© Crown Copyright and Landmark Information Group Limited (2016). All rights reserved. (1889)). It is unfortunate that there is not total coverage of LiDAR data (which focusses on valley floor) for the Blackdown Hills, which help us understand the broader pattern of mineral extraction (clay, marl, aggregates, iron ore etc).

Ordnance Survey maps of late nineteenth-century date (see Collings in Chapter 5), and LiDAR. The pits recorded on the First Edition Ordnance Survey are either marked as 'Old Clay Pit', 'Old Gravel Pit' or, to the south of Culm Davy in particular, 'Old Quarry'. Whether naming as such implies that extraction occurred within living memory of the date of the survey, or that the Ordnance Survey draftsmen were given names based on what local people understood to be the available resources, cannot be known, but it is clear from other sources that there are numerous pits within this landscape that the Ordnance Survey did not map.

The Environment Agency's 1m resolution digital terrain model (DTM) LiDAR data was scrutinised for the Blackdown Hills and immediate hinterland, in order to assess the potential for places where clay or iron ore might have been extracted in addition to those that have already been recorded (whether on historic mapping or discovered through archaeological fieldwork). It is unfortunate for archaeologists studying the Blackdown Hills that the existing coverage of LiDAR is largely restricted to the valleys, with the higher ground not surveyed (this is due to the primary hydrological purposes of the data for the Environment Agency) and, as such, we cannot map extraction on the higher slopes and plateaux in the same way. This would be particularly useful for exploring the extraction of iron ore from the clay-with-flints and Greensand. A step in the right direction is *The Blackdown Hills AONB and East Devon River Catchments National Mapping Programme (NMP) Project*, being undertaken by the Historic Environment Service of Devon County Council, the results of which were not available at the time of this book going to press. Importantly, this project has been able to commission bespoke LiDAR for the purposes of identifying archaeological features, and this new data will be considered alongside existing data and aerial photographs.

In order to contextualise the excavation results at Churchills Farm the raw data DTM data was combined and processed to create large area hillshade models which, by artificially casting a light source at different angles across the terrain model, highlighted earthworks associated with extraction. Whilst also showing as hollows those pits marked on the First Edition Ordnance Survey maps, the modelled LiDAR data shows numerous large hollows in areas that, in the late nineteenth century, were farmland (see Figure 132 for combined distribution in the Culm Valley, expanding

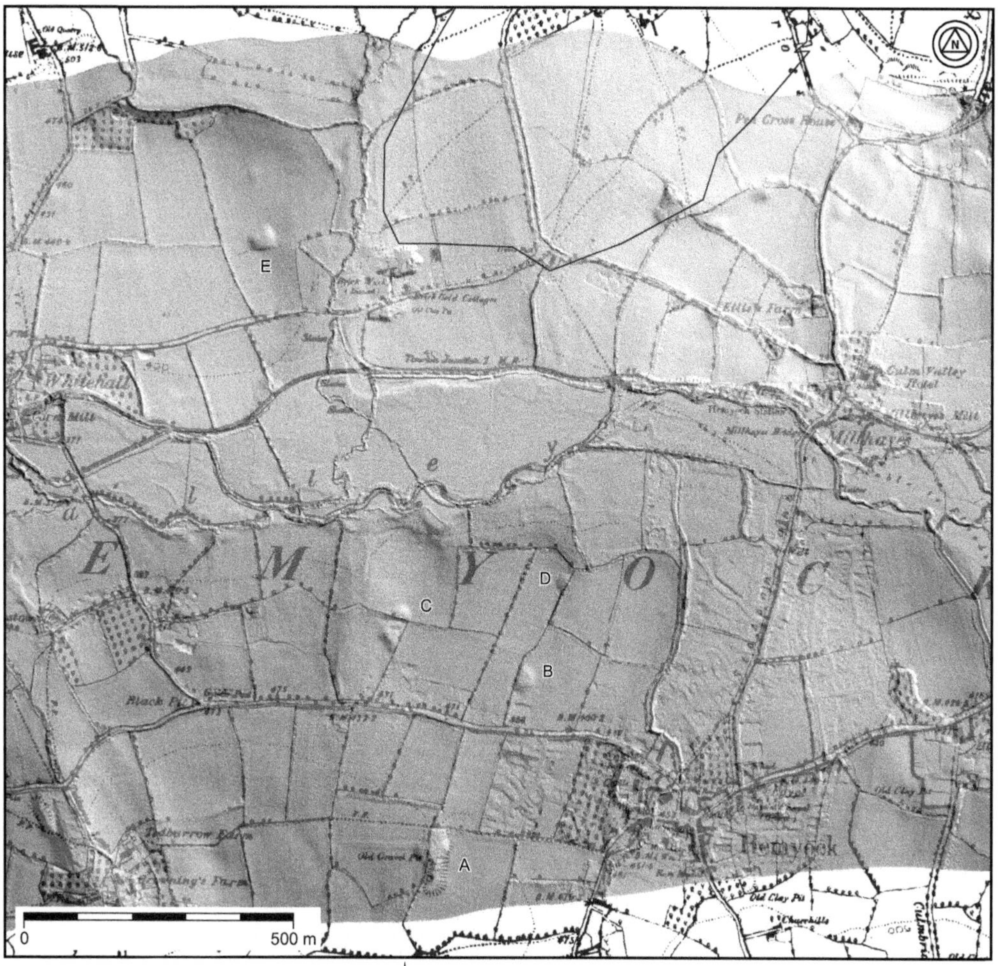

Figure 133. Detail of a hillshade model of 1 m resolution Environment Agency LiDAR data for an area west and north of Hemyock, shown against a backdrop of late nineteenth-century Ordnance Survey First Edition 6 inches to 1 mile mapping (© Crown Copyright and Landmark Information Group Limited (2016). All rights reserved. (1889)). The data shows that there are many examples of extraction pits, possible for the digging of clay, marl or gravel, at the edges of fields within the historic landscape. Whilst undated, the form of those not also shown on historic mapping is more muted, perhaps implying that they are earlier in date.

upon the initial mapping done by Tony Collings (Chapter 5; Figure 72). Whilst there is no evidence upon which to date these relict extraction pits, two observations can be made. First is that the earthworks corresponding to locations marked on the late nineteenth-century maps are more exaggerated, with greater definition, and a similar observation can be made of those unmarked examples that are situated within areas of orchard and woodland. The implication of this is that the unmarked examples visible on LiDAR that sit within agricultural fields have been heavily muted by agricultural improvement and that they are of an earlier date. The second observation is that of this latter group, most occur either at the edge of a field or are cut across by the field boundaries; few sit in the middle of a parcel of land (e.g. Figure 133, earthworks A-E).

We have already seen that large areas of the rolling valley sides are characterised by irregular and semi-irregular fields whose origins might be as early as the eighth or ninth centuries, though the overall pattern is likely to represent several hundred years or more of piecemeal adaptation. An important question – to which there is no certain answer – is whether pits were dug at the edges of existing fields in order to minimise disruption to farming, or whether the creators of fields set out boundaries to deliberately place existing pits at the edge of the new enclosure. Though it is safer to conclude that the former is most likely, it might be anticipated that more pits would occur in the corners of fields – many actually occur along one side.

Fuelling Industry: Trees, Heathland and Crop Species

Chris Smart

The environmental assemblage recovered from Churchills Farm, though limited in size and from non-domestic features, provides some important information that complements observations made about the character of the historic landscape, and its potential antiquity, as well as the integration of industry within the medieval countryside.

The variety of plant remains indicate that oats, rye, wheat and barley were all grown, both during the ninth/tenth centuries and sixteenth century, but the contexts from which they were obtained indicate their use within both iron and pottery production. The presence of cereal stems, chaff, grain and weed seeds within the furnaces suggested that those engaged in the production of iron had access to unprocessed crops, which were used as a packing for the charge of ore. The dominance of oats in these samples could either suggest that it was the favoured cereal for this purpose, or that it reflects the dominant crop available to the iron workers. The Danish parallels discussed in Chapter 6 evidenced rye and wheat used for packing, not oats, so one might conclude that the choice of crop was due to availability rather than individual properties. Analysis of the assemblage from sixteenth-century pit 627 also revealed a dominance of oat, which implies that this persisted as a favoured crop on the heavy clay soils prevalent on the lower slopes of the Culm Valley. The growing of oats and rye were a long-lived regional tradition, as is discussed by Julie Jones below, with good palaeoenvironmental evidence for this distinct dietary preference being recently published (Rippon *et al.* 2006b).

In Chapter 6 Julie Jones makes a keen observation in suggesting that the presence of mixed cereals, including attendant weed species, within the closed context of a furnace, might point to the cultivation of maslin crops. A maslin is a mix of cereal species cast in the same field as a means to ensure some degree of crop success despite weather conditions. This evidence is a useful and nuanced contribution to the reconstruction of regional agricultural regimes in the South West, where transformation is thought to have occurred during the 'long eighth century' and a system known as convertible husbandry employed (*ibid.*; Fox 1991). Convertible husbandry was a rotational system that followed two to three years of cultivation with six to eight years of grass ley. The evidence of mixed crops from ninth/tenth-century Hemyock suggests that as well as single crops sown in this regime, that maslin crops might also have been introduced as a way to 'hedge ones bets'. The presence of selfheal, grasses and dock in the Churchills Farm assemblage might also be linked to the ploughing of rough grassland prior to cultivation in this rotational system. There are some other lesser indications about land cover, and the types of plants used by the early medieval community. Gorse spines and bracken stems appear in some furnace contexts and might relate to the collection of this heathland plant from the unenclosed plateaux to the south of Hemyock for use as tinder. The presence of charred oak buds, hazelnut shell and bramble fruits might imply the gathering of hedgerow trimmings to use as fuel or packing and, importantly, might support the suggestion that the fields within the historic landscape might have origins prior to the ninth century (Rippon *et al.* 2006a).

An increased proportion of heathland taxa in the later pits, associated with waste material from the sixteenth-century Hemyock pottery industry suggest that gorse and heather might have played a greater role as a tinder or fuel in the associated kilns. Larger fragments of charcoal derived from gorse present in the sixteenth-century contexts might also indicate that whole bushes were cut and brought to the site. The evolving picture is, therefore, that the historic landscape depicted on late nineteenth-century Ordnance Survey maps might have been broadly familiar to the rural community of early medieval Hemyock, and certainly to the sixteenth-century villagers. Hedgerows surrounding fields of semi-regular type might have been established before smelting began on the Churchills Farm site, and the species within these managed and cropped for use as fuel, both for industry and domestic purposes. It has been proposed that ores from the Upper Greensand plateaux, potentially near Dunkeswell, were smelted at Churchills Farm, and it is in exactly these areas that we could envisage gorse, heather and bracken being collected.

The wood charcoal presents a similar picture of a diverse ecological setting. The range of species evidenced include those typical in an industrial context – oak, hazel, alder – but also a wider range of types that include poplar and willow, pear and apple, blackthorn, cherry and hawthorn. Oak was the dominant fuel used for the smelting of iron at Churchills Farm, accounting for up to 83% of an individual assemblage, but hazel and alder were also clearly favoured. If the calculation that 0.8 ha of woodland would be needed to smelt one tonne of iron, then we must envisage a carefully managed suite of woodland resources in the vicinity of Hemyock. If Dana Challinor's observations about the size of roundwood compared to the projected model of coppice rotation presented by Rowena Gale can be upheld, then stands of coppice or pollard might have been an obvious and important component within both the ninth/tenth- and sixteenth-century landscapes. There has been no work done to try and locate charcoal burning platforms in this landscape, particularly on the higher slopes where woodland must once have been more extensive, but it is assumed that fuel for the iron industry would have been a local product. The presence of willow and poplar suggests that trees adjacent to either the nearby stream, or the River Culm, were being cut, and perhaps managed in the same way. The presence of blackthorn, hawthorn, hazel, and perhaps wild cherry, in both early and later contexts again supports the assertion that the surrounding field boundaries were established prior to the operation of the furnaces, particularly as there is no physical evidence or cultural context for large-scale reorganisation of the lowland countryside in this region. The origins of the wood fuel used by the sixteenth-century kilns cannot be determined, but presumably included material cut from woodland proper, as well as trees and shrubs within the hedgerows. Our evidence suggests demand on wood for fuel over a period of at least 600 years and, whilst management would have been crucial, it might also provide the context for the ultimate clearance of woodland from swathes of the sloping valley sides to the south of the historic village of Hemyock.

The Role of Oats in the Regional Economy between AD 800 and 1400

Julie Jones

Analysis of the charred cereal assemblages from archaeological features associated with both iron and pottery production at Churchills Farm has indicated a dominance of oats in both the ninth/tenth, and sixteenth centuries. As such it seems appropriate to further explore the regional agricultural practices and preferences that influence this trend. The role of oats in the medieval economy was two-fold: human consumption and as animal fodder particularly, for draught animals due to its high-energy value. Documentary sources suggest that bread and meat formed the staple diet for many levels of society, with consumption of dairy produce, fresh fruit and vegetables of less importance (Dyer 1983). The basic diet of the peasant in the countryside consisted of carbohydrates from grains, mostly barley and oats which were baked into bread or brewed into ale (Hammond 1998). Oats were used in biscuits and as oatmeal in porridge and children were certainly given porridge made from grain and milk (Langland 1886), while oats were a common ingredient in pottage, a liquid broth also including peas, beans and other vegetables with herbs for flavouring. As well as bread, ale was an important source of nutrition and malting and brewing were commonplace activities. It appears that oats were the preferred grain for ale in much of medieval Devon (Fox 1991, 303-7). Accounts for Glastonbury Abbey in 1287 record that 825 quarters of oats, 328 quarters of barley and 364 quarters of wheat were collected from its estates for the making of ale (Hallam 1988).

The geology, topography and climate of the South West peninsula have very much influenced agricultural practises throughout this period. Much of the lower lying land of Cornwall and Devon comprises Devonian and Carboniferous sandstones which, together with the granites of Bodmin and Dartmoor, and high moorland on Exmoor in Somerset, typically produce acidic soils (Webster 2008, 3). Devon is characterised by rolling hills, but it is the granite mass of Dartmoor which dominates the central area and separates the poor soils of the Culm Measures in North and Mid Devon from the lighter more fertile soils of the South Hams and South Devon. Hemyock is situated in the northern part of the Blackdown Hills in Devon, close to the Somerset border, in an area of acidic greensand soils. The variety and contrast in the topography of the South West peninsula has given rise to distinct regional differences in past local economies and has influenced the way in which communities farmed the land. With regard to cultivation during the medieval period, Rippon's analysis of palaeoenvironmental data (2012, 258) suggests areas to the west of the Blackdown Hills were characterised by diverse cropping regimes including significant amounts of oats, whilst areas to the east are typically dominated by wheat, a pattern also reflected in the documentary evidence.

Cultivated oats are generally only thought to become commonplace from the later Iron Age onwards, though are rarely present in quantity until the Roman period andnot as a dominant crop. By the medieval period it was one of the four staple crops in cultivation. The main cultivar was the common oat (*Avena sativa*), with both spring and winter sown varieties, although spring sowing was more common as oats are less frost hardy than other cereals. Oat has the weakest stem compared with either wheat, barley or rye, but it is the most nutritious if used for fodder. The grain is also nutritious for humans in terms of protein and calorific value, although oat yields are less than other cereals grown in good conditions. Bristle oat (*Avena strigosa*) can tolerate the poorest soils and is very hardy, but most finds are restricted to Scotland. Wild oats (*Avena fatua* and *Avena sterilis*) are successful crop weeds and may have been tolerated by the farmer in the past especially when crop yields may otherwise have been poor (Moffett 2006, 50). Oats can thrive in conditions less suitable for other cereals, particularly on poor acidic soils, and so can be used on marginal land, and are able to cope with cool wet summers, which can be typical of the South West peninsula.

The recovery of palaeobotanical evidence for oat cultivation is very much influenced by the structure of the oat itself. Oats have a different growth habit to wheat and barley, with its spikelets in panicles with three grains in each spikelet enclosed in a floret. Harvesting occurs before the grain is fully ripe so the grain is not lost when the ripe panicle shatters. Oven drying prior to storage and processing for human consumption was sometimes necessary, resulting in some of the crop becoming accidently charred and, therefore, much of the archaeological evidence for oats comes from charred remains. However, in an archaeological assemblage, it is not always possible to tell from the oat grain alone whether this is from a cultivated or wild form unless the diagnostic chaff has been preserved. In addition, the archaeological evidence for this period is very much biased by the distribution of archaeological work that has occurred through England with most coming from the south and east of the country (Moffett 2014). Comparative data from Devon, Cornwall, and Somerset, is more limited although there are a few sites that provide some data.

The thirteenth- to fourtheenth-century rural settlement at Sourton Down, on the Culm Measures north of Dartmoor, was 'dominated by oats', with small amounts of barley and rye (Weddell and Reed 1997, 115). Corn driers, associated with longhouses and barns, were excavated at the medieval villages of Houndtor and Hutholes, lying at over 300m on Dartmoor, and deserted prior to the late thirteenth or fourteenth century. Ash within one of the driers included charred oats, the most suitable crop for the local poor exposed acidic soils and suggested to have provided nutritious fodder to replace hay in winter (Beresford 1979, 143). Pollen from a nearby peat bog included abundant cereal-type pollen, including oats and rye (Austin and Walker 1985). Wheat (78%) dominated an assemblage from a twelfth/thirteenth-century farmstead at Gaffers Membury, on the south-east side of the Blackdown Hills, with oats (16%) the next most commonly occurring grain in a mixed assemblage that also included barley and rye (Jones 2001).

The excavation of a twelfth-century granary at Lydford, 10 kilometres north of Tavistock on the west side of Dartmoor, provided rare evidence of a stored crop (Green 1980). The principal cereals stored here were rye and cultivated oats (*Avena strigosa* (bristle oat) rather than *Avena sativa* (common/cultivated oat), although there was also slight evidence for bread wheat/club wheat (*Triticum aestivum/compactum*) and Celtic Bean (*Vicia faba*). The rye and bristle oats were each stored in different parts of the granary. The low concentration of weed contamination (consisting of less than 2% of the assemblage), and lack of cereal chaff, suggests that these were 'cleaned' crops stored ready for use.

Other physical evidence comes from structural remains such as corn drying ovens where accidental charring of cereals prior to storage has occurred. These are mostly a Roman and later phenomenon with excavated structures often associated with large charred cereal assemblages but are often interpreted as being multi-functional structures (van der Veen 1989). Drying of fully-processed grain was also used to harden it prior to milling. Interestingly when looking at the more recent local history in Shetland and Orkney, two areas with high rainfall like the South West, grain was dried for several reasons. These included drying of crops that had not ripened properly, to dry grain sufficiently for the following seasons use, or to parch grain prior to milling, making this process more efficient. It is emphasised that 'damp grain tends to crush and smear between millstones rather than grinding to a flour' (Fenton 1997, 375).

Structural evidence, although with limited preservation of archaeobotanical remains, was identified at the medieval farm of West Wortha, situated in the Wolf valley northwest of Dartmoor, investigated as part of the 1980s Roadford Reservoir project (Rainbird *in prep*). West Wortha originated as an enclosed settlement of low status and excavation revealed that the original settlement was surrounded by a square, ditched enclosure, with a number of buildings including the remains of a double corn drier, with a stoking flue and one side of the circular oven surviving. The compacted clay floor immediately in front of the driers was baked deep red, a result of repeated raking out of ashes from the stoking flues, although unfortunately the only cereals from this building were two charred oat grains. Charred remains were also limited in a second building containing two corn driers/ovens, although here a well-preserved oat floret suggested that cultivated oats, with traces of wheat and rye were present (Jones 2014). The heavy clays and resultant poor wet soils which dominated the Wolf valley were more suitable for livestock grazing and some of the outbuildings, though not sampled, were interpreted as animal housing. Although the Culm Measures are traditionally seen as poor agricultural land, today oats tend to dominate cropping regimes here (Rippon 2012, 50). Evidence from West Wortha shows that parts of the medieval landscape were cultivated, and that the drying and possible storage of cereal crops occurred.

As well as human consumption, oats were used in animal feed and bedding. A rich sample of over 1500 charred oat grains was recovered from twelfth- to thirteenth-century marshland deposits at Welsh Back, Bristol (Jones 1996). As well as oat grain, well preserved husks provided confirmation of domesticated oats, while the presence of straw remains, suggested by pedicels (stalks) and awns, with some weed contamination, suggests this was an unprocessed crop intended for animal fodder. Its presence here suggests stalling of animals in the medieval city with the resultant sweepings, along with much other waste, being dumped into the marsh adjacent to the River Avon. According to medieval ordinances disposal of rubbish was a major problem and deposition into the marsh was commonplace in an attempt to keep the streets clean: 'no rubble, dung or timber was to be left on the streets, at the Quay or on the Back but all to be put in the Marsh and at other places appointed' (Ralph 1981).

During the early medieval and medieval period, as today, there would have been local traditions in the use of raw material for building. Straw would have been the natural roofing material in arable districts, supplemented by, for example, heathland plants or rushes where locally available. However, a direct association between possible material derived from thatch and association with a structure is difficult to demonstrate. Letts (2000) produced a major study on smoke-blackened thatch from rooves of early buildings and showed that oats may have been used, although combed wheat reed was preferred and evidence from documents, illustrations and from surviving old thatch shows that Devon has a strong local tradition of combed straw thatching, going back at least 600 years, using a method that was probably unique to the South West (Devon County Council 2003). Letts (2000, 55) refers to cultivated oats in the thatched roof of Tytherleigh Cottage, Chardstock – a former open hall dated to the fourteenth century – and also quotes Henry Best (1642, 226) who considers that mature *haver* straw to be 'as tough and lastinge' as wheat or rye when used in thatching, so there is no reason to suppose this tradition did not extend further back in time.

Cob is the term used in Devon for mud walling and was the traditional means of wall construction in Devon from the fourteenth to the nineteenth century (Beacham 1990). It was used not only for external walling but as an infilling in internal timber-framed partitions. The basic material used was the on-site sub-soil with the addition of straw to help overcome shrinkage problems. Dung was sometimes added as a plasticiser to help in the mixing and hanging of the wet cob. Mixing was sometimes achieved by using cattle to tread the cob as it was heavy and labour-intensive work (*ibid.* 21). There are some later examples of cob construction from Devon that show the utilisation of cereal crops, including some of the tenement buildings at Hennard Jefford in the Wolf valley (Jones 2014). Samples recovered from internal timber-framed partitions at Leigh Barton farmhouse, north of Kingsbridge, included dried cereal stem fragments, occasional grains and chaff from wheat, barley, rye and oats, that were interpreted as waste products remaining after processing, together with gorse spines, leaves and flowers of heather, and weeds from arable, meadow and scrub habitats. Preservation of oat florets suggests the presence of both wild and domesticated oats (Jones and Robinson 1998).

As one of the four principal cereal crops in cultivation from AD 800-1400, oats were of great importance and had many uses. It was used in food and drink in bread, biscuits and pottage, as well as ale and beer. Oat straw would have been used as animal fodder, bedding (animal and human), in flooring and building materials such as daub or cob, thatch, in the manufacture of baskets, mats and hen-roosts, as well as for fuel or tinder. As has been outlined above, and in Chapter 4, and paralleling the continental examples outlined by Mikkelsen (1997), the iron producers of early medieval Hemyock were also using oats in the furnace packing material.

Research Pathways: Unravelling an Industrial Landscape

Chris Smart

The excavations undertaken by Exeter Archaeology in 2008 at Churchills Farm opened a window into two industries operating in this rural landscape more than half a millennium apart. The extent of the remains, both for iron working in the ninth and tenth centuries, and the growth of a regional pottery centre in the sixteenth century, were not expected when five of the eight original evaluation trenches demonstrated a high degree of later disturbance, and the other three produced only a handful of features. It was only when stripping of the site for the construction of Churchills Rise began that the extent and potential became clear. Whilst the house-builder, Summerfield Homes, funded the fieldwork the strength of the analysis presented here owes existence to Historic England who funded the multiple strands of, admittedly, high-cost scientific and specialist analysis. It is not the intention to reiterate the thanks presented in the acknowledgements at the start of this book, but to highlight that without extraordinary funding and integration of the work of a large team of specialists, such work is not normally possible. Even with these resources, and the outcome of having perhaps the largest discrete collection of well-dated ninth/tenth-century iron smelting furnaces and the recognition of a new transition-period pottery production centre at the turn of the sixteenth century, there are many questions that remain to be answered and avenues for future work that can be highlighted.

Tim Young's pilot work on the analysis of iron ore samples – using evidence from Churchills Farm and Culmstock Road, Hemyock, and Dunkeswell Airfield – clearly has a lot to offer in answering questions relating to the organisation of this industry and the links between points of extraction and smelting operations. The work of the Blackdown Hills Iron Project in the 1990s and Devon County Council's aerial survey programme, furthered knowledge about the extent of ore pits across the greensand plateaux, but the sticky issue of poor dating remains a real problem. A programme of controlled excavation of a sample of pits might, with the benefit of some cultural material or that suitable for radiocarbon dating, make inroads into the spatial phasing of extraction. The same process would enable samples of ore to be removed from a secure context and this would provide a much larger collection of material for chemical analyses against which to compare slags.

There are, as Figure 131 shows, many isolated slag dumps or places in which stray slag has been found on the Blackdown Hills, both in open country and in the curtilage of historic settlements. Whilst large-scale excavations might be cost prohibitive, characterisation using geophysical survey methods and targeted evaluation would be a reasonable approach to better understand the resource currently in hand. It is now almost twenty years since the Blackdown Hills Iron Project's fieldwork came to a halt and a renewed phase of rapid field survey might reveal new spreads of slag. There is evidence from Hemyock, or within a kilometre or so of the village, for iron production in the Roman period (Tedburrow Farm), in the eighth century (Culmstock Road) and the ninth/tenth centuries (Churchills Farm). The undated slag from later features at Churchills Farm was also sufficiently different as to point towards another post-Conquest phase. Hemyock would, therefore, make an excellent focus for detailed fieldwork and further fieldwalking and geophysical surveys might pay dividends in piecing together the extent and chronology of the industry in this location.

One small but significant triumph of the radiocarbon dating programme has been to offer a secure date for the earliest known production and use of Upper Greensand-Derived pottery, which has a broad date range between AD 950 and AD 1200. Having identified it in a context dated *c.* AD 900-930 we are now at a point to revisit its use for dating at other sites in the South West. More pertinent to Hemyock, however, is that a collection of this material was used to date features excavated by Context One at Castle View, Culmstock Road Hemyock, and a critical review of that assemblage might offer revised dating for the building and trackways recorded there.

The scientific analysis of sixteenth-century Hemyock pottery undertaken for this project has been comprehensive and we now have a much clearer picture of the technology involved, and the markets which the kilns served. What we lack, obviously, are the kilns themselves. Were the kilns destroyed by the expansion of Churchills Farm, situated elsewhere in the village, on the periphery, or off-site altogether? We have seen the nearby place-name evidence for Potter's Farm, Crocker's Farm and Little Crocker's Copse and, whilst these could be an indication of the part-time occupations of a dual potter-farmer, or just an inherited family name, surely they should be a priority for some ground investigation? It was once thought that all products of this general type – domestic wares, roof and floor tiles – came from the kilns at Donyatt but now, with two other production centres at Hemyock and Pitt Farm, Culmstock known, the question should be raised as to whether other analogous potteries were in operation. Certainly, the raw materials and expertise were readily available across the north side of the Blackdown Hills. Given the richness of the manorial records for clay rents in medieval Clayhidon, one might suspect that this would be a good a place as any to search for new kiln sites.

The authors of this book, and all of those involved behind the scenes, have pushed for this detailed analysis precisely because of the huge potential that one excavation had to offer to such a wide range of issues. We can now only hope that future research, and development-led investigations, continue to offer new windows into the industrial heritage of this now rural landscape.

Bibliography

Manuscripts

Cornwall Record Office (CRO)

Arundell Papers AR/2/495-97.

Arundell Papers AR/2/500-03.

Devon Heritage Centre (DHC), Sowton, Exeter

Lay Subsidies, Z17/3/19.

Public Record Office

CPR 1377–81, 552.

CIPM 1399–1405, No. 105.

Printed works

Adams, B. and Garrett, R. *Excavations at Pitt Farm, Culmstock: a History of the Site*. Unpublished report, 2015.

Adkins, P. "Rook Hall." Current Archaeology 115 (1989): 262-3.

Adkins, P. *Archaeology North of the River Blackwater, Essex, United Kingdom*. http://adsl06805.freespace.surfree.co.uk/ (accessed 18/11/2015).

Allan, J.P. *Medieval and Post-Medieval Finds from Exeter, 1971–1980*, Exeter Archaeology Report 3. Exeter: University of Exeter Press, 1984a.

Allan, J.P. "The pottery; the glass" in D.M. Griffiths and F.M. Griffith, 'An excavation at 39 Fore St, Totnes", *Proceedings of the Devon Archaeological Society* 42 (1984b): 79–95.

Allan, J.P. "Cleeve Abbey: the pottery." *Proceedings of the Somerset Archaeological and Natural History Society* 142 (1998): 41–75.

Allan, J.P. "A group of early 13th-century pottery from Sherborne Old Castle and its wider context." *Proceedings of the Dorset Natural History and Archaeological Society* 125 (2003): 71–82.

Allan, J.P. "Post-Roman pottery: Gabbroic, Upper Greensand-Derived and later medieval wares; discussion." In *A Roman Military Complex and Medieval Settlement on Church Hill, Calstock, Cornwall: Survey and Excavation 2007–2010*, by C. Smart, 64–7, 82–3. Oxford: British Archaeological Reports 603, 2014.

Allan, J.P. [with contributions from Dawson, D., Blake, H., Gutiérrez, A., Hughes, M.J., Ponsford, M. and Taylor, R.T.] "The pottery", in S. Hughes, 'Excavations in George Street, Bridgwater', *Proceedings of the Somerset Archaeology and Natural History Society* (forthcoming).

Allan, J.P. and Blaylock, S. "Medieval pottery and other finds from Pigs Paradise, Lundy." *Proceedings of the Devon Archaeological Society* 63 (2005): 65–91.

Allan, J.P. and Keen, L. "The medieval floor-tiles." In *Medieval and Post-Medieval Finds from Exeter, 1971–*1980, by J.P. Allan, 232–42. Exeter: University of Exeter Press, 1984.

Allan, J.P. and Keen, L. "The medieval floor-tiles", in A. Passmore, 'Archaeological recording in the graveyard of the parish church of Ottery St Mary, 2005', *Proceedings of the Devon Archaeological Society* 64 (2006): 343–45.

Allan, J.P. and Langman, G. "A group of medieval pottery from Haycroft Farm, Membury". *Proceedings of the Devon Archaeological Society* 60 (2002): 59–73.

Allan, J.P. and Langman, G. "The pottery." In *The Archaeology and History of a Drowned Devon Valley and its People: A Report on the Archaeological Investigations, 1985-1995*. Exeter: Devon Archaeological Society, in prep.

Allan, J.P. and Silvester, R.J. "Newenham Abbey, Axminster." *Proceedings of the Devon Archaeological Society* 39 (1981): 159–71.

Allan, J.P., Horner, B. and Langman, G. "Seventeenth- and eighteenth-century pottery waste from the Stella Maris Convent School site, Bideford." *Proceedings of the Devon Archaeological Society* 63 (2005): 167–203.

Allan, J.P., Cramp, C. and Horner, B. "The post-medieval pottery at Castle Hill, Great Torrington, North Devon." *Proceedings of the Devon Archaeological Society* 65 (2007): 135–81.

Allan, J., Hughes, M.J. and Taylor, R.T. "Saxo-Norman pottery in Somerset: some recent research." *Proceedings of the Somerset Archaeological and Natural History Society* 154 (2011): 165-84.

Allan, J.P., Dawson, D. and Kent, O. "The post-Roman pottery." In *Glastonbury Abbey: Archaeological Investigations 1904–*79, by R. Gilchrist and C. Green, 250–78. London: Society of Antiquaries, 2015.

Allum, C. *Land to the east of 'Castle Dene', Culmstock Road, Hemyock, Devon. An Archaeological Excavation and Watching Brief Report*. Unpublished report: Context One, 2009.

Andersen, J.C.Ø., Rollinson, G.K. and Dawson, D. "Visualisation, quantitative methodology and matrix-inclusion separation of pottery using QEMSCAN: examples of medieval and post-medieval pottery from Somerset" in S. Coxon, B. Jervis and E. Sibbeson (eds), *Insights from Innovation: Studies in Honour of the Ceramic Legacy of Professor David Peacock*, Southampton: Highfield Press, 2016a.

Andersen, J.C.Ø., Dawson, D. and Rollinson, G.K. "Mineralogical report on ceramics" in C.J. Webster, *Taunton Castle: Archaeological Research 1998–2013*, Taunton: Somerset Archaeological and Natural History Society, 2016b.

Archaeological Surveys Ltd. *Dunkeswell Airfield, Dunkeswell, Devon: Magnetometer Survey Report*. Unpublished report: Archaeological Surveys Ltd report no. 510, 2013.

Ashmore, P. "Radiocarbon dating: avoiding errors by avoiding mixed samples." *Antiquity* 73 (1999): 124–30.

Astill, G. "Economic change in later medieval England: an archaeological review", In *Social Relations and Ideas: Essays in Honour of R.H. Hilton*, edited by T.H. Aston, P.R. Coss, C. Dyer and J. Thirsk, 217–47. Cambridge: Cambridge University Press, 1983.

Austin, D. and Walker, M.J.C. "A new landscape context for Houndtor, Devon." *Medieval Archaeology* 29 (1985): 147-52.

Austin, J. *Castle View, Culmstock Road, Hemyock, Devon. Results of an Archaeological Trench Evaluation*. Unpublished report: AC Archaeology report no. ACD315/1/1, 2011.

Baxter, M. *Exploratory Multivariate Analysis in Archaeology*. Edinburgh: Edinburgh University Press, 1994.

Baxter, M. *Statistics in Archaeology*. London: Hodder, 2003.

Bayliss, A. and Tyers, I. "Interpreting radiocarbon dates using evidence from tree rings." *Radiocarbon* 46:2 (2004): 957–64.

Bayliss, A., Bronk Ramsey, C., van der Plicht, J. and Whittle, A. "Bradshaw and Bayes: towards a timetable for the Neolithic." *Cambridge Journal of Archaeology* 17.1, supplement (2007): 1–28.

Beacham, P. *Devon Building: an introduction to local traditions*. Tiverton: Devon Books, 1990.

Beaulah, G.K. "Paving tiles from Meaux Abbey." *Transactions of the East Riding Antiquarian Society* 26 (1929): 116–36.

Beaulah, G.K. "A tile memorial and other medieval tiles at Whalley Abbey." *Transactions of the Lancashire and Cheshire Antiquarian Society* 49 (1933): 95–103.

Bellamy, B., Jackson, D., and Johnston, G. "Early iron smelting in the Rockingham Forest area: a survey of the evidence." *Northamptonshire Archaeology* 29 (2001): 103–28.

Bennett, J. and Pearson, T. "Kennedy's Yard, Excavations 1974." In *The Archaeology of Taunton*, by P. Leach, 82–90. Bristol: Western Archaeological Trust, 1984.

Beresford, G. "Three deserted medieval settlements on Dartmoor: A report on the late E. Marie Minter's excavations." *Medieval Archaeology* 23 (1979): 98-158.

Bertsch, K. *Fruchte und Samen. Handbücher der praktischen Vorgeschichtsforschung. Band 1*. Stuttgart: Ferdinand Enke, 1941.

Best, H. "The Farming and Memorandum Books of Henry Best of Elmswell, 1642." In *Records of Social and Economic History, New Series VIII*, edited by D. Woodward. London: Oxford University Press, 1984.

Birch, T. "Living on the edge: making and moving iron from the 'outside', in Anglo-Saxon England." *Landscape History* 32 (2011): 5–25.

Blair, J. "Palaces or minsters? Northampton and Cheddar reconsidered." *Anglo-Saxon England* 25 (1996): 97–121.

Blaylock, S.R. *An Architectural Survey of Hemyock Castle*. Unpublished report: Exeter Museums Archaeological Field Unit report no. 89.02, 1989.

Boardman, S. and Jones, G. "Experiments on the Effects of Charring on Cereal Plant Components." *Journal of Archaeological Science* 17 (1990): 1-11.

Boesenberg, J.S. and Hewins, R.H. "An experimental investigation into the metastable formation of phosphoran olivine and pyroxene." *Geochimica et Cosmochimica Acta* 74, no.6 (2010): 1923-41.

Bond, J. "Medieval charcoal-burning in England." In *Arts and Crafts in Medieval Rural Environments, Ruralia VI 22–29 September 2005, Hungary*, edited by J. Klápšte and P. Sommer, 277–94. Turnhout: Brepols Publishers, 2007.

Boore, E. and Pearson, T. "Red earthenware pottery from the Chandos Glass Cone, Bridgwater." *Proceedings of the Somerset Archaeological and Natural History Society* 153 (2010): 131–50.

Bowyer, P. and Keys, L. "Saxon iron smelting in Bermondsey? Archaeological investigations at 150-156 Abbey Street." *Surrey Archaeological Collections* 97 (2013): 43–58.

Brears, P. "Excavations at Potovens, near Wakefield." *Post-Medieval Archaeology* 1 (1967): 3–43.

Brears, P. *The English Country Pottery: its History and Techniques*. Newton Abbot: David and Charles, 1971.

Brock, F., Higham, T., Ditchfield, P. and Bronk Ramsey, C. "Current pretreatment methods for AMS radiocarbon dating at the Oxford Radiocarbon Accelerator Unit (ORAU)." *Radiocarbon* 52 (2010): 103–12.

Brodribb, A.C.C., Hands, A.R. and Walker, D.R. *Excavations at Shakenoak Farm, near Wilcote, Oxfordshire, III, Site F*. Oxford: privately published, 1972.

Bronk Ramsey, C. "Radiocarbon calibration and analysis of stratigraphy: the OxCal program." *Radiocarbon* 37 (1995): 425–30.

Bronk Ramsey, C. "Probability and dating." *Radiocarbon* 40 (1998): 461–74.

Bronk Ramsey, C. "Comment on 'The Use of Bayesian Statistics for ^{14}C dates of chronologically ordered samples: a critical analysis'." *Radiocarbon* 42 (2000): 199–202.

Bronk Ramsey, C. "Development of the radiocarbon calibration program OxCal." *Radiocarbon* 43 (2001): 355–63.

Bronk Ramsey, C. "Dealing with outliers and offsets in radiocarbon dating." *Radiocarbon* 51 (2009a): 1023–45.

Bronk Ramsey, C. "Bayesian analysis of radiocarbon dates." *Radiocarbon* 51(2009b): 337–60.

Bronk Ramsey, C. and Lee, S. "Recent and planned developments of the program OxCal." *Radiocarbon* 55 (2013): 720–30.

Bronk Ramsey, C., Ditchfield, P. and Humm, M. "AMS methods and developments - using a gas ion source for radiocarbon AMS and GC-AMS." *Radiocarbon* 46:1 (2004a): 25–33.

Bronk Ramsey, C., Higham, T. and Leach, P. "Towards high precision AMS: progress and limitations." *Radiocarbon* 46 (2004b): 17–24.

Brown, A.G., Hawkins, C., Ryder, L., Hawken, S., Griffith, F. and Hatton, J. "Palaeoecological, archaeological and historical data and the making of Devon landscapes. I. The Blackdown Hills." *Boreas* 43, no. 4 (2014): 834-55.

Buck, C.E., Litton, C.D. and Smith, A.F.M. "Calibration of radiocarbon results pertaining to related archaeological events." *Journal of Archaeological Science* 19 (1992): 497–512.

Burchard, A. "A Saxo-Norman iron-smelting site at 'Co-op', High Street." In *Excavations in Stamford Lincolnshire 1963–1969* by C. Mahany, A. Burchard and G. Simpson, 105–144. Society for Medieval Archaeology Monograph 9, 1982.

Cabboi, S., Dunikowski, C., Leroy, M. and Merluzzo, P. 2007, *Réflexions sur les formes d'organisation du travail du fer dans le nord de la France au Haut Moyen Age (l'apport des découvertes archéologiques récentes)*. Accessed at http://medieval-europe-paris-2007.univ-paris1.fr/S.%20Cabboi %20et%20al.pdf.

Campbell, B.M.S. *English Seigniorial Agriculture, 1250–1450*. Cambridge: Cambridge University Press, 2000.

Cappers, R.T.J., Bekker, R.M. and Jans, J.E.A. *Digital Seed Atlas of the Netherlands*. Groningen: Barkhuis Publishing and Groningen University Library, 2006.

Challinor, D. "Charcoal analysis", in S.R. Taylor, A.M. Jones and T. Young, "Smelting point: Archaeological Investigations along the route of the Avon Water Main Renewal, Plympton, Devon 2009." *Proceedings of the Devon Archaeological Society* 72 (2011): 254–6.

Cherry, B. and Pevsner, N. *The Buildings of England: Devon*, 2nd edition. London: Penguin, 1989.

Cherry, J. "Franks and the medieval collection." In *A.W. Franks: Nineteenth-Century Collecting and the British Museum*, edited by M. Cayhill and J. Cherry, 184–99. London: British Museum, 1997.

Clarke, C.P. *12a Churchills Rise, Hemyock, Devon. Archaeological Monitoring and Recording Archive Report*. Unpublished report: Arrowhead Archaeology report no. AA 157, 2012.

Cleere, H. and Crossley, D. *The Iron Industry of the Weald*. Leicester: Leicester University Press, 1985.

Coleman-Smith, R. "Excavations in the Donyatt Potteries: Site 13." *Post-Medieval Archaeology* 36 (2002): 118–72.

Coleman-Smith R. and Pearson, T. *Excavations at Donyatt and Nether Stowey; Interim Report*. Southampton: Donyatt Research Committee, 1970.

Coleman-Smith, R. and Pearson, T. *Excavations in the Donyatt Potteries*. Chichester: Phillimore, 1988.

Compton, A. "Notice of a decorative pavement in Haccombe church, Devonshire." *Archaeological Journal* 3 (1846): 151–4.

Cotswold Archaeology. *Land at Dunkeswell Airfield, Dunkeswell, Devon. Archaeological Strip, Map and Sample Excavation Report*. Unpublished report: Cotswold Archaeology report no. 14418, 2015.

Cramp, C. "Medieval and post-medieval floor-tiles at Weare Gifford church, North Devon." *Proceedings of the Devon Archaeological Society* 70 (2012): 133–46.

Crane, P. and Murphy, K. "Early medieval settlement, iron smelting and crop processing at South Hook, Herbranston, Pembrokeshire, 2004–05." *Archaeologia Cambrensis* 159 (2010): 117–96.

Cranstone, D. (ed.) *Historical Metallurgy Society Newsletter* 11 summer (1988).

Crew, P. "Bryn y Castell Hillfort – a Late Prehistoric Iron Working settlement in north-west Wales." In *The Crafts of the Blacksmith*, edited by B.G. Scott and H. Cleere, 91-100. Belfast: Ulster Museum/UISPP Comité pour la Sidérurgie Ancienne, 1987.

Crew, P. "Crawcwellt West excavations 1986-1989. A late prehistoric ironworking settlement." *Archaeology in Wales* 29 (1989): 11-16.

Crew, P. "The Experimental Production of Prehistoric Bar Iron." *Historical Metallurgy* 25 (1991): 21-36.

Crew, P. *Blackdown Hills, Devon: preliminary report on the slags from Sweetlands, Livenhays, Moorlands, Hemyock and Woodbury Great Close*. Unpublished report, 1993.

Crew, P. "Excavations at Crawcwellt West, Merioneth, 1990-98: A late prehistoric upland ironworking settlement." *Archaeology in Wales* 38 (1998): 22-35.

Crew, P. *Iron working in Merioneth from prehistory to the 18th century. Darlithiau Coffa Merfyn Williams Memorial Lectures No. 2, Snowdonia National Park/ Plas Tan y Bwlch, Maentwrog*. Unpublished report, 2009.

Daveau, I., Goustard, V. and Bahain, J-J. "Un complexe métallurgique et minier du haut Moyen Age. Le site des Fourneaux à Vert-Saint-Denis (Seine-et-Marne)." *Gallia* 57 (2000): 77-99.

Davey, W. and Walker, H. *The Harlow Pottery Industries*. Medieval Pottery Research Group Occasional Paper, 2009.

Dawson, D. and Dawson, N. "The pottery." In *Taunton Castle: Archaeological Research 1998–2013*, by C.J. Webster, 103-30. Taunton: Somerset Archaeological and Natural History Society, 2016.

Dawson, D. and Kent, O. "Reduction fired low-temperature ceramics." *Post-Medieval Archaeology* 33 (1999): 164–78.

Devon County Council. *Thatch in Devon*. Exeter: Devon County Council, 2013, available at http://www.devon.gov.uk/thatching.pdf.

Dyer, C. "The social and economic changes of the late middle ages, and the pottery of the period." *Medieval Ceramics* 6, (1982): 33–42.

Dyer, C. "English diet in the later middle ages." In *Social Relations and Ideas: Essays in Honour of R.H. Hilton*, edited by T.H. Aston, P.R. Cross, C.C. Dyer and J. Thirsk, 191-214. Cambridge: Cambridge University Press, 1983.

Dyer, C. *An Age of Transition? Economy and Society in England in the Later Middle Ages*. Oxford: Oxford University Press, 2005.

Dymond, R. "The history of the parish of St Petrock, Exeter, as shown by its Churchwardens' Accounts and Other Records." *Reports and Transactions of the Devonshire Association* 14 (1882): 402–92.

Eames, E.S. "The Canynges pavement." *Journal of the British Archaeological Association* 3rd series, 14 (1951): 33–46.

Eames, E.S. *Catalogue of Medieval Lead-glazed Earthenware Tiles in the Department of Medieval and Later Antiquities British Museum*. London: British Museum, 1980.

Emden, A.B. *Medieval Decorated Tiles in Dorset*. Chichester: Phillimore, 1977.

Erskine, A.M. (ed.) *The Devonshire Lay Subsidy of 1332*. Exeter: Devon and Cornwall Record Society, New Series 14, 1969.

Eschenlohr, L. and Serneels, V. *Les bas fourneaux mérovingiens de Boécourt, les Boulies (JU, Suisse)*. Porrentruy: Cahier d'archéologie jurassienne, 3, 1991.

Eschenlohr, L., Friedli, V., Linder, C. and Senn, M. *Develier-Courtételle, un habitat rural mérovingien 2. Métallurgie du fer et mobilier métallique*. Porrentruy: Cahier d'archéologie jurassienne, 14, 2007.

Espelund, A. "Bloomery ironmaking during the Roman period in mid-Norway." *Historical Metallurgy* 48 (2015): 16-24.

Exeter Archaeology. *Archaeological Evaluation at the Former Halls Engineering Works, Market Square, Hemyock, Devon*. Unpublished report: Exeter Archaeology Report No. 05.04, 2005.

Fell, D. *Archaeological Evaluation: Land at Wakerley, Northamptonshire, Volume 2: Appendices*. Unpublished report: Archaeological Services and Consultancy Ltd, 2007.

Fenton, A. *The Northern Isles: Orkney and Shetland*. Edinburgh: Tuckwell Press, 1997.

Field, J. *A History of English Field-Names*. London: Longman, 1993.

Finberg, H.P.R. *The Early Charters of Devon and Cornwall*. Leicester: University College of Leicester, 1953.

Fleming, R. "Recycling in Britain after the Fall of Rome's Metal Economy." *Past and Present* 217 (2012): 3–45.

Fox, H.S.A. "Farming practices and techniques: Devon and Cornwall." In *Agrarian History of England and Wales; III 1348*-1500, edited by E. Miller, 303-23. Cambridge: Cambridge University Press, 1991.

Fox, H.S.A. and Padel, O.J. (eds) *The Cornish Lands of the Arundells of Lanherne, Fourteenth to Sixteenth Centuries*. Exeter: Devon and Cornwall Record Society, New Series 41, 2000.

Freeman, S.P.H.T., Cook, G.T., Dougans, A.B., Naysmith, P., Wicken, K.M. and Xu, S. "Improved SSAMS performance." *Nuclear Instruments and Methods B* 268 (2010): 715–7.

Fyfe, R.M., Briwn, A.G. and Rippon, S.J. "Characterising the late prehistoric, 'Romano-British' and medieval landscape, and dating the emergence of a regionally distinct agricultural system in South West Britain.", *Journal of Archaeological Science* 31 (2004): 1699-1714.

Gale, R. "Appendix 2: Charcoal Fuel Analysis", in S.J. Reed, G. Juleff and O.J. Bayer, 'Three Late Saxon Iron-Smelting Furnaces at Burlescombe, Devon', *Proceedings of the Devon Archaeological Society* 64 (2006): 71–122.

Gallois, R.W. "The stratigraphy of the Upper Greensand (Cretaceous) of South-West England." *Geoscience in South-West England* 11 (2004): 21-29.

Gallois, R.W. "The origin of the Clay-with-Flints: the missing link." *Geoscience in South-West England* 12 (2009): 153-161.

Gibson, J. "Jane Gibson meets the potters of Bahla, Oman." *Ceramic Review* 211 (2005): 46–7.

Gilchrist, R. and Green, C. *Glastonbury Abbey: Archaeological Investigations 1904–79*. London: Society of Antiquaries, 2015.

Goffer, Z. *Archaeological Chemistry*, 2nd edition. New Jersey: Wiley Interscience, 2007.

Good, G.L. "The excavation of two docks at Narrow Quay, Bristol, 1978–9." *Post-Medieval Archaeology* 21 (1987): 25–126.

Gotch, J.A. *Early Renaissance Architecture in England: A Historical and Descriptive Account of the Tudor, Elizabethan, and Jacobean periods, 1500–1625*. London: Batsford, 1901.

Goustard, V., Leroy, M., Serneels, V. and Daveau, I. "La production sidérurgique en contexte d'habitat aux VIIIe/XIIe siècles : l'apport des fouilles récentes en France et en Suisse", in *L'innovation technique au Moyen Âge. Actes du VIe Congrès international d'Archéologie Médiévale (1-5 Octobre 1996, Dijon - Mont Beuvray - Chenôve - Le Creusot - Montbard)*, 139-44. Caen: Société d'Archéologie Médiévale, 1998.

Gover, J.E.B., Mawer, A. and Stenton, F.M. *The Place-Names of Devon, Volume* 2. London: English Place-Name Society, 1932.

Green, F. *Grain deposits from the 12th century granary, Lydford, Devon*. Unpublished report: Ancient Monuments Laboratory Report (Old Series) 3108, 1980.

Grieve, M. *A Modern Herbal, Volume 1 (A-H)*. New York: Dover Publications Inc., 1971.

Griffith, F. and Weddell, P. "Ironworking in the Blackdown Hills: results of recent survey." *Mining History* 13 (1996): 27–34.

Grime, J.P., Hodgson, J.G. and Hunt, R. *Comparative Plant Ecology*. London: Unwin Hyman Ltd, 1988.

Groenewoudt, B.J. and Van Nie, M. "Assessing the Scale and Organisation of Germanic Iron Production in Heeten, the Netherlands." *Journal of European Archaeology* 3 (1995):187-215.

Hall, D.W. "Excavations at the pottery production centre of Colstoun, East Lothian 1939, 1969, 1971, 1977, 1999 and 2000." *Medieval Ceramics* 28 (2004): 35–74.

Hall, D.W. "Recent excavations of pottery kilns and workshops at New Carron Road, Stenhousemuir, 2007." *Medieval Ceramics* 30 (2008): 3–20.

Hallam, A.D. "Decorated medieval tiles from Taunton." *Proceedings of the Somerset Archaeological and Natural History Society* 95 (1951): 63–71.

Hallam, H.E. (ed.) *The Agrarian History of England and Wales, Vol II, 1042-1350*. Cambridge: Cambridge University Press, 1988.

Halstead, P. and Jones, G. "Agrarian Ecology in the Greek islands: time, stress, scale and risk." *Journal of Hellenistic Studies* 109 (1989): 41-55.

Hammond, P.W. *Food and Feast in Medieval England*. Stroud: Sutton Publishing, 1998.

Hancock J.M. "Transgression of the Cretaceous sea in south-west England." *Proceedings of the Ussher Society* 2 (1969): 61–83.

Harcourt, J. "The medieval floor-tiles of Cleeve Abbey, Somerset." *Journal of the British Archaeological Association* 153 (2000): 30–70.

Harcourt, J. "Medieval floor tiles", in *Glastonbury Abbey: Archaeological Investigations 1904–79*, by R. Gilchrist and C. Green, 278-93. London: Society of Antiquaries, 2015.

Harrington, S. and Welch, M. *The Early Anglo-Saxon Kingdoms of Southern Britain AD 450-650: Beneath the Tribal Hidage*. Oxford: Oxbow, 2014.

Haslam, J. "A Middle Saxon iron smelting site at Ramsbury, Wiltshire." *Medieval Archaeology* 24 (1980): 1–68.

Hather, J.G. *The Identification of Northern European Woods: A Guide for Archaeologists and Conservators*. London: Archetype Publications, 2000.

Heaton, M.J. "Two mid-Saxon grain driers and later medieval features at Chantry Fields, Gillingham, Dorset." *Proceedings of the Dorset Natural History and Archaeological Society* 114 (1992): 97–126.

Henriksen, P.S. "Rye cultivation in the Danish Iron Age – some new evidence from iron-smelting furnaces." *Vegetation History and Archaeobotany* 12 (2003): 177-185.

Hinton, D.A. "Revised dating of the Worgret structure." *Proceedings of the Dorset Natural History and Archaeological Society* 114 (1992): 258-60.

Hjärthner-Holdar, E., Grandin, L. and Forenius, S. "Blästbruk – finns det en systematic mellan tid, rum och typ?" In *Ovnstypologi og Ovnskronologi I den Nordiske Jernvinna*, edited by B. Rundberget, J.H. Larsen and

T.H. Borse Haraldsen, 24-38. Oslo: Kulturhistorisk Museum, 2013.

Hodgkinson, J. *The Wealden iron industry*. Stroud: The History Press, 2008.

Hohler, C. "Medieval paving-tiles in Buckinghamshire." *Records of Buckinghamshire* 14 (1942): 1–49, 99–132.

Holdsworth, P. "Saxon Southampton: a new review." *Medieval Archaeology* 20 (1976): 26-61.

Hollinrake, C. and Hollinrake, N. *Carhampton, Eastbury Farm: Archaeological Works 1993-95*. Unpublished report, 1998.

Hooke, D. *Pre-Conquest Charter Bounds of Devon and Cornwall*. Woodbridge: Boydell Press, 1994.

Hughes, M.J. "ICP-AES analysis of South Somerset pottery and South Netherlands tin-glazed maiolica from Cleeve Abbey", in J.P. Allan, 'Cleeve Abbey: the pottery', *Proceedings of the Somerset Archaeological and Natural History Society* 142 (1998): 59–75.

Hughes, M.J. "Report on the analysis by Inductively-Coupled Plasma Atomic Emission Spectrometry (ICP-AES) of late 13th- to 14th-century pottery sherds from Haycroft Farm, Membury", in J.P. Allan and G. Langman, 'A group of medieval pottery from Haycroft Farm, Membury', *Proceedings of the Devon Archaeological Society* 60 (2002): 67–72.

Hughes, M.J. "Report on the analysis by Inductively-Coupled Plasma Atomic Emission Analysis (ICP–AES) of 13th-century pottery sherds from Sherborne Old Castle", in J.P. Allan, 'A group of early 13th-century pottery from Sherborne Old Castle and its wider context', *Proceedings of the Dorset Natural History and Archaeological Society* 125 (2003):79–82.

Hughes, M.J. "The analysis by Inductively Coupled Plasma-Atomic Emission Analysis (ICP-AES) and -Mass Spectrometry (ICP-MS) of medieval pottery from Pigs Paradise, Lundy Island", in J.P. Allan and S. Blaylock, 'Medieval pottery and other finds from Pigs Paradise, Lundy." *Proceedings of the Devon Archaeological Society* 63 (2005): 78–88.

Hughes, M.J. "The analysis by Inductively Coupled Plasma-Atomic Emission Analysis (ICP-AES) and -Mass Spectrometry (ICP-MS) of Saxo-Norman pottery from Somerset", in J.P. Allan, M.J. Hughes and R.T. Taylor, 'Saxo-Norman pottery in Somerset: some recent research', *Proceedings of the Somerset Archaeological and Natural History Society* 154 (2010a): 177–82.

Hughes, M.J. "Inductively coupled plasma emission spectrometry analysis of south Hertfordshire-type grey wares." In *Shelly-sandy ware and the grey ware industries: a dated type series of London medieval pottery. Part* 5, by L. Blackmore and J. Pearce, 273-77. London: Museum of London Archaeology, Monograph 49, 2010b.

Hughes, M.J. "Plasma spectrometry analysis (Atomic Emission ICP-AES) of post-Roman pottery from Calstock", in J.P. Allan, 'Post-Roman pottery: Gabbroic, Upper Greensand-Derived and later medieval wares', in *A Roman Military Complex and Medieval Settlement on Church Hill, Calstock, Cornwall: Survey and Excavation 2007–2010*, by C. Smart, 70-7. Oxford: British Archaeological Reports 603, 2014.

Hughes, M.J. "Inductively coupled plasma spectrometry (ICPS) analysis of tin-glazed pottery from Glastonbury Abbey." In *Glastonbury Abbey: Archaeological Investigations 1904–79*, by R. Gilchrist and C. Green, 268-70. London: Society of Antiquaries, 2015.

Hughes, S. *Land to the rear of Churchill's Farm, High Street, Hemyock, Devon. Results of an Archaeological Trench Evaluation*. Unpublished report: AC Archaeology report no. ACD87/2/0, 2009a.

Hughes, S. *Results of a trench evaluation at 3 Broadway, adjacent to Hemyock Motors, Culmstock Road, Hemyock, Devon. Interim Archaeological Statement*. Unpublished report: AC Archaeology report no. ACD133/2/1, 2009b.

Hughes, S. *Old Tennis Court Site, Station Road, Hemyock. Results of an Archaeological Trench Evaluation*. Unpublished report: AC Archaeology report no. ACD281/1/0, 2011.

Hull, G. and Taylor, K. "Archaeological sites on the route of the N21 Castleisland to Abbeyfeale road improvement scheme, Co. Kerry." *Journal of the Kerry Archaeological and Historical Society* Series 2 (6) (2006): 5-59.

Hurst, J.G. "Post-medieval pottery' in E. Greenfield, 'Excavation of a bombed site in Chapel Street, Exeter." *Reports and Transactions of the Devonshire Association* 96 (1964): 361–79.

Hurst, J.G. and Gaimster, D.R.M. "Werra ware in Britain, Ireland and North America." *Post-Medieval Archaeology* 39/2 (2005): 267–93.

Irving, A. *A Research Framework for Post-Roman Ceramic Studies in Britain*. Medieval Pottery Research Group Occasional Paper 6, 2011.

Isaac, K.P. "Tertiary weathering profiles in the plateau deposits of east Devon." *Proceedings of the Geologists' Association* 92 (1981): 159-168.

Jackson, D. "Iron Age and Anglo-Saxon settlement and activity around the Hunsbury Hillfort." *Northamptonshire Archaeology* 25 (1993-4): 35–46.

Jacomet, S. *Identification of cereal remains from archaeological sites*. Archaeobotany Lab IPAS, Basel University, 2006 (www.ipna.unibas.ch/archbot/pdf).

Jarrett, M.J.M. and Stevens, B. *Out of Dunkeswell – US Navy Fleet Airwing* 7th *and 479*th *Antisubmarine Group USAAF*. Devon: South West Airfields Heritage Trust, 2010.

Jensen, N.L. "A treatise on iron ore as found in the bogs and swamps of Norway and the process of turning it into iron and steel", Abridged translation of Evenstad 1790, *Bulletin of the Historical Metallurgy Group* 2 (1968): 61-65.

Jones, J. *5 Welsh Back. Environmental sampling programme*. Unpublished report, 1996.

Jones, J. *Charred plant remains from Gaffers Membury, Devon*. Unpublished report, 2001.

Jones, J. *Roadford Reservoir: plant macrofossil remains from West Wortha and Hennard Jefford*. Unpublished report, 2014.

Jones, J. and Robinson, M. "Plant macrofossil and insect remains." In "Recent building recording and excavations at Leigh Barton, Churstow, Devon", by S. Brown. *Proceedings of the Devon Archaeological Society* 56 (1998): 5-108.

Jones, P. and Hughes, S. *Hemyock Motors Workshop site, Culmstock Road, Hemyock. Results of an Archaeological Trench Evaluation and Watching Brief.* Unpublished report: AC Archaeology report no. ACD207/2/0, 2013.

Joosten, I. and Van Nie, M. "Vroeg-middeleeuwse ijzerproduktie op de Veluwe." *Madog* 9, 3 (1995): 203-211.

Joosten, I., Elburg, M.A., Jansen, B., and Kars, H. "Calculation of the output of an early historical iron production site in the Veluwe Area, the Netherlands." In Material Culture in Medieval Europe, Papers of the 'Medieval Europe Brugge 1997' Conference, Vol. 7, edited by G. de Boe and F. Verhaeghe, 43-51. Zellik: Instituut voor het Archeologisch Patrimonium, 1997.

Jope, E.M. and Threlfall, R.I. "The twelfth-century castle at Ascot Doilly, Oxfordshire: its history and excavation." *Antiquaries Journal* 39 (1959): 219–73.

Jouttijärvi, A. and Voss, O., "Drengsted/ Scharmbeck slaggegrube ovnen i Danmark og i Skandinavien." In *Ovnstypologi og Ovnskronologi I den Nordiske Jernvinna*, edited by B. Rundberget, J.H. Larsen and T.H. Borse Haraldsen, 83-92. Oslo: Kulturhistorisk Museum, 2013.

Keen, L. "A series of seventeenth- and eighteenth-century lead-glazed relief tiles from North Devon." *Journal of the British Archaeological Association*, 3rd series 32 (1969): 144–70.

Keen, L. "Medieval floor-tiles from Campsea Ash Priory." *Proceedings of the Suffolk Institute of Archaeology and History* 32/2 (1971): 140–51.

Keen, L. "The medieval decorated tile pavements at Worcester." In *Medieval Art and Architecture at Worcester Cathedral*, edited by G. Popper, 144–60. British Archaeological Association Conference Transactions 1, 1978.

Keen, L. "The medieval floor-tiles", in P.M. Christie and J.G. Coad, 'Excavations at Denny Abbey', *The Archaeological Journal* 137 (1980): 212–22.

Keen, L. "Windsor Castle and the Penn tile industry." In *Windsor: Medieval Archaeology, Art Architecture of the Thames Valley*, edited by L. Keen and E. Scarff, 219–37. British Archaeological Association Conference Transactions 25, 2002.

Keen, L. "The floor-tiles", in *Sherborne Abbey and School Excavations 1972–76 and 1990*, by L. Keen and P. Ellis, 118-30. Dorset Natural History and Archaeological Society Monograph 16. Dorchester: Dorset Natural History and Archaeological Society, 2005.

Keepax, C.A. "Charcoal from an ironworking bloomery at Ashdown Forest". In *Ancient Monuments Laboratory Reports*. London: Department of the Environment, 1980.

Kerr-Peterson, K. *New Aircraft Storage Sheds, Dunkeswell Airfield, Devon. Results of an Archaeological Watching Brief.* Unpublished report: AC Archaeology report no. ACD904/2/1, 2014.

Keys, L. *Assessment of iron slag and related high temperature debris from sites in Lyminge, Kent (Site codes: LYM 08, LYM 09, LYM 10 and AFL 10).* Unpublished Report, 2011.

Ladle, L. *Excavations at Bestwall Quarry, Wareham 1992-2005: Volume 2, the Iron Age and later landscape.* Dorset Natural History and Archaeological Society Monograph 20. Dorchester: Dorset Natural History and Archaeological Society, 2012.

Langland, W. *The Vision of William concerning 'Piers the Plowman'*. 1886.

Larsen, J.H. "Kittilbu, Dokkfløy og Norsk Jernvinneforskning." In *Ovnstypologi og Ovnskronologi I den Nordiske Jernvinna*, edited by B. Rundberget, J.H. Larsen and T.H. Borse Haraldsen, 11-23. Oslo: Kulturhistorisk Museum, 2013a.

Larsen, J.H. "Ovner med slaggrop i Sydøst-Norge – 400 BC–AD 800 – likheter og forskjeller." In *Ovnstypologi og Ovnskronologi I den Nordiske Jernvinna*, edited by B. Rundberget, J.H. Larsen and T.H. Borse Haraldsen, 59-72. Oslo: Kulturhistorisk Museum, 2013b.

Laurent, H., Laurent, S. and Raïssouni, B. "Zones de réduction et zones de forge ? La région de Berthelange et le Finage dolois (Franche-Comté)." In *La sidérurgie de l'Est de la France dans son context européen : archéologie et archéométrie, actes du colloque de Besançon, 9-13 Nov. 1993*, edited by M. Mangin, 189-200. Paris: Les Belles Lettres, 1994.

Le Patourel, H.E.J. "Documentary evidence and the medieval pottery industry." *Medieval Archaeology* 12 (1968): 101–26.

Leroy, M. *La sidérurgie en Lorraine avant le haut fourneau: l'utilisation du minerai de fer oolithique en réduction directe*, Monographie du Centre de Recherches Archéologiques 18. Calcaire: Centre National Recherche Scientifique, 1997.

Leroy, M. and Merluzzo, P. "Les ateliers sidérurgiques médiévaux de Saint-Dizier (Haute-Marne)." *Bulletin de la Société Archéologique Champenoise* 4 (1998).

Letts, J. *Smoke Blackened Thatch. A unique source of late medieval plant remains from southern England.* London: English Heritage, 2000.

Lowe, B.J. *Decorated Medieval Floor-Tiles of Somerset.* Taunton: Somerset Archaeological and Natural History Society and Somerset County Museums Service, 2003.

Lyngstrøm, H. "Slaggeaftapningsovne i Danmark, udgravninger og forsøg." In *Ovnstypologi og Ovnskronologi I den Nordiske Jernvinna*, edited by B. Rundberget, J.H. Larsen and T.H. Borse Haraldsen, 119-33. Oslo: Kulturhistorisk Museum, 2013.

Lysons, D. *Magna Britannia*, London: Cadell and Davies, 1822.

MacCaffrey, W.T. *Exeter, 1540–1640: The Growth of an English County Town*, 2nd edition. Cambridge, Mass. and London: Harvard University Press, 1975.

Mack, I., McDonnell, G., Murphy, S., Andrews, P. and Wardley, K. "Liquid steel in Anglo-Saxon England." *Historical Metallurgy* 34 (2000): 87-96.

Maddicott, J. "Trade, industry and wealth of King Alfred." *Past and Present* 123 (1989): 3-51.

Marguerie, D. and Hunot, J. "Charcoal analysis and dendrology: data from archaeological sites in north-western France." *Journal of Archaeological Science* 34 (9) (2007): 1417-33.

Maynard, D. "Excavations on a pipeline near the River Frome, Worgret, Dorset." *Proceedings of the Dorset Natural History and Archaeological Society* 110 (1988): 77-98.

McCarthy, M. and Brooks, C. *Medieval Pottery in Britain AD 900–*1600. Leicester: Leicester University Press, 1988.

McDonnell, G. and Young, T. "Chapter 5: Metalworking." In *Destined to serve: use of the outer grounds of St Augustine's Abbey, Canterbury, before, during and after the time of the monks. Canterbury Christ Church Excavations 1983-2007*, edited by A. Hicks, 167-183. Canterbury Archaeological Trust Occasional Paper No 11. Canterbury: Canterbury Archaeological Trust, 2015.

McDonnell, J.G. *The Ironworking Residues from Romsey, Hampshire.* Unpublished report: Ancient Monuments Laboratory report no. 72/88, 1988.

McDonnell, J.G. "Iron and its alloys in the fifth to eleventh centuries AD in England." *World Archaeology* 20 (1989): 373-82.

Mikkelsen P.H. "Straw in slag-pit furnaces." In *Early Iron Production – Archaeology, Technology and Experiments*, edited by L.C. Nørbach, 63-6. Technical Report no. 3 Historical-Archaeological Experimental Centre, 1997.

Mikkelsen P.H. *The growth of the field-agricultural systems and strategy of cultivation in the Iron Age agriculture. Archaeobotanical investigations of iron-smelting furnaces from the 1st to 8th centuries AD.* Unpublished PhD thesis: Institut for Forhistorik Arkaeologi, Århus Universitet, Denmark, 1998.

Milby, S. *Dunkeswell Parachute Club, Dunkeswell Air Centre, East Devon. An Archaeological Programme of Works: a Desk-Based Appraisal and Field Evaluation.* Unpublished report: Context One, 2010.

Mitchell, N. *The medieval floor-tiles from Wolford Chapel, near Dunkeswell, East Devon.* Unpublished MA dissertation: Department of Archaeology, University of Leicester, 1995.

Mjærum, A. "Ovnene i Breiveskaret – trekk ved jernproduksjonen i vikingtiden og middelalderen i et skar ved Hovden i Setesdalen." In *Ovnstypologi og Ovnskronologi I den Nordiske Jernvinna*, edited by B. Rundberget, J.H. Larsen and T.H. Borse Haraldsen, 134-44. Oslo: Kulturhistorisk Museum, 2013.

Moffett, L. *The Archaeobotanical Evidence for Saxon and Medieval Agriculture in Central England circa 500AD to 1500AD.* Unpublished MPhil thesis: University of Birmingham, 1988.

Moffett, L. "The archaeology of medieval plant foods." In *Food in Medieval England: Diet and Nutrition*, by C.M. Woolgar, D. Serjeantson and T. Waldron, 41-55. Oxford: Oxford University Press, 2006.

Moffett, L. "Arable Farming in Anglo-Saxon England, 1: The crops." In *Anglo-Saxon Farms and Farming*, by D. Banham and R. Faith, 19-40. Oxford: Oxford University Press, 2014.

Moorhouse, S. and Roberts, I. *Wrenthorpe Potteries: excavations of 16th and 17th-century potting tenements near Wakefield, 1983–8*. Wakefield: West Yorkshire Archaeology Service, Yorkshire Archaeology 2, 1992.

Morris, B. "The missing link – the Exeter Inn, Barnstaple: North Devon pottery in the 16th century." *Proceedings of the Devon Archaeological Society* (forthcoming).

Morton, A.D. (ed.) *Excavations at Hamwic: Volume 1.* York: Council for British Archaeology Research Report 84, 1992.

Mudd, A. "Early to middle Saxon iron smelting furnaces at Fineshade Abbey, Northamptonshire." *Northamptonshire Archaeology* 34 (2006): 81–95.

Mynard, D.C. "The Little Brickhill tile kilns and their products." *J. Brit. Archaeol. Ass.* 3rd ser. 3 (1975): 55–80.

Newstead, S. "Merida no more: Portuguese Redware in Newfoundland." In *Exploring Atlantic Transitions: Archaeologies of Transience and Permanence in New Found Lands*, edited by P. Pope and S. Lewis-Simpson, 140–51. Society for Post-Medieval Archaeology Monograph 8, 2013.

Newstead, S. "Cod, salt and wine: tracing Portuguese in the English North Atlantic World." *North Atlantic Archaeology* 3 (2014): 71–89.

Newstead, S. *The Oldest Alliance: a Material Exploration of Early Modern Portuguese–English Relationships*. Unpublished PhD thesis: University of Leicester, 2015.

Norbach, L.C. "An experiment using wood as fuel in a slag-pit furnace." In *Early Iron Production – Archaeology, Technology and Experiments*, edited by L.C. Nørbach, 59-62. Technical Report no. 3 Historical-Archaeological Experimental Centre, 1997.

O'Brien, R., Quinney, P. and Russell, I. "Preliminary report on the archaeological excavation and finds retrieval strategy of the Hiberno-Scandinavian site of Woodstown 6, County Waterford." *Journal of the Waterford Archaeological and Historical Society* 61 (2005): 13–122.

Orme, N. *The Church in Devon 400–1560,* Exeter: Impress Books, 2013.

Orton, C. and Hughes, M. *Pottery in Archaeology*. Cambridge: Cambridge University Press, 1993.

Oxford Archaeological Unit. *Clearwell Quarry Extension Phase 6, Stowe Hill, Gloucestershire, archaeological evaluation*. Unpublished Report: Oxford Archaeological Unit report no. 1265, 2002.

Papazotou, G. "Veria workshop production." In *Byzantine Glazed Ceramics: the Art of Sgraffito*, by D. Papanikola-Bakirtzi, 254–5. Athens: Archaeological Receipts Fund, 1999.

Parker, J.H. *A Glossary of Terms used in Grecian, Roman and Italian and Gothic Architecture*, 5th edition. Oxford: Parker, 1850.

Paynter, S. "Innovations in bloomery smelting in Iron Age and Romano-British England." In *Metals and Mines. Studies in Archaeometallurgy*, edited by S. la Niece, D. Hook and P. Craddock, 202-10. London: Archetype Publications in association with the British Museum, 2007.

Paynter, S. *Pre-industrial Ironworks. Introductions to Heritage Assets*. Unpublished English Heritage guidance, 2011.

Peacock, D.P.S. "Ceramics in Roman and medieval archaeology." In *Pottery in Early Commerce*, edited by D.P.S. Peacock, 21–34. London: Academic Press, 1977.

Pearson, T. "Medieval and post-medieval ceramics in Taunton." In *The Archaeology of Taunton*, by P. Leach, 142–4 and MF 7–153. Bristol: Western Archaeological Trust, 1984.

Pearson, T., with Dawson, D. and Ponsford, M. "Evidence of seventeenth-century pottery production at Wrangway, Somerset." *Proceedings of the Somerset Archaeological and Natural History Society* 158, (2015): 81–103.

Pelet, P-L. *Une industrie méconnue. Fer charbon acier dans le Pays de Vaud*. Lausanne: Bibliothèque historique vaudoise, 1973.

Peter, O.B. "Notes on encaustic tiles and the designs portrayed on them." *Archaeologia Cambrensis,* 5th series, 13 (1896): 307–14.

Pine, J., Allen, J.R.L. and Challinor, D. "Saxon iron smelting at Clearwell Quarry, St Briavels, Lydney, Gloucestershire." *Archaeology in the Severn Estuary* 20 (2009): 9–40.

Pleiner, R. *Iron in Archaeology: The European bloomery smelters*. Prague: Academie Vedceski republicky, 2000.

Rackham, O. "The Forest of Neroche and the kiln supply of the Donyatt kilns." In *Excavations in the Donyatt Potteries*, by R. Coleman-Smith and T. Pearson, 3-8. Chichester: Phillimore, 1988.

Rackham, O. *Woodlands*. London: Collins, 2006.

Radford, C.A.R. "Tiles and other objects found at Frithelstock Priory." *Proceedings of the Devon Archaeological Exploration Society* 2 (3) (1935): 198–9.

Rahtz, P.A. *The Saxon and Medieval Palaces at Cheddar: excavations 1960-62*. Oxford: British Archaeological Reports British Series 65, 1979.

Rainbird, P. (ed.) *The Archaeology and History of a Drowned Devon Valley and its People: A Report on the Archaeological Investigations, 1985-1995*. Exeter: Devon Archaeological Society, in prep.

Rainbird, P. and Young, T.P. "Saxon iron smelting furnaces at Culmstock Road, Hemyock, Devon." *Proceedings of the Devon Archaeological Society* 73 (2015): 279-314.

Ralph, E. *The Streets of Bristol*. Bristol: Bristol Branch of the Historical Association, 1981.

Rasmussen, K.L., Rahbek, U. and Voss, O. "Radiocarbon dating of the iron production in slag-pit furnaces in Jutland." *Journal of Danish Archaeology* 14 (2006): 127-138.

Reed, S.J. *Blackdown Hills Ironworking Project: Archaeological recording of an iron extraction pit, Broadhembury, Devon*. Unpublished report: Exeter Archaeology report 97.38, 1997.

Reed, S.J., Juleff, G. and Bayer, O.J. "Three late Saxon iron-smelting furnaces at Burlescombe, Devon." *Proceedings of the Devon Archaeological Society* 64 (2006): 71–122.

Reimer, P.J., Bard, E., Bayliss, A., Beck, J.W., Blackwell, P., Bronk Ramsey, C., Buck, C.E., Cheng, H., Edwards, R.L., Friedrich, M., Grootes, P.M., Guilderson, T.P., Haflidason, H., Hajdas, I., Hatté, C., Heaton, T.J., Hoffmann, D.L., Hogg, A.G., Hughen, K.A., Kaiser, K.F., Kromer, B., Manning, S.W., Niu, M., Reimer, R.W., Richards, D.A., Scott, E.M., Southon, J.R., Staff, R.A., Turney, C.S.M. and van der Plicht, J. "IntCal13 and Marine13 radiocarbon age calibration curves 0–50,000 years cal BP." *Radiocarbon* 55 (2013): 1869–87.

Reimer, P., Hoper, S., McDonald, J., Reimer, R. and Thompson, M. *Laboratory Protocols Used for AMS Radiocarbon Dating at the 14CHRONO Centre, The Queen's University, Belfast.* English Heritage Research Report Series 1-2015, 2015.

Rippon, S. "Landscape change during the 'long eighth century' in southern England." In *The Landscape Archaeology of Anglo-Saxon England*, edited by N.J. Higham and M.J. Ryan, 39-64. Woodbridge: Boydell Press, 2010.

Rippon, S. *Making Sense of an Historic Landscape.* Oxford: Oxford University Press, 2012.

Rippon, S., Smart, C. and Wainwright A. *The Living Past: the Origins and Development of the Historic Landscape of the Blackdown Hills.* Unpublished report: University of Exeter, 2006a https://ore.exeter.ac.uk/repository/handle/10036/4032 (accessed Mar 2015).

Rippon, S.J., Fyfe, R.M. and Brown, A.G. "Beyond Villages and Open Fields: The Origins and Development of a Historic Landscape Characterised by Dispersed Settlement in South West England." *Medieval Archaeology* 50 (2006b): 31-70.

Rippon, S., Claughton, P. and Smart, C. *Mining in a Medieval Landscape: The Royal Silver Mines of the Tamar Valley.* Exeter: Exeter University Press, 2009.

Rippon, S., Smart, C. and Pears, B. *The Fields of Britannia.* Oxford: Oxford University Press, 2015.

Rodwell, J.S. *British Plant Communities, Volume 3: Grasslands and Montane communities.* Cambridge: Cambridge University Press, 1998.

Russell, I. and Hurley, F. *Woodstown: a Viking-age settlement in Co. Waterford.* Dublin: Four Courts, 2014.

Ryan, S., Ruse, C. and Allan, J.P. "Seventeenth-century pottery kiln waste from Hillside, Plympton." *Proceedings of the Devon Archaeological Society* (forthcoming).

Ryder, L. *The Historic Landscape of Devon: a Study in Continuity and Change.* Oxford: Windgather Press, 2013.

Sauder, L. "Making steel in the 'Aristotle' furnace." In *Accidental and Experimental Archaeometallurgy*, edited by D. Dungworth and R.C.P. Doonan, 69-74. Historical Metallurgy Society, Occasional Publication no. 7, 2013.

Schairer, J.F. and Yagi, K. "The system FeO- Al2O3-SiO2." *American Journal of Science*, Bowen volume (1952): 471-512.

Schweingruber, F.H. *Microscopic wood anatomy*, 3rd edition. Swiss Federal Institute for Forest, Snow and Landscape Research, 1990.

Scott, E.M. "The third international radiocarbon intercomparison (TIRI) and the fourth international radiocarbon intercomparison (FIRI) 1990–2002: results, analyses, and conclusions." *Radiocarbon* 45 (2003): 135-408.

Scott, E.M., Cook G. and Naysmith, P. "The fifth international radiocarbon intercomparison (VIRI): an assessment of laboratory performance in stage 3." *Radiocarbon* 53 (2010): 859-65.

Scott, I.R. *Romsey Abbey. Report on the excavations 1973-1991.* Hampshire Field Club and Archaeological Society Monograph 8, 1996.

Searley, A.W. "Haccombe. Part IV. (The Archpresbytery)." *Report and Transactions of the Devonshire Association* 53 (1921): 180–200.

Shennan, S. *Quantifying Archaeology*, 2nd edition. Edinburgh: Edinburgh University Press, 1997.

Slicher van Bath, B.H. *The Agrarian History of Western Europe, AD500-1850.* London: Edward Arnold, 1963.

Slota Jr, P.J., Jull, A.J.T., Linick, T.W. and Toolin, L.J. "Preparation of small samples for ^{14}C accelerator targets by catalytic reduction of CO." *Radiocarbon* 29 (1987): 303-6.

Soil Survey of England and Wales. *Soils of England and Wales, Sheet 5 South West England.* Southampton: Soil Survey of England and Wales.

South West Archaeology. *The Site to the East of 'Castle Dene', Culmstock Road, Hemyock, Devon, Results of Evaluation Trenches.* Unpublished report: South West Archaeology report no. 050702, 2005.

Stace, C. *New Flora of The British Isles.* Cambridge: Cambridge University Press, 1991.

Stace, C. *New Flora of The British Isles*, 2nd edition. Cambridge: Cambridge University Press, 1997.

Starley, D. and Loveluck, C. 2009. "Ironworking debris and manufacturing process." In *Life and economy at early medieval Flixborough* c. *AD600-1000, Volume 2, the artefact evidence*, edited by D.H. Evans and C. Loveluck, 322-328. Oxford: Oxbow, 2009.

Stenhouse, M.J. and Baxter, M.S. "^{14}C reproducibility: evidence from routine dating of archaeological samples." *PACT* 8 (1983): 147–61.

Stoate, T.L. (ed.) *Devon Lay Subsidy Rolls, 1524–7.* Almondsbury: privately printed, 1979.

Stoate, T.L. (ed.) *Devon Lay Subsidy Rolls, 1543–5.* Almondsbury: privately printed, 1986.

Stoate, T.L. (ed.) *Devon Taxes, 1581–1660*. Almondsbury: privately printed, 1988.

Stopford, J. *Medieval Floor Tiles of Northern England: Pattern and Purpose: production between the 13th and 16th centuries*, Oxford: Oxbow Books, 2005.

Stuiver, M. and Kra, R.S. "Editorial comment." *Radiocarbon* 28 (1986): ii.

Stuiver, M. and Polach, H.A. "Reporting of ^{14}C data." *Radiocarbon* 19 (1977): 355–63.

Stuiver, M. and Reimer, P.J. "Extended ^{14}C data base and revised CALIB 3.0 ^{14}C age calibration program." *Radiocarbon* 35 (1993): 215–30.

Summerson, H. *Crown pleas of the Devon Eyre of 1238*. Exeter: Devon and Cornwall Record Society, New Series 28, 1985.

Tabachnick, B. and Fidell, L.S. *Using Multivariate Statistics*, 5th edition. London: Pearson, 2007.

Tabor, R. "A medieval building and metalworking debris on land to the east of 'Castle Dene', Hemyock." *Proceedings of the Devon Archaeological Society* 68 (2010): 199-208.

Tait, H. "Two Renaissance tiles from Lacock Abbey, Wiltshire." *Antiquaries Journal* 50 (1970): 347 and pl. LX.

Taylor, R.T. "Petrological study of the temper of pottery from Sherborne Old Castle." In Allan 2003, 77-8.

Taylor, S.R. and McLennan, S.M. "The composition and evolution of the continental crust: rare earth element evidence from sedimentary rocks." *Philosophical Transactions of the Royal Society* A301 (1981): 381-99.

Tebbutt, C.F. "A Middle-Saxon smelting site at Millbrook, Ashdown Forest, Sussex." *Sussex Archaeological Collections* 120 (1982): 19–35.

Thomas, G. *A chemical and mineralogical investigation of bloomery iron-making in the Bristol Channel Orefield, UK*. Unpublished PhD thesis: Cardiff University, 2000.

Thomas, G.R. and Young, T.P. "Bloomery furnace mass balance and efficiency." In *Geoarchaeology: exploration, environments, resources*, edited by A.M. Pollard, 155-64. London: Geological Society of London Special Publication 165, 1999a.

Thomas, G.R. and Young, T.P. "A graphical method to determine furnace efficiency and lining contribution to Romano-British bloomery iron-making slags (Bristol Channel Orefield, UK)." In: Young, S.M.M., Budd, P.D., Ixer, R.A. and Pollard, A.M. (eds). *Metals in Antiquity*, British Archaeological Reports International Series, 792, 223-226. Oxford: BAR Publishing, 1999b.

Turner, S. *Ancient country: the historic character of rural Devon*. Exeter: Devon Archaeological Society, 2007.

Tylecote, R.F. *The prehistory of metallurgy in the British Isles*. London: Institute of Materials, 1986.

Vandeputte, K., Moens, L. and Dams, R. "Improved sealed-tube combustion of organic samples to CO_2 for stable isotope analysis, radiocarbon dating and percent carbon determinations." *Analytical Letters* 29 (1996): 2761–73.

Van der Veen, M. "Charred grain assemblages from Roman period corn driers in Britain." *Archaeological Journal* 146 (1989): 301-19.

Vranch, R.D. "Fieldwork on eastern Mendip." *Proceedings of the University of Bristol Spelaeological Society* 182 (1988): 321–2.

Wagner, D.B. "Ancient carburisation of iron to steel: a comment." *Archaeomaterials* 4 (1990): 111-117.

Wakeham, C. and Firth, E. *St Swithun's Church, Woodbury, East Devon: Results of an Archaeological Building Survey and Watching Brief.* Unpublished report: AC Archaeology report no. 47/1/1, 2012.

Wall, W. "Middle Saxon iron smelting furnaces in Cambridge". *Historical Metallurgy Society News* 41 (1999).

Wall, W. "Middle Saxon Iron Smelting near Bonemills Farm, Wittering, Cambridgeshire". *Anglo-Saxon Studies in Archaeology and History* 17 (2011): 90-103.

Ward Perkins, J.B. "Late medieval tiles at Poundisford Park, Somerset". *Proceedings of the Somerset Archaeological and Natural History Society* 86 (1940): 124–8.

Ward Perkins, J.B. "A late thirteenth-century tile-pavement at Cleeve Abbey". *Proceedings of the Somerset Archaeological and Natural History Society* 87 (1941): 39–55.

Ward, G.K. and Wilson, S.R. "Procedures for comparing and combining radiocarbon age determinations: a critique". *Archaeometry* 20 (1978): 19–31.

Way, A. "Illustrations of Devices on Decorative Tiles traced or collected by Albert Way 1841–1851". National Library of Wales, Department of Maps and Pictures acc. no. P. B. 8271, no date.

Webster, C.J. "Introduction to the Project and the Region." In *The Archaeology of South West England*, edited by C.J. Webster, 1-22. Taunton: Somerset County Council, 2008.

Webster, C.J. *Taunton Castle: Archaeological Research 1998–2013,* Taunton: Somerset Archaeological and Natural History Society, 2016.

Weddell, P. and Reed, S.J. "Excavations at Sourton Down, Okehampton 1986-91: Roman road, deserted hamlet and other landscape features." *Proceedings of the Devon Archaeological Society* 55 (1997): 95-128.

Williams, A. "A metallurgical study of some Viking swords". *Gladius* 29 (2009): 121-184.

Worcestershire County Council Archaeological Service, Ceramic Research Centre. *Worcestershire On-*

line Fabric Type Series, available at http://www.worcestershireceramics.org.

Young, A. and Young, D.E.F. *The Bristol and Bath Science Park (SPark), Emersons Green, South Gloucestershire Archaeological Excavation (Excavation Area 1) and Recording Project 2010*. Unpublished report: Avon Archaeological Unit report, 2013.

Young, T.P. *Archaeometallurgical residues from Clonfad 3, Co. Westmeath (A001: 036 E2723)*, Unpublished report: GeoArch report no. 2008/17, 2009a.

Young, T.P. *Ferrous archaeometallurgical residues from Woodstown 6*. Unpublished report: GeoArch report no. 2009/22, 2009b.

Young, T.P. *Archaeometallurgical residues from the N7 Castletown to Nenagh scheme, Camlin 3 (E3580), Co. Tipperary*. Unpublished report: GeoArch report no. 2011/23, 2011.

Young, T.P. "Appendix 3 -. Exploiting the bog -: iron production and metalworking". In *Settlement and Community in the Fir Tulach Kingdom*, edited by P. Stevens and J. Channing, A3.1-A3.60. Dublin: Wordwell, 2012.

Young, T.P. *Evaluation of archaeometallurgical residues from Churchills Farm, Hemyock, Devon*. Unpublished report: GeoArch report no. 2013-06, 2013.

Young, T.P. *Archaeometallurgical residues from Culmstock Road, Hemyock, Devon (ACD591)*. Unpublished report: GeoArch report no. 2014-11, 2014a.

Young, T.P. "Chapter 6: Discussion of metalworking evidence". In *Woodstown: a Viking Age Settlement in Co. Waterford*, edited by I. Russell and M.F. Hurley, 103-113. Dublin: Four Courts Press, 2014b.

Young, T.P. *Report on Archaeometallurgical residues from Torr Quarry, Leighton, Wanstrow, Somerset*. Unpublished report: GeoArch report no. 2014-12, 2014c.

Young, T.P. *Analyses of ores and residues from Dunkeswell, Devon*. Unpublished report: GeoArch report no. 2014-31, 2015a.

Young, T.P. *Assessment of archaeometallurgical residues from Cefn Graianog, G1598 (2012-13)*. Unpublished report: GeoArch report no. 2015-09, 2015b.

Young, T.P. *Assessment of archaeometallurgical residues from Cefn Graianog, G1598 (2014)*. Unpublished report: GeoArch report no. 2015-19, 2015c.

Young, T.P. *Assessment of archaeometallurgical residues from Yorkley, Gloucestershire*. GeoArch Report 2015-24, 2015d.

Young, T.P. *Archaeometallurgical residues from Llandre, Ceredigion*. Unpublished report: GeoArch report no. 2016-36, 2016.

Young, T.P. *Assessment of archaeometallurgical residues from Lydney B North (LYF17)*. Unpublished report: GeoArch report no. 2017-16, 2017.

Young, T.P. *Archaeometallurgical residues from Folly court, Wokingham*. Unpublished report: GeoArch report no. 2017-09, in prep.

Young, T.P. and Thomas, G.R. "The cargo: iron ore analysis." In *The Magor Pill Medieval Wreck* by N. Nayling, CBA Research Report 115, 105-111. York: Council for British Archaeology, 1998.

Zikos, N. "Pottery workshop at Mikro Pisto in Thrace." In *Byzantine Glazed Ceramics: the Art of Sgraffito* by D. Papanikola-Bakirtzi, 243-4. Athens: Archaeological Receipts Fund, 1999.